How to Drive Into
ACCIDENTS

And How NOT To

Questions
Checker

ACCIDENT NOTES
KEEP THESE NOTES FOR YOUR RECORD - DO NOT MAIL THEM

ACCIDENT DATE	TIME	❑ AM ❑ PM
PLACE OF ACCIDENT		
POLICYHOLDER NAME	PHONE NO.	
POLICYHOLDER ADDRESS		
OPERATORS NAME	PHONE NO.	
OPERATORS ADDRESS		
VIN OF INSURED VEHICLE		
OTHER DRIVER NAME	PHONE NO.	
OTHER DRIVER ADDRESS		
OTHER DRIVER LICENSE NUMBER	STATE	
MAKE OF OTHER CAR	YEAR	
PLATE NUMBER	STATE	
OWNER OF OTHER CAR	PHONE NO	
ADDRESS		
INSURANCE COMPANY		
POLICY NUMBER		
DAMAGE TO OTHER CAR OR PROPERTY		
PERSONS INJURED - NAME - ADDRESS - PHONE NO.		
WHERE TAKEN		
OCCUPANTS OF OTHER CAR - NAME - ADDRESS- PHONE NO.		
WITNESSES - NAME - ADDRESS - PHONE NO.		

POLICE OFFICER NAME	BADGE NO.	❑ CITY ❑ STATE
POLICE DEPARTMENT/PRECINCT NAME		
WERE CITATIONS ISSUED? ❑ YES ❑ NO		
WHO RECEIVED THE CITATION(S)?		
CITATIONS(S) ISSUED		

- This page is not copyrighted.
- The front cover is made up of parts of the Massachusetts Accident Report Form.

How to Drive Into
ACCIDENTS
And How NOT To

by Robert A. Pease

Pease Publishing
San Francisco

LEGAL DISCLAIMER

I am not responsible, and I am not legally liable, for any driving mistakes you may make based on anything I wrote, or for any advice that I did NOT give. Whatever you do, DON'T break laws, and DO use good sense and good judgement, no matter what you read.

As we recognize the importance of preserving what has been written, it is our policy always to print books on acid-free paper.

♦ ♦ ♦

Library of Congress Cataloging in Publication Data:
How to Drive into ACCIDENTS – and How NOT TO.
Robert A. Pease, Author
Library of Congress Number 97-91601

Includes bibliographical references and index.
ISBN 0-9655648-0-0 (Hardcover) (paper: acid free) $28.95
ISBN 0-9655648-1-9 (Softcover) (paper: acid-free) $18.95
1. Safe Automobile Driving – How To Do It.

TL152.52.P42 – 1997
629.28

Pease Publishing
682 Miramar Avenue
San Francisco,
CA 94112-1232 USA
10 9 8 7 6 5 4 3 2 1

Printed in the United States of America

Editorial, design, and production services provided by
Shizue and Sai Seigel, San Francisco, CA

TABLE OF CONTENTS

....

FOREWORD

....

WHY???

Why did I write this book? I want beginning drivers to learn thoughtful, advanced techniques, for defensive driving, and for avoiding accidents. I decided to make the effort, to write about all the ways that funny little things become bad habits, and these habits can work together with other factors, to cause accidents.

For example, most people have figured out that "speed kills" is baloney. Yet, driving fast CAN compound or conspire with other factors that can get you in trouble, cause accidents, and get you killed – or, worse, get you badly injured....

WHY?

Why am I qualified to write this book? I have driven over 1,000,000 miles. I have seen other people's accidents, and talked about them. I think I understand the mechanical problems of cars, and the human nature of people. I think I know enough about cars. As for *people*, well, they are *very* complicated. I don't think *anybody* knows everything there is to know about people. But at least I am an adequate typist, and a good story-teller.

Why?

Why did I think I can write this book? I had already written one book. So I knew I could write another book. Word by word, paragraph by paragraph, topic by topic, file by file, I knew I could do it. Process those words. CRUNCH those topics. I was confident (as I checked my old notes) that by September I would have 90% of the draft typed up. The only minor problem was, I neglected to specify *which year*. I thought I'd be mostly finished by September of 1995 – but to get all the loose ends in, it was basically September of 1996 when I got it done.

WHO FOR??

Who is the book for? It is for any inexperienced or new driver. Now, a person who does not yet know much about driving – or does not drive – is not going to appreciate all this stuff, until later. That's OK. This is a good book for BEGINNING and INTERMEDIATE drivers. I do not think it will screw up the head of the non-driver, but it ain't going to do him a lot of help, either. I mean, if you have never held a tennis racquet in your hand, a book about "How to Play Better Tennis" is not going to sink in really well.

Who BUYS the book?

Who is going to buy this book? Obviously, that is where the mothers and fathers of the young drivers come in. THEY are going to buy a LARGE number of the books. What parent would not want to buy this book, for his kid?

THEN, after the kid starts to read the book, I got to keep his interest. With good writing, interesting ideas, and, MOSTLY, EXAMPLES. Examples of accidents and near-accidents.

$$$?

Where's the incentive for me to write this? Lots of $?? Well, I am going to contribute 1/3 of the pre-tax profits to safe-driving organizations, and 1/3 to safer-flying organizations. What's left (*after* taxes) will not be enough for me to retire from work on. But that's ok. My motivation is to save lives, save pain. Maybe in the long run, our insurance rates will stop rising!

Why Did I Get Started?

What was the first motivation for the book? My cousin Ellen Hubbard lost her 16-year-old daughter Christine to an unfortunate driving accident, a few years back. The official police report said that they did not know how the accident happened. But two young women died when their car was hit by a truck. The idea of a book began to grow, but I got sidetracked until the fall of 1994.

Why Safe Flying?

What's the big deal about safe flying? I lost 3 friends who flew into the ground.

Ron Brown was giving flight lessons to a student, up along the Connecticut River. Another pilot was not watching closely enough, and flew up behind Ron; his propeller chopped up the plane's tail. Ron could not control the plane, and it crashed. Ouch.

In 1991, Kathy Raphael was on a practice flight, practicing mountain flying with one other student and an instructor. They were all 3 good, smart pilots. They flew up a canyon in the Sierras, near Sonora pass. The canyon got too tight, and they could not climb out of it, nor turn. They tried to loop out of it, and crashed and were killed instantly. They all knew enough, not to try flying up a canyon. But somehow, inadvertently, they DID. Sigh. That accident got me thinking....

Chuck Everhart used to work for my company, National Semiconductor, back 18 years ago. He was a test engineer in our Linear IC group — he was programming one of our first Teradyne testers. He was flying up in the foothills, up near Groveland in October of 1994. All of his friends were confident that Chuck would be a long-term survivor, and would retire from flying at the age of 85. Well, he got too low in bad weather, and almost cleared a ridge – but clipped a tree. Killed instantly. Too darn' bad. That accident got me *mad*.

I'd like to write a book to save the lives of young pilots, but I am not wise enough to do that. I'll let somebody else do that. (See Appendix A on Flying.) But I CAN write a book to help young drivers. So I did. It just took all my spare time for a year.

HOW?

It's not exactly easy, writing for 16-year-olds, rather than engineers. You have to be very careful not to "write down to them". But I think I did OK. Hell, how can I "write down to" a young driver who has better reflexes than I do, and more power in his car, and is on the same road as me?

– The important thing I tried to put into this book is, stories about interesting accidents. How did it happen? What were the drivers THINKING? If YOU were in the same situation, could YOU avoid the accident by THINKING? Or, could you get out of that situation by knowing how to REACT? – and, if you are going to REACT properly, does that mean you have to think about these situations in advance? I planned this book to be as much about THINKING, as about driving. So I put in EXAMPLES. I sure as hell am not going to teach kids anything by being PREACHY, but I think I can teach them with EXAMPLES.

Who Will Buy?

The ordinary list price of this book is supposed to be not much more than 10 or 12 gallons of gas. Paperback. Affordable. No young driver can say he can't afford to buy my book. And no driver can afford NOT to buy this book.

Publishing??

I talked with about 8 publishers, who all sent me a nice rejection notice. This did not discourage me – it just made me wonder – why are they so foolish? And it inspired me to show them – hey – you goofed. So I decided to self-publish the book. I bought some books about how easy it is to self-publish. The first, hard part of self-publishing, is to get your ideas into print, and onto paper. Fine.

The second, harder part, is to inform and explain to thousands of ordinary people, why they ought to buy the book. Marketing. Advertising. Very challenging.

Theme?

Ah – yes – and what is the theme of the book? That quote from Otto von Bismarck, that was on the back cover of my first book, is displayed yet more prominently on the back of this book:

"Fools you are... who say you like to learn from your mistakes.... I prefer to learn from the mistakes of others and avoid the cost of my own."

What Next?

Is there a possibility of a sequel, a video, a CD-ROM? A comic book? Quite possible, if I get suggestions and encouragement from readers. But I want to get this book out promptly, and start saving lives.

As I say in Appendix O – Your comments, as always, are invited. Good luck and safe driving to you.

Robert A. Pease, Engineer and Wordsmith/
9 July 1996 / 2 June 1997.

ACKNOWLEDGMENTS

You had just better believe, I have had a lot of help from my friends, when I wrote this book. There are a lot of stories in here from my buddies, about accidents, and about ideas related to accidents and safe driving. I got about 25 of my friends at National Semiconductor, and about 20 friends across the country whom I wrote to by e-mail, who agreed to help review each of my Chapters as it came along. Some helped just a little, and others, a whole lot.

♦ ♦ ♦

Needless to say – if you have ever tried to write a comprehensive story about everything you know on *ANY* SUBJECT – when you show it to your friends, they'll say, "Why did you forget *THIS*?" and, "What about *THAT*?"

– Then you will realize that, YES, you did know about *THIS* – but you forgot to include it until they reminded you.

– Also, NO, you did NOT know about *THAT*, and you sure are glad they told you. Either way, you will be REALLY GLAD to have such good friends.

– Friends like Stuart Brennan and Stuart Smith and Roy McCammon, who REALLY know a lot about cars and driving, and gave me many good ideas and suggestions. Friends like Bill Kimmel and Ed Walker and Nick Grey and Shizue Seigel, who not only know a lot about cars, but put in the effort to check my writing, my typing, spelling, and grammar. I mean, I write a lot of good stuff, plus a small amount of stupid writing that is badly written, mi-spelt – and; poorly; punctuated. When I do that, I need the help of these friends who raise nasty and forceful questions about my dubious writing.

I have a whole bunch of friends who put in several great comments – John Powell, Helena Mullins, Jerrilyn Pease, Heidi Anderson, Jay Friedman, John Densem, Robin Shields, Jan Jopke, Les Earnest, Alan Tausch, Ellen and Emmett Hubbard, Geoff Harries, etc....

– And a lot of other guys who helped me by hollering when they saw something wrong, or remembered a situation: Mike Akers, Ann Berry-Gallegos, Bill Broach, Lynn Bowen, Sumer Can, John Christensen, Jon Cronk, Jim Diller, Kyndale Duelks, Wanda Garrett, Frank Goodenough, Carlos Huerta, Nick Johnson, Janis Knight, Kerry Lacanette, Jerry Latta, Carol Lewis, Alan Markow, Ion Opris, Zahid Rahim, Bert and Anne Raphael, Tim Regan, Marcello Salvatierra, Lisa Santillana, Roberta Silverstein, Bob Sleeth, Tom Spisak, Lee Stoian, George and Viola Taylor, John Trudel, Bob Whelton, Gerry Ziegler, and my sons Benjamin and Jonathan Pease.

I must also confirm my appreciation for Wanda Garrett, who first taught me how to do word-processing on PC Write Lite. Little did she realize how her instructions would lead not just to crummy reports, but monstrous books!

I'll put in here, a special mention of my old boss, Dave Ludwig, from whom I was really hoping to get a lot of good comments. But he had the bad luck to die of cancer suddenly in December of 1995. I not only lost a good friend, but a guy with a lot of experience and good ideas about driving, who would have heckled me properly when he saw me goofing off.

Also, my friend Frank Goodenough died in February of 1998. He had contributed several stories about his driving experiences. Too bad he never got to see the book, with his advice in it. We'll miss him.

Similarly, there were a couple other guys who would have been great contributors, but they had a lot of illness in the family and could not put in as many comments as they would have liked to.

– My long-suffering wife Nancy wanted to go on a long hike in Nepal in the summer of 1995. I told her, "Go ahead. I'll stay home and write this book." She went, and she came back. A year later, I was still putting in 40 hours every weekend, finishing the book. She put up with a lot of guff from me. Yet when I got through with a long day of typing, she always had supper ready for me.

When it was time to put my typed chapter drafts into a type-set format, my son's girlfriend Shizue Seigel volunteered to try it. She made it look great. When she ran out of time, her daughter Sai put in long hours on other chapters. She helped with the proof-reading, too.

Money is useful. Money is all very nice. But friends, like the ones who helped me on this book, are MUCH better than anything money could buy. This is especially true when you are trying to get your book out, and every publisher has turned you down. When your friends believe you have a good cause, their belief and confidence is a GREAT SUPPORT. If you ever try to write a book, I wish you to have friends as great as the friends who helped me on this book.

ABOUT THE AUTHOR – Robert A. Pease

I was born in 1940 in Rockville, Connecticut. I attended Mount Hermon School, and graduated from MIT in 1961 with a Bachelor's Degree in Electrical Engineering. Then I went to work at Philbrick Researches, in Boston, Mass. I worked as a circuit design engineer from 1961 to 1976, and I designed many industry-standard Op Amps and Analog Computing Products, including DACs and Voltage-to-Frequency Converters – mostly as little potted modules.

In 1976 I came out to work for National Semiconductor Corp., in Santa Clara CA – that is, Silicon Valley. Here I designed several industry-standard Integrated Circuits, including LM337 Voltage Regulators, LM4050 Bandgap References, LM34 and LM50 Temperature Sensors, and LM331 Voltage-to-Frequency Converters.

I've published more than 65 technical papers in various technical journals and magazines. I have 14 US Patents. I am a Senior Member of the IEEE.

So What? Who cares? Oh, not a big deal, but I mention all this, so you can see where I'm coming from. I want you to see that I worked a lot of years, to get enough experience, to be able to JUST WRITE about things... and NOW it gets interesting:

Writing

In 1988, I was asked to write a Chapter for a book on Troubleshooting for Switching Regulators. I wrote down a lot of notes, a lot of pages. The pages grew past 50. Then I kept on writing about every other kind of Troubleshooting for other circuits – just for the heck of it. The number of pages rose past 200. This collection got published as a series of 12 stories in EDN Magazine in 1989, and was very popular. Finally Carol Lewis at HighText (San Diego CA) got me to write these stories into a book.

In 1991 that book, titled "Troubleshooting Analog Circuits", was published by Butterworth Heinemann (Newton Mass). The hard-cover book has sold over 17,000 copies, and it is still in print in paperback.* It is still the best book on this topic.

In September of 1991 I began writing a column, "Pease Porridge", in *Electronic Design* magazine. This column has been widely praised as a thought-provoking forum for clear thinking and technical excellence. In other words, a lot of people agree with what I say, when I criticize silly ideas or pompous fools. I've gotten thousands of letters. In 1992, this column won a Neal Award from the American Business Press, for excellence in Editorial Opinion. My 125th column was published in March of 1998.

Anyhow, now you can see that I have gotten into a *habit* of doing a *lot* of writing, in a conversational style. Not nearly enough to fill up a 100 Mbyte hard disc, but enough to wear you out if you try to read it.

* *Robert A. Pease, TROUBLESHOOTING ANALOG CIRCUITS, Butterworth-Heinemann, Boston, 1991. Order from Robert A. Pease. Send a check for $32 to 682 Miramar Avenue, San Francisco, CA 94112*

Driving

Another thing I have done a lot of is, I have driven my cars – mostly old VWs – over 1,000,000 miles in conditions from desert to blizzard to flood, on freeways, on the two-lane, and on mountain dirt roads. I have driven many thousands of miles around England and Europe. I have learned a lot about driving my own cars, and rental cars, and I have always been a student of other drivers' problems. So, as I explain in the Foreword, when I decided to put together some stories about the problems of accidents vs. safe driving, I knew I could put together enough ideas to make a book.

Writing *About* Driving...

So I spent 30 hours, every weekend from May 1995 to August 1996, typing cheerfully on my PC – an old IBM XT. I used PC Write Lite*, for my word processing, and it really is user-friendly. I'll recommend that. I kept all my text on floppies.

I sent out copies of the draft of each Chapter to be reviewed by about 46 friends, some in California, and some by e-mail to various parts of the country, and I got a lot of feedback and comments. "Bob, did you forget *this*?" "Bob, I can't believe you said THAT!!" So, taking their advice, I made a lot of corrections, and added a lot of new advice and stories about accidents.

I talked to several publishers, who, foolishly, did not seem to see the wisdom of publishing this book. So I decided to publish it myself. After all, I've already written one book. I know there is a lot of work, after you have the final text ready, getting all of the type-setting work and formatting done, before you are ready to send it to the printer. But I know that computerized aids for publishing were quite good, even 5 or 10 years ago, and they are much better now.

Shiz Seigel and her daughter Sai did the typesetting, using Quark Xpress. Quite soon, it began to look quite neat and professional, in many Chapters.

However, some Chapters looked LOUSY, because I had not written them well. You may have noticed that a page of REALLY neat handwritten text can suddenly look terrible when you get it typed neatly, because your thinking and grammar were sloppy. Then after you revise the typed text so it looks good, then when you get it typeset, it can look really bad, all over again – as the neat format makes you more demanding of your own writing. This happened to me, several times! Anyhow, I got all the Chapters in good shape, and all the sketches, and wrote a contract with a printer – and – here we are.

I live with my wife Nancy up in San Francisco, and I commute about 85 miles per day in my reliable old 1970 VW Beetle down to Silicon Valley. For vacations, we often drive hundreds of miles up into the Sierras, to go back-packing with family or friends. My hobbies include driving, and designing little circuits, and Industrial Archaeology and Ferroequinology (that is, tracking abandoned railroad roadbeds). Also, hiking, backpacking, and trekking in Nepal, in Europe, or in the Sierras.

– All for now / Best wishes to you, and I hope you enjoy reading my book.
/ Robert A. Pease, Engineer and Wordsmith

* PC WRITE LITE *is word-processing software from Starlite Software, 360-385-7125; about $48.*

DEDICATION

This book is dedicated to the memory of some young flyers and drivers... nice people... people that I can't forget:

Christine Hubbard

Ron Brown

Kathy Raphael

Chuck Everhart

They will remain in my mind – always young.....

Chapter Zero. GENDER, GRAMMAR, UNISEX, and other GENERALIZATIONS

Hello to Young Men and to Young Women, and Girls and Boys, and Guys and Gals, and Kids, and everybody:

I could have written this book in the latest politically-correct format, with "he/she" in every darned sentence. I decided not to do that. That would just be TOO awkward. I am going to say "he" in every general place. Or, I will say, "guy". In this book, the word "guy" means a *person*, and if a "dumb guy" drives into an accident, that could be a dumb *male* guy or a dumb *female* guy. There is, alas, enough stupidity around to spread fairly evenly over men and women, too. And have some left over, too.... That is what I want to minimize.

So, Young Lady, if you read about the case when "he drove into a wall", don't assume that only men are stupid enough to drive into walls. Don't assume my advice to "him" is not applicable to *you*.

Aggressive Drivers?

Now, it is true that men and women do drive into some different kinds of accidents. Often, young men are more aggressive, and they get into certain aggressive situations that can result in accidents. But, some women are aggressive, too.

Sometimes women are cautious, and sometimes their caution and inexperience can lead to other kinds of accidents, too. But some men have this problem, too: if you are too cautious, you might cause other people to be frustrated, and they might have an accident you never even SEE.

There is an infinitely broad spectrum of good and bad drivers, aggressive and timid drivers. We should be careful about any rash generalizations. But certain types of accidents are more likely to happen to pushy drivers, whether men or women.

Sometimes I list an accident that really did happen to "Joe" or "Carol". In most cases, I may have changed the name of the unlucky person, or I may not have – but I have not changed the gender. Some men and women were willing to tell me about their accidents. Some were not. No pattern.

Young Drivers

SIMILARLY, when I talk about "Student Drivers", or "Young Drivers", I am likely to say, "Kids". One-syllable words work well, and do not destroy your train of thought. Politically-correct phrases are too bulky, and in general they will not be used. That's tough. Even you Kids will understand that. I am not trying to be disrespectful. Some of my best friends are Kids. Some of my smartest friends are Kids. Some of my NICEST friends are Kids. OK?

However, this book was not just written for KIDS. It was written primarily for any inexperienced driver, or for any driver who makes mistakes. Since I do not know ANYBODY who makes zero mistakes when driving (especially not myself) – then – this book is for EVERYBODY who drives. In fact, this book will still be of some use to

6-22-21

people who do not drive, but who have to deal with drivers, such as bicyclists.

Policemen, etc...

Likewise, when I write about a "Cop", I also mean, Cop = Policeman = Highway Patrol Officer = Law Officer = Peace Officer. I am going to use these terms more-or-less interchangeably – even though there are legal differences about *which one* is supposed to be enforcing *what laws*. I mean no disrespect to any lawman. But all the phrases except for "Cop" are just too long, too wordy. I will use the short word "Cop" a lot, as it makes the ideas flow better. I have a lot of respect for "Cops".

What Kind of Road?

Here is a similar topic: Turnpike = Freeway = "The Interstate" = Expressway = Throughway (= Motorway = Autobahn = Autostrada).

I apologize for any confusion that might ensue. These names are not exactly interchangeable, but I am using them interchangeably, to mean a multi-lane (at least 4 lanes) limited-access divided highway with no traffic lights.

– The terms "Parkway" or "the four-lane" are NOT interchangeable with *anything*, because there are a lot of crummy 4-lanes that are dangerous and have weird traffic patterns. When the Jamaicaway runs into the Fenway in Boston, is that a WEIRD parkway? For sure. So, I will not use those terms, unless there is a specific example where it makes sense.

What Kind of Car?

I am ALSO going to make the simplifying assumption that you will be driving a car with an automatic transmission, *or* a manual transmission with 4 forward gears. I will, in general, make comments on what happens if you have 3 or 5 or any other number of gears, or an automatic transmission. Four forward gears is a very common number of gears, these days – but there are a lot of cars that are set up otherwise.

THE Disclaimer...

Note – at the beginning of most Chapters, I insert my standard Legal Disclaimer, because I don't want anybody to make any rash assumptions that they can do something stupid, based on something they think I said. I didn't put it in this Chapter, as it was not needed here. But, you'll see it in 60 other places....

Who Wrote This Mess?

No politically correct references to "the Author believes..." *I* wrote this, it was written by *me*, and if you want to holler at the author, holler at "Pease" or "rap". /R.A. Pease

Statistics?

Some books use only accurate statistics. All the statistics in this book were made up by me, out of thin air. Don't bother to ask me to prove they are good, because they are all faked. /rap

Chapter 1. BRAKES

Why are we going to cover the brakes first? Because the brakes are the most important part of the car. If you can't get your car to GO, then you have one kind of trouble. But if you can get it to go, and then you can't get it to STOP, that is a more serious kind of trouble. If you don't know how to stop, you should not get started. First things first.

How Do The Brakes Work??

– When you want to slow down or stop, and you step on the BRAKE PEDAL, the pedal is connected to a lever that pushes on a piston, in the MASTER BRAKE CYLINDER, which forces a kind of oily hydraulic fluid (brake fluid) down through some thin tubing – the brake lines – that goes to each wheel.

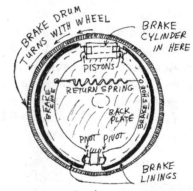

Typically, the rear brakes have another little piston which pushes on a couple brake shoes, which push on the inside of a brake DRUM. The brake shoes have just the right amount of friction, and they *rub* and *drag* and pull on the drum, and slow you down. In general, unless somebody has pulled off the brake drum in order to work on the brakes, you cannot see the drums or the other drum-brake parts.

– When the brake pressure increases, each Piston pushes on a Brake Shoe, forcing it against the inside of the Brake Drum. (Handbrake Linkage not shown.)

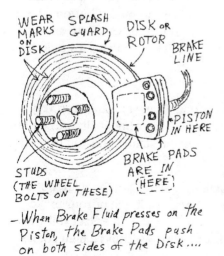

– When Brake Fluid presses on the Piston, the Brake Pads push on both sides of the Disk....

In most modern cars, the front brakes do not use drums; they use disks. Each wheel has a brake DISK or ROTOR connected to the wheel, and calipers, and pads, to go with the pistons. The caliper holds the brake pads. Refer to adjacent sketch. When you step on the pedal and increase the hydraulic pressure, the piston pushes the brake pads against each side of the disc, and this friction slows ya down. If you peek through the slots in your front wheel, you may be able to see parts of the disc brakes. When a front tire is being changed, you can easily see the disk brake parts. The design is similar to a bicycle's caliper brakes. But there is one significant difference: On a bicycle, the calipers squeeze on the wheel rim, right near the tire. If you ride a bike down a really long hill, the rims can get very hot. On a car, this would be unacceptably hot, so the disk is *separate* from the wheel. The disk can get very hot, without overheating the tire.

For about the first 50 years, cars had only rear brakes, and they were mechanically connected. Then in the 1930s, cars got drum brakes in the front and rear, and they were operated hydraulically. Then in the 1960s and 1970s, the front brakes on many cars – especially high-performance cars – were converted to disks, because they can handle the high power. Some high-performance cars even have disk brakes in front and rear. (Some of them have drums for the hand-brakes.) Planes and passenger trains have disk brakes, too.

Power Brakes

Now, most cars have power brakes. So long as the engine is running, there is a power BOOST from a vacuum booster that helps you put on a lot of force on the brakes without a LOT of force from your foot. If your engine is not running, you lose your power boost. So be careful if your engine stops – your brakes will start working badly. Not a disaster, but just be careful. If you have not checked this out, find a safe place – perhaps the back corner of a big empty parking lot – and get rolling at a speed of perhaps 20 or 30 mph. Shift into neutral and turn off the ignition key just a little; do not turn the key all the way to the left, or your steering could lock up.

Step on the brakes. They'll work just fine. Take your foot off the brakes and try again, and again. About the third time, you'll find that you need a lot more force on the brake pedal, to get your car to stop. You should be aware of this, as if your engine ever quits, you do not want to be too surprised by the amount of force you need on the brake pedal, to stop.

There are also "hand brakes". Here, we'll call them hand brakes – (even if they are operated by a foot pedal). These are often called "parking brakes" or "emergency brakes" or "mechanical brakes". When you pull on that long hand-lever, a long cable pulls on a little lever inside each rear wheel and holds the brakes on. These brakes have a ratchet so they will stay on when you park. You have to push a button or pull on a lever when you want to release the "handbrakes". But some cars have an automatic hand-brake release, when you shift into DRIVE. I think that's a stupid idea.

Now – What Can Go Wrong?

The brake shoes or brake pads will eventually wear out. Then you can't stop very well. The brake fluid can leak out – and your brakes may not work at all. But, do not worry a whole lot. Usually, these problems don't happen instantly, and you can tell that things are going wrong, and fix them before you get in trouble.

For over 20 years, all cars have had a dual braking system. No, there are not 2 brake pedals. Inside the master cylinder, there are 2 pistons. If one of your brake lines breaks or leaks, you lose half of your brake fluid – but the other half still works, and you do not lose all the fluid, so you can still stop fairly well, and a light comes on to warn you that something is wrong.

If you step on the brakes too hard (which is very easy to do in case of snow or sand or other cases of poor traction) then you may not be able to slow down, and you can also skid. (Refer to the Chapter on Skids.) So, it is worth a lot of study to learn to use your brakes properly.

General Comments on Brakes...

In general, I like to work on my car, because the more I understand what might go wrong, the more I can avoid problems. The only place I do not do my own work is on the brakes. I am willing to let other people, *professionals,* do the work on my brakes. Actually, let me back up: I do not mind working on the mechanical brake linkages; I just do not work on the main (hydraulic) brake systems. Keeps me away from asbestos, too.

If my hand-brakes get worn out of adjustment, I take some little wrenches, and adjust the hand-brake cables. If my brakes have gotten so far out of adjustment that my brake-pedal is getting low – too close to the floor when I step on it – I take a screwdriver and turn the adjusting wheels on my brakes. That is all mechanical. But I have never fooled around with the hydraulics, and I probably never will.

Meanwhile, I keep an eye on my brakes. So long as they work well, I don't worry about them. I do a lot of freeway driving, so I can put on a lot of miles between adjustments. I drive 30,000 miles per year, and I only adjust my brakes once or twice a year, and I only have to have the linings replaced every 2 or 3 years. Of course, most modern cars have self-adjusting brakes, so they don't need much attention. But they do need checking, because when they actually wear down too far, if you don't replace the lining pretty soon, it gets really expensive. A "brake job", which means just replacing the brake shoes or the pads, might cost $50 for each wheel, or in case the rotor or drum needs to be "turned" on a lathe, perhaps double that. But if you have to replace the discs because you neglected getting the brakes repaired too long, there's another $100 on top of that. And that $100 is wasted just because you procrastinated too long, before getting them fixed. So, don't ignore those grinding or rattling sounds.

Bad Brakes

There is one other thing that gets expensive. If your brakes really wear down, and the brake linings or pads are mostly GONE, the metal-on-metal friction is poor. Then when you need your brakes to work well, and they don't, you wind up in an accident.

Mr. Thomas Speier, the husband of one of our local legislators, (Jackie Speier, San Mateo CA) was driving along one day, minding his own business, and got hit by a car with bad brakes. In a well-publicized court case, the negligent driver, who kept driving even though he knew his brakes were lousy, was convicted of manslaughter. He got off without doing more than a couple years of prison time, but that does not sound like fun, being responsible for killing a guy because you did not take the time to fix your brakes.

On the other hand, you might be driving along with really rotten brakes – saying – "I'm going to fix them tomorrow – I really am" – and before you get to the repair shop, you could kill or injure yourself because of the bad brakes. Or your wife. Or your kids. Is that a better deal?

One time in 1967 I went skiing, and when I started home in my old 1962 Beetle, my rear brakes sort of "froze up". I tried to drive, and the rear brakes were dragging badly. Now, in most cases, it is your hand-brake cable that gets wet and freezes, that causes this problem. So, many drivers have wisely learned not to put on their handbrake when they park in the winter.

In that case, cutting your hydraulic line is NOT usually going to solve that problem. For that case, you get the car into a warm garage for a couple hours, and the problem goes away when the ice melts. But in this case, I convinced myself that it must not be the cable, it must be the main (hydraulic) brakes. I'm not sure how I convinced myself of that, but I did. So I cut the rear brake line – and the dragging problem went away! Of course, I did not have any foot-brakes.

I had to drive only a few miles, but I knew the road pretty well, and I knew the hills, and I was sure I could get home safely if I drove very carefully and just used my handbrakes a little. I went VERY carefully and fairly slowly – perhaps 45 mph on empty roads – on an early Sunday morning when there was almost nobody on the road, and I got home just fine. I stayed away from all traffic. I drove the car right to the repair shop, and then had my wife give me a ride home. The repairman fixed it all up, but said they could not find any problem. I never did find out what caused the problem. It never happened again.

Anyhow, if you have no foot brakes, or almost no brakes, you usually want to get them fixed before you go any distance at all. Get the car towed into the repair place. Or if you figure your hand-brakes are pretty good, you should know exactly what to do, and be prepared for the consequences if somebody pulls out in front of you. You might have to jam your car into a guard-rail, if your handbrakes do not work well enough.

The other thing that is worse than no brakes, is – brakes on only one side – brakes that *pull* to one side. That is a very serious deal – and if something gets out in front of you, you may hit the brakes hard out of sheer instinct – and skid sideways. Again, screwing around with poor brakes is not a good idea. Get them fixed *pronto*.

Handbrakes...

Here, we will still call them handbrakes, even though they are foot-operated. If your handbrakes do not work very well, (if your car will roll down a downgrade, even though you pull it on very hard) – then – they are trying to tell you something. Basically they are trying to tell you that your rear brake linings are no good, and consequently your front brakes are doing all the work. Even if your foot brakes SEEM to work OK, it is time to fix them, really soon, because your brakes are NOT as good as they should be. If you have to drive in this case, drive rather slowly, and very carefully until you can find the time and $ to get the car fixed. Preferably really soon, you cheapskate. And watch out in case another car pulls out in front of you. If you do not have the money to keep your car in a good state of repair, maybe you should not be driving a car. It may happen that the car can solve that problem – by wrecking itself – and you may not have any choice.

Of course, the *other* bad thing about having bad handbrakes is, you are likely to forget to take the handbrake *off,* and then you drive along, and they get really hot and really cooked and *really* bad. Since this heat is behind you, you may get MILES before you notice. REAL hot. That is REALLY time to get your brakes fixed. I did that, one time, in 1961 when I had an old Studebaker. I didn't notice the handbrake was on, for about a dozen miles. Fortunately, the front brakes were still working OK, and I eased home and got 'em fixed.

The solution to this problem (leaving your handbrakes on) is to have a warning light and/or a beeper that indicates if your handbrakes are left on. I have one of these on my Bus, but I do not have one on my Beetle. The Beetle does not need it. AND, I have a habit to protect me: Every time I shift into 4th gear, I reach down and grab the handbrake and lift it up and then set it OFF. About one time in 1000, I reach down and find that it was NOT all the way off. It's not a bad habit, checking the handbrakes. But I suppose I should put on a little beeper. It is not hard to rig a little switch, to turn on a little beeper and a light until I put the handbrake OFF.

Hey, here's what I will do: I'll put this circuit on my "OUGHT TO DO" list, and prepare to do it someday. I will hang up a plastic bag, and a list of all the parts I need to do that task. I need a little lamp bulb, and a small switch, and some small screws to mount it. Then when I have a little time, and all the parts, I can grab this bag, and go out and install the switch. Hey, the car only has 357,000 miles on it, so it is finally broken in. It's probably good for another 200,000 miles, so I probably should put on this fix. And if I ever retire this car, I'll be able to unscrew this switch, and take it with me and put it on my next car – which will surely be another 1968 or '69 Beetle.

Chocks...

When you do not have decent handbrakes, you may need a lot of bricks to put behind your wheels when you park. Or maybe, chunks of 2x4 – pieces of plank at least 2" x 4" x a foot long – or preferably 4x4's. Or, even some rocks. That is a lot better than nothing. You may only need one or two, at any one time, but in some cases you have to leave them behind, if you do not have anybody to run out and pick them up when you are driving away. So you should carry several of them. Hey, that is a lousy, temporary deal, but it's better than having no way to park at all. Better than having your car roll down a hill after you parked it.

Of course, if you are in a town, and there are sidewalks and curbs, you can put your front wheel against a curb, and that will hold you on a gentle grade. In San Francisco, the law requires us to do that. But on a really steep grade, that may not be sufficient. So you should have some stones or bricks or 2x4's.

"Park" Mode

Most cars have automatic transmissions these days, and the PARK position can help relieve the strain on the parking brake. But sometimes the PARK mechanism gets stuck, so you cannot get out of PARK. If you have this trouble, you can PARTLY avoid it by putting on the handbrake HARD before putting the shift lever into PARK. If you never make an error in this sequence, you may not get stuck.... If you do get really stuck in Park, you may have to get an up-hill push from another car, or a number of people. Or, if you block the front wheels *really, really well,* and jack up one rear wheel, will that help get you released from being stuck in Park? I don't know. Maybe. Just be careful to block things so the car cannot run away when jacked up.

Sometimes I used to get a rental car with brakes that were too touchy, as they had too high gain – they were too sensitive. When I stepped fairly lightly on the brakes – the car lurched badly because I put them on too hard. (This does not happen too much these days, because most cars are built to perform about the same.)

How do you solve this problem? I figured out how to drive these cars safely – take off my right shoe. Then if I pushed on the brakes, it would be easy to not push too hard. Because you can easily step much harder with your shoe than with your foot – and you can step more softly, with your shoe off.

On the other hand – or, on the other foot – some states require you to wear shoes while driving, presumably so that you can always step hard on the brakes, if necessary. Your state may differ. There are a lot of strange rules out there, in different states.

Using Your Brakes

Every driver has to learn how to put on the brakes. Most people who are learning to drive have ridden bicycles. Or tractors. Or riding mowers. Or golf carts. But if you have not, then you have to learn a lot about brakes.

> *I have always figured that if I take up flying, the first thing I want to learn to do, is to taxi, at moderate speeds – so I can learn how the plane feels. Then I want to learn how to LAND the plane. That is difficult, I know. After that, I can learn how to take off – but that is relatively easy. (Learning how to use all the radios would be, for me, the hardest part. The actual flying would be easy. I know how to do that; I learned from reading comic books.)*

So, with a car, if you do not know much about brakes, you really must figure out how to use them before you move. The first thing you have to learn, before you learn how to GO, is, how to STOP. The most important thing. You have to learn to ease on your brakes, when that is appropriate. And if you need to tromp on the brakes, you have to know what that feels like. And everything in between. Obviously, the art of using the brakes is a fine art.

Sometimes you just ease on the brakes. And just stop. Cars have been designed to be driven by anyone, in almost any way. But that does not mean there are not some *right* ways and some *wrong ways....*

One thing I usually do is touch my foot onto my brakes, lightly, and then lift it and then, 1 second later, hit the brakes again, and really apply them. This accomplishes 3 good things:

1. If your foot is not centered right on the pedal, you can put it on with better centering, 1 second later. It's a really good idea, not to be off-center.

   Bad footing: One day I was going to drive to a funeral service, up in the Sierra foothills. I started down a steep hill, near my house, and my foot slipped off the brake pedal. I nearly hit a car in front of me before I could get my foot back on the brakes again. My shoe had been a little muddy. Bad way to start a trip!

   I stopped and cleaned the mud off my shoe. After that, I was a little more thoughtful and careful, and I only went to one funeral that day – not to my own. I drove very aggressively on some mountain roads, with 500-foot drop-offs on the right, but my foot DAMN' WELL did not slip off the brake pedal again. (Ward's Ferry Road near Big Oak Flat is a glorious road, but not for the faint of heart.)

2. If your brake pedal is "low", sometimes it just needs to be pumped up. So if you hit the pedal twice, and then the brakes work a lot better, you have learned something. However, this is a sign that you need to get them adjusted – or repaired.

I went shopping for cars on one fine day in February of 1976. I found a 1970 Beetle that I liked, but if you just stepped on the brakes ONCE, the pedal was quite a way down. If you then hit the brakes again, they came up to an acceptable level. That is called "pumping up the brakes". I had never run into this before; my other Beetles did not do that. If they were low, they were low, and hitting the pedal twice did not make them get "pumped up". So I did not know what was involved.

It turns out, when I bought the car and got it home, I tightened up the adjustments on the brakes, and the pump-up problem went away. That was the right solution.

But in general, the need to "pump" the brakes means there may be a hydraulic leak, and you should IMMEDIATELY stop and check your brake fluid level. Then keep checking to make sure it is not getting worse, and plan to take it easy until you can get to a repair shop. (Make sure your handbrake or emergency brake is working really well. If it ain't, park it, and get your car towed or carted in to a repair shop.)

3. If you tap your brakes before you hit them, this helps the guy behind you notice that you are serious about slowing or stopping. Your brake lights turn on TWICE, and that reinforces. It is a good idea.

So I like to do this habit – even if it may seem kind of dumb.

Fuzzy Logic for Brakes

A couple years ago, I was studying a technical article* about a train in Sendai, Japan. It was claimed to be a very good, smooth modern train, and it used "Fuzzy Logic"** to do the controlling. I was studying some odd contradictory claims. The train was claimed to be smoother, and faster, and use less energy than a train without Fuzzy Logic. Then I looked at some of the plots of speed.

The authors claimed the train was very smooth on acceleration.*** Yet the controller started out by jamming the controller right into the highest "notch" of acceleration. Now, when you ride on a train or trolley or any smoothly-driven vehicle, you know that the acceleration does not start out instantly at full strength. It starts out rather slowly. But if you are in a car, and the driver NAILS the gas pedal, and you start at maximum acceleration, THAT is called "hot-rodding". That is not called "smooth".

Similarly, this train was rolling along at full speed, and, WHOOMP, the controller put the brakes on hard, and left them on hard, all the way to a stop. What the HELL is going on here?

After a while, I figured out that their claims of "smoother" relied on a definition that "smooth" means the smallest number of changes of acceleration.

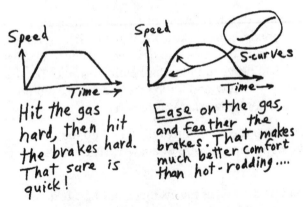

Hit the gas hard, then hit the brakes hard. That sure is quick!

Ease on the gas, and feather the brakes. That makes much better comfort than hot-rodding....

NOW, if you just put the brakes on hard, and leave them on until you stop, they claimed that was only ONE CHANGE. And they claimed that was a good example of "smooth". In fact, this was just an early computerized simulation of how to drive a train "smoothly". When they actually got the train moving, with people, they realized this definition was absurd. So they changed the definition and made the train run smoothly. See the second paragraph below.

---

* *An Automatic Train Controller by S. Yasunobu and S. Miyamoto, in Industrial Applications of Fuzzy Control, Elsevier, Holland, 1985.*

** *What's All This Acceleration Stuff, Anyhow? R. Pease, Electronic Design Analog Applications Issue, Nov. 7, 1994, PP. 63-64.*

*** *If you had a plot of the speed of a smoothly driven car or train, plotted versus time, it would show smooth curves, rather than sharp corners. These are called "S curves", because they look like an "S". If the "S curves" had sharp corners, that would show JERK. The derivative - the rate of change of speed - is the acceleration, and the second derivative - the rate of change of acceleration - is the JERK. If you have ever studied Calculus - and specifically, Differential Calculus, that deals with these "Derivatives", you may appreciate this is one of the most basic applications for derivatives - contrary to what you might have guessed, they are actually useful...*

The day after I learned about this absurd definition of "smooth", I was driving down the street to go shopping. I decided to hit the brakes the way these Japanese had originally defined as "smooth". I hit the brakes once, medium hard, and then kept them on, all the way to a stop. I did not ease up at 5 or 3 mph. Of course, when the car actually stopped, the brakes were still on hard, and the car LURCHED backwards at the instant of stopping. My wife said, "What the heck are you doing??? Why are you driving like a madman?" I explained that I was just driving according to the Japanese definition of "smooth". She said, "Well, cut it out, it's too rough," and of course I agreed.

◆ ◆ ◆

One of the excellent promotional films for the Sendai train showed a Japanese man sitting on a bench, with a goldfish tank full of water and fish resting on his lap. After a few seconds, the film shows that the water g r a d u a l l y surges off to the left. After a number of seconds, the water returns to center. Then after a few more seconds, the water g r a d u a l l y flows over to the right. Then the water slowly returns to center. This film was taken on the Sendai train, with the man sitting on a length-wise bench, to show that it was really smooth. An excellent demonstration.

The smoothness is not related to the way that the Sendai train does not have a good top speed – because it does. Speed never causes the water to surge badly. It is not even the acceleration – because the Sendai train has good acceleration. It is the RATE OF CHANGE of acceleration – the "JERK". That is a technical term: JERK is defined as the RATE of CHANGE of the acceleration – the derivative or d/dt of acceleration. If the rate of change of acceleration is fairly small, then the water won't slosh. If you sit in a car that takes off fast, from a stop, the water would go all over the place. The demo was filmed to show that on the Sendai train, the "JERK" was small – and thus the comfort and smoothness were very good. If the acceleration described as "smooth" in that old 1985 technical paper had ever been applied to the man with the fish-tank, he would have lost 3 fish and soaked his suit!! If anybody actually tried to run a train with that old definition of "smooth", half the train riders in Japan would fall down because of the bad JERK, and the other half would fall down laughing!

◆ ◆ ◆

So you should know how to drive smoothly. And you should probably drive smoothly, most of the time. We'll talk about acceleration later, but we'll talk about braking here.

If you just step firmly on the brakes, and leave them on at that setting until you stop, that may involve only 1 or 2 "changes of acceleration". But this is exactly what is uncomfortable. When you want to slow down, first you should *ease* your foot off the gas, and then *ease* your foot onto the brake, and ease on the pressure until it feels right. This is where judgement is required. Beginning drivers may be good at this, but if they are not, then they have to practice at it, until they get it right.

– In fact, every time you get into a different car – a rental car – a borrowed car – a demonstration car – you have to learn how the brakes feel. But, an experienced driver can almost always figure out what is the right way to use a strange, new braking system. For example, if you are starting out in a rental car, you should figure it out in the first 5 feet – get rolling just a little, and keep checking the brakes, until you know that they feel right.

◆ ◆ ◆

Then, as the car is approaching the place where you want to stop, you plan to *ease off* on the brakes. Lift your foot lightly. This is also known as "feathering" the brakes – the art of decreasing the braking just before you stop. When you are nearly in the right place, and nearly stopped, you should leave on minimum braking. The lurch after you actually stop will be very small. This is one of the marks of a good driver.

Think of driving your elderly Aunt Tillie and two of her old friends on a trip across town. There is a time for jack-rabbit driving – and that ain't it. You want to drive as smoothly as you can, so these people will all remember what a thoughtful driver you are. They sure won't remember you in their will if you jerk them around! This is a good time to be on your best behavior. *Ease* the brakes on, and *taper* them off. Of course, for best comfort, you might decrease the maximum amount of acceleration and braking a little, but at least you want to minimize the *JERK*.

Here are some other occasions when you want to accelerate and decelerate smoothly:

- You are taking a friend to the doctor, and he is hurting. Smooth driving will be appreciated. (Even if you have to hurry, smooth driving is a good idea.)

- When you are taking your driving test.

- When your mother has a big aquarium full of water and fish on her lap, and you are trying to get it home. Boy, she really must trust you!! Can you get her there, and keep the fish wet, and her clothes dry? I hope you do not have far to go. Otherwise you should tape some Saran wrap over the top!!

- When it is rainy – keep it a LITTLE smoother than usual....

- When it is snowy – keep it a LOT smoother than usual.

- When there may be sand or oil or some other substance on the road that may hurt your traction.

- When your brakes are lousy.

- When you are driving a heavy load. (You have no idea how much fun it is to discover that a car with 1200 pounds of bricks on board – or 7 people – needs more room to stop!)

- Of course, there are times when you have to make some speed, save some time. Hot-rodding may be a bad idea when a cop is looking right at you, but it is *not* illegal to start your acceleration sharply, after you have made a legal stop, and sharpen up the "S-curves". It is not illegal to keep the brakes on hard, when you come to a stop. But, judgement is required. You don't want to skid to a stop when the cop is lookin' right at you! Nor burn rubber.

There is one more reason to decelerate gently and "feather" your brakes. If you are coming up to a corner and you plan to decelerate at a constant rate down to a stop, if there is any error in your judgement, you may have to put on your brakes REALLY HARD, to avoid going past the stop sign. If you plan to *ease off* on the deceleration at the end, and "feather" your brakes, then you have a safety margin. If you have put on your brakes a little too late, this safety factor may let you stop without jamming on your brakes hard at the last second.

THIS is one of the hardest things for a new driver to learn. If you took 1000 drivers and told them to roll along at 55, and at the last moment, hit the brakes hard and come to a stop at a STOP line, I bet you would see drivers ALL OVER THE PLACE!!! Most drivers think they are pretty good, AND, most drivers cannot drive as well as they think they can. Some might stop short, some would stop beyond the sign, and some would skid and lose control. It is a really difficult thing, involving a lot of judgement. If you are a beginning driver, and you find that you are not very good at this, don't feel too bad, because it is NOT easy. Practicing will help. Understanding that it is NOT easy, will make you feel better. AND, easing your brakes on early, and planning to ease them off near the end, is the right technique to help you. Even when you are experienced, you'll usually want to drive smoothly, most of the time, with these S-curves. It tends to put less wear and tear on your car. It is one of the marks of a good driver, to not spill those goldfish.

> *I once heard of a flight from Oakland CA to Los Angeles, when one of the passengers got on the plane with a fish-tank half full of water! This was many years ago; that would not be permitted today. Anyhow, he tilted the tank JUST RIGHT during takeoff. The plane did not hit any turbulence, and he was careful (and lucky) during landing – and did not spill any water. And all the passengers cheered and applauded! We'll never see that one again!*

Practice Driving Roughly

NOW, when are the times to NOT brake smoothly? I know a guy who was a very good driver, and he drove VW Beetles for many years. But when it snowed, he did not go out and practice skidding. He said he almost NEVER skidded at all. When the traction was lousy, he never hit the brakes hard! I discussed this with him. I argued with him. I could barely understand this!!

Because I ALWAYS went out on the first snowy day, and practiced some little skids, on acceleration, on curves, and when stopping. I wanted to see how my brakes felt, and my tires, and my traction, and I wanted to know that my reflexes were good to "catch" a skid, and recover almost automatically. Often I would make sure I had a good reason to go shopping, and I would go over to the back corner of the store's parking lot, with no cars around, and practice my skids. I would practice putting on my brakes so I would not quite skid on the snow, and then I would practice putting them on so I skidded a little, and then, put them on hard, so I would skid a LOT. And, I did this on roads, too, but of course, I would do this with virtually no other cars around.

Watch Your Tail!

Many years ago, I knew a guy named Lenny. He had a pretty strong '53 V-8 Ford, and he did used to, well – drive a little *aggressively*. He maybe did go a little *fast* at times. In other words, he had a reputation as a hot-rodder. One winter, he was driving down through town, in the first snow of the season. He came down to a stop sign, and E A S E D on his brakes. As he came to a stop, WHACK, another car came up behind him and hit him. Mr. T., one of the most respected, conservative, mature gentlemen in town was not paying much attention to the fact that you can't JUST tromp on the brakes and STOP, in the snow. So Lenny was driving very conservatively (for a change) – and got whacked in the tail by a "conservative" driver. We all laughed at that. Fortunately, no great harm or damage was done – except to a bruised ego. Poor Mr. T.

Greasy Wet Pavement...

Here in California, we often get no rain for months. Then when it rains, the streets are kind of oily, and they get very slippery. So on the first rainy day, I usually try to go up a freeway ON ramp and feed the gas hard, and practice skidding. This calibrates not only my tires, but the road surface, too. It reminds me that it is rather slippery out there. I use this little skid to remind me that I should not hit my brakes very hard, out on the freeway. If I see that there is a lot of HARD BRAKING going on ahead of me, I had better ease on my brakes, *early*.

But I do NOT come into a freeway EXIT ramp too fast, and hit the BRAKES too hard, and check out my braking traction there. That is a BAD idea. Practicing your skids while braking is much too dangerous, except for the most experienced drivers.

Of course, if you drive so gently as if you were driving your Aunt Tillie, or as if it were snowy – and it is NOT snowy – then you may waste a lot of time, getting from here to there. And perhaps you would make a lot of drivers frustrated, if they cannot pass you. So unless you have a good reason to drive very gently, you'll probably want to pick a moderate rate of "JERK". If you wanted to use ZERO JERK, you could only do that by never starting! So you just want to use your judgement by picking the appropriate amount of JERK. If you are accelerating, you can usually tell if you are accelerating too hard if your engine starts to ROAR. On braking, there's not any such a sign, so you just have to use your judgement. (If your tires start squealing under extreme deceleration, that is usually MUCH too much braking – and a sign you are on the edge of a skid.)

Dragging the Brakes

What else do you need to know about braking? You certainly do not want to drag the brakes. This is also called, "riding the brakes". If you leave your foot on the brakes, while driving, it can overheat the brakes, and fry them. It can waste a lot of gas, and greatly reduce the life of your brakes, too. Yet we do see people who drive along with their foot on their brakes. A bad habit. Of course, when you are driving through a tricky parking lot, or down a hill, you probably *have to* leave your foot on the brakes a lot. Just know that you are doing it on purpose. Or, if your brakes get wet and you lose a lot of braking effort, you may be justified to "ride" your brakes until they dry out and the brakes get better.

Stopping...

You do need to use your brakes, to stop, almost every time (except on a strong upgrade). That's just about a definition of what brakes are good for. Even in Florida or other flat country, where there are hardly any hills, you need brakes for stopping.

You also need some parking brakes, for when you park. Especially on a slope or hill. It may be a hand-brake, or a foot-brake; it may be on the left of you, or on the right. Different makers put them in funny places. (I am not sure why they are permitted to hide the handbrake so as to drive you crazy. If they could standardize a little more, it might make driving safer....) If you try renting a car at night, you can have some very tricky problems finding the handbrake!! And you have to know where to find the hand-brake RELEASE, too. Fortunately, many cars now have a light to remind you that you have not released the parking brakes. (But in the daylight, you may not see it, so a beeper or buzzer is not a bad idea.)

Downhills and Braking

The place where brakes get REALLY interesting is on downhills and downgrades. You really need them! So, let's talk about this.

Yes, you CAN just drive down hills and just step on the brakes, to keep from going too fast. Most cars have good brakes these days. But that is not always the best way to drive.

NOTE: people with manual transmissions gotta read this next section, too. Because it has good basic ideas. And, besides, you will probably be driving a Slushbox sometime, too.

Automatic Transmissions and Downgrades and Steep Hills

Let's first talk about cars with a Slushbox – oh, excuse me, an automatic trans-mission. Most automatic transmissions have sort of a free-wheel in Drive, which means that when you are going down a hill in Drive, you get no engine braking. The engine's drag cannot help you slow down the car. And sometimes the engine's drag is *exactly* what you want.

For a slight downgrade, it is not normally reasonable to shift down. For high-speed highway driving, you will not usually shift down.

– Even on a 5% downgrade, the amount of power generated by letting your car roll downhill, will NOT make you go too fast on a highway. Most cars have tire losses, and wind losses, and other transmission losses, so you do not have to worry about that. If you are on a 10% or 15% downgrade, that begins to get a little different... then you might go too fast. You might need to use your brakes.

You might just *touch* the brakes, to keep from going too fast on a downhill. But if you are on a big, steep hill, you usually want to slow down, and also you probably want to shift down, to a lower gear, to prevent excessive wear on the brakes. Before you shift down, you want to make sure you are not going too fast. Consult your Owner's Manual. If this is hard to remember, put a little dot of tape on your speedometer, to mark the speed where it is reasonable to downshift. For example, it might be *permitted* to down-shift at 55 – but it is *better* to use your brakes to slow down to 45 or maybe even 40 before you shift, to minimize the wear and tear on engine and gearbox.

> – What if you don't have an Owner's Manual? You can figure out a maximum speed for down-shifting, by flooring the gas when accelerating, when you are getting onto a high-speed road. If it roars up past 55 mph, and then shifts to top gear at an indicated speed of 60, then you could probably downshift comfortably at 50.

◆ ◆ ◆

In some cases, you want to downshift before you start down the hill. Other times, you may get part of the way down the hill and then downshift. Hills are different. Drivers are different. Road and Traffic conditions are different. You gotta use your judgement. The general rule is, brakes are cheaper than engines. Use your brakes for slowing down in general, and only use "2nd gear" or "2" for long downgrades. Avoid shifting at high speeds; don't make the engine roar excessively. And if you are going too fast, and you have to use the brakes a lot, slow down with the brakes until you are going slow enough, and *then* shift to the lower gear. Then you can rest your brakes.

Let's say you are working your way down a long steep hill, and even though you shifted down to 2nd, (this is marked as 2 on most automatic transmission shifters) the grade keeps the car going faster than you like, and you have to use the brakes a lot. Basically, you got two choices: USE those brakes, good and hard. Or, slow down to 25 mph and shift into LOW. This can then rest your brakes. Maybe that is a little TOO slow, so after a minute, you might decide to shift back up to "2". Again, this is a matter of judgement, and of driving style. If you know where the steep places are on the hill, that will help you decide. If there's a cop on your tail, all you need to do is drive as if your Aunt Tillie were aboard, and he won't ticket you for being too aggressive. He might pass you. Or he might pull you over because you are driving TOO carefully... too slowly, and perhaps impeding traffic.

Brake Fade

A couple dozen years ago, most cars had LOUSY brakes. The brake drums would get too hot, and the shoes would be too hot, and you would have to step on the pedal harder and harder, and the brakes would work less and less well. This is called *brake fade*. This is bordering on real trouble. These days most cars have disc brakes, at least on the front wheels, and most cars are lighter, and it takes a LOT of work to get your brakes to fade. But you should recognize the signs of *fade*, and be prepared to do something about it. Why am I telling you all these things, about situations that do not happen any more on modern cars? Well, some day you may have the privilege of driving an old car – or a truck. And you would certainly want to know how to do that, gracefully. Further, if you understand the limitations of cars, you won't wear out your new car so fast!

So if you are driving down a long, fast hill in 2nd, and you have been using your brakes a lot, and you notice that you have to push harder and *harder* on the brake pedal, to get the braking you want, then you are detecting a little *fade*. Now, you are probably not in serious trouble, BUT unless you are about at the bottom of the hill, you will want to do something about it. For example, if you are still rolling at 45 or 50, use your brakes pretty hard, once, to slow down to about 25 or 30, and then shift down to LOW. That should rest your brakes a lot, and let them cool off.

Or, if you smell that the brakes are getting pretty hot, shift down to LOW before you have to – and prevent fade before it starts.

> *Note, when I was running down Ward's Ferry Road, back in December of '94, I was really driving fairly hard. Not racing, but pushing hard. Not on a steep hill, but a really shallow downgrade, perhaps 2%. I fed the gas pretty hard, even on downgrades. And when I came to corners, I would just use my brakes hard. There were DOZENS of corners. After a couple miles of this, at the bottom of the hill, I wanted to stop at the bridge, to look at the river. And I noticed my brakes were starting to fade a little.*

> *NOW from that point on, the road was up-hill, so I did not have to baby my brakes, but if I had to do any more downgrade, I would not have used my brakes much; I would have just eased down the grade, in a low gear without any need to use the brakes, and they would have cooled off and recovered from their fading, just fine.*

Note – I am still driving my old 1968 VW Beetle with drum brakes. If I got a new car with disks up front, that would avoid the fade, but the brakes I have are still perfectly adequate for most rational driving. Now, if I had to drive on steep roads like that, very often, I would probably just ask my mechanic to put on metallic or extra-heavy-duty, high-temperature brake shoes. They might cost more, and they might wear the drums more, but if I drove fast on steep hills very often, I would like to have a little more safety factor.

NOW, if you are going fast down a hill, and you find that you STILL need to use your brakes a lot, and you think that you are going to get some more fade, the only safe thing is to stop. Find a good, safe place, and stop. Rest your brakes. Let them cool off. Maybe 2 or 3 minutes is enough. And then start up, really slow, in LOW range. NOTE, a hill that you might roar down at 30, in LOW range, that causes you to really overheat your brakes A LOT, might be really boring at 5 mph. But when you go 6 times slower, the brakes would NOT get too hot. So one solution that WORKS, is to just go a *lot* slower and take it easy on your brakes. Or, stop more often, and rest 'em.

So, all this downhill stuff involves judgement and thinking. If in danger or in doubt, slow down, use a lower gear, and, as a last resort, stop, and think, and let the brakes cool off.

Fade of Disk Brakes

I got some comments from a guy who was driving a Jaguar XJS in England, on a flat road. Every 2 or 3 miles, there would be a "traffic circle" – a rotary – or a "roundabout", as they call it in England. Tom was driving at 115 to 120 mph, along these flat, straight roads. Every time he came to a rotary, he would use the 4-wheel disk brakes HARD, to pull the speed down to 55, so he could merge his way through the rotary.

Surprise, surprise – the brakes got very hot. They got EXTREMELY hot. So when Tom noticed the brakes starting to FADE, he used the disk brakes *HARD* one more time, and then took it easy on the brakes. He cruised a couple miles, at only 100 mph, and then took his foot off the gas early, and slowed down a lot without touching his brakes, and rested his brakes.

UNFORTUNATELY, the brake disks were *cooked*. They were of different thicknesses, at different places, and the nonlinear heating caused distortion of the brake rotors. This caused excessive shuddering, every time the brakes were applied. This was an expensive lesson that cost more than $500 to replace the rotors.

Manual Transmissions and Downgrades and Hills...

NOW, here is the story for cars with a MANUAL transmission, but guys with Slushboxes can read this, too. Most cars can indicate what is a good maximum speed in any gear. Either the car may have a tachometer, or little marks on the speedometer, to indicate where to shift, the maximum speed in any gear. (If they did not put the marks on your speedometer, YOU put 'em there.) If you don't have a good number for downshifting, err on the side of caution. If you can't find the Book, the Owner's Manual for your car, ask the local car sales office, and they can tell you. If you avoid making the engine roar or scream too loud, that's a good rule of thumb.

Just as with a Slushbox, if you are starting to use your brakes a lot, to keep from going too fast, use your brakes to slow down to a safe speed, and then shift down to a lower gear. (Refer also to the Chapter on Manual Transmissions, and the Appendix on Double-Clutching.) (And the Appendix on Heel-and-Toe, too.)

If that gear ain't low enough, use another, lower gear. Mostly, in conditions like this, you'll shift by ear, to make sure you do not abuse the gearbox or the engine. If you are roaring along down a steep hill in 3rd, and the brakes are trying to fade, don't just shift to second, because that could over-rev the engine and cause expensive noises. Rather, hit the brakes hard, slow down a good bit, and THEN shift into second. That should let you rest your brakes.

If you get into first, and the engine is still screaming at full revs, and you have to keep hitting the brakes, then that hill is TOO steep. Slow your speed down to a crawl. The brakes will now be doing almost all the work, but at a very slow speed, they will not get so hot*.

Or stop for a while. As with a Slushbox, you have to use your judgement. If it is a road you have travelled before, you will usually know what you want to do. If you have never been on that road, and you cannot see what is ahead, you want to apply all appropriate caution. SLOW THE HELL DOWN!!

There is one grade that I know that is really steep – Old Priest Grade on California 120, up at the foot of the Sierras. This grade runs between Moccasin and Big Oak Flat, about 150 miles east of San Francisco. It ascends about 1000 feet in 1.4 miles, and it is really hard work. Route 120 bypasses this old grade. That is a much easier grade, but it is also very curvy and slow, so I usually take the old steep grade. I can go up a lot of it in second gear, but some of it I have to go up in first, and a lot of it I go down in first, just to save wear and tear on the brakes. It is still 4 or 5 minutes faster than going up or down the main highway. We do this 2 or 3 times per year, as this is the main route to Yosemite Park and many routes east. So that is one of the steepest grades I drive very often. But, some of the hills in the city of San Francisco are pretty steep, too!

If it gets any steeper than that, I am not concerned about my brakes, but I get cautious about traction. There are still a lot of steep gravel roads in the world, and if I do not know the road, I will stop and walk down the road to see if I can get down safely, and get *through* – or if I could get back up, if I had to. (If it is really steep, I could put on chains. But I don't like to rely on chains to get me INTO trouble; I like to only use chains to get me OUT of trouble.)

Sometimes I hear Tom and Ray Magliozzi explain that downshifting is a bad idea, because wearing out your engine is more expensive than wearing out your brakes. Well, that is all a matter of opinion – and judgement. Obviously, I am not going to drive down Jones Street (a 25% downgrade) in San Francisco in 4th. I usually go down at about 25 mph in second, but it is only as steep as 25% for a couple hundred feet. If I had to go down a mile as steep as this, I'd surely shift into first.

Y'see, if I get going down a hill that is just right – let's say I can go down a hill at 45 mph in 3rd, without using my brakes, but with the engine revving briskly at 3400 rpm. If I tried to go down this hill in fourth, I would have to use my brakes a LOT. Dumb. If I tried to go at 30 in 3rd, it would mean a little less wear on the engine, but a lot more wear on the brakes, and it would take me a LONG time to get down the hill. If I tried to go down at 18 mph in 2nd, it would be less wear on the brakes, because the engine is not revving fast – but that would take a really long time. So if the road isn't too curvy, I use my judgement and scurry down the hill, with the engine revving cheerfully. (That way, the air drag will help slow me, too! Especially at 55 or 60 in 4th....) My car will run nearly forever at 45 in 3rd gear, uphill or down, so the amount of wear caused by providing the engine braking is not a big deal.

*Physics explains: Power = Force x Speed. If the brakes are providing all the stopping FORCE, but the speed is small, then the power will be small, and the brakes should not get very hot at all.

So, I like to downshift a lot for downhills, and I even downshift to 3rd for most stops. I don't usually downshift to 2nd for a stop sign, but I may downshift to 2nd when I am coming to a light that is turning green, if I know I will need to accelerate in 2nd. And I try to downshift before I have built up too much speed, on downgrades, so the engine does not have to rev excessively. Slowing down before you start down a steep hill, and downshifting at slow revs, will NOT wear out your car or engine or transmission. That is a lot better than shifting at too high revs. The Magliozzis can say anything they want, but downshifting like that, at slow rpms, at the right time and place, is BETTER for your car and your pocketbook, than not. I agree that downshifting that causes high revs is NOT a good or economical idea.

Now, when I mentioned that Mr. T. whacked Lenny's Ford in the tail, I did mention that it was snowy, and there was a stop sign. I neglected to mention that this stop sign was at the foot of a downgrade. Maybe Mr. T. would not have whacked him, if the downgrade had not compounded the problem of braking.

> Anyhow, if you are coming down a downgrade with snow, you have to go a *lot* slower than normal, and use your brakes as gently as possible, most of the time. (You might touch them hard, momentarily, to see if you have any traction to spare. Do this at a place where a little skid won't cause an accident.) Now, mostly a beginning driver should not be storming down a steep hill with snow on the road. But, hey, everybody's gotta start sometime! Still, until you are sure you are safe, take it *really easy*. OK?

Now that we have gotten down that steep hill, safely, what else do we have to know about brakes? Ah – we gotta be ready to do a

Panic Stop.

Sometimes you have to stop really fast. Sometimes you do this to avoid hitting something. Sometimes you do this to minimize the speed that you are going when you do hit something. This may be expensive, but it is better than hitting *hard* and getting really hurt.

Sometimes, to stop fast, you just stomp on those brakes. You might do a lot worse. If you are at high speed, you might PUMP the brakes, stepping on the pedal hard for a couple seconds, and then off for a second, momentarily, which gives your brakes a chance to cool off momentarily. Modern disc brakes usually do not need that. But the real problem in a panic stop, is that one wheel may lock, or one may not brake properly, and your car may swerve, skid, or spin. If that happens, and you veer off in a bad direction, or if you just cannot steer, then you may get into a different kind of accident, that might be worse than the others. So in a panic stop, it is a good idea to be very careful. Being careful in a panic stop, when you do not have much time to think, is an oxymoron, and it is improbably hard to do. So, let's see what the angles are.

Somewhere else in this book, in the Chapter on Reflex Response, I will explain that if something jumps out in front of me, maybe a panic stop is not the best solution. Let's say a child jumps out from behind a car, right in front of me, about 100 feet in front of me!!! Let's say I am only doing 40 mph, but there is not space enough to stop. I can get on the brakes, but the 0.6-second delay before I get my foot on the brakes means I do not have time enough to stop.

– If the oncoming lane is clear, I will surely dodge into that lane.

That is MUCH better than trying to stop. (Well, maybe not if the kid keeps running to that lane!)

– Or, I might brake as much as I can, and at the last minute, steer into that parked car and hit that. There is some chance I can do that and not hit the kid. If there is traffic oncoming, nearby, and I cannot expect it to stop, then that is my best bet.

– OR if there is a chance the kid will run back behind the car, then maybe I should prepare to go on straight. But you don't want to count on that happening.

– OR, if you can just about stop, and you would hit the kid at only 1 or 2 mph, then that might be the least painful possibility. But that is nearly impossible to judge.

– Meanwhile, if you can get your thumb on the horn, blow the horn and leave it blowing, if it does not interfere with your primary task.

– On the other hand, if a DOG wanders out in front of me, I will try to dodge – but at a lower level of priority. If I can dodge to a clear lane, fine. But if it comes to wrecking a car compared to hitting the dog, I'm sorry, but the dog is going to be the loser. I will hit the brakes – but I really am not going to choose to wreck my car.

There are all sorts of reasons for a panic stop. Dogs or people or other animals jump out in front of you. You come around a corner and there is an obstruction. The road is washed out. A car from the other lane comes over at you.

In each case, well, you put a little wear on your brakes, and perhaps a LOT of wear on your tires. If your brakes are really GOOD, you can ruin an $800 set of tires, by locking them up at 65 mph. But that may be less painful than hitting that object in the road. (In a couple more paragraphs we will come to the Anti-Lock stuff.)

There is one other problem with a hard stop or a panic stop. If you hit the brakes *HARD*, you may find the guy behind you draped all over your rear bumper. He may have gotten absent-minded or sleepy. He may have been too close behind you. He may have lousy brakes – heck, probably 2% of the cars on the road have lousy brakes, or lousy tires. Just because YOU know that YOU can stop, does not mean that you do not have a problem.

Whatever the reason, if the guy behind can't slow down as well as you do – BAM. NOW, technically, the guy who was following too close behind you, and did not put on his brakes well enough, is to blame if he hits you. It is, technically, his fault, according to the rules in every state. But, if you don't WANT a lot of hassle, try to avoid hitting the brakes really hard, if you have any choice. If you are heading into a difficult problem, and the guy behind you is *riding* your tail too close, pull over and let him pass. It's better to do that, than have the guy *whack* you in the rear. If the guy behind you wants to crash into the guy ahead of you, pull over and *let him do it.*

– ABS...

For several years, the Anti-Lock Braking System (abbreviated as ABS) has been recommended as a safety feature, to keep you out of certain classes of accidents. You can just step on your brakes HARD, and you should not skid. In many cases, you can stop faster. Therefore, everybody should buy the ABS for a mere $1000. And we will all be safer, and we will save money due to fewer accidents. Right? Well, not necessarily.

Recent studies have indicated that cars with ABS do *not* have fewer expensive, damaging collisions than cars without. I am still trying to get more data on this, but I suspect that people with ABS are driving more aggressively, and they are more pushy, and despite having better brakes, they still get into accidents. Personally, I find it a little hard to believe that all cars with ABS, the Fords and Chryslers and GMC cars, too, and the VWs and the Mercedes and Volvos are ALL having the same amount of collisions. Maybe one of those systems is better? But, we shall see.

One of the things that can easily happen when you hit the brakes hard is a skid. Most of the debate on skidding, and how to deal with it, will be covered in the Chapter on Skidding. But I can mention here, that any time you hit your brakes hard, you can get a skid. Even a teaspoon of sand, or a half-teaspoon of oil, can cause a first-class skid, if you hit it just wrong. A tiny bit of glare ice or snow can get you started, too. Even if you hit your brakes just right, and the road is not sandy or slippery, but there is a little bump on the road, your tire can start hopping after it hits that, and the skid can turn into a spin. This may lead to a first-class accident – or a first-class scare. So, just be aware that with hard braking, you can get into some very interesting skids. Which we will study later.

NOW, not all cars' brakes work or feel exactly the same. If you get out of one car, and into another, and the brakes feel weird, that does not necessarily mean they are bad – but it might. Get some knowledgeable person to check if they seem reasonable. If I were driving a friend's Mercedes, I might need to get the opinion of a knowledgeable Mercedes driver, to see if those brakes feel right for a Mercedes. Conversely, I know when a VW's brakes feel right. After 1,000,000 miles, I damn' well ought to.

Braking for Pickups

Here is a related story, and I'll include it here: I was driving down Route 280 at 9 A.M., headed into town for a meeting. There were 4 lanes rolling down the hill, and everybody was doing about 60 mph. Suddenly I saw a whole lot of brake lights about 100 yards in front of me, and smoke, and dust. A lot of people were on their brakes, really hard. Suddenly out of this big collection of cars, a pickup truck emerged – just like a watermelon seed, it squirted out – right across the lanes, off to the right. It rolled, majestically, BACKWARDS, at about 10 mph, across 3 lanes and over into the ivy, and stopped – unharmed. By this time, everybody had slowed down a lot, and I slowed down a lot, and

I pulled over to the right to see if there was anything I could do to help. But then everybody began speeding up again. Apparently, everybody avoided hitting everybody else. And the guy in the pickup truck just sat there. He must have been in shock. I looked at him, and he looked like he did not need any help (except, perhaps, a clean pair of pants) so I just eased along and kept on going.

The point is, when a pickup truck starts to brake really hard, you just cannot be sure the rear end will not swap around and skid and spin. Pickup trucks with no load in the back are really pretty scary that way. So if you have a pickup, either put a couple hundred pounds of sand in the back, or take it easy. You must KNOW that it can't stop hard, not at all. I am told that even ABS on the rear wheels of pickup trucks does not necessarily prevent skidding like this – though it might help in some cases.

Refer also to the Chapter on Engines, to learn how to stop in an emergency such as, when your gas pedal sticks. That is a little different.

But, what if you want to stop, or slow down – and your brakes do not work???

PANIC???????

No, not panic, but concern. If you step on your brakes, and the brakes do not work, that would normally lead to panic. But, a MAJOR function of this book is to get you pre-educated so that this is NOT a matter for panic. We want to save you from EXACTLY that panic.

IN this case – If you step on the brakes, what if there is NOT as much braking force as you want?? That could be FADE, if the brakes are too hot. This does not usually happen instantly, with no warning. So, even if the brakes do not work well, you can STILL usually slow down and stop. If you have been driving too fast, you can shift down to a lower gear, as described above. If the brakes are working at all, use them. After all, we do not usually buy a car with 1-wheel brakes. If a brake cylinder starts leaking, and SPRAYS brake fluid all over the brake shoes, (which ruins their ability to provide much stopping force), that does not ruin the other 3 wheels and their brakes. Not right away. So, brakes do not usually fail, disastrously, completely – not with no warning.

NOW – let's say – you step on the brakes – and the pedal goes to the floor. Kinda serious! Yes. But not yet a disaster.

What To Do? Feet, Hands, and Head...

First thing: hit the brakes AGAIN, fast. Pump them up. Sometimes that works. That gives your foot something to do.

Meanwhile, let's give your HEAD something to do. Start thinking – where are you? Are you headed into a dangerous intersection?? Or are you headed into a flat area, where you do not really need your brakes? You start PLANNING. Fast.

Then give your hands something to do. The next thing to do, that is sure to help, is to put on the hand-brakes. That can help you a lot. If they are as good as you think they are, you should be able to stop pretty well. I mean, even TODAY, I wanted to slow down, so I put on my handbrakes, rather than my foot-brakes. They slowed me down about as well as I expected. Damn' well they had better....

The other thing you can do, is get ready to down-shift. If you are rolling at 70 mph, that may not be a good time to downshift. But if you are heading for a solid wall, maybe downshifting could save your life, so, if you think you should do it, then, go ahead and do it. If it wrecks your engine, or your gearbox, well, I am warning you to make a decision in advance. I mean, if you hit a parked car, or a wall, at 30 mph, you are likely to be hurt a little, (presuming you *do* have your seat belt on), but you are not likely to die. So you have to plan what to do. If you think that jamming your gearbox into 2nd at 70 mph will help you get down to 30, even if you wreck your engine – if that will save your life – then – go ahead and do it. Got the picture?? I am suggesting that if you plan ahead, what if something really scary happens – if you pre-plan – then you may be able to pick the right action. (Note, I cannot recommend that you check this out in advance, but some automatic transmissions, if you try to down-shift at a high speed, will NOT shift. They are trying to protect you from expensive repairs. Normally that makes good sense, but if you NEED that downshift to save your life, and if it REFUSES to shift, well, I have warned you it might fail to shift....)

NOW, of course, this is a bit silly. 99% of you readers will never have any brake failure, in *your* million miles of driving, because brakes are really pretty reliable these days. So, I am only trying to save the life of YOU, the unlucky 1% guy. Okay, all you other guys can stop reading this, right? If you know that you are a guy who is going to NEVER have a brake failure, YOU do not have to keep reading. But if you think that you would rather be protected against that remote possibility, keep reading. YOU are the guy I want to protect. (Actually, I am not trying to JUST save your life once. I am trying to get you to THINK.)

Now, in addition to PUMPING your brakes, and hauling on the hand-brake, there are a few other things you can do, to slow down.

You can turn off the ignition key. This is slightly illegal and bad for the environment, as it will pump raw gas into your catalytic converter. But if it saves your neck – and can prevent any crash at all – then it is probably OK. Now, you have to be VERY careful of two things:

– 1. If you have downshifted from 4th to 3rd, and if you may later wish to shift down to second – if the key is off, you may have trouble shifting down. I am not an expert on this, but I bet you can still horse the gearbox into a lower gear. We are NOT talking about a way to help your transmission last forever. We are talking about how to save your life. Of course, if you are heading for a red traffic light at 50 mph, but it is all up-hill, and you know the car will slow down even without brakes, then you can, luckily, ignore this section, if you know you are slowing down OK, EVEN if your brakes have failed. Got the picture? IN other words, even in a desperate situation, you may have no problem. When the car comes to a stop on an upgrade, with no brakes, and no problem, then you can walk into town, and call the local garage to tow it in... then you were smart – and lucky. But, if you are on a downgrade, then the rules are all different. You slow yourself down as well as you can. And,

- 2. Make sure not to turn the key too far, as that would lock up the steering. Turn the key just far enough to leave the ignition off. You can check that any time you turn off the ignition.

SCRUB OFF Speed...

Next step: If all the tricks listed above here are not working, get your fenders against a guard-rail, if there is one. GRIND your car's metal into energy-expending modes. Now, some cars are very pretty, BUT that same sheet-metal that makes it look nice, can be TRADED – SACRIFICED – to save your ankles. Don't *slam* that guard rail, but ease onto it, so as to grind off speed.

If there is not any guard rail, you may decide to ease into rocks or trees or shrubs.

One time I was driving along US 101, down in Sunnyvale. There was a sudden slow-down of traffic, and the guy ahead of me slammed on his brakes and slowed to about 4 mph. Then his car kept rolling. As I watched, it ROLLED and ROLLED, over to the left of the high-speed lane. It rolled into the bushes – the huge long thicket of rose-bushes. I think what happened was, the guy hit his brakes so hard, he fell off his seat and fell on the car's floor. Because, as the car rolled at about 3 mph into the rose bushes, he did not make any attempt to hit his brakes. Anyhow, not a big deal. When the big car CRASHED into the rose bushes at 3 mph, it slowed down very gradually, and nobody was hurt.

Years later, I confirmed that those rose bushes have been all removed. So, it is unfortunate that you cannot slow down along that stretch of road, by driving into the rose-bushes, because they are relatively forgiving. You may have to scrub against a guard-rail. Or, against a rock. If there is a smooth rock wall, you ease against it. But, if your rocks are the way mine are, you may have to hit a sharp edge. You may have to choose to wreck your car SOONER (at 34 mph) rather than later (at 49 mph). So, this is an area where, if you have lost your brakes, you have to use your judgement, to guess how to stage one EARLY accident, to avoid a later accident that could be a lot worse. It's all your move. But, if you think about it early, you have a better chance to avoid that late pain.

Let's say – at 20 mph you discover, on a steep downgrade, that your brakes have suddenly faded badly. If you STUFF the gearbox into LOW GEAR, quick, you may not wreck your engine, and in first you may be able to stop. If you try to let it roll in second, you may also survive – or then – how can you predict if you can get through the next curves?? But, brakes do not fail often, and they do not fail with no warning. That's the good news. If your brakes are fading a *little* now, you should start to baby them, to make sure they do *not* get a lot worse, in a minute or two. OK?

Time to Fix...

How do you know your brakes need work or repair?

- If they do not feel right... do not feel like they used to.

- If they are spongy, or if you have to hit the pedal 2 or 3 times to get the pedal off the floor. (Stop and check the reservoir right away, to see if it needs more brake fluid. That is usually a plastic bottle up in the engine compartment, somewhere above the driver's ankles...)

- If the brakes PULL to one side.

- If they make a lot of noise. (Note, modern cars are arranged so the brakes make a loud vibration or squeal when the pads need to be replaced.)

- If they don't work very well – if they do not slow you down properly.

- If the pedal is too close to the floor.

- If the hand-brake travels TOO FAR, before it works.

- If your handbrake will not HOLD the car on a hill, without extreme force on the hand-lever. (Or, will not HOLD at all).

- If the little red BRAKE WARNING light comes on.

- If you have to keep adding brake fluid, or if you find any drips or puddles of brake fluid around a wheel or under a wheel.

If your car has capability for mechanical adjustments, as mine does, you might adjust to take up the slack. Other than that, I recommend that you get a qualified repairman to fix your brakes, PRONTO. Myself, I like to adjust my brakes so the brake pedal is moderately low. Then I can easily do my heel-and-toe work. (Refer to the Appendix on Heel-and-Toe.)

OK, I have told you just about everything I know about brakes and braking.

Chapter 2. STOPPING – and PARKING

···

One time I went to a show – a convention – at the Cow Palace. This big old hall, which most people think of as being in San Francisco, is actually in Daly City, just across the city line from S.F. One of the Sales Representatives of our company had a car, and he loaned it to a friend, who then came back and returned the keys to the Rep. All very fine. When the show was over, at 9 PM, the Rep realized – he had the keys – but the guy who borrowed the car had forgotten to tell us where he parked the car. If you have ever visited the Cow Palace, you know it has parking for several thousand cars. You would KNOW it is much too big a place to ever find a car, without information on where it was left.

So the Rep and I went over to a lounge area and had a beer, and we sat and thought. Finally we saw a guy we knew. We bought *him* a beer, too. We explained our predicament. And this other guy agreed to drive us around the parking lots until we found our car. We went out, and since many people had left, there were not so many cars left. We found the car in about 20 minutes. But we never made that mistake again.

When you are stopping, you might just turn off the key and walk away. Depending on where you are, it may not be important to lock the car, or turn on the alarm, or even remember any particular details about where you parked it. Fine. But in some cases, all these little factors may be important.

We started out with a Chapter on using the brakes. That's pretty dumb. Next, we follow it with a Chapter on Stopping and Parking. That sounds pretty dumb, too. But, not really. Because as soon as you get started, you know you will have to plan a place to stop. After all, would you want to take off in an airplane, if you did not know how to land? So, before we get started, we have to know how we will stop.

First Things First

First, you have to find a parking place. This may be no problem, if you are in your own back yard. But it may be a significant problem in a city. You may have to pass over a place that is legal, if it is in a scary neighborhood in a city, to find a safe place. You may have to skip places if they are too short, or too steep. I'll let you keep track of these details.

Sometimes you have to try to find a good parking place, with special features. Maybe you need shade, so your dog won't get too hot. Maybe you need to find a place at the top of a hill, if you are not sure the starter will work. Maybe your parking brakes are poor, so you want a flat parking place, or a good curb to put your wheels against. That may take you more time, to find a place that suits you.

27

Other times, you may pick a place where the snowplows will not throw a lot of snow on your car. Every part of the country has little problems that may affect how *you* drive and where you *park*, that other drivers do not have to worry about.

Parking

After you have found a parking place, ease on your brakes, and slowly get your car centered in the parking place. Let's presume you can just pull into this parking place. (Parallel parking will be mentioned at the end of this Chapter.) Make sure you are close enough to a curb, not too far out. In some cities, you must park with both wheels no more than 6 inches from the curb, but in San Francisco, the spacing allowed is 18 inches! Make sure you are not too close to the sides or ends of the parking place, to avoid getting up too close and inconveniencing another car – or yourself.

Turn Off the Key

If you have just come off a high-speed road, your Owner's Manual may warn you to not just stop and turn off the key. If you have a car with a turbocharger, the manual will tell you to let it idle or run at slow speed, for about a minute, so the turbocharger can slow down and cool off. My 1985 VW bus also tells me that for best results (i.e. best reliability), let the engine cool off for a minute, by idling or with low-speed driving, before you turn off the key, after high-speed driving. So things ain't as easy or simple as they used to be.

For the same reason, when I come off the 65 mph freeway to a traffic light, I do not turn off my Beetle's engine until after I have driven a mile, or waited a minute or two. I figure letting the engine idle for a minute is a cheap investment, compared to turning the engine off when it is quite hot. When I get a mile down the street, and the engine has cooled down, turning off the engine at a red light is fine.

A lot of people used to *gun* the engine – tap the gas pedal – just before they turned off the key. I think that is because in *OLD* cars, back in the 1930s, the carburetor would leak and run dry, and the car would start better if you *gunned* the engine as you shut off the key. Sometimes my father used to do that in his old 1936 Ford pickup. These days, there is no need to do that. It wastes only a tiny bit of gas – but does not do any good. Fuel injection does not need that.

I mentioned in the Appendix on Economy that there is a sign for "Scottish Rite Parking", down by the local Masonic temple. Well, I turn off my key about 100 yards up the street, and roll down the hill, and roll right into my favorite parking place. If that isn't a frugal rite, I don't know what is.

Set the Brakes

In general, put your manual transmission in first gear, or put your automatic in PARK, set your front wheel against the curb, and put on the handbrakes. But if it is cold and wet, it is sometimes a bad idea to set the handbrakes, because the brake cables may freeze before morning. So you may prefer to set your wheels against a curb or a rock, instead of setting the handbrake. Pick a place that is safe. If you are just in a big broad parking lot, you may be able to pick a parking slot that is transverse with the hill, so you are not just pointed downhill. You may be able to turn your wheels so that rolling either forwards or backwards would be uphill. Then you probably do not need to feel bad, if you do not set your handbrake.

Take the Keys

It is important to take the keys with you. Even if you are just walking over to pay for some gas, there are stories about car thieves sneaking up and stealing cars. If you don't take the keys, you may not only lose the car, but you could be sued for leaving an "attractive nuisance". So, it is important to take the keys with you. Because the thief that steals your car is MUCH more likely to have an accident in one day, than you are in a year. The best way to avoid that accident is, take the keys with you.

I have a spare key which I keep in my wallet. I only use it every couple months. It has been many years since I had to break into my own car, using a coat-hanger. Other people have a spare key that is hidden around the car. Either way, it is a good idea to keep a spare key, in case you lock your keys in your car.

Lock it Up.

In many cases, it is important to lock the car, depending on where you are, and depending on what is in the car. In other cases, it is foolish to leave anything in your car, because that is just a temptation for thieves. And in other cases, nobody ever cares what you leave in your car, and it is safe. Unfortunately, there are not so many places where this is true, as there used to be.

In fact, I have heard of places in Hawaii where hikers are warned to take everything out of their car and leave it unlocked, to avoid car thieves that break in. That doesn't sound like a nice place to me.

Set the Alarm

Some people have car alarms. You may want to set yours. For a long time, I didn't even have an alarm on my house or car. But the guy next door had his house broken into, one day, when he forgot to set his alarm. And he was a Burglar Alarm Salesman! So I built up one. One for my car, too. If you lock your doors to keep thieves out of your car, you may also prevent a mugger from hiding in your car, waiting for your return.

Parking Lots and Garages

There are lots of place such as parking lots for malls, where the areas are HUGE. As I mentioned at the top of this chapter, it can be disastrous if you do not keep a good mental note of where you left the car. In some cases, you should write down on a slip of paper that you carry with you, a note on what row or parking space or what floor of the garage your car is at. If you are a good navigator, a mental note may suffice.

Another problem in broad parking areas arises because a small number of people cruise across lots at high speeds – and even cut across at an angle. Be very careful to watch out for cars driving at strange angles across the lot. Don't assume that all other drivers are driving rationally or in the marked lanes. I know a woman who pulled into a Motor Vehicle Department parking lot. She was hit by a woman who worked for the DMV, and made an illegal turn – and who did not have any insurance! Hey, you can't hardly be too careful, these days!

Backing into Parking Spaces

As I will explain in the Chapter on Starting, I like to *back* into a parking place, to make it easier to start out. Even if they post a sign instructing you to not back in, I prefer to back in. It makes it much easier to get out. If you have a driveway that fronts onto a busy street, you may find it MUCH safer to stop along the street and, when there is a good break in traffic, *back* into your driveway. Then when you want to leave, you can just drive ahead, with good visibility. If you pull in and try to back out, that's often a *lot* harder – and more dangerous.

Every once in a while, I see a parking lot with little signs: "Do not back into parking spaces". I usually ignore that. Backing in is safer for me, as I do not then have to back out. I don't really know why they tell you not to back in. One person said he thought it was because some people are not good at backing in. Another guy said maybe it was because if a person backs in, and then lets the car idle for a long time, his exhaust pipe may leave a black mark on the wall, which looks ugly. Either way, I am not impressed. But the next time I see those signs, I will inquire. But, if the insurance company required them to put up those stupid signs, to protect them from drivers who are no good at backing *in*, what do they expect to have for problems when those people are having trouble backing *OUT*?

Parallel Parking

This is something you have to learn from your teacher. I'm not going to draw any sketches, or tell you what you should do. Every car is different, every driver is different, and many parking spaces are a lot different. I'll just try to give a little advice to keep you out of accidents:

- Are you parking on a hill? That's a problem.

- Do you have a passenger who can climb out and show you (by holding his hands at the right distance) how far you can back up? If not, that's a problem.

- Is the parking spot pretty short? That's a problem.

- Do you have a manual transmission? That's a problem.

If you have more than one "problem", you should probably park somewhere else, to avoid bumping into a car. Anything over two problems is hard even for experts!

Chapter 3. VISION and VISIBILITY

···

I have a VISION – a wonderful VISION – I just close my eyes and see that driving this beautiful car is such an ineffable pleasure....

NO, that is not the kind of "Vision" or dream I am talking about. We get too much of that crap, these days. No, I am talking about, can you see where you are going? And, what's coming at you. If you can't see, you can't drive safely.

Most of us get to see through a windshield. If it's not very dirty on the outside, and not very dirty on the inside, that gives us a chance to see what we need to see. But there are other details that can be important.

- Windex*, Windshield wiper fluid.
- Wipers with good blades.
- Good eyeglasses, spare glasses.
- Glare and sunglasses.
- Cracks or pits on your windshield.
- Scrapers vs. snow or frost.
- Mirrors: not too high, too low, nor too shaky.
- Rain, Snow, Sleet.
- Snow over car – remove it before you move.
- Defroster, ventilators.
- 500-watt defroster, with interlock.
- Peripheral Vision.
- Fog and smoke, dust and white-out.
- Swing your head, vs. blind spot.
- Night driving, night vision.

Windex, Windshield Washer Solution, and other Glass Cleaners

If your windshield is grubby, and you get any glare at all, sometimes your ability to see is just RUINED. But if you have some paper towels, and some kind of glass cleaner, you can get the windshield clean – for a while. My wife always keeps a bottle of Windex in her car, and some paper towels, and that works pretty well. You can minimize glare and smear on the inside. And in many cases, windshield-washer fluid is quite adequate for washing off the outside.

◆ ◆ ◆

But I recall a few times when the temperature was about 10 degrees, and the solution of alcohol, soap, and water in the windshield-washer bottle would not thaw out. Yet the sun on the pavement caused the snow to melt, and the cars ahead of us kicked up a lot of salty, icy spray – right on our windshield. It was getting white and smeary, real fast. NOTE: a strong solution of salt and ice can stay wet down to about 0 degrees F, and most of us do not keep a strong-enough alcohol mixture in our

Windex is a Registered Trademark of S.C. Johnson & Son Inc.

windshield-washer tank, to keep it working at zero degrees F. Fortunately, we kept our Windex in a warm place in the heated car, and were able to reach out and spray it on the windshield. That helped a lot.

> When you are washing or cleaning your windshield, be *sure* to clean the wiper blades, too. Very important.

I did mention this in the paragraph on snow, about 4 pages further along, but this is a good place to mention it, too: you have to make sure your windshield defogger is working well, too. Even without snow, a rainy day or even a dry cold day can cause a lot of condensation on the inside of your windshield and other windows. Paper towels or clean cloths can help clear it off. But the defogger (de-mister, in England) is the only way to *keep it off.* Opening up your vent window can help a little, though.

Wiper Blades

The other thing you have to have is good wiper blades. I usually buy one wiper blade at a time, and put the new one on the driver's side, and put the older one onto the passenger's side, just before that one falls apart. Most of the driving I do in my Beetle is just commuter driving, with no passenger, so if the RH side is not wiping perfectly clean, that does not do any great harm. But for our Bus, I usually buy 2 new blades.

Here in California, we get very little rain in the summer. So I usually leave the ratty old blades on, all summer, until the fall. Then I buy a new wiper blade, or two, for each car – whether they need it or not. That way, I will have new blades for the rainy season – blades that have not been sitting around on the car and drying out all summer.

> And, as I just said, every time you clean your windshield, be sure to clean the wiper blades, too. Very important!! Similarly, in case of any snow or ice, when you are scraping off the windshield, make sure your blades are not frozen to the windshield, because you may blow fuses or wreck the linkage, or burn out the motor. If you forget, and turn on the wipers, and the motor stalls, sometimes you can shut off power to the wiper motor, by turning off the ignition key, fast. Or, if that does not work, run outside and pull the blades off the windshield, to keep the motor from being stalled.

◆ ◆ ◆

> It is important to be able to grab your windshield wiper control very quickly, when you need it. For example, if you are driving along, and you suddenly hit a big puddle, can you grab the wiper controls and turn them on instantly, in less than 1 second? Can you do it at night? Can you do it in your rental car? Because if you are in a tricky place, and you suddenly get a big splash of water on your windshield, you do NOT want to be driving blind, waiting until the water drains off by itself.

◆ ◆ ◆

I want to mention one gripe, about recent General Motors cars. As I said, when I see I am going to hit a big puddle, I want to have my wipers start *instantly*. But when you hit the switch on a GMC car, in the 1993-1995 era, there is a small delay before the wipers start to sweep. This may be only 1/2 or 3/4 second, but it is unnerving when you really want the wipers on *FAST*, yet you begin to doubt if they are going to start. In 1/2 second, you begin to wonder – did I hit the right switch?! I do NOT like this delayed CRAP, and I guess I will have to remind General Motors Corp. that they should not lightly put mindless computerized delays into important functions.

Eyeglasses

The other thing YOU may need is to keep your eyeglasses, if any, up to date. If your eyes change, and you cannot read road signs until you get close – you may need to get your eyes checked and get new glasses. The good thing about that is, you get a new set of spare glasses. Sometimes I keep my spare glasses in my car, and other times I keep them in my briefcase. Either way, when I want to go for a ride, they are not far away. If I misplace my glasses (as I do occasionally), I just grab the spares.

Now, if I misplace the spares, *too,* I have a problem. Legally, my vision is *just* bad enough, that I cannot drive without glasses. But actually, on roads where I know all the signs, and all the lights, and all the traffic patterns, I can drive fairly safely, if I just go along the normal route to get home. If I wanted to take a new route, I would not be very safe. Fortunately, I do not have to do that. And I do not have to drive without glasses, more than once a year.

◆ ◆ ◆

One time I fell while skiing and lost one lens from my glasses. I tried driving with one lens missing, but with both eyes open. That was *awful.* I found that closing one eye and just looking through one lens was better. One friend says he has driven with one lens for distant vision, and one for up-close vision. He got used to it, and liked it. But I don't think I would ever like that.

◆ ◆ ◆

I read that in Sweden, if you are required to wear glasses for driving, you are also required to keep a spare pair in your car. That sounds a bit awkward if you have 2 or 3 cars....

Glare and Sunglasses

I have a simplifying factor: I do not often have to drive in snow. But when I do, that can be really tough, even with sunglasses. Right now, if you asked me where are my nearest sunglasses, I'd have a hard time finding them. Maybe I'd just go down and buy another pair of clip-ons.

Other times, when the sun is just wrong, the glare off the road can be very fierce – especially when it is wet. Sometimes you just have to hold up your hand to shade your eyes from that glare – which may be from above – and may be from the ground or the road, below. In other words, the sun-visor may help a little – but not a lot. Your hand may work best.

Now, just in case you are wearing some fancy, expensive sunglasses, because they make *you* look good, let me remind you that Polaroid™* sunglasses are really much better for glare than any other sunglasses I know. If you have to drive in glare situations, be sure to keep at least one pair of Polaroid sunglasses in the car.

> Sometimes, *you* do not see any glare, but if you think about it, you can realize that cars travelling in another direction can get a lot of glare. I was conversing with a bus driver about safe driving. When it was his turn to start up at a green light, he started out *EXTREMELY* slowly. Sure enough, a car on his left was getting so much glare, he ran right through a red light, until he saw the bus. Then he promptly stopped and backed up, allowing us to proceed. If you are travelling with the sun at your back, wet or dry, you can assume that oncoming traffic may have trouble seeing the entire picture, and you should cut them some slack – give them some extra room in case they goof because of poor visibility.

Sun Visors

Recently I noticed that a lot of people have sun visors that are flopping down. Then the little plastic clips that hold up my sun visors broke, and *my* visors began flopping down. I replaced the stupid plastic with coat-hanger wire, and that should last forever. No problems.

> Make sure you know how to use your visor over on the left of your head, too. Sometimes when you go past a row of trees, the sun and shadows shining on your head can be *really* distracting, and the visor can protect you from getting an epileptic fit! One of my friends suggests, try wearing a baseball cap with the visor set sideways. Neat idea – I bet that would work.

Mirrors

Almost constantly, unless you are on an empty road, you have to keep checking the view of traffic behind you in your mirrors. Usually, you'll use your left mirror, outside the car, and your rear-view mirror at the top of the dashboard. (And also, if you ever carry huge loads, or tow a trailer, you'll need a third mirror on the right-hand side of the car.) The art of using a mirror will be treated in the next few paragraphs. But, if the mirrors are old, or faded, or dingy, or vibrating, or drooping down, you cannot properly see things in the mirror. You should first plan to get the mirror fixed or replaced.

Then, you have to learn how to aim the mirror, and what to look for. This is part of your early education in learning to drive. I'll let your primary teacher show you what to do, but I'll list a few of the general rules:

- The left mirror should show a little bit of your rear flank of your car. It should then show any car that is behind your rear wheel – at least a

---

* Polaroid is a Registered Trade Mark of the Polaroid Company, Cambridge MA.

part of it. You can start adjusting your mirror while parked, but you usually have to get it just right when rolling on a straight road.

- The inside mirror should generally show all of your rear window. You want to see as much of your right rear corner as possible.

- The right-hand mirror will normally be adjusted by a passenger. If you don't have a passenger, you will have to walk around the car a lot, or clamber across the front seat, to get it just right. (Inside adjustments and/or power mirrors are now available, on some cars.)

- Make sure you understand the day-night switch on your inside mirror. The flipped-down position puts a glare filter in your view, so cars behind you cannot blind you, at night.

◆ ◆ ◆

After your mirrors are adjusted, you should glance at them, basically all the time. You should scan and notice, roughly, who is there. You should notice, how many cars are there, and how fast they are coming up on you – or, you should be aware if you are clear. When you want to start to pass, you have to make *really sure* there is nobody on your left. I almost always give my neck a quick turn to the left, so I can *SEE* that there is really *nobody there* in my blind spot. I do not literally trust my mirrors, but I use them to convince me that when I do look, there will not be a car there.

Then when you are through passing, you need to know you are well past the other car, so you can pull back into line. You have to learn to judge spaces and distances and speeds. For a beginning driver, this is tough stuff to learn! Especially, as everything in your mirror is, by definition, a mirror image.

Make sure your teacher explains all this, to your satisfaction, and trains you to do the right things. And make sure you know the right way to set your mirrors to suit your height. Fortunately, everybody at our house sits about equally tall, so we rarely have to make significant changes in our mirrors, when we swap drivers.

◆ ◆ ◆

When you start driving in England, you will be amused that you glance up to your right, where you expect the inside mirror to be – but it is up on the *left,* by the center of the windshield. After a while, you will get this sorted out, but it is quite tricky to have to break a habit.

Windshields

If your windshield is old and heavily sanded or pitted, it may make a lot of glare under ordinary sunny conditions, or at night with headlights shining on you. Surprisingly, my windshield, the original one for 365 K miles now, is not too badly sanded. Not like the ones I had in Massachusetts. If you find the glare is pretty bad, you may consider getting it replaced.

6-30 m

Right now, my windshield has 2 little cracks down at the bottom, on the left, not in my line of view, and four big nasty cracks on the right side. They have been there 10 years, and have not gotten worse. I figure if I bought a new windshield, it would soon capture a big rock, right in the middle of the driver's side, and I'd have to replace it. As it is, it looks pretty rough, over on the right, but the vision is quite good on the left half, and I am very unlikely to get a rock on the driver's side. So I will stand pat, and let Murphy's Law go to work for me. If I do not change this windshield, I will not get a rock in it. I can make Murphy's Law go to work FOR ME.

◆ ◆ ◆

What is Murphy's Law? It was derived by US Air Force researchers, who named it after Captain Ed Murphy, a development engineer at Edwards Air Base in 1949. Murphy first stated, "If there is any way he can do it wrong, he will", regarding a particular test technician who could be counted on to botch the wiring. Later it was re-formulated to "If anything can go wrong, it will." This can be easily applied to almost any automotive or electronic system. In the case mentioned here, it means if you have 2 windshields, an old one and a new one, the rock will wait until the new one is installed, and will then go through the new one.

Snow Scrapers

Even here in San Francisco, we get heavy frost on our windshields, a few times every year. So we have to keep a good scraper in the car. If we go on a trip up to the mountains, we had better have at least two, so two people can work at it and get it done fast. Or, in case one gets lost, you have a spare. Tom and Ray Magliozzi recently ran a Puzzler – if aluminum is much softer than glass, how can you make big mars and scratches on your windshield if you scraped the frost off with a soft-drink can? Their answer was, the aluminum gets oxidized into aluminum oxide, and THAT is harder than glass. So, you sure do not want to use a soft-drink can. A plastic credit-card would be much better! The next time somebody sends you a useless credit card, find some way to disfigure it, and scratch its face, and scratch its magnetic stripe, and then keep it in your car, as a spare scraper.

Do NOT throw warm water on your windshield. Yes, that may wash off the frost or ice, but it can also crack the glass. Yes, I have done this, without cracking the glass, but I was lucky. If you have to use water, use COLD water. That is unlikely to cause a crack – unless the temperature is 10 below. Then it would STILL be a bad idea to put water on the windshield, because it might freeze up really bad.

Rain

Rain can cut your general visibility, but it is not usually a big deal. If your wipers are running pretty well, you just have to be aware of your blind-spots. Normally, you can see around your windshield's posts (pillars). Your 2 eyes can see a pedestrian or a car trying to hide there. But since the wiper blades usually leave some glass not wiped, then your blind spot may be a little bigger than normal, and you have to be careful not to let people or things get INTO that blind spot.

The other problem that happens with rain is, that rain is usually cool, and cools off your windows until the moisture in your car starts to condense on the windows and windshield. In other words, they FOG UP. To a large extent, there are 4 main defenses against this.

1. Paper towels, or clean rags. Use these to mop off the worst of the moisture.

2. Turn on your defroster to blast warm, dry air to blow the moisture off the windshield. This is the most important thing for forward vision. Even if your heater has not warmed up, this can help a lot.

3. Open each window and vent, a little, to let a little moving air suck the moisture off, and out. This can help a little.

4. Turn on your rear-window defroster. Most of these are made with resistive materials. That can help a lot. (Be careful not to scrape at these resistive stripes when washing the rear window.)

There are some special chemical substances that are supposed to prevent condensation from settling on your glass – perhaps based on glycerine? I have not tried these, but you might check them out if you have this problem a lot.

Snow

SNOW can make life really *very* interesting. There are so many kinds of snow that we have to be careful about making generalizations. There is dry snow, wet snow, snow that has piled up and drifted, and snow that is still falling. Eskimos supposedly have 117 different names, for 117 different kinds of snow. That's a good thing, as if they didn't, they would not have a lot to talk about.

◆ ◆ ◆

Some authorities are always hollering over the radio or TV, "It is snowing, so you should not go out for a drive unless it is absolutely essential." Well, in some parts of the country, you would never get anywhere if you followed that advice. I mean, if I decided I would go to the store after lunch, and it starts snowing, that will *not* prevent me from going to buy groceries. There are, admittedly, times when you might decide not to go out in deeply drifted snow, or other severe weather. But I'll assume you will use good judgement. If you have been around snow all your life, you know what that means. If you just moved into a snow belt, you have to figure it out as you go along, and be a little cautious.

FIRST, before you go anywhere, take a stick, scraper, or shovel, as appropriate, and carefully remove all the snow from your HOOD, so you can see over your hood. Then, use a good scraper, and get all the snow off the windshield. Also get the snow off the spray nozzles for the windshield washers. Get the snow off the wiper blades, too, and make sure they are not frozen to the windshield. (That can blow a fuse or kill

7-6-21

your wiper motor, if you neglect that.) Make sure all the ice is off the wiper blades, if possible.

Then get the snow off the rear window and the trunk, or whatever you call the back of your car, so you can see out the rear window.

Next, scuff all the snow off the headlights, and off the tail lights and brake lights, and also the license plate.

Then, remove the snow from the top of your car. It may not directly affect your vision, but it's not really safe to leave a big slab of snow or ice up there, because it could fly off in another driver's face. (You might not want to dump all this right beside your car – you might want to drive slowly over to an unused corner of a parking lot and dump it off there.) Then you touch up the windshield, and rear window, and start the engine, and turn on the defroster, and get ready to roll.

◆ ◆ ◆

NOW, did you leave your wife and kids (or, your friends) sitting in the car, all this time, while you were shovelling and scraping? Fine, but I hope you told them NOT TO BREATHE. That's what we always say, in our family. If they were permitted to *breathe*, they would start to really steam up and frost up the insides of the windows. So we tell them to NOT BREATHE.

Usually, if there is a big amount of shovelling, we do not even bring the other passengers out of the house (or, out of the store, or other building) until the car is cleared off. But, sometimes there is no choice, and it's too cold for them to hang around outside – so they just have to get in the car, breathing or not. If they are breathing, they can also be helpful by scuffing the steam off the windows.

◆ ◆ ◆

Now, let's get rolling.

If the snow is still coming down, the snow can be swept off the windshield by the wipers, but after a while there may be a big pile of snow under the wipers, and you have to stop and shove it out. Sometimes you have to sweep off the rear window, too. You just have to play it by ear. It all depends on the type of snow. When it is cold, and you are getting powder, the snow is likely to just blow off the car. When it is wet and heavy and coming down fast, you may need to stop every mile or three, to remove the accumulation. It's true, that stopping on the side of a snowy road may be slightly dangerous. But if you can't see, and if the wiper blades are starting to *bend* when pushing on too much snow, then you have to balance the risks. Just try to pick a place where it's pretty safe to stop.

◆ ◆ ◆

Now, you guys down South may say, Boy, I am glad we do not have to put up with all that snow stuff, what a HASSLE! But, driving in snow is not bad – it is really quite fun. If I went back to live in the cold areas, that's the least of my worries and problems. I'll explain later, how to drive ON snow. This section was just about, how to SEE WHERE YOU ARE GOING in snowy conditions.

Sleet and Freezing Rain

Now, if you want BITCHY (pardon my French) driving conditions, let's see how we handle SLEET. Basically, sleet is a kind of freezing rain, and it freezes on your car and on the road, and can make everything really miserable. It freezes on trees, and bends them over until some of them break, and it weighs down power lines until, with a 2-inch crust of ice around them, they can break.

♦ ♦ ♦

So if you lose power and your house is getting cold, you might decide to go over to visit your sister, because her house is less likely to lose power, and she has a coal furnace. And all you have to do is drive 15 miles across town, in these rotten sleet conditions – !!

♦ ♦ ♦

The first, BEST (Zeroth) thing to do would have been, to note that it is starting to sleet, and put a big slab of cardboard on your windshield, under the wiper blades. If you are really smart, you can PREVENT the sleet from forming on the windshield. But I've never been that smart.

One guy said, "Gee, Bob, that cardboard sounds like a good idea, but how do you see through it or around it?" Okay, I must admit, I did not spell out that you should put the cardboard on the windshield only when your car is parked, and THEN remove it before you start driving. But, yes, that is what you do with the cardboard.

♦ ♦ ♦

So the first thing I do, is to just get out there, with my scrapers, and scrape away until I get the ice off. Get the wiper blades clean and free of ice, too. Make sure both blades are un-stuck, because if they are frozen to the windshield, you can blow a fuse, or burn out the motor, or the shaft may even twist off! Meanwhile the sleet is still coming down. Then you get your family and stuff in the car, and get rolling.

The problem is, even if you get your heater going, the ice still accumulates on the windshield. First around some edges, then the patch of ice grows, and then the little patch of VISION is shrinking. You have to stop and scrape off the ice. Sometimes, I just take one hand out of my mittens, and hold it against the windshield, and the heat from my hand melts the ice off the windshield, and helps maintain a small area of vision. If I swap hands, I can melt away enough area to keep peering out, and keep going. I may be able to get 3 or 4 miles before I have to stop. There's no point in scraping off the whole windshield, because it's just going to freeze up again. And I have never found much point in squirting windshield-washer fluid on it, because it just frosts up into mush. So, get back in and make a few more miles of progress. Watch out for fallen trees and wires, because they often come down across roads. And when you get to your sister's house, or get home, or wherever you are going, put some cardboard over the windshield, because in the morning, it's likely to freeze really hard, and the less ice you have to remove, the better. The only good thing about driving in sleet is, there are not too many people out there, so if you are reasonably careful, you may have clear roads. I have mostly seen sleet fall on top of snowy roads, and that is not really viciously, dangerously slippery. And after the sun comes out the next day, the ice on trees and wires can be very beautiful!

BIG Defroster

I recently heard a good solution for the problem of defrosting your car in the morning. And this solution would even remove the sleet from the windshield. But, you have to have a driveway beside your house – you cannot just park your car by the sidewalk and do this:

> Get a long heavy-duty extension-cord, and a 500-watt heater with a fan. Mount it carefully on a board or plank, above the front seat of your car. Aim this at the driver's windshield, and position it back a couple feet away, so it will not blow too vicious heat on the glass. Apply some power, when you are parked in the evening. Then go in the house and unplug the extension cord.

> In the morning, when you are almost ready to leave for work, plug in that extension cord, into the socket in your house. In 10 or 20 minutes, any light frost will be melted away, and the car will be warmed up, too. Even in case of heavy frost or ice, the heater can melt away a decent amount of ice from your windshield in half an hour. Any ice that does not melt off, will come loose, and is ready to nudge off. I must say, if I ever went back into the snow-belt, I would try this, and see how well it works for me.

You do, however, have to rig the extension cord going to the car, in a way that people do not trip on the cord, and the plugs and sockets do not get wet. For a 500-watt heater, you need a really heavy extension cord, say, 50 feet of 14-gauge wire. Also, you have to set up some kind of an interlock, so you do not forget and drive off with the extension cord still linked into the house!! Maybe you want to clip your car keys on the plug, in the house?

◆ ◆ ◆

Still, for a nickel's worth of electricity, you can get some very nice defrosting done, and save a lot of time and struggle. A lot more than a nickel's worth of trouble.

Peripheral Vision

Next, I will mention the role of peripheral vision. This long word simply refers to, how much you can see, 'way over on the left and right, without turning your head *or your eyes*. Even if you are looking straight ahead, you can see *a little bit* of what is going on, on the right or left. When you notice *that something* is over there, then you can swing your eyes to that side, and turn your head, too, to see what is really going on. It is pretty important to have good peripheral vision. You have to be able to tell when a car is easing up beside you on your left – or right. (I mean, mirrors can do just so much.)

◆ ◆ ◆

If *you* have lousy peripheral vision, that is not a disaster, so long as you are *aware* that you have poor peripheral vision. Maybe you should get an extra mirror, or a wide-angle (convex) mirror, to help you know what is going on. A driver who has only one eye can still be a safe driver, but he has to keep turning his head from side-to-side a little, to compensate for what he can't see in a straight-ahead position. Note, *every* driver should be turning his head a little, from side-to-side, most of the time – to minimize boredom, and to see things in his mirrors – and to augment his peripheral vision.

◆ ◆ ◆

There are other drivers who have other kinds of vision problems. There are some people who have had problems with their neck and backbone, and have had all their vertebrae fused. They typically cannot drive an ordinary car, so they get a milk-truck converted to private use, in order to be able to drive standing up. The problem is, they cannot turn their necks. So they rely on their peripheral vision. And they get into all sorts of accidents, because they cannot see what is coming from the side – they get hit on the side a *lot*.

◆ ◆ ◆

The other class of people who *used to* have this same kind of accident, was nuns who wore cowls. These days, most nuns are not required to wear a cowl, and they don't wear them, at least not when driving. But when they *did*, years ago, they got into ALL sorts of accidents, because their cowls blocked their view of anything coming up on their left or right. Thank Heaven for enlightened dress codes.

◆ ◆ ◆

Next, let's talk about poor vision in fog, smoke, or dust.

Fog

Every year, you read about a 90-car pile-up in fog, somewhere in the US – or maybe in England. People go rolling along at 60 or 70 mph, and when they come to fog, they drive right on into it. People do that about every day. Often, they keep on rolling, and seem to get away with it.

> But you should NOT just drive on into the fog. In fact, you should hit the brakes a couple times, HARD, and slow down somewhat before you enter the fog, so the car behind you can see you are slowing down a lot. Because there are sometimes *TEETH* in that fog. Sometimes a slow

7-1-21

truck, sometimes a stopped car. Sometimes a bunch of people climbing out of a wreck. NONE of these places is a good thing to discover, *just 100 feet in front of you,* when you arrive on the scene at 60 mph. So even if a lot of other people want to go fast, you should slow down some. You might slow down to 35 or 40 mph, or perhaps 15 mph slower than the most of the traffic. You don't want to creep along at just 20 mph, unless you know the guys behind you are slowed down likewise, because the guy behind you may be going at full speed, and might not be able to stop before he slams you. If the fog gets REALLY bad, you might need to get off the road for a while. Not just on the shoulder, but 'way off the road. I mean, 'WAY off.

◆ ◆ ◆

Another thing you can do, in moderate fog, is get behind a car or truck that has good visibility, and follow him at a suitable distance – not really close, but far enough back so you can just see his tail-lights. I usually find that if the guy is going 10 mph faster than I would have gone, I don't feel too bad about following him, say 150 feet back. The only thing is, if the guy ahead of you hits the brakes, (as if he just sees a problem, or a wreck) then you have to be able to get on your brakes really quick, really hard. The other possibility is that he might not get on his brakes, and he might hit something. Then you have to be ready to stop as soon as you see him crash. Can you stop in 100 feet at 50 mph? Probably not. But you might at least be able to slow down. The alternative, slowing down to 35, might be risky if the truck doing 60 cannot stop when he sees you. You have to estimate your own risks. If you lose the tail-lights of that guy cruising through the fog – you may have to slow 'way down and give up on trying to follow him. Sometimes I have to do that.

◆ ◆ ◆

I was driving my VW Bus one time on route I-495 near Worcester Mass, and there was some fog, and it was mostly kinda *low* fog. I could see over the fog, more or less. I passed an Oldsmobile that was quite low. He was doing about 35, in good caution. I was up just high enough that I could see a lot better, so I was going about 45. And as soon as I passed the Oldsmobile, he sped up and followed me about 15 miles, about 120 feet back. Then the fog ended, and he blinked his lights, and went right by me. I had helped save him some time and add some safety to his trip. I was happy to give him a free draft.

This is especially true because he was adding some safety to my trip, by protecting me from the possibility of a fast truck coming up behind us. Actually, a truck's driver would be up even HIGHER, so maybe he could have seen out OVER the fog, and he could perhaps have safely gone 55 – and I would have followed *him* at 55 – at a good distance. But if I saw a car doing 55 or 65, I would have suspected that he was flying blind, and I probably would NOT have followed that guy.

◆ ◆ ◆

Other notes on FOG or other poor-visibility situations: In fog, don't drive
with your high beams, as the light reflecting back usually gives LOUSY
visibility. You can try it and see for yourself. If the visibility gets *really*
bad, drive with your blinkers on, so other people have a better chance
to see YOU.

I'm not sure what people do in places where there is SERIOUS heavy fog, many
days a year. Such as the "Tule Fog" in Northern California, or the "Valley Fog" in the
Central Valley. You can start with my advice, and ask some of the locals, and see if
you like their stories. (You do not have to believe everything they tell you, and you
do not HAVE to assume they are a safe or sane driver....) Some people get fog lights
with yellow lenses, and they do not reflect the glare back so badly as other lights do.
Sometimes you can get fog lights mounted under the front bumper, which can shine
under the fog. I know some guys who say they can make a *big* improvement. Ask
your friends, which fog lights work best for them.

But, sometimes the only safe thing you can do, with heavy fog, is stay home. Or,
just get off the road. 'Way off the road.

◆ ◆ ◆

Here's another angle: if you are IN or NEAR a pile-up, with fog or poor
visibility, get the hell out of the road, AND out of the breakdown lane, as
far off the road as you can. Get FAR away from the scene. Because if I
am coming up behind you, and I see your car blocking my lane, I am
likely to veer right and try to stop in the breakdown lane. I am aware
there may be people there, perhaps injured, or perhaps walking around
like idiots. So, if YOU are smart, YOU will NOT stand around in the
breakdown lane. You will not just stand behind a guard-rail. You will get
as FAR off the road as you can, and quickly.

Perhaps the safest direction to go is, up along the road the way you came. If you
do that right, you may be able to wave your arms, as you walk near the shoulder of
the road, and try to get people to slow down – so they may be able to slow down
and stop before they smash into cars or people. In most accidents, where visibility is
OK, that may not be critical, but if there is bad traction (snow or ice on a
downgrade, or sharp curves) or bad visibility, it is not only the polite, neighborly
thing to do, but it may also be the safest place to stand. Even if you are walking on
the shoulder, or in the breakdown lane, and prepared to wave your arms at any car
that comes down the pike, you must be prepared to jump out of the way if a car is
coming up the breakdown lane – right at you!! Still, it is probably safer to do that,
than to stand by your car and wait for the next car to plow into it. Got the picture?

If both lanes are blocked, on a foggy 2-lane road, you may have to guess which is
the better direction to go and flag down traffic.

If there are injured people, try to make sure that people do not stand or stay in
the most dangerous places. If there is a 5-car pile-up, and if you have to stand or sit
by the first car, that is typically a lot safer than staying around the last car. This is true
whether or not there is limited visibility. I mean, if you think about it, you'll admit
that probably 1 out of every 90 cars on the road has LOUSY brakes, and there are

always a few heavily loaded trucks. If they are going to run into my car, I just don't want to be in it, or beside it, or anywhere near it. OK? Got the general idea? There is no way to cover every possibility, so you have to use your judgement, especially when visibility is poor.

Dust and Smoke

Sometimes the threat to visibility is dust. Just last year they had a 50-car pile-up on I-5, in California's central valley, because the dust got too heavy, and some people slowed down, and others did not. To a large extent, it's the same problem as fog. When heavy smoke goes across the road, same idea. Hit your brakes a couple times, HARD, before you enter that patch of smoke, so the guy behind you will see that he must slow, too. Help him get the message and slow down, so HE can protect your tail.

White-Out

Here's another topic I almost forgot: If you are out on a snowy day and the wind really begins to blow the snow around, you can't see a darned thing. This can happen in the dark, but is even more annoying in the daytime, because there ain't no shadows! It really is almost impossible to see what is going on, because everything looks the same. You can't see the snowbanks, or the ruts in the road, or the road. That is a white-out. Maybe you can see the front end of your car, but that is not a big help. Now, it may be unsafe to keep going, but it's not exactly safe to stop in the middle of the road, either. Try to find a safe place to stop off the side of the road, and, if you have any choice in the matter, get a long ways off the road, if you can do that without getting stuck in a drift.

Night Vision

Finally, let's talk about night driving, and night vision. In some cases, driving at night can be quite safe, because you can see who is coming along a road, much better than in the daytime. You can boom down a little one-lane road or 1-1/2 lane road at 30 or 35 mph, and ease through curves at 25, and be really quite safe. However, that might be pretty unsafe, if there could be bicyclists on the road, or deer, or people, or other big animals. If there are, you would have to hit the brakes, and try to slide into the side of the road, to dodge whatever is in the road. So if you like to "speed" at 30 mph, beware about the costs if you might have to hit an animal, or to dodge it.

Not all people have good night vision. Your eyes have "rods" and "cones", and some of them don't work at night as well as other people's do. So night vision can vary a lot. Also, the rate at which a person's night vision recovers from bright lights, can vary a lot. So some people really do like to avoid night driving – and partly because they recognize they are not very good at seeing what is going on. Other people point out, wearing sunglasses on a bright shiny day can help prevent your night vision from being degraded. Good point.

Driving at night on a 55 mph road is not any more dangerous, in general, than in the daytime. Because anything that is out there is just about as easy to see, at night, as in daytime. But there are a few exceptions.

♦ ♦ ♦

An old friend, Jack, was driving along in the Central Valley near Bakersfield CA, late at night, returning from a date, 30 years ago. He had a V-8 Ford and was driving fast, probably about 85, on a perfectly straight, flat road. He was speeding as he was trying to stay awake, trying to get home. There was one car a mile ahead of him, and he could see its tail-lights.

Suddenly there appeared in his headlights – RIGHT in front of him – a dark brown mule. If he tried to dodge right, he knew there was a deep ditch. If he tried to dodge left, he might miss the mule, but he might go off the road into the telephone poles. So he just ducked. That is probably the wisest thing you can do, because you KNOW the animal is going to come through the windshield, more or less.

He hit the mule. The mule caved in the whole engine compartment, and also hit the left side of the car (but, amazingly, it did not come through the windshield). The car did go off to the left side of the road, and stopped between two telephone poles. Jack was not badly injured, but his arm did hurt, and he knew he was not going to see much help for a while, on a *very* lightly-travelled road. It was going to be a COLD night. Then, amazingly, a car came up the road and stopped. The driver in the car ahead of Jack had seen in his mirror when Jack's headlights went out, and had suspected that the car had hit the mule (which he had seen). So the guy had thoughtfully stopped and turned around and went back to the scene, and took Jack home. (And the insurance had to replace the car.)

Could Jack have avoided this accident if he had some high-intensity driving lights? Maybe. Probably not. If I had to drive a lot at night, on roads that are not limited-access, that would be worth a try. The alternative is to take the risk of out-driving your headlights, and I don't like to do that.

♦ ♦ ♦

One time my son was attending school out in a desert area, at Deep Springs California, near Dyer Nevada. Sometimes he had to drive at night to pick up arriving students at the nearest bus-stop, 40 miles east at Lida Junction. Now, this was a pretty good road – a good 70-mph road in the daytime. But at night he had to drive at 50 mph, because the open range had cows – and they often stood or sat on the road – and they were *black* cows. The only safe way to drive this road at night is at 50 mph – even though you could otherwise cruise safely at 65 or 70. The drivers all knew not to out-drive their headlights.

♦ ♦ ♦

Maybe if the guy ahead of you was doing 60, you might follow him at 60, a couple hundred feet back. The risk of a cow stepping onto the road just after that car – and the chance that you would not see the blockage of the tail-lights of that car – would be minor. Risky but minor. Hey, all of life is risky. Try to pick reasonable risks, not unreasonable risks.

I can also observe that when you hit a cow, or a deer, the authorities can pretty much figure out how fast you were going. If the deer just *wrecks* the whole car and winds up in your lap, you were probably going about 65 or 70. If just the front of the engine compartment is damaged, maybe you were doing 35. So if you were really going 70, and you try to tell the cop (or the insurance agent) you were just doing 35 when you hit the deer, don't be surprised if they do not exactly believe you. (Further, if you hit the brakes and skidded 100 feet, hit the deer, and careered another 80 feet up an embankment, it is going to be pretty hard to pretend you were just doing 40....)

♦ ♦ ♦

Anyhow, running into animals is another case where speed can be a MAJOR contributing factor to the cause of an accident, even though the bad visibility at night is the primary cause. You can argue with a cop – although it may not do much good. But arguing with a cow is a LOSING deal. There are some times when speeding is a reasonable risk – and other times when it is just NOT reasonable. The price and the payback are just NOT worth the risk.

VISION considered overall

Why are we worried about all these picky details about poor visibility? Because any one of these factors can, if you goof, cause an accident. Even if *you* do NOT goof, the bad visibility could cause an accident. If somebody or something gets into a place where you cannot see it, that can cause an accident. You might run into a car – or a rock – or a tree. So try to minimize these factors.

Conspiracy

If any one of these factors is bad, what about any TWO? Obviously, snow *and* darkness, or rain *and* fog, or smeary windows *and* bright glare, can really hurt your ability to stay out of accidents. When you are being hit by a DOUBLE WHAMMY, you should be aware of this conspiracy, so you can keep an extra watch on the road. For example....

♦ ♦ ♦

Ursula was trying to drive into the UPS yard, but it was dark and rainy and not easy to see where she could park. She eased along at about 2 mph – and felt a thump – and then some hollering. She stopped. Half under her car was a UPS worker, very indignant, but unharmed. He was wearing a black jacket and a black slicker and black rain-pants, carrying a black flashlight. (No, he was not a black man.) In the rain, it was almost impossible to see this guy, who had been assigned at the last minute, to help people park during the Christmas rush.

The next day, Ursula had to go back to the UPS office again. The yard was now lit up with 3 big floodlights, and the guard who was directing people where to park, was wearing a yellow slicker and an orange vest and a reflectorized belt and shoulder straps, and one of the biggest flashlights you can carry. So, they got smart *really fast*.

It took several months for the UPS lawyers and Ursula's insurance company to stop saying bad things about each other, but eventually all lawsuits were dismissed. It was fortunate that UPS was taught a lesson, with no serious harm done to their unfortunate employee. But, anybody who has to work in a dark area with cars around, has to be aware that wearing a black costume is really playing a dangerous game. Ursula was wise enough to proceed *veeeery* slowly, but maybe she should have opened her window and peeked out? Every driver must be extra-cautious in such cases.

◆ ◆ ◆

So, in general, be very careful what you are doing when the visibility goes to pot and you cannot see where you are going. Because you can assume that other people are going to have trouble seeing *you*. Fair warning?

Chapter 4. STARTING

What is the definition of a chauffeur? These days, a chauffeur is a person who drives you around in a car. But originally, a *chauffeur* was a guy that you hired to light up the fire under your steam boiler in your steam car, a few *hours* before you wanted to go on a drive. He was a *fireman,* for pity's sake. A Combustion Engineer. (*Chauffeur* is the French word for *fireman,* or *stoker.*)

When the Stanley brothers invented their famous Stanley Steamers, 80 years ago, their key invention was *not* that their car could go fast. Rather, they invented a flash boiler so you could get your steam engine running in just a few minutes. Much better than old boiler technology. If we all had to fire up our boilers several minutes before we wanted to start out for a drive, that would not slow us down much on our commute to work. But it sure might cut down on frivolous little trips!

Even in the 1920s, most cars had to be hand-cranked to start. Boss Kettering, working for General Motors, pioneered the electric starter motor so that even a person who was not big and strong could easily start his engine, in the late 1920s.

These days, our cars start really easily and reliably, for our convenience. Still, planning our trips and getting started should be a serious part of the trip. Refer also to the Appendix on Checklists.

- If you are just going to drive down a mile, on a rainy evening, to buy milk and bread, it's not a big deal – but you'd feel really stupid if you forgot your money – or your shopping list! Do you have your shopping list? Even if the primary objective of your trip is NOT shopping, it is still reasonable to buy those few things you need, and this may save you a separate trip, later. Try to co-ordinate your trips together, so you can cut down on your short trips. This can save you a lot of time and money, and wear and tear on your car.

- On a simple commute to work, if you have your wallet, including driver's license, and money and credit card (or handbag or purse) and your briefcase, hey, that is routine.

BUT, for any trips longer or more serious than that, you should do some serious planning, as appropriate:

- Do you need glasses? Will you need sunglasses? Bring 'em.

- If you are going on an errand, to *take* something to somebody, be SURE to pack that in the car. Don't leave it behind.

- If you are going to pick up something, from a place you are not familiar with, you will want to be very certain to keep a copy of the ADDRESS, and the PHONE NUMBER, and the DIRECTIONS to get there, in your wallet, and/or on a clip-board, and/or taped to a piece of cardboard, so they will not blow out of the car, or get lost! Or –

* Make notes on a Post-it™ and stick it on your steering wheel....

• And if you have a baby, don't forget the baby. Don't forget the baby's food, as appropriate, and don't leave the diapers on top of the car and drive off! (I know several people who have done that.)

• When you turn on the key, FIRST note if you are low on gas. If you are, do you have enough $$ for gas?? Do both the Idiot Lights (Oil and alternator) go ON?

• When you turn the key to START, does the engine sound right? Do both the Idiot Lights go OUT?

• Good. Let's go!

(NOTE: The CHECK-LIST for all this stuff is in an Appendix, and you are permitted to make photocopies of that, for the benefit of you and your friends.)

Start the Engine

If you are starting from a cold start, a lot of cars are supposed to start best if you step on the gas pedal once before you turn the key. This is to set the automatic choke. Some cars actually start better when you step on the gas twice. Some cars tell you in the book, to not step on the gas pedal at all, before you turn the key. Your Owner's Manual will recommend a procedure. Of course, this is with the engine "cold". This usually is applicable, even on a hot day, if the engine has not been running for a good while. Because the engine then is *still* a lot cooler than if it was running. Anyhow, you figure it out, what works best for your car.

So, step on the clutch (if you have one) and turn the key – and it starts. *Blip* the gas only enough to make sure it is idling fast – but not very fast. Of course, if the engine is threatening to stall, you may have to *blip* the gas some more, or get it idling faster so it won't stall. Do NOT race the engine. Give the engine a chance to get its oil flowing, and its oil pressure up.

When the engine is *hot* – if it is well warmed up – you usually have to use another procedure – refer to the Owner's Manual. Often, it tells you to depress the gas pedal at least partially, to give it enough gas. It is almost *never* a good idea to step on the gas pedal 3 or 4 times. This is likely to flood the engine – get too much gas in. If you get it flooded, the procedure to get out of it is in the Chapter on Gasoline.

A friend of mine pointed out that if you rent a car in Europe, it may not have an automatic choke. If you try to start that car, and it barely starts, or starts badly, or runs *really rough*, look for a little knob that has a label like a butterfly valve (see at right). When you pull that out, it will run a lot better. Then be SURE to push that knob *in*, after a few minutes as the engine warms up. If you didn't, it would waste a lot of gas, and perhaps harm the engine. A lot of old cars in the U.S. used to have a manual choke, and they need the same treatment.

CHOKE KNOB
– PULL OUT FOR
COLD STARTING.

7-18-23

Warm It Up?

NOW, some people will let their engine idle for a while. Sometimes the guy next door lets his engine idle for 3 or 4 minutes before he starts out. These days, and for the last 30 years, cars are designed to just START and RUN and GO, and not need a long warm-up period. Now, you should not floor the gas, and roar down the street, and flog your car at high speed when it is still cold, not warmed up. The engine is much happier if you drive slowly and gently, and let it warm up gradually, for a mile or two, before you have to go fast. My house is almost a mile from the freeway, and the engine is warmed up just about enough when I have to accelerate onto the freeway. But just letting your engine idle is not doing any particular good. And it does waste gas. A big V8 engine can easily waste 1/4 gallon if you let it idle a couple minutes, when it is cold. That's equivalent to wasting 4 miles worth of gas. Sigh. Don't waste gas like that!

Cold *Cold* Starts

Now, there is one case where idling the engine does work better. First, let me mention that when you start a car with a manual transmission, it is a good habit to step on the clutch, even if the gearbox is in neutral. This is a good idea – *except* when it is VERY COLD – and then it is ESSENTIAL.

I remember a few times in Massachusetts, when it was 20 degrees below zero, Fahrenheit. I went out and got in my Beetle, stepped on the clutch, hit the gas pedal twice, turned the key, and the engine started. The engine ran a bit rough, because gasoline does not vaporize very well at such temperatures. After a few seconds, the engine was idling nicely, and I figured I could let out the clutch, in neutral, as I usually do. I let out the clutch. The engine just stalled! After a while I figured it out: The grease in the gearbox was SO COLD that the engine could just barely turn over the gearbox, IN NEUTRAL!! After a couple tries, I learned that I wanted to first get the engine warmed up pretty well, maybe for 10 or 15 seconds – which is 8 or 12 seconds more than I usually do.

Then I could just barely, by blipping the throttle, and slipping the clutch *gradually,* get the engine to turn over the gearbox IN NEUTRAL! At this point, the gears in the gearbox were throwing that cold grease into every corner, and getting it out of the gears. After another 20 seconds of fast-idling there, blipping the gas just a little, I was just able to put the gearbox in first gear and start out. After a quarter mile in first, I put it in second. Everything was so cold that, even in second, it would just barely accelerate on a flat road in second. But, the engine was warming up, and the gears were warming up. After a mile, I was able to get into third. After another mile, I made fourth – not that I got going very fast.

So, putting the gear shift into neutral is not *at all* identical to depressing the clutch. If you try to start at zero or at -10 or -20 degrees without stepping on the clutch, your engine probably won't start! The starter will NOT turn the engine over! And the battery will be drained down in just a few seconds. So, I almost always step on my clutch before I turn the key. It's a good habit.

If you are trying to start your car at really cold temperatures, and it will crank (perhaps weakly) but refuses to fire, then you may be able to get it to start using a spray of ether – also called "starting fluid". I wrote about this in the Chapter on gasoline. Look in there.

If, for any reason, you can't even get it to crank, or it cranks very weakly, you may be able to get a jump-start from a friend. Or maybe a push start. Or roll down a hill. This is all covered in the Appendix on Jump Starts.

If the engine cranks OK, but will not fire, and there is no obvious reason, it may be flooded. Look in the Chapter on Gasoline for a fix.

One of my buddies points out, it is sometimes a good idea to turn off your air conditioner before you turn on the key. I asked him why, since there is a relay to turn off the air-conditioner when the starter is cranking. He replied, "If your engine is running badly, as soon as you release the key from the START position, the air-conditioner can cut in, and your engine may stall. In that case, you are better to turn OFF the air conditioner until you are rolling." Good point. It may not be a big deal, but this is the kind of problem to watch for, in case your car is running badly.

Know Where To Go

There is one situation where we start out, and I drive a block up the street, and I just stop and wait. Why? This is the case where we have all agreed that we want to go out to eat. But we haven't agreed *where*. There is no point in keeping going, if we do not know what direction we want to go in. So I stop, and turn off the key, until we can agree. Our first question is, "Asian or Not Asian?" And since the answer is usually "Asian", 87% of the time, then we begin the serious debate. Thai food, or Chinese? Hunan or Szechuan or Mandarin or Hong Kong style? Burmese or Indian or Laotian or Cambodian? Indian or Korean or Rijstaffel?

After we have gotten some agreement, I then turn on the key, and we proceed. But it would be silly to keep the engine running, if we do not know to which restaurant we want the car to take us.

Starting onto the Road

When you have your engine started, you want to get moving. If you are coming onto a road, you have to make sure the road is clear. If you look to the left, to see if there is any on-coming traffic, and it looks clear, are you sure there is nobody coming up your lane (in his passing lane), over on the right? Perhaps, passing another car? OK that's clear – now look back to the left again. Because a car could have come "out of nowhere". Or a jogger may have come around the corner and may be on the point of running in front of your car. RE-check that the way is still clear. If you have to wait for a car, you will probably want to RE-re-check that the way is clear! OK, now you can get moving.

7-/8-21

Backing Out

What if you have to back out of a parking space? Then you have to be even more careful. Unless you KNOW there is nobody there, you have to *KEEP* checking and re-checking, on left and right, as you back out. Look over *both* shoulders. Make sure no kids are jumping behind your car. Or critters. Or joggers. Or bicycles or tricycles.

One friend said she was in a parking lot, ready to back out. She looked left and right behind her, and it was clear. She backed up. *Bam*. It turns out that a car had just gone *past,* and decided that he wanted to get *her* parking space, so he backed up to a good place to get her parking space – right where she was backing up. Unfortunate. That is a tough kind of problem to guard against. Or is it?

FIRST of all, when you are backing up, you have to keep looking back and forth, over each shoulder, alternating left and right, repeatedly. Since I first wrote this down, I notice that when I am backing, and I do keep looking left and right, I do feel safe. If I just give it a peek, I do not feel safe *unless* I am in a place where I know nobody will come by.

Secondly, I always like to *back* into parking spaces, so I can just pull *forward* when I want to leave. That way, I have much less chance to have problems of backing into things. If there is a choice of backing OUT of a parking space, or backing IN, I will always back IN.

Every once in a while, I see a parking lot with little signs: "Do not back into parking spaces." I always ignore that. Backing in is safer for me, as I do not then have to back out. I don't really know why they tell you not to back in. One person said he thought it was because some people are not good at backing in. Another guy said maybe it was because if a person backs in, and then lets the car idle for a long time, his exhaust pipe may leave a black mark on the wall, which looks ugly. Either way, I am not impressed. But the next time I see those signs, I will inquire. But, if the insurance company required them to put up those stupid signs, to protect them from drivers who are no good at backing *in,* what do they expect to have for problems when those people are having trouble backing *OUT?*

Best of all, I like to stop in a big parking lot where I can pull through one parking space and into the second one. And when I want to leave, I can just start straight ahead. I never have to back up at all. Of course, we do not always have a choice of doing this.

Anyhow, how you *stop* partly determines how you *start*. If there is a big MOB SCENE when you are parking, you may be best off to just pull in and get parked and get out of everybody's way. On the other hand, if you know it is gonna be *chaotic* when you come out and want to get going – such as at a sporting event, or a Town Meeting – then it is wise to plan for your exit. If you can back in when it is not too hectic, you will be able to pull out when you leave and traffic is messy.

Chapter 5. ENGINES and ACCELERATION

The Gas Pedal or "Accelerator Pedal"

I was just typing away on the very initial concept for this book, and I decided to start typing on a chapter, to show what a chapter would look like. But, which chapter should I start on? Just then, the newsman on the radio said that a car had driven onto a busy sidewalk of people in Reno, Nevada, killing 3 and injuring 12. The driver was quoted as saying that he had had trouble with a sticking gas pedal. OUCH!! That was a *sign* that I had better get started writing.

Obviously, one of the things that every car must be able to do, is STOP. If it won't GO, that is one problem; but if it won't STOP, that is BAD. Part of the deal is that when you take your foot off the gas pedal, the engine must cut back on its power – should cut back to an idle. If it doesn't, you have a SERIOUS PROBLEM. If you suspect that your car's gas-pedal linkage is acting sticky, that is an important item to get fixed, *really soon*.

What if it Sticks?

Meanwhile, if you are still rolling down the road, and your gas pedal sticks in the DOWN position, what do you do? First, *do not panic*.

1. Even if your gas pedal is stuck all the way down, and the throttle is wide open, you can stop just by putting on the brakes. On every good car, the brakes are a LOT more powerful than the engine. So, depending on whether you are headed for trouble, or you are just trying to slow down when you start down a hill, hitting the brakes is the first option. You will also, of course, want to get the engine to stop pulling, so go on to steps 2 and 3. NOTE, if you have to use your brakes to pull you down from 55 mph, while the engine is still pulling, you may be able to do this ONCE, but you don't plan to do this again, because brakes were not designed to do this – they may start to fade. If you can't get the engine to stop pulling, PARK IT.

2. If you have time, jiggle the gas pedal with your toe. Tap it once or twice. It may come unstuck. But even if it does, that is still pretty dangerous, and it's time to get it fixed. Maybe if you are on a broad open freeway with no sharp curves and no traffic and no stop lights, it may be safe to continue to the next exit. But if you are on a curvy mountain road, or in city traffic, *park it* right away.

3. If the "quick jiggle" doesn't work, TURN OFF the KEY. This is the absolute solution. No matter how hard the engine is pulling, if you turn off the key, it will stop pulling. Now, you must check this out in advance, because you do NOT want to turn the key too far and let it LOCK UP THE STEERING. You do NOT want to pull the key out of the ignition, because then you are just about certain to lock up the steering (except on some very old cars). So, turn the key just a little

53

bit, to shut off the ignition. This gives you time to stop and find out why the linkage is sticking, or jammed, or whatever.

4. It is probably NOT a good idea to just step on the clutch, or shift into Neutral, because if the engine is trying to rev high, it could over-rev and blow up. If you keep it in gear, that's the better thing, in general, at least until you are stopped or nearly stopped. Even if you shut off the key, keeping the engine in gear can help keep the power steering and power brakes running OK.

5. If you find that you can control the speed by turning the key ON and OFF, ON and OFF, you may be able to drive a little further. But it's still not a good idea to do that any further than essential, because it is not good for the car, and might damage the catalytic converter, or other parts, too. Park as soon as you can, as soon as it's safe, and put in a fix. Note, if you have a high-powered car, like a Corvette, you probably won't be able to do this, as it would accelerate too hard.

6. If your gas linkage is sticking occasionally, intermittently, and you are really stuck and forced to drive a little more, before you can get it fixed, there are a few things to do about it. Do NOT floor the gas-pedal and then hope it will slow down when you take your foot off the gas-pedal. Even if you do not wreck the car, you might blow the engine. Feed the gas as little as you possibly can, and ease off on the gas very early as you approach a curve or stop-sign. If you take your foot off the gas, and the engine keeps pulling, then – make sure your right hand knows how to find the key, really fast and surely, and your right foot should be on the brakes.

Some cars have levers and push-rods for the gas linkage; others have cables. Sometimes these things get stuck or frozen or jammed. Other times you might have some junk stuck under or around the gas pedal, and it's just a little excess friction. That is not a joke; don't let junk accumulate under your pedals. Clean it up.

So you may not have to climb under the car, or wallow around in the engine compartment, depending on what is stuck. Sometimes it may just be that the return spring is broken, so you can rig a couple rubber-bands until you get to a hardware store or gas station where they can sell you a spare spring. (NOTE, rubber bands tend to degrade really quickly in the presence of gasoline, so don't expect a rubber-band fix to last very many hours. Get a real spring in there, quickly.) So if your gas pedal sticks DOWN, it is very serious, but it may not be a big deal to get it fixed – so long as you don't let it slide you off the road.

Gas Pedal Won't Go Down

One time I had a 1972 VW bus, and it started to have its gas linkage jam up – NOT jamming so the gas pedal would not come UP, but jamming so that I could not push the gas pedal DOWN more than half way. It turned out that one of the carburetors was sticking, jamming, and you could put your foot half-way down and then it would go no further. If you jiggled it, it might go further – but it might not.

Of course, this popped up about 100 miles into a 1000 mile vacation. I fiddled and diddled and finally I lived with the need to go up hills at 1/2 throttle. And even at half-throttle, it would go 55 mph on the flat, quite nicely. Fortunately the roads were not heavily traveled, so not TOO MANY drivers were cursing my slow speed on up-hills. When I got home, I got the carburetor fixed – I had it rebuilt. Still, even while this was vexing, it was not dangerous or life-threatening, as it never had any tendency to stick at FULL POWER.

Engine Does Not Respond – a Different Mode.

One time I was driving in Berkeley, and the gas pedal of that same VW bus fell to the floor. Of course the cable for the accelerator had frayed and broken, after 120,000 miles. I gripped a set of vice-grip pliers onto the carburetor linkage in the engine compartment, and tied a piece of nylon cord onto it, and I set my 14-year-old son Benjamin back in the luggage compartment, to pull on the cord. We rehearsed the instructions I would yell to him – "LET GO" and "Pull a little more", and a few other phrases. We teamed up just fine, and he fed the throttle as much as I asked for. We drove home across the Bay Bridge, which is a 7-mile span, where you would be embarrassed to break down. But we had no problems. We got home just fine, and he was tickled that he had been able to do such a good job of helping with the driving. It wasn't really dangerous or scary, but it was tricky. If I had been driving by myself, I would have walked to a hardware store and bought a few pulleys. But I always keep some nylon cord in my cars, so I can tie things up or down, or pull on things....

How to Keep Your Engine Happy...

Despite the importance of the brakes, the windshield wipers, and the cup-holders, if the engine does not run well, that is seriously disappointing to most drivers, and if it runs badly, that may cause dangerous situations which could result in accidents.

- Keep enough oil in your car. Know how to read the dip-stick, even in the dark. Don't let the oil get too low, AND don't over-fill it.

- Keep an eye on your oil-pressure light, especially when the engine is cold, and especially when you go around a corner hard, especially when cold. When my oil gets low, it shows up by turning on the green light when you are cornering hard, and it goes on easier when the engine is cold. (After the engine warms up, the oil drains down faster, and does not run dry on oil.)

- Keep enough water and anti-freeze in the radiator.

- Don't run out of gas. (That's covered in the next Chapter on Gasoline.)

- Follow the instructions in your owner's manual.

- If your car starts to run badly, it could just be a clogged fuel filter. Go read the Chapter on Gasoline. Or it could be bad spark-plug wires, or dirty plugs, or a cracked or dirty distributor. Check the Appendix on Spark. If cleaning or replacing these things does not help, you need a GOOD repair shop. Because driving around in a car that loses power, can be pretty dangerous. When you want to pull out into traffic, or make a left turn across traffic, and it won't GO, that is pretty serious. Get it fixed, and drive very gently and cautiously until you get it fixed.

Chapter 6. GASOLINE

Gasoline is an amazing substance. If you have an efficient car, you can take 3 or 4 friends and travel as much as 30 or 40 miles on one gallon of gas – just 7 pounds of gasoline – and maybe more, if you take it easy on the gas pedal. That's pretty impressive. A mere $1.25 investment can provide a LOT of person-miles. Even my old Beetle can provide about 120 people-miles for 120 pennies, at 1998 prices. And when you fill up the tank – with perhaps 70 pounds (10 gallons) of gas – you can easily drive 300 miles. If you ever studied electric cars, you know that it's hard to get even a very good electric car further than 80 or 100 miles, without running your battery down. (Unless you had some expensive experimental batteries.)

Chemistry

First, let's talk philosophy and chemistry. If you had a car that could run on dynamite, and if you had a 20-gallon fuel tank full of dynamite – you would not be able to drive very far. A tank of gasoline is MUCH better, and has MUCH more energy than a tank full of TNT or dynamite or nitroglycerine. That is because those explosives do not need air to burn or explode – they bring their oxygen with them. (If they had to get oxygen from the air, they could not explode as fast as they do.) So, gasoline carries a lot more energy, per pound, than those explosive substances, because it does not have to carry its air with it. When you drive along, your car brings in a lot of air to burn with the gasoline.

Further, if you do not mix up gasoline with a lot of air, it does not burn very well, and is not very dangerous. It takes about 10 or 15 pounds of air to burn one pound of gasoline well. If you put that in terms of *volume* that says that 1/7 of a gallon – about 1.1 pints – needs 1500 gallons of air to burn with it. That is one of the nice things about gasoline. One could also observe that 1 gallon of gasoline is able to POLLUTE 10,000 gallons of air, but let's set aside those pollution debates.

When I work with car parts, I sometimes do this, just as a sanity check: I take a pie-pan full of gasoline that I have been using for cleaning greasy parts. I stand up, and, in a safe place, such as out in the middle of my driveway, with nothing else around, I drop some lighted matches into the gasoline. About 9 times out of 10, the match simply goes out when it hits the gasoline. It does not ignite the gas. And if the gas *does* catch fire, it just sits there and burns very quietly. It does *not* explode. Then I put another pie-pan over the fire, and it goes out. Of course, there are not a lot of weeds or dry grass or flammable stuff along my driveway.

Let me tell you what I will NOT try. (Refer to the Appendix: "What's all this Stupid Dangerous Stuff, Anyhow?") I will *not* drop lighted matches into an "empty" gallon gasoline can. Because about 6 drops of gas in a can will make a rather explosive mixture, and I do not want to find out if that gas can will send shards of metal into my legs. That is a bad gamble. I could be wrong, but I do not want to find out. I am NOT gonna screw around with that, because 6 drops of gasoline could cause you a LOT of trouble. Do NOT fool around with gasoline and matches – or even sparks!

Too Little Gas

You already know that when you run out of gas, you don't go much further. So it is important to keep checking your gas gauge and not run out. Sometimes I don't mind if I run out of gas, because I am on a road with lots of gas stations, and if the engine quits, I can just roll into a gas station and buy more. But usually we cannot count on that. Now, I do carry a spare gallon, so I can run a lot closer to empty than most people can, and not worry too much about running out.

> When the gas level is very low, I keep very alert. I am careful not to get caught in the left-hand lane, and to not go any place (like the Golden Gate Bridge, or any other big bridge) where there is not a breakdown lane. As soon as I hear the engine cough, I am prepared to instantly kick in the clutch, and turn off the ignition, and roll to a safe parking place along the road.

> (If I let the engine keep running until it is really dry, then it does not like to start very well. The mechanical fuel pump works a LOT better if I leave the engine with a little gas for when I try to start it, so the engine will fire and draw the fuel from the gas tank. But if you have an electric fuel pump, that may not be important.)

As soon as I am parked safely, I pour enough gas from my spare gallon into the tank, to get me to the next gas station, plus a little to spare. Then I get going pronto. But storing a spare gallon of gas in your car SAFELY is *not* trivial; see below.

One time I saw a guy with a VW bus, broken down, and I tried to help. He said his gas gauge showed plenty of gas. But, we could not get it started. I left him a self-addressed envelope with a stamp, and later he sent me a note to explain what the problem was. He had just bought the bus, and the gas gauge was broken, so it would show that he still had a lot of gas, when his tank was actually dry. The previous owner was not very helpful and did not warn him about this. So if your fuel gauge seems to be taking *forever* to drop to "reserve", or "empty" – and then the car quits – maybe the gauge is broken.

If you drive a Diesel car, look at the last paragraphs before the end of the chapter.

Bad Fuel Filter

> When your engine starts running rough and very short of power, especially at high speeds – this can easily be caused by a dirty, clogged fuel filter. This may seem partly intermittent, but tends to get worse and worse, gradually. After a while, you can't even cruise along at 50 mph – and then, 40 mph. So when you have an old fuel filter, and you want to put on a new one – buy *two* new filters. Install one, keep the other in the car – and save the old one, too. Don't throw it away. If you then

x

have a problem when the second new one clogs, the old one will probably save you – it may even work better. And if you have a *really* dirty supply of gas, your new filter can clog up fast, too. And that can happen almost any time!

One night I was driving my wife's 1969 Beetle up Route I-5 toward Mt. Shasta, and the engine began to run a little rough at 60 mph. I stopped at a roadside rest area, to check it out. And then I couldn't get it started! After some checking, I found that the fuel filter was REALLY badly clogged with rust. Heck, you should be able to BLOW through a good fuel filter, pretty easily. If you can't blow through it, that explains a lot. No, my wife did not know where she bought that gas, but we shoulda gone back and griped. Anyhow, after I fooled around for an hour, the car finally decided to start, but it did not want to run faster than 50 mph. The next day, I bought a new fuel filter. And since that time, I do not throw away my old fuel filter. Actually, I never even did throw away that rust-filled one, because a bad filter is better than nothing. Worst case, you can flush it out with gas, or poke a hole in it, and get it working better, at least for a while.

◆ ◆ ◆

When I bought that fuel filter, I was accustomed to buying a little transparent plastic one. But the dealer at this NAPA* auto parts store in Redding CA only had metal ones. I asked why. He said the plastic ones can catch fire and burn, so the metal ones are safer. But, hey, the fuel lines are made of fabric and rubber, and if you had a fire, wouldn't they burn, too? I dunno. Since I had no choice, I bought the metal one from the NAPA guy. It was a big one, probably suitable for a big Chrysler with 300 hp. I figured it would last a long time. Come to think of it, I just walked out to see, and that old metal filter is still on there. It hasn't filled up in the last 4 years. Not a bad deal.

◆ ◆ ◆

The other thing I keep in my car is a piece of plastic tubing, about 3 inches long and 1/4 inch diameter, that will fit inside the fuel line – the right size to substitute in, *in place of* the filter. You might get a lot of sludge, but you are still likely to be able to keep going. The other thing you can do with a clogged fuel filter, if you have no choice, is to take a piece of coat hanger wire and just poke a hole through the clogged filter element. Then rinse out the worst of the dirt, before you re-install it. This is not a great move, but it's better than being really stranded. You may have to get your carburetor cleaned out later, but it's better than being completely stuck out in the boondocks.

If your fuel filter fills up often, maybe it's trying to tell you your gas tank is rusting badly.

---

* Note, NAPA is an acronym for North American Parts Association and has NOTHING to do with the Napa Valley where they grow such nice grapes, 50 miles north of San Francisco. But if you are up there and need some car parts, you'd go to the Napa NAPA store.... I think NAPA sells mostly Chrysler parts. But, FORTUNATELY, they sell fuel filters on a Saturday morning, that fit JUST FINE on a VW.)

Fuel Injection

If you have fuel injection, it obviously requires the gas to be clean and well-filtered. The Owner's Manual should indicate where you have to clean out the fuel filter, in case it gets clogged. The in-line gas filter is just to keep the grit from getting in to fill up that final filter.

Gasoline – Too Much.

Let's talk about it. There is such a thing as the right amount. If you get too little – if you run out of gas, or if your filter will not let the gas through – that is a bummer. But if you get too much, in the wrong place – like, it all dumps out of the tank on you, all at once – that is pretty dangerous, too.

If you discover that some gasoline is dripping down from the bottom of your car's gas tank – it may have gotten rusty, and it may be ready to rust out. Do NOT poke at that leaky, rusty spot with a screwdriver, and do not even poke at the rust with your fingernail. Because you are likely to poke a big hole in it, and then you are really in trouble. No, you *can't* patch it with chewing gum. Instead, park in a safe, isolated spot, OUTSIDE, preferably with a big pan under that leak, until you can get to a repair shop and get the tank replaced. Note, on my VWs, the tank tends to rust out after about 24 years.

Be VERY CAREFUL, working with gas tanks. A full gas tank might catch on fire – but it can't explode. An "EMPTY" gas tank can be easily exploded by any spark, any cutting, even a hack-saw. I guess a gas-tank filled really full with water might be safe. Still, you don't want to attack one with a cutting torch. Leave that to experts. They know how to flood the tank with non-flammable stuff, such as nitrogen.

Storage

You want to be really careful about gasoline. Would I want to keep a car in a closed garage under my house? Heck, no! Even if the gas tank did not leak, the carburetor might leak, or a fuel line, or a fuel pump, or my spare gallon.... I don't want a car full of gasoline anywhere *near* my hot water heater and its pilot light!! Even the spare gallon I keep for a lawnmower, I keep in a ventilated place. NOT in my house.

Too Much Gas – Another Way to do it...

There was one time my car was running, and I wished it would not. I was driving home, and I started to smell a lot of gasoline fumes. I drove another half mile past a complicated area of interchanges, and then turned off the key and rolled to a stop on the shoulder. I looked at the fuel line. The fuel line was NOT connected into the carburetor. The metal tube that sticks out of the carburetor – the place where the fuel line clamps onto – had pulled out. The fuel hose was still clamped tightly onto the tube – but the tube fell out of the carburetor. I thought that was not very nice. Your fuel line should *not* come loose, causing the gasoline to spill all over. I mean, there was gasoline spilling ALL OVER the engine! Yet it did not catch fire.

Now, if the engine had stopped, then the fuel-pump would have stopped. But apparently there was so much fuel squirting up AT the carburetor, that enough gas went INTO the carburetor, and it kept running! And I would have been much happier if it stopped! Anyhow, I first shoved that tube back into the carburetor, and that was a fairly tight fit, so I figured it would not fall out in the next 5 miles. Then when I got home, I wired it up *really securely* so it could not ever fall out again. Now, no problems.

Cars with fuel injection have a special case, because all of the high-pressure fuel hoses have to be clamped very well, or they will come off. You need the right kind of hose clamps.

(But, one time on my '72 Bus, the oil started pumping out the dip-stick, because of a clogged PCV valve. The oil pumped out onto the muffler, and the oil started to burn. Fortunately, I had my fire extinguisher, and put it out. Surprisingly, oil on a hot muffler is bad – whereas gasoline boils off so fast, it does not tend to catch fire!)

Too Much Gas - Flooding

I am not an expert on "flooding", as my cars do not seem to have this problem. I think it is not a common problem now, but older cars may still have this problem.

> When your engine is cold, it needs a rather rich mixture to get started – lots of gas to go with less air. The "choke" was used on older cars with carburetors, to provide this rich mixture. But if the engine does not start right away, the gas can splash over the spark plugs, and then the engine can refuse to fire. The more you crank, the unhappier it gets. It is "flooded".

> There are two things to do to solve this problem. One is to just *wait.* If you wait a while and the gasoline dries off, that can help a lot. The other thing is to step on the gas pedal, all the way to the floor – just *Once.* Then crank the engine, and see if it will start. You might have to crank it for 10 seconds, maybe 3 or 4 times, to "un-flood" the engine. Then it may start. This lets in a lot of air, and defeats the attempt of the choke to provide a lot of rich gasoline mixture. This can help. But it depends on how the car is in a good mood. If you have this problem a lot, it's probably a good idea to get it fixed.

Fuel-injected cars are supposed to not have this problem, but I bet if you get an older car that is not well-tuned or well-calibrated, you may have the same problem. Consult your Owner's Manual, for advice on starting under difficult conditions. Or get the advice of a good mechanic. Or, see if flooring the gas pedal and cranking the engine *once* doesn't give the correct command to the fuel-injection computer, and solve the flooding problem.

Yet Another Way...

When you buy gas, you may pump your gas tank "full". But, after the nozzle clicks OFF the first time, you may be able to squeeze in another 0.3 or 0.4 or 0.5 gallons. If you are driving on the road, then the extra 5 or 10 or 15 miles of range may be useful. In most states, it is illegal to "top off your tank" that way. But some people do it.

However, if you are filling up just before you park, this may be a really bad idea. The gas you pump from underground is cold, and if you put it in your gas tank and park it in a warm place, the gas will expand and can overflow onto the floor. If this happens in the basement of your house, that's a *really* bad idea. Even if it is in an empty parking area, and even if nobody throws a match on the ground, it is a bad move, because a quarter cup of gas, unburned, causes a lot more air pollution than the same amount of gasoline when you burn it. So, please try to avoid over-filling your tank, and avoid spilling gas.

A Spare Gallon and Safety

Now, I have carried a spare gallon of gas, in my car, on at least 80% of the last 1,000,000 miles I have driven. Yet many books and experts tell you to never carry a spare gallon in your car. Why? Well, if you get in certain kinds of accident, that gas can could bust, and send gasoline all over. THEY think you should not take that risk. Well, that is a small part of the problem. You should not just ignore that possibility. You should STOW your spare gallon can in a place where a small accident cannot cause it to bounce around and get broken. Strap it or tie it down securely where it is not likely to get loose. (More on this later.)

The bigger problem is that if you carry a spare gallon in your car's trunk, it could easily fall over and start to leak. If you got even 88 drops of gas in your car's trunk, and this mixes well in the air, then that can be a very explosive mixture. Any little spark could set off a rather significant explosion.

So if you are going to carry a spare gallon of gas, you must take VERY good care, to make sure that it does not roll around and bust, or break, or fall over or leak. And, if it does start to leak, you must detect it, pronto. I solved this problem by keeping my spare gallon behind the driver's seat, *not* in the trunk. If it falls over, or starts to leak, I notice the smell of gas, pronto. I set it where it will not leak, or, on a piece of newspaper where it will not make a big mess. If it ever did leak, I would replace it with a new can that does not leak. One guy suggested that it might be illegal in some states, to carry a gallon of gas in the passenger compartment. Sounds unlikely. And the chance that a law like that would stop me from doing it, is also unlikely.

And then if I see a guy out of gas, I can give him a spare gallon, to get him out of trouble. Or, if the gas station is just a couple miles down, I'll give him a half gallon. I tell the guy, don't pay me a buck for the gas, but, pass along the favor, and carry a spare gallon so you can help someone else.

Some people say they *never* carry a spare gallon of gas, as they think it is not safe. Whatever. But you might at least carry an empty gallon can, so if you run out and have to go to a gas station, you will be all set to buy gas. Just make sure it is very dry, inside, without any significant fumes.

Gasoline – Just Right!

So, if your gas tank is not empty, and your fuel-injection computer is not goofed up (or, your carburetor) and your fuel filter is not clogged, and your fuel pump has not quit – then your car is NOT going to stop running for lack of gas. So your car runs cheerfully, 'most all of the time.

How Can You Tell??

But, what if your engine has stopped running, and does not want to even start and fire? How can you tell if you have a fuel-feed problem, or, if it is a case of no spark??

> It's really pretty easy. With a carburetor, take off the air-filter. Pour a tablespoon of gas down the middle of the carburetor. Then crank it, and if it fires momentarily, and dies, you know that your spark is OK, and you have a fuel problem. If you have fuel-injection, the deal is the same: take off the air filter and pour that tablespoon of gas into the "throttle" area. Hit the key. If it fires and dies, that is a good CLEAR-CUT indication, that your fuel injection is not working well. Maybe it is out of gas, or the computer is not working (is its fuse blown?) or the filter is clogged, or the fuel pump has quit.

If your fuel is not getting to the engine, there are several trouble-shooting procedures you can do. Are you really Out Of Gas? Faulty Gas Gauge? Clogged Fuel Filter?

One thing to try, IF you are in a safe place, is to undo the clamp on the hose from the fuel-pump to the carburetor. If you have an electric fuel pump, just turn on the key briefly. (If the fuel pump is mechanical, crank the engine over for a second.) If the gasoline spurts out, at least you know the gas has gotten that far. Or if no gasoline comes out, you may be out of gas, or the fuel pump is bad. In either case, you have narrowed it down a lot.

Is your fuel pump bad? You might tie a can of gas to your roof rack, and run a long hose to siphon the gas down to the engine. This can get gas to your carburetor, even without a fuel pump. A friend of mine who is a VW nut did that. It's an *old* trick.

Or maybe you have a bad carburetor? That's usually a job for a specialist.

If you have a bad fuel-injection computer, you may have to replace it, but it might be just an intermittent connection. Or a blown fuse. Or a bad fuse-holder. Or a shorted wire. Try wiggling the connectors of the computer, while somebody cranks the engine. Admittedly, this is grasping at straws, but it's worth a try. If that doesn't fix it, you'll probably have to tow the car into a good repair shop. It's worth a reasonable try, because if you cannot tell that it is NOT the fuel-injection computer, then the repair shop will probably start replacing things, whether a system is bad or not, just to try to find out what is wrong. You may be charged hundreds of dollars to replace a computer even if there is NOTHING wrong with it, just because that is the easiest way to trouble-shoot the problem. These days, it is not easy to work on cars and actually repair them, but it is worth-while to do some preliminary evaluation, to

7-24-21

help narrow down the cause, and to help avoid getting ripped off on unnecessary repairs.

Still, the art of troubleshooting a fuel-flow problem is REASONABLY well-known – so long as it is not a rotten intermittent problem. And the rules to avoid having gasoline making a mess, or catching fire, or causing an explosion, are pretty easy to remember, too.

When Hell Froze Over...

One final situation. Let's say we are getting gas to our engine, and a pretty good spark – and it won't start. It started yesterday – but it won't start now. What do we do?

First of all, let's be fair and explain the actual conditions.... Yesterday the temperature was +7 degrees F – and NOW it is -20 degrees. And the engine won't start. It cranks, but it won't start. And if you try 3 more times, it won't even crank, because the battery is pretty strong, but it won't crank forever. OKAY, wise guy, Pease, how do you get it started? I know how. I've done it.

> I go down in my cellar and get the bottle of ether spray. Open up the hood, and reach over to the intake vent to the air-cleaner. Squirt a 1-second squirt into the air intake. Then RUN to the drivers seat (step on the clutch if you got one) and hit the key. Rur, rur, cough, r'm, R'M. It started! Keep your foot on the gas, and let it rev just a little, and don't take your foot off the clutch, because that would stall it.

Why does the ether get your engine started? Very simple: a mixture of ether and air needs a much smaller spark to ignite it – *much* less spark than a gasoline mixture. If your spark is anything but really strong, then at very cold temperatures, it may not fire the gasoline mixture. As soon as the engine fires, the voltage goes up a lot. After all, when your battery is trying to crank a very cold engine, you will be lucky if it puts out 8 volts – or even 6 or 4 volts. As soon as it fires, and you disengage the starter, the voltage will quickly go up to 10 or 11 volts, and then rise higher. So if you get it to fire once, it will almost certainly start.

After your engine has warmed up for a few seconds, and you get the gearbox turning over in neutral, stow the ether bottle in a safe place. You may need it tonight! But, do not leave it in the car all year – it would get too hot in summer.

Diesel Fuel

If you have a car with a Diesel engine, you have fuel problems that are different than with gasoline. Diesel fuel is not as flammable as gasoline, so carrying a spare gallon securely strapped down is not such a bad idea. And in some parts of the country, it's not very easy to find Diesel fuel, so carrying one or two 5-gallon cans may be a good idea.

On the other hand, Diesel drivers have one problem, which I learned from my Uncle Roger many years ago: if you let a Diesel engine run dry of fuel, it is the Devil's own job to get it started again. And the Owner's Manual typically does not warn you about this! Actually, one guy told me that VW Diesels do not have that problem, and are easy to re-start, but almost every other Diesel car has this problem. If you have a Diesel, make sure you know how much problem you'll have if you run it dry.

Tie Down Your Spare Gallon

What is a good way to tie down your spare gallon of gasoline? Some VWs come with a special round can that fits in the middle of the spare tire. They are pinned into place so they can't move. I used to keep a spare 2-gallon can, strapped to the upright next to the spark plugs on the left side of the engine of my 1965 Bus. I strapped it down with some ingenious coat-hanger clips, and it didn't even get warm under hot driving conditions! But if it ever got loose, there'd be hell to pay!

In my Beetle, I put it behind the driver's seat, in the foot-well for a rear-seat passenger. I pile tools and oil cans around it so it can't wobble or fall. Admittedly, that's not very secure if I flip the car over, but I don't do that often.

In *your* car, you may be able to find a corner of your trunk where you can wedge it in or tie it down, so it won't move under hard braking or cornering or acceleration. (Not all gas cans have the same shape.)

TECHNICAL NOTE:

A gallon of water is really close to 8 lb., but a gallon of gasoline is about 7 lb., so the density of gasoline is very simple to compute – about 7 lb. per 231 cubic inches, or about 875 grams per liter.

Now – some scratch-paper work: 1 milliliter of dry air weighs (has a mass of) 1.19 milligrams, under conditions of normal atmospheric pressure, at 77 degrees F. (This is per the CRC Handbook of Chemistry and Physics, p. 2137. I am writing this down, because I can't derive this.)

So 1 LITER of air will weigh about 1.2 grams. And since 28.35 grams weighs 1 ounce, then 1 liter of air weighs about 1/24 ounce. So it takes 24 liters of air to weigh 1 ounce. And about 16 x 24 = 384 liters of air to weigh 1 lb. AND it takes about 2700 liters of air to burn one gallon of gas. 1 liter is 0.264 of US gallons. (1 Liter is 61.025 cubic inches, and a gallon is 231 cubic inches). So, 100 gallons of air weighs about 1 lb. And it takes 15 times that much – 15 pounds of air – to combust properly with 1 pound of gas. That's 1500 gallons of air to make a good, efficient burn with 1 pound of gas. And, 7 times that much, or 10,500 gallons of air, to burn with 1 gallon of gas. And it may take 15 or 20 or 30 minutes of normal driving to burn up that gallon of gas. OK? Yes, I double-checked this.

Next, I computed, HOW HIGH would you have to stack up this air, at this density of 1.19 grams per liter, to make 14.7 lb per square inch?? This is a number I can always use, to derive the density. The answer is 28,600 feet. If a column of constant-density air one inch square and 28,600 feet high weighs 14.7 lb, then you can easily back-compute how much its density is: you can derive the 1.2 grams per liter.... Now, it may be hard for you to remember 28,600 feet, as a standard number. But you can remember that Mt. Everest is about 29,141 feet high – or perhaps 29,002 feet. Anyhow, this is only a couple percent different from 28,600 feet. So now you know that a simple column of air, at normal sea-level density, stacked up about as high as Mt. Everest will weigh – that magic number – 14.7 lbs. per square inch. (Why so high? Maybe because the air is cold, up there.)

One of my buddies said, "Oh, is that why you cannot drive your VW to the top of Mt. Everest?" and I agreed, he is right, I would run out of air before I got to the top. Hey, most cars will run out of power LONG before they get to 20,000 feet! Every car I have driven at 14,000 ft. or even at 10,000 or 12,000 feet is very much short of power.

Chapter 7. *"PING"*

....

This was *going to be* just an Appendix, rather than a Chapter, because problems with your Spark or Ignition do not happen every day, and they are not likely to cause a collision or accident. *However,* problems with ignition can be serious, and can lead to expensive engine damage, which you want to avoid. So I rearranged this into a Chapter about *Ping,* which is kind of important. I put the rest of the information about Ignition into the Appendix on Spark. If you seem to be having ignition problems, or the engine is running badly, take a look there, as well as in the Chapter on Gasoline. This can be important...

What Can Go Wrong?

...because if you keep driving when your engine is running rough, and your spark is working badly, you can do hundreds of dollars of damage to your engine, or your catalytic converter, or both. That's not a *collision,* but if we called any error that causes over $100 of damage, an "accident", that's not too misleading. NOTE ALSO that if your ignition is failing intermittently, it might cut out right when you were counting on some power, thus putting YOU into an accident. If your engine is running badly, get it fixed fast. Until it's working right, take no such chances.

"Ping"

If the "timing" of your ignition is out of adjustment, your spark plugs might be firing too early. OK, what's wrong with THAT? Very simple: when you are working your engine hard, it may start to *ping.* A tiny bit of *ping* is not too bad, but if it starts to *ping* for more than a couple seconds, or *pings,* or "knocks" or "raps" loudly, that is bad, because the spark is firing (or, perhaps the gas is exploding without any spark) before the piston gets to the top. This can cause overheating, and can burn a valve or burn a piston. It can cause *hundreds* or *thousands* of dollars of harm to your engine. And you can hear this because it really does sound like a rapid, insistent *"pinging".* Some people say it sounds more like a "rap" or engine "knock" – a knock on the door, maybe with a hammer. It can vary from car to car. It occurs mostly in cars with manual transmission.

If you start getting serious *ping,* the first remedy is to ease your foot off the gas pedal, because the *ping* depends on the speed and the gas-pedal setting. If the *ping* goes away, that tends to confirm it really was *ping. Pinging* mostly starts when the engine is fully warmed up, and when you are on an up-hill, working the engine hard. Sometimes, stepping on the gas a little *harder* can help, but usually, taking your foot *off* the gas helps the most. Shift to a different gear. Shift to a lower gear – that may help a lot. Let your revs get higher, and don't tromp on the gas so hard – that is likely to help. Take it easy. Don't work the engine too hard. Don't let it *ping* a lot. Plan to get it fixed, soon.

7-16-21

Secondly, if you just bought some gas, maybe it is too low in octane. Stop buying that low-octane stuff. Buy some high-test gas, soon, and add it into your tank, and this will help cut your *pinging.* It may be easier to buy a half-tank of high-test, to go with a half-tank of low-test. Or, sometimes the mid-octane grade is cheaper and better. Some gas stations' low-test is higher in octane than others'. If your tank is full, stop in at an auto-supply store or a hot-rod shop, and get a little can of octane-booster, to add to your tank.

There are other things that can cause *ping,* and increasing the octane won't help. A bad EGR valve (Exhaust Gas Recirculation valve) can do that. So it may take serious repair or trouble-shooting effort.

If somebody re-timed your ignition recently, take it back and let him re-time it. If you did it yourself, plan to re-check your timing shortly.

◆ ◆ ◆

Modern engines with modern computerized ignition systems are supposed to not have *ping* – or at least not very much. They are supposed to use computers and sensors and tricks, to prevent *ping.* But if they are not working right, then you have to do whatever is necessary, to prevent a lot of *ping.* Change to a different gear, ease off on the gas, all the tricks listed above. Whatever you do, don't let your engine *ping* a lot. Baby it until you can get it fixed.

Damage Caused by Other Spark Problems...

– AND if you have any other ignition problems, or if the engine is running rough, and it does not seem to be a fuel supply problem, look in the Appendix on Spark, because your engine or catalytic converter may be getting damaged. An engine missing on one cylinder (with one bad spark plug) can dump a lot of raw, un-burned gas onto your catalytic converter, and it will overheat *fast.*

Chapter 8. AUTOMATIC Transmissions

What is an Automatic Transmission?

Historical: Manual gear-boxes have been around for over 100 years, but the Automatic Transmission (from here on in, let's call it an AT, to save ink) has been around really only 60 years, and the sales of ATs got only up to 10% of all cars, by 1951. However, ATs got better, and were much improved, whereas manual transmissions were pretty lousy for a long time. And the ATs gradually became a lot more popular, and now are up at 77% (estimate).

Just as with manual transmissions, front-wheel-drive cars have the AT and differential gears all grouped together, right near the engine. This is called a TRANS-AXLE – a combination of the Automatic TRANSmission and the drive-AXLE . Many rear-engine cars have the transmission and differential right in FRONT of the engine. That, too, is a *TRANS-AXLE*. In old-fashioned front-engine, rear-wheel-drive cars, the AT is right behind the engine, and then a drive-shaft carries the power back to the differential, mounted at the middle of the rear axle.

How Does an Automatic Transmission Work?

Automatic transmissions often have 3 or 4 forward gears, plus reverse. (Cheap ones used to have 2 forward gears, sometimes.) They consist of a torque converter plus some clutch-bands, to connect the output shaft to one of the internal gears.

When you start out at zero speed, the action of pumps plus impellers plus fixed vanes, means that if you get *some* torque from the engine, you can get 2 or 2.5 x as much torque coming out. This is called a torque converter. As the output shaft turns faster, less torque multiplication is provided. But, that's OK.

As the car goes faster, the transmission computes that it is time to shift. These computers used to be hydraulic, but now electronic ones are working well. As the speed again increases, another shift can take place.

These days, many best-performance ATs have a lock-up, so no slippage can occur. The series losses can be quite small. There still can be shunt losses – pumping friction, etc., but these losses are usually acceptable. The early automatic transmissions had poor efficiency – they had all kinds of losses. But over the years, they have been improved to where they provide substantially the same performance as a good manual transmission. The reason is, the wide range of slippage permitted by the torque converter lets the manufacturer put in a very *long* rear axle ratio, so the AT can provide good efficiency at highway speeds, compared to a 3-speed manual transmission. However, many modern cars have a 4-speed or 5-speed manual, and this permits a long gear ratio in top gear, too.

67

Shifting Up

The automatic transmission has neat capabilities to up-shift, as you accelerate. The modern ones are very smooth. Not perfect, but pretty good. If you floor the gas pedal, the engine will roar up to high revs, and shift at high revs, at each shift. If you just step on the gas moderately, the shifts will be at much lower RPMs and at lower speeds. This puts a lot less wear on the engine – and less wear on the AT.

Shifting Down

The AT can also do automatic downshifts, when you need one. If you are just going up a hill, and you get slowed down, the AT will eventually decide to downshift, and give you more power and acceleration.

Also, on the flat, even if you are not slowing down, you can get good acceleration for passing, by stepping hard on the gas-pedal. A little switch at the bottom of the gas pedal's travel, indicates that you want a downshift, and the AT will give you one. You get "passing gear" really quick, and at nearly full throttle too.

Engine Braking?

What does the AT not do well? Well, you cannot get engine braking, in "Drive". If you want engine braking, you have to shift down into "2" gear, by manually pulling the shifter to 2. Likewise, to get to an even lower gear, for engine braking on steep downhills, you wait until you are slowed down enough and then pull it into "LO". The debate of when you want to do this, is covered in the Chapter on Braking.

Fuzzy Logic?*

The Saturn got an improved AT for 1994. It got a new capability for automatic downshifts. If you are an Electrical Engineer, you may have heard a lot about Fuzzy Logic. This AT uses FL to decide when to shift. Actually, FL is capable of much more complicated functions than is needed here.

When you are driving a Saturn on a down-grade, and you don't feed the gas, but just hit the brakes 2 or 3 times, at a moderate speed, such as 40 or 45 mph, the AT Computer decides that you are on a downgrade, and you ought to have a downshift – even if you are not bright enough to shift down into second, yourself. So, after it checks all the right clues, it downshifts for you.

At first, I thought this would be dangerous, on a snowy downgrade, because a sudden downshift might cause a surprise skid. But then I learned that the downshift is properly double-clutched – in other words, the throttle is fed a little more gas, so you do not get any jerk when this downshift occurs. That sounds like a pretty good idea.

It was also stated (on Marketplace Radio) that the Fuzzy Logic was used to improve the shifting on upgrades. From what my friends told me, the 1992 Saturn had a lousy shift computer on upgrades. If you got on a long, steady upgrade, and just stepped on the gas, trying to go up a steep upgrade as fast as

*Fuzzy Logic, D. McNeill & P. Freiberger, Simon & Schuster, 1993.

the engine would pull you, the AT would shift down into second – and try to rev up – and then shift UP into third. It would shift up, and down, back and forth, incessantly, up and down.... This is called, "hunting". The transmission is "hunting" back and forth, trying to find the right gear. And not finding a good decision! If you think it was boring to read that, think of how wearying it would be to drive a car that actually shifted like that! So, the Saturn engineers realized they had met every function on their list of Things To Do, but they forgot to teach the computer to avoid Hunting. They went back and re-designed the AT to NOT do Hunting.

But an author of a book on "Fuzzy Logic", Mr. McNeill, said that the Saturn engineers used Fuzzy Logic to avoid Hunting. I read in an industry newsletter, that the Saturn engineers did NOT use FL for this improvement, because they did not have to. It was easy not to. I have been having many arguments with stupid people making dumb arguments why Fuzzy Logic is great. Actually, Fuzzy Logic is very good and powerful, but its promoters are so much addicted to hype, they brag about things that are not real.

Anyhow, the guy who plunks his money down for a new Saturn gets a better AT. It may not make any difference exactly what technology is used, but I thought you would be amused to hear about this debate over what technology is useful for which improvements.

How To Be Nice To Your AT...

My pappy taught me the right way to drive an AT. He had driven manual-shift cars and trucks, all his life, but he bought a 1955 Packard Clipper that was really a pretty good turnpike cruiser. He pointed out, if you don't feed the gas much, you will put minimum wear on the AT, but it will take a long time to get going. If you just tromp on the gas, hard, it will accelerate briskly, but that will put a lot of wear on the bands (the clutch bands) when it decides to shift.

He told me to feed it pretty well – about half-throttle – until the speedometer shows 30 mph, and then take my foot off the gas. The computer (a hydraulic computer, at that time), sensing decreased demand, will decide to shift, at a time when there is not much power coming from the engine. Then as soon as it shifts, I should *feed* the gas again, (don't floor it) up to 55, and then slack off again, and wait for the shift to high gear. It works! It gives good acceleration, yet minimum stress on the shifting components. It's not quite the same as double-clutching a manual transmission, but it's the same concept – feed the power to it, when it's not shifting; then ease off and make a clean shift, and then feed it more power.

Downshifting

When you just push the shift lever of an AT up into "2" – what happens? The engine has to speed up – but the car jerks because the road has to speed up the engine. After that you get engine braking. The friction of the engine is able to slow your car down, on a flat road – or to prevent it from going faster, if you are on a downgrade.

What if the owner's manual says you can safely shift down into second, up to 55 mph – but you are going 65? You are beginning to lose your brakes. So, what if you pull the shift lever *anyhow*? In some cases, in some cars, the AT will refuse to shift until you get the speed down to 58 or 57. In other cases, it might shift down when you do it, but it might over-rev the engine somewhat, and overstress the AT. I don't know which of these *your* car will do. I certainly do not recommend that you try this, until you absolutely desperately need it.

Often, I rent a car, and I take the Driver's Manual in to my hotel, and read it. The manuals tell me all sorts of odd things; sometimes they were even well written, and sometimes, of course, they had been translated (not-too-well) from Japanese.

But on some of them, they said, if you stall the transmission (put the car's nose against a brick wall, or hook it up to a BIG trailer) and *floor* the gas for 10 seconds, you are likely to cause a MELT-DOWN of the automatic transmission. I do not want to buy one of these cars. I have heard that some of the manufacturers have put so many plastic parts into the "Hydraulic computer" that are sure to melt in the first 11-seconds of full-throttle operation, that I'm not favorably impressed to buy such a car.

What Can Go Wrong With An AT?

If you let the AT Fluid get too low, that will let the AT overheat, due to not enough fluid. If you work it too hard, it could also overheat. Can this cause an accident? Not likely. It just can cost you money, or cause a breakdown. I don't care who built it.

Ah – there is one little detail you should know about an AT – if you just leave it in "Drive", and try to drive in snow, or ice or any other slippery conditions, the AT will shift down into LO gear, for starting, and will try to put out too much torque to the drive wheels. For better results, shift from DRIVE to "2" before you start. Then the AT will put out less torque. This is MUCH better than staying in DRIVE.

"Semi-Automatic Stick Shift"

I bought a 1970 VW Beetle with "semi-Automatic Stick Shift" (ASS). I was a little skeptical, but some VW experts told me that it was not a bad system, with good performance and reliability. And actually, it worked very well, for 170,000 miles. I was not dissatisfied with the performance. I was able to go up 20% grades for some hills in San Francisco, in top gear. Not a *great* gearbox, but – pretty good. When the engine began leaking a lot of oil, I retired the car. It did not owe me anything.

Four-Wheel Drive (4WD)

I am not an expert on 4WD. But even if I were, I would not tell you everything I know, because this is not the right book. Still, I'll throw in some brief comments.

The best part about a 4WD car is that you can drive it just like an ordinary car. You can just leave it in 2-wheel drive and leave the transmission in HIGH range, and DRIVE. Whether manual transmission or automatic, you can just drive it like any other car. If you want to know anything more about 4WD, go look in the Appendix on 4WD. To a large extent, a study of 4WD is not relevant to this book, but the types of accidents you can have with 4WD vehicles are listed in that Appendix.

Chapter 9. Manual Transmissions

WHAT is a manual transmission? How does it work? A manual transmission, which *used to be* called "Standard Shift", is a set of gears to connect the power and torque of the engine to the wheels, with a set of different gear ratios. The gears are all sealed up in a *gearbox,* with some heavy oil or light grease. A shift lever is connected to the transmission, to let you select the correct forward gear – or Reverse gear – and ALSO, neutral. The Lowest gear (first gear) is for starting, and ascending steep hills. Second gear gets you going faster. High gear is for driving at speed on the open road. These days, transmissions often have 4 forward gears, but some have 5. Many years ago, most cars had only 3 forward gears.

The *clutch* is located between the engine and the transmission, to disconnect the engine for shifting – and for starting. While the clutch is essential for driving with a manual transmission, it will be discussed in the next chapter.

The *differential* is connected between the transmission and the drive axles, to permit power to flow evenly to both drive wheels, even when they are rolling at different speeds – such as when you are going around a corner.

Some cars have 4-wheel drive, and many of these have Low and High ranges, for ascending steep grades and pulling stumps. We'll treat this topic in an Appendix, because it is quite specialized.

> *Most front-wheel-drive cars have the transmission and differential gears all grouped together, right near the engine. This is called a TRANS-AXLE – a combination of a TRANSmission and a drive-AXLE. Many rear-engine cars have the transmission and differential right in FRONT of the engine. That, too, is called a TRANS-AXLE. In old-fashioned front-engine, rear-wheel-drive cars, the transmission is right behind the engine, and then a drive-shaft carries the power back to the differential, mounted at the middle of the rear axle. This is considered old-fashioned for a passenger car, but if you need to go 200 mph, as in Grand National Stock-Car racing, this is still not a bad arrangement.*

Shift Patterns

In the old days, "standard shift" meant 3 forward gears – First, Second, Third – and Reverse, in a conventional "H" pattern. See Sketch A. In the 1930s, the gear-shift lever extended out of the car's floor, right up from the transmission, which was under the floor-boards. Cars were built TALL, back then. Then, in the 1940s, to provide better comfort for the passengers, car makers moved the shift lever up onto the steering column: "Three on the Tree". Then in the 1960s, many cars put the front seats down *beside* the transmission, and the shifter was on the top of the transmission, (the center console), right by

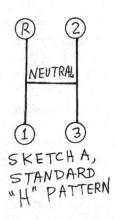

SKETCH A,
STANDARD
"H" PATTERN

the driver's elbow. Thus, "Four on the Floor". Now, many cars have a fifth gear. Where did they hide reverse? See sketches B and C.

How does the manual transmission work? The drive shaft from the engine (by way of the clutch) turns several pairs of gears. Not all the gears are connected to the output shaft, which goes to the differential, to drive the rear wheels. Depending on which gear you select, you can connect up any one set of gears. Normally, you start in first gear, and shift later into second, etc., up to high gear. In many cases, the manual transmission is quite efficient, and a smooth driver can get excellent performance and drive smoothly, too.

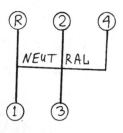

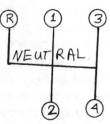

What Can Go Wrong?

If you are not a good, skilled driver, you can "grind the gears" or make the gearteeth or synchronizer teeth clash against each other. After the transmission gets old, the bearings can get worn and make a bad humming noise. If you try to shift too fast, eventually you can wear out the synchronizers, and then it is hard to shift without unfortunate grinding noises. If the transmission is badly designed, or abused, you may get stuck and unable to get the transmission out of gear – or into a gear – without struggling. If you "miss your shift" – if you don't get the gears completely engaged – then when you step on the gas, you can over-rev your engine. And you may be in trouble in traffic, because you were planning to accelerate, but you wind up decelerating, just when you are trying to merge into traffic. The guy behind you might have to brake hard, and be quite unhappy at your driving!

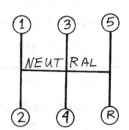

SKETCH B, TYPICAL 4-SPEED SHIFT PATTERNS

Synchronizers – usually called – "Synchros"

When you "shift gears", you are not really engaging or dis-engaging the gears (except for reverse). When you "grind the gears", you are not really crunching the gear teeth (except for reverse). All the forward gears are always in mesh, but some of the gears are not connected to the shaft they are rolling on. There are little "synchronizers" that connect the gears to the shafts. They act like little "clutches", so if the gear and its shaft are not at the same speed, the synchro

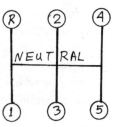

SKETCH C, TYPICAL 5-SPEED SHIFT PATTERNS

forces the shaft to come to the right speed. If you are trying to shift very quickly – "speed-shifting" – this puts a lot of wear on the "synchros". They may last 100k or 150k miles, but if they wear out because you shifted too fast, don't be surprised.

To avoid wear on your synchros, you should shift at a slow or moderate rate, on up-shifts, and double-clutch on down-shifts. Refer to the Appendix on Double-clutching. This minimizes wear on the synchros, and the clutch, too. It can minimize wear and stress on the entire drive-train. More later.

◆ ◆ ◆

Historical: before 1935, most cars did not have "synchronizers". So to be an adequate driver, you HAD TO know how to shift by ear, and to double-clutch on down-shifts, or else make horrible GRINDING noises. But synchronizers made life a lot easier. Most US cars in the 1940s and 1950s had synchronizers on all forward gears EXCEPT FIRST. VW only re-designed their gearbox to put in a synchronized first gear in 1962. When modern US cars got 4 forward gears, they got synchro in all 4 gears. But on any old car, you may find that first gear is NOT synchronized. To get into first, either you stop, or you learn how to double-clutch. So, this is a good reason to learn how to double-clutch – to be able to drive an old car gracefully.

Trucks often have a "crash-box", a transmission without synchronizers. These gearboxes can be stronger and more efficient. Some sports/racing cars likewise have a "crash-box", for the same reason. So it is a good idea to know how to drive a manual transmission, and also to know how to double-clutch – then you could quickly learn to drive a truck or racing car, competently.

◆ ◆ ◆

How do you drive a car with a manual transmission? Very carefully – until you learn how!

First of all, you need to get the engine started, with the gearbox in Neutral. Let's presume you have figured this out – or, refer to the Chapter on Starting. Second, you have to check the gearshift pattern to make sure you know where the gears all are, if you are not used to this pattern. There are several semi-standard patterns.

If you already know how to drive this set-up, you know the procedure is deceptively simple. Assume you are on a flat road – you check the road for a clear road and not much traffic – and keep checking it.

Step on the brakes. Step on the clutch, all the way down. Ease the shift lever into first gear. If the way is still clear, take your right foot off the brake, hit the gas pedal *just a little,* and start letting up on the clutch, *slowly.* As the clutch begins to engage, don't let up the clutch pedal much more. Then as your speed picks up, let the clutch up a little higher, and feed a little more gas. When you are rolling pretty well, you can let the clutch out (up) all the way. Now the clutch is up all the way, feed it some gas.

When you are going "fast enough" in first, kick in the clutch, all the way down. Snap the shift lever out of first – and stop in neutral. And simultaneously, take your foot off the gas pedal. Wait a second – or at least half a second. Then, after the engine is slowed down nicely, ease the shift lever into second. Let out the clutch. If you have judged it right, there will be no jerk, and no change of engine speed when you let out

9-2

the clutch. If there is a little lurch, you should notice that you mis-judged slightly. See the following paragraphs.

◆ ◆ ◆

If you are shifting from first into second, or from ANY lower gear to the next higher gear, and when you let out the clutch, the car lurches back, because the engine was going too slow, there are 3 basic things you can do.

1. It may be because you accelerated to too high a speed in the lower gear. If you do not wind out so much in first – if you do not get going so fast in the lower gear – then the engine at idle will not be going too slow. When you are on a flat road, and in no rush, this is a good solution. For beginning drivers, where the timing is hard to get right, this is one of the best solutions, until you get your practice in.

2. It may be you shifted too slowly. If you shift a little faster, the engine will not have slowed down so much, and you will get less jerk. This is good to do when you are on an up-grade, or in a hurry in traffic. This is appropriate for an experienced driver.

3. It may be that, for an uphill or upgrade, you HAVE TO shift at higher RPMs. Then the method in paragraph 1 is not appropriate. Therefore, feed the gas just a tiny bit – don't let the engine speed come all the way down to a slow idle.

4. If you are not getting the timing or the co-ordination right, you might let the clutch out a little more slowly. This is a Band-Aid. This causes a little wear on the clutch, and is a symptom of bad driving. It may lead to bad habits that cause expensive repairs. But if you only do it rarely, it is not so bad.

5. If you are driving under easy conditions, you can listen for the engine when its revs start slowing down, after you take your foot off the gas. If you listen, that should help you get the speed right. If your radio is on too loud, and that is causing you to shift badly because you can't hear the engine, maybe you should turn down the radio. A radio is all very fine, unless it distracts an inexperienced driver. Then that is time to turn it down, or shut it off. If the gravel road makes too much road noise, that can't be helped. It's hard to expect any but a skilled driver to drive smoothly on a rough gravel road. If there is a lot of noisy traffic, well, you can't do much about that. So when you cannot hear your engine, it is hard to shift smoothly. Just concentrate, and try not to rev too high, and do the best you can. If you really do not have much experience, and you are shifting roughly, don't feel too bad, because it DOES take a good bit of practice. After just a few dozen miles, your techniques should get DEFINITELY better, and after a few thousand, you should get really smooth, most of the time. Don't be too discouraged.

SIMILARLY, if you are shifting up, and you let the clutch out, and the car LURCHES forward, there are a couple simple solutions.

6. You may have forgotten to take your foot off the gas. It's easy for a beginner to forget that, but it is also easy to learn to do it right. Keep practicing, and listen to the engine. If the engine is still revving when you are ready to let out the clutch, get your right foot up before you let out the clutch. It's like a kind of DANCE. Some kids learn to dance pretty naturally, and others need lessons, and some need MORE lessons. Putting the left foot DOWN on the clutch, at the same time you lift off your right toe; and waiting, and putting the shift lever over, and then lifting the left foot up, and putting the right toe down – that's just a little kind of DANCE. You can learn it.

7. If you let up the clutch too quickly, that could cause a jerk, too. So you might wait just a small part of a second longer, to let out the clutch. Your teacher can show you what is right.

◆ ◆ ◆

Why all this emphasis on shifting properly? If you do it wrong, eventually it will become not only EXPENSIVE, but you might bump into something, like the car ahead of you. The classical problem is, you can't figure out where you are in the shifting process, so you look down at the gearshift. And while you are glaring at it, you bump into the car in front of you (because he stopped, and you weren't looking). Or perhaps you nudge into the car on the left or right, because it's hard to keep centered in your lane, when you are looking down at the floor. So, it really is important to get a lot of practice in, on *empty* parking lots, and then on *empty* roads, before you get into any traffic at all. And your teacher knows this. Even if you are slow to learn how to shift, don't get too frustrated, because when you have it right, you are all set for many years. You'll never forget how to do this.

I used to shift 320 times per day, to go to work. These days, it's more like 150. So let's say I have only put on an average of 150 shifts per day, ever since 1961. That's only about 1,900,000 shifts. And I won't say I never make a mistake and miss a shift. I won't say I never let out the clutch with a little jerk. Just, not very often.

◆ ◆ ◆

NOW, make sure your foot is off the clutch, and gradually feed the gas – step on the gas pedal slowly and smoothly, to accelerate appropriately. (That is a matter of judgement, as your teacher has taught you.) When you are going "fast enough" in second, repeat the up-shift procedure as listed in the previous paragraph.

When you are going fast enough in third, etc. you may shift up again.

When you are going as fast as you want to go, you don't have to shift up any more. For example, at 30 mph, in traffic, you usually do not shift into high gear. You might be in 3rd or 2nd. That's fine. Just stay in that gear.

◆ ◆ ◆

When I am at rest, and want to get going, after I step on the clutch pedal, my usual procedure to get into first gear, is to shove the shift lever into SECOND, and THEN into first. Then I start to let out the clutch. This causes less wear on the first-gear synchronizers – and a little more wear on the 2nd-gear Synchros. I figure that is fair, because I will probably never wear out the synchros on 2nd gear. On old cars that did not have any synchronizer for first gear, this was important, to avoid graunching the gears. On modern cars, this is still a good habit, if you are not in a hurry. If you are in a hurry, then just go right into first.

I have a similar habit, going into fourth: after I shift into Fourth, or top gear, I reach down and lift up the handbrake, and set it OFF. This is just a reminder, to make sure the handbrake is off. About one time out of every 500, I find that the handbrake is NOT all the way off.

One of my buddies pointed out that modern transmissions are so efficient and low in drag, and have such thin grease, that when you kick in the clutch, the gears continue to spin for a few seconds. So when you then try to shift into Reverse (which does not have any Synchros) you get a graunch. This is not disastrous, as the gears are designed to survive a lot of this. But for best results, if you have time, even a second, shift into any forward gear, where the synchros will get all the gears and shafts STOPPED. THEN shift into Reverse. If you can do this, this will decrease the amount of tiny metal flecks floating around in your gear grease. It's a good habit.

◆ ◆ ◆

NOTE – when you drive in reverse, you hear a whine from the gears. That's because the gears are straight-cut. Reverse is the only gear where the gears actually move and engage or disengage. As this is true, you cannot use spiral-cut gears, because it would force the gears apart. In an old car, you will ALSO hear that whine in first, if first is non-synchro. But you do not hear that whine in other gears because the gears are spiral-cut. I'll provide a little sketch.

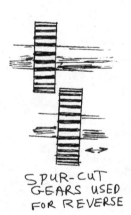

SPUR-CUT GEARS USED FOR REVERSE

SPIRAL-CUT GEARS USED FOR 3RD GEAR (BEARING DETAILS NOT SHOWN)

When your REVERSE gears are not engaged, the gears do not even TOUCH. When you put them in gear, their gear teeth make a noise – just like gears!

When you are not using second gear, the gears are still meshing and turning every time you drive along – but the lower gear is not connected to its shaft. It is just rolling freely around the shaft. When you DO shift into second gear, the lower gear is connected to its shaft. The spiral gears are efficient and quiet, but they put out some end-thrust along the shafts. The bearings are designed so this is OK. But you could not use spiral-cut gears like that for reverse, because that thrust would pop you out of gear. THUS, in reverse, you get a lot more noise.

◆ ◆ ◆

After I came out with my column on Double-clutching, a guy pointed out that race cars may indeed NOT have Synchromesh, but that does not mean the gears are disengaged. They just have no Synchros, because the transmissions get so hot that the Synchros don't work very well, anyhow. Trucks, I am not so sure about.

◆ ◆ ◆

NOW, this whole procedure of shifting with a manual transmission is something you are not going to learn from this book, or from any other book. This is what you learn from your teacher. After you have learned it, it makes sense. And it should be pretty much as I wrote it.

If you find that your teacher is teaching you something different from what I write, you could ask your teacher, "Why?" He might say I am wrong. He might say Pease is right, but it is not critical in YOUR CAR. It might lead to useful and educational discussions. You have to use your own judgement. If you think I am wrong, you could write me a letter and explain. Please include a return address. I might like to debate with you, and I might need to learn more about your car.

Further, this procedure, as written down, is something that sounds awfully messy – but once you learn how to do it, it is pretty neat and natural. In other words, shifting is easier than it sounds!

◆ ◆ ◆

Back there, where I said, you should shift when you are going "fast enough" – how fast is "fast enough"? This is something you also learn from your teacher. But let me list some of the guidelines.

- Normally, you decide when to shift "by ear". When the engine "sounds about right", that is time to shift.

- Normally, the engine will not be screaming when you shift. Not usually above 3000 rpm, unless you have a reason to be in a hurry.

- Normally, the engine will be turning over pretty well, SO THAT when you get into the next higher gear, it will not be lugging. "Lugging" consists of making the engine turn over slow, and feeding it a lot of gas, so it runs rough, and you can feel every piston stroke. The whole car shudders. This "lugging" is not good for the engine, and not comfortable, either. You do NOT want to run at 1100 rpm in 4th gear unless you are on a downgrade.

- Your shift points – the speeds when you shift from one gear to another – will depend on whether you are headed uphill or down. If you are trying to get started up a steep upgrade, you will shift at a slightly higher speed than normal (48 mph into top gear?) If you are on a downgrade, you can shift at a little slower rpms (perhaps 35 or 40 mph ?) and still not have to feed the gas too hard.

- Your shift points will depend on the traffic. If everybody wants to get up to speed pretty quickly, you will usually shift into High, rather on the high side, to get accelerating well. (45 mph? 50?) If traffic is very light, or very slow, you could shift slower, and there's nobody to complain. Maybe 35? If I am in fairly slow traffic, and there is nowhere to go, I could shift into high gear at 26 or 30 mph, and just ease along. So long as I do not need to accelerate, I won't be feeding the gas – and then easing along at 30 or 35 is just fine. But if I needed to then start accelerating, I might have to shift down into 3rd, to get moving. If I got slowed down *a lot*, I might have to shift down *two* gears to be able to accelerate properly.

The Joys of Shifting

So – whenever and wherever you like to shift – then that is one of the nicest things about a manual transmission – you can shift *when* and *where* you want to.

If you want to skip a gear – you can do that – just wind it out in second – and shift to fourth. You can shift at low revs – or high.

One time I was bicycling through Cambridge Mass, and came to a stop light. A shiny new Alfa Romeo was at the light. When the light went green, the car wound out nicely in first, at about 3/4 full throttle – right up to about 5000 rpm. Then he snap-shifted into second, fed it a couple seconds, shifted to third, fed it hard for 2 seconds, shifted to 4th – and then, off in the distance, after a couple seconds, he shifted into fifth – and cruised off into the west. Neat! I was impressed!

One time, I wanted to see if I could start my Beetle in 4th gear. I started out on a flat road, and slipped the clutch gently, at low revs, and gradually I got it up to 23, and then I was able to just let out the clutch and proceed. It was not doing any great amount of harm, not particularly a lot of wear on the clutch. (It would have caused a lot of wear if I slipped the clutch at high revs.) But I have never bothered to do it again. Never needed to.

I recall reading that a 1975 Corvette has so much power and such close gear ratios, that the time for 0-to-100 mph was about 11 seconds going through all 4 gears – and just 16 seconds in 4th gear only. But, that is putting a *lot* of stress on the clutch!!

I also recall reading, in a boy's magazine from the 1930s, that a young man should not be considered a good driver, until he can slip the clutch and move a car's rear wheels up on top of a 2-by-4 – in third gear! I don't think that is a great idea – and it would be an abuse of the clutch. But in concept, one could do that. I just don't want MY kids doing that with MY clutch.

Down-Shifting

Now that you are moving, eventually you will want to stop. There are some old books that tell you, just take your foot off the gas and put on the brakes, and step on the clutch when you are going pretty slow. If you are in second gear, this is quite reasonable. But, what if you are in high gear? It is literally true that you can just take your foot off the gas, and your brakes will not wear out excessively fast. But it is better to down-shift at least once – at least on any competent car that has a decent gearbox.

Let's say you are rolling in high gear on a flat road at 55 mph, and you see you are approaching a stop sign. You slow down to, say 35, and kick in the clutch and *blip** the gas pedal a bit. Then you ease the shift lever fairly quickly from 4th to 3rd, and let out the clutch. If you got the speed right, the car does not jerk at all when you let out the clutch. Then when you get down toward 15 or 10 mph, you can kick in the clutch again, and pull the shift lever out of 3rd, into neutral. Then you use the brakes down to a stop. After you stop, wait in Neutral, with your foot off the clutch, until the way is clear to start. Then one second before the way is clear, you depress the clutch, and shift into first and proceed. THAT is a good way to downshift and stop.

It is absolutely not essential for you to down-shift for a stop sign like this – but you SHOULD know how to do it. HOWEVER, it IS essential to be able to do this, if you are slowing down and approaching a red traffic light. Because soon that light will turn green. You have to be able to shift down, smoothly, and then start to accelerate. In fact, you should also be able to shift down from 3rd gear to second, the same way, in case you need to accelerate at low speeds on a moderate upgrade.

◆ ◆ ◆

There are a couple other places where down-shifting smoothly is *essential*. The first is on a snowy upgrade, where you are running out of power in High gear. You need to shift down SMOOTHLY, or you will lose traction. If you just shove it into 3rd, it would tend to JERK and you could lose traction and start skidding, and not make it up the hill.

The other place for smooth downshifting is, after coming over the top of a snowy hill, when the downhill grade starts to get a little steep. If you just shove the shift lever into third, and let out the clutch, it may jerk, and you could lose traction, and start skidding. If you *blip* the gas before you let out the clutch, the car will not have to speed up the engine. Downshifting smoothly is part of driving safely.

When to Downshift

Downshifting can be done under many conditions. You might do it at a nice high rpm, because it is fun to do. OR, because you need a lot of engine-braking, on a long steep downhill. OR, you might do it at a low rpm. You might even downshift at an excessive rpm, in an emergency, if your brakes were failing. Or you might just do it at a moderate rpm – not just because you want a lot of engine braking, but because you are going to need some power pretty soon, and you want to get down into your lower gear, in advance of coming out of the sharp curve.

7-27-21

Blip is a technical term – that is, you just tap the gas pedal for a half a second, so the engine revs rise up briefly.

If you shift at rather high speeds, only on rare occasions, that will only wear out your car a little bit. But if you downshift only at moderate or low rpms, it will not cause excessive wear on the car, nor the engine. Nor the clutch nor the synchros. Just be neat, and don't miss your shifts!!

– And, this is also true for heel-and-toe shifting, too – you do not *have to* do this at high rpms – and if you do it at moderate rpms, it will not cause wear on the car.

When is Downshifting Not Stupid?

Several of my buddies have pointed out that downshifting is stupid and not cost-effective, if you try to use it for the effects of engine braking, because wearing out your engine or your clutch is a LOT more expensive than wearing out your brakes. This is generally a true statement. Replacing a clutch is generally more expensive than just re-lining your brakes.

But there are several cases where it is NOT true that downshifting (while decelerating) is foolish or expensive. Such as:

- Where there is a long steep hill, and you want to go slow and not abuse your brakes.

- When you downshift at fairly low RPMs, this is not abusive to the engine.

- When you downshift cleanly by double clutching, this does not put any significant wear on the clutch.

- When you are slowing down in traffic, or for a curve, and you downshift in anticipation that you will soon want to accelerate.

- When you are in trouble and you need engine braking to get out of trouble.

- Just for practice.

- Just for fun.

- And, Note: you DO have to know how to downshift when you run out of power on a steep hill, and you need a lower gear.

Speedshifting

If you are really in a hurry, accelerating – say, on a really steep, long upgrade, you may find it justifiable, to rev the engine 'way up there. Then you do not have to make a slow shift. In fact, if you are REALLY trying to get up the hill as well as you can, just punch the clutch, shove the shifter into the next higher gear, and let the clutch out. Meanwhile you DID take your foot off the gas, while shifting. As soon as the clutch is out, you feed the gas again. If you do that all the time, it is bad for economy, and bad for wear on the engine, the clutch, and the synchros. But it will help you get going up that hill. I just don't recommend you do it all the time. Just once in a while.

Similarly, to downshift when ascending a big hill, where you really are running out of power, (as soon as you have slowed enough in 4th, so you would not be over-revving in 3rd), shift quickly into 3rd (for example) and just feed the gas hard, as soon as the clutch is out. Again, if you do this all the time, you'll wear it out faster.

◆ ◆ ◆

For best results, I recommend double-clutching it. This is a semi-advanced technique. But if you know how to shift, now, you can learn it. It's good for you – it will help you drive more smoothly, and put less wear on the car's parts. *Your parents will be impressed.* Refer to the Appendix on Double-Clutching. Good stuff.

◆ ◆ ◆

Then there is another advanced technique – heel-and-toe braking. As I keep my brakes adjusted so the brake pedal is moderately low, then I can easily do my heel-and-toe work. This is not a main-stream topic, as it does not usually have much to do with avoiding accidents. But you should read the Appendix on Heel-and Toe, at leisure, for general interest.

◆ ◆ ◆

Many years ago, I was teaching my wife to drive, down in Barnstable Mass. We were sitting at an intersection, with the engine idling, debating and deciding where to go next. We decided. She shifted into first gear. Now, she forgot to put in the clutch. But she did it so NICELY, that the gearbox went into first, without any graunch. Away we went. I suggested she might want to put in the clutch next time! Now she does. NOTE: the cars SHE drives never have any trouble with their gearbox wearing out.

What Else Can Go Wrong?

If you are driving about as hard as you can, and you make a speed-shift – and miss your shift – fail to get it in gear – with your foot firmly on the LOUD-pedal, you can over-rev the engine. With a really hot engine, you can cook the engine. Most engines are not that hot, not that free-revving – so you probably cannot instantly ruin the engine, not on any car you can buy. But you should try not to abuse the engine that way. On a racing engine, you could ruin it doing that. Don't be too pushy.

◆ ◆ ◆

If you let out the clutch just as the synchros are just ready to get the gears engaged – you might bust the synchros. There is no guarantee that abusing the gearshift like this will not do harm to the synchros or gears, or whatever. Lean how to drive consistently, before you get pushy or aggressive.

◆ ◆ ◆

One time my son Jonathan was driving his Beetle back from a long trip in Pennsylvania. He was getting very sleepy, so he let another guy drive for a ways. This person knew how to drive on a slush-box, but had not driven with a manual transmission. Jonathan got him started, and took a nap. After a few dozen freeway miles, they slowed down for an exit. The driver decided to shift down at about 30 mph. Unfortunately he shifted NEATLY into reverse. This did not destroy the gearbox – but the clutch blew out. You could not any longer shift gears by stepping on the clutch. You could not slip the clutch.

Jonathan called me up at 2 AM, and explained his predicament. I told him he had 2 main choices. One was to wait in town until the repair shops opened up the next morning, and get it fixed. That was what I recommended. OR, he could try to drive it back on the highway to Ithaca NY., about 150 miles – with no clutch. At some times of day, that would be messy, but at midnight, at least it was unlikely to be unsafe. He had recently read my column on Double-Clutching – see at Appendix M.

Four hours later, he called from Ithaca. Apparently there were not many bad hills on the roads to Ithaca, so he learned the art of shifting with no clutch. He figured it out. Needless to say, after that small nap, he had a lot of adrenaline flowing, and he made all his shifts with no clutch, and stayed awake. The next week, it cost a few hundred dollars to replace all the clutch parts that were busted. But, the gearbox ran on and on.

Driving in England

When you go to England and rent a car there – you climb into the driver's seat on the right side of the car. Do you find the clutch pedal on the right, and the gas pedal on the left? NO!! Fortunately. It sure is a good thing, because if I had to learn to depress the gas pedal with my left foot, and STAB the clutch with my right foot, that would be VERY difficult. Fortunately, we do not have to learn this cross-functional mode. The pedals are just fine for us Yankee drivers. And it is a good thing, because a car with automatic transmission in Europe costs a lot more – about 30 to 60% more – than a car with manual transmission. So, it is a good thing to be competent at driving with a manual transmission.

However, when you start out in this little rented Ford Fiesta, or Vauxhall Corsa, or whatever, you start out in first – and as you get up to the speed to shift – your hand naturally reaches out – your RIGHT hand – and all there is over there, is – a door handle. No, put that hand back on the wheel, and reach over with your LEFT hand – and the gearshift lever is there. Works just fine. After a few hours, you really get used to it.

Fortunately, most cars in England are RH-drive cars, and the driver sits on the right seat, with his RIGHT elbow near the center-line of the road. If I had to start in France, with a LH drive car, and drive over to England, that would be REAL trouble. When I am in a RH-drive car, I can easily remember to drive on the left side of the road. If I had to drive a LH-drive car in England, that would be too confusing for me – and dangerous, too. I had better not do that. It's just too vice-versa of a problem for me.

FourWheel Drive (4WD)

I am not an expert on 4WD. But even I were, I would not tell you everything I know, because this is not the right place. Still, I'll throw in a brief set of comments.

The best part about a 4WD car is that you can drive it just like an ordinary car. You can just leave it in 2-wheel drive and leave the transmission in HIGH range, and DRIVE. Whether manual transmission or automatic, you can just drive it like any other car. If you want to know anything more about 4WD, go look in the Appendix on 4WD. To a large extent, a study of 4WD is not relevant to this book, but the types of accidents you can have with 4WD vehicles are listed in that appendix.

Now, I wrote a nice column about Double-Clutching, and it was published in Electronic Design magazine, about August 1993. Should I upgrade What's All This Double-Clutching Stuff, Anyhow? from an Appendix to a Chapter?? NO, because double-clutching does not normally have anything to do with accidents. It does not cause or prevent ACCIDENTS. However, I recommend that you *ought to* read the Double-Clutching Appendix, to know how to shift without any clutch, and, to understand how to go up and down thru the gears without a clutch. This is not to avoid accidents, but to get around breakdowns.

This covers almost everything there is, about manual transmissions. But be sure to read the Appendix on Double-Clutching, too.

Chapter 10. THE CLUTCH

This Chapter is about the clutch, and is mostly of interest to people who use a manual transmission. This Chapter has information that is sort of interleaved with the information on manual transmissions. I think if you read that Chapter first, and then this, it will make the best sense.

What is "The Clutch" and How Does It Work?

In a car with a manual transmission*, there is a clutch pedal on the left of your brake pedal. When you "step on the clutch pedal", there are levers (or cables, or a hydraulic linkage) going to the clutch, to disconnect the engine from the transmission.**

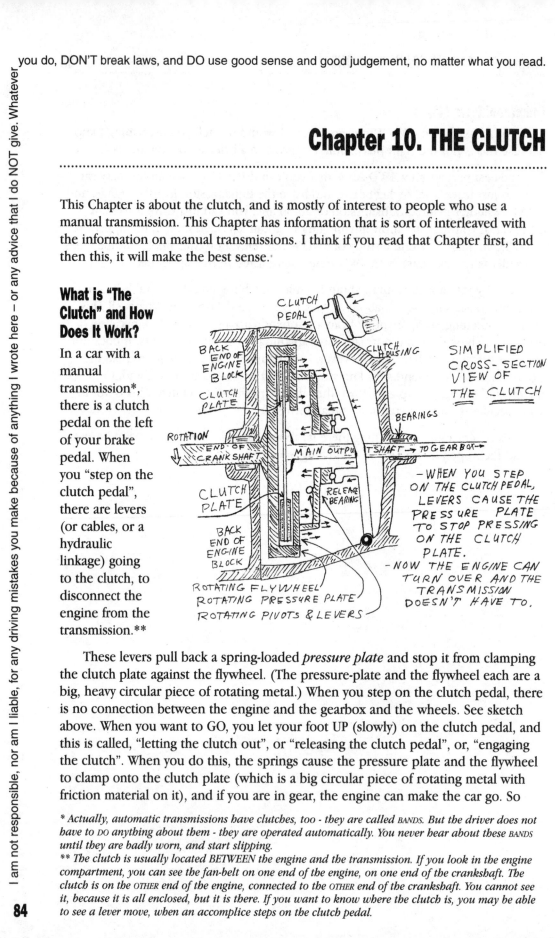

These levers pull back a spring-loaded *pressure plate* and stop it from clamping the clutch plate against the flywheel. (The pressure-plate and the flywheel each are a big, heavy circular piece of rotating metal.) When you step on the clutch pedal, there is no connection between the engine and the gearbox and the wheels. See sketch above. When you want to GO, you let your foot UP (slowly) on the clutch pedal, and this is called, "letting the clutch out", or "releasing the clutch pedal", or, "engaging the clutch". When you do this, the springs cause the pressure plate and the flywheel to clamp onto the clutch plate (which is a big circular piece of rotating metal with friction material on it), and if you are in gear, the engine can make the car go. So

Actually, automatic transmissions have clutches, too - they are called BANDS. But the driver does not have to DO anything about them - they are operated automatically. You never hear about these BANDS until they are badly worn, and start slipping.

**The clutch is usually located BETWEEN the engine and the transmission. If you look in the engine compartment, you can see the fan-belt on one end of the engine, on one end of the crankshaft. The clutch is on the OTHER end of the engine, connected to the OTHER end of the crankshaft. You cannot see it, because it is all enclosed, but it is there. If you want to know where the clutch is, you may be able to see a lever move, when an accomplice steps on the clutch pedal.*

now we have two modes for the clutch: step down on the clutch pedal, and it disconnects the engine. Let your foot off, and it connects the engine to the gearbox. See sketch below.

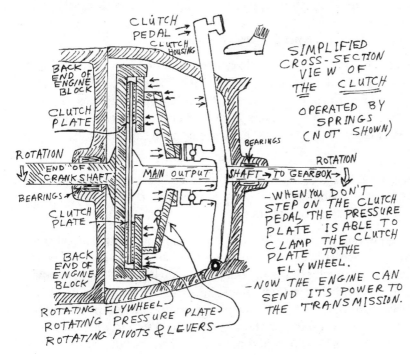

There is one other important mode of operation for the clutch: controlled slipping. When you want to start the car, usually you put the car in first gear, and slowly "let out the clutch" – lift up the weight of your foot on the clutch pedal – fairly slowly and gradually. As the friction first starts, the car begins to move slowly. Soon, the clutch slips less and less, the car begins to move faster, and soon you can let the clutch up a little further, and then all the way up. That is what is called, "slipping the clutch". You normally do it every time you start. When the car is moving, you do not normally want to let the clutch slip any. The clutch pedal is normally depressed, every time you shift. But there are other special cases, which we'll discuss later.

What Can Go Wrong?

If the clutch cable or clutch linkage happens to break, you can step on the clutch *pedal*, but it does not do any good. You cannot get the clutch "OFF", or "disengaged". This makes it rather hard to drive, but not impossible. See Appendix M, "What's all this Double-clutching Stuff", for procedures on how to drive without any clutch.

If the clutch plate wears out, it will slip, and while you may be able to drive a little, *very carefully* and *gently* on level roads, you will probably not be able to go up hills because the clutch will slip. A good driver should be able to get 50,000 to 100,000 miles before he has to repair the clutch. A hot-rodder may get considerably less.

If there is an engine malfunction, it may cause some oil to get onto the clutch, and that can make it slip. If things are not right, the clutch can CHATTER as you are trying to let out the clutch smoothly. This may cause rough driving, even though you are trying to drive smoothly. Other than these little problems, clutches are quite reliable, and rarely work badly. Driving well with a clutch and manual transmission IS a fine art, and it can be a tricky art, and a lot of people who drive with a slushbox have not learned it. (Woops, "slushbox" is just a slang name for an Automatic Transmission, and since it's much shorter and easier to pronounce or type, I may use that term occasionally. Or, I may type: "AT", to save space.)

It's like a secret club, where those who have been admitted are good guys, and other people who are not in the club are left out. In the US, it's not a big deal. Most rental cars come with an automatic transmission. But in Europe, you have to pay 30 to 60% extra for a rental car with a slushbox. I have never rented a car in Europe with a slushbox; the manual transmissions in most European cars are quite competent and fun.

When you start a car, it is a good idea to step on the clutch, even if the gearbox is in neutral. This is a good habit, except when it is VERY COLD – and then it is ESSENTIAL. Refer to the Chapter on Starting.

What else can go wrong about the clutch? If you absent-mindedly put your foot on the clutch pedal, as you drive, and the clutch starts to slip, it can get frying hot. In a short time, you can take a lot of the life out of the clutch plate – perhaps ruin it. That is called, "riding the clutch", and it is almost never a good idea. The point is, your engine can easily put out 50 or 100 horsepower or more. If you put that into making your car go, you are warming up the wind and the tires and the bearings. But if you "ride" the clutch, a large part of the energy will go into the clutch plate and the flywheel – and they are MUCH too small to take in that amount of energy for more than a few seconds. Clutch plates are made with the same excellent high-temperature-resistant materials as brake pads – but after a few seconds of severe abuse, they just get too hot. If you don't quit slipping the clutch, you will go nowhere, except by a tow-truck to the repair shop. Replacing a clutch plate costs only a couple dozen dollars of parts – but the labor is not cheap.

Now, when you are accelerating in first, and you know you will be shifting to second gear very soon, it is not TERRIBLE if you leave your foot on the top of the clutch pedal, at the top of its travel, JUST BARELY TOUCHING the clutch pedal, for just a couple seconds. But any more than 2 seconds is a bad habit. Please do not reinforce your bad habits!! Minimize them.

What else can go wrong? If you step on the clutch, you might get certain odd noises, as there are some bearings that only work when you step on the clutch. It might be the *throw-out bearing*, or a pilot bearing. Small noises are rarely serious, right away; noises that get louder are often serious. Get some knowledgeable person to check out those noises. (The Chapter on Noises may give you some help.)

Clutch is SLIPPING!

How do you notice if the clutch is slipping? That is, slipping when it is *not* supposed to be slipping! Normally, you first notice this when you are accelerating, or going up a hill. You step on the gas – and the engine revs rise *right up*. Hey – that's not supposed to happen! In a manual-transmission, the engine speed is only supposed to rise, *proportional to* the ground speed, in any given gear. (The other exception to this is, in case of a wheel spinning or slipping on oil or ice. You want to watch out for that, because that spells trouble, too!)

As soon as you notice this, ease off on the gas. (This is true for wheel-slip, too.) If you can still get the engine to pull up the hill, at a lighter power setting, you have a little margin. Or, if you still get some slippage, shift down to a lower gear, which will put less stress on the clutch. But still, you have to *baby* the clutch, and you must plan to get it repaired, or adjusted, *soon*.

Normally, when you step on the clutch pedal, the first half inch of its travel has only a light spring force. The clutch linkage is not changing at all. Then, as you push the clutch down further, as the linkages hit more springs, there is more force. There is (normally) no slippage in that first half inch. While your clutch is working perfectly, check this to see if that travel is about right. Some time when you are parked, with the handbrake securely set, get out of your car and push down on your clutch pedal with your hand, so you can feel the increase of force, which should start about 1/2 or 3/4 inch down, or, check your owner's manual. Then if the amount of that "travel" changes, you will recognize that it is wrong.

If the cable has gotten out of adjustment, or if the clutch disc has worn thin, that half-inch of travel shrinks to nothing, and the clutch can start to slip, at the top of its travel. If that's what has happened, get it adjusted *soon*. I don't know about YOUR car, but on VWs, the nuts and bolts for this adjustment are in a difficult, nasty location, and rather hard to do. I bet it is, on your car, too!

Clutch Does Not Release Completely

The other aspect of the mis-adjustment problem is, if you start getting grinding noises when you try to put the car into gear, even though you have pushed the clutch pedal all the way to the floor. This is not disastrous, but you want to get it adjusted or fixed as soon as possible, because you are wearing out some parts of your gearbox. Follow the procedure in the Double-Clutching column, to minimize the grinding.

Specifically, let's say the gearbox starts making graunching or gear-grinding sounds when you try to shift into first or into any gear.

Let's say you are coming to a stop sign or stop light. Slow down to about 3 mph, *then* shift into first. Stop, with your left foot on the clutch, and your right foot on the brake. If the engine keeps turning, there maybe some poor friction, but this is fixable.

Then you can let out the clutch and start without any graunches. That is much better than waiting until you are stopped.

Or, if you forget, and you stop in neutral, and you KNOW it will grind badly if you try to get into first – here is the solution: turn off the engine, shift into first, and then re-start the engine, and go on your way. As you shift up to second and to higher gears, let the engine slow down to about the right speed before you push the lever into gear. The "right speed" is the one where you don't get any graunch. Best yet, use the double-clutching procedure in my Column on this topic, in Appendix M.

What if there is *chatter*? That's for an expert to fix. Clutch chatter will not by itself usually cause an accident, but it might distract you and cause you to not pay attention to traffic. However, on a snowy road, it might cause you to skid when you didn't want to, so it's a good idea to get this fixed.

Clutch-Related Accidents – ??

Why are we so interested in the clutch? Partly, if you understand these problems, you will avoid expensive repairs, and place minimum wear and tear on the clutch so it lasts a long time. But if you started to get clutch slippage on a big uphill, you might find yourself unable to go up. Can you back down safely without an accident? Using only your brakes? Will the cars behind you understand and get out of your way? That doesn't sound like fun to me.

The other problem is, when you decide to cut a left turn across traffic, and your clutch starts to slip. Does that on-coming truck have good brakes? I DON'T WANT TO FIND OUT. If my clutch starts to slip, I will baby it and drive carefully, straight to the repair shop, and get it fixed – adjusted or replaced. I've done that a couple times.

All other aspects of the clutch and its operation are treated in the previous section, that covers driving a car with a manual transmission.

I do know that there are some roads, from Lake City, Colorado to Silverton, up in the old mining districts, that are quite steep and difficult to drive. I ran up those hills in our 1972 VW Bus. That bus never had a lot of power, and it never had a lot of *torque* – even at low altitudes. But at high altitudes, it was even a little more *wimpy*. But by careful planning, I was able to keep my revs up, and ease up those roads and not have any serious problems – even though the switch-backs were, at times, quite severe.

I mean, if you are going up a road, and there is a curve, and you cut your wheels as hard as you can – and the curve is so sharp, you can't get around the corner – what do you do then??? Well, you may have to back up and try again. And, what if it is very steep? You may have to slip your clutch a lot, to get started. And if you do that too much, your clutch might start to overheat, and smoke, and to slip a lot. What do you do then? Well, you might get out your shovel and dig a little, to ease the grade. And while you do that, the clutch will be cooling off, and you have a chance of getting up the hill. Otherwise, you may need to retreat and not go up the hill. I always hate to give up on a road, but sometimes you just have to.

NOTE, a garage man in Silverton told me that he has to go up on those roads, occasionally, and tow down a car that has a burned-out clutch. If your clutch is, for ANY reason, kind of old and worn, and you go up into the mountains and try to work your way around some of these hills and curves, your clutch might start to slip, and fail. This might not be your fault. It may just be, the time for fate to give you a failure.

(Note, if your clutch is giving any signs of slipping, and you go up in severe hills, and the clutch fails – don't get mad at *me* – and don't be surprised – I warned you.)

Now, right now, our VW Bus is sitting in the driveway. What if somebody asked me to drive east, and drive over that pass from Lake City to Silverton – would I *hesitate*? ?? This car has 99,756 miles on it. And it still has the original clutch. And as you may have noted, I live in San Francisco, where there are a lot of hills. Surely, I would not trust my clutch? Surely by now it would be fried.

Wrong. I would start right away, except I have to pick up my wife at the airport next week. So, this week I would not go driving from Lake City to Silverton. But, maybe next week. Or maybe I will wait until you readers tell me some more interesting roads to drive on.

Baby Your Clutch...

If you ever notice ANY significant slipping of your clutch, when your foot is off the pedal – well – then – take it very easy, and plan to get it into the shop, to get the clutch adjusted or replaced. Note, if the car is warmed up good and hot, you may get *worse* slippage. So, if it is cold, you may get *less* slippage, and then you may be able to drive carefully and travel a few miles without significant slippage. The clutch may give you enough service to get to the repair shop. No guarantees. Baby it. Pick a route that does not have hills. It can save you $80 or more of towing charges. Do I cry about an $80 tow job? No, but I hate to waste $80, if I didn't have to spend it. Also, I prefer to get the car in to the shop at the time I choose, and schedule my own time.

I have always been impressed by the low-speed capabilities of VWs, because they can potter along at about 4 mph. But, when a hill gets really steep, if you cannot go up the hill at least 10 mph, you run out of torque, and either you go faster, or you stop. I mean on STEEP hills. So, with any stick-shift car, your ability to go up hills, is partly limited by your ability to keep up your speed so that you do not run out of torque. On most cars, if you get on a steep hill, you run out of traction. But first of all, my old VW bus will run out of power. It cannot get through. I would have to stop, walk around, and decide to go back down the hill.

Slipping the Clutch Under Various Conditions

NOW, When you are starting up – depending on the car – the clutch – the road – and the conditions – you may slip the clutch MORE or LESS, while you are revving the engine MORE or LESS than normal. This is an area your teacher has showed you how to do it. This is NOT the kind of stuff you learn from this book or any other book. This write-up is just a sanity check, on what your teacher told you.

- Case Number ONE: – under normal, quiet conditions, on a level road – when you are not in a hurry – rev the engine a minimum above idle, and slip the clutch just enough to get the car's speed up to idle speed. Then let the clutch all the way out, so the engine will slow down to a nice idle speed. Then feed it some gas. If your clutch is not grabbing, it's pretty easy to do this easily and smoothly. In my Beetle, I usually get rolling and stop slipping the clutch after about 3 feet.

- Case Number TWO: If you are in HEAVY traffic or NOISY traffic, and you definitely do not want to stall, you will want to rev the engine a little more than usual, because you cannot hear if it is revving properly, or if the clutch is slipping properly. So, in this case, rev the engine a little more and slip the clutch more.

I remember driving through Luxembourg in a little rented Peugeot, and the engine was running rough and did not have any power at slow rpms. The light turned green, and I looked in my mirror to see a big NOISY cement mixer rolling up behind me at about 15 mph. We ALL really wanted me to get started – but I could not hear my engine. So I revved the engine more than usual, and slipped the clutch plenty, and got going just fine.

A couple of times, I heard the Magliozzi Brothers (who run the *Car Talk* program on National Public Radio) say that if you never stall the engine when you are slipping the clutch, then you are a lousy driver. I asked them why they said that. I was really curious why they said that. I sent them a letter by registered mail. Never got any answer. I don't stall my engine very often when starting. Maybe about once every 2 or 3 months. And I don't think I am a lousy driver.

SLIPPING the Clutch??

A guy I know was on a long vacation trip, and one day he was feeling tired and starting to get sick. He asked his girlfriend if she could drive for a while, even though she had always said she was not interested in learning to drive with a manual transmission. But she was a good sport, and she agreed to try.

She got started, with a little lurch, and after she got the car going, she seemed to be doing okay. But every time she had to start from a stop, the car lurched a lot. Why?

Her friend watched EXACTLY what she was doing. She was letting her foot slip OFF the clutch pedal – which would obviously cause the car to lurch. No, she made a mis-interpretation of the phrase, "slip the clutch"... – she thought it meant, "slipping your foot off the clutch". When she learned that the right procedure is to just EASE your foot upward, slowly, while you keep it on the clutch pedal, to let the CLUTCH do the slipping, then she was okay. She never had any trouble driving with a manual transmission, after that.

- Next – Case Number THREE: to get started on a little UPGRADE – put on the handbrake, move your right foot from the brake pedal to the gas pedal – get the engine up to moderate rpms – release the handbrake – and slip the clutch a moderate amount, until the car's speed comes up to where the engine has enough torque – and a little more, to have a safety margin. THEN ease off on the gas, let the clutch all the way up – and then feed the gas hard. This is the kind of situation where your *teacher* has to show you what is right, FOR YOUR CAR. On a little upgrade, you may consider you did a good job if you slipped back not at all, or only a few inches. You should be able to do this consistently. If the car rolls back more than a foot, then you ought to improve your co-ordination. Because if there were a car just a few feet behind you, you would not want to roll back and hit him.

FOR example: here in San Francisco, sometimes the only place available to park is on a moderately steep grade. If there is not a lot of space, I try to stop with my front wheel against a curb, so I do not have to worry about slipping back when I start. Or, I might check the bumper height, and if my bumper is a perfect fit against the bumper of the down-hill car, I might actually rest my bumper against his. It's a lot better to do that, than to slip back a foot and BANG the other car!

- Case Number FOUR – for reasonably quick acceleration in moderate traffic – use the procedure just about the same as for Case Number THREE above, but you probably do not have to use the handbrake at all, as there is no possibility of slipping back.

Now, after your teacher has gotten you pretty well trained and educated on starting the car, on the flat, he will teach you how to get started on successively steeper hills:

- Case Number FIVE – For SEVERE up-hills – VERY steep hills: Hold the car from rolling back with the handbrake AND the foot-brake. Get ready to release the handbrake. Lift your foot off the brake pedal, momentarily, to make sure that the hand-brake is holding OK. (If it isn't, set the handbrake tighter, *or*, refer to the example at the end of this chapter.) Now, move your foot over from the brake to the gas pedal, and idle the engine GOOD and HIGH. Start slipping the clutch moderately, and feed the gas even MORE, to keep the engine rpms up even while the clutch is trying to slow it down – and let off the handbrake, ALL AT THE SAME TIME. As soon as you are up to a good moderate speed in first, let the clutch all the way out, and keep feeding the gas *hard*, to make sure your revs do not get too low, so you will not run out of torque. This is an advanced technique, and requires very good co-ordination, and your teacher has to show you how to do this. This also puts very serious wear on your clutch. You should generally avoid this. You certainly do not want to do this every day, and not every week, either. It's worth some planning, so you can avoid getting *into* this situation.

Example – when I go to church at Grace Cathedral, I usually drive up Taylor Street, which has a steep 24% grade. I do not even start up the last block of this street, from Pine St. to California, unless the traffic is light and well-organized, and unless I am pretty sure the light will be green when I get to the top. If I see a whole MESS of traffic, I will avoid Taylor Street, and take another, longer route. But if I see that traffic is light, and I have a 95% probability of making it up without having to stop and then start, I will proceed up the hill in second gear. If I get near the top, and I will have to slow down for slow traffic, I shift back into first, and drive slow, and hope that all the traffic keeps moving until I have made the light. Otherwise, I may have to stop and slip the clutch

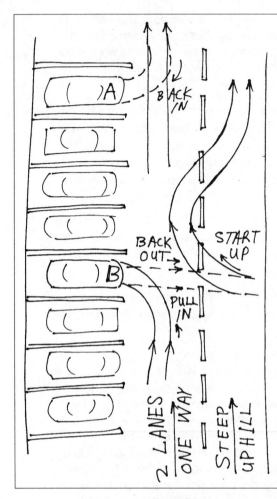

When I drive up a steep street such as Taylor Street, I prefer to back into a parking space (A). That makes it easy to pull out. But if you are not good at backing up, that's probably a lousy idea for you.

– If you pull forward into a parking place (B), then when traffic is clear, you can back straight across the street. Then you can start up the hill from a nearly level starting place. Much better than trying to start on a steep upgrade.

heavily to get going when the light goes green. But usually, no troubles. And I almost always get my clutch to last more than 120k miles before adjustment or replacement. My wife is pretty gentle on the clutch, too.

NOTE – if you are slipping the clutch as hard as this, your tires may break loose when you do this. Not a big deal, as this feels rather similar to the clutch slipping. But if your tires do slip, the rear of the car might slide sideways a little – or a lot. Sometimes a car on Taylor Street hill may lose traction, and cannot get started up the hill, especially if it is wet, or if there is any oil or sand on the road. I have seen cars back down the hill because they cannot go up. Lots of fun!

When I go up that last, steep block of Taylor Street, there is sometimes a parking place, over on the left, where the cars are parked perpendicular to the road. Do I drive into one of those parking places? Heck, no, because if I did, I would have to back out and get started up the hill, by slipping my clutch severely. Instead, I go up past the parking place, and then slowly roll back INTO it. Then when I want to start out, I just drive ahead on a flat grade, and when I am rolling, I turn left and go up the hill. Much easier than backing out....

- Case Number SIX: Acceleration under EMERGENCY or racing conditions: Let's say you are stopped at a light, and you look in your mirror and see a runaway truck headed right for you, blowing his horn and blinking his lights at you. Then you accelerate just as stated above, in Case Number FIVE, except you probably can ignore the handbrake: Floor the gas, slip the clutch HARD until the car gets up to good speed, then let out the clutch all the way, and floor the gas. Then pull over to the side as quickly as you can, to let the truck go past. I must admit, I haven't done this in the last couple years, but I know I will be able to do it if I have to. Note, the Case SIX is a little easier than Case FIVE, because it's almost impossible to stall, whereas in Case FIVE, if you are not pretty well co-ordinated, you might roll back a lot, or you could stall the engine, and then you have to jump on the brakes FAST, and re-start, and try again.

- Now – Case Number SEVEN – to get started downhill – you don't even have to slip the clutch at all. Just let off the brakes, kick in the clutch, and put the car in gear. As soon as the car is rolling more than 2 mph, you can let out the clutch gently, and then feed the gas. No slipping, no wear.

- Lastly – Case Number EIGHT – to get started on bad snow or ice – if you try to start in LOW gear, you may have too much torque, too much power, too much acceleration. If your drive wheels slip when you try to start in first (especially on an upgrade) – try putting it in second, and slip the clutch gently – not viciously. That often works better. That can decrease the jerk of letting out the clutch too fast. One of my Buddies who had a Jaguar XJS with 265 hp was given some good advice by the shop's chief mechanic: when it snows, start up in second gear AND put on the handbrake just a little, about one or two *clicks* of real braking, to put a little drag on the engine and clutch, until you get going. Makes sense to me.

♦ ♦ ♦

NOW – what does all this advice have to do with accidents? If you are trying to start up on a hill, and you botch it, you might just stall the engine. That is not a disaster. But if you really goof, and get flustered or absentminded and step on the clutch when you shouldn't, you might roll backwards several feet, before you can get your right foot on the brakes, and you might hit a car behind you. Or if you are near a dangerous edge, you might roll over the edge. So it really is important to know how to start on a steep hill. It is also important to know how your car is going to work.

Too Close to an Edge?

I got a story from one of my friends, Sam, who was once driving a truck in Antarctica. He went up a steep hill in a BORROWED truck to look at some kind of accident site at a cliff. At the top, he drove over near the edge of the cliff and tried to turn around. Unfortunately, the engine was running kind of rough; and did not want to put out any torque. AND, he discovered, the handbrake was not holding at all. And he was stopped on a fairly steep downgrade, about 10 feet from going over the cliff.

First of all, if you are going to BORROW a truck, it's a good idea to figure out what is working and what's NOT. Like, minor details – like the handbrakes. Secondly, it is really smart to NOT get pointed right toward a steep cliff. Third of all, what the hell do you do when you need your handbrake, and the handbrake does not work???!!!

As you can see, this is one of these situations where a CONSPIRACY of bad equipment PLUS bad judgement can get you in serious trouble. Sam knew if he tried one more time to start up, and failed to get the truck to back up the hill, and slipped forward a few more feet, he was going to have to open the door and leap out, as the truck went over the edge. So he sorta had one more try.

Sam figured out the right trick: He got his left foot on the clutch, and the gearbox in reverse. He left his right toe on the brakes, REALLY HARD, and got the engine revved up REALLY HIGH, using his right heel on the gas pedal. Then he slipped the clutch HARD, and started to ease his right toe off the brakes, while he kept his RIGHT HEEL on the gas. And the engine was revving so well, it did not stall, and he backed out OK. But he sure scared some sense into his head.

Anyhow, the procedure Sam used is basically the same as the "Heel-and-Toe" technique that I explain in Appendix N. This is an Appendix, rather than a Chapter, because it is an advanced technique, and does not normally necessarily have anything to do with avoiding an accident. But, as Sam pointed out, in his difficult case, using Heel-and-Toe is useful for getting out of a certain set of problems, and avoiding an accident. So I guess you ought to read that Appendix, too.

That's all on this topic. But, if it makes sense, you might go back and re-read the Chapter on Manual Transmissions, to see if that now makes more sense. Remember, I never said that this was an easy topic. I never said it would make sense, unless you already knew how to use the clutch, and to slip the clutch.

P.S. Try to avoid leaving your car in gear, with your foot on the clutch, for a long time, at a red light or a stop-sign. This may cause only a little wear on your clutch or your throw-out bearing. But it's important, because if your foot slips off the clutch, you would tend to lurch into traffic and get in trouble. It's better to shift into neutral, and wait until the light is about to change, or until traffic is clear and you can proceed. This is especially important if your shoe is wet or slippery.

P.S. I finally figured out what Tom and Ray meant, when they said you are a bad driver if you never stall when slipping the clutch. On many cars, it takes a lot of energy and a good bit of skill to get started in first gear. If you are careful to *never* stall, that means you are revving the engine too much, and slipping the clutch a lot – and you are probably putting excess wear on the clutch. In that case, it may be true that if you never stall, you are abusing the clutch. In my Beetle, I typically slip the clutch for about 2 feet, at about 900 rpm – NOT excessive. In a car with a low gear like that, it's not a crime to not stall. I stall it every 2 or 3 months, typically. In a heavier car with a LONGER first gear, Tom and Ray may be nearly right. / rap

Chapter 11. STEERING

How Does Your "Steering" Work?

Every car has a steering wheel. When you turn the wheel, there are levers or gears that pull on strong metal links called tie rods, that pull on the "steering arms", the levers connected to each front wheel, that make your wheels turn left or right. Under normal conditions, when you turn the wheels, the car goes where you point it. Jolly good!

These days, most cars have power steering. There is some hydraulic fluid that goes through a pump and into cylinders and helps you steer. When you try to turn the wheel, the power steering helps you turn them. When something pushes on the front wheels, it is not just your arms resisting the force.

What Can Go Wrong?

Fortunately, steering gear is very reliable. So you never have to worry about the steering linkages breaking. Those "tie rods" are made of very strong metal that almost never break. But if you hit some road debris or rocks, they can BEND. If that happens, you can still steer, but your front wheels may start pointing in odd directions, and the tires can wear out. You gotta fix that. If your power steering does not work well – typically because the fluid leaked out – you gotta fix *that*.

If your engine stops running, your power steering will not work, and your wheel will feel really *heavy* and you have to allow for that. If you have not experienced this, find a big wide parking lot and get going at a gentle speed. Put the gearbox in neutral and turn off the key, just a little. You will find the steering wheel is kinda hard to turn, but not impossible. If you work really hard, you should be able to make a moderate turn. You should just be aware that if your engine quits, your power steering won't be helping you, and you have to be prepared to put your shoulders into it.

Steering Problems...

The basic problem with steering is, if you go "too fast", or if you turn the wheel "too far", or if there is "not enough traction", the car does NOT go where you thought you were pointing it. This is greatly influenced by weather and road surface. Rain makes some problems. Snow makes big problems. Ice makes very bad problems. So does oil. We will talk about Skidding in a special Chapter on that topic.

Lots of Curves

For over 25 years, I have been improving my ability to count curves when driving. When I first drove up Mt. Hamilton, which looms on the northeast of San Jose CA, I was impressed that there were about 430 curves to get to the top. For example, when you turn left, that's "78", and then if the road goes

95

8-9-21

*right, that's "79", and if you then go straight again, and then go right again,
that makes "80", and on and on... I can usually keep a true count without
losing the count. Sometimes I count out loud – usually I just count in my head.
And, at the top there is a NICE view across San Jose, and all of Silicon Valley,
and out across San Francisco Bay, and up to San Francisco, too. If the weather
is clear, you should be able to see the peaks in the Sierras. Very nice at night,
too.*

*Further, if you then take the road down the far side of Mt. Hamilton, there are
another 400 curves to get down to Livermore. Or if you go down Del Puerta
Canyon Road, to the Central Valley at Patterson, then there are about 700
curves. A pleasant road. You will, if you ever drive those roads, drive at your
own pace. If you go too fast, your wife (or spouse, or passengers, if any) will
probably complain. Throw them out and speed on! (No, you probably can't do
that.) Eventually, if you drive too fast, your car will complain. I have never
heard of anybody driving himself so fast, that HE got car-sick. If a passenger
complains of being car-sick, as a passenger, he will be able to go faster,
WITHOUT complaining, and WITHOUT being car-sick, if you let him drive.
That is because, when driving, he knows he is under control. Holding onto the
steering wheel really helps a lot.*

*On time we went on a backpacking trip up just north of Mt. Shasta. We
decided to come back from Weaverville CA on the back roads through the tiny
towns of Hayfork, Zenia, and Alderpoint. This was in our old 1972 VW bus –
which did NOT have power steering. I counted curves that day. From
Weaverville to Route 101 at Garberville, there were 2200 curves in 150 miles.
VERY interesting roads! I would recommend that anybody might try that,
once. I enjoyed it. The rest of the family – well – they survived it. But they did
not get car-sick.*

Straight Roads

By comparison, I have even counted the curves on Interstate I-5 which goes up from
Davis to Redding, right near Weaverville – that is the *normal* route to go to (or
return from) Weaverville. That has about 55 curves in 120 miles. Let me assure you,
that is B O R I N G. I've driven that stretch about 8 times. I can do it, but it does take
some effort to pay attention. To keep from getting excessively bored and sleepy. It
takes as much effort, to keep from being bored, as it does to turn the wheel through
2200 curves on the alternate route.

When I was a kid, the Maine Turnpike had just opened up. It was straight and it
had a 65 or 70 mph speed limit. I rode up there, from Boston to Portland, with my
family, several times. It was surely the smoothest and straightest road I ever had been
on. Actually, it probably had about 4 curves per mile. But it was still much easier
than any road I had seen. A very nice road... except....

The problem was, a lot of drivers kept falling asleep and crashing into the
bushes or guardrails. It was *too* smooth, TOO straight. There was not enough to do,
to keep you awake. Be careful what you wish for – you might get it! After a while,
drivers figured out how to stay awake on boring roads. They never did pass a law to

add more curves on the Maine Pike, to keep people from falling asleep. But if it were any other state than Maine, they might have put that on the ballot. Folks in Maine have too much sense for that.

When I first drove out west, I found some AMAZING roads. When you come over the crest of a hill – you can see the road stretch out S T R A I G H T in front of you and that is as far as you can see – and that can be 5 or 10 miles. When we came over US Route 93 in Nevada, just north of Las Vegas, we were impressed. Then when we angled NW on Nevada Route 375 towards Warm Springs Nevada on Route 6, we were really impressed. The sun was setting, and we could see about 14 miles of straight road. I'd never seen such a straight stretch as that. It's a very pretty countryside out there – kind of stark. No trees. No houses. No gas stations, either. Come to think of it, that was about 1965, and I have not been on routes 93 and 375, by Hiko, for 30 years. Maybe the next time I drive East, I should go a little out of my way to go that way. I'll put that on my list.

The other amazing place is on I-80 east of Wendover Nevada, toward Salt Lake City, Utah. There is a 50-mile stretch of straight road, across the salt flats. Actually, if you look *really* closely, I think there is a 1-degree bend in the middle, so it is two 25-mile straight stretches. Or, maybe my eyesight was warped, from the heat? But it is eerie and unearthly to go so long without any curve. It is hard work to keep your attention, when your brain does not have to work on any curve at all. It is a little boring. It is the exact antithesis of the 2200-curve road!!

Driving on Curvy Roads

NOW – let's talk a little about ACTUALLY driving on a curvy road. If you are on Mount Hamilton Road, with 430 curves in 20 miles, you almost never get going too fast – because there are too many curves. (It is not really very steep). You just cannot build up much speed, in most cars, even on the down-grades. So it is EASY to judge your speed. Thus, after a very short time, you can judge the right speed for each corner you come to.

But if you are on a long straight road, and you are doing 55 – and you come to a curve – how do you judge how to slow down for the curve? This is one of the things most new drivers figure out pretty fast. You take your foot off the gas – at *about the right time* – and you may touch your brakes *in about the right place* – and you touch them *just* hard enough – and you ease around the curve – *at about the right speed.* Well – how are these right places and speeds defined? Ah – that is the art of driving. And what's right, today – when you are driving Aunt Tillie to tea – may be the wrong speed tomorrow.

Learning about Curves

If you are learning to drive, what you have to learn, is to look at that curve, and estimate when it is getting close, and then take your foot off the gas a little *early,* and make sure your speed does fall off as you expect – a little bit. Then as you get closer to the curve, slow down a little *more* and keep slowing down to a speed that seems right. Mostly, you want to decelerate *before* you get to the curve. If you find that you have to decelerate more, as you are *in* the curve, well, then *decelerate –*

8-9-21

ease ON the brakes before you go off the road. But, that's not quite right. You should have done most of your braking *before* you got in the curve. Because if you brake very hard at all while you are cornering hard in a curve, that can make the car skid and slide off the road. Refer to the Chapter on Handling.

If you are rolling through a curve about as fast as you comfortably can – and then, for whatever reason, you have to slow down (maybe because the curve tightens up? or there is some obstruction?) – be careful when you take your foot off the gas. When you "lift" – lift your foot off the gas – your tail end may start to skid out. If you were really going too fast, that skid can cause an accident. Even if you do not skid, the rear end can sway out more than you expect, as a form of oversteer. You have to be very careful not to get in trouble when you do this. Of course, if you are in a tight curve, and you take your foot off the gas, and hit the brakes – this, again tends to cause oversteer, and the rear end may tend to drift out or skid. This is because when you put on the brakes, the weight of the car tends to transfer off the rear wheels and onto the front wheels. With the same braking force, and less weight on the rear wheels, that can cause oversteer and skidding. And even "lifting" on the gas pedal can cause this. So you have to watch out for it.

Conversely, going into a curve a little slow and then *feeding* the gas does help improve the stability, and cuts out oversteer.

If you slowed down a little too much, then you can speed up until it feels right. Accelerating through the curve and accelerating out the exit of the curve is fine. Of course, if you are driving VERY CAREFULLY, that's fine, but if you collect a big tail of cars behind you (more than 2), then you should pick a time and place to pull over and let them pass. That's only polite. And of course if you are at the stage of being VERY SLOW AND CAREFUL, you should be doing this with your teacher. By the time you are on your own, you should have some confidence and judgement, so you don't have to go too slow. You should know what a curve looks like, and what it should feel like. On the other hand, if you are driving a car – or truck – that is very different from what you are used to – then you have to feel out how this new vehicle feels in corners, just as a beginner does.

Sometimes you can choose a straight road, and avoid the need to turn a lot. Other times, you don't have much choice, and you are stuck with a road where you have a lot of turns. If you have to go fast, the turn forces AND the jerk are high, going through those turns. If you want to avoid the high side-forces, and the JERK, all you have to do is slow down.

◆ ◆ ◆

A SMALL PHYSICS LESSON

If you have a nice smooth curve and you go around at 20 mph, you generate a certain amount of side force. If you want to go 40 mph, that would cause twice as much side force – WRONG. At a fixed radius R, the formula for lateral (sideways) acceleration is: $A = V^2/R$. If you go around the curve at 40, you will have FOUR TIMES the side force. If you wanted to have just twice the side force, you would go around at about √2 x 20 mph, or about 28 mph. That's why "speeding just a little bit" sometimes has a dramatic effect. Physics may seem dumb and obscure, but when you are trying to get around a curve a little faster, it is a real-world subject, not just something in a book.

◆◆◆

Comfort versus Discomfort

As I mentioned in the chapter on Brakes, if you are driving your elderly Aunt Tillie to a special occasion, you would not want to *jam on* the brakes and make the car lurch. WELL, even if you never have to put on the brakes hard, all the way to Aunt Tillie's friend's tea party, you may have some curves. If you CUT the wheel really hard, or corner severely, you may make Aunt Tillie just as uncomfortable as if you jammed on the brakes. Discomfort is not necessarily related to the transverse acceleration caused by cornering hard. Usually it is caused by the RATE OF CHANGE of sideways (transverse) acceleration – the JERK. If you go through curves really slow, the transverse acceleration forces are small, and also the *rate-of-change of acceleration* is not uncomfortable. NOW, if you start going faster on this same road, the (transverse) acceleration has to increase. And, the *rate-of-change* of acceleration increases, too.

NOW, let's pretend that the route to Aunt Tillie's tea party was on a *circular* road, and you gradually went faster and faster, around and around, on that smooth circular road. Your Aunt Tillie would probably get used to it, and she would not complain a lot, even if you went a little faster and faster. A constant Acceleration, *by itself,* is not really that bad, when you get used to it. We all are used to 1 g of acceleration, *STRAIGHT DOWN*. A mere 0.05 or 0.1 g of transverse acceleration is usually not a big deal. But a lot of transverse acceleration above 0.2 g gets complaints. Even then, Aunt Tillie might not complain until you started squealing the tires. (Even my wife has an increased awareness of speed and acceleration, and she tends to complain when the tires start to screech.) As we discussed, in the chapter on brakes, it is not the acceleration that is discomforting, it is the JERK – the rate-of-change of acceleration – that makes you uncomfortable. (Or, if you are hot-rodding – that is what is FUN!!) I mean, after you drop off Aunt Tillie at her tea party, you will feel perfectly justified and comfortable if you decide to accelerate and brake and take the curves BRISKLY, on the way home, because, after a while, the idea of driving slowly, even for a good reason, gets *awfully* boring.

Still, now you understand how to drive gently and "politely", without tromping on the brakes, and without cornering too vigorously.

◆◆◆

Steering Force

Many cars with power steering have very little steering force required. Without power steering, your shoulders have a lot more work. (Note, those 2200 curves in one afternoon were without power steering – a good work-out.) I have heard people brag that their power steering is great, because almost no effort is required – only a couple pounds. Well, if you had a shoulder operation, or a bad arm, that might be essential, but for good driving, it's not such a good idea.

The reason is, force feedback. It's good to have a little feedback – especially if you are driving in snow. If you have no force feedback, you cannot tell how slippery things are. It's very hard to tell if you are starting to skid.

When I tried out my "new" 1985 VW Bus (Vanagon), I was a little skeptical of this newfangled power steering, but it *did* seem to work well, on test drives. The first weekend we had it, we went up to Concord CA, and there were some *fierce* crosswinds, and I just *knew* it would have been awful if I was still driving my old 1972 Bus without power steering. There was *some* force feedback, but not too much. Later, we went up in the Sierras, and I found that on snow, I could still feel through the power steering, the difference between driving on pavement, on snow, on slippery snow, on ice – and when one of the wheels was starting to slide. So I am really very favorably impressed with that power steering. The engineers back at Wolfsburg sure did some good work. I would like to recommend this type of power steering, with moderate force feedback.

One time I was riding with a friend in his Peugeot 403, which was a very good car – but its steering was a little *dead,* and it had some friction in it. It had much less "road feel" than my VW. We went up a hill, and suddenly came upon some glare ice. He went into a slow spin and we L A Z I L Y slid down the road and slowly bumped into a guard rail, with minor damage.

I've always thought that if we had gone in MY beetle, I would have felt the steering get *light,* at the first bit of ice, I would have *touched* the brakes earlier, to check and see how slippery it was, and we could have eased out of there without spinning out. My friend was a good driver, but the steering was too stiff to let him feel the ice. And this was not power steering.

Steering Ratio

If you have a slow steering ratio, it may take a whole turn of the wheel, or more, to get you around a sharp curve – and then it takes you a lot of effort to return the wheel to center. Many cars with power steering have a faster ratio. Faster is usually better. Older cars without power steering had a slow ratio, because otherwise, turning the wheel would be just too hard.

Back before I could afford a VW, I had an old 1950 Studebaker whose steering took 4.5 turns lock-to-lock. That was pretty slow – pretty bad. I put on a "Spinner" – a little knob that clamps onto the steering wheel – so I could turn the wheel *over* really fast, and bring it *back* fast. One time I took the car in to a Massachusetts safety inspection. The tester made me take the spinner off – because spinners were illegal. I took it off. After I got out of his sight, I put it right back on. (Spinners were supposedly illegal, because if they broke, you would lose control of your car. Sounds like a dumb reason. I think they should have written a law to make sure spinners were designed so they could not break....)

Now, 4.5 turns lock-to-lock is just too slow a ratio to be safe. If you have to turn quickly, to avoid something, it's almost impossible. My VW Beetles at 2.6 turns are about right for me. A lot of cars are in that range, these days.

Soft or Hard Springing

If you go into a corner in a car with very soft springs, it will tend to lean a lot, and you will decide not to go so fast. A car with stiff springs sort of encourages you to drive more aggressively in corners. That's why a lot of people like sports cars. Of course, the soft springing tends to give a softer, more comfortable ride.

Anti-Sway Bars

Many cars these days have an "anti-sway" bar, that is sort of a torsion bar between the two front (or rear) wheels – actually a link between the axles. All this does is let you go over a bump (a bump that both wheels hit together) with soft springs, but in a turn, you have more stiffness against rolling or leaning or tilting. (NOT, "swaying" – the term, "sway" is not used quite correctly, but nobody worries about that....)

Other Problems with Steering

If you drive over really difficult terrain, it is possible to drive over rocks or junk that can hit your tie-rods and other steering parts, and bend them or break some part. This is unlikely to cause you to be unable to steer at all. But it may cause your steering to feel WEIRD, and start causing bad tire wear. Any time your car starts handling WEIRD, drive slow and get some advice on checking it out.

> If you see your front tires just wearing really ODDLY, get some expert help, from a good tire expert, at a tire store. Your front end could be out of alignment, Or you might have a bent tie rod. Either way, you want to get a PROFESSIONAL car repairman involved. Get it fixed. It is not HIGHLY LIKELY that this problem will get you into a bad accident – but it is a big waste of money. So get it fixed soon. And keep your speed down until you do. NOTE: if a tie-rod is bent, it should not be un-bent; it should be replaced. If a tie-rod were "straightened", it would be unsafe, unreliable.

I used to live next-door to a guy who had a crummy old Chevy, and he had gotten a guy to pass the car through the Massachusetts inspection, even with a busted front suspension. Apparently the "A-arm" – the frame that carries the front axle – had gotten cracked. Legally, this was very bad and unsafe to drive. But he figured if he drove really slow, he would not be too unsafe. Maybe. I think he drove it for a month and then got enough money to junk it and buy another car.

NOW, let's get into the good stuff. HOW TO STEER.

More Notes on Steering Ratio

Some people say that a steering wheel with 2 turns lock-to-lock (limit-to-limit) travel is too fast a ratio. Sports cars are in this range. A car with much more than 3 turns lock-to-lock is really hard to drive, because you have to turn the wheel too long for a sharp corner – and then you have to turn it back! But before the days of power steering, a heavy car might have 4 turns, to minimize the steering forces. Trucks could have more than 5 turns.

But a bicycle has about 1/2 turn lock-to-lock. Nobody ever says a bicycle's steering ratio is "too fast". I think it's just a matter of what you get used to. I bet that a bicycle with 1/4 turn or 2 turns would feel weird!!

Power Steering

Most cars have power steering these days. It helps you get around corners without much effort. That's good because if they did not have power steering, they would have 4 or 5 turns, lock-to-lock. But the bad news is, you don't get much feel of the road. No force feedback. Which I think is important. Sigh.

> If the power steering fluid runs out, you can hear nasty noises every time you turn the wheel. So, go down to the car-parts store, or a gas-station, soon, and buy a bottle or two of power-steering fluid. Put some in the correct place. (The correct place for filling in the power-steering fluid is not always labeled well, as it is not used very often. If you have any questions, ask a knowledgeable person.) If you get a leak, it is probably in the power steering's rack and pinion assembly. This is kinda expensive. When it happened to my VW Bus, I was kinda pissed off (that is a technical term, that applies to cars) because it cost about $850 to replace it. But I paid.

When I first came out to California on trips, I would rent a car. Then, sometimes, I would be easing through a parking lot. I would see a parking space, and *cut* the wheel hard, and dive into the parking place. Yes, the power steering had a fast ratio. But, I discovered that I could not turn the wheel fast, because the power steering did not help, if you turn the wheel very fast. When the engine is at idle – at low rpms – the power steering pump does not pump fast enough to help turn the wheels fast. So I had to learn to slow down when I spotted a parking place, and not count on turning the wheel fast. I never hit a parked car, but I sure scared myself, when the power steering didn't work as I expected! I must say, I have not seen this problem on cars I have rented recently, so maybe they are engineered better.

When I first came out to California on business trips, I discovered curvy roads. I mean, serious curves, such as Page Mill Road. If you start at El Camino Real in Palo Alto, and head up Page Mill just a mile, you can visit the Hewlett Packard guys. Then if you keep on going, the road starts bending – and curving. By the time you get to the top, at Skyline Drive (Route 35) there are about 206 curves. Some are very TIGHT. I mean, you find that in some places, you are looking out the side window, to see where you are going. I know a couple guys who have been commuting down Page Mill every day for over 20 years. How many does that compute up to? 5000 days, 10,000 trips, 2 million curves??)

But I must say, if you are pushing along as fast as you want to go, most of the curves on Page Mill are very FAIR – they do not tighten the radius after you get into the curve. In fact, that is one of the toughest parts of driving – coming into a curve with a pretty good radius, and getting your speed matched for that radius – and then *discovering* that the radius gets *tighter*. This is kind of – challenging. Or, not helpful.

My son says there are several places up on Route 49 near Downieville CA where the curves start in at one radius – and then tighten up. So be careful about stuff like that. Highway engineers don't *like* to do that – but sometimes it would be too expensive to avoid that.

Curves and Signs

I wrote a big section on signs for curves, and I moved it all into the Chapter on Signs. Good place for it. The point is, usually you count on your vision to tell you when you have to slow down for a curve. You rarely trust the sign. But there are a few exceptions. So when you get over to the chapter on Signs, you can read it. Meanwhile, for a beginning driver, if you start out believing the recommended speed on the signs, you will be a little slow, but not too far wrong.

What else do we need to know about steering?

"Sweepers"

When you are on a high-speed road, there are often sweeping curves. Usually these present no problem. There are a lot of roads with these sweeping curves, and they keep life interesting. Of course, any time you are on a road which is new to you, and you start into a curve, you must be aware that the curve may suddenly tighten. If you are going into a "45 mph" curve at 45, that is not usually a big deal. But if you are headed into a "45 MPH" curve at 55, you must be VERY careful – because sometimes a 45 mph curve really is a 45 mph curve. That is where you have to look at the curve, as you go, and use your judgement.

Admittedly, in *many* parts of the country, the road engineers try to never put in a "fooler". But, sometimes it happens. And you can't get mad if a curve tightens up just when you are hurrying down the road. If you are really pushing it to the limit, the sudden need to brake to a slower speed, for a tighter radius, is the kind of thing that sends you into a guard-rail – if you are not very alert. This is covered largely in the next Chapter, which is on Handling.

Of course, driving 600,000 miles on Freeways does NOT necessarily qualify me – or you – as a good driver on curvy roads. But I have done hundreds of thousands of miles on 2-lane roads, and curvy roads. I am not an expert – but I know enough to teach you the basics. If you come from back east, and every road with a 1-foot slant beside the road is protected by a guard-rail – as you know they are – then you will be AMAZED when you come west, and there are drop-offs of 10 or 100 or 1000 feet – with no guard rail – YOU will be ASTONISHED. Or, horrified. How can the authorities have such a dangerous road, and

NO GUARD-RAIL???????

It's really very simple. If there is a guard-rail there, at the edge of the drop-off, that's nice, but you are not going to drive into it, are you? Well, if you are not going to drive into the guard-rail, then why bother to put it up? – So, they did not put it up. Saves some funds.

One time my wife Nancy was driving my mother down a steep scary road that looks down on the Golden Gate, just a mile north of San Francisco, in Marin county. That is Conzelman Road, which looks down from an 800-foot hill on the 750-foot towers of the Golden Gate Bridge. A great road. But, when you start down the far side, it is steeper than any road in the east, and it has no guard rails. I bet if you got 100 VW Busses or Beetles going *really fast* down that road, and cut the wheel so as to roll them off the road, I bet you could put 40 of them into the ocean.

My mother said, "This road is so scary, I am going to close my eyes; I just can't look." Nancy said, "I brought you up to this road because it has such a great view. If you close your eyes, I'm going to close mine, too."

Why do we have sharp curves? Simple. If there is a hill, and we want to get around the hill, there may be a lot of places where it is *reasonable* to make a sharp curve in the road. If we had enough money, we could make straighter roads. We would have to pay for a lot of digging. But I do not know anybody who has so much money that he can straighten out every road. Now, we do have a lot of freeways, and a lot of good fast highways. Even Route 120, up in the foothills, does have some new straight stretches. (I want to check out the old road.) But, until a TRANS-infinite amount of money appears, we shall never run out of sharp curves.

The other reason we have sharp curves, even where there are no hills, is to get around property lines. Roads run straight – until they want to get around the lot lines. Curves are not necessarily bad – we just have to respect them, and slow down as required. Okay, guys? A sharp curve is not a big trouble – unless you forget to slow down.

NOW, let's suppose that you are driving on an interstate highway, and a sign says "25 mph" with a left-hand arrow. HEY, you might complain that an Interstate Highway is not SUPPOSED to do that. And you are right. If somebody were to SPLICE a chunk of 25 mph road into a piece of the Interstate Highway system, that would be unfair. Every driver has a right to expect the roads to not get tooo silly. Most roads are expected to meet that rule – and mostly they do. NOW, if any reader wants to tell me about the weirdest, wildest roads, anyplace across America, I will be interested. I may drive around and check them out.

I do know that there are some roads, such as from Lake City, Colorado to Silverton, or between Idaho Springs and Central City Colorado, up in the old mining districts, that are quite steep and difficult to drive. I have driven over some of these very twisty roads, without any serious problems – even though the switch-backs were, at times quite severe.

I mean, if you are going up a road, and there is a curve, and you cut your wheels as hard as you can – and the curve is so sharp, you can't get around the corner – what do you do then??? Well, you may have to back up and try again. And, what if it is very steep, too? And what if the traction underfoot is rough, with rocks and gullies? Well – you may not get around the corner. You might get out your shovel and dig a little, to ease the grade. Get the worst rocks out from under your wheels. You have a chance of getting around this corner. But after another mile, the road may get even worse! So you may not get up the hill. Otherwise, you may have to admit, an ordinary car should not try to get over a Jeep road, or "4WD road". Then you must retreat and not go up the hill. I always hate to give up on a road, but sometimes you just have to.

Straights – Driving on Straight Stretches

There are a LOT of straight roads. I will not philosophize a LOT about the need for careful driving on straight roads. Part of the problem is that there is not a lot of need for correcting your steering on a straight road. Part of the problem is that you can get bored, and inattentive. If you get sloppy, that is not nice. So, please try not to drive badly.

A good driver will not get sloppy very often. He will drive in the good or excellent category, most of the time. A good driver will rarely do dumb things. We should all try to be good drivers, as much of the time as possible. Actually, we should try to be excellent drivers, but as that does not always work, we should still keep trying.

Am I a great driver? No, probably not. But I am a *good* driver, and I do not get into accidents very often. The main question is, am I good teacher? I hope so. You tell me.

Mostly I have learned – if you tell the straight facts, you may get people bored. But if you tell the straight facts *plus* some stories about what happens if you are thinking the wrong stuff, then people may learn the right stuff, by saying, "I'm not as stupid as this story, pronto. (Right now it is 4:54 AM, as I type this – it happens to be July 2, 1995) and I am just driven by adrenaline to type up this story, and Ill probably keep on typing a few more hours. I may take a nap at 8 AM, but right now I am on a roll. Keep telling stories.

Parenthetical...

An old friend of mine, the late Ed Barrett, once had a lot of bad luck in his cars. One time, he was coming around a freeway ramp and a trailer truck fell on top of him! But the problem I want to mention today is, he once had a car whose steering linkage broke, and left him stuck in the middle of the road. I bet you don't know anybody whose steering gear has broken. I don't know any other person – because the car makers figured out, more than 50 years ago, that it was JUST UNACCEPTABLE to have your tie rods break. To have your steering not steer. So the manufacturing and forging procedures to make steering parts are VERY good.

> What would you do if YOUR steering broke? Would you ease on the brakes as soon as possible, and drive very slowly to the edge of the road, and stop? That's what Ed Barrett did – and that is what I would do – if I could. It's better than just stopping in the middle of the road. – NOTE: if one tie rod breaks, the other one is usually still connected, and

you may be able to steer, just a little. So if your steering starts to feel *WEIRD,* slow down and take it easy and stop and check it out.

Historical stuff. When cars were first being invented, 100 years ago, inventors had neat ideas how to do things. Inventors often want to do things differently – just to be different. So some early cars had tillers, or other ways of steering. But the wheel became obvious, fairly quickly, and standardized. Good thing!!

NOTE: in the 1920's, there was not yet any standardized pattern of having the gas pedal on the right, and the clutch pedal on the left, and the brakes in the middle. Fortunately, the old patents ran out, and that pattern became standard. Damn' good thing!!

What else can go wrong with Steering? How about shimmy? That is when your wheels twist back and forth – left and right – at a pretty fast speed. The exact cause may be a loose front end – or bad power steering. Or badly imbalanced tires. NOTE: your tires can be balanced *statically* and still shimmy badly.

> A tire with bad balance – static or dynamic – can cause bad shimmy or wheel vibration. This can ruin the tire – or wear out the shock absorber. And when the tire is ruined, it can then HELP ruin the shock absorber. Then if you replace the tire with a good balanced tire, and the shock was ruined, the new tire will also start bouncing. If the tire does not stay on the road, you cannot steer. So, the tire and its balance and shock-absorber are a kind of *system,* and you have to have all parts of the *system* working well. If mama ain't happy, ain't nobody happy!

If your car seems to have gotten a lot of shimmy or imbalance, suddenly, that might be because a piece of your tread has been cut, or fallen off. Maybe a bad "bubble" is developing. Or maybe you parked on some soft black-top, which stuck to your tire. Or some mud got stuck on the inside of the wheel, which causes an imbalance. No matter what, it's a good idea to check it out.

If you ever did a good panic stop from over 45 mph, with the brakes locked, you may have worn all the tread off one spot – making a flat spot. This probably makes enough imbalance to cause bounce and shimmy. If a tire is out of round, slightly, you may not be absolutely required to junk it. Many tire stores have a procedure to cut the excess rubber off and make it closer to round – with a sort of lathe. It's worth asking.

VW Beetles and Busses have one more item that has to be working right. There is a "steering damper" to cut down shimmy. It is a little shock-absorber, connected transversely – that prevents the steering wheel from getting too much vibration. If that gets old and worn, and you get shimmy, you have to replace that, too. But that is only $12, not like the need for a $500 power-steering repair. I have only had to replace 2 or 3 steering dampers, on all my VWs.

One time, my old blue Beetle developed a shimmy. I tried all kinds of things to fix it. I swapped tires, checked the balance, checked the shocks, and the steering damper. It only happened at 55, so for a few months I just ducked the issue and drove above 65, or below 45. Then I looked at the front suspension one day. The front frame that carries the torsion bars and all that stuff is held on by 4 big bolts, with 4 big lock washers. I noticed that one of the lockwashers was missing! I put a wrench on that bolt and tightened it up and the shimmy went away! Later, I went back and put a good lock-washer under the bolt head. Anyhow, it just goes to show how much trouble the loss of one STINKING lockwasher can cause. This never did cause an accident, but it wasted SEVERAL hours of my time, trying to trouble-shoot the problem.

Anyhow, if you have significant shimmy, this is kinda dangerous. Spend the money to get it fixed, as soon as possible. Drive slowly (or, at a faster speed, if the shimmy goes away up there) until you can get it fixed. If you didn't, you might get a LOT of tire wear, and ruin your shocks, too, and get into an accident, perhaps.

One time I bought a Beetle at 47,000 miles. It ran very well, but there was a little *hitch* in the steering, on hard left-hand turns. If you turned the wheel to the left, you had to push a little *harder* to get past one point, and then it was OK. But, if you had to drive at just the radius where that hitch was, it would be lumpy and awkward. But, that was a very severe, slow left curve, and I rarely drive on that hard a curve, except at very slow speeds. So it did not make much harm. I ran this about 260,000 miles more, and then I noticed that the steering was in one position, slightly right of center, when I started driving in the morning, but later in the day, the steering wheel was pointed left of center. I decided that if the steering box had two different modes like that, I would junk it and put in a new (rebuilt) one. Then I am going to bust it open and see what was wrong, inside the box.

If you steer too hard, and the car refuses to go where you point it, that's a form of skid. If you are in snow, or rain, and turning the wheel doesn't work right – that's not just a problem with steering – that's still a skid. Or, if you are going too fast, and turn the wheel. Check out the Chapter on Skids. Meanwhile, that's about all there is about Steering.

NOTE: In my whole Chapter on Steering, I have gotten a little feedback from several people, but nobody yet has reminded me that I forgotten to explain, how to hold onto the Steering Wheel. So I'll write a couple brief paragraphs here.

How to Hold the Steering Wheel

When you are driving under easy, straight conditions, you may think you can just hook one thumb over a spoke, or just one finger on the wheel. Yes, if you have power steering, you can get away with this. You may not have any problems. But it is still wrong. Driving with one arm out the window is not usually a good idea, except for a short time.

HOLDING YOUR STEERING WHEEL AT 10 O'CLOCK AND 2 O'CLOCK IS A LOUSY IDEA...

In general for ordinary driving, on mostly straight roads, it is best to drive with your left hand at 9 o'clock on the wheel, and your right hand at 3 o'clock. This gives you the best ability to respond to any strange requirements that may happen.

I recall old books that said, hold the wheel at 10 and 2 o'clock. That always bugged me. If you start getting side forces, the weight of your body will tend to pull you above the wheel. If you are at 9 and 3, you are better balanced. If I try holding the wheel at 10 and 2, it just feels *wrong*.

–9 AND 3 IS MUCH BETTER....

OR, you could hold the wheel at 8 and 4. That's generally bad, for the same reason. Holding it at 7 and 5 is worse. At 6 and 6 is worse yet. Holding it with your knees is not right, either.

Just hooking your hands onto the spokes is not as good, because you cannot hold on as strongly, and you cannot turn it very far. But every once in a while, that is one of the positions which is restful, and heaven knows, when you are on a long drive, you need some alternative positions. You would just want to do this, mostly when the road is fairly straight, and there is not much traffic. The same is true for resting one arm on the windowsill.

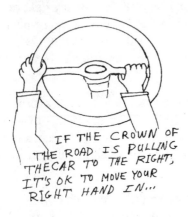

IF THE CROWN OF THE ROAD IS PULLING THE CAR TO THE RIGHT, IT'S OK TO MOVE YOUR RIGHT HAND IN...

In case of crosswinds, or a steep crown* or slant of the road, you may want to rest your hands with special positions, to provide torque against the wind forces. Sometimes, to work against a crown, I keep my left hand on the rim of the wheel, but let my right hand come half-way in on the spoke. Then the weight of my arms makes it natural to not have to push on the wheel. If there is a heavy crosswind from the right, I reverse those positions.

I like to sit, not too close to the wheel, and not too far back. Maybe some people like to drive with straight arms, but not for me. Maybe for racing....

Even when you are just on a straight road, it is preferable to keep both hands on the wheel, in a good, reasonable (9-and-3 o'clock) position. Why? Because you might have to dodge something. A car coming at you. A big rock in your lane. A chuck-hole. A strong gust of crosswind. In the winter you might need to be prepared to quickly correct for a skid. Or, at any time, you might have a blow-out, and you would need all your skill *and strength* to keep the car under control. Is that enough reasons? I am not saying, you never want to goof off and drive with only one hand. But that should normally be only for best-case driving conditions, and with light traffic.

The "crown" of a road refers to the way it is slanted down from the center, in both directions, to let the rain run off. Many roads are designed with 1/4 inch per foot, but sometimes more....

Steering in Curves

Now let's get into curves. For very shallow curves, you may just keep your hands on the wheel, and turn it a little. Maybe as far as 8-and-2, or 10-and-4 o'clock. But for harder curves (at least for ones that last more than a few seconds), it is best to go "hand-to-hand". For an example:

Let's say we have a moderate right-hand curve. You start into the curve, and your left hand moves up toward "noon". As you *know* this will be a moderate curve, your right hand comes up to "noon", and grabs the wheel, and pulls it down toward 3. Then put your left hand back to 9 o'clock. Now you can go around this curve, and if necessary you can turn the wheel a little further, or turn it back. THAT is why this is the best technique. When you are coming out of this curve, you reverse the motion – use your right hand to push the wheel back to noon, and pass it to your left hand to bring back down to 9.

Sharp Corners...

Of course, for very sharp corners, (or for cars with very slow steering ratios), you may have to pass it over, hand-to-hand, several times. It sounds like a lot of work, but, that is the right way. The more you hurry, the more important it is to do it right, so you can turn more or less, as needed.

For occasional corners, if you know the corner pretty well, you may just, after putting in 1 or 2 hand-to-hand moves, just turn the wheel a little more – so long as you are not hurrying, and so long as you know that you have judged the corner properly. For example, for a right-hand street-corner, after passing the wheel over once to the right, you might then turn the wheel with your left hand all the way over to 12:30, and your right hand down near 5. This will work OK, for a very short time – just a second – but only if you are very sure, because if you had to turn it further, you couldn't. This is not an ideal way to steer, but if this lets you get around the corner crisply, and not slop around in your lane, and not get too close to the center of the road – then this is not too bad. But only for a second! And only when you are not hurrying, and only when you are sure you have judged the turn correctly.

After I wrote this down – I checked to see if this is or ain't what I really do, when I steer.

Later – Yeah, the procedures I really use for steering are pretty close to what I wrote – ! / rap / 6 viii 95

Chapter 12. HANDLING

About 10 years ago, I saw a car with a bumper-sticker:

"STEERING IS NOT ENOUGH".

NOW – what the heck does *that* mean? Without hollering to the driver to stop, I could not find out what this was about. Then a few years later, I was driving down on Alemany Avenue in San Francisco, and I saw a car with this bumper sticker. I stopped and read the fine print, which sort of explained that this was sent out by some kind of society for smarter, safer driving. I do not remember who that was, and I never figured out exactly why this society was saying this.

But, the main point is, that STEERING is not the only part of driving. Steering is quite important. But, it is not the only important thing.

What is "Handling"?

First of all, when you turn the steering wheel gently, or at low speeds, and the car goes exactly where you point it – that is Steering. But when you are going faster and *faster*, and the direction the car goes is affected by the speed, by tire inflation, and by other factors – *that* is Handling. If you always drive slowly and sedately, and you never turn the wheel very hard, and you never get into high-speed curves or turns – then you are not using the car's Handling, and the car's Handling is *almost* not important to you. For example, if you are smoothly driving your Aunt Tillie to a special party, you might never notice how your car handles. If you keep it polite and slow and gentle, you won't get many surprises.

BUT if you ever get into a difficult or emergency situation – if you enter a curve a bit too fast, or, if a curve tightens up on you – or if you have to swerve to avoid an obstruction on the road – a rock – or a dog – *or* if one of your tires is going flat – then you may have problems, and you really should understand about Handling. Because you can get into an accident, if you do not understand the strange things that can happen. And that is what I am going to explain in this Chapter.

Handling – How Does It Work?

The basic problem with "steering" is, if you go "too fast", or if you turn the wheel "too far", or if there is "not enough traction", the car does NOT go where you thought you were pointing it. This is greatly influenced by weather and road surface. Rain makes some problems. Snow makes big problems. Ice makes very bad problems. So does oil. We will talk about Skidding in a separate Chapter on that topic – though it is often closely related to handling. Your car's Handling is also affected a lot by car design, by tire design, and by proper tire inflation, or, errors in tire inflation.

UNDERSTEER versus OVERSTEER

This is the heart of the topic of Handling. These can best be explained with a thought-experiment. You don't exactly have to *do* this experiment, but you could, if it's convenient. Let's say you are on a curve of constant radius, driving around in a circle marked on an empty parking lot. As you go gradually faster and faster, if your car has *understeer*, you find yourself cranking the steering wheel over further and *further*, to hold that radius. Eventually, when you can't go any faster, the front wheels will be cut over pretty hard, toward the inside of the circle, and the front end is "plowing". It's a sort of skid. (We'll talk more, later, about skids, and what to do about them, in the Chapter on Skids.)

Conversely, if you find you have to turn the wheel over *less far* at high speed, that is *oversteer*. When you go as fast as you can, the rear end of the car is "hanging out" and the wheel may be turned nearly straight ahead. This, too, is a kind of skid. It's often called a "drift", where the rear end *drifts* out. Porsches and VWs and other rear-engine cars tend to do this. Many sports and racing cars are set up this way. Any car with an under-inflated or nearly-flat rear tire can do this. If you are not prepared for this to happen, you can get a bad scare, a spin, or an accident. But if you are expecting it – if you are used to it, it's not so bad.

When you have a high-powered car, understeer *or* oversteer is not so bad because you can control it with power – with your right foot. You can "feed it" some more gas, and if you "feed it" too much, then ease off on the gas, just a little, to recover stability – to get out of the little skid. In a VW Beetle, you cannot do that on pavement – it does not have nearly enough power – but you can on gravel or snow. That's one of the reasons I enjoy driving on gravel and snow – I can drive just like a Porsche pilot, and hot-rod around, and if I goof, I'm not going 85 mph, I'm doing 25 or 35. And when I do this, I'm the fastest guy on the road!

"Neutral" Steering?

If your steering wheel stays at almost the same angle, to stay on that fixed radius, at slow speeds and fast speeds, too, that is called "neutral" steering. That's pretty good. This is sometimes called a "4-wheel drift". Many sports and racing cars are set up for this. To get good handling, tire pressures are adjusted to be "just right"....

Ideally, a car with "neutral" steering would stay neutral at all speeds. But in actuality, a car's handling can change from neutral to understeer or oversteer at different speeds, or at different radii. A VW may be nearly neutral-steering at 45 mph, but not at 65.

Transients

Or, if you go over a little bump, the rear axle might slide out more than the front, (or vice versa) and this could cause a spin or skid – or at least a surprise. In other words, if your shock absorbers are lousy, your handling will be degraded. Or if you had lousy tires... the car might not handle as you expect, on a bumpy road, compared to a smooth road. Or on a wet road, compared to a dry road.

8-11-21

If a car has nice neutral steering in a curve of constant radius – but it lurches when you ask it to change directions suddenly – that says its handling is not as well-behaved as it seems. Any idiot can design a car that will be well-behaved for slow changes, or for constant curvature. But a car that responds properly and safely when you need to make a sudden change – that is a car with good handling. CONVERSELY, if a car can be driven fast, with high cornering forces, and it behaves well for an experienced, expert driver – that sounds good – but if it is hard to drive and squirrelly for an inexperienced driver – like a high-powered sports car, that may be hard for a driver to control under less-than-favorable conditions – that is NOT a car with good handling for young, inexperienced drivers. Got the picture? The car that has "good handling" for one driver, may not be a good or safe car for another driver. Hey, some of you guys who have not driven a VW might think my Beetle has LOUSY handling. But it's just about perfect for *me*.

Where Does Handling Get Interesting?

If you are on a long straight road, and you are holding the speed limit – and you come to a curve – how do you judge how to slow down for the curve? Most new drivers figure out pretty fast, how to get around curves, gently but safely. You *look at* the curve, and use your judgement – you take your foot off the gas early, and you might touch your brakes a bit – preferably *before* you get into the curve – and you ease around the curve, at a safe, moderate speed.

Ah – but, what if you keep pressing through that curve, faster and faster? – What if you make a mistake and come booming into that curve faster than usual – faster than you are used to doing – faster than is really safe?

Ah – *that* is related to Handling, and is closely related to the art of driving. And what was right, yesterday – when you were driving Aunt Tillie to tea – may be the wrong speed today, when you are trying to stay with the traffic. And tomorrow, if you are really in a hurry, may be a lot different yet.

To a large extent, if you are just beginning to drive, you are not very interested in "Handling". You want to first learn to drive smoothly and safely and consistently, as you get around curves.

BUT, as you get a little more experienced, you'll learn more about handling — by mistakes — by trial and error. I won't argue that it is a disaster to make a few mistakes, and wear a little rubber off your tires, as you are learning. I just want you to *recognize* what is happening, as you go along....

Learning About Curves

Normally, you should decelerate *before* you get to the curve. If you find that you have to decelerate more, as you are *in* the curve, well, then you had better *decelerate* – hit the brakes before you go off the road. But, that's not really right. You should have done most of your braking *before* you got in the curve.

If you slowed down a little too much, that is fine – then you can speed up until it feels right. Accelerating through the curve and accelerating out the exit of the curve is a very good idea.

You should learn to judge what a curve looks like, and what it should feel like. On the other hand, if you are driving a car – or truck – that is very different from what you are used to – then you have to feel out how this new vehicle feels in corners – to figure out how it *handles*, just as a beginner does.

Not All Young Drivers are Bad

In the 1950s, Jackie Stewart was a young Scotsman, living on a large estate. He learned to drive on the back farm roads of his parents' estate. He learned to drive – what shall we say – rather fast? – quite fast? – let's say, BLOODY FAST. One day when he had only been driving on the highways a short time, he was driving his mother home from a shopping trip... reasonably smoothly and slowly. However, at a few corners his youthful exuberance cut in, and he began to take the curves a little – shall we say – aggressively? Jackie's mother complained that he was taking the curves a little too fast for comfort.

Young Jackie responded by STOMPING *on the gas, and FLUNG that little British sedan through the curves at such great speed and acceleration that his mother was too shocked and astonished to say anything. Not only that, he did* NOT *go off the road and crash. So, let's consider that there is a MAJOR difference between the rates and speeds that we normally consider comfortable, where we normally drive, and, the speed where the car can just barely hold the road without sliding off. And we rarely explore that area. Jackie Stewart did.*

Jackie Stewart started out driving competently at the age of 12. He kept driving more and more interesting, powerful cars. He drove in his first race in a Porsche in 1962. He ran his first full season as a Grand Prix driver in 1965.

Good news: Jackie Stewart went on to become world champion of Grand Prix racing, in the years 1966-1973. For years, he was the best. His record of 27 Grand Prix victories remained unmatched for many years.

Good news: Jackie Stewart, after many years of racing, retired and is still living at the ripe old age of 56. He did not get killed in any accident, on or off the race track.

◆ ◆ ◆

Where are all the great racing drivers? – Living a cheerful old age? Dead in car crashes? Well, some of each:

Jim Clark	– died April 1968, crash at Hockenheim
Bruce McLaren	– died 1970
Graham Hill	– died in plane crash
Phil Hill	– retired
Juan Fangio	– retired in 1957, and died of old age in 1996.

Jochen Rindt	– died during practice at Monza, 1970
Niki Lauda	– retired in 1985
Jack Brabham	– retired
Stirling Moss	– retired after he nearly died in a bad crash.
Mario Andretti	– survivor, retired
Alberto Ascari	– died during practice at Monza
Al Unser	– survivor
Bobby Unser	– survivor
A. J. Foyt	– survivor

– If I had as much talent as those drivers, I would never just give up auto racing because it was dangerous. Auto racing is just too fascinating and attractive, and it would be silly to pretend I could walk away from it. But despite all the flash and allure – it's still pretty dangerous. It's one of the most dangerous sports – until you come to flying....

Handling of Airplanes...

Chuck Yeager was probably the greatest pilot of this century. He flew a lot for the US Air Force, in the 1940s and 1950s and 1960s. He has written a couple books, and made videos and all that. He was the first man to exceed the Speed of Sound, in the X1 in 1947. He flew P-51 Mustangs during World War II. He shot down just 13 planes over Germany. BUT, the number of planes he shot down is *not* important – *not* at all the point.

Mr. Yeager was one of the wisest, best, hottest pilots in the 1950s. When the US Air Force captured a MiG-15 during the Korean War, Yeager was invited to evaluate that plane. He went up along with another pilot in a USAF F86. Yeager went into mock combat with the F86, and "shot it down" 3 times.

After they landed, the other pilot complained that Yeager had an unfair advantage. Yeager simply said, "Let's go up again, and YOU take the MiG-15."

When they went up, Yeager in his F86 "shot down" the MiG-15, 3 times in a row. As they said in the USAF, Yeager "waxed" the MiG-15. The point I am making is – a really excellent pilot can drive a F86 better than a MiG-15 – and he can also drive a MiG-15 better than an F86. A really good driver "can beat you with *his* car, and he can beat you with *your* car".

To be fair, we must point out that before he climbed into that MiG-15, Mr. Yeager had studied both the F86 and the MiG-15 more than any other pilot in the world. He had studied every book and every manual and every pilot's report and story on each plane. He was one of the best students and studiers of airplanes. He knew that in certain situations, one plane could have a neat little advantage over the other plane. During a dog-fight, the F86 was in trouble in a climb, and the MiG-15 was in trouble in a dive. The MiG could get around corners faster than the F86, but when Yeager was flying the F86, he was able to avoid situations where he had to turn much.

Good news: In 1998, Mr. Yeager is still alive. He's an old man at 75, with bad hearing due to many hours in EXTREMELY noisy cockpits, and he doesn't fly much any more. But if he did, he might still have the instincts to be THE BEST. And since he knows his reflexes are not so good, he refuses to fly.

Read the BOOK

Mr. Yeager always read "the book" – the pilot's manual – on any plane he was going to fly. If there was any trouble, he wanted to know all about the special character-istics, and back-up systems and emergency equipment. If you want to drive a car competently, you should read the Owner's Manual, and the reports and books about that car, too. I mean, I used to read *Car and Driver* magazine a lot. I've been a loyal subscriber for over 30 years. I read about all sorts of cars. I learned that if you drive a Porsche pretty fast, you have to be very careful in corners, because the tail may swing out, and you can skid or spin out. (i.e. oversteer...) I read *C & D* a lot. When I drive a Porsche, I am pretty careful, and I am aware, as I climb into the car, that I should not let the tail hang out tooo far. I can assure you that when I drive a Porsche, it is a *lot of fun* to let the tail hang out just a *little*.

When *C & D* said that VW Beetles are awful cars and VW Busses are even worse – because they are too slow, underpowered, and have lousy handling – that's partly true. I did not like what they said. But I did not junk my VWs. Yet, I did not ignore what *C & D* said, either. I took care to drive as smoothly, quickly, and competently as possible, to avoid slowing up traffic behind me. And when I come up a long upgrade, and I cannot hold a good speed, and I see any cars in my mirror, if I am slowing them down, I find a good place to duck to the right and let them pass me. I really despise people who go too slow, yet refuse to pull over, to let you pass.

So, Mr. Yeager was one of the wisest flyers of the century. It's NOT so important whether you are in the best plane (or the best car), or if you can fly *faster* or *farther*. What's important is how you *think* about the process. I want you guys to THINK, too.

A Small Physics Lesson...

If you have a nice smooth curve with a specified radius, and you go around at 20 mph, you generate a certain amount of side force. If you want to go 40 mph, that will cause twice as much side force – Right?? – NO, WRONG!! At a fixed radius R, the formula for lateral acceleration A is: $A = V^2/_R$. If you go around the curve twice as fast, at 40 mph, you will have *4 times* the side force. If you wanted to have just twice the side force, you would go around at about $\sqrt{2} \times 20$ mph, or about 28 mph. That's why "speeding just a little bit" sometimes has a dramatic effect. Physics may seem dumb and obscure, but when you are trying to get around a curve a *little* faster, it is a real-world subject, not just something in a book.

Now – what else does that formula tell us? If you want to get through a corner as fast as possible – the force can be decreased a little, if you increase the radius a little. So instead of staying *right* in the middle of your lane, you can start the curve near the outside of your lane, and swing *inside* a little at the center, or "apex", and then ease back to the outside as you exit. This increases the effective radius *r* of the turn. If you watch race cars, they do this, for best speed coming out of the corner. This is sometimes called "curb-to-curb" or "curb-to-curb-to-curb" cornering.

Curb-to-Curb Cornering

Just one little problem: If YOU try that, if you make ANY error, you'll start hitting the curb, and you can blow a tire, or get in a wreck. If one edge of your line is near the center line of the road, you might cross over into the on-coming lane if you made a mistake. Even most experienced drivers are not very good at this. Race drivers are pretty good, and after a lot of practice, they get better. But that does not say it is easy. This is normally recommended on the highway, only if you are absolutely DESPERATE – such as trying not to crash when you lose your brakes. Or if the Mob is after you. Or, if you are on a race-course – that is the right place. The correct way to drive *on the road* is to keep NEAR the center of your lane, all through the curve. You can cheat a few inches, but if you hit a bit of sand or snow or ice, you want to have some safety factor – some space to recover from the bad traction – or from the driver error. From *YOUR* error....

Race drivers do not just drive around a corner *once*. They do it repeatedly, in practice, until they get it about right. And if you want to be an excellent driver, *practice* is a good idea for you, too.

Further, if there is a crash, the racing driver often explains, "I hit a little oil, and lost it in the corner." When engines are being run at racing speeds, if they fail, they usually dump a lot of oil on the track. The guy who went through a tight corner at 70, on the last lap, may discover an oil spill that causes him to do 70, *right off the track* and into the hay bales. If you try to push through a corner at the same speed you did last weekend, how can you be sure there isn't a little sand? (or oil?) And if you are going about as fast as you can, how much are you going to skid when you hit that sand? And, what are you going to hit? Something painful and expensive? Note: the way you went pushing through a curve, *last* weekend, may not work *this* weekend....

The other thing about race tracks is, they have fire extinguishers, emergency rescue teams, and ambulances in case you goof up. So if you want to play "boy racer", and race through a corner as fast as your tires will allow, just remember there are a *lot* of differences between a curvy road, and a real race track.

Handling on Different Cars

Many books and articles have been written on "handling". The definition of what is "good" handling, and "inferior" handling, will be debated forever. But if you only have one car – what you got is what you get.

Then if you then start to drive a different car, you may not notice much difference on a straight road, until you come to a curve, where you discover that the "handling" may be a *lot* different from what you are accustomed to. Maybe better – maybe worse! Let's discuss briefly, the aspects of handling, and comment on what they have to do with steering and curves.

Steering Force?

Many cars with power steering require very little steering force at the steering wheel. Very easy to drive. But for competent driving, it's not always such a good idea.

The reason is, force feedback. It's good to have a little feedback – especially if you are driving in snow. If you have no force feedback, you cannot tell how slippery things are. It's very hard to tell if you are starting to skid. As I mentioned in the Steering Chapter, if you get on glare ice, and you can't *feel* how slippery it is, you can get in a bad skid before you even recognize it.

If you have any choice, to get a car with just *partial* power assist in the steering, that is much better for a good driver than low-force power steering – and especially in places where you'll be driving on snow. Similarly, if you have any choice in the steering ratio, you may find some good advantages in a car with fast steering ratio; 3.5 turns, lock-to-lock, can be a LOT worse than 2.5 turns.

Soft Suspension?

Similarly, if you are buying a car, and you have a choice of soft springing, or a stiffer, "sporty" suspension package, with a bigger "anti-sway bar", take enough test-drives of the car (or a demonstrator) to make sure you are going to like what you get. Stiffer springs may provide *great* handling and cornering, but after a while your rump may decide it's just too harsh a ride. Conversely, some cars with soft springing just don't go where you point them – they wallow too badly. Other modern cars with soft springing can actually handle pretty well. Good tires can make a lot of difference, too. YOU figure it out....

Check out YOUR Car

How do you find out how your car "handles?" Well, first of all, don't try it on a crowded road. If you are on an empty road, you can try changing from one lane to another, to see if it feels good, and is not out of control. When you have that all figured out, change lanes a little faster. Cut the wheel a little harder, a little more crisply. Do this until you understand what your car would do in an emergency move – to avoid a rock in the road, for example.

If you want to try this on a wet or snowy road, be EXTREMELY careful, because a simple maneuver that's OK on a dry road, may get you in trouble on a wet road. So "back off". Take it really easy. And, of course, if that car half a mile back is a cop car, you may have to explain what you were doing!

Squirrelly?

How do you check if you suspect your rear tire is deflating and the car may be squirrelly? *Don't* jerk the wheel. You should probably slow down, and then turn the wheel a tiny amount, and see if the car keeps swaying or wallowing or cork-screwing – acting different from usual. If it is, slow down considerably, and stop to see if you have to change a flat tire.

Oversteering Caused by Low Pressure

A car with oversteer can be fairly dangerous – very difficult to drive. Last month I was driving my son's '74 Beetle on a Throughway, and it felt LOUSY, even on the straights. The rear end felt *squirrelly*. That is a technical term — the rear end tends to sway back and forth. Even without a gust of crosswind it was doing it, but with any gust, I had to fight to prevent it from swaying in a cork-screwing motion.

I stopped at the first rest stop, and checked the tires. Three tires were inflated just right, but the left rear tire was at 18, not where it should be at 28. I chewed my son out for letting it get so low, and for not recognizing it was so squirrelly. When I put it back up to 30, it felt great. (The book says 28, but as it was warmed up, 30 was about right. Your tires when warm *should* have a little higher pressure than when cold. Don't bleed off that extra pressure.)

Oversteer Caused by Stupid Inflation

The first time I met up with oversteer, I had my new 1962 VW Beetle about 7 months, and I decided, like a devout little follower of the Owner's Manual, to rotate the tires. (I do not rotate my tires very often, these days.) I put the front tires on the back, and the back on the front, and started into town to get some groceries and some air. MAN, I nearly lost it on the third curve. I don't know why I did not notice it earlier, but I was *breezing* into a 35 mph curve at 40 mph, and my tail came around in a messy skid, right up to the white line of the road, and I just *barely* caught it. The rear tires at 17 psi, and the front tires at 27 gave just AWFUL oversteer. I eased on down into town, and got some air, and things were fine. BUT, I should have noticed it earlier. And, I should have known this would happen. AND, the owner's manual should have warned me this will happen, when you rotate the tires.

> SO YOU ARE HEREBY WARNED: NEVER let your front tire inflations get too high, and NEVER let your rear tire inflation get too low. And this is especially true on a rear-engine car. But true in general.

What I *should have done*, to avoid the severe understeer, was to over-inflate my front tires to 27 psi, on the way home before rotating the tires. Then after I swapped the wheels, I could have just let out the air from the new front tires, and I'd be all set. Ain't it great, all this free hindsight?

The Corvair and Oversteer

This outrageous oversteer that I discovered while rotating my tires, is what old Ralph Nader was talking about in his 1965 book about the Chevrolet Corvair, "Unsafe at any Speed". Actually, the Corvair was a pretty good car for its day, and I know several people who owned them and liked them a lot. (Heck, I wanted to buy one, once. If I could buy a new one now, I'd be tempted.) But one day a Corvair driver asked a mechanic at the local Chevy agency, "How much air should I put in my tires?" And the dumb mechanic said, "Oh, put in 25 pounds pressure all around, because that's good for all Chevys". And the driver did.

> NOTE, for at least 25 years, the correct inflations for your tires, front and rear, have been listed on a little sticker that is on your car's door

jamb, or in the lid of your glove compartment, or some similar obscure place. If you have to check the tire pressures on YOUR car, or on ANY car, search it out and follow its advice.

Actually, the Corvair, with its heavy engine in the rear, needed about 30 psi in the rear, and 15 in front – roughly the same inflations as a Beetle. So, that poor Corvair with equal inflation on all 4 corners was just as horribly squirrelly as my Beetle when I was in the middle of rotating my tires, with too much air in front, and too little in the rear. The Corvair inevitably spun out, into an accident, and after all kinds of publicity, and all sorts of weird happenings (Chevrolet tried a cover-up, and then sent investigators to find out if Nader could be black-mailed in case he had any dirty laundry – and he didn't!) Ralph Nader wrote his book, and that was the start of Nader's highly-publicized career.

Nader complained that a good car should not care if it has incorrect pressure on some tires (WRONG, Ralph) and that GMC should not be telling people to put in equal pressure (he's sure right there) and that the Corvair was a lousy car, and some rolled over, and *overheated* their spare tires, (well, the Corvair was really no worse than a lot of other cars of that era) and a bunch of other gripes. However, he *was* correct that if you ever got the front tire inflation up too high, OR the rear pressures too low, yes, it was AWFULLY dangerous. But if that one mechanic had not given out the wrong info, Ralph would still probably be griping about mediocre soap and bad washing-machines.

– Recently I spotted some *bad* advice in a popular magazine.* They recommended that you keep all your tires "fully inflated" to the maximum recommended pressure marked on the tire. Wait 'til Ralph Nader gets ahold of them – that is TERRIBLE advice!!! Follow the advice in your Owner's Manual, or on the sticker on the door-jamb. And don't believe everything you read in magazines!

Review of Oversteer

Oversteer is less common these days. Very few cars have it. If you don't buy a Porsche 911 or an old VW, you won't run into it – except ... in any car, if a rear tire is going flat, the steering can get squirrelly, and you should be quick to recognize this. Also, some cars with snow-tires can feel squirrelly, even with the right inflation. You should be aware of that. Another case is, if you get a blowout in a rear tire, *suddenly* you get a bad oversteer condition. The car can get really squirrelly – can "fishtail", which means the rear of the car tends to veer from side to side. It's almost like a dog wagging his tail, but not so quickly. If you have some experience with oversteer, you will be better prepared to turn the wheel GENTLY, and not make any violent correction. You may be able to "damp out" the oscillation. A fishtail is a kind of skid, and you can tame it just like you handle a skid.

Some experts point out that a VW and "other inferior cars" can go from understeer at low speeds, to oversteer at high speeds. They imply that is rather bad.

*HEALTH *Magazine, March/April 1994, states on page 98: "(IF) YOUR TIRES ARE TOO SOFT: The* SAFEST *bet is to keep your tires filled to the maximum air pressure shown on the tire's sidewall." – WRONG!!! TERRIBLE advice!! Don't do that!!! Keep the* FRONT *and* REAR *tire pressures just as high as your car's manufacturer recommends – and* NOT *any higher! More ain't better! As I've observed,* MORE *can be quite dangerous.*

8-11-21

I say, the oversteer would be dangerous if you did not know about it – or if you let the rear tire inflation get low. The shift from oversteer at high speeds to understeer at low speeds is not a big deal.

I'll mention here, that there's a broad transition region between driving a car with oversteer, through a corner, fast, and getting into a skid. There's no clear demarcation line. So, don't be surprised if you start getting pushy, and wind up in a little skid. If you are driving aggressively, you must be prepared *at all times* to use the procedures in the Chapter on Skidding, to catch and stop that little skid, before it becomes a big one.

Review of Understeer

Understeer is normal on many American cars. It is probably safer for most drivers. That's what the manufacturers think. But I am not in favor of boredom. You turn the wheel and not much happens. I prefer responsive steering. Of course, there are a lot of good responsive cars in the US, these days. Most of them have very little understeer in most normal driving conditions. Damn' near neutral.

It's hard to get really good neutral steering under every condition. But it is fun to try. Note, you do NOT have to drive fast, or skid, or race, or dodge obstructions, or drive through corners fast, to need to know about understeer and oversteer. But those are the places where it is most noticeable.

Understeer caused by a Flat Tire

Converse to what happens when a rear tire goes flat, if a front tire goes flat, or has a blowout, you suddenly get a lot of understeer. The front end tends to *plow*. You have to be pretty careful, and prepare to turn the wheel more than normal. If the wheel comes off the rim, or loses all its air, it can get much worse. If you did not have power steering, you would have to turn the wheel pretty *hard*, too. In the old days, with no power steering and lousy tires, having a blowout on a front tire was a real concern – even a strong driver might have trouble holding the wheel straight. And a small driver might have real trouble, especially if he was not paying attention – or just holding onto the wheel with a couple fingers.

Mixed Tires

If you just change a tire, even with the correct inflation, the handling may change considerably. Most books tell you not to mix radial and bias-ply tires on the same axle. Sometimes I do, and sometimes I don't. I never found much of a big deal, not much change in handling, on my Beetles. On my 1972 Bus, I found that radial tires made it feel squirrelly, and so I went out of my way to buy bias-ply tires. They felt better, somehow.

Any time you are buying tires, you must be aware that the new tires might feel bad – squirrelly – in terms of stability. Check the Chapter on Tires....

If you have some tires that feel squirrelly, even though they are apparently well inflated – is that because the rear tires feel funny? What if you carefully rotate the rear tires to the front? Or, what if you over-inflate those rear tires a little? Check your tire pressure gauge – it could be wrong. Hey, I'll shut up, on this topic.

Signs?

Many times there's a road sign warning you, "SLOW, CURVE", with a curvy arrow, sometimes with a "recommended maximum speed". Even if you have convinced yourself that you can usually boom through most such curves at 5 or 10 mph over the "recommended" speed, just be careful – sometimes you can't. Sometimes the curve tightens up. Or, there could be an obstruction in the road – a rock, or a car wreck, or an animal, or a pack of bicycles. Or maybe an on-coming car in your lane. So, no matter what happens, you have to be prepared to respond to those circumstances.

> *One time, 34 years ago, I was driving down a road in northern Kentucky – maybe US Route 25, or Route 68. I was steaming along in my almost-new 1962 VW. I came to a sign that said "CURVE, 15 MPH". Well, I was a pretty hot driver, so I slowed to 25. The first curve came up, and then the second curve came up, and the third was even tighter. I came out of the third curve and looked down at my speedometer and it read – 15 mph. Ok, I got the picture. This was not JUST a game – because the road engineers had to drop the road down off a high plain, down to a low bridge across a river. So the road made a hard left to descend along the river bank, then a hairpin right to descend further, and then a hard left onto the bridge. Perfectly logical. And, for a change, 15 mph was not a lie. But, maybe they could have said 12 mph, to wake us all up?*

What else do we need to know about steering in hard curves?

"Sweepers" with a Tightening Radius

When you are on a high-speed road, there are often sweeping curves. Usually these present no problem – there are a lot of these "sweepers", and they keep life interesting. But, any time you start into a curve on an unfamiliar road, you must be aware that the curve may suddenly tighten. If you are going into a "45 MPH" curve at 50, that is not usually a big deal, because if you just "lift" your foot off the gas, you'll be able to slow down to 40 or 35 pretty easily, if necessary. But if you are headed into a "45 MPH" curve at 55 or 60, you must be VERY careful – because sometimes a "45 MPH" curve really is a 45 mph curve. That is where you have to look at the curve, as you go, and use your judgement. If it looks fishy, get off the gas, and if it looks REALLY FISHY, use the brakes.

Admittedly, in *many* parts of the country, the road engineers try to never put in a "fooler". But, sometimes it happens. My son Benjamin says there are several places on California Route 49, up in the Sierra foothills near Downieville, where you start into a "sweeper", which then suddenly tightens its radius. And you can't get mad if a curve tightens up just when you are hurrying down the road. If you are really pushing it to the limit, the sudden need to brake to a slower speed, for a tighter radius, is the kind of thing that can send you into a guard-rail, if you are not very alert. You just have to keep looking at the road, and if the curvature appears to be tightening up, slow down before you get in trouble. This is especially true on roads you have never driven before.

Planning for Hard Curves

An old friend of mine, Sam, used to drive his old 1958 VW Beetle rather fast. He told me he never went faster than 126 mph. (That's *clocked*.) There was one road he used to drive down from New Hampshire, which had a tough "45 MPH" curve that tightened up into a "35 MPH" curve. Sam had good Michelin X tires. He would come down the road at 85, and slow to 65 for the first curve, and then slow to 52 for the slow part, before accelerating out of the curve. He finally stopped, one day, to nail up a little white board to one of the fence posts, so he would know when to nail the brakes for the "slow" 52 mph section. Then, as he came down that road, when he saw the white marker, he would hit the brakes hard, to get down near 52. This worked for a long time.

But one night, he came steaming down that road, and slowed down for the first curve, and then – he realized – the white marker was gone!! He hit the brakes, and got the car half-sideways to scrub off speed, and he nearly lost it. But he did not wreck the car. Did not hit the guard rail, nor anything else. But it scared him properly.

Note, Volkswagens, like Porsches and most other rear-engined cars, do tend to oversteer, especially at high speed, especially while braking. When Sam realized he was too deep into the corner, and much too fast, he knew that when he hit his brakes, his tail would hang out severely... and he allowed this to happen, but he survived.

Braking-Induced Oversteer

Here is a good place to explain – even if your car is running through a fast curve very stably, or nearly "neutral", and you hit the brakes, the weight of your car tends to transfer *off* the rear wheels and *onto* the front wheels. This is good for the front wheels – but lousy for the rear wheels. Just as you are hitting the brakes – the rear wheels have less weight on them. The car tends to over-steer – and if you were using all the traction you had, then you are likely to skid – the rear end can walk right out there – and if you are not extremely careful, it can walk right out into the guard-rail – or into a lane of oncoming traffic. That's basically what *almost* happened to Sam.

> SO: If you are cornering hard, and you have to hit the brakes for any reason, you are likely to skid with your tail out. And you do not have to be driving extremely fast, or cornering extremely hard. You do not have to be on snow or sand. You do not have to be driving a VW or a rear-engine Porsche. (Although, all of these factors can contribute to the problem.)
>
> If you are cornering hard, and applying a lot of power, and you have to lift your foot off the gas – even THAT can cause a little rear-end skid or

"drift". So driving "aggressively" can cause problems – even if you are not going really fast.

So, be ye warned, here and now: Hitting the brakes in a curve – OR even lifting your foot off the gas – can cause a big surprise – and quite possibly, a skid.

Conversely, going into a curve a little slow and then *feeding* the gas does help improve the stability, and cuts out oversteer, as it tends to transfer weight onto the rear wheels.

A buddy pointed out to me – sometimes there is ice on the road – or oil – or sand. This is still true at night, when you can't see it. And it's still true, on curves – where you can't see around the curve, until it's too late. So, when you are hurrying, cornering hard, you have to be prepared for difficult changes. You have to be prepared for *anything*. Maybe that's a good reason to take it easy!

Steering in Hard Curves

As I said in the Chapter on Steering, it's important to hold your hands in good positions on the Steering Wheel. If you try to drive aggressively, and you get sloppy about where you hold your hands on the wheel, you are putting yourself at a serious disadvantage, in terms of staying on the road and avoiding accidents. So – keep awake. Keep alert. Keep alive. Be sure to practice your "hand-over-hand" steering, to make sure you do not develop sloppy habits. Because if you are cornering aggressively, you need to keep your hands in a position to recover from any of your errors – or from transients in the driving conditions.

Have I ever gone off the road, or hit the guard rail, on a curve? Lemme think. I think not. I have only gone off the road, by mistake, a couple times. NOT on a curve. Nope. I never did.

Just remember, "Steering is Not Enough"....

Chapter 13. SKIDS and SKIDDING

This is gonna be fun, because here I am trying to describe something that is pretty hard to explain, unless you have already done some. I mean, does reading a book on Playing Better Tennis help you a lot, if you have never held a tennis racket in your hand? Or, a Sex Education book? Skidding is something we generally do not do every day. Well, something that YOU do not do every day. I try to keep my skills up.

There are several types of skids:

- Front-end skids, also called *plowing*.

- Rear-end skids, where the rear end swings out, and

- Side-skids.

- There are power-on skids, when you are trying to accelerate with a front-wheel drive car.

- There is also the rear-wheelspin skid, for cars with their drive-wheels in the rear. This often leads to "fish-tailing".

- And there is also the straight-ahead braking skid, such as when you lock your brakes, straight ahead.

- There are also skids when your 2 right wheels are on sand or snow, and your 2 left tires are on good pavement. (Or, vice-versa.)

Most skids are a simple case of, too much demand for traction, and, not enough traction. On ice or snow, it's pretty hard to avoid all skids, but if you are alert, you can keep your skids small, and make sure you can recover from them.

Why are we so concerned about skids? Because when your front wheels are skidding, and the wheels are not turning, YOU CAN'T STEER. You are basically out of control. If your rear wheels are skidding, you can steer a little with your front wheel, but if the rear end of your car goes off where it wants to, you are probably 'WAY out of control, and headed for an accident.

Let's talk about a few basic EXAMPLES of skid.

CASE 1. A guy is driving a new front-wheel-drive Chevy at a fairly reasonable speed, let's say 45 mph, on a straight snowy road. He comes to a right-hand curve followed by an uphill. This klutzy driver decides that if he slows down, he will not make it up the hill, so he does not slow down. He just turns the wheel to the right, to go around the curve. But there's not good traction, and when he turns the wheel too far, the car sort of plows almost straight ahead, right across the center line. If there is on-coming traffic, he may slide right into it. That is really tough, as the on-coming car might have been minding his own business, and along comes this idiot and hits him! Not nice.

CASE 2. Next, a big Ford sedan with rear-wheel drive comes along the same road, at the same speed, with the same amount of snow. The driver slows down for the same corner, and gets around the corner OK, and then steps on the gas and tries to accelerate up the upgrade. The rear wheels spin loose, and the tail of the car fish-tails, left and right and left, and his tail goes over and hits the next on-coming car!!

CASE 3. Next, along comes an old VW Beetle. It is going as fast as the other guys. The driver enters the corner and feels the front end skid a little, and he corrects, and keeps feeding the gas. Then as he is applying full torque on the upgrade, the rear end starts to skid – it drifts out a little – and then the driver eases off on the gas momentarily, and catches the skid, and corrects, and gets right through the corner and up the hill, where the other two guys skidded and crashed. This is possible – because that driver is ME.

CASE 4. Next, along comes another VW Beetle and he was trying to go 5 mph faster than all the other guys. His rear wheels lose traction, and his rear end skids out on the left, almost like the Ford's, but an even stronger skid. He slides tail-first into the left-hand guard-rail.

CASE 5. Finally, a guy in a Subaru pickup comes along, and he goes through the corner, just as fast as the VW that spun out, and runs right up the hill.

Let's look at each of these examples, and see what we can learn from them. Before we do, let's list the old rule: – if you are in a skid, steer in the direction of the skid. Let me repeat that:

In a skid: STEER in the DIRECTION of the SKID.

STEER in the DIRECTION of the SKID.

Okay – we just made a statement three times – "Steer in the direction of the skid". It is a cute phrase, and easy to remember. Now, what the heck does it *mean*?

If you are trying to turn to the right, and you turn the steering wheel to the right, and the car does not go right, but goes straight ahead – as if you were on ice – the front end is skidding *to the left of where you would like to go*. To recover from the skid, or to prevent it from getting any worse, turn your steering wheel back to the left a little, for a short while, until the front wheels stop skidding. We'll study this more in the discussion of Case 1.

If you are trying to go straight – but your rear end slips off to the left – this can easily happen when you are running out of traction, or applying too much power. The rear of the car is trying to go left of the way the car is pointed. As you sit in the car, you can see the car is pointed to the right of where you want to go, but the car is *moving* to the left of where it is pointed. This is a way to say, the skid is to the *left*. Turn the wheel to the left to recover from this skid. Details when we get to Case 2.

If you are trying to turn to the right, and you turn the wheel to the right, and the car does start to turn right, but the rear end swings too far to the left – the rear of the car is trying to skid to the left. To recover, turn your wheel to the left a little. Maybe a lot. Details when we get to Case 4.

Now, when I tell you statements like this, you can *think about* them and *say* them and *memorize* the words and *repeat* them any time you are asked. BUT, that does not mean you *recognize* a skid as it happens, or as it starts, nor do you *know* what to do when a skid happens. You have to go out, preferably with your teacher on a snowy day, to find out how to learn *intuitively* what a skid feels like, and how to respond *automatically* as a reflex. You have to do hands-on stuff. You have to learn about skids, in the real world, how to detect them, and how to correct them, *instinctively* and *intuitively*. See the section on Practicing Skids, at the end of this Chapter.

Now let's take a look at each of these five cases.

CASE 1. The *first* driver had a car with a heavy front end. On snow, as on pavement, it basically tends to understeer. (Refer to the definition of understeer, in the Chapter on Handling.) *That* means, turning the steering wheel *further* may not help the car turn more. But, if you turn it *less*, you may be able to recover from the skid.

If you get in a skid in this kind of car, while trying to turn right, and it just tries to plow straight ahead to the outside of the desired curve, it is skidding OUT to the LEFT. Turn the wheel OUT a little – turn it LEFT a little, in this case, or at least turn the wheel not so far to the right – even though you really want to go right.

Now this sounds like you are steering OUT into the other lane – right toward that on-coming car. Yes, you are *temporarily* steering in the wrong direction. BUT, you must not wait until you are already in a big skid, and all the way across into that lane. You must turn your wheel back nearly straight, as soon as you detect the skid. You must "catch" the skid, and catch it EARLY.

As soon as you feel or see the skid to the left starting, turn the wheel back to the left, a little. If you have your foot on the gas, take it off a little, so you decrease the forward speed a little. If your foot is already off the gas, you may even consider touching the brakes a little. After all, your rear wheels are still rolling. They may be able to slow you down, without ruining your front wheels' traction. Touch the brakes just momentarily – maybe 1 second – and then get off the brakes.

But, if you are already ON your brakes, you should consider, taking your foot OFF the brakes, momentarily....

Why Add Less Braking? Why Add Less Gas??

– This sounds *stupid*!! Why should you, in some cases, take your foot *off* the brake, and in other cases take your foot *off* the gas? The answer is simple: Whatever you were doing may have contributed to the skid – whether *braking* – or *accelerating* – and if you stop doing it, or decrease it, you have a better chance of getting out of the skid. If you do not *STOP* doing what you were doing, you may *NOT* get out of the skid. Okay?

Very shortly – after about one second – see if your front wheels have stopped skidding. They may start rolling true. NOW is the time to slow down a little more, and then start easing the wheel to the right, to get back toward the middle of your lane. If you are sharp and alert, you should not even skid out of your lane. And you should learn to do this automatically, in barely one second.

Mistakes Made in CASE 1.

Now, the actions of the first driver were pretty bad. He tried to keep on going at a constant speed, much too fast for the curve, and he did not recognize the skid and "catch" the skid. If you are not good at "catching" your skid – if your car is big and heavy, with no "feel" in its power steering, and if you are not alert, then you had better not be going too fast. You had better slow down for that curve. By definition, if you got around the corner and up the hill, you were not going too fast. If you crash, or skid outside your lane, you were going too fast.

So if you own this kind of car, you should get out in the first snow and practice your little skids, such as in an empty corner of a parking lot, so you can recognize the skids, and "catch" them fast. Now we know a little bit about how to recover from an over-steer skid.

Look at Sketch 1A. The view from above shows that the front wheels are turned fairly hard to the right, but the car is not going where the front wheels are pointed, because the front wheels are not rolling. The front wheels are plowing straight ahead, sliding on the snow, and the rear wheels are following. This skid has been going on for a few seconds, and the car is well on its way into on-coming traffic – or even to the left guard rail. If you wanted to avoid an accident, you should have "caught" this skid quite a while ago. If you don't notice the skid and turn the wheel left rather promptly, you are not going to avoid a crash. Here and in the five following sketches, the grey shading indicates the road's

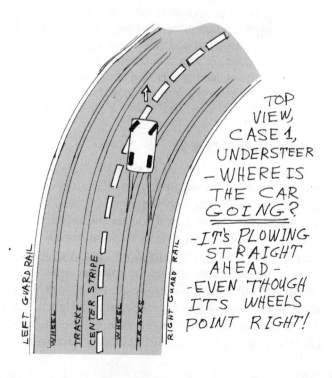

TOP VIEW, CASE 1, UNDERSTEER – WHERE IS THE CAR GOING?
– IT'S PLOWING STRAIGHT AHEAD –
– EVEN THOUGH ITS WHEELS POINT RIGHT!

LEFT GUARD RAIL WHEEL TRACKS CENTER STRIPE WHEEL TRACKS RIGHT GUARD RAIL

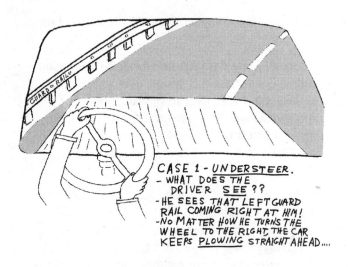

CASE 1 - UNDERSTEER.
- WHAT DOES THE
  DRIVER SEE ??
- HE SEES THAT LEFT GUARD
  RAIL COMING RIGHT AT HIM!
- No MATTER HOW HE TURNS THE
  WHEEL TO THE RIGHT, THE CAR
  KEEPS PLOWING STRAIGHT AHEAD....

pavement, with perhaps an inch or 3 of snow on it, and wheel tracks of other vehicles indicating where most drivers want to be in their lanes.

That means that in Sketch 1B, if you have turned the wheel a lot, and nothing is happening, and you see that you are headed straight for that left-hand guard rail, it's kinda *late*. You must detect the earliest signs of the skid, and stop the skid early. The longer you wait to correct a skid, the harder it is to stop it.

◆◆◆

CASE 2. The second little pig went to market, no, wrong story. The second driver was wise enough to slow down, and got around the corner OK. But when he tried to accelerate up the hill, he did not have enough weight on his rear wheels, and he applied a little too much power. The rear end skidded and "fishtailed" and finally skidded into the far lane. (To "fishtail" is to have the rear of your car skid alternately, left and right.) If you keep your foot on the gas, there is just about *no limit* to how far your tail can swing out to the left or right. You might spin all the way around and go off the road backwards. If you stop tromping on the gas, you have a chance to recover just fine. Turning the wheel in the direction of the skid can help recover, too. BUT if your tail comes back to the right place, you have to be quick to straighten out your wheel, OR the tail may swing the *other* way. That's how a fish-tail skid is perpetuated.

Mistakes Made in Case 2.

The second driver neglected to slack off the power when he felt a skid or fishtail. If you *feel* the rear end slipping, or *see* the car pointing in the wrong direction because the tail end is skidding 'way out, or if you *hear* the engine revving up because the rear wheels are slipping, or if you *see* the speedometer needle go 'way up, or if you *hear* the rear wheels whining as they spin too fast – and you *still* keep your foot on the gas – you really are a dumb *klutz*, and you should get off the road. I mean, if you ease off the gas briefly, and let the wheels catch traction, you have a good chance to get up that hill. But, you *must* be alert to ANY of the five signs of a skid, as listed above – not like this guy who ignored all 5 signs!! You *must* detect the first sign of a skid, and slack off the gas, and then bring the gas back to a reduced power setting. Otherwise, if you are not smart enough to take yourself off the road, the car will take care of that for you. Your car will take you right off the road, into the oncoming lane or into the ditch or guard-rail. If you want to be out on the road on a snowy day, you *gotta* get out of the klutz mode.

So, let's look at Sketch 2A. While the road is straight, the driver was applying so much power that the rear end skidded out to the left. In this case, this is a skid to the left, so the driver must turn the wheel to the left. He must also take his foot most of the way off the gas, to give the rear tires a chance to start rolling and stop spinning. The earlier he does this, the better the chance of getting out of the skid and continuing straight ahead. Otherwise, he could go off the road to *either* the left *or* the right, depending on how the tires get traction.

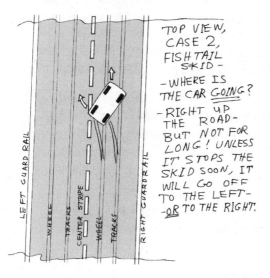

TOP VIEW, CASE 2, FISH TAIL SKID –

– WHERE IS THE CAR GOING? – RIGHT UP THE ROAD – BUT NOT FOR LONG! UNLESS IT STOPS THE SKID SOON, IT WILL GO OFF TO THE LEFT – OR TO THE RIGHT.

So when you see the snow on your left coming toward you, as in sketch 2B, turn your wheel to the left. If your foot was on the gas, take it off. If your foot was on the brake, take it off – at least for a little while, until you have recovered from the skid.

Absurd??

You may think I am picking some pretty dumb examples out of thin air. Well, a car plowing straight ahead happens every day, when an un-thinking driver hits his brakes too hard in snow. And the second example, with the car fish-tailing, happened RIGHT IN FRONT OF ME.

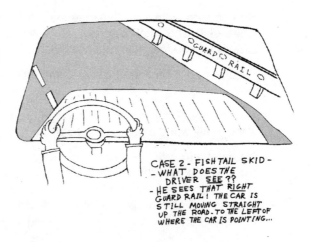

CASE 2 - FISH TAIL SKID – – WHAT DOES THE DRIVER SEE?? – HE SEES THAT RIGHT GUARD RAIL! THE CAR IS STILL MOVING STRAIGHT UP THE ROAD - TO THE LEFT OF WHERE THE CAR IS POINTING...

On January 6 of 1976, I was running about 50 mph down Mass. Route 128 on the way to work. It had been snowing a good bit, but the plows had knocked the snow down to perhaps an inch of hard-packed snow. I passed a diaper truck who was doing 45, and I noticed that he then followed me out into the passing lane. HEY, trucks are supposed to be prohibited from the high-speed lane on these roads.

As I approached Mass. Route 9, near Newton Upper Falls, I looked over on the right and saw a car trying to accelerate up the entrance ramp from Route 9 (east) to Route 128 (south). I noticed he was fish-tailing a little on the up-hill.

Suddenly, this klutz swung left across all 3 lanes, and crashed into the center divider – right in front of the car in front of me! As we saw this absurd situation unfolding, I and the car in front of me both eased on our brakes and stopped. However....

However, that damn' diaper truck did not do a very good job of stopping. He was still doing about 20 when he hit me, and gave me a good SHOVE forward. Fortunately, I was not too close to the car ahead of me. I steered to the left, and shoved my nose into the snowbank before I hit the other car. But my engine got crunched. I had to get a ride to work, and had to buy another car.

Anyhow, beware of fishtailing drivers. Any guy who lets that kind of fish-tail skid continue is REALLY STUPID – stay away from him!! I guess I might have figured out a way to stay a little further away from that car, and I might have gone a little slower until I got well past him. But I figured if he was going to goof up, he would goof up over on the far right, not across all 3 lanes. Wrong.

If I had slowed down, I might have forced that diaper truck to slow down. But, if I had to hit my brakes at all, he STILL would have been right on my bumper. He really must have been hoping that he could PUSH me to go a little faster. Unfortunately he did.

◆ ◆ ◆

CASE 3. What did the third driver do *right*, in his VW?

- He had a car with sensitive steering, so he could FEEL any front-wheel skid, and catch it *quickly*. Cars with power steering do not usually let you feel this, nearly as well.

- He also had a car with quick steering ratio, so he could *correct* for a skid quickly.

- He was alert – he knew you don't get around a snowy corner and up a tough hill without paying attention.

- He had a car with good balance. I mean, having the engine and the most weight over the drive-wheels gives you the best traction on the hill. If the hill is steep enough, that old Beetle had the best chance of any of the 3 cars of getting up the hill. (Note, front-wheel-drive cars can go up shallow hills nearly as well as rear-engine cars.)

- Further, I just happen to know that he cheated by having studded snow-tires on all 4 wheels. I always did that, when I lived back east. I have checked, and studded snow tires are now illegal in many states, and legal only for a short snowy season in the states that DO allow them (such as Oregon), because they put a lot of wear on the road surface. But if I had to drive in snow, I would definitely have them.

- Just in case he could not make it up the hill on the first try, he had a shovel, and chains that he could put on. There is *no way* that hill would stop him.

Mistakes Made, Case 3.

NOW, what did that third guy do WRONG?

– He was pushing as fast as he could go. When you do that, you may avert *some* skids, and you may avoid *some* crashes, but when you are cocky, and *pushy*, you do not have much safety margin. If there were a chuck-hole or a bump in the middle of the curve, he might have lost control, or skidded to the edge of his lane, before he caught the skid. So, if the third driver were wise, he would blast through that curve as fast as he could, ONLY if there was no on-coming traffic. I mean, I KNOW I can survive a crash if I glance off a guard-rail at 40 mph, but I really do not want to go smashing into an oncoming car. VW drivers do not survive that kind of crash very well.

– What else did the third driver have as a dis-advantage? Well, the Chevy and the Ford are heavier cars. A heavy car has a good chance of pressing down hard *through* the snow, and getting better traction than a light little VW with its wide tires. So, if the VW did not have studded snow tires, it might be able to get over that hill just barely as well as the other cars. If the other cars had good studded snow tires, they would do a lot better, too. BUT, neither that Chevy nor the Ford would get up the hill with a stupid, dumb *KLUTZY* driver. Every driver has to understand when to stop doing the stupid thing that got him in trouble.

– Do we have any sketch for Case 3? No. But the third driver *did* have to detect the tiny front-wheel skid, as the front wheels started to slide, and he had to cut the wheels to the left, momentarily, and prevent the skid from continuing – EARLY. And when he applied a little too much power, he had to detect the rear end starting to lurch sideways a few inches to the left, and immediately take his foot half-way off the gas, and cut the wheel to the left, just a *little*, and then apply more power only after the rear end was rolling true. In other words, the third driver got into both kinds of skids, but by keeping them small, he was able to stay in his lane and continue at almost full speed.

◆ ◆ ◆

CASE 4. The fourth driver was too pushy, and he was just trying to go too fast. You can have a lot of fun in a VW, but if you go too fast, and you LOSE IT – that is, let the rear end get into a wide skid – you usually cannot recover.

If you come into a corner too fast, you just *have to* look at that corner and decide to slow down. What the posted speed limit says,

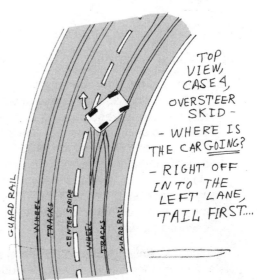

TOP VIEW, CASE 4, OVERSTEER SKID –

– WHERE IS THE CAR GOING?

– RIGHT OFF INTO THE LEFT LANE, TAIL FIRST....

GUARD RAIL   WHEEL TRACKS   CENTER STRIPE   WHEEL TRACKS   GUARD RAIL

8-14-4

just does not matter, when there's snow or ice on the road. You have to use your judgement.

Mistakes Made, Case 4.

When a car is going a little too fast, and the rear wheels break loose, they tend to skid out very quickly, very far. This guy was just going too fast for the conditions; he didn't use good judgement, and he didn't slow down.

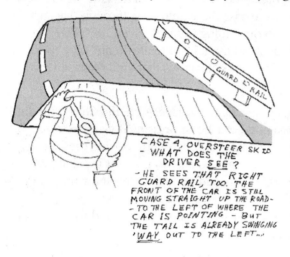

CASE 4, OVERSTEER SKID
– WHAT DOES THE DRIVER SEE ?
– HE SEES THAT RIGHT GUARD RAIL, TOO. THE FRONT OF THE CAR IS STILL MOVING STRAIGHT UP THE ROAD – TO THE LEFT OF WHERE THE CAR IS POINTING – BUT THE TAIL IS ALREADY SWINGING 'WAY OUT TO THE LEFT...

So, what did the fourth driver see, just before he went into the left guard rail? He saw the right guard rail. He didn't take his foot off the gas at the first sign of the rear end drifting left. Maybe he was going so fast, it was not going to do any good. I mean, if you are really going MUCH too fast, you may have zero chance to recover from a skid.

◆ ◆ ◆

CASE 5. The fifth guy was pretty smart. He wanted all the advantages, and he got his money's worth. The Subaru had 4-wheel drive. He added a couple hundred pounds of sand in the back of his pickup. He had 4 mud-and-snow-tires, and he knew how to drive carefully. He was probably going a little too fast, too. But he had a little safety margin. Consequently we have no drawings of him getting in trouble, because he didn't...

◆ ◆ ◆

Let's talk about other kinds of skid, such as a skid while BRAKING on snow.

CASE 6. In any car, the driver can put on the brakes in a curve on a snowy road, and *plow* straight ahead. If you see that happening, you should respond quickly, and ease off on the brakes, because the car is starting to skid out of its lane. Give the wheels a chance to start rolling. Also, STEER IN the DIRECTION of the SKID – toward the outside of the curve. Shortly, in perhaps 1/2 second, when you have slowed down a little, and the wheels are rolling again, *then* you can try to steer back onto your desired course. And you hope that meanwhile, you haven't gotten too close to the guard-rail – or to the oncoming lane.

Would ABS (Anti-lock Braking System) help you in this case? Yes, there is a good chance that it will help. It would help prevent your front wheels from locking and skidding. It will slack off on the braking, and let your front wheels keep rolling. So ABS can help keep you from a bad skid. ABS does not *just* keep you in a straight line when you want to go in a straight line. It can help you stop or slow down in a curve, when you are driving in a curve. It would let you remain able to steer out of trouble, while you are braking.

Would ABS help the guy with the Chevy, back in example 1? Probably not, because he was too dumb to hit his brakes. ABS can only help if you are using your brakes.

What if a VW is coming around that snowy curve in example 6, and puts on his brakes – is he likely to have the front wheels PLOW, or the REAR END hang out? I think the front-end PLOW is a little more likely, but either can happen. Ya gotta be prepared for both.

Detecting and Catching a Skid

Now, I said that a good driver should "catch" the skid – should detect the skid and then prevent it from getting worse. How do you do that?

When you are suspecting a front-end skid, you may notice, (on a car without power steering) that the wheel starts to feel *light*. You notice that when you turn the steering wheel, it takes very little force – and that is about the time when you turn the wheel and nothing happens, and the car still goes straight ahead. So, a car without power steering may have advantages in avoiding skids. It can help you *detect* little skids, just before they begin to get serious. You may still be able to feel this on a car with power steering, but you probably can't catch it so early.

As soon as you detect the possibility of these front-end skids, you probably want to slow down and be alert to use all the strategies you will use to avoid a real, serious skid. See if there is a lot of traffic headed toward you. If there, is be extra careful.

If there ain't, well, you may want to *fling* the car around. You may not want to JUST go into a skid-avoidance mode – you may want to get *into* a small skid, and see if it feels about right, and confirm that you can recover. Of course, you'll only do this where there is not heavy traffic, and no big drop-offs beside the road. And, keep watching the roadway for things that will affect your stability. If you are on the verge of a skid, and you hit a little pile of snow thrown up by a snowplow, that may start you spinning.

Similarly, if you suspect that you are getting near a rear-wheel skid, or fish-tail, you will probably slow down and minimize your skids, and sharpen your senses for the five signs of fish-tailing or rear-wheel skids. Is your rear end sliding and slithering on every tiny rut? Does it point off to the left or right, behind you? Does your engine rev up when one tire gets loose? Does a rear wheel start to *whine* when it spins too fast? Does the speedometer jump up from 30 to 60? You may want to turn off your radio, so you can listen for those signs. You might take off your parka's hood, and even open your window a crack, so you can hear when the tires let loose and start to spin. Be alert!

Then, if the road is kind of empty and safe, you may decide to check out your ability to handle those rear-end skids. Feed the gas a little more, and watch what happens, and be alert so if the skid starts, you can let off the gas. That is how to "catch your skids"!

Best Climbing Ability in Case of Poor Traction

Which cars are going to have the worst trouble with drive-wheels slipping, while climbing a hill? Which ones will have the best chance to avoid skids?

– Heavy cars will do a little better. Like that big Ford. Lighter cars will do worse.

– Cars with their engine NOT over the drive-wheels will do worse – such as that rear-wheel-drive Ford. However, there are really NOT a lot of rear-drive cars that you can buy new these days. There are still a lot of rear-drive cars on the road, though.

There is such a good choice of good front-wheel drive cars these days, that if you plan on doing some driving in snow, you can easily pick a good front-wheel-drive car. Or, a four-wheel-drive car. Only 20 years ago, the choice of 4WD cars was pretty small – Jeeps and a Subaru, or a Ford Bronco. Now, there are LOTS of good choices. Audis, Toyotas, Explorers, Eagles, in addition to all the other old models. (More information on 4WD is in the Appendix on 4WD.)

– There are other kinds of cars that would have trouble on that scenario. Yes, a Porsche 911 has its engine over the drive-wheels, but it has much too much power. A hot Mustang or Camaro would be in the same trouble. Only a VERY careful driver could get one of those cars up the hill. However, a Corvette would have a slightly better chance, because the new models have a switch where you can cut back the maximum power, to a fairly low power level. The Corvette normally has much too much power, but in its low-power mode, it has a better chance.

– Cars with large-diameter wheels have an advantage. Tiny little econo-cars with small 12-inch or 10-inch wheels have a disadvantage. Trucks with LARGE wheels have a big advantage.

– Conversely, cars with W I D E tires will have big disadvantages. A Camaro with 10-inch wide wheels is going to have more trouble. Narrow snow tires work pretty well.

– Cars with power steering may have a little more trouble sensing the onset of a skid; cars without power steering have a minor advantage.

You may or may not have much choice in what car you drive. But you will want to know which car will be able to move – which lane to bet on, on a slippery upgrade.

Give a Guy a Nudge...

One time, I was trying to go to work on Route 128, and there was heavy slow traffic because there was a couple inches of snow. I pottered along, and came to the heart of the problem. There was a brand new Ford Pinto, struggling up the hill. That was the first year Pintos were out, and he obviously had his original tires on, and did not have snow tires. He was spinning his tires, and wallowing and struggling, and was JUST barely making progress up the hill. He was not *stuck* but he was just barely able to go slow. He was the cause of the slow-down. Even though he was not blocking all lanes, very few people were able to get past him.

I eased up behind this guy, and got my bumper against his. It was not a bad fit. I fed the gas in first, and got him moving, up to about 14 mph. After all, I did have my studded snow-tires on. Then I shifted into second, and sneaked up behind him again, and shoved him up to about 25 mph. By that time, we were nearly at the top of the hill. I had done about as much for him as I could. Then I passed him, and wound out to 60 mph. The road was quite clear ahead of the Pinto, because almost nobody had been able to pass him. So I had a couple miles of clear sailing at 60 mph.

Meanwhile, if YOU have a crummy little car, and the engine is NOT over the drive wheels, you should be sure to buy some good snow tires, so you will not get bogged down in a simple little snowstorm on an easy upgrade.

"CHAINS REQUIRED – Whips Optional"

If the traction just gets too poor, or the snow too deep, or the grade too steep, you can put on chains. I generally like to not put on chains to get *into* trouble – I prefer to put them on to get OUT. But sometimes you have to.

When I bought my first VW Bus in June of 1965, I went down to Sears and tried to buy a set of tire chains. It took a couple of weeks to get them back-ordered out of a warehouse. The clerk asked me why I was so concerned, at that time of year. I had to explain that I was headed for Colorado, where they still had all sorts of snow on mountain roads and passes, and mud, and dirt roads, and sand and gravel, too. I only used the chains every other year, but it is good to have them.

Many times in California and other western states, a mountain road is posted, during a snow-storm, "Chains required. 4WD OK." Unless you have a four-wheel drive car, you must put on chains, or go back. Even a VW with good snow-tires has to put on chains.

On the other hand, sometimes it is left to your discretion to put on chains, and you have to use good judgement. One time we were coming up Route US 395 in our '85 VW Bus, with fairly new tires, in heavy snow. We came up from Bishop to Bridgeport just fine. I kept checking my traction, and we had some safety margin of traction. But when my wife saw the car ahead of us, *with chains on*, slide off the road, she hollered at me to put our chains on. And I did.

Note, even if you put chains on your drive wheels, in the rear, you may not be able to steer very well if you don't have chains on your front wheels. So, even though the chains will let you GO, or STOP, you may not be able to STEER very well. Take it easy.

On the other hand, if you have a front-wheel drive car, and you put chains on the front, you may be able to go, stop, and steer, but it may still feel weird. I know one guy who was very displeased with how his front-drive SAAB felt, with the obligatory chains on the front. So the next time he was required to put on chains, he put them on the rear wheels! It still steered and accelerated OK, and it did not feel so bad. But the highway patrol guy let him go, because he DID have chains on. So he was happy.

Skidding on Rainy Roads

Skidding on rainy pavement is similar to snow, but you may be going faster because you are not expecting it to be so slippery. Just as with snow, the major types of skid are the same – oversteer, understeer, and, WOOPS, lost the whole thing sideways. You have to respond to a rainy skid the same way as with snow – by turning into the skid. Turn the wheel *in the direction of* the skid.

Here in California, we often have a couple months with no rain, and then on the first rainy day, the ramps and roads are slippery with rain *plus* a little oil. That can be very treacherous, because just before the tires let go, they do not necessarily feel very slippery. When you start sliding on that, you can "lose it" quite badly. So on the first rainy day, I like to check out a few freeway entrance ramps to see how slippery they are. I get into second and feed it fairly hard, so long as there is not much traffic around. I usually find it is quite slippery indeed, and I had better take it easy. I steer toward the inside of the curve, and feed the gas. Sometimes the front end slides out – and sometimes the rear end slides out. In either case, I take it easy on the gas, and steer in the direction of the skid, and slow down, and then get back onto the middle of the ramp.

Recently I was riding on a bus going up to Boston, with about 1/2 inch of hard packed snow on the road. The bus driver was not very talkative, so I was talking with another passenger on the topic of skidding. She was fairly knowledgeable about driving, and she said her mother had taken a course in skidding, on wet *and* dry *and* oily *and* snowy pavement. I was impressed. But the bus rolled on, straight and level, and there was not any traffic around. Suddenly the rear of the bus slipped 5 inches to the left. *I* looked at *her* and *she* looked at *me*. We knew a skid when we saw it. We did not need any engraved invitation to know when a skid was happening. I don't think anybody else on the bus noticed, except for the bus-driver.

She said she had not had many accidents, but one time she racked up on a turnpike's slippery exit ramp, when the curvature tightened up and she could not brake fast enough. She agreed, skidding on an *exit* ramp is quite risky. It is not recommended except for experts, and even then it can be quite scary. That is much more likely to cause an accident than a skid on an *entrance* ramp, while accelerating.

Hydroplaning

There is one other marvelous way to get into trouble with rain. If the rain is heavy, and you get a heavy run-off, you can get big puddles or little streams of water

8-16

running across the road. If you drive through a couple inches of rain at 10 or 20 mph, you just make a big splash. But if you hit this at 30 or 40, your tires are not going to touch the ground. The tires ride right up on the water. You are in a skid, know it or not. You will soon know it. The car can easily skid, any-which-way.

Snow tires or rain tires, with a deeply-cut, aggressive tread, will help minimize this. Smooth tires are headed for trouble. Wide tires are worse than narrow tires. But, at 40 mph, everybody is in trouble. It's a matter of the *degree* of trouble.

The main procedure to avoid hydroplaning, is to slow down before you hit the deep water. If you are plowing through a shallow puddle at 45 mph, it is pretty hard to PROVE that it will not get deeper in the next 50 or 100 yards. So it is probably wise to slow down and not push your luck.

I have done a little splashing through puddles – puddles that get deeper. I was greatly amused when I actually started to hydroplane, at about 30 mph. (VWs have fairly wide tires, and are so light that they can get in trouble at lower speeds than most cars.) I learned that I was not completely out of control: If the front of the car started to veer to the left, I was able to cut* the steering wheel to the right, HARD, for a short time, and use the front wheels as a rudder, to bring the front end back towards the center of the lane. This worked. But, you must be prepared to QUICKLY return your wheels to center, when you are starting to get pointed in the right direction. This, again, is a good advantage of having a fast steering ratio! For this steering, I do not turn the wheel hand-over-hand, but I just turn the wheel as far as I can, without taking my hands off the wheel. I get my arms crossed. That makes it easy to turn the wheel back *very quickly*, when I need to.

This same technique, using the front wheels as a rudder, is also useful when you are driving in deep rutted slush – or very wet snow. This often happens when the snowplows have not been doing their job. You can see when you are going to hit big stacks of slush, and if you start to skid, you turn your steering wheel to get the "rudder" effect. Just remember how to bring the steering wheel back to neutral, to the center, really quickly.

Skidding on Ice

Now, there is ice made from packed melted snow, and there is sleet or freezing rain. Each of these can be *extremely* treacherous. You have to be alert for any change of the traction. If it gets too bad, park it, and walk, or put your chains on.

Ordinary snow tires do not give you any safety margin. That is why I used to get studded snow tires – they really dig in their toenails. Still, you have to be a LITTLE careful because most of the other cars on the road do not have studded tires, so they do not have full control. I remember one time I was driving up a bridge that ascended over Route I-93, and I was in 4th gear. It was so slippery that even in 4th gear, at 40 mph at full throttle, my rear wheels kept breaking loose. And this is on a gutless old VW! Now, that is *slippery*.

8-17

---
* To "cut" the wheel does not require a knife, it just means you turn the wheel really hard and fast.

In Germany, there are signs on most of the Autobahns, as you approach a long bridge: "Glatteisgefahr", which means "Glare ice danger". Here in the US we occasionally see a sign, "Bridge Surface Freezes Before Roadway." A fair warning, as freezing mist can be very sneaky.

One time I went on a trip with my friend Mike in early December in his Peugeot 403, which was a very good car – but its steering was a little "dead" – it had some friction in it. It had much less "road feel" than my VW. We went up a hill on Mass. Route 2 near Ayer, and apparently we arrived at some glare ice – frozen mist – but it did not LOOK icy. The car, with no warning, went into a slow spin and we L A Z I L Y slid down the road and slowly bumped into a guard rail, with minor damage to one fender. And right behind us, 10 other cars came over the hill and did about the same thing. Fortunately, we got the heck out of that bowling alley quickly and did not get hit by any of the sliding cars. None of them slid as far as we did! I've always thought that if we had gone in my Beetle, I would have felt the steering get *light*, at the first bit of ice, and I would have *touched* the brakes earlier, to check and see how slippery it was. Then we could have eased out of there without spinning out. Mike was a good driver, but the steering was too dead to let him feel the ice.

This kind of ice is sometimes called "black ice". Black ice is not necessarily black, but it tends to be transparent, so it does not look appreciably different from the roadway. It can be very sneaky and slippery, especially as you may not notice it – because it is NOT WHITE. That's why they call it "black".

In a similar incident, a friend was driving along Route 20 near Worcester Mass, and the road had been properly sanded over the glare ice. When he came over a hill, he started to slide and skid – just like all the other cars – just like a skating pond – because the sander truck had turned off on a side road! Everybody *assumed* that the sander would stay on the main highway. But he didn't. So be careful to watch that the sand on the road does not suddenly stop! If it does, you have to *notice* that the sand has disappeared, and slow down a lot.

Skidding on Mud

Some dirt roads can have very good traction. But when they get wet, anything can happen. You can slide on the mud just as easily as any snow. Mud can be very unpredictable. And sometimes *very deep*. Be careful.

One time I was wandering around the San Mateo area, before I moved out to California. It was December, and I walked up old Alpine Road, which was a dirt road, closed to traffic in the winter. I came across a pickup truck stuck in deep mud. He was not supposed to be there. He was mired, and could not go up, and could not go back. But the driver figured he was OK, because he had his chains. He started to put them on his rear wheels. I walked on up the hill.

An hour later, I hiked back down. The pickup was still there. The driver, soaked in mud, had just discovered that he could NOT move the truck. I stood around and watched as his friends gave him advice and encouragement. THEN he discovered that he had carefully put the chains on *over* the emergency brake cable, so of course he could not get the wheels to turn. *THEN* he discovered that the clasp on his chains had gotten bent, and he could not even undo the chains. And all this time, he had been lying in the mud, putting on the chains, and struggling with them, and the truck was axle deep in mud, and the sun was going down, and it was getting cold. Well, there was nothing I could do to help, so I walked quietly away. I went back there a couple months later, and the truck was not still there. So I can only imagine what he had to do to get out.

One of my buddies, Ron, grew up in Texas. He says they have a "caliche" clay in many areas, which is very slippery when wet. He learned a *lot* about driving and skidding by practicing in an old car on wet caliche roads. He learned to do his sideways driving on mud, not on snow.

"Positraction" or Similar Limited-Slip Differential

"Positraction" is Chevrolet's name for a "Limited-Slip" Differential. Ford makes the same idea, and so do Chrysler and most other manufacturers, but they call them different names such as "limited slip" or "locking differential" (even though it does not really "lock" at all).

If you are trying to go up a hill, and you have your 2 left wheels on pavement, and your 2 right wheels are on snow or ice, you normally cannot get up that hill – you normally cannot accelerate. The function of the Differential (which is connected between the 2 drive wheels) is to let one of your drive wheels turn a little faster than the other, when you are going around a corner. Fine. But when you are trying to accelerate, or go up a hill, if one wheel had no traction, the differential usually lets all the power go to the wheel with no traction. And it just spins.

The function of the limited-slip differential (costs an extra $300 or so) is to let the outside wheel turn a little faster, if you are going around a simple curve, but it then can use extra friction to feed some power to the wheel with good traction, even if the other wheel is on glare ice. So in certain kinds of road condition, the Limited-Slip Differential can help you get up the hill. (Hot-rodders and Drag-racers like this, too.)

Skids while Braking

Now, let's say you are going *down* that same kind of hill, and 2 of your wheels are on glare ice. As soon as you touch the brakes, the 2 wheels on ice will lock up. But the other 2 wheels will still apply some braking and you can still steer a little, if you are very gentle. So the key to this situation is, to recognize this problem, and to not brake very hard, but get slowed down while keeping under control. And "Positraction" will not help you. Every car descending this half-slippery hill will have the same problem. (Unless he has ABS.)

What if you DO hit the brakes HARD, and the whole car warps over to the left, because the center of the car wants to go straight ahead, but the only braking force is on the left? WELL, as with any skid, if you got into the skid by hitting the brakes hard, then you should get off the brakes to try to straighten out. In this case, you might not have to steer right, if your direction returns correctly when you get *off* the brakes. So this is a special case of a skid. Could ABS help you here? Yes, it would probably help you avoid a bad skid.

Slippery Metal

If you are driving in a city, and riding along trolley tracks or railroad rails, it is generally a good idea not to drive *right on top of* the rails. Because sometimes, when a tiny bit of water or oil is added – even when there is no precipitation but just a little condensation on the cold rails – the rails can be VERY SLIPPERY. If 2 of your wheels are on the rails, and you hit the brakes, the car can slew or twist or skid badly. So if you are in any traffic, stay off the rails. (When no traffic is around, I often drive down the rails, grinning like an idiot and saying "Toot-toot".)

Similarly, if you are on an old-fashioned bridge with steel grid paving, that can be very slippery when wet, and pretty slithery even when not wet. There are not so many of these around any more, but you may find one in a strange city. Assume it is slippery, and take it easy, and you'll survive it. Even when it's dry, the rear of your car is likely to feel very *squirrelly* on this kind of metal surface. No, you are not imagining things.

Skidding on Normal, Dry Pavement

Most of our skidding is on slippery roads. But there are times when we skid on dry pavement. Examples, when you get into a curve and find you are going too fast. A curve may tighten up to a tighter radius than you expected. Or, you have to cut the wheel hard – turn it fast and hard – to avoid a hazard or some potential accident. In each of these cases, you have to be prepared to detect and recover from a little skid. A skid on dry pavement starts out quite similar to skids on any other surface, but you have to expect it to happen more quickly, at a higher speed, than on snow or ice. You have to be very alert to recover from such a fast skid.

In the early days of automobile racing, the experts cautioned that every driver must "avoid the dread side-slip". In those days, the design of suspensions and of wheels and tires was quite primitive, so if you got into a skid, you probably could not recover. A skid was pretty sure to cause an accident. But modern tires, modern suspensions, and good driver skills mean that a skid, whether on wet or on dry pavement, is not necessarily a bad problem. You do, however, have to be prepared for the skids.

Four-Wheel Drifts

I think I mentioned this in the section on handling, that modern cars can skid or "drift" very nicely – skidding just a little bit on all 4 wheels, when cornering very hard. Good drivers can control such a drift nicely. This is one of the reasons people like to drive sports cars – they are fun to "drift". Of course, it is quite important not to go out of your lane and get other people in trouble. And if you "overdo it" and slide off the road, well, you are not supposed to do that. Still it is fun to try *drifting* a little, when the road is not cluttered up.

To *drift* properly, it is best to have plenty of power. VWs do not have nearly enough power to *drift* on dry pavement (unless you are descending a hill and coming into a curve, which is *not* a good place to practice your skidding). But on a wet road, VWs have almost enough power; and on snow or on gravel, VWs are *exactly right*. They have just enough power – but not too much power – and are just right for *drifting* on the drifted snow.

STRAIGHT-AHEAD SKIDS

One of the most common form of skid is when a driver just steps on the brakes *hard* to make a panic stop, in an emergency. In many cases, you roll and skid, straight ahead, to a stop. However, if there is any foreign matter on the pavement, you may start veering or skidding to the left or the right, depending where the debris is. Just as with a skid with 2 wheels on snow, you must be prepared to ease off on the brakes, to prevent the skid from taking you too far out of your lane or your intended track. Or, if you see that you are going to hit a guard rail, maybe you *still* want to keep on the brakes, because scraping your fenders on the guard rail may be less painful than slacking off the brakes and hitting the car or the kid right in front of you. So, judgement is likely to be needed. The best way to avoid this problem is to not need to make so many panic stops.

ABS – ???

ABS – the Anti-Lock Braking System – can help keep you straight on your path, as we mentioned above. If you have ABS, you should be aware that your brake pedal will rattle and vibrate under your foot. Just hold your foot down, and keep it down. With ABS, "pumping" the brakes does no good, and only degrades your ability to stop.

ABS can also keep you from skidding during hard braking on a curve. You can still steer. This is significant, because one of the biggest problems with skidding is, you cannot steer when the front wheels are locked up, not turning.

However, do not count on ABS to save you from having any accidents. Recent reports indicate that cars with ABS have about as many accidents as comparable cars without ABS. Apparently people count on the ABS, and drive in a pushy way, and get into different kinds of accidents.

> One of my neighbors, Art, was driving in his econo-box behind a BMW on Route 17, on a sweeping curve. Suddenly they had to hit their brakes hard, as all traffic was stopped ahead. The BMW braked as hard as he could, but skidded and hit the center divider. Art hit his brakes but did not skid, and did not hit the center guard rail. The Bimmer Pilot stood there in tears, as his car was badly scraped. And then he was incredulous. How could this inferior car stop without hitting the guard rail, when he hit it? Art just shrugged. He did not bother to explain that he had better tires than the BMW did. He did, after all, start 80 feet behind the BMW and ended up just 8 feet behind the BMW. But the major technique he used, to stop faster than the BMW, was, just before he hit his brakes hard, he cut his wheel to straighten out his path, so he could stop in nearly a straight line, whereas the BMW really was on a curve. That

*was his major secret. That's a pretty good technique. Did the BMW have ABS?
Probably not.*

◆ ◆ ◆

*One time I was rolling down a grade on I-280, right near Stanford Linear
Accelerator, in the next-to-left lane of 4 lanes. I saw a slow work truck pull out
from the right lane, 'way out in front of me, and he got up to 50 mph. Then he
started cutting left across 4 lanes of traffic – and cut in front of me – and
started putting on his brakes. I realized he was planning to stop along the
center island, to do some work. Well, the way he was doing it was all wrong. I
got on my brakes fairly hard, and slowed down to 35 mph, and let the work
truck cross left ahead of me. I heard the shriek of brakes in several places,
around and behind me. I started looking around.*

*First I noticed that a pickup truck, who was passing me on the left, was on his
brakes really hard, trying to avoid this truck that was now stopping in front of
him. The pickup's wheels were jumping up and down, and the truck was
pitching and rocking. Note, un-loaded pickup trucks do not have very good
stability, so they are liable to bouncing and wheels skipping and being VERY
unstable, under hard braking.*

*Then I looked in my mirror. I saw the brake lights of a 1958 Chevy. Why the
brake lights? That car must have had such badly skewed brakes that when he
hit them hard, he just spun around. At that point, there was nobody in front of
me. I shifted down into 3rd, and tromped on the gas and got the heck out of
there. I figured there was not too much good I could do by staying around. In
retrospect, I shoulda pulled over and stopped, and chewed out the driver of
the work truck, who caused a very dangerous situation. I never heard a big
WHAM behind me, so I figured there was not any collision. But, next time I
would go back and make sure that truck driver got educated, because I saw
the whole stupid mess, right in front of me. I did not hit the brakes hard
enough to cause the guy behind me to slam me, but it was pretty close.* /rl

Practicing Skidding

If you are sure you will NEVER skid, then you don't have to practice skidding. Since I
do not know ANYBODY that can say that, then YOU have to put in some practice.

Many kids learned to skid by putting on the rear brakes of their bicycles and
skidding down a grassy slope, or along a patch of sand. Of course, if you tear up the
lawn, your father would grouch like heck, so don't overdo it. When you have
practiced this a little you will learn that a rear-end skid is not anything to fear. You
just learn to steer in the direction of the skid – and this is good practice for what you
will do in a car.

Where to Practice

Obviously, when you are first learning how to skid, or learning how much traction
you have on the first snow of the season, you want to do it in a safe place. Many

shopping centers are nearly deserted on a snowy day, so the back corner of their parking lot is usually a good place to start practice. Or if the Mall's lot is crowded, a church's parking lot is usually empty. Of course, you still have to watch out for other cars, lamp posts, etc., but usually this is not a big deal. It's usually MUCH safer than on a road.

How to Practice

With or without a teacher, you can usually learn a lot by just fooling around on an empty snowy parking lot. First try just easing along and then *hit* the brakes. You'll be surprised how nicely it slides. Then, just tromp on the gas for a second. Your drive wheels may do some amazing things!

The next basic thing is to try to go as smoothly as you can, and then go just a little faster, until you just start to skid a little. Then, stop doing what you were doing to cause the skid – *catch* the skid. If you were accelerating, take it easy on the gas and recover and then accelerate again. If you were braking just a little, notice the feel of the car as it started to skid. Ease off the brakes, and let the wheels start rolling, and brake some more. Get a *feel* for the brakes – and the snow. Not all snow is the same. Some is very slippery; some is barely slippery. Practice *easy* turns, and then turn just a *little* harder, and go just a *little faster*, until you start to skid. Then ease the wheel, and turn *in the direction of the skid*, and recover. Practice skidding while turning *and* accelerating, and turning *and* braking. Left *and* right. Practice accelerating as hard as you can in a straight line without much skidding, as if you were trying to get moving up a hill. Practice skidding at fairly low speeds, and then at faster speeds.

Then you should also get into some slow but wild skids – all the time trying not to get too close to other cars or obstacles. Get up to 20 mph and hit the brakes hard. Slither around. Observe that if your tail gets 'WAY out, you cannot recover very well. Floor the gas and see how bad a fishtail you can get into. Then see if you can recover.

All this time, you should be learning what it means to turn the wheel "in the direction of the skid", so it becomes natural and automatic. When you start to get in a skid, out on the road, you never want to have to *think about*, "NOW, what is the direction of the skid? Which way should I turn the wheel?" It should be *automatic*. However, out on this empty parking lot, you should even see what happens when you turn the wheel THE WRONG WAY. You will be amused to see what wild skids you can get into. Just don't get too close to anything you might hit. Don't get stuck, either!

After you have done your practice in the parking lot, and you head out onto a road, you should be aware that the snow out there has probably been packed down by traffic, and may be somewhat slipperier than the parking lot. It may be less deep. It may have been sanded a little. It is really DIFFERENT. Still, there is some similarity in how your car handles on the different surfaces. So take it easy, and keep studying for signs of skids. Keep well away from other cars. Don't follow other cars closely, especially on downgrades or approaching a stop.

When you come to a corner or start up a hill, be especially watchful for signs of skids. An empty entrance ramp for a freeway is an especially interesting place to get a clue if the main road is going to be very slippery.

As mentioned above, here in California, we often have a couple months with no rain, and then on the first rainy day, the ramps and roads are slippery with rain *plus* a little oil. That can be very slippery. So on the first rainy day, I like to check out a few freeway entrance ramps to see how slippery they are. I just check on an entrance ramp to see if it is empty, and then I see where things break loose, at fairly low speeds.

One nervous would-be Editor told me, "Bob, it is not a good idea to tell people to try skidding on entrance ramps. They should practice on an empty corner of a parking lot." Well, for snow, I do like to do my preliminary practice in an empty parking lot. But for a rainy oil-slick highway, that parking lot is not realistic, because it may have rougher pavement, and it will not be nearly as oily or slippery as an entrance ramp. The packed snow on an entrance ramp is NOTHING like an empty parking lot. A little practice skid at 15 or 20 mph, on an empty entrance ramp, is the safest way to learn how slippery the highway is. The alternative is to go out on the road and PRETEND that it is not slippery. I'll repeat, that is not a good idea. That is much more dangerous than a small practice skid on an entrance ramp (with no cars right around you).

Okay, Pease, where *else* do you like to practice skidding? One good place is on an EMPTY 4-lane road. If I have to turn from one 4-lane road onto another, I try to take that corner pretty hard, in the snow, and if I skid a little, there is a spare lane for me to slide into. I don't usually slide more than a foot or two, from my intended line. When I start out from a traffic light, on snow, I usually try to out-accelerate the other traffic, and of course with a VW, that is easy. I usually try to do just a little bit of wheel-spin, but not let my tail drift off to the side. If it starts to slide too far, I just ease off on the gas pedal – and I still walk away from all other traffic.

What if you live in an area where it doesn't snow? You might try some practice skids on some sand, or wet sandy pavement. Or a little mud. It's too hard on your tires, to do your learning on dry pavement. Ask your teacher to show you how it is done – how to recognize a skid, and how to respond. If you have to do it yourself, you can, but it's much better with a teacher. My father never gave me a specific lesson on skidding, but I figured it out by watching what he did and what other drivers did.

Miscellaneous

What else can make you skid? Wet leaves, in the fall. A little oil – so little you cannot see it. Brakes that grab. Brakes where one wheel does not provide as much braking as the other wheels. Situations where you have one or more tires that have very little tread. Situations where one tire has much *better* traction than the others. In other words, anything asymmetrical.

Driving Sideways?

After all these years of driving my VWs in various skids, I did finally figure out a reason why maybe I should not skid so wildly and flamboyantly. I mean, I have covered a LOT of miles, sideways, skidding, on highways. But there is one good reason to take it easy.

Let's say I am scurrying along, at 55 mph on packed snow with patches of glare ice. And for some reason, I get in a big broad skid. Usually, I figure that if there is no traffic around, that is no problem, as I will eventually get straightened out. BUT – what if I hit a patch of bare pavement? I could easily roll my car over!! I bet that if I tried hard enough, I could roll a VW bus at 25 mph, or a Beetle at 35 – or darned near any car at 40 or 45 mph, if I really got it crosswise before I hit the dry pavement. So while I have done my share of skidding, I am willing to admit that there are times when you and I really do NOT want to get sideways. Reasonable?

Recently I saw a little Honda that had rolled over and was lying on its roof. Traffic was at a walk, to get around it, but I figured out what had surely happened: The road was half wet, and half dry where cars had dried it off. The car must have gotten into a skid on the rainy pavement, and must have spun sideways. Then it must have hit the dry pavement, and the sudden increase of friction must have rolled it over.

So if you are taking a chance of skidding at high speed on a snowy road, be sure not to get sideways when you are approaching an underpass where there might be no snow under the bridge!

Star-Wars Technology for Skids

I had an old friend, Mr. Raymond, who was a very smart inventor. He invented a scheme for stopping quickly on a very slippery road, or under any other emergency conditions:

Let's say you are on some very slippery road, and headed for serious trouble. Going over an embankment? Headed into the path of an oncoming car? With this invention, you push a little button on the dashboard. This fires a kind of armor-piercing shell, that sits in a box in your trunk. This blasts a spike into the pavement. Asphalt or concrete or whatever, it just fires this spike until it is embedded into the ground. THEN this little box pays out a sort of chain, which sort of stretches and takes up energy, and slows you down. The metal of each chain link stretches and is deformed as you stretch it out. This can take up a LOT of energy. You soon stop, quickly and safely.

Now, you are anchored to the ground, back at that spike. How do you get away? As soon as your car is safe, you can just take a special tool and SNAP off the head of that spike, and go on your way. When it is time for the road to be repaired, the paving company digs out the spike and notes the code on it, and makes sure that you are billed a fair charge, on your account. Ha. It might even work. But not very well if you are on a railroad track. Or a bridge. Or maybe a dirt road. Also, it would not be the right thing to use, unless the car behind you had the same kind of emergency equipment. I haven't seen Mr. Raymond in several years, as he moved away. I'll have to look him up and see if he has done any such inventions, recently.

A Note to Warm-Weather Drivers:

NOW, all you drivers down South can gasp and chuckle and say, "Boy, I am glad I do not have to worry about all that stuff about skidding in the snow!" But youall should read this chapter, too, because someday you may have to drive somewhere in the north, in the winter. Or you may come across a frosty road up in your hills, and you want to know how to drive smoothly, then. The news reports I just heard about the "Blizzard of '96" indicated that there was a lot of snow on the roads of Alabama, Georgia, and South Carolina. And these rules and procedures that apply to skids on snow, are also applicable to sandy roads, or to oily patches. So, if you read all this *stuff* about skidding, that is good for you. That's what I recommend.

P.S. – What is Under You?

At the last minute, one of my friends reminded me that one of the major ways that a driver knows about skidding, is from his *rump*. When a car starts to slide, you may notice this from the feeling on your rump. If your rump were anesthetized, you'd have a *much* harder time knowing when your skid is starting -- or stopping. So that is another important way for you to be aware of the skid you may be in. (Experiments have shown that a pilot whose rump has been anesthetized finds it quite difficult to fly, and he has to trust his instruments.)

Reckless??

A friend said he went out on an empty snowy school parking lot with his father, for skidding lessons, and learned a lot. Later he went out there again -- and got a ticket for reckless driving! Maybe the empty back lot of a mall would be a better place, as the local police may not have any jurisdiction over that area. At least I have given you a caution about this.

Skid Vid?

Maybe one of my next projects would be to make a video of skidding and skidding lessons? I'll think about it. Is there anything you can see today that shows this? Probably not. Your comments are invited, using the address in Appendix O.

8-14-21

5P

Chapter 14. TIRES

Cars did not always have nice pneumatic tires, as we have today. In the very early 1900s, many cars had solid rubber tires. If you see pictures of trucks or ambulances from World War I, they had solid rubber tires. Must have been a very rough ride!

Pneumatic tires were invented for bicycles, and were applied to most cars, early in this century, 80 years ago. They provide good comfort. But actually their big advantage is in safe, predictable steering and handling. If you had solid rubber tires, and you turned the steering wheel, it would be really hard to be sure where the car was going to go. Tires have been refined so much, it is amazing. A lot of tire research was done for racing, as they always say about the Indy 500. And this really *has* gone into improved performance, at reasonable prices for passenger cars. The cost per mile for tires has been improving several percent per decade, for a long time, and the tires now are much better tires, too, with better fuel economy and better handling.

How Do They Work?

A tire is not just a rubber bladder or tube full of air. Tires have belts or layers or "plies" of cords. Most of these belts are located along the tread, but some cords are wrapped around each part of the tire. Older tires had *bias*, or angled, plies. These are generally not as good as the more modern radial belted tires. Steel belts are also excellent for most heavy-duty or high-performance tires. They have less internal friction, and do not wear out much due to heat. They are also more efficient, with less rolling friction, and are helpful for the improved gas mileage that car makers and drivers like. Even though they cost a little more, they pay for themselves in better fuel efficiency, and longer tire life.

What Can Go Wrong?

About 70% of tire troubles are related to tires going flat. If your car is starting to feel unstable or "squirrelly", low tire pressure is quite likely the cause – and probably in one of your rear tires. Slow down, take it easy, and pull over in the first safe place to check if you have a flat. Usually you had better change the tire right away. Avoid driving on the tire when it is flat. If you did that, you would damage it – ruin it – and the rim, too, whereas it may be repairable if you change it right away.

If you feel that the steering is getting heavy and slow, or if the steering wheel seems to be *pulling* to one side, you may be getting a flat in the front, so stop and check that out. Or, if you have power steering, you might notice this low pressure first because of excessive squealing noises when you go around a hard curve.

These effects of underinflation are mostly explained in the sections on understeer, and oversteer, in the Chapter on Handling. And the changing of tires is discussed in the Flats chapter, which comes up soon.

> If tires are over-inflated, they may start bouncing. They may bounce off the road and make driving unstable. You might get *slightly* better gas mileage, but poorer tire life, and poorer over-all economy. Driving with your rear tires overinflated is dangerous. Driving with your front tires overinflated can cause very unstable handling, and can be VERY dangerous.

Underinflation

You should buy, and keep in your car, a good tire pressure gauge. In general, don't trust gauges at gas stations. They are often *quite* inaccurate.

And looking at your tire may not tell you if its pressure is getting low. This is especially true if your tire is parked on a lumpy place in the road, or on a curb, or on a slant.

> Radial tires don't look much different if the pressure is low. One of the best clues about low pressure is if the car feels squirrelly (due to low rear tire pressure) or requires excessive steering force (due to low front tire pressure). Most guides on tires point out, do NOT let air out of your tires if they are hot. The recommended inflation pressures are for cold tires, and the pressures will properly rise when they get hot during normal driving.

> If you suspect one of your tires is getting low in pressure, and you don't have a gauge, you can check the tire's temperature. Just put your hand on the tread. If you have been driving fast, a slightly under-inflated tire will get warmer than its mate on the other side. A *badly* under-inflated tire can get quite hot, and that is bad. Slow down to avoid this over-heating, and get the pressure back up where it belongs, as soon as you can.

There is one place where under-inflating your tires can be advantageous: If you are on very soft soil or sand, and you are sinking in a little too much, if you let "quite a bit of the air" out of the tires on your powered wheels, you have a chance of getting better support – you will sink in less. But this is usually a marginal idea, and may cause a lot more trouble than it is worth. Your tire might go flat! And even if it doesn't, you would have to drive VERY slowly to where you can get more air, or else pump it up yourself. Still, in a desperate situation (the tide is coming in!!!), letting out some air might get you out of the sand. But if you have already sunk into the axle, that's too late for this technique to do any good.

Pumps

Recently I bought a cheap little electric pump – "Made in China". I paid all of $8 for this little pump that is supposed to have a list price of $12. But I set it to work, and in just 4 minutes it added 8 PSI of pressure into my spare tire (185SR14). Better than I can do by hand. But if I needed something better than that, I'd buy a decent pump.

One of my friends says he can use just 16 strokes of an old-fashioned fat tire pump to add 2 PSI into his 175-13 tires – but that is a much smaller tire. I can assure you that a high-pressure bicycle tire pump is a LOSER – a VERY slow way to add pressure to a tire.

Tire Damage

Tires can get very unhappy when driven over debris, junk, metal, nails, etc. – or scraped against curbs, or banged over a sharp edge of a pot-hole. They may go flat instantly – or they may develop a leak, and go flat later. Or, they might be badly cut and blow out later....

> If you think you may have a damaged tire, pull over and check and inspect the tires carefully, preferably in good light. If you park in a quiet place, on a little downgrade, you can get down on your hands and knees and check the tread *and* the inside sidewall – the part you cannot normally see, under the car – on all 4 tires. If the light is not excellent, use a flashlight. Then let the car roll forward a foot, set the brakes again, and do it again – and again, until you are all the way around the tire, and you have checked all four tires, too. Look for any kind of cut or abnormal wear or damage. This is a very good thing to do before you go on a long trip, too. It could help you avoid having a blow-out on a heavily-loaded car, in case the tire is really damaged before you start.

And sometimes tires fail without any particular abuse – with no provocation. Years ago, some manufacturers sold tires with poor quality that failed often. Goodyear's "7-2-1" tires attracted so much notoriety that the Feds complained. These days, nobody can make tires that just fail at a high rate – it's not acceptable.

Types of Tires

> Here's an important rule: avoid mixing radial tires and other types (bias ply) tires on the same car, and especially not on the same axle. Mixing different types may cause squirrelly handling – but it is not guaranteed to. If it causes bad handling, check your tire pressures, and go slow until you can get this resolved. Even tires that are supposed to be similar, from different manufacturers, can act funny.

I always used to put bias-ply tires on my '72 Bus because they felt less squirrelly. Even tires from different manufacturers can feel squirrelly. If they do, find a way to swap them around to a different axle. Or, if the dealer just put them on, he should take them back, if he cannot adjust the pressure to make them stop feeling squirrelly.

Rain Tires

If you do a lot of driving in the rain or wet, you can get rain tires that are especially good for that. They have deep, "aggressive" tread patterns. They have good traction, in general, and resist hydroplaning, at least when new. Any tire salesman will be happy to explain and make recommendations.

Snow Tires

Snow tires can provide *tremendous* advantages in the snow, for traction, hill-climbing, cornering, and sheer safety, compared to ordinary tires. But they can also feel squirrelly, even when properly inflated. I was riding in the back seat of a friend's station wagon, and I warned him that he must have a tire that was flat, or nearly flat, because the ride felt so squirrelly. The back of the car was really swaying very uncomfortably. He stopped and checked the pressure, and the back tires were inflated correctly. I forgot to ask him to see if the front tires weren't over-inflated. But I still think it was the snow tires on the rear wheels that were to blame. If you buy some tires like this, you may have to wear them out to get your money's worth. But before you buy your next snow tires, ask the salesman if he can recommend any snow tires that will not feel squirrelly like that. Because, even if the tires are brand-new, it is unsafe to drive with such oversteer. Your car could become quite unstable and skid or spin out in a very easy curve. It is *not* a joke.

When I am taking off my snow tires in the spring, I store the good tires with lots of tread. But if I have some older tires which are badly worn, I just leave them on, all summer, and wear them out. Because a snow tire that has poor tread is not worth a thing in the winter. I may as well wear it out in the summer, when the amount of tread is not very important.

Studded Snows

When I lived in Massachusetts, I always had snow tires for my winter driving. I usually got retreads, which were perfectly adequate at moderate speeds. (I rarely got up to 70 mph, anyhow.) I WISH I could recommend studded snow tires, but there are a lot of states where they are not legal. Still, if I lived in a snowy place, I would be tempted to smuggle them in from a state where I could buy them, because the ice conditions and the hard-packed snow always made it a little scary without studs. Massachusetts, Minnesota, and California used to permit studded snow tires during winter months, but they are now prohibited. Oregon does still permit them. *You* check it out in *your* state.

Oversized Tires

Tires that are *slightly* over-sized can be safer, and can provide more safety margin on a fully-loaded vehicle. Many cars are barely able to carry 5 passengers (and no luggage), without exceeding their tires' ratings. Tires that are slightly bigger, and of good quality, can be a *lot* safer.

However, low-profile tires that are TOO wide tend to hydroplane on a rainy road, and may work badly on snow. Low-profile tires can give better handling on dry pavement, and may give good sporty response – but may not survive chuck-holes or other road-hazards. Also, over-sized tires may not fit in your spare-wheel compartment. It is very hard for me to find 175SR14 tires for my VW Bus, so I bought some 185SR14s. That is not an excessive size, but they just *barely* fit in the spare-tire compartment.

Over-sized tires may not fit well in your wheel-wells, either. If you buy some over-sized wheels, and they just do not fit – if they rub when you hit a bump, or when you turn your steering-wheel 'way over – you have to be able to go back to the guy that sold you these tires, and negotiate a refund or replacement. I mean, if he did not caution you that these tires might not fit, he was not serving you well. Sometimes he may be able to adjust the "stops" on the steering so the tires will not hit the car at the full lock of the steering wheel.

Other times, over-sized tires may fit OK *until* you need to put on your chains – and the chains will not fit on the tire – *or* the chains start to hit the frame – or the wheel-wells. Ouch!

On the other hand, sometimes you see cars or pickup trucks with HUGE tires. These are often set up with the car 'way up high off the ground. These vehicles are often wobbly and top-heavy, and rather unsafe. I am sure anybody who has one will not pay attention to claims of caution or danger. But these cars should be driven very carefully and gently and slowly in corners, lest they tip over.

Tiny Spares

Here is a word of caution about tiny spares. If your car is FULL, and you have a flat, and you install your tiny spare tire, where do you put the flat tire, if it won't fit in the trunk? Are you supposed to strap it on top of the trunk? Or leave it behind? Or put it on the passengers' laps? The Owner's Manual does not have any good advice on that. So the cute "tiny" feature is cute – only if you do not need it.

If you put on a tiny tire, your differential has to do a lot more work than usual, feeding power to both wheels while one is turning faster and the other one slower. Of course, you are not going to travel a long distance before you get your flat fixed, and you are not going to drive really fast – the Owner's Manual warns you about that.

But if you have two tires of *slightly* different sizes on your drive axle, that can cause a lot of extra work for your differential, and this can be bad. You may not notice this condition, until some wear has set in. Here is a way to notice it: If you hear a low whining noise from the rear axle or transaxle, and if you curve slightly to the left (or to the right) on an easy curve, and the whine goes away, that indicates that your tires may be of slightly different diameters. Check into this, and if one tire is definitely undersized, swap around some good tires until you have two of the same size on your drive wheels. The wheels that are not on the driven axle are more tolerant of different sizes.

Tubeless Tires vs. Tires with Tubes

Tires used to have tubes inside. But in the 1960s, car manufacturers found that tubeless tires could be made to run cooler, and give better gas mileage (and they could buy them *cheaper*) than tires with tubes. In the last 30 years, most tubeless tires are now made not only cheaper and more efficient, but they are generally better in quality, reliability, and performance.

Bicycles still have tubes. Large trucks still have tubes. And 4-wheel-drive vehicles often have tubes, because if you nudge a tubeless tire too hard, you can't fix it if the tire pops off the rim. A tire with a tube in it is less likely to lose air, and if it does go flat, it is easier to repair. So people who do off-road driving often install tubes inside tires that do not normally need tubes.

One time I was driving very slowly and carefully in my '70 Beetle, on a badly rutted road. The front wheel bounced off a rut – and lost all its air! I had to put on my spare. I suspect I had let the pressure get too low.

Balancing

Your tires may get out of balance. Then you may need to have them re-balanced. Maybe some of the wheel-weights fell off? If you scrub a tire against a curb, that can happen. You will notice this if you feel your steering wheel wobble or shimmy at high speeds. Time to get it fixed. Or this vibration may occur if your tire develops a "bubble", where the outer rubber separates from the cords. Sometimes you can see this. Drive *real slow* until you get that one fixed.

Your tires might be out of round. If they are slightly out of round, a good tire store could get them trimmed or cut or ground down to be true. Racers need good balance, so if they do not buy specially true, round tires, they take ordinary tires and trim them to be very precisely rounded, for best tire response and balance. NOTE: if your wheel or axle or bearings were not perfectly round or *true,* the wheel can be out of balance on your car, even if it is balanced on the wheel-balancing machine. Get the advice of a wheel-balancing expert.

If you lock up your brakes in an emergency stop, you probably developed some flat spots on your tires, especially if you were going much faster than 35 mph. After that, the tires are basically ruined. There's not much of a way to put a fix on those tires, unless the flatting is very minor. You might get them re-trued, or cut down in diameter, if the flat spots are not too deep.

One of the major tire manufacturers has a home page on the "WEB" – the trendy new computer network. I looked at it and found it full of all sorts of truisms and platitudes and useless advice. "Avoid hitting chuckholes, as you may ruin a tire." Heck, if I worried about their advice, I'd just have to stay home!! It is true, they did warn about the dangers of overinflation, underinflation, and mixing different types of tires on an axle.

Bald Tires versus Enough Tread

I neglected to include, in my first draft, any comment on bald tires. My reviewers did not catch this, either. Nobody noticed this! Bald tires, or tires without adequate tread, can cause a lot of trouble – and accidents. If you are on snow, it is OBVIOUS that you do not have much traction. When snow season comes around, you had better have *at least* good tread on your normal tires; snow tires have great advantages. And your spare should have plenty of tread, too.

Here in California, many of us do not see any appreciable snow, but when the rainy season begins, it is important to have decent tread. You may drive around all summer on bald or nearly-bald tires, but on the first rainy day, you had better get some decent tires on. One VW driver told me he spun badly on a wet freeway, around and around, as his rear tires were nearly bald. The general rules for safe driving say that your tread depth should be *at least* $^2/_{32}$ inch ($^1/_{16}$ inch), but if you are going into a rainy season, you would be better off putting such a tire in as a spare, and buy enough good, new tires so you will have GOOD traction in poor conditions.

Bald tires often pick up nails or just go bad – they go flat. It's poor economy to try to keep rolling on tires without enough tread.

I am not responsible, nor am I liable, for any driving mistakes you make because of anything I wrote here – or any advice that I do NOT give. Whatever

Chapter 15. WHEELS (also known as RIMS)

How Do They Work??

A car's wheel consists of a set of round *rims* that holds a tire, and a central section that has 4 or 5 bolt-holes, so it can be bolted to the brake drum. Almost always the wheel has a big hole in the middle, to provide clearance for various bearing parts. It just has to sit there and go around.

What Can Go Wrong?

Basically, only one thing can go wrong: if you hit a curb or some other junk in the road, you can bust the rim so hard that it gets bent, and the rim goes out of round, or the tire loses air pressure. Then you just about have to throw the wheel away. A couple times I have had a minor dent on the rim, that bent it just a little. I hit it with a *big hammer* and banged it back a little. No problem.

A couple other times, I tried to beat a dented rim back into shape, and the tire would still not hold air. I guess this is a case where a tube inside the tire would hold the air OK. But I do not want to fool around with that, because if a rim has been bent that much, I ought to retire it. It is not really *unsafe,* but it is not as safe as I prefer to run.

A steel rim can take a lot of banging, but an aluminum rim is more likely to be seriously weakened, or broken. Even if it is only bent, if you try to bend it back, it is likely to just fall off. You know how aluminum can be, when you abuse it too much. If you are going to do rough driving, aluminum wheels might be a bad choice.

But if I were far from home, and short of cash, and bent a rim a little, and could not easily find a replacement wheel, I might buy a tube and install it. I have heard that if you are going to go off-road driving, or down to Baja California, it is a good idea to put tubes in your tubeless tires, and bring along a good patch kit, because even if you are driving carefully, you may hit some junk – or some cactus spines – and then wish you had a tube.... A tubeless tire is much more likely to go flat, than a good tire with a tube. And a tube can be patched. Not an easy thing to do, but if you are 27 miles of dirt road away from the nearest town, it's better to be able to patch a tube, than to walk back to town pushing 2 flat tires.

> I reiterate: many fancy aluminum wheels are nice and light, excellent if you want to reduce your un-sprung weight for racing, and sexy and stylish – but they are not very rugged. So if you hit a rock, the aluminum wheel is more likely to bend badly or get crunched, compared to the conventional steel wheels.

8-20-21

Two-Piece Suit?

One time, in one state – I think it was Hawaii – some legislators got ticked off and decided that people should not be able to buy these fancy aluminum wheels. So some silly legislator wrote up a law: "In this state, nobody can buy a fancy wheel that is made in 2 pieces; you can only buy 1-piece wheels." AFTER this law was passed, and went into effect, somebody LOOKED AT IT.

Then a tire expert confronted the lawmaker. "Here are 2 rims. This fancy aluminum one is what you are trying to outlaw, right?" And the law-maker said yes. "And here is a rim that came with my Ford, and this is OK, right?" And the legislator said, right.

The expert pointed out, "This aluminum wheel – the one you don't like – is cast in one piece. The way you wrote that law, this is still perfectly legal." (Ohhh.) "And this tire that came with my Ford – it is made in 2 pieces that are welded together. Every Ford, Chevy, and Toyota comes with wheels built that way. You just made 97% of all the wheels in this state, illegal – with the exception of the fancy aluminum wheels that you don't like. Those are the only ones that are legal." (Ohhh....) So within a short time, they repealed that law.

The point is, most people do not realize that most of our car wheels or "rims" are actually made of 2 pieces of steel welded together. Recently I took off an old wheel from my 1972 VW bus – one of these welded together from 2 pieces – took off an old tire, and put on a new one, and put it on my 1985 Vanagon. I checked, and it fit perfectly. So that is one of the accessories that is REALLY compatible.

(Unfortunately, the 1957-1967 VW Beetles had a wide 5-bolt pattern that does not fit the "newer" 4-bolt wheels that VWs have had from 1968-1995. One of the few places where VWs are not compatible.)

◆ ◆ ◆

Most of the other ideas about Wheels, Rims, and Lug Nuts have been moved into the Flat Tires Chapter.

Chapter 16. FLAT TIRES

I am not really the best person to write this chapter from personal experience, because I have had rather few flat tires. And in the last 1,190,000 miles of driving, I have *never* had a blow-out.

I have *read* about other people who are driving along, and – KA-POW, wump-wump-wump – a tire has a "blow-out" at 65 mph. The tire loses all its air, suddenly. The car starts to swerve and fish-tail, and then the poor driver hits the brakes, and the car swerves and skids and crashes into a bridge abutment. No, I'll prefer to just read stories about that. But the stories do all go on to recommend: If you have a blowout, try to keep your car in its lane, as the first priority, and take your foot off the gas, and DON'T hit the brakes. The main reason behind that is, when you have 3 good tires and one flat, if you apply the brakes, and the tires' traction pulls unevenly, the car will tend to pull or swerve or veer, to one side or the other. So, if possible, wait until you are slowed down and *then* ease on the brakes a *little*, and then pick a good place to stop and change the tire.

Braking?

Of course, if you are on a curve, and the blowout has steered you right toward the guard-rail, and you are pretty sure you are going to hit the guard-rail anyhow, because the steering does not have much effect, well, if you can ease on the brakes, you might be able to pull off a little speed. You are already in BIG trouble, and putting on the brakes fairly hard and smoothly might not do much more harm – it might even do some good. This is one of the places where you have to use snap judgment – make the best guess you can. And meanwhile, continue steering as carefully as you can, to try to stay in your lane.

Another place to break that old rule – don't use the brakes – is if you are coming to a stop, and you are going to be using your brakes, and then you discover you have a flat tire or blowout. You cannot just decide to not use the brakes then!! So the thing to do is to put on the brakes *carefully*, and feel what happens. OK?

Oversteer?

As we have mentioned in the Chapter on Handling, if your rear tire pressure gets low or goes flat, the car feels "squirrelly". That is the slang phrase for bad *oversteer* – the car's rear tends to sway alternately to left and right. This is also called "fish-tailing". Refer to the Stuff on Handling. If you have a flat, and the car sways like this, you know what you got. Turn the wheel gently, and be prepared to correct. For example, if you turn the wheel left a *little*, and the car's rear starts skidding and wallowing to the right, be prepared to steer back right, as this is a kind of *skid*. Read the Chapter on Skidding. Yeah, even people who never see snow have to learn how to deal with skids.

Understeer?

In case of low pressure up front, or a flat on a front tire, the steering can get slow and heavy – that is *understeer.* You may have to turn the steering wheel further than usual, and it may be very heavy. This, too, is very close to a skid.

After you get down to a safe speed, look for a safe place to park and change the tire. Sometimes this is easy – sometimes not. You want to find a level place with firm ground to stop on – and preferably well away from traffic. You figure it out.

Of course, in some places you cannot easily change a flat. On the Golden Gate Bridge, they won't let you. They send a tow truck fast.

Changing your Flat Tire

Next, get ready to change the tire. Get your tools and the spare tire ready, too. Does it have enough air? If it doesn't, there is no point putting it on! (When you take the tire out of the trunk, *bounce it* a little on the ground. It ought to bounce pretty crisply if it has enough air to drive on.)

> Get your spare tire out and adjacent to the flat. Do this ahead of time, before you jack the car up, because when the car is jacked up, it is not very stable, and if you have to struggle to get out the tire, you don't want to knock the car off the jack.

Jacks and Jacking

I used to have a 1962 VW Beetle, and the Massachusetts salt caused it to get quite rusty after only 5 years. The jack-points on a VW are right in front of the rear wheel, and they are cleverly made of sheet-metal that is very light and strong, *until* it rusts through. About 1966, I realized that if I had one more flat tire, and I put the jack into its socket, the jacking force would rip the socket right through the floor of the car. So I went out and bought a scissors jack, to jack on the frame of the axle. That way I could jack up the wheel without jacking up the whole car – and it worked fine.

Whatever jack you have, make sure that you know that it works, and can lift up the wheel and the appropriate parts of the car, without making a mess. If your jack is in poor shape, or the bracket it hooks onto is damaged or rusted, or you are suspicious that it is weak, go out and buy a suitable jack that can get under a reasonable place under your axle or suspension sub-frame. Most of the auto supply stores sell these for only $10 or 20. Usually a scissors jack can get under a good place. Make sure that you know how to position the jack, so that even in the dark, you can find the right place to do it safely. You want to make really sure you do this so the car cannot slip or fall off the jack. Because even if the car does not fall on you, if it falls off the jack, it usually falls ONTO the jack, and then you really ARE stuck.

Don't *just* look at the jack and the jack-points; you should actually get out the jack and prove that the jack does fit, and can jack up the car. If you only discover the jack does not work, on a dark rainy night, well, I warned you....

8 - 21 - 21

If the ground is soft, you may want to use a chunk of 2"-by-4", or preferably, a 2-foot-long chunk of 2" x 6" plank, so the jack will not sink into the ground. You may need to stack up a couple 2x4s if the reach of the jack is not enough. Conversely, if the tire is really flat, there may not be enough space for the jack. You may have to drive the flat tire up onto a couple 2x4s to get the car high enough to fit the jack in. So, you should always carry *at least a* few chunks of 2x4 and a slab of 2x6, or equivalent, along with your jack. Every few years, you will be glad you did. I mean, you cannot always choose the place where you get a flat. The side of the road might be pretty soft.

> *One time I got a slow-leak flat, so I pulled out my jack and tried to fit it under the axle. But the jack had been left kind of high. So I turned the crank to get it lower. Meanwhile, the air kept leaking out of the tire, so when I had the jack lower, the car had settled even lower, and I could not put the jack in. I had to drive up onto the 2-by-4s to make room for the jack. So NOW when I am through with using my jack, I crank it back down to its lowest level before I put it away, so it will be ready when I need it. But one of my buddies cautioned me that the jack may be hard to stow in its correct place, if it is not cranked down to exactly the right level....*

I was once talking to a guy who went with friends on a camping trip. They drove up a long logging road to a trailhead and hiked for a few days. When they got back to the car, they had a flat tire, and no jack, and nobody for many miles that could help. What could they do?

I said, "Aha, I bet you looked around and figured out what to do." He said, "Yes, there were some old trees, and we brought over some logs and some short chunks of log, and we levered up the car high enough to put on the spare tire."

Yes, that was the right answer there. A jack is one good way to jack up a car, but it is not the only one. You could build up a pile of rocks and a pile of dirt, and drive the flat tire up on a big pile of dirt. Then you set the pile of rocks under the frame, and then dig the dirt out from under the tire, so you can swap the tire. Of course, this may not work so well on city streets. But it indicates, there is more than one way to change a tire, even if you have no jack, or if your jack breaks. It may take a while, but it may save you a visit from the tow-truck, *or* a long walk.

◆ ◆ ◆

Now that you have the jack under (or, hooked onto) the car, just lift it a few strokes. Not far at all. Make sure your hand-brakes are on tight, and put the car in low gear (if manual transmission) or in PARK (if automatic). If you are at all skeptical about the handbrakes, or if the grade is at all steep, find something to chock up the wheels. That's why it's good to have *several* 2-by-4s, to put some in front of, or behind the wheels as chocks, and some under the jack, to support its base on soft soil – and several more to drive the flat tire up onto.

Removing the Hub Caps

Maybe your car has hub caps – maybe not. If it does, you may need a screwdriver or lever to remove it. Sometimes those things are very tricky. Make sure you know how to do it – and make sure your tools work. Don't gouge yourself with a screwdriver!

Loosening the Wheel Lug Nuts

Now, before you jack up the car any more, you have to loosen all the lug nuts or bolts. Sometimes, this merely takes all your strength. Other times, the lug nuts cannot be loosened by any ordinary amount of force.

The first possibility is that your car has left-hand thread on the lug nuts on the left side of the car. What kind of cars do this, or used to do this? I'll make a list.

List of Cars with Left-Hand Threads:

– Old Chrysler Motors cars,1924-1973.

– ???

Barring the problem of left-hand threads, if you have been able to remove one of the lug nuts, but you can't loosen the others, then you have this basic problem: the lug nuts were tightened too tight. Or, they were last tightened so long ago that they are "frozen" or seized up or rusted a little.

> *Once upon a time there was a very thoughtful guy running a tire company, in Baltimore, I think I recall. He realized that a lot of people with flat tires were stranded because they could not loosen their lug nuts. So he instructed all his employees not to use the rat-ta-ta-tatta impact wrenches to tighten up the lug nuts, but to tighten them by hand. He started a big advertising campaign: "We torque your nuts by hand". After a short while, a number of prudish people got an injunction to prevent him from using that phrase. Personally, I liked his thoughtful style, and I liked his ad.*

No matter how you got your lug nuts too tight, you will need extreme torque to loosen them. A very good way is to carry a 3-foot length of 2-inch iron pipe in your car, to act as an extra length of torque arm. Even better is to carry two of these 3-foot pipes, so you can add torque on both sides of the wrench. Recently, I stopped to help a guy, and we could just barely get 4 of his 5 lug nuts loose. When both of us pulled together on the lug wrench, we began to twist the wrench's shaft! We finally got it loose, as I torqued the wrench, and he hit the wrench, right where it fitted over the nut, with his hammer. So now I carry a hammer. Better yet, make sure you are able to break loose your lug nuts before you need to. Best, you might ask the tire store to tighten the lug nuts by hand, not with an impact wrench.

Jacking

After you have all the nuts loosened a little, now you can jack up the car. Jack it up good and high. When you have it jacked up enough for the tire to not touch the ground, that is *almost* enough. Remember, the flat tire does not have much air in it. If you get the car up high enough to get this tire off, you might have to get it even *higher* to get the spare tire on – because that has air in it. (If you have a tiny spare, that is not a problem.) You don't want to be jacking the car while it has no wheel on, because if it slips then, and falls off the jack, you got a REAL MESS on your hands! It might do some real damage to the car – or to you – or to the jack. So jack it up a little higher than necessary, before you get the wheel off. (Nobody else warns you about this.)

Almost Ready to Swap

Now, get all ready to change the tire. Have the spare tire out of the car and ready, right adjacent to where you are. (One of my buddies recommends that you place it under the car's frame, until you need it. Not necessarily a bad idea.) Loosen up and remove all but one of the lug nuts. Put them in a safe place, where you can find them, and where they will not get dirty. The hubcap is usually a good place for that. Check the threads on the studs or lugs or bolts. Are they kind of dry or rusty? You might get your bottle of oil, so you can add a dab of oil on the threads before you put them back on.

Start to loosen the last nut – but before you remove it, first there are some things to check.

> Look up the road. Are there 5 trucks coming up the road at 60 mph, that might just whip you with a gust of wind and wobble your car on its precarious perch? Maybe you want to wait until those trucks are all gone by.

> Are there any passengers in the car? Tell them to sit still and DON'T wiggle. EVEN the kids. Not for a couple minutes.

> Is the jack secure? If you are really skeptical, try wobbling the car just a little. If you can wiggle the car, and give it a small shove, and it falls off the jack, well, it's a lot better to do that, than to have it fall off when the tire is *off.* If it is stable enough, then you are ready to make the swap.

Time to Swap

NOW – get your toe under the flat tire – remove the last nut – and ease the flat tire away. Set it where it's stable – so it won't roll away. Get the spare, and ease it onto the lugs. Sometimes it works best if you wedge your toe under it, to ease it up to the right height. This can be tricky in the dark – with only a flashlight, or with just your emergency flashers *blinking.* Now, promptly, put one lug nut (or bolt) on. Get 2 or 3 turns on the nut, by hand. At this point, you are pretty safe, because even if there is an earthquake – even if the car falls off the jack, it probably will land on the tire and be safe. If you do this procedure right, the car is only without a tire for 20 or 30 seconds. Even if you don't live in California (or some such place where there are earthquakes) it's wise to minimize the time when the car is only supported by the jack, with no tire on the wheel. The next time I change a tire, I'll time it, and see how long it takes me. (Yeah, about 30 seconds.)

Now at leisure, tighten up the first lug nut a little. Put 2 drops of oil on the threads, if needed. Put on the other 3 or 4 nuts, and get them hand-tight. Then use your wrench and, even though the tire is not on the ground, get the nuts wrist-tight.

Special Caution on Lug Nuts

One of my buddies, Jim, sent me a special caution – with a story to back it up:

"Bob: Wherever you talk about lug nuts, I suggest including a STRONG warning on how they go on. Most nuts have a flat side and a "coned" side. Make sure the cone is installed toward the wheel and the flat side is out. As I'm sure you are aware, the cone centers the wheel rim so it does not tend to wiggle or move around on the brake drum."

And here is Jim's story to explain why the proper orientation of the LUG NUTS is very important:

"Several years ago, I was driving a rented van on a long trip with several colleagues. We rented a new van that had only a few hundred miles on the odometer when we picked it up. Prior to leaving, one of the guys took the van to a local store to stock up on food for the trip. While driving back, he had a flat tire on the left rear. He and a couple buddies who were with him changed the tire.

"About 4 hours later, I was driving on a steep downgrade, driving in a lane next to the slow (truck) lane, passing a 10-wheeler, when the truck suddenly slammed on his brakes and started blowing his horn. At the same time, the car behind me started flashing his headlights.

"The next thing I knew, the left rear of the van was sliding on the road. We had no brakes, and it was starting to swerve (actually turning somewhat broadside) into the slow lanes. At the same time, I noticed a tire pass me on the left side, cross in front across all lanes, and end up in the ditch.

"Luckily, the car and truck behind me were able to jump in and slow the traffic coming from the rear. By driving the van as if it were in a skid (turning in the direction of the skid), I was able to keep us from rolling over. After about 1/3 mile of a bucking-bronco ride leaving a trail of sparks that looked like the 4th of July behind us, we finally stopped.

"I got out and examined the axle. The road had ground away the brake drum and half the axle housing. The axle drive shaft was exposed on the left side. It left a deep rut gouged in the road that I noted is still there, years later. In looking at the brake housing, I saw that there were no wheel studs left; it appeared all had broken off.

"We got a ride back to the previous town and called the owner's emergency number. His first statement was, 'Oh, no, not the new van!' It turned out that the van's manufacturer had to replace the whole axle and brake assembly under warranty, believing the unit to be defective.

"However, the real story I only found out weeks later: The guys had a discussion on which way the nuts went on when they changed the tire. They put them on on backwards. The conical shapes were AWAY from the wheel. Then they put on the hub cap and nobody could see if the nuts were backwards.

"The guy driving the car behind us said that things were flying off as he watched the wobbling rear wheel; one of them hit his car. I found a lug nut wedged into the front grill of the car. The studs were broken off by the wobbling tire as it eventually came off after several hundred yards. If the studs were defective, the lug nut I found would still have had the stud in place.

So that is what can happen, if you put the lug nuts on backwards. There were 10 of us aboard that van, and it could have been a real mess."

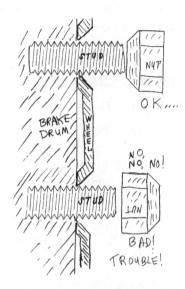

After I read this, I thought about my VW Beetles. I have put on about 1,100,000 miles on my old Air-cooled VWs. And they do not have lug nuts that can be put on any "WRONG WAY". They have BOLTS that go through the wheel and into the brake drum.

What Instead of Lug Nuts?

For a long time, I have thought – why is VW so different? Why didn't VW do it like everybody else, and put nuts on studs?? And just now, I realized – why doesn't VW do it like everybody else? Because VW is RIGHT, and Everybody Else is WRONG. If you try to put in a BOLT, the wrong way – it obviously does NOT go into the hole. You cannot mount the wheel on the brake drum, unless you put the bolts the RIGHT WAY. Unfortunately, this is not true for a nut....

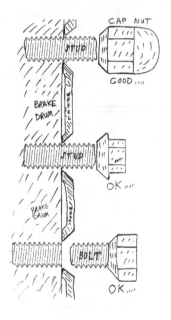

What Kind of Lug Nuts?

I checked some automobile agencies. Most new cars had lug nuts on studs, not bolts. Refer to the *sketch*. In most cases, they had cap nuts – a nut with a closed cap, so you could not put them on with the cone facing the wrong way. But in some cases, these lug nuts can be put on the right way *or* the wrong way. Not so good.

I checked a BRAND NEW van that my company had bought, just in the last month. I peeked under the hubcaps. The lug nuts had a single taper on one end, and square cut on the other end. If you put them on the wrong way – you could have "technical problems" – as my friend described above.

Should the car's manufacturer be obligated to replace all these single-taper lug nuts, to be of a safe type? I think so. What is a safe type of lug nut? Well, some cars have lug nuts that are cap nuts, so they can not be put on the studs backwards – they are closed off. That's a pretty good solution. Other cars have a nut that can start to screw onto the stud at either end – but they have a flare built in, sort of a washer, on the coned end, so you cannot put on a wrench to tighten the nut, unless it is the right way. I have seen these on some VWs. Or, one could have nuts that taper evenly on *both* ends. That would look silly, but that would work.

Anyhow, it is very important that you put the lug nuts on the RIGHT way, not the *wrong way.* If *you* have a car with lug nuts that could be put on backwards, you might put a little tag on the jack-handle to remind you about this. YOU might never have a problem with this. Your spouse might not. But how can you be sure you will never loan your car to somebody who does not understand this? A month after I passed this story around, one of my reviewers drove in to a gas station to get a tire changed. The young employee started to put the nuts on backwards – and then stopped – and asked my friend, "What is the right way, anyhow??" And my friend was able to tell him that story. I bet the kid never forgets! And I hope you won't, either.

Finish Up

Next, lower the jack until the tire is just touching the ground. Use the wrench to tighten the nuts a little more – but not just in a random pattern. Don't just tighten one nut all the way, and then another, all the way. Tighten each nut a little tighter, in a sequence. If you had 5 nuts, going around in a 5-point star pattern is good. See the adjacent *sketch*. If you have 4 nuts, it is better to go N, S, E, W, than to go in a circle.

Get the nuts a little tighter, and then go around again and get them a little *tighter.* (This is probably unnecessary, these days, but in the old days you could warp the brake drum by tightening each nut tight; and then the brakes would squeal.)

Now you can lower the jack most of the way, and make yourself comfortable. You can tell the kids they can

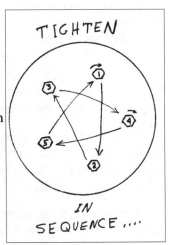

wiggle. Stand up. Stretch. You are almost through. Take the lug wrench and go around one more time, and use your shoulders to get the nuts *good and tight* – but not TOO tight.

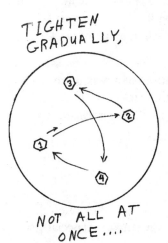

Put the jack down – not just enough to get it out from the car, but "lower it" down even a little lower than that. Stow the jack and the lug wrench. Stow the hubcap, as it is often a better idea to leave it off, than to put it on the wheel. Stow the oil. Stow the old tire. (You might inspect it, to see if you can tell what made it go flat.) Make sure you have picked up all your stuff

– even the screwdriver and the flashlight. And you can start thinking about where to get your flat tire repaired – or replaced.

Meanwhile, it's a good idea if you kept a 6th wheel and tire – a second spare tire – at home. This is quite valuable for the case when you come home with a flat, and you want to go out, but you don't want to go without any spare tire. Also, in case you come out of the house and find a flat tire and have to change it before starting. Now, if you have 4 extra rims with snow-tires, then you are in pretty good shape.

Slow Leaks

Sometimes tires get porous – they have a slow leak. Sometimes even a nail makes a slow leak. If you find that a tire has low pressure, it might have a nail that is just starting to cause a little leak. That is a good time to inspect your tire, as mentioned above. And if you find a wire or screw or nail, do NOT pull it out, unless you are AT a service station and have a guy who agrees he can fix it – or – unless you are prepared to change the tire! Because if you pull out that nail or screw, the leak is likely to not be a slow leak any more!

Tire Gooo?

One of the things you can do, if you just have a slow leak, is use an instant-inflation bottle. These cost $3 or $4 at most auto-supply stores. They are filled with a compressed gas and a sealant goo, so small leaks and minor punctures can be sealed while you re-fill the tire on the road. The good news is, a small leak can be sealed in just a couple minutes.

The bad news is, while these used to be filled with Freon (which may have been wrecking the earth's Ozone layer), *now* they are filled with propane or some similar flammable gas. So if you use one of these to inflate a tire, you have to put on a label, to remind the tire repairman that the tire is full of flammable gas. I have heard that if you don't let all the gas out of the tire and refill it *at least* 4 times, you will either risk an explosion, or the tire man may bill you $20 for disposing of such a dangerous substance. So now you are warned.

I never used to use these, years ago, as they were fairly expensive. Now they are cheaper – but more dangerous. I have used them successfully about 4 times, and unsuccessfully twice. If the leak is bigger than just a tiny leak, it may not work at all, and you just wasted $3....

The other problem is, the cans are only rated to be stored at a maximum temperature of + 120 degrees F, so you can't JUST leave it in the back of a car. But if I leave it in my little icebox, it is very unlikely to get as hot as 120 degrees. So that's what I do.

Tire Repairs

I won't explain all the details of how you can patch your own tires, because it is not easy. I've tried the plugs that you can poke into a tubeless tire, and they often do not work well. So I won't recommend them. Let an expert do the repairs, especially on tubeless tires. On a tire with a tube, it is VERY hard to change a tire, or get at the tube, but after you get access to the tube, it is not that hard to patch a tube. So that is another reason why off-road drivers prefer tires with tubes.

do, DON'T break laws, and DO use good sense and good judgement, no matter what you read.

I am not responsible, nor am I liable, for any driving mistakes you make because of anything I wrote here – or any advice that I do NOT give. Whatever you

Chapter 17. JUNK on the ROAD

Every once in a while, there is *something* on the road. This stuff may cause a terrible accident. Or it may be of value. If you stop to pick it up, you could get in an accident. You could be hit by another car and killed. What to do? Well, it depends on the traffic, and the importance of getting that stuff off the road.

One time, on Route 128 north, 100 yards south of Highland Avenue, I came across a big traffic slowdown and a big mess. Everybody was slowing down for some junk in the road – the remains of a baby's playpen, in the middle lane. It must have fallen off a car's roof rack, and splintered into a big pile of sticks and junk.

I decided to stop and help. Traffic was so slow, I could only make things better. I pulled over, parked, and walked out in the middle of the road and held up my hand, for traffic to stop. Most cars were reasonable, and stopped. But one foolish guy in a Pontiac kept on easing through the debris at about 4 mph. I held up my hand some more, and he kept on coming. I continued to hold up my hand, requesting him to stop – because there was a big armful of busted wood, and if he would stop, I could take the whole armful off to the side. But this damned cretin kept on coming. When he got about 40 feet away, I stepped out of the middle of the lane, but with my hand still held up. He kept coming, at 3 mph, and climbed right over the pile of debris. Finally he bounced off a stick which flipped up and gouged a little hole in his radiator. The antifreeze began to piddle out on the ground. He kept on driving ahead. I hollered at this idiot, "Your radiator has a hole in it; better fix it." I did not watch to see if he pulled off at the next exit. I was busy picking up 90% of those sticks and carrying them over to the side of the road. And, I must say, every other driver slowed down and stopped when I gestured them to stop, because I was just trying to clear up the road. And, hey, it was not even my playpen. I am sure that 1 hour later, the traffic was flowing smoothly.

Anyhow, if that dummy who persisted in driving over that wood and debris would read this, he would be very unhappy. But I doubt if he is able to read. Meanwhile, I could not wish for better luck to happen to such a nice guy. I just wonder if he woulda stopped, if the baby was still in the playpen????

Valuable Stuff...

Every once in a while I find other interesting stuff on the road. One time I found a big long heavy "breaker bar" that is used with socket wrenches. It was worth about $11.55. I knew this because the previous week I had finally broke down and bought one exactly like that, and that's how much I paid. Now I have *two* breaker bars....

Sometimes I have found money along the road. One time I was walking along the road and found $4 in change – mixed in with the cigarette butts when the slob dumped out his ash tray. I've also picked up venetian blinds, shovels, and heavy chains. Rakes and ropes. Wrenches and trowels. Planks and screwdrivers.

Dangerous Stuff...

If you see boards or wood or plywood in the road, it is usually worth some effort to avoid driving over them, because they often have nails sticking out of them, and you don't want to get a flat. But the thing that I picked up that was most likely to cause an accident was a 6-by-6-inch beam, 10 feet long, that could easily blow a car's tires.

And one time out on I-93 I saw 10 people stopped, all fixing flat tires. They were all worrying about their tires – but none of them went back to remove the debris from the road, that had caused their flats. I went back and found a 10-foot-long chunk of 5-inch by 5-inch steel angle iron. Nice sharp edges to blow tires! I pulled it off the road and set it behind the guard rail, as it was too long and awkward for me to carry with me. I went back the next day and looked for it, but it was gone.

BIG Stuff...

One time I was coming up I-280, on a dark and stormy night, and I saw several cars 'way up ahead, jamming on their brakes, and skidding and fish-tailing. I slowed down and put on my emergency blinkers, and eased along – and saw a camper shell in the second lane! I went up a couple hundred yards further, and parked. I ran back, watching for skidding cars that could come at any time, from any direction. After I got just beyond the camper shell, I waited until I saw a couple cars stopped, behind the shell. *That* is what you have to have, to make sure you can walk out in the middle of a high-speed road safely. Then I ran out and waved my arms, to make sure everybody stayed stopped. When I was sure all traffic was stopping safely, I dragged the camper shell off to the side of the road. And I threw it over the guard rail, to make sure the wind did not blow it back onto the road. After that, all traffic began to move just fine. But I bet when the pickup got home, the driver sure was puzzled where his camper shell went!

Awkward Stuff...

A buddy said he was driving along with a friend, who ran over a mattress. The mattress apparently snagged on the underframe of the car, and was dragged along. Soon, it caught fire due to contact with hot exhaust parts. The driver finally got smart, and stopped. He was able to get off the mattress, by backing up. A good thing, or he would have been in real trouble!! Other times, cars *do* burn up, if they can't get off the burning mattress!

Scary Stuff...

One other time, down on Route 128 (right across from the playpen incident) I spotted a full-sized concrete block, right on the lane markings. I figured I'd better stop and pull that off the road. I drove down 100 yards, and ran back, and waited for a break in traffic.

Just then, KATOW, a woman in a station wagon hit that concrete block and busted it all to pieces. It didn't do her front tire or wheel a lot of good, either.... She pulled over and stopped.

I waited for a break in traffic and got all the big pieces of the concrete block off the road. Then I went over to see the woman with the station wagon. She was kinda shook up. I think she was a little suspicious that it was MY concrete block, but I explained that it must have fallen off a truck. I certainly wasn't carrying it on the top of my Beetle! I figured, I was already stopped, so I changed her tire for her.

Nasty Stuff...

There were some car repair shops down in Texas, that got caught throwing old mufflers out onto the Interstate highway, a mile or so before the exit for their shop. Finally after a lot of accidents, the police got suspicious, and caught these guys, drumming up business!

Okay – What Should *YOU* Do About This?

Anyhow, if you see trash or debris on the road, you may not feel that you have to move it out of the road. But it might be a good move, if you can do it safely. If you hold up your arms, with your hands flat and facing the other drivers, they usually get the message and slow down. You may be able to get other drivers to stop, and that will protect you from other traffic. And it may be a good move to prevent other cars from having an accident – either from hitting the debris, or hitting other cars when they try to avoid hitting it. The other drivers may think it is YOUR junk, so they will *usually* be helpful and co-operative.

A couple of my buddies said *they* would feel pretty nervous, standing out in the highway, trying to get other drivers to stop. Well, if the cars were going at full speed, I sure agree. But if they are already stopped, or nearly stopped, in all lanes, I do not feel too nervous about walking out there with my hand held up. Of course, I watch to see what the cars are doing. If it is dark, or dangerous, and the car heads right for me, I'll be sure to get out of his way.

If the traffic is really moving at speed, and I just want to rescue something that is not too important – like a $10 wrench, or a $20 chain – I am willing to wait a few minutes for a break in traffic, and then just run out one lane, and grab the stuff. But if there is not a break in traffic – I will not try to get speeding traffic to stop, unless there is something really serious or dangerous. I mean, a friend of mine said a young neighbor of his was hit and killed while trying to direct traffic around some junk in the road. I never said it was safe. Be careful out there!

A Wireless Solution...

My buddies observed, this is a good place for a guy with a cellular phone, or a CB radio, to call the Highway Department (or the State Cops, or the Highway Patrol, or whatever they are called in your area) and tell *them* to come out and clean up the dangerous junk. That's a pretty good idea, in general. So, keep their phone number handy.

How Do You Warn Everybody?

A friend said she was driving along rather slowly, in murky, rainy conditions, and her husband said, "Watch out for this idiot standing in the middle of the street". He was waving his arms in a random way, and shining a flashlight in odd directions. She slowed down some more, and found that the guy was trying to warn them about some wires down in the road. Now, if you stay in your car, driving over wires may not be terribly dangerous, but it's better if you can avoid them. So she was glad she was able to take this guy's advice, and stop. But she wished he had used a better technique to flag them down.

There are two main procedures that are recommended:

If traffic is slow, and you are pretty sure you can get the cars to stop, you stand right near their lane and hold up one or both hands, just like a traffic cop will do. You do it in a way that shows you know what you are doing, even if you are just bluffing. People respect the show of authority. After they have stopped, you can go up and explain why they have to stop or wait or whatever. If it is dark, and you have a flashlight, you should shine it on yourself, so the other driver can see you. That's better than shining it at the driver, shining it in his eyes. (Sometimes you can shine the flashlight in a swoop, from the driver's eyes, down past your yellow raincoat, to your ankles.) And all the time you are holding up your arms, you must keep your eyes on the other drivers, to make sure they see you and are going to stop. If you cannot get them to stop – well, at least you tried.

And all the time, your highest priority is to make sure that car, and all other cars, do not hit you. You make sure you can get out of their way. Not just the one car, that isn't bright enough to stop. But out of EVERYBODY's path. It is worth some effort to keep trying to slow them down. Maybe you'll find one driver smart enough to catch on.

Another, related technique, is to stop your car in one of the lanes, turn on its emergency blinkers, and stand near the car. Leave the door open if that makes sense. Hold up your arms and then sweep them down toward the ground. See sketch at right. This is to signify, "Get your speed DOWN!" Most drivers will figure this out pretty quick. Just the other day, I saw a guy standing out in the high-speed lane of I-280, near Cupertino. He motioned for us to *slow it down*. Very shortly we saw why – there was a very big puddle, across all 4 lanes. It looked like he had hit the puddle and spun and bent his car, and the cop asked him to go back up and get everybody slowed down, and he was a good sport, and he did it. He got us all to slow down. He may have even done himself some good, by making sure none of *us* skidded into *his* car.

Meanwhile, *you* keep near the FRONT end of your car, so if a guy is coming too close to your car,

5-24

and won't slow down, you can dodge behind the front of your car. You do NOT want to stand *behind* your car, because if another car runs into it, he will cut your knees off. I'm not going to stand there. And all the time, you keep watch so that nobody is going to run over you.

As soon as you get a couple cars slowed down, that is half the battle. You can talk to the drivers, and explain why they have to stop. Soon, you will have enough cars stopped, and you will have things under your control.

Stopping Fast Traffic?

But those procedures are suitable only if traffic is already going pretty slow.

> What if traffic is coming along fast, and you have to flag them down, because there is an accident with injured people, right around the curve? Or what if there is a bridge out, or a truck blocking the road? Well, you have to use some combinations of the above techniques. Hold up your arms and your hands, and push them *down* – repeatedly. And keep an eye on all these cars, so they will not hit you, whether or not they see you. Hey, so long as you do not get hurt, it is worth a try, to keep them out of a bigger accident.

> What if the visibility is *LOUSY?* Well, you stand over near the breakdown lane, and try to slow down any cars that come along – and you keep watch, to make sure that no car – not even a car coming down the breakdown lane – is going to hit you.

Dead Car in the Middle of the Road

A couple times, I have found another car stalled in the middle of a freeway. My normal procedure, when traffic is slow, is to pull over into the lane behind that car, and stop behind him. (Whereas everybody else is trying to get OUT of that lane.) In each case, I get out and talk to the driver, and I can usually give his car a little push with my car, over to the side of the road. If the grade is too steep for me to push him up the hill, I will just direct traffic around him, and let him roll back until he is off the roadway. This can clear away a pretty bad and potentially dangerous road hazard, and clear up a bad slowdown. And if you do it thoughtfully, it is not dangerous. Specifically, if you have a LOT of cars behind you, already slowed down, it's pretty safe, and you are very unlikely to get a car running you over. And, it's a neighborly thing to do.

Dangerous Debris *IN* Your Car

A guy told me of a time when he was driving along, and he tried to step on his brakes, and the brake pedal would not go down. It turned out, there was a soda bottle that rolled around under the driver's feet until it got wedged behind the brake pedal. Fortunately, he was able to use the handbrake to get slowed down. From that time on, he was very careful not to let any trash accumulate under the driver's feet. I often keep a lot of stuff and junk in my car, but not on the driver's floorboards.

Chapter 18. BUMPS and BUMPY ROADS

I must admit, I like some smooth roads. But sometimes a road with lurches and bumps can be very interesting, and fun to drive on. I remember I was once scurrying down an easy downgrade, eastbound, in the Pennsylvania Dutch country, in my old 1962 Beetle. The road was probably good for 40 mph, and I was only doing 50. Suddenly I crested a little bump, and the road dropped off and took a sharp bend to the right. I almost took off into the air, and I turned the wheel just right, and came down in a very neat 4-wheel drift. I was impressed that they left such a nice, *interesting* curve in the road. It's a good thing I was alert; if I "lost it" – lost control – in a case like that, I coulda rolled my car into a ditch. Refer to the Chapter on Handling.

When I was a kid, my father would drive us up on a woods road, an old dirt road, up behind Griswold Road. Perhaps that was Abbey Road? We would come down this road, and there was a nice curve, and then a big HUMP in the road, more than 2 feet high. Our car would *leap* over that at about 30 mph, making a nice LURCH. My father said that was called a "Thank-you-Ma'am", because it was originally called a "Kiss-me-quick", and after you got your quick kiss from your girlfriend, then you should reply, "Thank you, Ma'am." So the notion that a lurch in the road was a pleasant surprise, got into my head at an early age. I am not saying that we HAVE TO have lurchy roads, but if you have one, you ought to enjoy it. You do not have to drive terribly fast – you do not have to go so fast that you PITCH your car up in the air – but it would be a crime to drive over it at a boring speed.

Here in San Francisco, there used to be a NICE "Thank-you-Ma'am" on Gough (pronounced Goff) Street, just a block east of Geary. When we were driving home from church, if you come down the street at about 27 mph, it was a really nice lurch. But if there were no cars parked in the curb lane, and you drove down *that* lane (which was legal at certain times of day), you would get a really NICE lurch, not too bumpy, as the road dropped out from under you. A VW Beetle always got a nice ride on that bump. But in a VW bus, you are sitting in front of the front axle, and you get a little too strong a lurch, unless you are in a good mood, or else you would have to slow down a little.

All these bumps are not a disaster, unless they take you by surprise. I suppose they could throw you out of control, if you were not paying attention, or if you were not a good driver, or if you were going too fast. So, by definition, if you want to drive fast, pay attention, and concentrate on being a good driver. And don't let a little lurch in the road throw you out of control.

Lurches Causing Accidents?

– When does a bump or lurch cause an accident? Not very often. One time, we heard the roar of a powerful motorcycle, and then a bad crunch, about 100 yards down the street from our house. This motorcycle apparently came around a little traffic circle at about 30 mph, and was accelerating very hard – probably up to 65 mph on a quiet suburban street – and hit a bump in the street. This threw him out of control.

– When you think about it, if a motorcycle is accelerating VERY HARD, and its front wheel is JUST BARELY on the ground, if the front wheel hits a bump, it could easily bounce 'way up in the air. And the rider would lose control.... That's what happened – he lost control and crashed into a parked car. It nearly killed the guy, and wrecked the back of the car. So, it is uncommon for a bump to cause a car to crash, but, never say never....

If you were driving very fast and aggressively on a curve, and you hit an unexpected bump, that might cause you to skid – maybe only a little – but maybe enough to lose control, or slide over to a sandy part of the road where you'd be in trouble.

So, watch out for bumps when you are cornering hard. When I am cornering hard, and I see a bump ahead, I try to turn a little harder before I get to the bump, and then I ease off on the steering wheel just when I get to the bump, to straighten out my line; and then I resume a tighter radius after the bump has settled out.

Other Problems...

While bumps rarely cause a car crash, a bumpy or lurchy road may cause car-sickness. Some people just don't agree with that kind of road, especially at "too fast" a speed. Nausea is something that can not be "cured" by reasoning or arguing. Usually the only thing to "cure" it is to slow down. Sometimes when I get a little too exuberant, on a twisty road, my wife tells me to slow down. Sometimes I slow down. Other times I tell her, "OK, *you* drive." When she drives, it does not bother her so much because she has the steering wheel to hold on to, and it helps her feel more comfortable. She drives just about as fast as I do, on these roads, and does not feel uncomfortable at all. So, that is one way to help avoid that kind of "accident" in your car. If you look outside the car, rather than reading stuff inside, that can sometimes help.

Dropping off the Pavement?

One time I was camping up on Prince Edward Island, in Canada, and I was talking with a guy in the next campsite. He said he really liked his new Citroen, because when he drove off the edge of the pavement, it was easy to keep control and drive back onto the pavement. I think about that occasionally. I mean, I rarely drive off the pavement, so, how do I know if his Citroen is better to get back on the pavement than my Beetle, or my Bus? So, a few times, I went out of my way to drive a little bit off the pavement, when there was not any traffic around to be worried. In general, I had no trouble driving back up onto the pavement, even if there was an inch or two of drop-off. Of course, if you did this all the time, you would abuse your tires. But I guess in those days there were some cars that did NOT smoothly ride up back onto the pavement, from an inch or two of drop-off. I have no idea what kind of cars they were.

That was over 25 years ago. Maybe there were a lot of lousy cars with lousy steering, back then. Maybe a heavy old car without power steering would have a problem. But my Bus weighed 3000 lb. empty, and when fully loaded with people and camping gear, it was not a light car. And it did not have power steering. And I never had any trouble with that. Or perhaps, cars with lousy tires... or cars with tiny 12-inch wheels? I never was able to figure out why that guy thought his Citroen was so superior to *what*. But if *your* car handles kind of funny, *you* should be aware if you are likely to have trouble, driving over a little lurch – or an edge of pavement, dropping off to a shoulder.

– Obviously, if your right wheels drop down over an edge, and you have to cut the steering wheel *really hard* to get back on the pavement – and if the car then swerves viciously toward the centerline and lurches into oncoming traffic, before you can get the wheel straightened out – that's not a joke. Instead of cutting the wheel *hard* to the left, maybe you would be better off to *slow down* a little, before you try to cut back onto the pavement. Or, wait until the drop-off is a little smaller?

But you may not have that luxury. Still, if you have to turn the wheel *pretty hard* to the left, to get back onto the pavement, you have to know in advance, that you must be ready to turn the wheel *back* sharply to the right, briefly, to get straightened out, as soon as you are in your lane. Don't be slow to *correct,* and let the car take you too far left!! This is not a skid – but you have to be quite alert, and react as if you were in a skid. Plan this move in advance.

This is obscure, but, still worth thinking about – worth considering in advance....

you do, DON'T break laws, and DO use good sense and good judgement, no matter what you read.

Chapter 19. LOADS on your CAR

There are several ways to load large objects onto your car. You can get a roof-rack. You can put them in your open trunk. (Well, I can't very well do that in my VW Beetle!) Or you can just pad the roof and set the large object on the roof. A table or small mattress can easily ride on top of most cars, if they are not a convertible.

On the Roof

One time I saw a car with a mattress on its roof, rolling along a busy freeway at 50 mph. The mattress was only held on by a few strands of light cord around the middle of the mattress. And the air had lifted up the front of the mattress so it was flopping up in the air. I did not like the looks of that at all! I passed him and got out of there. Then I looked in the mirror – just as the cord broke, and the mattress launched itself into heavy traffic! I think nobody crashed, but I just kept going. There was nothing I could do better than to get out of there.

> For Pete's sake, if you are going to tie on a load, use appropriate rope or heavy cord, and use enough of it!! Don't try to just hold the load on with your hands! I've seen that, too....

Sometimes I carry a canoe on my roof. I use a lot of straps and ropes to tie down my load, and lots of padding. I've never had any problems with loads falling off my car. But that's because I tie them down with a LOT of rope.

Roof Racks

One time I had to bring home a large dresser. It was 6 feet long by 5 feet high. It would not fit in any car. Not even in a VW bus. Of course, it would fit pretty well in a pickup truck. But I put my roof rack on my Beetle and had my friends hold it the dresser up high, and I drove under it, and they set it down on the roof rack. Fortunately I only had a couple miles to go.

Back in 1976, I had to bring home a mattress from San Jose, about 7 feet square. I figured I could fold it over double, and it would fit easily on my roof rack. But the label on the mattress said, do not fold it like that.

I went to the lumber store next door, to buy some 8-foot 2 x 4s, to help support it. I got the whole thing loaded on and secure. But a VW is barely 5 feet wide, so it hung over a full foot on each side. I got within 2 miles of home, when a Highway Patrolman pulled me over and explained that that's too much overhang. But he let me go up the side-streets to get home. In the future, I knew better than to carry such a big load.

◆◆◆

Back in 1975, my buddy Jim gave me a computer – the computer from the nose-cone of a Minuteman I missile. It was two feet tall and 4 feet in diameter. With the help of 3 people, I got that up onto my roof rack. Afterwards, we figured out, it weighed 152 lb., with all the Printed Circuit Boards in it. No wonder it was a beast to get it down!

Another time, I bought an old computer for $50 – one of the earliest work-stations. It weighed 250 lb. That one just fitted in the passenger's side of my Beetle, after I removed the front seat, and I got the door closed – well – almost, give or take an inch.

◆ ◆ ◆

When I was active in the MIT Outing Club, we used to go skiing. One guy started up to New Hampshire with a full roof rack of skis. When he got there – there was no roof rack. Ouch. What can you say?

> What *I say* is, always tie a rope from the roof rack, or the load itself, to the front bumper – just to be safe. I mean, you'd feel bad if you saw your ski rack fall off your car, but you'd feel worse if you looked in your mirror and saw the next 3 cars behind you crash into the load and each other. The rope will not only hold the roof-rack stable, and keep it from falling far, but it will remind you that you have a roof-rack, to help you remember not to drive under a low overhead. This is a good reminder for canoes, too.

◆ ◆ ◆

One time my son was going on a backpacking trip with a Natural Science Organization. About 100 miles up the freeway, people began honking and waving to them, to tell them that packs were falling off the big roof rack. They went back to salvage the packs, but in the few minutes it took them to get back, somebody had picked up the packs and they were all gone. The insurance company had to pay for replacements.

Yes, this really happened...

My best story on this topic was a guy who bought a new 1958 Ford, and a new roof rack, and a pair of new Head skis. He went on a ski trip, up to New Hampshire. UNfortunately, he lost control and rolled the car into a ravine. Rolled and ROLLED. The car was totalled. The roof rack was totalled. And the skis were totalled. Fortunately the guy was not badly hurt.

When he got home, he put his skis in a vise, and beat them with a big hammer, until they were more-or-less straight. He bent enough curvature out of them, until he was able to slide them into the box they came in. He sent this box back to Timonium Maryland, the headquarters of Head Skis, with a note: "THIS should not have happened to *these* skis."

Two weeks later, he got a box with a shiny new pair of Head skis, with a note, "We agree, THAT should not have happened to THOSE skis." In other words, they were good sports, and were willing to replace the skis, but they did not want to admit that this kind of disaster was exactly covered by their warranty.

> No matter what you do, if you have STUFF on top of your car, or in your trunk, or in the back of your pickup truck, do not let it get loose. Tie it down securely. Also, use coats, rugs, or blankets, for padding so the load is not wobbling around and lurching or falling. Pad it so the load does not harm the car, and so the edges of the car do not harm the STUFF.

◆ ◆ ◆

For that matter, as a buddy pointed out, stuff *in* your car can be very dangerous. A rally team was racing across the countryside of Australia, and they had a relatively minor accident at 85 mph. Unfortunately, the driver and co-driver were killed. The crash alone, they would have survived. But they had so many replacement parts in the back of the car, they were killed by flying parts, despite rally rules that all spare parts had to be lashed down. So, try to avoid large, heavy, dangerous loads. If you can tie it down, you should. Even if you can't tie it down, you still should. I think Volvos are one of the few makes of car that provide good tie-down points for cargo in their station wagons. Good for them. And when you have a heavy load, drive more slowly, and brake early.

A friend of mine said she never had an accident, except for one time when she had some flowers on the passenger seat. She had to put on her brakes hard. The flowers began to slide and lurch forward. She reached out her hand to catch them – and lost control and crunched her car.

> So her advice is, if there is something *big* or *awkward* or *valuable* in your front seat, tie it down, or put a seat belt on it – so it won't flop around when you put the brakes on. Or, put it on the floor in front of the seat. You could slide the seat forward to help pin it in place. Sometimes the smaller area of the floor behind the front seat is better so items can be wedged in securely.

Obstructed Visibility?

If you have a lot of STUFF in your car, it may obstruct your view through your rear-view mirror. If you open your trunk to put a large object in there, that is likely to obscure the view, unless you are able to pull the lid almost closed. (String or tape or "bungee cords" may help.)

> In the case of obstructed visibility, try to get a passenger to help you watch out for traffic on your right, so he can tell you when it is safe to pull over to the right. That's even better than a right-hand mirror (which many cars do not have). Or, if you don't have a spare pair of eyes, and you can't see what's back there, just stay in the right-hand lane, and don't do any passing.

Proper Balance

As I mention in the Appendix on Flying, a plane can become quite unstable and can crash if it is too tail-heavy. That reminded me that cars, too, can be unstable if loaded with too much weight in the rear. Try to load a heavy load so the weight is not all in the trunk. If the car is still squirrelly or not stable, go slow. Maybe a little more air in the rear tires will help; check your Owner's Manual for advice. At least make sure your tires are not *under*-inflated.

If you rent a trailer, there are reminders to NOT load all the weight on the back of the trailer, but put more than half of it ahead of the axle. Otherwise, the trailer can get very squirrelly and hard to control. This applies to loads on pickups, too.

Don't Lose Your Load

Maybe your state does not yet have regulations on this, but in just the last couple years, California laws require any animals in the back of a pickup truck must be tied down, so they cannot fall over the edge. Makes good sense to me. Since human beings are animals, maybe they ought to be strapped in, too, for their own good, but the law was not written that way. Also, most states require that any material loaded on a truck must not fall off and scatter across the road. There are two exceptions – one is a feather, from a truckload of chickens. The other is – a drop of water – ?? It sure ain't a match or a cigarette butt.

– As I mentioned back in Chapter 3 (Vision), be sure to remove all the snow from the top of your car before you go out on the highway. Campers and trucks, too. Don't dump a load of snow onto the car behind you!

Twenty-five years ago, gravel trucks in Massachusetts did not have to be covered. One day a large boulder fell off the top of a full load of a gravel truck. It bounced and landed on the head of a woman in a sports car, who was driving beside the truck. She remained in a coma for months before she died. Meanwhile the legislators of Massachusetts were so incensed, they passed a law requiring gravel trucks to be covered by a tarp. Now all gravel trucks are covered. Good idea. Keep *your* loads secured properly, too.

I am not responsible, nor am I liable, for any driving mistakes you make because of anything I wrote here – or any advice that I do NOT give. Whatever

Chapter 20. DRUGS – And Booze

....

- First of all, there are "legal drugs", such as nicotine, caffeine, and alcohol.

- Then there are medical drugs such as antihistamines, aspirin, or Quaaludes. Some of these are prescribed, and some are "over-the-counter" drugs.

- Then there "illegal" drugs, including such mild drugs as marijuana, and also stronger drugs such as hashish, cocaine, "crack" cocaine, heroin, angel dust, and other synthesized mood-altering drugs.

- Let's also throw in comments on pills such as benzedrine, "uppers", and "downers", which people use for mood-changing and stimulants.

– Every person is different, and the effect of drugs on each person can be VERY different. But the general law is, whatever drug you take, if it makes you feel strange, then you probably shouldn't be driving. Yet a major reason why people take drugs, is to feel strange. I'm not going to preach. But there are some general rules I think I can pass along.

1. If you start feeling weird, try to avoid driving. Avoid getting into these situations where you just about have to drive. Select a designated driver, and make sure he stays sober. Let him drive.

2. If you are trying to drink a cup of coffee to help stay awake, or smoke a cigarette, that is a well-known kind of *stimulant.* Everybody knows that if you are a little tired or bored, a cup of coffee can help you be more alert. BUT, if you are really tired, and are relying on another cup of coffee to get you through the night, that coffee is just a "bandaid"* and the coffee will not REALLY keep you safely awake for very long.

Sometimes, a short stop and a little water to wash your face can help you keep refreshed and awake. Sometimes a short walk is a good break. Sometimes turning on the radio or a tape can help keep you alert and awake. But sometimes a 10-minute nap is the better solution.

A month ago, I was coming down from a hike, and I felt really crummy, because there was so much pollen that my nose was clogged, and my eyes were very itchy. And I was feeling SO sleepy, it was NOT gonna be safe for me to get out on the freeway. I pulled over and took a nap. 15 minutes later, I was really surprisingly refreshed. Could I have made it with a cup of coffee or a cigarette for stimulation? Maybe, but the nap was probably better. An antihistamine pill might have made my eyes less itchy and swollen – but antihistamines make you even more sleepy! That would have been a lousy idea!!

178 *Bandaid is a registered Trade-Mark of the Johnson & Johnson company.*

It's American lore that some truck drivers take "Uppers" or Bennies (Benzedrine) or similar stimulants to stay awake on long runs. I wish they didn't, because some of these pills can turn you into a Zombie. You are awake – but you aren't. Your eyes are open – but are you seeing anything? If a dangerous situation happens, can you react? Anyhow, most of these pills are illegal for drivers to use, and probably a really bad idea, and I have to agree that the authorities are correct to condemn their use. I sure hope you can avoid them. Especially while you are driving.

But, if a cup of java makes you feel alert enough to make the last 50 miles home, and you think it will, then maybe that is a good idea. (But a nap might be better.)

Booze... Alcohol

I once saw a movie, that showed some people who took some fairly large, controlled amount of booze – about 6 drinks, I think. And then they went out to drive on a course marked with cones on a parking lot. They drove like madmen!! They whooped and hollered and slurred and staggered. They skidded and spun and knocked over cones. So this film proved that if you had a few drinks, you would drive along a street like a madman, and hit pedestrians on either side of the street, and knock over lamp-posts and stop signs. So, you should not drink and drive....

This was one of these propaganda films, that was intended to tell you why you should not drink and drive. It was insulting. It was bizarre, and counter-productive. I know a number of people who drink more than one drink, more than 2, more than 4 – and sometimes, alas, more than 6. And they NONE OF THEM drive like that. They all tend to get a little more careful after 3 drinks. So the concept that you will drive wildly and crash into things is just an insult to our intelligence. It is unfortunate that the makers of this film chose to tell these actors to drive wildly and stupidly, after 6 drinks. Because if you had told those people to drive as if they had just come out of a bar and were trying to get home, without drawing attention to themselves, they would have driven RATHER carefully and cautiously, and most of them would not have crashed into any cones, even if they did have to slow down to do it.

It was unfortunate that this film was made. It was counter-productive. Because any person can say, "Hey, last weekend I had 5 beers at a picnic, and I KNOW I do not drive like THAT when I am feeling high". So they think they are safe to drive after 5 beers. And THAT is not true, either.

I would like to recommend against that thinking – that you are safe to drive after you have had 5 beers, even though a propaganda movie might make you all pissed off. The movies are wrong, but if you just think you can drink and drive, YOU are wrong, too.

First of all, alcohol is a very insidious, sneaky drug. If you are taking some controlled tests, where you take a drink of alcohol, and then try to drive a specified test – such as a course of cones on a parking lot, as fast as you can – it is well known that, after one drink, most people typically can go a little *faster,* a little *better* than before that drink. And after the *second* drink, you still *think* you are faster and smoother. After 3 or 4 drinks, your performance goes downhill, but your judgement is lousy, and you can't tell how sloppy you are. And these controlled experiments are supposedly a reason why you should not drink, if you are going to race in a sports-car race.

Blah. Bleah. Bullshit.

Now, if I go to a picnic and split a bottle of wine with a friend, or have a couple beers, I ALWAYS get back in my car and start racing back to my house – Right??

NO, the ability to race – or the inability – is NOT why I do not drink.

You, or I, or many other people, might react completely to different amounts of booze. I know a guy who agreed that everybody was right when they called him Ted "One Beer" Johnson. After one beer he was pretty sloppy, so he knew better than to drive – or even talk with friends, after having a beer. Other people might take 6 or 8 or 20 drinks to get to that state of sloppiness. But when you get there, that is still a bad place to be. Even if you can "hold your liquor", it is wrong.

Dumb Promises...

I remember being with a young guy named Tom. We had all had a few drinks. Tom was driving, to take us all home. And I told Tom, "If you go over 70, you should stop driving." Hey, he drove 69 mph all the way home, curves and all. Maybe we were not too bright? Maybe our thinking was – impaired? Not just Tom's – but my judgement, too. Heck, I bet Tom didn't even *see* the road all the way home – he was probably staring at the speedometer.

Can I Just Get Home??

If you can drink a few drinks, and drive home safely and cautiously, once or twice or three times, or 98 times in a row, that is NOT an argument why you should or shouldn't drive after drinking. But on the 99th time, if some kid pulls out in front of you, and if you can't even see the kid, or you can't stop, or your foot falls off the brake pedal, THAT is a reason to not drive home drunk, not even one time. Definitely not 99 times. I mean, how many times do you want to play Russian Roulette? With some kid's life? And, with your conscience?

Have you ever driven home, sort of drunk, once? It is possible that you said, afterwards, "Gee – I wonder – how did I get home last night?" Did I take the freeway? Or, did I come up the back road? Gee – I cannot even recall. But the car is in the driveway, and my shoes are in the bedroom.... I must have gotten home OK. I guess if I had to do that again, I could do it again...."

Let me recommend, don't do that. Don't do it again. You would NOT want to explain to yourself for the next 20 years, why you were stupid enough to do that again. To drive into a tree. To drive into a car, and have to recover from a wreck. To drive into a kid. One of the most painful ads I have heard was the guy who says, on the radio, "I was too drunk to see that kid, when he ran out in front of me, that night. But I will be able to close my eyes and see that boy, every day of my life." It is just not quite worth it, to have a few drinks and drive, and take the chances of hitting something very PAINFUL, and regretting it every day of the rest of your life.

Here is a tough angle, which I thought about when I started to write this book. How can I tell you, "Don't speed"? How can I tell you, "Don't drive when you are sleepy"? How can I tell you, "Don't drive when you have had a couple drinks"?

I cannot just say, you must never do that. Preaching is a bad way to tell you what to do. But I'll just try to explain. If you do something and you shouldn't have done it, you might think you can do it again. You might think you can do it again and again. Until – ooops.

If you keep on driving WHILE UNDER THE INFLUENCE OF ALCOHOL, until you get into trouble, then all you are doing is postponing the inevitable. Get into an accident, or hit a car, or hit a kid.

The Old Mr. Pitcher Circle

There was a guy who used to pitch for one of the Boston baseball teams. Let's call him Mr. Pitcher. He'd pitch 8 innings, and go into the clubhouse and have a beer. And another. After he left the park, he would go to a bar and drink with friends. After about 8 hours of drinking, he would head home, down Route 1. He would fall asleep, about 6 miles down, and his car would NOSE into the shrubs at a little rotary near Roslindale. The cops would come along and say, "Oh, there is that good old Mr. Pitcher again", and pack him up and cart him home. Well, those cops were not exactly doing him a favor. Even if the Ballclub needed every good pitcher they could get. Meanwhile, for many years, that little traffic circle was known as "Mr. Pitcher Circle", because it was the same circle every time, at the end of a long straight stretch, that collected poor, sleepy, drunken Mr. Pitcher.

I do not know if Mr. Pitcher is still alive, or if he ever got into any serious accident. Surely we cannot print bad things about a person. But I wanted to show that at various times, driving under the influence of alcohol, or Driving While Intoxicated (DWI) has been treated like a joke. This book is NOT gonna solve the problem. But I want to point you in the right direction.

A Better Solution...

I recommend: get yourself a Designated Driver. I really don't care how many drinks you have – that is none of my business – so long as you do not try to drive after you drink. It is NOT that hard to negotiate with ONE person who will not drink, and will stay alert and awake, and cart you and all your friends home. Even if it is inconvenient.

Reasons...

The next good reason not to drive drunk, or not to drive after drinking: If the cops see you driving sloppily, and pull over, they are likely to handcuff you, and take you into the police station. They will give you a test for alcohol. If you ask for a breath test, and you flunk it, they may ask you if you want to take another test for alcohol in the blood.

Don't be stupid. If you failed the breath test, you will probably fail the blood test by an even worse margin. The blood test is the legal standard. Recently, that standard in California was tightened from 0.10% of alcohol in the blood, to 0.08%. Probably a good idea. If the breath test says you fail at the 0.09% level, the blood test will probably fail you at the 0.12% level. So, if you are just a *little bit* drunk, you can take a re-test, and that will PROVE you were *really* drunk. So maybe the re-test will be a bad idea.

If you decide to not allow the police to take any alcohol test, you are likely to lose your license for some months. It may be different in your state. But pretending you are stupid, and refusing to give a few drops of blood, is *not* a great idea.

After they sober you up, and let you out of the drunk-tank, then the worries begin. Will your Insurance Company find out? Will they double your insurance rates? (I don't know ANYBODY who wants to have their automobile insurance rates doubled – but it can happen.) Will they try to cancel you as a bad risk? Assign you to a Bad Risk pool? Gee, that is a lot of fun. Maybe you should have thought of this before you decided you could make it home, after just 4 or 6 or 7 drinks....

Anyhow, I apologize for sounding preachy, but there are some stories that have to get told, and I have to explain to you, the most rational reasons for not driving drunk – – and the best reasons for not driving after *only* 2 beers, or *only* 4 whiskeys, or *only* 6 glasses of gin-and-tonic – which is the time your own reasoning processes are the most likely to be impaired.

A Public Demonstration...

Ginny Prior was a broadcaster on KYA radio. One time, around New-Year's time, they got Ginny to do a public service. She would start announcing her radio show, with news and music, and take a drink every 15 minutes. For the first hour, she was every bit as charming and bubbly as usual. Then, going into the second hour, she was really getting in bad shape, slurring and slobbering. I respect her for having the guts to go on the air, and explain why, "if you drink like I am doing, don't go out on the road." She had guests from the Highway Patrol, to talk with and explain this drinking problem – that people think they are OK to drive – when they are not. And they had another Disc Jockey, Gene Nelson, to act as co-host on the show, to make sure she did not fall off her chair and get hurt. She had a good sense of humor.

For years after that, every once in a while, Gene would talk with Ginny and remind her of how she had done such a good job of drinking her breakfast that day. The next time you are going to drink a lot – think about how much fun it would be, to be doing your job, and to get higher and sillier, and be on the radio. Then you go out to your car, and pull out onto the road – and try to explain to the cop why you keep a-falling down, and slurring. It was amusing when Ginny did it, because we knew the Highway Patrol guys were going to be very nice to her – and drive her home after her show.

For the rest of us – well – just get yourself your own designated driver. If you don't, you might have a cop give you a lift, when you did not want it. And, perhaps to a place you did not want to go to. Now, alcohol is a drug. And, more or less, it is a legal drug. But if you over-do it, and try to drive, it is a pretty bad and illegal drug. And its effects are well known. It can be a lot stronger than other illegal drugs.

Legal Penalties...

Additionally, if you are arrested for driving while drunk, that is prosecutable as drunk driving. But if you crashed into a car, or mowed down a fence, or even knocked over a mailbox, that is *felony* drunk driver, and the penalties are more severe. Probably different where you are, different than the laws are here. But the fines can go up to *thousands* of dollars, plus weeks in jail. Or you could lose your driver's license for *months.*

If you are driving along, sober, and a kid jumps out from behind a car, and you could not avoid hitting him, that may not be your fault. But if you are Driving Under the Influence, that can be counted as MURDER. You are likely to get locked up, even if it was the kid's own fault for jumping out in front of you, in the first place. Alcohol can turn a bad incident into a *crime.*

Marijuana

Marijuana is illegal, in most parts of the world. I have heard a lot of people argue that marijuana is not *nearly* as bad for you as most other strong drugs, not nearly as bad as alcohol, and not even as bad for you as smoking tobacco. That may be true, but it's still illegal. It is alleged that smoking marijuana makes you mellow, not aggressive. So your driving might get better. Yeah, but it is still illegal. The easiest way to not get caught smoking pot in your car is – don't smoke pot in your car. If you have to do it – do it somewhere else. Cars are easy places to be spotted with drugs.

Hard Drugs

Some drugs are quite strong, and, unlike alcohol, are illegal whether you are driving or not. A man's home may be a "castle", at least until a judge approves a search warrant. But a man's car is not legally such a good, strong, safe place to carry, or use, your drugs. Hey, it's got a lot of windows! A friend told me he often sees a police car ease up into the blind spot of another car, and watch it for a mile or two. I've almost never seen that, but I suppose it could happen. Personally, I never let *anybody* get into my blind spot and stay there. But if I were using some illegal stuff, that sure would be an un-nerving thought!

I wonder what would happen if I were smoking some illegal drug, and a cop pulled me over, and I just rolled up my windows and refused to communicate. I'm sure they would bring in a locksmith and open up the car, shortly. I don't think it would be a very good tactic....

Stimulants

I am not very knowledgeable about stimulants such as benzedrine or ephedrine that some drivers take, as UPPERs – a drug to wake you UP and get you UP in a good mood for driving more, when you were previously very tired. I understand that they seem to work well for a while. But they do not really keep you as alert as real rest and sleep does. Further, when you have driven the trip you want to, you may be WIDE AWAKE, and you have to take DOWNERs, or depressants, so you can get to sleep. Getting into a *cycle* of UPPERs and DOWNERS does not sound like fun. And, while you are just doing it to keep awake, driving, it is still illegal, even though it may not be illegal if you are a student, trying to study. So, try to avoid that illegal stuff. Taking a nap is better.

Alternative Solutions

If you started out with good intentions, to not drink very much – and you goofed – what can you do? What if your "designated driver" got drunk?

You may be able to get your father or mother or friend to come down and drive you home. Some kids have a signed agreement, with their parents, that they will not drive home drunk, but will call up their parents, who will lug them home safely, and the parents have to promise not to complain until the next day. They can't gripe on the ride home! That sounds like a pretty good deal. I never did that with my kids, because they do not drink much, and they did not have cars until they were over 25. But it's still a good idea.

Many times if you are at a party, the host can help you. I know a couple people who run big parties, and the invitation suggests that you should bring your sleeping bag, so if you get really sleepy or Under the Influence, you don't have to drive home. THERE is a thoughtful host.

You could take a cab. If there is no cab, you might phone for a limo. Expensive, but if there are no cabs, it might be a good investment. If there is public transportation, you could take a bus. Or a train. Admittedly, that is not applicable in most cases. Maybe your host would rather drive you home, than keep you around the house. Maybe another guest can get you home, or get you to a place where public transport does work. Maybe a hotel or motel. Sleep is one of the best ways to dispel too much alcohol. Conversely, a shower is one of the worst ways, because if you give a drunk a shower, all you get is a wide-awake drunk. Bad idea.

Sometimes the best solution is to find a bed, or car, and sleep it off, on private property, before you start home. Here is a TECHNICALITY: if you are sitting in your car and sleeping off a heavy dose of too much alcohol, a policeman may not be able to arrest you for drunk driving *unless* your keys are in the ignition. If the keys are in the ignition, the law will presume you have an intention to drive. So put your keys in a safe place, nowhere near the ignition. Maybe under a seat. Out of sight. But, that's a technicality.

What if you get part-way home, and you realize you feel really drowsy and drunk? Can you stop any old place? If you stopped and parked outside an all-night diner, or an all-night grocery, a cop could still come around and inquire why you are sleeping in your car. If he smells alcohol on your breath, and if your keys are in the ignition, there you go.

Take A Nap?

Can you stop at a park? If it were 5 PM, you might, but at 2 AM, cops have the responsibility of checking out people in cars, as sleeping in a car may also be illegal.

If you stop at a motel or hotel, and take a room, that is one of the few really safe, smart things you can do. That may be a really wise, cheap investment.

If you are really mostly sleepy, but maybe you had one beer, you are in a similar situation. Whereas, if you are sleepy and you *haven't* had anything to drink, sleeping at a rest stop along a highway or at an all-night restaurant, or near a gas station, is not a bad idea. The point is, if you had a few drinks, you have to be careful not to let a cop even *think* you were driving, or, planning to drive.

There are several other ideas in the Chapter on Sleepy/Bored. Read them, too. Still, being *drowsy* is really different from being *drunk*, and what you can safely do will be *different*.

Chapter 21. DISTRACTIONS...

Food In The Car – and Eating

I recall, back in 1959, we all laughed, because Ben drove his car into a telephone pole, while he was trying to eat a submarine sandwich. Now, submarine sandwiches were new in those days, and their dangers were not well known. Ben was driving along, trying to eat the sandwich, and a piece of tomato started to dangle down from the sandwich. Ben drove along with his left hand on the wheel, and held the sandwich 'WAY up high with his right hand – and cocked his head up, to try to bite that piece of dangling tomato. And he went off the road and hit the pole. I mean, if you think it is easy to try to take a bite of dangling tomato, while you are trying to watch where you are driving – it's not easy to do it right. It's POSSIBLE – but not easy.

At the time we thought that was funny. But the more I thought about it, the less funny it was. First of all, it was stupid. Ben did NOT have to take his eyes off the road. But he thought he could get away with it for a short time. The sandwich was just about the sloppiest kind of food you would dare to try to eat in a car. But he was a cocky guy, and he thought he could eat on the road, because he was in a hurry.

Well, his ribs hurt for months. He lost a good car. His insurance bills went up. People laughed at him for a LONG time. And MY insurance bills went up, too, because when one guy has an accident, everybody in town has to pay. So, no, I do NOT think it was very funny. But, maybe if we all learn from it, the cost was not too excessive.

Coffee? HOT Coffee?

How many ways are there to get in trouble, trying to eat while driving? Lots of them. For example, consider the woman who sued McDonald's for 2.7 million dollars because she put a cup of hot coffee between her legs – and it spilled – and it was HOT. Well, I don't know what she expected, but I hope she is condemned to drink luke-warm, room-temperature coffee, the rest of her life. I will not even comment on the legal aspects. But I will say, that there is one thing worse than trying to sip a little HOT coffee from an open paper cup, in a swaying, lurching car, and that is, trying to sip HOT coffee through a straw. When that hot coffee comes up through the straw and hits the roof of your mouth, that hurts worse, in my opinion. So, beware of hot coffee. Do not use a straw. Let it cool down. And, while it is cooling down, do NOT hold it between your legs.

◆◆◆

Plan Your Meal

Now, if you insist on driving and eating by yourself, you must plan very carefully, so all the food is convenient for your munching, and you won't have to take your eye off the road. If the road is curvy – or even if it is not – you must have a secure place so the food and drink will not slide – or slosh. You don't want to have your sandwich leap off the seat and spread itself all over the floor, just because you have to hit the brakes. If that happens, it does not taste so good....

An Accomplice

Or if you have a passenger, that person can pass you the food – "Nancy, please gimme one more cookie." ALSO, that person must be prepared to take the food BACK. "Nancy, take this shake BACK" – or, "Nancy, *hold THIS*" – in case you get into a sticky traffic situation. You should also keep plenty of paper towels handy in the car, so if you do plunge your fingers into the sauce, you won't be a sticky mess, and you won't drive off the road, trying to un-stick the steering wheel. Always keep a big roll of paper towels in the car – for greasy food – or for greasy engine work – or for cleaning windows, or for general usage.

After you have all these plans sorted out, and if the road is clear, and you are sure you can drive safely with one hand, then, well, munch away. But, if you are going to try to eat a chunk of dangling tomato from the bottom of a sandwich – make sure you know *how to do it*, without taking your eyes off the road.

◆ ◆ ◆

The Radio

The next topic is the radio. Push-button radios, as introduced 50 years ago, have been quite valuable in letting you change stations without distracting your eyes from the road. But new, modern computerized radios have so many weird features that you have to look at them to see what is going on. The controls are all different. The sequencers on the SEARCH button are STRANGE. Every manufacturer's radio is STRANGE, but a little differently, so if you rent different cars, you can assume that you cannot figure out how to run it. It's enough to make you want to go back to a tuning knob – which some radios are bringing back. Hell, *looking at* the radio is not enough – you have to stop and read the instruction book, before you get even some basic functions to work. One of my friends had her car totalled by some foolish guy who was trying to figure out how to work his radio.

Tape Players

If you are out where the radio does not pull in a good station, you may enjoy your tape player. But sometimes the controls for that are not entirely familiar. If you have to fiddle with a control, slow down or better yet, stop. Or peek at the thing when there is nobody else on the road.

Just 10 years ago, a young woman was driving along, and she wanted to get some tapes from a pile on the back seat. She reached back, just as she was going to pass several bicyclists. UNfortunately, she veered to the right and hit 3 of the bicyclists. Two were killed and one was crippled. She sure did pick a bad time to veer off the road. If you are going to get distracted, do it when you are not right in conflict with other cars or bicycles or guard rails or rocks or ice. Got the idea?

Cellular Phones

I see a car cruising along a highway, and the driver is talking on the phone. Sometimes the driver is going fast. Sometimes slow. But usually the driver is pretty careful. I mean, it's usually not a hard task to drive safely on the freeway.

But what if you have to write down some notes? While holding onto the phone and driving, too? I won't say that is really very hard, but you have to be very careful not to get too distracted, just in case traffic gets weird. The portable cellular phone has great potential as a safety feature, as the driver can report a dangerous condition. Like the old CB radio, only better. But you still have to be careful not to get distracted.

Recent studies indicate that using a cellular phone can increase your chances of having an accident by a factor of 4. Now, if you are rolling on an empty highway, $4 \times 0 \cong 0$. But if you are on a crowded, busy road, a factor of 4 is just what you don't need. It might be better to park, and then make your call.

Other people have noted that a driver whose blood alcohol level is up near the "legally drunk" level of 0.08 or 0.10% is also 4x as likely to have an accident. Nobody should drink that much, and drive. Yet cellular phones are *different*, eh?

◆ ◆ ◆

Rodney... and Helen...

Next, I will insert an excerpt from a book.* The setting is in 1944....

> She was a honey, all right, Helen was, he thought. But if he didn't get to her tonight, he was going to tell her to go blow. There were too many other girls eager to hook up with a good steady civilian, one with plenty of money and a decent car.

> With the idea of "getting to Helen" foremost in his mind, Rodney stopped at a liquor store on Concord's Main Street and bought another fifth of rum. Helen "just adored" rum when it was mixed with Coca-Cola. In addition to the rum, he had six pairs of black-market nylon hose in the glove compartment of his car as extra persuasion.

> "Oh, what're these!" cried Helen a few moments later as she held up the stockings.

> Levers to pry your pants off, thought Rodney, but he said, "Pretty nylons for pretty legs," and the inanity of it was lost on Helen, who had a nature as acquisitive as a squirrel's in autumn.

Reprinted with the permission of Simon & Schuster, from PEYTON PLACE by Grace Metalious. Copyright 1956 by Simon & Schuster, Inc.

All in all, the two spent a highly pleasant evening. By ten o'clock they were both feeling very rum-warmed and comradely.

"You understand me so well", purred Helen, smoothing the fingers of one of his hands with her own.

"Do I?" he asked, circling her with one arm, and resting that hand just under her breast. "Do I?" he whispered, against her cheek.

"Yes," said Helen, snuggling up to him. "You understand about the finer things in life. Books and music and all that."

Helen's biggest trouble, thought Rodney, was that she had seen too many movies. She tried to talk and act the way she imagined a motion picture actress would, after a hard day on the lot. His kisses left her unmoved if they were not of the expert, no-noses-bumped variety. Too bad, thought Rodney, that they had not yet begun to make the sexual act a part of every motion picture, for then Helen would have fallen into his hands like an overripe grape. He sighed and thought of the girls he had known, who had not been movie fans. Getting to Helen, he was afraid, was going to be a long, hard process, and he was not at all sure that the game was going to be worth the candle, as someone or other had put it.

"Hm-m," murmured Helen, against him. "We go together like peaches and cream."

"Ham and eggs," he said, beginning to massage her breast with his hand.

"Pie and ice cream," she giggled, moving a little under his touch.

"Hot dogs and football games," said Rodney, putting his other hand on her thigh.

"Speaking of hot dogs," said Helen, jumping up, "I'm hungry. Let's go get something to eat."

And that, thought Rodney, was that. He'd buy her a goddamned hot dog, a dozen if she wanted, but he was goddamned if he was going to bother with her again after tonight.

Helen giggled all the way down the stairs from her apartment to the car, and she giggled nerve-rackingly as Rodney drove to a drive-in a short way outside of the city. He did not speak.

"Oh, honey," giggled Helen, chewing the last of her hot dog. "Is my little old honey mad at poor little me?"

Unaccountably, Rodney thought, he was thinking of Betty Anderson. He could almost hear those same words coming from a contrite Betty on a summer night of long ago.

"I guess not," he said, and again he had the eerie feeling of having spoken those words before.

"Don't you be mad at me, doll," whispered Helen. "I'll be good to you. Just take me back to the apartment, and I'll show you how good I can be. I'll be the best you ever had, baby, just wait and see."

Playing at hard to get, in his turn, Rodney looked down at her and smiled. "How do I know?" he asked.

And then Helen did the most exciting thing that Rodney had ever seen in all his twenty-one years. Right there in the car, with the lights of the drive-in shining all around them, and people sitting in cars not six feet away from them on either side, Helen unbuttoned her blouse and showed him one perfect breast.

"Look at that," she said, cupping her breast with her hand, "no bra. I've got the hardest breasts you ever played with."

Rodney raced the car motor violently in his eagerness to be gone from the drive-in's parking lot. Helen did not rebutton her blouse, but leaned back in her seat, leaving her breast exposed. Every few seconds, she inhaled and sat up a little, running her hand sensuously over her bare skin, flicking her nipple with a snap of a fingernail. Rodney could not keep his eyes off her. She was like something that he had read about in what he termed "dirty books". He had never seen a woman so apparently enamored of her own body before, and there was something wicked, forbidden, exciting about it.

"Let me," he said, reaching for her as he sped along the highway toward Concord.

She snapped her head away from him quickly. "Look out!"

It was a scream of warning, uttered too late. When Rodney recovered enough to look up, the brightly-lit trailer truck seemed to be right on top of him.

◆ ◆ ◆

– You want a *distraction?* I'll show you some *distraction.* Obviously, there are many kinds of sexual distraction. I'm not going to tell you what to not do in a car, but you had better not let yourself get *distracted* like that. My father used to have a saying, that driving and paying attention to a woman are each two-hand, full-time jobs, and you should not insult either task, by trying to do either one in a one-handed way. When you are gonna do ONE, you should do it right. When you try to split the difference, you can get into a problem like Rodney did.

Ah – yes, and who was Rodney? He was the mill-owner's spoiled son, in *Peyton Place,* by Grace Metalious. Yes, that was a pretty *racy* book when it came out in

1957. You must admit, it is a pretty good argument for not splitting your attention. Otherwise, your car might get split by a trailer truck – or a snow-plow.

Hey, *RODNEY!* You just CANNOT take your eyes off the road like that. Now, if you think you can caress a woman while NOT taking your eyes off the road – can you do that properly, and do justice to both tasks? You figure it out, for yourself. As for me, I think I'm better off, parking somewhere.

Before I consider this Chapter complete, I will add a few comments to "Helen". I mean, *HELEN,* it is not exactly in the best interest of your health, to DISTRACT old Rodney that way. If you want to get home in one piece, stop being so distracting along the road. Wait till he turns off the key, OK? And also, Helen, remember the old saying, "Accidents don't just HAPPEN – People cause Accidents"? Well, Helen, remember, "Accidents cause People, too."

Note, I sent this chapter FIRST to a friend who had his car smashed by an idiot in a pickup truck. He suspected that the idiot was paying attention to something else other than the road – such as, the two girls in the front seat with him....

◆ ◆ ◆

Smoking

Smoking cigarettes is not a great habit. But some people do it in their car, on a long trip, because nicotine can help you keep awake and alert. Tobacco is partly a drug, and partly a stimulant – but also partly a distraction.

Be sure you do not drive dangerously, or swerve out of the middle of your lane, or take your eyes off the road, when you are lighting up. And be careful not to set the car on fire when stubbing out your butt.

One of my buddies told me about a driver/smoker who had a lit cigarette dangling from his lips. He felt it slipping from his lips, so he quickly reached up to catch the cigarette, but ended up stuffing the lit end up his nose. As reported, he never saw the truck he hit.

Sneezes

One other problem is when you have to sneeze. When you *have to* sneeze, you *have to*. There is not much you can do to prevent a sneeze. But you can be careful, to perhaps slow down a little, if you are on a fast or scary road. And plan to open your eyes QUICKLY after the sneeze is over. When I am not driving, I usually close my eyes *early* before a sneeze, and wait 3 or 4 seconds after the sneeze, before I open them. But when I am driving, my eyes are closed for only about 2 seconds, which is not TOO bad in most cases, if you plan for it.

Bumblebees...

Wasps or Bumblebees can be very distracting when they fly in your window. You don't just want to swat at them, or get them mad. You don't just want to use your hand to try to shoo them out a window. If you have a passenger who can take a magazine or cloth and shoo them toward an open window, that's one of the better things you can do. Or, you can stop and open the window and door and let him go out. Usually this happens when you are out in the country, so it's not hard to find a safe place to stop.

I heard about a guy who was driving erratically, and a cop pulled him over. The guy tried to explain, "I was swatting at a bumblebee, officer, and I got him – see – here he is." But the policeman observed that the bee was all dried out. Apparently the guy had been carrying the dead bee around for several months, and produced the bee's carcass as an alibi for his sloppy driving. The story did not work. The guy got a ticket anyhow. "Nice try".

Scenery

When you watch out windows at the scenery, that can be very distracting. Sometimes the countryside is just so beautiful that you have to stop and take in the view. It's better, stopping, than staring away from the road so long that you drive out of your lane and scare everybody. You might slow down, if you don't want to stop. Sometimes you might want to stop and take a picture. Just be careful to get far enough off the pavement – but not too far off. Don't get stuck in a soft shoulder.

I often slow down and hold my camera or cam-corder at arm's length and just take a picture without stopping. I just sort of *point it*. But, sometimes I stop.

I like to watch old abandoned railroad roadbeds that may run beside the road. I have never run off the road, or crossed into the other lane, while staring at the roadbeds. I turn my head, back and forth between the road and the distraction, and I usually do not go more than a couple seconds without looking back at the road. Actually, if the road is wide, and straight, and empty, I may stare off to the side for 3 or 4 seconds. But if the road is NARROW or CURVY, or if there are cars coming along, I keep my viewing down toward $1/2$ or $3/4$ second.

Maps

Sometimes I want to see where the map says I am going. I love maps. So I just hold the map up over the steering wheel, and then peek down at it, for a couple seconds. But, as I mentioned in the last paragraph, I only do this when there are no curves and no cars around, and the road is wide. I do not do it on any crowded LA freeways! Usually I just let my passenger do the navigating, or I stop occasionally to check the map properly.

Whatever...

– Whatever distracts you, be careful it does not keep you from paying attention to traffic conditions, brake lights, and such. Not even for a second....

Chapter 22. PASSENGERS... and their Obligations

If you have a passenger in your car, he (or she) has several main obligations. If the passenger is a grownup, he can help with planning, navigation, and watching for signs. This can be VERY helpful, depending on how complicated the roads are. He can also help watch for cars putting on their brake lights, and other strange traffic hazards.

The passenger also has an obligation to not distract the driver too much. 55 mph on the highway is NOT a good place to start smothering the driver with kisses. On the other hand, the passenger *can* help hand the driver a cookie, or a snack, or something to drink. And sometimes a little back-rub feels good, on a long drive. (This was mostly covered in the Chapter on Distractions.)

Sharing the Fun

If the passenger is a driver, it may be useful to let him drive some of the time, depending on how long a drive. Years ago, when I drove across the country, I would drive all the way – even though my wife was a pretty good driver. I was piggish. I wanted to have all the fun. After a long time, she talked me into taking turns. Perfectly reasonable. It is also safer, if that helps the driver avoid getting bored or sleepy. I recommend it.

Kids

If the passenger is a child, he still has some obligation to not goof off too much, and to stay in his seat-belt. It is not reasonable to expect a kid to never distract the driver – because that is what kids do best. Still, the driver has to know how to lay down the law to the kids. If the kids are too rambunctious, unhappy, or messy, the driver may have to stop. He may have to explain to the kids: "No more hollering (or goofing off or whatever) or we are not going anywhere." After a little while of going nowhere, the kids usually get the message, and figure out that you are serious.

If the passenger is a baby, then the driver has the obligation to strap him down safely, so he does not have to worry about the baby getting loose in case of heavy braking. Or moderate turns – or evasive action. In most states, it is required to have car seats for babies. But be sure that these baby seats are safe if you have air bags in your car. If you want to be really safe, get the opinions of *both* the car's manufacturer and the car seat's maker.

Hotter than Hot...

There is one other problem about passengers in your car. Every so often, you read about "Dog Dies In Car On 95-Degrees Day". Or, sometimes a baby will die – when left in a parked car just a few dozen minutes. The point is, a dog or a small person can survive 95-degree weather, for a couple minutes, pretty well – in the shade – but

193

a closed car sitting in the sun can get MUCH hotter than the nominal in-the-shade temperature. A dog or baby or small helpless person can overheat much faster than an adult, and overheating can cause death surprisingly quickly.

> – So – don't leave your dog – or your kid – in a closed car, with the windows closed. Especially not in the sun. Even with the windows open, sitting in the hot sun can be terribly uncomfortable. You can get a burn from just sitting on the seat-covers! So, don't fool around in the hot sun. OK?

Well, at least this was a short chapter. If I had to, I could rearrange these ideas and sprinkle each idea into another chapter, each in its best place; but this short chapter is not a terrible idea. I think I'll keep it....

Chapter 23. LANES and MULTI-LANE ROADS

These days, most of us sure see a lot of multi-lane roads. How do they work? Well, it just goes without saying, that drivers have figured out that everybody can have a lane to do what they want to. One guy can stay in the left lane and go fast, and another can slow down and angle down the exit ramp. A third guy may stay in the middle lane and not be bothered by any of the others. So, in our permissive society, that is wonderful. Everybody can do what he wants to do, and nobody has to worry about anybody else. Ah – but it is not quite that simple.

Are multi-lane superhighways always better than mere 4-lane parkways, 3-lane roads, 2-lane roads, and 1-lane roads? I sure don't think so.

The worst thing about a great wide multi-lane road is that it attracts so much traffic that it eventually gets clogged. Or, in case of one little skid or one little accident, all lanes of traffic get tied up and everybody is late getting to work. So, the advantages of a multi-lane road are not without drawbacks.

The other worst thing about these fast, open roads is that many drivers feel they can safely go as fast as they want. And they do drive fast, until some other driver makes a mistake. Then that guy who has just driven "safely" for 80 miles at 80 mph, discovers he is not going to get to mile 81 today. Every other type of road has its own advantages and disadvantages, and we'll discuss each type.

Four-lane Roads

Let's start with the basic 4-lane road, that is *not* a divided or limited-access highway. Originally these were just an extension of the main street in town. These can be, marginally, better than a 2-lane road, because you can pass a slower car, or you can slow down to make a turn and other drivers still can get by you. They can carry more traffic than a 2-lane road. But the main problem is, these old 4-lane roads *attracted* more and more traffic until they became inadequate. Crowding at rush hour or on a summer afternoon soon showed the limitations and drawbacks of the 4-lane road. If one car slows in the high-speed lane, to make a left turn, and ANY of the cars braking behind him does not have a working brake-light, then the guy behind him is likely to either hit him, or brake at the last second and get hit by the car behind *him*. If a car is trying to turn left across traffic, and he misjudges the speed of the on-coming traffic, or if his car loses power as it cuts in front of a fast on-coming car, then you get another crash. The Fenway and the Jamaicaway in Boston are old 4-lane roads still in use, and they curve and swoop and have no center median. There are also several miles of Route 2 and Route 16 on the north end of Cambridge. It's a miracle there are not more crashes, especially on snowy days, on these un-divided roads. There are not many 4-lane roads I know in California, where there are such marvelous opportunities for accidents. But, a few....

Bad Alignment...

I can name another problem with some of these old roads. The roads were laid out with the lanes aimed at each other. The passing lane of the north-bound lanes would start up, when the light went green, with their left wheels lined up with the left wheels of the south-bound lane. These cars would have to dodge each other, or else hit. There was a full 18 inches of overlap of the lanes, as Route 16 crossed Huron Avenue, on the west end of Cambridge, Mass. And there was another 14-inch overlap, on US Route 1 at Lechmere Square, in East Cambridge. It sure would be nice if the traffic engineers could align each lane, so it does not aim us right at the cars in the on-coming lane – and it would be nice if THEY were not aimed at us. But I'm sure, that's too much to ask. If they were TRYING to cause an accident, maybe they would have aimed a 32-inch overlap???? You tell me.

Then I realized, after I had written this down, I did not have to go 2500 miles just to find a place where the lanes face each other. About 80 yards up the street, at the corner of Monterey Boulevard and Plymouth in San Francisco, there is a 9-foot offset, so the lanes face each other with a huge overlap. Any driver going north or south has to veer 10 feet to the right, or else be aimed right at the opposing traffic. Actually, I think that is safer than a 20-inch or 30-inch overlap, because it is so big, you can't help but notice it. Still, it is silly, and it may cause an occasional accident, or a near miss – especially in cases of bad visibility.

Divided Highways

There are so many limitations and problems with the basic 4-lane roads that planners started making improvements. Such as, putting in broad median strips. Then, if you want to turn left, you do not just have to wait in your lane for a break in traffic. You can turn left and wait in the median – in the center island – for a break in traffic.

And if you have to cross 4 lanes of heavy traffic, you are a lot better crossing the *first* half, and then the *second* half, and you can wait in the median while you wait. If the median is only a couple feet wide, you can't wait there, but soon "parkways" were designed with 15 or 20 feet of median strip. This was not only pleasant to look at, but encouraged safer driving patterns.

Sometimes, a car waiting by the median might be nudged by other traffic, pushed out into the high-speed traffic. When a car is suddenly nudged into high-speed on-coming traffic, great harm can happen.

It was accidents of this sort that led people to discontinue undivided highways, back in the 1930s. If *you* are crossing an old road and waiting in the median, be sure to keep your foot PLANTED on the brakes. Be SURE to keep a watch that you are not edging or slipping out into traffic. That is probably the *only* thing we can do to prevent this kind of accident from happening again – aside from not driving on that type of road.

Divided Highways with Barriers

The "Worcester Turnpike" started out as just an extension of Huntington Avenue in

Boston and Boylston Street in Brookline – all the way to Worcester, in the 1930s. But while it did have some overpasses, it still had traffic lights, and access for cars to turn off at stores, streets, and houses. After a while, this became a busy commercial strip. As it was the best road into Boston from the west, it attracted really heavy traffic. Not a terribly fun road to travel, though at midnight you could roll right along, and the traffic lights were not bad. But at rush hour, just a heavy commute.

Notwithstanding these problems, this road did offer some real advancement over city streets. It was a divided highway with a guard-rail all the way down the middle. This means a minor fender-bender in the other lane will NOT throw a bunch of cars into YOUR lane. Yeah, I like *that* improvement.

The other improvement was, the use of some overpasses and "jug-handle" intersections – and virtually no left turns. This cuts down greatly on the conflict and clash at intersections – and also means nobody sits there in the left lane, blocking traffic when the light turns green. If you want to make a left turn, you turn off on a ramp to the right, and then curve left and wait for the green light, to go left. That is a "jug-handle". At some more important cross streets, they had overpasses with exit ramps, where you could ramp off and wait at a stop sign, and then turn left to cross the bridge. THIS was a real advancement in safe, smooth traffic flow, for safer driving.

Now, I was only born in 1940, so when I began wandering over these Massachusetts roads in the 1950s, I saw how they were in those days – but not how they were when first built. I have looked up these roads in old books. Boy, they were acclaimed as great roads in those days. And they were pretty good, compared to other roads which were badly laid out, and usually not even paved. There were a LOT of 2-lane gravel roads that never got paved until later in the 1930s.

Shunpiking

These days I like to drive the old Worcester Turnpike – now called Route 9 – occasionally, because it carries me to some places where I want to go. And it does not carry so much traffic any more (except at rush hour) because the parallel Massachusetts Turnpike carries most of the traffic. These old roads are still challenging and tough to drive, due to all the entering and turning traffic. And the traffic lights force you to do a lot of stop-and-go. I won't say these are really dangerous roads, but you have to be pretty careful about the strange traffic patterns. And when you get a road like that, with several long hills, on a snowy day, that can make some very challenging driving. Usually they do plow Route 9 well, and salt it and sand it heavily, so it is possible to keep safe from a fender-bender. But you need to keep a reasonable space behind the car ahead, and you have to move along slowly – and keep very alert.

NOTE: most of these old-fashioned 4-lane roads still exist – but thanks to the Interstates, these old roads are more-or-less adequate, because they do not have to carry so much traffic. Still, at rush hour, or on a busy Holiday afternoon, these old roads fill up, and can be JUST AS DANGEROUS as they ever were. In fact, they may be a little more dangerous now because most drivers are not really familiar with these ancient kinds of problems. That's where this book comes in.

Limited-Access Roads

Next let's consider the next level of improvement, the limited-access 4-lane roads. When these were pioneered in the 1930s, they were called grand names such as "Merritt Parkway", and the "Hutchinson River Parkway" from New Haven Conn to New York. Or the "Pasadena Freeway", going down from Pasadena to Los Angeles. They eliminated all left turns and all cross traffic, and all stop lights. These roads also cut all the access to businesses and houses, and to most streets, too. Thus they cut out a lot of the entering-and-turning traffic, and a lot of the traffic-light congestion. But they had some very difficult, abrupt entrance ramps, and cars were not able to accelerate and merge easily. In most places, you had to STOP and WAIT for a break in traffic, and then accelerate from a stop, to get into traffic. The cars of the '30s and '40s did not perform well, and it was not easy to accelerate and merge. And when I ran down the Merritt Parkway, 20 years ago, that was a really *lousy*, narrow, curvy old road. A real challenge for a good driver. But it has recently been completely rebuilt, and is now a pretty good modern road – safe, but boring.

When the first plans were made for Interstate Highways in the 1950s, the planners looked at these old roads, and realized they had to engineer them a lot better. So they built in long zones for acceleration and merging, and wider lanes, and easier curves, and smoother entry into curves. Most of the roads in the Interstate Highway system are consistent, adequate, safe, and reasonable to drive. But let's look at the exceptions.

Freeway Problems

When the planners decided they could EASE Route I-91's north-south traffic through Hartford, Connecticut, and ALSO Route I-84's and I-86's east-west traffic, they built some very nice main highways, with good interchanges, right on the banks of the Connecticut River. Everything went fine, until they put *cars* on the roads. You see, the one little fly in the ointment was the other roads, *such as* Route 2 and Route 44 and Route 6 and Route 5, and several major city streets. There were a LOT of different on-ramps and off-ramps in a one-mile stretch. And the planners discovered one thing they HAD NOT REALLY THOUGHT OF: There were a lot of cars getting on Route 91, and then trying to get over to a left-hand exit in about 1/4 mile. Other cars were coming in where two large roads merged together, and the cars coming in on the left side were wedging over to get off at a right-hand exit – within just a few hundred yards.

Under light traffic conditions, this interchange just requires great care and agility. Under heavy traffic, it just makes a slow, tangled mess. It tended to jam up badly, with slow weaving traffic. They called it "the Mixmaster". Now several towns have one. Seattle, I recall, and Providence's Route I-95 have zones where a LOT of cars try to angle across from a right lane to a left lane, and vice versa. Now I won't say that it is *easy* to design roads without this problem. But first the planners should study the traffic patterns, and anticipate *who* is going to want to cut across *what*. If you can avoid most left-hand exits, or places where traffic from 2 equal roads merge, that is a good idea. Of course, sometimes it would be excessively expensive to avoid a left-hand exit. So if you are driving around such places, be aware and be alert. Plan to change lanes as early as possible, if you are getting near your exit.

An Example of a Mixmaster

Just last month, we were driving across Providence, Rhode Island, trying to get from old US Route 6 on the west side of town to Route I-195 on the east, to get to Cape Cod. The first problem is that Route 6 turns into a small city street, so you have to jog a mile right to get on Rhode Island Route 195, which is not I-195. In fact, Rhode Island Route 195 does not even connect to I-195. In fact, RI Route 195 just comes to an end and you have to guess whether you want to go north or south on RI Route 10. And there didn't use to be any sign to indicate whether you might want to go north or south. (Fortunately, you can get there OK if you go either north *or* south, but you soon realize that you are not getting a lot of help from signs.) Then if you go north, you are suddenly dumped off a small, quiet road onto a ROARING Route I-95, with 4 lanes of speeding trucks in various lanes, and lots of cars at various speeds. And the first thing you see is a HUGE sign, "Route I-195, CAPE COD, LEFT LANE EXIT, 1/4 mile." – !!

We were expecting this, and we merged at speed as quickly as possible, and started cutting across the lanes of traffic. Fortunately, we KNEW this was going to happen, so we were all psyched up. My wife was driving, and I was riding shotgun, and I helped her plan for all the open spots, and we got across just fine. But a driver who was alone, or was not prepared for merging across 3 lanes in a big hurry, might have some real problems there. I am sure you have seen it, when a driver just panics, and starts cutting left despite traffic. Everybody tries to avoid a crash, which is not easy. I have seen a really unnerved driver slow down to 35 mph, or STOP in the middle of the 55 mph road, and wait for a break in traffic to open up. THERE is the reason why you have to be able to do panic stops. THERE is a good reason to not go 65 in 55 mph zones.

I was always impressed with the ramps from the George Washington Bridge, down to the old Henry Hudson Parkway, in NYC. They had exit ramps on the left AND the right, so you could get off without a wholesale lane-switch.

Other Highways

Some of the roads that are NOT Interstates, can be JUST as smooth and safe and easy to drive as any Interstate – except when they are not. They may go from straight and smooth and wide, into crummy little roads with strange traffic. You may steam around a corner and find a stack of traffic waiting at a light. Or a herd of cows. Or an accident. No matter where you are, you have to be prepared for anything, anytime.

Changing Lanes – and Merging

The major problem for beginning drivers, in thick traffic, is when they need to change lanes – to know when it is clear. They are often unsure of where they are on the road, and they are nervous about whether what they see in their mirror is believable. They are not sure if it is safe to crane their neck out the window to see if they can safely change lanes. If they look to the side too long, the car in front of them may hit the brakes, and that's one of the most common causes for a crash. Beginning drivers must be very cautious about heading into a bad jam of high-speed traffic. And, even though they know it's tricky – sometimes they have to do it.

Freeway Navigation

Another problem for *any* freeway driver, is navigation. The exits come so fast – and soon, you can forget exactly what you are looking for. Have I missed the East Topeka exit? Was I looking for the exit for Route 84, or was it 86? Is exit 6 beyond exit 5, or is it on this side of it? The most scary problems are probably on the Los Angeles Freeway system, because there are so many roads, and so many exits. And if the traffic ever gets going, there you are at 70, 6 lanes wide northbound, trying to guess whether you want the next left exit, or the next right exit. And you can't possibly look down at your map, or stop to read the map.

The first solution is to get help from your passenger, if you have one. Put him to work as a navigator. That person can read the map, read the signs, and tell you when you are getting near the correct exit. However, some passengers have no map skills, and would be worse than no help at all. You figure that out pretty fast. If you ask a person in LA, "Are you good at reading maps?", they had better KNOW. And if they hesitate, they are probably not very good at it. Still, if they can READ, they can still be of some help.

The other thing to do, if you are by yourself, is study the map before you start into this mess, and list the major freeway exits you want, and the 1 or 2 names that you will recognize, just before you get to your exit. Put this list on a clip-board, or tape it to a heavy piece of cardboard, so it won't fly around or get lost. After you go through 4 or 6 interchanges like this, you may plan to stop again, and re-check ahead for your next navigation. Even if your passenger is a non-navigator, or a kid as young as 7, he can be helpful by reading the list of exits in sequence. Of course, at night, it can be hard to read that. Turn on the map light. Or just memorize the sequence. Because if you miss your exit, sometimes it's quite a few miles before you can get off and turn around.

On the other hand, if you just passed the exit, you should NOT back up. We do see this occasionally. Sigh. Keep on going to the next exit – and check your maps before you turn back.

Merging Onto Highways

The other thing that is not easy to learn for beginners, is to accelerate and merge, when trying to enter a high-speed road. When you are just a beginner, sometimes just getting the car going is a major accomplishment. Then, just when you get going about 40, you have to accelerate to 55, and merge with the cars on your left, and shift, and not hit the car in front of you, and look in the mirror, to watch out for the car behind you – all these complicated, interacting things. I mean, if you miss your shift, on a manual transmission, you can't very well accelerate. This is one of the places where an automatic transmission is really very helpful – and especially for young or inexperienced drivers. So, you just have to plan to get all the teaching and experience you can get, and then do minimum amounts of freeway driving without a teacher or navigator, until you can get your competence and confidence up.

The major trick you have to learn is how to get your speed up right near the speed of other traffic, AND then as soon as you are right behind one car that is passing you, start merging left, right behind him, and keep accelerating until you can match his speed, a second or two behind him. So long as there is not a car *right on his tail*, or coming up *really fast*, this technique generally works very well. Thus, you have to look in your mirror or turn your head to the left, *just briefly*, to see if there is anybody in that space. Then, as SOON AS you are behind that first car, your priority is to stay off his tail. Don't get too close – but if you get too far back, somebody will fill in that space with another car. Ideally, you should be back 6 car-lengths at 60 mph. If you can get back 100 feet, (4 or 5 car-lengths) you will probably be OK. 2 seconds

If you are beginning to drive, your teacher should surely have taught you how to accelerate and merge onto a freeway. But if the busiest freeway in Missoula, Montana does not ever have heavy traffic, then perhaps the best training you can get there is pretty skimpy training for LA freeway driving. You'll just have to adapt as well as you can, when you get to LA. And either have a good car with fast, trustworthy acceleration, or be aware that you can't accelerate properly. For example, if I had to drive an old VW with a top speed of 65 mph, or a car with a sick engine, I would be VERY careful about how I wedge out into traffic.

On the other hand, you cannot just start down that ramp, and then *stop*. The guy behind you will not be expecting it. You have an extremely good chance of getting POONED in the tail. (That's a technical term.) If you think that traffic is too heavy to merge with, or your engine starts to run rough, slow down *before* you get to the merge point, so the guy behind you can see you slowing, and you can watch him slowing, too.

Hey, there are entrance ramps, and there are entrance ramps. On the old Pasadena Freeway, the merging zone was about 60 feet, after about 60 feet of acceleration zone. The better modern roads have about 8 times that much distance.

If you don't have a hot high-performance car, try another route. Some entrance ramps have a tough up-grade, and if you just pick another ramp, you may be able to select one with a down-grade, or a longer merge zone. It can make a big difference.

Merging, in General...

Sometimes two lanes are required to merge into one. Just as with your merge to get onto a highway, you have to fit in with other people. Usually they give you some warning. But if traffic is heavy, it can be quite difficult. In some areas, drivers are very polite and you all can merge, one car from the left lane and then one from the right, alternating, just like a zipper. This works best if you all match your speeds and pick a spot behind the other guy, before you have to merge. In other areas of the world, if you try to align yourself like that, some pushy guy will try to squeeze past. You have to use your own judgement. But, in merging two lanes, at least you are at roughly the same speed, so it's usually much easier than merging with a lane of fast cars as you enter a highway.

Anticipate...

Try to anticipate the need for changing lanes. If there is a slow truck in your lane, don't wait until the last second to change lanes, but merge into another lane *before* you have to hit the brakes.

Lane Etiquette

Unless you are the only car on the road, you should signal your change of lanes. (Even if you are the only guy on the road, it's still a good idea, a good habit.) Turn on your directional blinkers. Then other people can see that you are coming. Then when you get *just* into that lane, turn the blinkers off, so traffic behind you will understand that you are not going to move over 2 lanes – unless you really are trying to move over further.

Just as you ought to stay properly spaced compared to the car ahead of you, and the cars on your left or right, you should stay well-centered in your lane. A good driver can usually stay centered within 4 or 6 inches of the center of his lane. After a few months of driving, this becomes an automatic reflex, that you do without conscious thinking or worrying. You just *do it*. This should not be a matter of *paying attention* – you should just be able to stay well-centered, at all times, and not bounce off the edges of the lane. Even if your eyes stray over to the countryside, or to your instruments, or to signs along the road, your eyes are ALWAYS returning to the road and keeping track of where you are, and where you should be, and keeping you there.

Sometimes you see a driver veer gradually over to near the left edge of the lane, and later – over to the right. He has just no lane discipline. You watch this guy – you wonder – "how come this guy is drunk before NOON?? Or, is he just a really poor driver??" Pretty sad. You would not be surprised if I told you that the police will pull over a person driving like this, at any time, but especially, late at night, because that is one of the symptoms of a suspected drunk driver, or a sleepy, dangerous driver.

Crosswinds

On the other hand, if you are driving a big, heavy car with power steering, and you do not even *recognize* gusty crosswinds, you might not understand that a small car that is not holding to the exact middle of its lane may be struggling against severe crosswinds. Don't condemn the little guy, if you are simply ignoring the problem by pouring gasoline over it!! I have driven a lot of miles with heavy crosswinds. Driving all day long across the state of Kansas, working your shoulders all day long against crosswind forces, is a forbidding task. I will not ask you to feel sorry for me; I just recommend that you might want to do it once, but not very often, not for long.

A buffeting crosswind from one side is a fair challenge. For instance, my friend

Ed said that he nursed the steering-wheel on his VW Bus, by listening to the gusts in the side-vent window. Whenever he heard the wind scream, he worked harder against the steering wheel. Not a bad idea.

But when the wind hits you alternately from the left and right, those buffets are indeed tough, in any small car. A VW Beetle or Bus, with a lot of cross-section ahead of the center of gravity, is especially susceptible. Don't feel sorry for me; I knew this when I bought the cars. I don't mind working against such gusts. It just keeps me on my toes. When the wind gets *really strong*, and the gusts are *really nasty*, I may decide to slow down a little, so the wind won't blow me out of my lane.

Off-Center?

There are a couple good reasons why you may, at times, want to NOT stay centered in the middle of your lane. One is, you may wedge over to the left side of your lane, so you can see around the cars ahead of you, and keep an eye on cars 6 or 8 cars up, and watch for brake-lights. That is usually a pretty good idea.

Small junk on the Road

Another reason to move out of your lane, is to dodge junk in the road. If you see rocks, or pieces of tire, or boards with nails in them, it is reasonable to try to dodge these, if you can do it without going out of your lane, or scaring your neighbors. Refer to the Chapter on Junk on the Road. And, Yes, dodging a dog is usually worth the effort, if you can do it without endangering anybody else. (Refer to the Chapter on Reflex Response.)

Chuck-holes

Sometimes it is reasonable to dodge around chuck-holes or "pot-holes" that have been eroded in the road. It depends on how big the chuck-holes are! I know some places where there is a pattern of chuck-holes, and on this stretch of road, I have learned to first veer left a little, and then back to center, and I avoid two whole rows of pot-holes. If you drive on roads with pot-holes, you will figure out how many chuck-holes you want to dodge, and how deep of a chuck-hole you want to drive around. Then if you can do it, good. You will soon learn to recognize a BIG chuck-hole, and whether you can get around it safely and easily. The veering might make Aunt Tillie unhappy, but hitting a really deep, bone-jarring chuck-hole might also bother her, so you have to use your judgement. If you watch a little over 120 feet ahead, you may be able to recognize a chuck-hole and ease around it without a lot of lateral acceleration – not much *jerk*. If you are only looking 60 feet ahead, it will take a lot more transverse acceleration.

You Can't Stay In Your Lane If You Fall Asleep

It is hard not to get bored on a long drive – especially a long, straight road. Here in California, we have Botts Dots*, named for their inventor, Elbert Botts (1893-1962). These are little spots of ceramic or plastic, with reflectors, that will rattle your tires if

* *"Caltrans Plots to Erase Lots of Botts Dots," San Francisco* CHRONICLE, *January 18, 1997, p. D7*

you start to stray to the edge of your lane. You should not hear that very often, except when you are changing lanes on purpose. If you notice that you are drifting out of your lane – refer to the Chapter on Sleepiness, for ways to stay awake.

Recently I noticed, on the Massachusetts Turnpike, some rumble strips. If you start to get sloppy or sleepy, and you start to veer left or right off the 3 main lanes onto the shoulder, the vibration of your tires on the rough blocky pavement will alert you to your foolish error. Wake up, man! There are several other stories about sleepiness, and I have put them in their own Chapter, "Sleepy and Bored"....

Keep a Good Watch

As soon as you have learned how to stay in your lane, the next priority to learn, in general highway or freeway traffic, is to keep scanning the road ahead for problems, and likewise, keep scanning the mirror for odd things.

One of the most important parts of scanning ahead, is to watch for brake-lights up ahead. If traffic is light, just watch a couple cars ahead. If the traffic is closely spaced, the old rule says you should stay one car-length back, per 10 mph. Thus, at 60 mph, you should stay back at least 120 or 140 feet. It may be almost impossible to do this, because another car will squeeze in there!   *2 sec = 176 ft*

But, you can compensate for that by keeping an eye on the brake lights of cars 6 or 8 or 10 cars up. If any of these cars starting hitting their brakes, you should get your foot on your brakes, and touch them lightly, just in case. For full details, refer to the Chapter on Following Distance.

Blind Spots

Avoid staying in the blind-spot of another car, right behind or beside his rear wheels, on either his left or right side. That is where you do not show up well in his rear-view mirrors. He might check his mirrors and assume there is nobody there, and then make a quick lane change. Always drive out of the other car's blind spot. Get up along-side him, so he is sure to see you, even if he has *lousy* peripheral vision. (Refer to the Chapter on Vision, for more comments on peripheral vision.) Or, fall back to a safe distance behind him.

If you are changing lanes, go out of your way to avoid pulling into another car's blind spot. If you have to go into a driver's blind spot *from the side*, plan to accelerate or slow down so as to *get out of there*, soon, because if you pulled from the side, he can't guess you are there.

Likewise, don't let a car get into *your* blind spot. When you are actually ready to change lanes, it is wise (just as you start signaling) to turn your head for a quick sanity check, to make *sure* there is no car – or motorcycle – in your blind spot, or anywhere over there. If you see a car easing into your blind spot, ease off and make sure he continues to pass, so he does not stay there in your blind spot. If you didn't see a car get into your blind spot, that doesn't mean he is not there. He might have eased into it from the side.

For example:

Trap Play

There is a classical problem that occurs on a 6-lane freeway (with 3 lanes in each direction) when there are several slow drivers on a fast road. See sketch below.

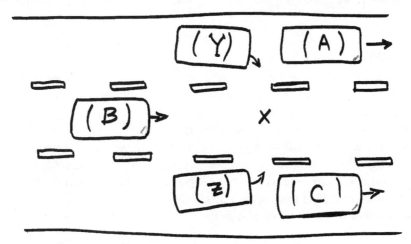

– Drivers A, B, and C are proceeding slowly toward the right side of the page at perhaps 53 mph. For a long time, A, B, and C were abreast, blocking the road – this is called a "rolling blockade". But just now, driver B has just started to fall back. This will let faster traffic past.

– Drivers Z and Y have been frustrated by these slow drivers. So when driver Y sees B falling back, as soon as the way is clear, he is going to pull RIGHT and pass.

– Likewise, driver Z is going to pull LEFT and pass, as soon as he can. And guess where drivers Y and Z CRASH? Right where x marks the spot. I have not seen this happen, but I have seen people come awfully *close*.

– So the general rule is, if you see a lane, and you think you can signal and then take that lane, be VERY careful that somebody else is not going to take it. In a case like that, ease into that lane slowly enough, so that the other guy can see that he should not make a DIVE for it. And if he *does* make a dive for it, back off and let him have it. There are times when you can be pushy, but lateral moves are a bad time, because it is hard to watch what is going on over there, yet keep properly in your own lane.

Lane Markings

Most multi-lane roads have lane markings, stripes painted between the lanes, and a big yellow stripe down the middle of the road. When the paint is new, that is *good stuff*. But what happens when the paint wears down – AND the night is dark – and the weather is rainy – how do you see that worn-out paint? It can be very hard. If you are not really sure where you are in your lane, you should probably slow down. If any or all of those conditions apply, take it easy.

One thing that can help is, Botts Dots – the little plastic or ceramic blobs, with reflectors built in. Here in California, on roads that are not in snow country, these are set in between all the lanes, along the lane-marking stripes. And the reflectors really do help you see your lane, at night. In snow country, they can't cement those onto the road, but they do have little rubberized ones that can be recessed into little gouges that are ground into the road surface, and the snowplows can go right over them.

Snow Problems

Of course, when it is really snowy, you can't exactly see where your lane is. You have to put some trust in the wheel-tracks ahead of you. I recall one time, it was snowing hard and drifting fast. One driver thought he could see his lane – and drove out across a rye field for a few hundred yards before he found his way back to the pavement. The next driver followed him, and the next. It was several days before the snow-plow opened up the road. Meanwhile, everybody took that detour across the rye field. If you really can't see where you are going – as in a white-out – you may have to stop and park. Wait until some guy comes along who really knows where he is going. Then follow him at a safe distance.

Braking On Highways

Sometimes, you have to brake just a little, out on the 4-lane, to slow down, or avoid going too fast down a hill. But other times you really have to stop hard – a panic stop, or nearly that hard. First of all, if you were watching the car ahead of you, and he hits his brakes hard – you are already in trouble. You should have been watching the cars 6 or 8 or 10 cars ahead, and when they hit their brakes, you start touching yours. At that point, you want to be *ON* your brakes, before the guy ahead of you hits his. You want to start opening up a little distance between his car and yours. You want to hit your brakes LESS HARD than he does – yet still not hit him. And you have a good start on this, if you are *ALREADY TRAVELLING SLOWER THAN HE IS*, when he hits his brakes. OK?

From there on, you just have to use your judgement. If a huge crash has taken place in front of you, you MAY have to hit your brakes as HARD AS POSSIBLE, to minimize the crash speed. Or, you may just touch the brakes and gradually slow down a little. Or, anything in between. You just have to use your judgement. But if you are studying the cars 8 and 6 cars up, and they are all hitting their brakes – you watch them, and decide how hard to brake. If they are starting to skid and weave, and you hear SHRIEKS of rubber because they are braking so hard, you may have to do the same. But you are still in good shape. You have a good chance of not hitting them, and not getting hit, yourself.

I remember one time I was coming down Route I-95 from New Hampshire. The guy ahead of me was hitting his brakes, every 20 or 30 seconds. He was *pushing* close on the tail of the car ahead of him. I guess he must have been thinking that if he pushed harder, he would get home faster. I looked at his style, and I decided I didn't like him. I decided to stay back a full 150 feet. I kept a wary eye on this guy.

Suddenly, I saw some brake lights up ahead. The guy put his brakes on, ONE MORE TIME, and he was STOPPED. If I had not been suspicious, I would have nailed him. As it was, I hit my brakes in a timely way, and got right down to 5 mph, and then I decided to roll up onto the median, onto the grass. I figured, if the car behind me was going to bump into the guy ahead of me, I was not going to stand in the way. But he did not hit the guy. I did not like this junk, so I got off at the next exit and drove down old Route 1.

Slowing Down

While panic braking is not a good idea on the highway, neither is it safe to just take your foot off the gas and slow down a lot. A guy might not notice and might hit you. Even if you ARE just slowing down, with your foot off the gas, it is wise to tap your foot on the brake pedal, 2 or 3 times, to wake up the guy behind you. Got the idea? If all lanes are slowing down, it may be safe for you to slow down in the left lane. If *you alone* are slowing down, you had better get to the right lane or the breakdown lane, and get out of other drivers' way.....

Choice of Lanes

In many kinds of traffic, it does not make much difference what lane you are in. Sometimes the left-hand lane is too fast. Sometimes it slows down more than other lanes, so it may be a loser.

And often the right-hand lane gets a LOT of merging traffic, so you are better off in a middle lane. Of course, if you cannot hold speed, for whatever reason, you should get over to the right lane, and if you cannot even hold 40 or 45, put on your emergency blinkers.

In general, don't hog the high-speed lanes, if other traffic is trying to go faster – not even if you believe you are over the speed limit. Pull over and let them go. It's *OK* to have these guys faster than you, because if there is a cop, he'll talk to them rather than to you. Don't try to enforce them to go at your speed, because it just makes them unhappy. There are more comments on choice of lanes, in the Chapter on Heavy Traffic.

55MPH Speed Limits????

Right now, somewhere on the Kansas Turnpike, somebody is getting a speeding ticket for doing 79 mph. It's a little sad, because for 20 years the road had an 80 mph speed limit. The road was designed for 80, and if everybody else were going 75, then 80 is a perfectly safe speed. So why are we limited to 55 or 65 on good high-speed roads?

- Some people say it is in the interests of safety, because the highway accident rate and death rate are lower when everybody drives 55. That is a joke, because I never see "everybody" doing 55.

- Well, other people say that the 55 mph is for economy. We will save more money on gas, if we go 55. It is true that my car will save a few dimes on a 5-hour trip if I drive 55 rather than 66. That gas I burn and the money I waste are gone forever. True. But if driving at 55 takes me another 45 minutes, the time I waste at the lower speed is also *GONE FOREVER*. Time cannot be bought nor replaced. I am willing to consider paying the extra dimes, if I get my 45 minutes back.

– Maybe it is for National Security. If we burn up all our gas at 70 mph, the OPEC countries can blackmail us. Well, gee, how come the cars in England and France are going 70 and 80, and in Germany even faster? Are they trying to get blackmailed? Meanwhile the average true cost of a gallon of gas in the US (as measured by the time you have to work to buy it) is lower than it was 10 years ago. No, it's a little hard to justify that argument.

– Let's reconsider safety. Are you really safer at 55 mph, and falling asleep, or at 70, watching in your mirror to see if you can spot a cop car back there somewhere? (Isn't it funny how that black Chevy back there has a white roof? Oops – ease your foot off the gas....)

– Wouldn't we be safer rolling at 65, with a 65 mph speed limit, watching the road instead of the rear-view mirror? Naw, the Federal Safety Nazis know what is best for us.

– No, when you think about it, the real reason for the 55 mph limit is easy to figure out. It's *Revenue Enhancement*. If we gave up the 55 mph limit, a lot of cities and towns would run out of funds. And the hypocrisy quotient would never be the same again.

Now, I am not going to talk much about high-speed driving, as that will be in the Chapter on Speeding.

Exit Ramps

Now, we have been driving along a fast highway for 20 kilobytes, up near the speed limit, and it is time to get off at the next exit. We are going to get off and cruise over to some 2-lane roads. We know it is the next exit, because we have been watching the exit signs for several minutes. We should be getting over near the right lane. Sometimes in light traffic, it is not critical what lane you are in, 1/2 mile or 1 mile before the exit. Sometimes, it takes a long time to work your way over from the left lane – especially if there are 6 or 8 lanes on your side. It all depends on traffic, and your judgement. If you are not sure, get over to the right, *early*.

Sometimes I boom along in the left lane at 60 or 65. Then when I see a little break in traffic, just before the exit, I ease off the gas and ease over to that slot, and just 100 yards before the exit, I am all ready to depart. BUT, I only do this on roads where I know the traffic patterns, and I know that if I cannot politely get into the exit lane, I will go on to the next optional exit, which will take me only a few seconds longer. I do NOT like to be pushy or wedgy about getting into my exit lane or exit ramp. Not like they drive in some places – like Long Island. I mean, if I wedged my way into the exit line, that might not cause an accident, but it might scare people, or make them angry. It's not nice to scare people, or wedge in front of people who have been waiting patiently in an exit line. As they say, "Drive Mellow".

If this ramp you are approaching is a ramp you know, or similar to ones you know, and you can see where it is going, ease on your brakes, and slow down, using your judgement. But, it's entirely too easy to slow down from 65 mph to 50, and think you are slowed down properly, and then come to a 30 mph curve. A seasoned driver is not likely to get in trouble with a ramp like that, but a beginning driver can be fooled, up to the point that he has to hit the brakes hard, to avoid skidding on a bad curve. If in doubt, check your speedometer. It's better to be a little bored, than to have to NAIL your brakes at the foot of the ramp. Some exit ramps are labeled 25 mph or 15 mph, and they ain't kidding. Then, as you approach the first intersection, slow down as required – whether it's a stop sign, YIELD, or traffic light.

If you know this is a hard ramp to brake on, and there is not too much traffic, you are justified in taking your foot off the gas before you get to the exit. And you might even touch your brakes before you are out of the travel lane. For example, on the old Pasadena Freeway, there are mostly very abrupt ramps. If I had any doubt, I would probably slow down *gradually* to 45, before leaving the travel lane, EVEN if there is a car on my tail. In fact, *especially* if there is a car on my tail, I would do that. It's better than hitting your brakes *hard*, with the car right on your tail, just before you go down the exit ramp. And that might happen, if the exit ramp was nearly full of cars!

> Caution: When you start off in ordinary traffic again, take it easy, and LOOK at your speedometer. If you had been doing 70, you might get up to 50 before you realized that you are not exactly obeying the local 30 mph speed limit. Some cops hang around in places like that, because they know they can find suckers like you, to help with their Revenue Enhancement.

Other Problems at Exit Ramps

One time I was bicycling legally along the edge of a 4-lane highway, US Route 5 in West Springfield Mass, over in the right-hand breakdown lane. I heard a whirr of air, and a *scrich* of rubber, as a guy cut right behind me, entirely too close to suit me. He went down the exit ramp, and – halfway down the ramp – he *banged* into the left-hand guard-rail – then, a bit slower, crunched into the right-hand guard rail – and stopped. The guy either had a heart attack, or he was the drunkest guy I had ever seen. I suppose these days I'd go over to investigate, but at that time, I did not want to get into a fight. Anyhow, that's one way to go down an exit ramp, completely *wrong*.

Here's another problem: Sue was driving North in the rain on a busy 8-lane freeway, US 101, in Marin County. She was in fairly heavy traffic at about 55 mph, in a middle lane, that is, lane 2 out of 4. Minding her own business. Suddenly she noticed a car in the far left lane, about 200 feet ahead of her, that suddenly hit his brakes and cut to the right, making an ill-considered dive toward an exit. UNfortunately, this car began to skid and spin. She figured she had better get on her brakes. UNfortunately, in *her* effort to avoid the other car, *her* car began to skid. She managed to miss the first skidding car, but she skidded and slid into the median guard rail, damaging her car heavily.

This is a case of trying to avoid one problem and causing another. If she had hit the first car, she probably could have been covered by the other car's insurance. But she might have been hurt. So she used her judgement and made a strenuous effort to avoid that contact – and wound up in an accident where her own insurance had to pay – a less desirable situation. Most drivers do have to make, occasionally, a quick judgement on what to do. Sometimes you are wise – or lucky. Other times you get the result that you are unwise – or unlucky. Sue had one bad piece of luck – but at least she was not hurt, and she did not crash into another car. Maybe good judgement after all – and just a bit of bad luck.

The real problem was the foolish person who decided, at the last second, to make a desperate dive for an exit. You see this, every once in a while. When somebody does this, right in front of you, you have to VERY QUICKLY recognize what is happening, and try to figure out how much effort you should make, to evade the accident. (Be sure to read the Chapter on Reflex Responses.)

Lane Usage

On Multi-lane highways, some Driver Ed teachers and some books tell you to drive in the right-hand lane. They say, only use the left-hand lanes for passing. This may have been true at some times, and it may still be true in some places. But it ain't necessarily true now.

Especially when you have more than 2 lanes in each direction, the right-hand lane is usually a *transition* lane or *merging* lane. It is often busy with people merging and getting onto the highway, and other drivers slowing down to exit. Sometimes this lane backs up and stops as it goes down the exit ramp! Kinda scary! This lane sometimes has slow trucks and slow cars in it. So it is not necessarily the best lane to drive in.

The far left lane is usually the best lane for passing and going fast. But some- times that is an exit lane, for a left-hand exit. So, if you have 4 lanes in each direction, that leaves a couple lanes in between. THESE are often the best lanes for driving.

Trucks are often permitted only in the two right-hand lanes. They are usually prohibited from the left lanes. So the lane 3rd from the right is often a better place to cruise, better than the second from the right – fewer trucks there.

These are general guidelines about where it may be best to drive. When you see a lane being used in one of these ways, you should recognize it – even if it is being used differently than the names listed here. The point is, if you are in a lane that is doing what you want to do, fine. But if the lane is not doing what you want to do, then maybe you should try a different lane. If the fast lane is slow, it may be a good lane to ease out of, carefully. If the "slow lane" is too erratic or gets too much merging traffic, try another one that may be less hectic.

When traffic is light, I sometimes get out and cruise in the far left lane, because it often has smoother pavement than other lanes on the right where the trucks have beat up the pavement.

Two-Lane Roads

There are hundreds of thousands of miles of Two-lane blacktop (and a little bit of concrete road, too.) You find the two-lane in towns and villages and cities, and in the country and the mountains. It serves us well for a lot of driving. But it does not always serve us well, if there are slow cars and fast cars and slow trucks, and lots of heavy traffic in both directions. Because it may be very hard to pass. It may be very frustrating, if a guy won't let you pass. Or if there is too much on-coming traffic to pass, or, if it is too curvy or too hilly to pass.

Here in California, there's a law that if you have collected as many as 5 cars behind you, you must pull over and let them pass. Unfortunately, some of the worst and slowest drivers never heard of this law, and even if they did, they are too stupid to notice the cars stacked up behind them, and too stupid to do what's right – PULL OVER. Often these miserable people are driving Campers or RVs (Recreational Vehicles) up in the hills, and they can collect a line of a couple dozen frustrated drivers behind them. More on this, in the Chapters on Passing and on Rude Drivers.

Of course, one of the major disadvantages of 2-lane road is that you have to be alert for the possibility that some guy will cross the center line and start to encroach on your lane. He may be asleep, he may be drunk, he may be skidding, he may be crazy. Or, he may just be turning left into his driveway. Can you stop? Or, can you get out of the way?

One night in Wilmington Mass, on old curvy Route 62, I came around a curve, and there was a car out to pass another car – coming right at me, up my lane. I could tell instantly he was not going to be through with his pass, by the time he got to me. I got my thumb on the horn, and jammed on my brakes, and spotted a good place to pull onto the shoulder. I also downshifted into 3rd, before I came to a stop, and the cars went thundering by. And I think, after I downshifted, I blinked my headlights at them, too. And the horn stayed on. I wasn't really scared, but I sure was cross at these idiots.

In retrospect, the driver who was being passed should have stopped or slowed, to let the passing car go by. But he sure didn't. Maybe he was even speeding up. I must also say, this was a pretty short passing zone, about 90 yards, and the guy being passed had probably got the other guy mad by driving slow for many miles. When he found this tiny passing zone, he just got mad and went out to pass – even though he saw my lights coming!!

Three-Lane Roads

Some 2-lane roads have a passing lane on the right – a "climbing" lane, so faster vehicles can pass slower cars and trucks – and hay wagons, which are supposed to stay on the right. So, you might say that this kind of 3-lane road is a variation on a 2-lane road.

In other places, there used to be, 40 or 50 years ago, 3-lane roads, where the center lane alternated between being for one direction to pass, and then for the other. The only problem is, just a little lapse of judgement gets TWO cars into that lane, and there were some VERY messy head-on crashes. One guy used to call that middle lane, the "HOCL" – the "Head-On Collision Lane". Or the "Suicide Lane".

To a large extent, most of those old classical 3-lane roads have been converted to 2 lanes or 4 lanes. For example, old US Route 20 between Westborough and Auburn, just south of Worcester, Mass, was a LOUSY 3-lane road. It has been converted to 2-lane. But it has been mostly bypassed by the 6-lane Mass Turnpike, and the 6-lane I-290. Thank heavens.

5-Lane Roads??

Another variation on the 3-lane road is the 5-lane road – a 4-lane street with a HOCL lane in the middle, for various left turns. On a good day, this works pretty good, whether you are making a left turn *onto* this street, or *off of* this street. We have a lot of these in Silicon Valley, such as Kifer Road, which is right out in front of National Semiconductor, where I work. It's not a bad road. But you always have to be careful that somebody is not also grabbing for that lane at the same time you are. I always edge into that lane very gradually and tentatively, about half-way, so everybody can see I want that lane, and the on-coming driver will not take that lane. I usually find light traffic on these streets. I just go out of my way not to be pushy. It's a bad place to be *pushy*.

Two-Lane Gravel

When you get down to the 2-lane gravel road, now, this is getting *interesting*. 'Most every road in this country has been a 2-lane gravel road, at one time or another. There are still HUGE stretches and networks of 2-lane gravel, across the country – in the east, the mid-west, the west. And some of these are good 55-mph roads. I enjoy cruising at 55 on these, where they are reasonably straight and smooth and wide. Of course, if you get up above 40 mph, don't keep going faster if your car starts feeling squirrelly. And be careful when you come to curves, until you know how the car will handle, going around the curve.

When you are drifting around these corners at 55, it is NOT polite to STAB your gas pedal and send gravel into the face of an on-coming car. I mean, some unpleasant people think it is FUN to break the other guy's headlights – or windshield. Not really nice. It is NOT recommended. If some guy tried it on me, he might have some problems a little further down the road.

One basic problem is traction. Gravel roads, and especially dirt roads, can be slick in wet weather, and tricky on steep upgrades, downgrades, or even sidehills. Especially if your tires are a little short on tread. Especially if there is a little *washboard* effect, when you come to a corner. Especially when wet. Especially if there are deep puddles. So don't get going too fast. And be prepared to slow down promptly, when traffic conditions call for it – such as when a car is approaching, and it's hard to be sure if there is enough room to get past. After all, there isn't any center line down the middle of a gravel road!

And if the road is not muddy, it may be dusty. Now, it's no fun to get stuck behind a car on a dusty road. Sometimes you just have to stop and take a break, if there is no way to pass that car. That's why I always like to carry along something to read, in my car, in case I want to take a break and let the other car get far ahead of me. Maybe I should open up my Hymnal and sing a couple hymns. But at least, if you are on a straight road, you can easily see any approaching car coming up the dusty road, for a long ways off.

One of the minor drawbacks of Anti-Lock Braking Systems (ABS) is that it can provide *worse* braking distance in gravel. Sometimes locking your wheels is a quicker way to stop, on a gravel road. So some ABS systems have an on-off switch, so you can turn them off for gravel conditions.

One other problem with gravel roads is, there can be a patch of sand, where you start skidding despite yourself. There is an excellent stretch of 60-mph gravel road, running from Eureka Valley down to Death Valley. But at the south end, there is a patch of very soft sand. Geez, they ought to put up a sign to warn you about that!

– And the count-down continues:

One-And-a-Half Lanes...

If there is anything worse than a 2-lane gravel road, it is probably a 1-1/2 lane road. By that I mean a road where there is sort of 2 lanes, but actually everybody drives with their left wheels right in the middle of the road. When there is no other car on the road, you can drive pretty comfortably. But when you come around a corner and you see another car coming around the corner at you, and his front wheels are aimed at the exact same place yours are – then you have to slow down and/or do some fancy dodging. Most times you make it. But it gets kind of messy if you hit the other guy – or if you spin out as you try to get over off the center-line. These *really narrow* 2-lane roads can be a little dangerous. Be sure to slow down for curves and for on-coming traffic.

One time I was surprised by a jeep that came over a hill-top. I am not sure if we just misjudged it, or whether he made a small last minute skid, as he suggested. Our mirrors kissed, BANG. No great damage, but I had to pay $30 for a new mirror. He probably had to pay $20 for his. An expensive lesson. I've never hit anybody at speed, worse than that.

One-Lane Roads

Mostly, a one-lane road is a narrow dirt road, out in the country. When there has never been enough justification (or money) to pave it, or widen it, that's what you get, from the old days of horse-and-wagons. Personally, I like driving on 1-lane roads. They are kind of fun. Especially at night, as you can convince yourself that it is safe to speed along, when no headlights are coming.

Of course, if there is a deer around that next corner, maybe I will wish I had not done that.

The major problem with old one-lane roads is on-coming traffic. Even if you see the driver coming, and look for a place to back up and move over for the other driver to squeeze through, that is not always easy. And if you come around the corner, to find the other car almost *right in your LAP*, well that is not very nice. So, unless you are driving at night (when you can see the headlights approaching) then you have to keep your speed down so you are sure you can stop quickly enough. That means, slowing down for corners if you can't see around them.

One of the other problems of 1-lane roads is, it is sometimes hard to pass a car or truck when you catch up with it. Fortunately, some drivers are very polite, and will cheerfully pull over and let you by, after a short while. But other drivers are not very perceptive, or polite. Even if you bip your horn, or turn on your lights. Or BLAST your horn, or blink your HIGH BEAMS. Anyhow, if anybody wants to pass YOU, YOU would not be so inconsiderate, would you?

When a one-lane road gets its ruts too deep, your car may start to scrape or drag its under parts on the high center part (the crown) of the road. When the dragging gets too much, you may want to drive a little left or right of center, so your wheels ride up a little onto the crown or the side. Then you won't drag so much. If the ruts get TOO deep, you may need to stop and get out your shovel and fill some dirt into the ruts. I never go anywhere without a shovel. The further out in the country you get, the more you learn about how not to get stuck in the boondocks. You have to learn to drive carefully on narrow, rutted roads. After all, it is not just your transmission that is hanging down low. It is your oil-pan – and your gas-tank. Puncture one of those, on a rock or a stick, and you may be in for a LONG walk.

Other One-Lane Roads...

Now, not every one-lane road is an old dirt road. Many times, a city street has just one lane, between parked cars. Often these are narrow, quiet streets – and with all those parked cars, it's hard to see if a kid will jump out in the middle. So, these paved 1-lane roads are not really very free of danger. The street in front of my house has one lane in each direction with a center island (plus, occasional parked cars). If you want to park, you should be careful to not block the traffic, as there's no way for other cars to get around. When the garbage truck goes down our street, people usually just detour to another street.

There is one more kind of 1-lane road – and it is FUN – the 1-lane roads of Scotland. There are hundreds of miles of these, wandering on and on across the rather barren countryside. They are almost always paved. Every couple hundred yards, there is a small passing zone – a wide spot in the road – known as a *layby*.

As I am always driving in a rented RH-drive car, with the steering-wheel on the RIGHT, I find it easy to remember to pull over to the LEFT when I come to a layby, to let the other car pass me. And if I see that a driver behind me has caught up and really wants to pass, I'll signal and pull over and just about stop, and let him by.

Sometimes you come around a corner – and there is a car – and no passing area between you. Then you just have to stop, and figure out which car has the shorter or easier distance to back up, to get back to the last layby. Everybody always tries to be polite about, which driver should back up. I mean, you wouldn't ask the driver of a trailer-truck to back up – even if he *could* do it. You wouldn't ask him to back up, because a truck's reverse gear is rather slow, and it will take more time than if *you* back up.

The real fun is when you see an on-coming car, and you are each an equal distance from the layby. Usually you can just *cruise* into it, and twitch the wheel to the left, and just tap your toe on the brakes, and ease on through without hardly slowing down. You just sort of *dodge* the car, at the wide spot. After a little practice, you get pretty good at that. Or, if you are closer to the layby, you slow down so that you get there, and out of the way, just as he comes rolling through, and you don't have to slow down very much. That's the kind of *sport* you can get, driving in northern Scotland.

Ah, but there is one baffling problem on these one-lanes. If you are backing up, you may look over your shoulder – or you may look in your rear-view mirror. But either way, as you are backing up, when you get to the layby, which way do you go to pull over and let the other driver by? I mean, there is just too much mirror effect. I cannot figure out, while looking over my shoulder, which way is LEFT or RIGHT any more. I just don't CARE any more. I just don't even TRY to figure out which way to go – I just tuck my little car into one side, and let the guy go by on the other side.

No Lanes At All

Now, if you are going to drive on anything less than one-lane roads, you are on your own. I will just caution you that driving cross-lots across fields, there can be rocks, or tree-trunks, or ditches. Or patches of soft sand. There are all sorts of problems, ways to get in trouble. You have to be REALLY careful. At any point, if you are not *SURE* about what is out there, you should stop and walk across, to make sure there are no bad surprises. Otherwise you may have to walk back to town. Also, in some areas, it is not legal to drive off roads, because wheel-tracks can damage a fragile environment. Please don't drive across those park meadows, because it looks messy, and it might be expensive if you get caught.

There's a *third* caution about driving across meadows – or even, pulling off into the weeds to park. Most cars these days have a catalytic converter, which gets rather hot. If you park with your cat converter above some dry weeds or grass, they can catch fire. Pretty embarrassing, and perhaps very expensive, if you are found guilty of starting a big fire. Or, even if you start only a *small* fire that burns up your car.... If you have to park along small roads, be *sure* to park with your cat converter over gravel or dirt.

Breakdown Lanes

By definition, the breakdown lane is a place where you are supposed to park, only for emergencies. You are not supposed to drive there, or do sight-seeing there. Except....

EXCEPT –

– Except – in some suburban areas, there are posted signs – such as the ones along the Southeast Expressway, south of Boston, Mass: "Driving in breakdown Lane Permitted 4 PM – 7 PM". It is mind-boggling, but sometimes there is such driving permitted.

Danger in the Breakdown Lane

If you did break down, you should avoid walking around in the breakdown lane, because sometimes a driver gets absentminded or sleepy, and drives down the breakdown lane. For example, it is not very smart to stand behind your car, if it is broken down, because sometimes a car will come down the breakdown lane and cut your legs off. It's safer to stand behind the guard-rail, to avoid this. You may even find it is safer to stand behind the guard rail, rather than sitting in your car, because of that thin possibility that your car may be rammed from behind. However, if it is cold or rainy, it is not realistic to expect everybody to stand behind the guard-rail, rather than wait in the car....

In many parts of the country, you can find a decent shoulder beside the road, to pull over and stop, in case of a breakdown. But sometimes you see a sign – "SOFT SHOULDER". It may be too soft to stop there. Or, "LOW SHOULDER" – the road may drop off several inches, at the edge of the pavement. Heck of a lurch. Or, in Pennsylvania, "LOW BERM" – same thing. In some parts of the world, (like Virginia) there is a deep drainage ditch beside the road. Sometimes that makes me nervous! I mean, these ditches are 3 or 4 feet deep, with almost no margin between the narrow shoulder and that ditch! So be careful about the shoulder beside the road! It may not be a safe place to drive – or even to park! – or even to walk!

Car Pool Lanes...

Here in California, we often see these Car Pool Lanes labeled as "HOV" or "High Occupancy Vehicle" Lanes. Sometimes you have to have 3 people in your car – and other times, 2 people. Sometimes you have to know what time it is. I know a guy who flies in from New York and sets his watch so he can pretend he is ignorant of the real time, and he drives his rented car right down the HOV lane. He doesn't get caught very often, and when he does, he talks his way out of it. What the heck, he's a lawyer.... I wouldn't recommend that *you* do that.

If you are rolling along legally, in a lane beside the HOV lane, and a car shies into your lane – you might have to veer into the HOV lane, to avoid an accident. But you had better ease back into the travel lanes, really soon, to avoid a cop pulling you over. Here in California, the fines START at $270, for driving down that lane, if you do not have enough people in your car. It's enough to make you want to take a couple of the neighborhood kids along, when you go on an errand.

I advise you, in the Chapter on Passing, not to pass other cars by a relative speed of more than 15 mph. In general, that's a good idea. But if there are 40 cars behind you, in a Car-Pool Lane, and the normal traffic lanes are stopped – should you go faster than 15 mph? I would find it hard to go faster than 30 or 35 mph. But I have talked with some guys who have figured out how to do 55 mph in that high-occupancy lane. If I were in that position, I think I would pull over to the left-hand breakdown lane, and let somebody else go down the lane at 55.

That's all for now, on LANES. We just ran out of LANES.

Chapter 24. INTERSECTIONS

....

Driving can be very simple when you just cruise along one road. But life sure can get complicated when you come to an intersection and have to make choices. And that is so, even if there are no other drivers around to confuse the issue.

If you know exactly where you are going, and you have memorized all the turns, then at any intersection it is a minor challenge to steer over to the correct side of the road, as you approach each intersection, and make your turns.

Do You Know Where You Want To Go??

If you have not decided where you want to go, you may have some difficult choices when you come to an intersection, deciding whether to go left or right or straight. You should make your decision in advance, if at all possible. But sometimes you can only make up your mind after you have arrived – and look at the street names. If you have to slow down like that, you may need to turn on your blinkers, and pull over, and stop. So that is one mode.

Another mode is when the signs are before the intersection. You *have to* figure out your plans before you get past the sign. Just last week, I was coming down a small street, and the signs 20 yards before the intersection told me what my choices were. I thought I knew which turn I would take. When I got to the intersection, nothing looked right, so I had to walk back 20 yards and look at the sign, before I could decide.

The week before that, I was up in some hills, and after I started down the right fork, a sign said "Narrow Road Next 10 Miles". I had to back up a couple hundred feet to see if I really wanted to be there. The sign was well before the intersection, but it was a little misleading.

Navigation...

So in the real world, just planning how to navigate, and how to choose the road you want, can be complicated. What if you *think* you want to turn right, and then decide you really want to take one of the other roads? You have to be careful to change your lane so as not to get everybody else unhappy – in case one of the people behind you is expecting you to continue to the right. And you want to plan your navigation carefully, to minimize these last-second changes. As I said in the Chapter on Lanes, if you can get one of your passengers to help with the Navigation on a Freeway, or in a city, that's a very good idea. Even if your passenger is not very good at navigating or map reading, he can be helpful by reading signs, making notes, and reading a list of which road or street you want to take next. Even a kid can be very helpful. Of course, it helps a lot if he can read! — ✗

A Standard Route...

So let's say your route today consists of a route along city streets, then some freeway driving, and then some miles out on country roads. If this is a route you do all the time, those turns will usually come naturally. You barely have to think. You know that your next turns will be left and right and left, so after your first left turn, you ease over to a right lane, so you will be in a good position to make the right turn. And after that right turn, you start getting over on the left, to facilitate your next left turn, etc.

A Tricky New Route...

However – let's say your route *tomorrow* will be quite similar, but it involves city streets that you have never been on before, and new freeways, and wandering along country roads you have never seen, to go out to a farm and pick up some special fruit basket. You have to consider that trip a little differently! You should make some plans.

Directions...

You probably need some instructions – "get off Route 77 at the Mile Hill Road Exit, turn right, take the first left onto Quinnipiac Street, and go 3.5 miles to the blue sign for Johnson Orchards." You have to be sure not to misplace those instructions! You might want to bring along a map. Then if you decided to CONTINUE along Quinnipiac Street to the next main road, the map can confirm that that is a reasonable route. Also, as I mentioned in my CHECKLISTS, you might bring the phone number of the people you are going to see, in case you get lost. In other words, planning a little jaunt of this type is not trivial. Because you KNOW that one little slip, one false turn, can get you lost and waste a lot of time. So, planning the route and the intersections can be pretty fun and challenging.

If you are not an experienced driver, you can be confused by odd traffic patterns, and strange intersections. This does not mean you should not go on strange roads – it just means that when you are travelling on strange roads, be careful and be alert for intersecting things. And be especially alert when you come into intersections. Taking trips into strange places is part of your education.

Intersections *with* Traffic Added!

Now let's consider these trips with traffic added. When there is a lot of other traffic – or even just a little – that makes your trip VERY INTERESTING. You KNOW which streets you want, and you KNOW exactly where you are going. But there are other drivers, and some of them get in the way. You may want to get in a left-turn lane. As soon as you can get in the left-turn lane, you can *easily* make your left turn – but there are several cars in that left-hand lane – so you have to wait and plan, to merge into that left-turn lane. Life gets very complicated. Sometimes it is fun, and other times it can be *frustrating* if it is really hard to get into that left-turn lane. You have to plan, and you have to be patient, because if you try to force your way, and the other guy does not want to give you the lane, or if he is not noticing, an accident could happen. So be reasonable and patient.

Planning...

So a lot of driving involves the planning and the give-and-take of negotiating through the other traffic, and getting to your intersection, and flowing smoothly with the other traffic, and not getting mad, and not getting other drivers mad at you. It is really an art. That is a lot of the challenge and the fun of driving. When you were a kid, growing up, if you often went on trips with your mother or father, as I did, you realize that every trip requires the appropriate amount of planning. If you were just going a mile to visit a neighbor, not a big deal.

But if you are going to drive 10 miles into town, you will plan all your errands so you can get everything done in one trip. You line up all your ducks and shoot 'most all the ducks with one bullet. You try to plan things reasonably efficiently. You are also likely to plan so that you do not take the worst roads, or have to go through the worst intersections, nor at the wrong time. I mean, a trip that takes 20 minutes, at noon, can take over an hour, if you try to go at rush hour. And if you pick the wrong intersection, that can waste 2 or 4 minutes right there. I often plan my cross-city trips just to avoid certain messy intersections. There are some routes that I often take SOUTH across San Francisco, that I almost never take NORTH, because the routes work better one way than the other. Seventh Street, for example, has 2 lanes south-bound, and one lane north-bound, and the lights are all synchronized to help south-bound traffic. So I rarely take 7th Street northbound.

Cross-country Trips in England

I remember a very enjoyable drive across London one evening – I had to pick up a package to bring to somebody. If I had tried to do this in the daytime, it would have taken HOURS. And I would not have made the trip. And if I hadda go in the daytime, I would not have enjoyed it. But I decided to go about 11 PM, and it was a very enjoyable trip, as there was very little traffic, and the frustration of getting stuck behind a slow truck on a fast road was just GONE. We ZAPPED along the main roads, and slowed briefly for roundabouts, and had a great trip on the challenging secondary roads of England.

Back to that Tricky Route...

Now, let's think about the "second kind of trip" – that trip you have never done before. You have to fight your way through some traffic to get on the freeway. Then you HOPE there is not a lot of stop-and-go traffic on the freeway. Then you HOPE there are not too many slow cars or trucks on Quinnipiac Street. And if you want to stop and read your map, you HOPE there is not a big truck on your tail, when you want to pull over and stop. So, again, added traffic can make any familiar trip challenging – or miserable. And for a new trip in unknown territory, the challenge can be much greater. It can even be dangerous.

Let's say you remember that you want to do a left, right, left turn. But after the left turn, there is a sign, "Quinnipiac Commons, Next Right". Hey, you try to get over from the left lane to the right – and some car blares his horn at you, because you were trying to cut into his path. At least he did not crash into you. But it can be unnerving and upsetting, to try to get across these lanes – and realize – hey –

Quinnipiac Commons is just a stupid housing development. You are not going to go *there*. It is Quinnipiac *Street* that you want. So the need to wedge across the lanes of traffic was perhaps – unnecessary? Maybe so. I think I will not write a lot more about this. But just remember – when you are on the road, anything may happen. 7,000 people may just decide to go down Quinnipiac Street, to the back entrance to the rock concert! That street might be closed. Or the farmer might be bringing his cows across the road. Wishing for the cows to hurry is not a very useful kind of worrying.

Let's get back more into the intersection business. If everybody KNOWS which direction they want to go, at every intersection, then you all line up and take turns. The guys turning left have to wait for oncoming traffic. The guys turning right can ease through. The guys going straight across may have to stop, but at least the way is clear. BUT, how about other factors? Poor visibility. Rain. Darkness. It all adds up to this: that intersections are really pretty dangerous. Even if you are very careful, they can be potentially dangerous.

Dangerous Interactions

The US Air Force once ran some surveys, on why their pilots were having accidents. What was the leading cause? Take-offs? Bad landings? Engine failures? No. It was car crashes at intersections. The Air Force had every possible safety procedure for flying. But when these hot pilots got out of their RATHER SAFE flying environment, and climbed into their cars, hey, they just had every kind of accident.

I am not going to belabor this, and list 877 things to do to avoid accidents at intersections. I am not even going to tell you that 41% of all car accidents happen at intersections. Hey, did you know that 47% of all these statistical things that people put in books, are just made up out of people's heads, anyhow? Well, in this book, 100% of all statistics are made up out of my head.

But I do want to remind you that there are a LOT of dangerous things about intersections, and there are some precautions. First of all, one of the most important things about intersections is, that when you get on a superhighway or freeway, there are NOT any left turns, no turns across traffic. It's true that you gotta merge, and then to branch off, but the primary reason for these freeways is,

NO LEFT TURNS ACROSS ONCOMING TRAFFIC .

Left Turns

So when you are on any ordinary road, and you have to turn left across traffic, you know by now that can be very dangerous. If you have to cut through a break in traffic, and you misjudge, or if your car loses power, and the other guy neglects to hit the brakes, CRUNCHO. OR, if you do not see the other guy coming, or if he does not see *you,* again, cruncho. You can get killed or badly hurt, and this left-turn stuff is a major cause. Another thing that is nearly as bad, is to slow down or stop, in the middle of the road, planning to make your left turn, and get hit from behind.

Example: Sue was driving along in city traffic, and came to an intersection where she wanted to turn left. She waited there in the left-turn lane, for several seconds.

Suddenly, she felt a BAM-BAM. She had suddenly, inexplicably been hit from behind – *and also* from in front.

In review, the problem was simple: She sat in the left-turn lane, and as she waited for a break in traffic, she cut her wheels to the left. When some sloppy driver came up behind her and hit her, her car then was pushed into the oncoming traffic stream – and she had no chance not to not be hit by one of the oncoming cars. It's bad enough to be rear-ended by some dummy who forgets to stop – but it's even worse to be forced into oncoming traffic. Fortunately, she was not badly hurt, but the car was heavily damaged. Expensive.

AND, some good books on driving DO tell you about the danger of sitting in the left-hand turn lane with your wheels cut, for exactly that reason. So, it may be a good idea to consciously leave your wheels set straight ahead.

Cut Your Wheels The Right Way...

On the other hand, I have talked with a guy who says *he* stops, in city traffic, with his wheels cut RIGHT, and his car in reverse. If some thug comes up to his window, and points a gun at him, he figures he can tromp on the gas, and run over the guy with his front wheel. I am not recommending this strategy to everybody, but it's an example of how people do plan what to do if something unexpected happens. Maybe that guy *expected* to have a mugger show up....

In Sue's case, if she happened to have her foot on the brakes, HARD, maybe the car would not have lurched so far forward. So that is one advantage for having power brakes that only take a small amount of pressure.... Still, that's a marginal advantage.

Or, let's look at this way: if you have an old car *without* power steering, and you cut your wheels left before you stop, that's one way to plan your turn carefully – but it is also one way to NOT avoid trouble. If you were not such a cheapskate, and if you bought a decent car with power steering, you could stop with your wheels pointed straight ahead. Then when the traffic gets clear, you can easily turn the wheels at the last second, and make your turn. So, can one argue that Power Steering is a safety feature? Yes, in some cases, and, depending on how you drive, it is a fair statement that power steering can be an anti-safety feature, if you do a lot of driving on snowy roads. We discussed power steering in Chapter 11, Steering.

Can You Avoid Left Turns?

Anyhow, there are 1000 things that can go wrong with a left turn. It is often worth the effort, to plan your route, to avoid left turns. When I am on a busy road, and the oncoming traffic is really bunchy, I will sometimes go PAST my left turn, and drive along waiting for a break in traffic. Then I'll turn left into a store, or another road, and then come back, so I can get to my road and turn RIGHT onto it. Sometimes the left turn situation, at a traffic light, is so messy, I'll turn RIGHT, and go down the side road, and then make some kind of a legal U-turn, and come back so I can go straight across. Sometimes when the line of cars waiting to make the left turn is really long,

I'll do that right turn and U-turn, just to save time, and to relieve congestion for everybody else.

Sometimes when I want to turn left into a driveway, and there is light traffic in both directions, I'll just stop and wait – on the right-hand shoulder, NOT in the middle of the road. Then when all lanes are clear, I make my left turn.

I am not going to say, never make a left turn, because that would be silly. Often a left turn is perfectly routine. No danger. No problem. But other times it can be very scary.

No Left Turns...

There are 3 streets I can name, that have almost no left turns: Market Street in San Francisco, 19th Avenue in San Francisco, and the Champs Elysees in Paris. If you are not familiar with these streets, you can drive along them, in the left lane, for a LONG way, looking for a left-hand turn. After a while, you realize there have not been any left turns, and there are not likely to be any for a long way. So then you just make 3 right turns, and get across that major street, and then you are OK. There are probably streets like that in several of the cities you know. And surprises like that in other towns that you have never yet gotten to. So, when you find one, don't be too surprised.

(Actually, there are left turns on Market Street after about 2 miles, and on 19th, after about 3 miles. And on Champs Elysees you come to some big traffic circles after 3 km. But it is still an uncommonly long stretch.)

Roll On Through...

A friend Tom said he used to have an old pick-up truck, and the engine ran rough. He figured out that if he just stopped in the middle of the road, to make his left turn, and waited for a break in traffic, he was gonna get killed, because the truck would lose power right when he wanted to get across traffic. So he started making "momentum turns". He would be moving at speed, and then when it was clear, he would cut neatly across traffic, and if his engine coughed or cut out, that would not get him in trouble.

If you have a car where the engine is running poorly, and you cannot get it fixed, you should consider that a "momentum turn" is a lot safer than just hoping your engine does not run rough, when making a turn across traffic.

So, if you often have to do any number of left-turns, and if there is much traffic or congestion, think about how to avoid them.

"Points"

In my old town of Wilmington Mass, there were all sorts of odd intersections. At each intersection, there were accidents, occasionally. And all the accidents were added up. After any intersection had collected enough "points", the safety department would agree that they could put up a warning sign or blinker. If you waited long enough, every intersection in town would get a complete set of warning signs and blinkers. But it was taking a long time. And, how would you like to be the last person who had an accident at a dangerous corner and tipped the balance?

You should assume that every intersection is potentially dangerous. Every intersection holds the potential for some very messy accidents. Even a 10-mph crash holds the potential for getting a person severely injured or killed. (Of course, in the old days before we had seat belts, the odds of serious injury were much worse.)

Compound of Poor Visibility – at Intersections...

The other ingredient that makes intersections so deadly, is poor visibility. You look left, it looks clear. You look right, it's clear, and you start to pull out – and there is a car on the left, bearing down on you.

WHERE THE HECK DID HE COME FROM??? – Maybe he was right there, but you were not watching very carefully. Maybe that car was a dull grey, and hard to see. Maybe he was in a blind spot. Maybe behind a pillar, behind the frame of your windshield. Maybe he was coming up faster than you expected. That's one of the problems with people speeding – other drivers look to see where a car should be, and when that space is empty, they think it is safe to proceed – and then the speeding car "comes out of nowhere".

In the Air Force study I mentioned, they found that a lot of accidents occurred at square intersections, because the drivers did not see each other. Apparently they did not obey the stop signs.

I don't know how it is where you are, but in San Francisco, there are a lot of intersections with no stop signs. It is quite challenging to be driving around in some of these neighborhoods and realize that, even if you do not have a stop sign, neither does the other guy! There is one square intersection that has just two stop signs – but they are not opposite each other. Quite tricky.

So, to be anywhere near safe at an intersection, don't just look once in each direction – look at least twice. Look once, and then re-check as you start out.

There are many other kinds of intersections. There are Tee intersections, and Y-intersections. Sometimes there are multiple stop signs. I know some 5-corners. There are city streets where one big diagonal street intersects with a 4-corner on a grid. There is no simple solution that will magically get you through every intersection. The general rule is:

If you are not sure as you enter an intersection,

- try to figure out in advance which direction you want to go.

- if you are going to turn, switch on your blinkers, preferably before you get into the intersection.

- slow down appropriately before you get to the intersection.

- take it easy.

- watch what is going on. Watch left and right, and then left and right again.

6-4-22

- see where it is safe and legal to go.

- consider following somebody who seems to know what he is doing.

- follow marked lanes, if possible.

- be polite, and not too pushy; and

- yield the right-of-way to somebody else who seems to really want it.

"Gerade Aus"

One time I was riding with a salesman in northern Germany. They were having some elections, and there were signs and posters on various walls. One of the posters exhorted the voters to vote: "Not Left. Not Right. Straight Ahead!", or, in German, "Nicht Links. Nicht Rechts. Gerade Aus!" We drove along until we came to a tee intersection. There was this same poster – on a brick wall – at the Tee of the TEE intersection. I was quite amused, because we obviously had to go left or right; we could not drive straight ahead. I did not, alas, get a photo of this sign – I was too slow with my camera. I hope the German political worker who put up that sign enjoyed this joke as much as I did. I still giggle....

What else do we know about intersections?

Rotaries or Traffic Circles or Roundabouts

In some parts of the country, they do not have many of these. But in New England, there are quite a few. And in Old England, also. That is probably why.

On a good day, a rotary is a wonderful way to get people around each other. A 5-way or 6-way rotary intersection is not necessarily any worse than a 4-way or 3-way intersection. If people are polite and co-operative, the rotary can work very well. You can get through pretty fast, and nobody has to wait very long.

On the other hand, if people are sloppy or inconsiderate, rotary traffic can lead to poor progress or nasty disagreements or assorted accidents. Massachusetts used to follow the rule, "The man on the RIGHT has the right of way". Thus, a car entering on the right would have the right to enter, even if you could not leave. And your inability to leave, might cause a jam-up. So, about 3 years ago, Massachusetts changed the laws so that the car that is IN the intersection now has the right of way. This seems to be working much better. That is how it works in England – quite well – as the car that is IN the rotary has the right of way to get out.

There are still weaknesses in the Rotary system. If one of the outlets is clogged, there is not a lot you can do to avoid a general jam-up. Sloppy people can still cause accidents. But in light traffic, it can save everybody a lot of time and effort. The time you spend waiting for a green light, is usually not wasted at the rotary.

BIG Rotaries...

There are some super-rotaries that are 100 or 200 yards across. Sometimes a big rotary is draped across both sides of a superhighway – see the sketch. These often work very well.

Then there are some tiny ones that are 6 feet across at the hub. But here in San Francisco there have been some experiments to convert these tiny ones to a 40-foot inner diameter. I don't know if these experiments were considered successful.

When I was working in Dedham Mass, I used to go to a dentist, Dr. Frolik, whose office was up in Jamaica Plain. The route went up Turtle Pond Parkway and a few other odd roads, and up Route 1, and it went past (or around) 7 traffic circles. I made my plans to leave work at the *last possible minute,* so I had to drive as fast as I safely could, up these curvy roads

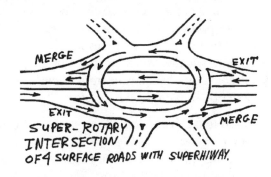

SUPER-ROTARY INTERSECTION OF 4 SURFACE ROADS WITH SUPERHIWAY.

and around these rotaries, to get to my dental appointment. This not only saved time, but if a policeman asked me, "WHY are you driving so fast?", I would say, "I am just trying to get to my dentist's office – SEE, here is my appointment slip." But in 8 years, a policeman never asked me why I was in a hurry. So I just had a good time, hurrying up around these 7 rotaries.

British Roundabouts...

Note, the Rotaries in England work very well. Their signs are very carefully done, to indicate where you want to exit the circle. If you have never driven in England, do not be nervous at all. You can, after you wait your turn, definitely get into the rotary, and after that, you can definitely get out. The mirror image effect is not a serious problem. If there is not much traffic, but you keep the passenger side of your car near the curb, you will NOT get in trouble. You will NOT get confused about which side of the road to drive on, left vs. right. If there is a lot of traffic, just pay attention to how other people get out of the rotary, and do like they do, and you will not have much trouble.

Driveways

A driveway is similar to a street, where it enters a roadway. But when you come out of a driveway, you are not subject to exactly the same set of rules as a street. If you come out of your driveway, you must be very careful, and you should probably go slowly, but you are not really obligated to STOP, as if it were a street, unless there is traffic. Yet, you must be as careful as if you did stop. Similarly, when you come down a street and want to turn in to a private driveway, you have to be just as careful – even if you do not have to follow every law that applies to streets and roads.

One day my little sister observed, "Isn't that too bad about the poor Doctor that lives next door?" We inquired, "Why do you say that?" And she said, "Oh, I feel sorry for our neighbor, poor Blind Dr. Iveway". We soon explained that it was not Doctor Iveway, but, a badly-painted sign warning about a BLIND DR IVEWAY. Ohhhh.

Stop Signs

Alas, stop signs cause a lot of grief. They make us stop when we really should not
have to stop – such as at night when there is no traffic, and you can see perfectly
well without stopping. Conversely, when a guy comes right through a stop sign
without stopping, that sometimes causes bad accidents. Sometimes the police
enforce things strictly. Sometimes not. It is always a good idea to stop. But whether
you stop, or whether you slow down to 1 mph or 3 or 11, at least be *sure* to look at
what is going on. If a kid runs from behind a car because he thinks you are stopping,
you better be *stopping*.

I used to be able to get off my street and go down Monterey Boulevard, all the
way to the freeway, with no stops. I could ease through 3 traffic lights, no problem.
But then somebody added a stop sign at the bottom of the hill. Then a school moved
in, and they added another stop sign. Then the school moved out. But they never
took out the stop sign. I finally got mad and found another alternate route. Literally I
can get to work with about 3 traffic lights plus ONE stop sign, on any one of 3 or 4
different routes. Sometimes I pick a route with 6 or 8 or 12 lights, but those lights
are usually semi-synchronized, and there is not any waiting. But it is still a lot better
than 12 stop signs, I think.

Yield

I was about 10 when I first saw a YIELD RIGHT-OF-WAY sign. That was 1950. I was
impressed. Because there are a lot of places where just slowing down to 14 mph and
checking that the way is clear, is exactly the right thing to do. NOW, not ALL stop
signs can be safely replaced by YIELD signs. But I'll swear, almost 1/3 of them
probably should be. It would make less of a hypocrite out of us. Personally, I can
choose routes to work that have *so few* stop signs, that I do not feel bad about
stopping at a full stop at each of them. But there are other neighborhoods where
there are 8 or 9 stops signs in 10 blocks. That sure annoys me.

One-Way Streets

A one-way street is, usually, a less complicated place to drive than a 2-way road. You
do not have to worry so much about oncoming traffic. But if you want to park on the
left side of the street, that can be tricky.

When you come to an intersection, you may want to turn right or left onto
another street – and that may or may not be a one-way street. So you have to plan
that carefully. In California, if you are at the left lane of a one-way street, and there is
no traffic, you may be able to make a legal left turn, while the light is red, onto
another one-way street. This may not apply to other states.

A Perfect Interlocking Impasse

One late evening I was returning to my house in Cambridge MA, and was walking
past the intersection of Cottage Farm Bridge (better known as BU Bridge) and
Commonwealth Avenue, in Allston, which is the west end of Boston, where there
were no traffic lights, but just blinking red and yellow.

I looked at the traffic.

- The west-bound cars were blocking the north-bound cars.

- The north-bound cars were blocking the east-bound cars.

- The east-bound cars were blocking the south-bound cars.

- The south-bound cars were blocking the west-bound cars.

It was a perfect impasse. BUT, it was late at night, about 12:30 AM, and there were not a LOT of cars. There were only about a dozen cars in each of the 4 legs. But for about a minute, it was a perfect impasse, and nobody moved. Nobody honked. And very few new arrivals showed up.

After about a minute, one driver saw that he could back up and let a car through. So he backed up – but he let just one car through – and then he zoomed ahead, back to the place he had been. Everybody waited another 40 seconds. Then that same key car decided to back up and let another car go. This time he let 2 cars go. Then he zoomed ahead. And waited. By this time, it was possible for a couple cars to move and get out, and then the impasse broke up. But my friend and I just stood there with our jaws hanging open – and we laughed and laughed. What a bizarre way to run an intersection!! But, if you ever read, "Wild in the Streets: The Boston Driver's Handbook",* you will agree that this is consistent with the Boston driver's mentality: "Screw you, Buddy, I'll do what's best for me" – and the guys all kept doing it – even though nothing was best for anybody!!

Until I figure out what I forgot, this is all for this topic.

You can look up this book in the Appendix on Book Reviews... easy to buy it.

Chapter 25. TRAFFIC LIGHTS

Traffic lights are probably one of the necessary evils of Western Civilization. We like green lights, but we gotta put up with those other colors.

How Do They Work?

The old ones ran off mechanical timers, with timers and motors and cams and relays. Newer ones are electronic, and often computerized. They often have computerized sensors in the pavement, to tell when the lane is empty of cars, and the lights can change. Modern lights can easily give different cycles and times, at different times of day.

What Can Go Wrong?

Fortunately the lights are pretty reliable and fail-safe. So we rarely get a case of the lights lighting green in both directions! But there are other philosophical problems.

Green, Red, and – Pink?

The major problem with traffic lights is that drivers get sloppy or pushy, and go through a light some time after it has turned red, or before it turns green. This is often called a "pink" light – that is a red light when you wish it wasn't red, even though it is red. This is a definite cause of many accidents, which we will discuss below.

Do I *Have To* Stop?

First comment: while it is true that we are not supposed to drive through a red light, it is NOT true that we have to *stop* for a red light. We may be able to just *slow down*, so we do not run the red light. If you dislike stopping, as I do, then you will prefer to slow down in advance. As I mention in the Appendix on Economy, it's advantageous to slow down early, so you then wait at low speed for the light to turn green. Then you avoid having to stop, which saves money and time. But, be careful not to sneak across the intersection before the light is actually green, because other people may be sneaking across at the end of their green light, or, on the yellow – or on the "pink". Drivers running the light "on the pink" are a major cause of accidents.

By necessity, if the light is green for YOU, it is probably red for me and all of us poor slobs waiting at the cross street. But if it is the middle of the night and YOU are not there, the light may still stay red for ME. In the old days, even if I wanted to turn right, I had to wait for the light to turn green. Fortunately, the laws of California have permitted us to turn right on red, after we STOPPED, for many years. And other states were recently required to match this. People have waited billions and billions of hours, for the light to go green, even for a right turn, before all those laws were rationalized.

Synchronized Lights

The next improvement to discuss is *synchronized* or "timed" lights. If you are on a main street, and the traffic is flowing smoothly, it is possible to keep a smooth flow by having the timing and pattern of the lights moving along like a ripple. The majority of the traffic can keep rolling along. We used to have some timed lights on 19th Avenue, and we could drive from one end to the other without stopping. But they improved that. Now we have to stop every 6 or 8 blocks. Sigh. Because if the lights were properly synchronized, it could save us a lot of time and fuel.

If the cross-streets are spaced wrong, it is hard to get the lights properly synchronized for drivers in both directions. But if the traffic planners fiddle around, it is not impossible.

Trip Lights

The next improvement was the "trip light". If I ain't there, and it's midnight, then the magnetic sensors built into the road will sense that I am not there, and will then give YOU the green light. Trip lights save us a lot of time, waiting for that green. However, while the San Francisco *Peninsula* has lots of trip lights, the City of San Francisco does not have any trip lights. So much for progress, and progressive thinking. (I may have discovered the first and only trip light in San Francisco, brand new, last month, at Alemany and Bayshore Boulevard....)

The next problem with the "trip light" is that sometimes the trip light does not trip. Down in Silicon Valley, they have lots of trip lights, mostly for left turns. But we may show up at the left turn, and get there in plenty of time, and wait 4 seconds – and then when the lights are supposed to change, the left arrow does not turn green. Often, the sensors have a 4.4 second delay. So you have to wait another 2 minutes for the lights to cycle around, so you can turn left on the green arrow. I understand why they have to have delays, but if you show up for a green arrow 2 or 3 seconds before the light should turn green, I don't see why they can't let you have your green arrow.

Then after you sit there and cool your heels 2 minutes – the light sometimes *still* does not give you the green arrow. So you decide that the light is broken – and you wait until there is no traffic – and you ease along to go straight ahead – and then a cop shows up and gives you a ticket for not going left at the left-turn lane. I had that experience once. I wish the cop had given a ticket to the signal computer, for insubordination – but the cop is not interested in that. He's just following his rules. He's *assuming* that the light is not broken. Thanks a lot for being helpful and protecting us from bad computers, officer.... The judge may be sympathetic, but there is no guarantee on that....

Running The Yellow (Other people)

The major problem with traffic lights is that when we see a green, we assume that everybody is stopping for us. But when a guy runs a red light, or runs through on the yellow light, or "on the pink", we can have a – well – a *conflict*. Like, a CRASH.

So in many places we have learned that a green light is merely a license to look VERY CAREFULLY to make sure nobody is coming through on the red.

(Note, some engineer once told me that if you just drive fast enough, the red light is blue-shifted by the Doppler shift, and doesn't look red at all. But I have never been able to get my Beetle going fast enough to see this.)

When a light turns green, and I am the first driver, I spend the first 2 seconds – even as I am starting up – looking to see if the other drivers in cross traffic are going to stop. I am learning to look left, and right – even more intensely than I ever did before – and left and right again. Swivel your neck! What I am looking for is to see if the first car in each lane is stopping. Once I see that, I am willing to stop worrying about that.

When the light turns green, I do not blast my horn if the first guy in line at the light does not start up in the first second of green. But after about 1.3 seconds, if he is still on his brakes, I do bip my horn, just a light brief *bip*, just to make sure he is awake and watching.

Running The Red Lights (the Receiving End)

Here's a classical story: My friend George was waiting at a red light, waiting at a side-road to cross Route 1, in Norwood Mass, a 4-lane divided highway with traffic lights in 1960. The light changed green. George started out in his new Renault Dauphine. He crossed two lanes. As he entered the next lane, a truck rolled through the red light – about 6 seconds after the light had gone red for him – and his cab wheels hit the front of George's small car and flipped it over, like a big dog grabbing the snout of a small duck. Then the trailer wheels hit the small car and spun it around. George climbed out, woozy but unharmed. He did NOT buy another small car.

But, George was very lucky. If he had gotten 3 feet further into the intersection, he would surely have been killed by the heavy truck. Also, George was also unlucky, because if he had looked right AND left, he might have seen the truck, and stopped short, and avoided the accident.

NOW, LOOK: Even if some other guy is trying to cause an accident, you are not obligated to help that accident happen. You can look and think and stop before the accident happens. Especially if that causes less pain to fall on your tail.

I will not recommend that the first guy in line when the light goes green should dawdle, and take a lot of time. If he sees that all the traffic coming in on the right and left is slowing down so as to stop, then he ought to proceed, and I will surely follow that driver through the intersection. Let's increase our productivity, and minimize waste, by moving along. However, if the guy ahead of me sees some idiot who does not have any plans for stopping, then I will slow down and not try to pass him and beat him into the accident. OK?

As for the poor trucker – maybe he lost his brakes. Maybe he fell asleep. Maybe he decided to try to run the very late PINK LIGHT. Hey, all of you drivers, watch out for all those guys – whether they are in a car or in a truck. It is worth a LOT of effort for you to avoid those severe accidents, especially as it can save you a lot of PAIN AND SUFFERING. When the light changes green, do not just GO. Start out at a moderate pace, at the same time as you watch to make sure the oncoming cars and trucks are probably going to stop. Otherwise, what are you going to do, try to chicken out a truck with no brakes???

"That's How We Do it In Our Family..."

There is a great old story about the famous racing drivers Bobby and Al Unser, who come from Albuquerque New Mexico. One of Al's old friends comes to visit, so Al picks him up at the Albuquerque airport. They start into town. As they come to an intersection, the light turns yellow and then red. Al sees this and FLOORS the gas, and ZOOMS through the red light. The visitor is terrified. A little further along, the light turns red again, and Al really *flies* through that red light. The visitor is slumped down in his seat, from sheer terror. He says, "Al, why do you do that?" Al replies, "Do what?" And the visitor says, "Why do you go through red lights like that?" And Al accelerates through another red light, and replies, "Oh, it's an old family tradition. We always do that."

Just then they approach a red light, and it turns green. Al puts on the brakes hard and stops. The visitor asks, "Now, why did you do *that*?" And Al replies, "Oh, I heard that Bobby is in town today."

◆ ◆ ◆

Anyhow, I have seen cars roar through red lights, and I have no idea why they thought they could do it, but they got away with it once. Other times the car just loses his brakes, and does not have a lot of choice. (But if I lost my brakes, I would get on my horn, at least, and I have never seen anybody come through a red light with his horn blowing.)

◆ ◆ ◆

So, in general, when a light turns green, be extra careful that nobody is running on the yellow – or the "pink light".

Here in San Francisco, almost all lights are set for a 1-minute cycle. Down on the peninsula, the trip lights are set up for a 2-minute cycle, in the day time. Some are even set for a 2:20 cycle, at rush hour. But late at night, they are set for some fairly short cycles. If you are coming down an empty street, and the light ahead of you is red, perhaps 90 yards up, it may easily turn green as you approach. However, if you go just a little bit slower, it may change green and then red again! The computers sure are hard at work at midnight. You can't assume that a red light will stay red – or a green one, green.

How Long Will That Light Stay Yellow?

One time I got a ticket for entering an intersection on the red, perhaps (according to the cop) a half second after the yellow went off. I went back and checked. That light was timed for a 2-second yellow. I had just come up from Sunnyvale on the

Peninsula, where, even on slow city streets, some of the lights had a 3-second yellow. After I explained that, the judge dismissed the case, with a warning.

> So, be ye warned: just because you know how long it takes for *some* traffic lights to go from green to red, does NOT mean you are safe from variations. All traffic lights are NOT the same. Not all traffic signals give you a fair time to get across the intersection. In a city, there are often roads more than 150 feet across, and there is no simple way to enter on the green, and get out before the light turns red. But at least if you avoid entering when it's red, you are pretty safe.

Give 'Im the Lights

One time, when I was a very inexperienced driver, I was coming along old Route 16 in Watertown Mass, and there was a blinking yellow light that I knew very well, because I used to bicycle along that route a lot. That blinking yellow light turned red. And I went right through it! And why? Ah – because the guy ahead of me went right through it. I followed him through it. Well, I learned, that just because the guy ahead of you does something stupid, you may be wise if you do not ALSO do it.

And here's the point: if *you* are coming to a light, and it turns yellow, and you decide *you* have time to go ahead through the yellow, *you* should reach over and blink your lights on and off, once or twice. (At night, blink them *off* and *on*.) The point is, the guy behind you will notice that you are doing something out of the ordinary. He may think you are going to stop, which is a good thing to help him to think. And a car on the side street may notice you blink your lights, and will also not be worried that you are coming through on the yellow. But the main point is, you are helping the driver behind you decide not to just blindly follow you through. We call this, "Giving him the lights". Blinking your lights off and on has other purposes, but this is a very useful one.

(As I mentioned in my Chapter on Car Lights, I always make sure my light switch is not so recessed that I cannot grab that knob, quickly and easily, even in the dark.)

In some parts of the country, there are still places where there is no yellow light, but the red and green both stay on to denote the lights are changing. That's the old pattern, before they invented the yellow light. Then some parts of the country use the combination of red PLUS yellow, to indicate a walk light. One of my friends said he has never seen the use of "red-plus-yellow means walk" anywhere other than in Massachusetts. But we have them here in California, too. I bet some other places do, too.

Strange Traffic Lights

A friend, Kate, was driving east on old Route 9 near Framingham Mass. She was moving along in traffic. Minding her business. SUDDENLY the guy in front of her slammed on his brakes! Kate hit her brakes, and just had a heck of a time, making a panic stop, completely unexpected. She made her stop and did not hit that car, and did not slide into the adjacent lane where other cars were still doing 50. She made it. She stopped.

WHY did that guy stop? As he approached an intersection, (just west of the Carling brewery, just south of the old Jordan Marsh store) that guy looked up and saw the traffic lights. It looked like a red light. He thought he was going to go straight through the red light, so he hit the brakes hard and stopped.

The little problem was: at this intersection, there was, for each straight-through lane, a big red light with a little green arrow pointing straight ahead. (There were also a couple lanes of red lights over on the left, with red arrows to tell you that you should not turn left. But that was way over on the left, and nobody was looking at that. That was all stopped.)

So this guy saw so much red, he was sure he had to stop. Kate knew this intersection, and she knew the little green arrows were there. She saw those arrows, and figured she was doing fine. So she was going to sail right through this intersection, along with all the other cars – until that guy stopped in front of her! Needless to say, traffic light patterns like that can drive you crazy. I must say, I have never seen that pattern of traffic lights elsewhere. That was 25 years ago. Have they changed those lights? Possibly. Have they gone to a more rational plan for the lights? I'll inquire.

(Note – normally the plan is to have JUST the green arrows on, and the red lights only go on after the green arrows go out, and the yellows go on.)

Blinking Lights

When you see a blinking yellow, you are supposed to be cautious. When you see a blinking red, you are supposed to stop. I always thought that if you see a blinking yellow, the other guy has a blinking red. The first time I nearly got killed, I was bicycling through Watertown Mass, late at night, and I sailed through a blinking yellow light at about 20 mph. And a car came sailing through the cross street at about 40 mph, and did not even slow down. He missed me, but not by much. I went back to check. That light was blinking yellow in all 4 directions!! I never saw that one before. And from that time on, I have always been a little skeptical about blinking yellows. I gotta assume that the other cross traffic is not going to respect my so-called "right of way".

Lights Missing?

For example, maybe the other red light has burned out. Whenever I see a burned-out green light, I try to report it. Whenever I see a yellow or red light burned out, I am SURE to report that. NOW, here in San Francisco there is probably not just a single traffic light, standing alone. There are always 2 traffic lights at any intersection. So if one red light burns out, there is still another lit up. I don't yet know why they do not have ultra-reliable light bulbs with 2 or 3 filaments built in, as spares. But I don't think they do. Anyhow, the phone number in SF is marked in my phone book. It is 550-2736, from 7 AM to 4 PM on weekdays, and 695-2020 on weekends and after 4 PM. If that corresponding number for your town is not listed in your phone book, get it added, so you can easily report it. Maybe you could just call the local police, and they can tell the right people in a small town. Because in small towns, there is often just one light to be seen at any intersection, and if it burns out, you got a very serious potential problem.

Right-of-Way????

One guy pointed out that in his state, there is no such thing as a "right-of-way". There are situations where one driver is supposed to yield, but in no case does the law give any driver the "right of way". I guess that indicates a difference between some of our Olde English thinking, in eastern states, such as Massachusetts, versus certain more enlightened states.

What was the old poem? About a guy who thought he had the right-of-way, and barreled into an intersection. The other driver was "dead wrong", but this driver wound up dead – even though he was "dead right". So, be careful about assuming that you have a "right of way", because the rules indicates you should. It does not always actually happen.

– Anyhow, that's all I can think about, on the topic of traffic lights.

Chapter 26. SIGNS

There are all kinds of signs. Recently I was going down to lunch at a local Pizzeria. A couple guys asked, "How can I find this place?" I told them, the sign for the place is impossible to see, so go down El Camino about a mile east, and look for Scherba's Auto Parts, a big Yellow sign with Black letters. Turn in there and park. Get out of your car. Then if you stare really carefully, you may be able to see the sign for the Pizza place.

When I got there, I looked at the sign, which was nearly perfectly camouflaged. I decided to tell the owner, what a difficult sign it was to see. The owner threw up his hands – "I just paid $20,000 to have that sign repainted". I told him that it was a beautiful sign, but it was very hard to see. I explained that fortunately the Scherba's sign is easy to spot, and we know how to find Fiorillo's excellent pizza that way. He cried a little. I think somebody just chose colors for that sign, that were beautiful, but not very *noticeable*.

Fortunately, while commercial signs come in every strange color, the black-on-yellow traffic signs are much easier to spot. Hey, when I was a kid, all the stop signs were black-on-yellow. It was only in the 1950s that stop signs were made red. And, back then, there were no YIELD signs!

There are advisory signs, and signs to tell you how to navigate (often in green and white) and then there are signs that you have to obey, like STOP signs.

The driver training courses and the Motor Vehicle Dept. driving manuals do excellent work at explaining what each sign is good for. I am not going to spend much time on that. I will just caution you about the problems with signs that might relate to accidents.

Stop Signs

Sometimes on a city street, you come to a corner and you don't see a STOP sign. Then when you are just about in the intersection, you see a STOP sign hidden behind a tree. (And in some towns, there is a cop ready to pounce.) My point is, just because you do not see a STOP sign, that does not mean it is not there. So if the intersection *seems* to need a STOP sign, then you should be prepared to stop, even though you cannot see that sign.

Ah, yes – I recall that in one state – I think it was Massachusetts – about 25 years ago – there used to be a rule that if a series of three cars in a row stop at a STOP sign, all 3 can proceed, and only the *fourth* driver has to stop again. But if there ever was such a rule, you can assume it is gone, now.

Problems...

One time I was down by the airport, and stopped at a STOP sign. There was a cop 'way over on the left. The car ahead of me slowed down and eased past the STOP line, which was about 25 feet from the actual intersection. He finally stopped just before the intersection, to see what the traffic was doing. I pulled up to the stop line and stopped right behind that car.

Shortly, he decided to proceed through the intersection. And I followed him. And the cop pulled *me* over! Hey, the cop was about 100 feet away. He probably could not even see the stop line where I had stopped, quite legally.

The cop accused me of going through the STOP sign. He was not interested in hearing my story. And he was not interested in the car that went right through the stop sign and only stopped beyond it!! I was considering explaining this to the judge, but I decided to go to Traffic School.* I learned what kind of argument you have to use, to show that you are not guilty, in a simple case like that, and how to convince the judge that you really did stop in the right place. Taking a photograph is a good idea. Since that time, I carry a camera in my car. I keep it in an ice chest, so it stays cool.

Anyhow, I never did get to argue with that cop, nor to explain to the judge. But if I had to do it again, I would argue it out, with photographic evidence.

Troubles...

Here is another way to get in trouble at a stop sign. Jim stopped, quite legally and correctly, at the stop line, which was about 30 feet before the actual intersection. From that location, he could not see if it was safe to proceed. Then he pulled up 30 feet and stopped, so he could see if it was safe to actually go into the intersection. Wham! – the guy behind him *assumed* that he was going to keep going. That is really hard to defend against. I guess the best you can do is proceed very slowly, and keep pumping your brakes, so the guy behind you will *know* you are not going very far nor very fast. Don't zoom up 30 feet and then stop.

Advisory Signs – for Curves

When you approach a curve, there is often a "helpful" sign, advising you how fast you can safely go. For example, if you are driving along at 45, the sign might show an arrow left: "35 MPH". Big deal. Most times you do not have to even slow down, unless you have Aunt Tillie aboard, and you think she might be grouchy about the transverse acceleration forces.

So these signs are a complete waste of time – eh? No, maybe not. If it were rainy, and you were not trying to test your tires, you might actually slow down near 35. And if it were snowy, and you were doing 35, you might slow down to 25 or 20 – and you would be watching, in case you had to slow down even more.

---

* *Here in California, if you have a good driving record, you are often permitted to go to a special "Traffic School" in lieu of punishment for a minor driving infraction – and thus avoid getting a bad driving record. Your state may do other obscure procedures....*

But if you were steaming along at 55, you might slow down to 44 – and you might still be able to get through that "35 MPH" curve, although not really safely. So everybody has to use his own judgement.

Myself, I consider a "35 MPH" sign as an advisory that I can probably ease through at 40 or 42. I can usually make it safely at least 5 mph faster than the signs say. Even my wife goes through about 4 mph faster than the posted speed. She accuses ME of being a cowboy – but she is not much slower than I am.

If you start south from National's plant in Santa Clara CA, you start down a 6-lane road, Lawrence Expressway. After a while it gets smaller, 4 lanes, and then 2. About 8 miles south, you come to a sharp curve, and a sign "21 MPH". Yes, you might get through at 24 or 25 – but if your Aunt Tillie is aboard, 21 is not a bad speed. I talked to the guys who put up that sign, and they pointed out how they wanted it to be thought-provoking. They wanted people to THINK about this curve, as it is NOT just an ordinary 20-mph curve, and it is NOT a 25-mph curve. Saying that it is a 21-mph curve is *about right*. On the way north it's 19 mph.

Surprise!

A curve that starts right in at a constant radius, without any warning, is not fair. For example, if you come off route I-280 in San Bruno CA, and head east on the little connector, I-380, and then keep bearing right to get on US 101 to go to the airport, there is one bad curve, just as you enter the last ramp. One second you are going straight – and *suddenly* you have to turn fairly hard right, without any entry curve. That is not nice, and it's bad highway engineering, because you have to immediately start your curve at a constant radius. There is a significant amount of *jerk,* to do that. And if it were foggy, or if drivers were sleepy, they might not see it until they were well into the curve. It is a challenging piece of road to drive well, because it was planned so poorly. Fortunately, I think not many accidents occur there.

"Sweepers"

When you are on a high-speed road, there are often sweeping curves, and an advisory sign suggesting that you should slow down. Whether or not there is a sign, you have to be prepared to slow down safely for the curve. And as mentioned in the Chapter on Steering, if the curve tightens up, that is a real challenge. Especially if you are driving faster than the speed limit. Especially if the traction is not good. I have heard that while exceeding a posted highway speed limit can get you a ticket, exceeding the recommended speed for a curve may not necessarily get you a ticket. But if the curve caused you to have an accident, then that's bad. Don't let that happen – whether there is a warning sign or not.

Sometimes on a road, you might see a caution sign: "SLOW CURVE" with an arrow pointing *right* – while you are in a curve that is a sweeper to the *left*. Ha! Keep awake, guys!

Anyhow, if you drive enough, you will find every kind of curve. And a small fraction will tighten up in a sneaky way, after you enter. And some are marked by a sign – and some are not. No matter what happens, you have to be prepared to slow down enough to follow the road.

Yield

I talked about YIELD signs in the Chapter on Intersections, so if you want to see that, go read over there.

Street Signs

In a city, you can navigate pretty well if you know what street you are on. Some cities put a sign only on the cross street, so if you do not know what the main street is, it can be hard to find out. Some cities put the sign on one corner, and if you are at the farthest corner, you can be 100 or 200 feet away, so it is pretty hard to read. Especially at night.

A good partial solution is to make a list of not just the street you will turn on, but the 2 or 3 streets *before* that, so you can count down to the right place. And also, the next 2 or 3 streets *after* your street, so you will know if you went too far. A serious problem is, if you are looking for street signs, you might veer out of your lane, or hit a car that stops suddenly. So don't get sloppy!

NO Parking

Some cities and towns do a good job of putting up NO PARKING signs. Others do not. Hey, it is all a matter of Revenue Enhancement. I liked the ones in Needham Mass: "Don't Even THINK Of Parking Here."

One Way – Do Not Enter

Sometimes these signs are well placed. Other times, it is harder to see where to stay out of.

Other Signs

What other kinds of signs are interesting, or can cause or be related to accidents? I looked and thought and tried to remember, and never did find much. So this is a fairly short chapter.

Chapter 27. LIGHTS

Even in the daytime, you need some of your car's lights. But at night, it is a lot more important. Losing a light bulb, or two, can get you in real trouble. Many accidents are caused just because lights are out.

Headlights

Let's start with the BIG ones, the headlights. You have your HIGH beams and you have your LOW beams. In most states, by about 1/2 hour after sunset (and up to 1/2 hour before daybreak), you have to turn your lights ON. But, there are other times when it is a really good idea to turn your headlights on. When it is dark and rainy, or dark and snowy, or dark and foggy, even in the daytime, you want to help the on-coming traffic to see you. If they can't see you, they might do something dumb like turn in front of you. So it's pretty important to put your lights on, in the daytime, in these cases. In some states it is required.

Also it is important to NOT put your high beams on, when there is on-coming traffic. Because if you blind the other guy, he also cannot see where you are going. I know a guy who was just learning to drive, and realized his mother did not know what that little blue light on the dashboard meant. She just did not know about high beams. She had no idea how to turn them ON or OFF. So he explained it to her. Then she finally stopped driving around with her high beams on.

Are your HIGH beams just brighter and higher intensity?

No, they are bright *and* they point higher along the road, for better visibility at distances. Your LOW beams are aimed lower, and not so far to the left, so they won't shine in the other drivers' eyes.

Don't Blind the Other Guy

When you are driving in very sparse traffic, you may turn on your high beams when there is no on-coming traffic. But if a car is coming over a hill, and you see its headlights shining up into the air, it is nice etiquette to flip your lights down to low beam *just* before his headlights hit you. And, it is fun to notice that *he* dipped his high beams, at the same time as *you* did!

If a car comes around a corner on *your* left, his headlights may be aimed at you for a while. If he comes over the crest of a hill, his car may be pointed *up* in the air, and may seem "bright". Don't get mad at the other driver in those cases, because as soon as his car straightens out, the lights may be just fine.

On-coming Glare?

What if the on-coming driver leaves his high beams on? You might flip to your high beams for a moment, to remind this person that he forgot to dim his lights. I prefer

6/8/22   7P   20 mi

to turn my lights *off* for just 1/2 second. If that doesn't work, try blinking them off *twice*. If that doesn't work, you might try the high beams for a second. Or, just be aware that it might be somebody like my friend's mother, who has *NO CLUE* that she has her high beams on.

If the glare is really bad, you may have to slow down, to give yourself more time for guessing where you are in your lane. You have to know how to do that. If you are going slower, you may be able to hold up a hand and shade your eyes, and see where the center line is... and meanwhile, make sure to keep right of the center line – and preferably, to the right side of your lane. Make sure that on-coming car stays properly on your left, so you do not get into his lane! (And make sure that you do not have *YOUR* high beams on, too.)

> WHAT IF the on-coming driver thinks *you* have left your high beams on? He may flash his high beams at you. At this point, you may reply by flashing your lights to high beam, for just 1 second, too. When the on-coming driver sees that your other beams are HIGH, he will not complain so much about your low beams. However, if a *LOT* of guys think your low beams are too high – maybe your car is mis-aligned, with your front end high. Maybe you have a few hundred pounds of junk in your trunk? If that is not the obvious cause, then maybe you should get your lights checked out. The next chance you get, drive into a parking garage and see if the lights *seem* to be aimed reasonable correctly against a wall.

◆ ◆ ◆

Another time to *not* keep your high beams on, is when you are behind another car. It really is annoying, to have a driver behind you with his high beams on. On a long straight highway, a driver might be 1/2 mile ahead for many minutes, and even 1/2 mile ahead, your lights can make him uncomfortable. But if it seems to be a mile, that's not usually objectionable.

Another time to not turn on your high beams, is in fog. You can try it, and you'll usually find that the high beams just send back more glare than anything else! So, go back to your low beams.

Drivers who have to drive in fog a lot, can buy fog lights. They are supposed to shine under the fog. I've never tried them, myself, but some friends say that the good ones can help a lot. I have heard that in Germany, some cars have an extremely bright red light shining to the rear, to help other drivers see you in fog. Sounds like a pretty good idea.

Missing Headlight?

What if one of your headlights burns out? Well, you might not notice it right away. Then, if the other light burns out, you might say, "Gee, isn't it a funny coincidence how both lights burned out at once??!!" But actually, one burned out early, and then, later, the other bulb. So if you suspect that your lights are a little dim, you might check to see if both beams are throwing out light. If one isn't, get ready to replace it. Or, you might see if both lights seem to be lit, when you pull up behind a car at a light. It's worth a peek, if you think your headlights are dim.

What Else Can Go Wrong?

If your front end has been in an accident, your headlight could be pointing in some absurd direction. You may get away with this for a little while, if you don't do much night driving. But if that headlight is shining in other drivers' eyes, you should get it fixed pronto, before the police have to remind you.

These days, headlights have so many different patterns, it may require a very special source to get a replacement for a burned-out bulb. Sometimes you can install the replacement yourself. Sometimes, it's hard to do. If you are changing any bulbs, whether a halogen headlight bulb, or even a brake-light bulb, do not leave any fingerprint on the bulb, as that can cause an early failure. Handle with a clean cloth or paper, and polish off any fingerprints on the bulb.

If you neglect to clean off your headlight lenses, they can get plenty dim, due to mud, in muddy conditions, or due to salt in winter driving. So you have to clean them off when you clear off your windshield, too.

Ooops...

The other thing that can go wrong with headlights is, if you leave them on. If you leave them on for a few hours, you may still be able to start your engine. Maybe 3 or 5. But after 4 to 8 hours, your battery is likely to be so low, it won't crank. (On the other hand, if your battery goes nearly dead after just an hour of headlights, that is telling you that your battery is pretty nearly shot, anyhow.)

I cannot say I have never had this happen to me. I have a little $ 3.00 buzzer that is connected between the parking lights and the ignition, with a diode pointing toward the ignition. If the parking lights are on, and I turn off the ignition, it beeps at me, good and loud.

You just need one little diode, 1N914 or 1N4001 or similar, (.1 ampere, 50 volts) and a little 12-volt buzzer from Radio Shack. I went out and bought 4 of the 8 different buzzers that Radio Shacks sell. The 273-027, 273-055A, and 273-059 are all adequate, and the 273-060 is a little louder than the other ones. These all have a list price of $2 or $3. There are several other buzzers they sell that are rated to run on 12 volts, and I am sure any one of them would be adequate.

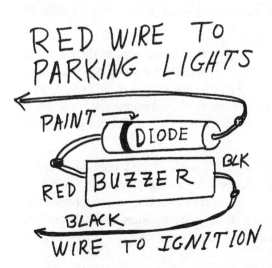

RED WIRE TO PARKING LIGHTS

PAINT — DIODE

RED BUZZER BLK

BLACK WIRE TO IGNITION

This circuit is quite easy to make up, and not very hard to install. Solder or crimp the wires, and tape over any exposed wires. You clip the black wire onto the ignition or to some voltage that is "ON" only when the ignition

6/9/2

switch is on. Clip the red lead to one of your parking-lights' wires. If your car does not have a buzzer like this, I recommend it. You only have to put in this $4.00 rig, and save your battery ONCE, to make a 10:1 return on your investment.

> Note, if your battery gets low, you should get it charged as soon as possible, because a battery loses its capacity quite quickly, and its life is cut short, if allowed to hang around in a low discharged state.

If you have left your lights on, and your battery is so low you cannot get the car started, refer to the Appendix on Jump-starting.

Parking Lights

I used to drive in the dusk, between sunset and 1/2 hour after sunset, with my parking lights on. But then I discovered that this is illegal, here in California, so I don't do it much. You should know if that is true in your state. Personally, I never found anything wrong with this. I guess the reason they have this law, is so you won't turn on your parking lights, and then look at the dash lights, and forget to turn on your headlights.

Tail Lights

Tail lights are pretty important, so people can see you, especially in conditions of poor visibility – snow or rain or whatever – even in the daytime. So if you find that it is hard to see other cars – maybe they are finding it hard to see *YOU*. So put on, at least, your parking lights. (Even here in California, I think that is legal in the daytime.)

Brake Lights

Brake lights are REALLY important, because you want the guy behind you to know you are slowing down or stopping. If one brake light burns out, and you tap your brakes, the guy behind you might think you are turning. If both brake lights burn out, other drivers may find it hard to guess you are braking – until too late. (This is another good reason to watch several cars ahead – if the guys 2 and 3 cars up are hitting their brakes, you will be watching them and slowing down, *even if* the car in front of you has no brake lights.)

But if you check your own lights, you can walk all the way around the car – and you won't see your brake lights unless you have an accomplice stepping on the brakes! When I lived in Massachusetts, we had to pass inspection twice every year, spring and fall. But in California, all we have to get is a lousy smog test, every 2 years. Therefore, we have to take responsibility for our own tests for things like brake lights.

One way is to look at the patterns on a wall, if you back into a parking garage. If one light is missing when you step on the brakes, you can see that pattern pretty well. Or if you are backed up near another car. Or, if you send a passenger back to check. Otherwise, you may not figure it out UNTIL I wave my sign at you. I take one sheet of paper: "YOU HAVE NO BRAKE LIGHTS" – and another, "YOU HAVE ONLY

ONE BRAKE LIGHT" – and glue them to the front and back of a heavy 9" x 12" envelope. I fold this once and leave it in my car's map pocket – one for each car (plus a spare that I bring along for rental cars.)

If I see a car with only one brake light, I bring out this placard, and hold it up and beep my horn. Sometimes, the car may turn off before I get his attention, or, he may refuse to pay any attention to a guy blowing his horn. That's really pretty dumb. I mean, what if I was trying to tell him, "YOUR CAR is ON FIRE" – ?? Some people are so ALOOF, they just try to ignore a guy beeping his horn. Really cool guys. Yeah. Really stupid. Some women, and some men, too!

Anyhow, in the last 6 years, I have seen about 1000 cars with only 1 brake light, and I was able to notify about 70% of them. And I have seen about 140 cars with NO brake lights at all, and I have been able to notify about 90% of them. That's well over 120 cars who might be driving around with no brake lights at all, and I got them to fix it. So I think that is a useful thing for us all to be able to do.

Thus when you get to Appendix W, that includes pages you can photocopy, as they are NOT copyrighted. Glue or tape those copies onto an old envelope, and you can show it to people who don't have enough brake lights.

If you learn that *your* brake lights are not working, then until you get them fixed, you can blink your parking lights ON and OFF, when you use your brakes, so the guy behind you has a chance to guess that you are hitting the brakes. But in a panic situation, you may not have time to do that, so it is important to get the brake lights fixed, pronto. Note, it may not be a brake-light switch that is bad – it may just be your bulbs that burned out. Or it may be a fuse.

Directional Signals

Your blinkers are pretty useful, so people will know which way you are going to turn. It gives them a chance to slow down and get out of your way. If you are on a multi-lane road, you can use your blinkers to request a lane, and many drivers (but, alas, not all) will be polite enough to give you the lane you asked for. Please remember to turn them off when you have completed your turn. Not all signals are self-cancelling. Especially if you are on a straight road.

Sometimes you see a guy with his blinkers on, mile after mile. Technically this is slightly illegal. But you may try to tell this person that he should turn off his blinkers.

One way is to get in front of them, and turn on your blinkers, alternately left and right. Maybe 1/3 of the time, they will catch on, and turn off the blinkers. Another way is to drive beside them, and beep your horn, and then point your first and second fingers at your eyes, as if pointing at YOUR "lights". This, too, works barely 1/3 of the time. Sometimes you just have to give up.

How do you tell if one of *your* bulbs is burned out? Many blinker circuits can detect if a bulb has failed, because the circuit draws less current. The blinker may blink twice as fast - or twice as slow as normal - or, it may not blink at all. If your blinker signal in your dashboard does one of these things, on one side, but not the other, your car is trying to tell you something.

4-Way Emergency Blinkers

I don't need these very often, but they are good to have in case of a breakdown. Or, in case you have to park in a tricky place. Or if you cannot keep up speed on a high-speed road – it is correct to turn on your blinkers if you cannot keep up a minimum speed, such as 45 or 40 mph. Just one caution – after a few hours, these may drain your battery, pretty quick. So don't leave your blinkers on for a long time, if you can help it.

Dash Lights

My wife rented a car. Going up Boston's Southeast Expressway, she reached to do something – and the dash lights went out. She was very uncomfortable about this, because when you are accustomed to having your speedometer lit up, it really feels wrong, if it is not lit. It took her a minute to fish around in the dark to find out how to put on the dash lights.

When she told me this, I said that I had rented that same miserable car, up in Seattle. And the same thing happened to me. It was a bad piece of human engineering. If you move to make a signal to the right-hand lane, if your hands are not tiny, they will bump that dumb big switch, and turn off the lights. I don't remember exactly what kind of car, but they certainly had a Cavalier Attitude about their cars and their drivers. So, make sure you know how to turn the dash lights ON and OFF – even in a rented car. That control may be different from the headlight switch.

Other Lights

The WARNING lights (or "Idiot Lights") for your oil pressure and alternator are really parts of your engine systems, but they are light bulbs, and we will mention them here. When you first turn on the key, they really must come on. Then when the engine is started, they must go off promptly. If they do not, stop immediately, and find out if there is a problem.

The MAP light or "Dome Light" is useful so you can find things in your car, at night – as well as, look at maps. If they are left ON for a few days, they can drain your battery. Don't let that happen!

Troubles with Lights

Sometimes your lights may go out because of a bad fuse. It's not *necessarily* the case that the bulb just burned itself out. Sometimes it is a bad wire – or a bad connection – or a bad switch – or a bent or dirty socket. Any of these is pretty easy to fix – so long as it is not intermittent. There's nothing tougher than an intermittent problem! Anyhow, you may want to get professional help on problems where you can't just fix it by replacing a bulb. Sometimes a little volt-meter can tell you how far the voltage or current is getting. I usually do that; many little multi-function electrical testers have an OHMS mode, so I can tell if the bulb is open. For sure, I don't throw away the "old" bulb, unless I am sure the new one works well.

> NOTE: if a problem is intermittent, you can't just count on a professional – a good guy at a car repair place – to fix it – because it may only go bad when you have the car. So it is reasonable for you to help gather the information that puts the finger on the trouble.

Lights and the Battery

I will not HERE talk a lot about the battery and its charging system. But if I did, I would say – this is surprisingly complex. The alternator can make the battery unhappy. The voltage regulator can make the alternator AND/or the battery unhappy. If your battery gets old and unhappy, it can make the alternator and/or voltage regulator look bad. The symptoms are sometimes a little contradictory, and you may need some clear thinking to figure out which clues are valid. There are many things about the charging system that you cannot measure yourself, and you will probably need help from a good repair shop. Even then, they sometimes make a guess at what is wrong, and after you spend well over $100, they give it back to you, and it is still not fixed. That's not right, but at least I have warned you that that can happen.

The Voltage Regulator

One night I was riding down to Connecticut with a friend in an old 1949 Chevy. We noticed that the headlights seemed to be getting dimmer – and dimmer. We deduced that the battery was not being charged. One of us said, "What if we bang on the voltage regulator?"

We stopped briefly, banged on the voltage regulator with a wrench, and it began to charge. The lights came up to full voltage. We had no more trouble on the trip. Fortunately, the replacement voltage regulator only cost $5.95. Unfortunately, in those days, $5.95 was a lot of money, about 30 gallons of gas, and we could not easily afford that.

Fortunately, these days, voltage regulators are mostly electronic modules, and they are very reliable. UNfortunately, these are quite pricey – and they still cost as much as about 30 to 50 gallons of gas. The electronic circuit only costs a few dollars to manufacture, but they get marked up by the parts distributors, warehousemen, etc.

Old electro-mechanical voltage regulators used to get old and refuse to charge (until you banged on them with a wrench). The newer electronic ones are, conversely, capable of failing full-on, so your battery voltage gets too high. If you notice several light bulbs burning out, and the bulbs that are ON are *much* brighter than usual, better check your voltage. Voltage much higher than 14.6 volts is not only bad for your bulbs, but bad for your battery and any other part of your electrical system.

$$6 \times (3 \times 10^{-2})$$
$$= .18$$
$$2.4 + .18 = 2.58$$

$$6 \overline{\smash)2.6}$$
$$\underline{2.4}$$
$$.20$$

6-11-22

Lights and Etiquette

We have already said – make SURE your lights are not on high beam, when you are approaching on-coming traffic, or when you are behind another car. But there are times when it's correct to use your lights – to signal.

If you see a car coming your way, at night, and he forgot to turn on his lights – it is appropriate to BLINK your lights, ON and OFF, about 2 or 3 times, to warn him that he forgot his lights. A year ago, there was a CAUTION message going around, on the "Internet", that some gangsters were having initiation procedures for new members. The new kid was supposed to get in a car at night, and start out with no lights on. When a car blinks his lights, to warn him he has no lights, the kid is supposed to reach out his window and take his pistol and shoot out the windshield of the car that blinked at him. After a few days, authorities decided that this was a hoax, and quite untrue, and they put out their rebuttal on the Internet. An "Urban Legend". Anyhow, I have always blinked my lights ON/OFF, when I see a car with no headlights on. I never stopped doing it, just because of some bizarre story. Now, a year later, I have not heard any confirmation that young gangsters are doing that. And if they had, I would have heard about it. So I am pretty sure that is not true.

"Give 'Em The Lights"

My father was a truck driver for about 30 years. He pointed out that it is good etiquette to blink your lights (ON/OFF/ON at night; ON-and-OFF in the day) when a truck starts to pass you, and, as soon as the truck's tail is past your nose by a fair margin, "Give him the lights" again. Turn your lights OFF/ON, for just 1/2 second – this tells the truck driver that it is OK to pull back in. It's a helpful thing to do.

The other place to "give 'em the lights", is if you see an accident in the other lane, and then in the next mile or two, you see trucks in on-coming traffic. You turn your lights OFF/ON/ OFF/ON/ OFF/ON, at night. This procedure, 3 blinks, warns him that there is trouble ahead. A heavily-loaded trucker may not put on the brakes right away, but he will be IMMEDIATELY ALERT to any problems ahead – such as a breakdown or accident or slow-down up ahead. He will be able to stop much better, and he will be greatly appreciative of your warning. Even if there are not any trucks, it may still be a good idea. Some drivers will understand that you are passing along a general warning.

Another place where it is useful to "give 'em the lights" is when you are entering an intersection on the yellow, and you want to warn the driver behind you to NOT follow you. See in the Traffic Lights Chapter.

I have driven VWs a lot, and every time I buy one, I notice that the light switch is cleverly recessed into the dashboard, so if you hit your head against it in an accident, it will be cushioned. I always unscrew the knob, and add 3 or 4 washers under it, and put the knob back on. That way, it is not recessed very much, and I can grab the light switch in a hurry, more easily.

Note, some cars have a special connection to the high-beam lever, so you can FLASH the headlights quickly. This is a nice feature. But it does not turn on your tail lights. I like to be able to turn on my tail lights quickly, too.

Can't Blink the Lights?

I recently rented a newish car, some kind of Corsica, one of the GMC products. Actually it had 21,000 miles on it. It was perfectly adequate and competent – even if a bit boring. But I started out from the airport and saw a car with no lights on. I tried to blink my lights at him. But this car has its headlights ON, all the time you are driving, day or night. You cannot turn them off or blink them off. You can only flick on the high beams. Well, I don't like that. It may be better for the general public's safety – but I don't like somebody taking me out of the control of my car. If I had this car, I would at LEAST install a push-button so I could blink my lights OFF and ON.

I finally figured out, if you turn off the key for a second, THAT will make the lights blink off. But on a rented car, it's just not worth the struggle, to take that risk. Still, on PRINCIPLE, I want to find out how to defeat these mindless computers that will not let us do what we want to do.... Screw the damn' computers!!!!! And throw them off the roof. (Well, I must admit, it would have taken me a long time to write this book without a word-processor.) A friend recently rented a Geo Metro (sold by Chevrolet) and he found that while the lights normally stay ON all the time, they do go OFF if the parking brake was put on. So, that is one other possible way to blink your headlights, maybe.

Lights – In Conclusion...

If some of your lights are not working, you can get in trouble because people cannot see you, or you cannot see where you are going. If a policeman sees some of your lights are out, he may stop and politely ask you to fix them. If you do not have a guilty conscience, and do not panic just because a policeman wants to talk to you, then you will just have to get that bulb replaced. If you get really nervous, the policeman may ask a lot of questions. So, it is a good idea to replace any bad bulbs before our friend the policeman has to remind you to.

See also, the Appendix on Jump-starting, in case your lights run your battery down.

P.S., And when you get to a photo-copy machine, make a few copies of Appendix W – you can make up a placard for each car that you drive.

It will say on one side: and on the reverse:

YOU HAVE YOU HAVE

NO ONLY ONE

BRAKE BRAKE

LIGHTS LIGHT

Chapter 28. RAIN, SNOW, & PRECIPITATION

I bet you thought this would be a really long chapter. But we cheated. We put the problems of visibility in bad weather in the Vision Chapter. We put the problem of insufficient traction in the Skids Chapter. So there is not all that much to discuss here. This should be another short chapter.

Rain

Let's say you want to go for a ride in the rain. Go ahead and go. Now, in these conditions, it will be a little more important than usual, not to run out of gas. So be careful about that. And you want to make sure that your wiper blades are adequate – not falling apart, or wiping poorly. If they are, stop off and buy some new blades before you get too far. And you may want to go a little slow in some places, if it is hard to see, or if there is a lot of water underneath the tires. We discussed that under "Hydroplaning", in the Skids Chapter. Now, go and enjoy your ride. I mean, it is not a big deal to go for a drive in the rain. After all, you will bring a raincoat or parka to keep you dry when you get to your destination. If you have to buy gas, or if you have to change a flat tire, your raingear will keep you – well – almost dry. Not too wet. So, have a nice drive.

However

However, if you have to drive through a low valley, subject to flooding, the rules all change. If there are places where water flows over the road, be careful. Any region can have heavy rains that cause the rivers to rise out of their beds. You have to plan what it will take, to make you decide to stop, in case the river rises too high.

Flash Floods

Out here in the west, we sometimes have a "flash flood", where a brief but fierce rainstorm can dump a lot of rain in one spot, and the water can rush down a dry stream bed and surprise you, even several miles away. I saw a little flash flood, one time, in southern Utah. I never really got wet from the rain, as the rain fell several miles to the north. But, as we drove along the parallel road in the sunshine, we saw the water rushing down the adjacent stream bed. It was fascinating. Then we drove another mile – and the stream bed was dry. How could that be?? We stopped and waited a couple minutes – and along came the little flood – and filled up the "dry" stream bed – quite quickly. THAT was impressive.

If you were sitting in your car, in that "dry" stream bed, you could probably start the engine and drive out of there. But if you were camped in a dry wash, and heard this small torrent of water coming down the valley, you might be able to run to your car and race out. But you'd lose all your camping gear! So, don't fool around. Don't camp, or park, or hang around, in a "dry" stream bed. Water can rise VERY fast. Such

6/12/02

as 3 feet in just 10 or 20 seconds. From a downpour that happens so far away you cannot see or hear it!

Deep Water – Deep Sauce

If you see a road under water, and you can't be *sure* that there is only 4 or 5 inches of water running over it, you probably should not cross it. How can you be *sure* the pavement is not washed out a couple feet deep? How can you be *sure* the water won't rise a foot while you are crossing? There are all sorts of stories of people whose car was swept away in flood waters. Or their car stalled in deep water and it was ruined. Of course, there are millions of people who drove through shallow water and got through just fine. You just have to judge the advantages of pressing on through that water, vs. the drawbacks of how painful or expensive it will be if you can't get through. I have some friends who drove their VW through a puddle 3 feet deep, and it floated just fine. They got through just fine. But I can't recommend it. One guy tried to drive his VW across the English Channel. He made it on the second attempt. (The first time, it sank.)

> And when you get out of the deep water, your brakes will probably work very badly – especially if they are drum brakes. Even the disks may take some drying out. So as soon as you are out of the water, step on your brakes, and ride the brakes until they get dry, and begin to work properly. That is one time that "riding the brakes" is exactly right.

Standing Water vs. Moving Water

A friend from Texas gave me some specific cautions about driving through water on the road. If the water is *still* – such as a huge puddle of standing water – you can take some risk. If the water does not get too deep, and the water does not splash too much onto your ignition – or into your air intake – you have a good chance to get through. Even if you don't, you may not get killed.

But if the flood water is *moving* – flowing across the road – and if there is any chance that it may get deeper as you go along – and if the water is even as deep as the bottom of your floor pan – even 5 or 6 inches deep – then you had better not try it. Too often, moving water can sweep a car off the road – especially if the water level gets up onto your door – even 3 or 4 inches. If you are lucky, you could get marooned overnight in a tree. Or you could get drowned, and your car ruined, and everything in it. This explains the difference between moving water and still water. If you see a number of other cars going through, and you are sure your car is heavier than theirs, you might take a chance – but it's really hard to be sure. You may be wise to wait.

Fords

One time I was camping up in the Pemigewasset Wilderness of NH, to hike up to Mt. Hancock. We had to ford a little stream, with our old 1965 VW camper bus, to get to the trailhead. The ford was barely 6 inches deep, and not flowing very fast. Crossing a ford is not exactly the same as crossing flood waters that are moving, but you still have to use your judgement.

We had a nice hike and decided to spend the night in our bus, up at the trailhead. At 1 AM, it began to rain. I got up and climbed into the driver's seat, because I knew if it rained very much, the river could easily rise a foot. I drove down the woods road and got across the ford, easily. It only rained 10 drops, but if I had stayed put, Murphy's Law says it would have rained a couple inches, and I would be stuck at that ford for *days*.

NOTE: of course, a ford always crosses *moving* water, and we just warned you not to. But a ford is, by definition, a place where people have decided it is *usually* safe to cross. On the other hand, in case of heavy rain, almost every ford can get so deep – or so fast-moving – that it is impossible or dangerous to try to cross. You gotta use *Judgement*.

The easiest way to get an idea if it will be safe for you to cross, is to watch somebody else cross. If you have a big, heavy car, and a little car gets through safely, you can decide it will be OK for you. Or, if you have a small car, and you see a big car get wet barely up to the bottom of its body, you might decide to go. Or you might decide to wait. Or, to go around. If you DO decide to follow another car across, follow in the same path, to avoid the possibility of falling into a wash-out on the left or right. If no other car comes along, and you are really nervous, you might take off your shoes and roll up your britches and *walk* across, to prove it's safe.

As for myself, if the water seems pretty slow, I don't mind getting the water 1 or 2 inches up onto the body of my car. If it's *fast,* I don't want it to hit the body of my car *at all.* Good rule of thumb? And, when I start out onto a flooded road, I always cast a wary glance upstream, to see if a wall of water is headed down at me....

K

Snow

Likewise, as we discussed, if you have read the Skidding Chapter, and practice your skids, you have a good chance to keep rolling through moderate amounts of snow. If you read the Vision Chapter, you will know how to see where you are going. That is half the battle. Heck, that is 4/5 of the battle. If you have that stuff down pat, you are in pretty good shape.

However...

However, there are other circumstances, when it is NOT so simple to get through the snow. While there is no known example of an infinite amount of snow, it is quite possible for there to be so much snow, it might as well be infinite. I mean, whether you have 4 feet or 6 feet of snow, that does not make much difference – you are not going to get through. Not to mention, the 200 inches at Donner Summit, at the summit of the Sierras, or the 15-foot drifts at Tioga Pass. Or the 1500 feet of compacted snow piled up on the Greenland ice pack.

Now, there are some places where a big blizzard can drop 4 feet of snow on the roads, and the plows will open it up in a few days. But in many other places, that snow is going to stay there until spring. Even a foot of heavy snow can stop you. And while a foot or two of dry powder snow may not stop you, you will be stopped when the wind blows that powder into 5-foot drifts. Even with your chains on, you might

1/13/19 K

not get through. Or, you might not be able to even find the road. So, while you can get through any normal snow, there are certain conditions that you must KNOW you are not going to get through.

For example, if you go on a hike, or go hunting, up at the end of a long forest road, and Saturday is nice, you might walk several miles up into the wilderness. Then you wake up on Sunday morning, and there's a foot of snow on the ground. By the time you hike down to your car, there's well over 2 feet of snow on the ground. Are you going to be able to get out? Not without chains!! And the more you think about it, the more you realize, that road will be snowed in until May. Is it going to be fun to walk 14 miles to the nearest highway? I hope so. Because this storm may quit in 10 minutes – or it may go on for a few *days*.

Deep Snow – Deep Sauce

- So – *first* of all, if you live in a cold climate, try to avoid situations where you can get marooned, miles from anywhere – such as, at the end of a long dirt road.

- Second, be sure to bring tire chains and a shovel. Make reasonable precautions so you do not get marooned. Leave a message with friends, explaining where you are going, in case you need to be rescued by helicopters.

- Third, bring warm clothes and blankets or a sleeping bag, in case you get marooned. I mean, if you drive daily on a long lonely road, up north, you KNOW there are some days when you will be stopped by snow. So keep your car well-equipped. Keep a little food in the car. (You can chew on snow, for water.)

- Fourth, wear (or *bring*) clothes that you can walk out in. Warm boots, warm coat, hat, and mittens. For a complete discussion, see in the Appendix on 4WD.

- Fifth, if you are on the road, and the snow is getting deep, stop at a town. Maybe you can rent a room. Or at least warm up with a good meal at a restaurant.

- Sixth, when you stop at that town, fill up with gas. You are much better off with a full tank of gas.

- Seventh, before you head out on the road again, check and see if the plows are going through. If they are, you can probably get through just fine. Worst case, you can get through by following a plow. But if the plows are not going out, or not getting through, well, unless you have a 4WD, you will probably not get through.

- Eighth, if there is one direct road that goes where you want, but there is another, longer route that is more likely to stay open, give serious consideration to taking that heavily-travelled road – even if it is longer.

- Ninth, in some states, if you are doubtful of what highways are open, there is sometimes a good official phone number to call for road conditions. Here in California, our state Transportation Department, Caltrans, has a good set of computerized phone numbers you can call. In San Francisco, call (415) 557-3755. Or, outside San Francisco, call 1-800-427-7623. THEN if you have a push-button phone, you just punch in the number of the route you are interested in, followed by #. If in future years, these numbers are changed, ask the Directory Assistance Operator for Caltrans' Road Conditions Line.

6/14/22

Or, if you do not have a push-button phone, call 1-916-445-1534 (not a free call). The recording at that number will give you a whole *LITANY* of all the roads that are closed or under suspicion of closing. Of course, the status of any road can change, but at least you have a chance if they say the road is open. And if they say the road is closed, the odds are good that it will not get opened up really soon!

Best of all, if you listen to the pattern – that in the last 6 hours, several of the roads and passes are closing in the north area, you can tell you had better go south. This is especially valuable if you are trying to drive in the Sierras, in any winter month, and you want to know if the roads are open – or closing. For example, you just KNOW if Route 50 has closed, then Route 80 will be very crowded and slow – *if* it stays open!

Of course, you are wise enough to recognize the tell-tale signs of a building storm. If you listen to the forecast, and every few hours the expected amount of accumulation gets bigger and bigger, that means the forecaster is being fooled, and is just telling you that the amount of precipitation keeps getting bigger than he expected. You don't learn that from listening to a single forecast.

Maybe in *your* state there is a corresponding telephone number. If you are planning to go on a trip and the weather is threatening, find out the good number to call. A friend says that in Massachusetts, the phone number is 617-374-1234 (or *S on a Cellular phone) and you can call up specific route info from your touch/tone phone. If you ask the local police, or look in the phone book, you may be able to find the number for highway conditions.

- Tenth, all things considered, you can still ask the state police or highway patrol if traffic is going through. Of course, their advice should be tempered by your car's condition. Is it heavy or light? Do you have good snow tires? Four-wheel drive? Chains, if push comes to shove?

Marooned? Stranded?

If you do get marooned, don't burn all your gas right away, just keeping the car warm. You might run the engine several minutes every hour. Don't let the snow clog around the tail-pipe, so you will not get carbon monoxide in the car. People do get poisoned when a snow-drift covers the car too much.

When we started going on winter trips, my wife made me buy HER a shovel, too. That way we can each shovel at a leisurely pace, to keep warm, rather than just taking turns. You may be able to get through a bad drift. And the exercise can help keep you warm. But don't get over-heated or over-tired. Maybe if you get through one big drift, there may be clear sailing after that. I've seen that.

Or, you may be able to get turned around and go back the way you just came. After all, you got as far as you did. If you don't wait too long for snow to drift, you may be able to retreat along your old tracks. I'm a stubborn old SOB, but even I know that there are times when retreating is the better plan.

I mean, even in "civilized places" like eastern Massachusetts, you can get marooned or stranded – perhaps along with another 900 drivers. Right on an

Interstate Highway. In that case, the roads are closed because there are too many cars stalled, and the plows cannot get around them. In fact, those cars usually get stranded because the plows never got out of the yard!

This is especially likely if you get a storm before Thanksgiving, because a lot of people don't think about putting on their snow tires until Thanksgiving. I've seen some *marvelous* jam-ups the week before Thanksgiving, because some cars could not even make it up a 2% grade.

Down in Washington DC or eastern Virginia, they have the same basic problem, but there aren't any plows. Almost nobody knows how to drive in the snow, and nobody has snow tires, anyhow. So even an inch or two of snow gets everybody bogged down. It's probably a good idea to not even start out, in conditions like that. Stay home if you can.

Same thing in many other southern areas: it may only take one driver who doesn't know how to drive in the snow, to crash into a couple cars and close the whole road – with just an inch of snow, or a tiny glaze of ice. SO, almost anywhere in the USA (well, maybe not at low altitudes in Hawaii) you can have enough snow or ice to get stranded or hung up for *hours*. Or *days*. Having warm clothes, warm mittens and a hat, and good boots can make it an almost-enjoyable experience. In a pinch, even old newspapers can be stuffed into your shirt, and keep you warm. Socks or other cloth can serve as mittens. That will help keep your hands warm, if you cannot keep them stuffed in pockets. Sitting in a cold car for a couple days is not NEARLY as much fun.

Stuck?

If you do get stuck in snow, the best move may be to dig your way out – even just a little digging can make a big help. First, make sure that if you move the car, it will not just slide into a place where it gets worse. Usually, if you get stuck in snow, it is worth a couple minutes of shovelling, before you try to drive out. Just rocking may get you stuck deeper. Instead, dig a little ahead and behind all four wheels. If you can't easily go ahead, you may be able to go back and *then* go ahead. Sometimes you are wedged onto a snowbank, and you have to shovel some snow out from under the car, or the car will just stay hung up on the snow, with no weight on the wheels. And, as you are shovelling, be careful to stand where other traffic cannot hit you.

After you think the wheels are cleared away adequately, you can get in the driver's seat, and try to drive slowly back and forth. Try to avoid letting the wheels spin, because that just ruins your traction.

Rocking

Or, you may be able to "rock" the car to get it out. Sometimes you are stuck at a low point, and if you try to go forward or back, either way is uphill. A possible solution is "rocking". You put the car in first, try to go ahead a few inches, then quickly put it in reverse and try to back up. Repeat this, alternating forward and back. Sometimes you can build up enough amplitude of motion to get out of the hole you were in. You may just get free. Or you may have to shovel again.

In an automatic transmission, shift into D or 2, and try to ease forward. Then, avoiding wheelspin, shift into R and try going back. If the wheels spin, wait to shift until after the wheels' motion stops, or you might do some damage to the transmission. Don't let the engine *scream*.

Pushes

Sometimes if you have enough people around, they can just push on the car or pull it out of where it is stuck. I won't say that 4 people can pull a small car out of ANYTHING, but often even 1 or 2 people can make a big help, and get you broken free.

> If you are the driver, be very careful not to run over anybody. And get your signals clear. If you want to go back, and they are pushing ahead, you are not likely to make much progress! If you are going to *rock* the car, make sure your helpers understand this. And, try not to spin the wheels, as it can throw snow and mush all over your buddies who are pushing. If you are pushing, make sure to grab carefully, and don't get where the car can run over you.

If you see another guy who seems to be *just a little* short of traction, you might go over and help him out. As I said, just 1 or 2 people pushing can make a big difference. I did this last week....

Going

In a slushbox car, you may make better progress by using "2" range, instead of L or D, because the engine will have less tendency to spin the wheels. Look in your Owner's Manual, and that should confirm this advice. One guy with a Jaguar (265 hp) was told that starting in "2" and putting on his hand-brake a click or two, to add a little friction, can help a lot.

Likewise, in a car with Manual Transmission, try starting in 2nd, and slip the clutch gently, a good bit. This may get you started better than in low gear, if conditions are really quite slippery.

Barring excessive snow accumulations, you can get through most snowy roads. A drive on a snowy day can be a very beautiful experience. Or a challenge. Or some real problems. Maybe a killer problem. Just plan carefully. And use precautions, in case you see that you are getting into trouble. Well, that was *going to be* a short chapter. But, still, that's not too bad.

Chapter 29. BACKING UP

Sometimes you have to back up your car. There are a lot of places where you have to. Many parking places let you pull in, and then you have to back out. Other cases require you to do more complicated backing. You can often choose places to drive that minimize your backing. But you can't avoid it altogether.

What Can Go Wrong?

If you are in tight quarters, you might back into another vehicle or some object. But if you have some time to stop and get out of your car, and walk around and check that you are doing OK, you can minimize the chance of doing that. Watch out for kids, animals, and junk on the road. Or, if you have a passenger to climb out and tell you how you are doing, that's often a good help.

If you think you are in Reverse, and you are not, that can cause problems. Or, maybe an accident. So, if you are not positive, take it easy.

Backing up your car is easy enough for many people. But other people have problems. They don't like to do it, or they say that they are not good at it. Or they can't visualize it.

Good Teachers

I'm not going to tell you that this Chapter can solve your problems, except by steering you to a good teacher. I mean, for some people, the way your head is organized can help you learn how to back up easily. This is sometimes called "structural visualization".

If your head is organized differently – some people call this "abstract visualization" – which is equivalent to a lack of "structural visualization" – then it may be difficult for you to back up. Nothing to panic about – it's just a different way that your head operates. There are teachers who are good at teaching people who do not have a lot of "structural visualization". If you ask any driving teacher, they will either say they can teach this, or they will refer you to somebody who can teach this. I mean, learning to back up does not have to be as hard as learning to play tennis. Because in tennis, the ball doesn't wait, whereas if you are just driving a car, you can go slow and easy, or stop and check your clearance. That helps a lot.

Mirror Images

Part of the problem with backing up, is the mirror effect. If you can handle this, fine. If not, that's OK, too, but you have to handle that case differently. And if you have a *lot* of trouble backing up, maybe you want to be very wary of driving in England, where every driving pattern is *backwards,* reversed compared to our "normal" side of the road.

c/15/2

Part of the art of backing, relates to how well you can turn around and look back over your shoulder. If you can look back easily, that helps a lot. I find it easier to put my right arm over the passenger's seat-back. That makes it easier for me to keep my balance, and easier to turn my body and neck, and look back.

The next thing about backing up is: you want to go slow. An automatic transmission will let you go as slow as you wish. You can make the car *creep* backwards. With a manual transmission, you cannot easily go really slow, unless the area is fairly flat. It really helps to know exactly where you are going. So, if you aren't very good at learning to back up, maybe an automatic transmission will help a lot.

Should you practice backing up toy trucks? Or trailers? It is well known, that an ability to handle one more dimension or variable (backing up a trailer, not just a car) can help you do a better job when you go back to fewer variables. Maybe you should practice with a couple markers on an empty, open parking area.

I just saw an ad in a magazine for a remote-control trailer truck, only $13.95. At first glance, this would be fun for practice at backing up. But then you look at the description of this product. It does NOT say that you can steer it. It says it can go backwards, and forwards, and also has "turn-around action". It does not sound to me like a real toy truck that you can steer properly. The "controller" does not seem to have any steering wheel or joy-stick. So let's forget that one.

I peeked in some toy-store catalogs. They seem to have a lot of radio-controlled racing cars that can zip around, but they did not seem to sell any such cars that can be steered precisely and backed up slowly. Then I went to the Radio Shack, and they had several different radio-control trucks that can be steered, and have a fast and slow speed, forwards and backwards. I bet one of those could be a good learning tool. After you learn how to back it up, add a simple trailer, made with coat-hanger wire and simple wheels.

Backing Up and Brakes

When you are backing up, your brakes don't work quite as well as when going forwards. This is partly because your weight – your *inertia* or your *momentum* – tends to pull you off your seat, and onto your brakes when you are driving forward. When you are backing up, it's a little harder to get your weight onto the brake pedal. Further, brakes are often designed with more braking power when going forward (when you need a lot of braking power) than when backing. This has to do with leading shoes and trailing shoes, in the brake drums. So, don't expect your brakes to work exactly as well in reverse, versus going forward. Because they were not designed to be equal.

A car with rear-wheel drive loses some traction when backing up a steep hill, because the weight transfers off the rear wheels onto the front wheels. I know some hills in San Francisco where I just avoid backing up, as they are so steep. I don't try to back up on the Jones Street hill, between California and Pine, because it's so hard on the clutch, and the tires slip, too. Fortunately, that is not often a requirement. Conversely, a car with front-wheel drive can go up hills better in reverse, because there is more weight on the front wheels.

Backing Up with a Trailer

If you are pulling what we call a trailer (i.e. a semi-trailer, with just one axle), it is an art to back up. But truck drivers do it all the time. It is just a knack. Most drivers who are good at backing up can learn this art. Of course, a long trailer is a lot easier to back up than a short trailer. But if you have a little time, and a little room, it's not that hard. If you practice with a toy truck with a trailer, and figure out how to back that up, then backing up an actual vehicle with a trailer will not be so hard.

Why do you see so many trailers on the road with a wheel fallen off? Well, first, most trailers have small crummy wheels, and they have to turn pretty fast at highway speeds. But the major case when wheels fall off is, wheels on boat trailers. And boat trailers get *backed up* into lakes. And if you back a trailer into water when the wheels are warm, the hot air around the wheel's bearings gets cooled off and shrinks, and tries to suck water into the bearings. The water corrodes and wrecks the bearings after a while, and the bearings overheat, and seize up, and then the extra friction causes the trailer wheel to fall off. The bearings for new boat trailers have been designed better, to have no air inside, but just pressurized grease. And if you allow time for the trailer wheels to cool off before you back the trailer in the water, that can help. But at least there is an explanation why. Because you want to minimize the cases where your trailer wheel falls off. It can do a lot of damage to the trailer, even if it does not cause you to lurch into an accident. If you are pulling a trailer, stop after half an hour to make sure the bearings are not overheating. Check them every time you stop. And be careful – don't burn your hand.

When Can't You Back Up??

If you are towing a double trailer, with one trailer following another, you may not be able to back up any appreciable amount. If you are towing a car on a towbar, you can't back up more than an inch, because the car's front wheels will caster, and jam up. So you have to be careful not to get into places where you'd have to back up. Otherwise, you waste a lot of time rearranging your trailers to a place where you can then proceed.

In some parking areas, they tell you "Do not back in to the parking spaces". I back in anyhow, because it's safer for me. This is because backing out can be a lot more stressful than backing in. See additional comments in Chapter 2 (Stopping) and Chapter 4 (Starting).

Parallel Parking

When you have to park along a street, parallel along the curb, between other cars, that is called "parallel parking". This normally involves pulling up beside the car in front, and then backing into the parking space. This is all mentioned in the Stopping and Parking chapter. But doing that does require you to know how to back up. So even if you live out in the country and never have to do parallel parking, when you go into town, you have to be prepared to *back up* and park parallel.

This is all for Backing Up.

Chapter 30. PHILOSOPHY

As Tom Magliozzi says, "Don't drive like my brother," and his brother Ray responds, "And don't drive like my brother." They make a lot of jokes, but they do tend to agree, there are a lot of serious things that are good to joke about. That does not mean you do not take them seriously. You just do not take them SO seriously, that you can't make a joke. By accusing each other of unspeakable (but nameless) driving flaws, they like to point out that driving nasty is not nice.

There's another way to put it: "Drive Mellow." Don't be aggressive, don't be pushy, and if someone else is pushy, let him go through. Hey, back in the Chapter on Drugs, I pointed out that many people feel that smoking marijuana makes you mellow. If it weren't illegal, maybe we would have more mellow drivers and less accidents? Maybe legalization would have some advantages, on the highway. Still, for the next 34 years before legalization happens, we gotta achieve mellow driving by *thinking*, not smoking.

Etiquette

The main point of driving etiquette is just like a lot of the rest of life:

Do unto others, as you would have them do unto you. Be as nice to people as you can. If you can help it, don't wedge in front of other people. Don't slow other people down. And, don't intimidate other people. Don't try to scare them.

This is related to, "RUDE, NASTY drivers," because rude, nasty drivers DO tend to get you angry. If you are really mad, so mad you can't see straight, just screaming and furious, then maybe you should not get in your car. If you are in the car, and you are getting REALLY ANGRY, maybe you should stop and take a break. I mean, there are many degrees of angry, but the most extreme cases are probably not a good condition to be driving in.

I sometimes drive when I am angry about something, but I try to not let it affect my driving, I use the driving as therapy to let me cool down. I try to stay as alert as ever, and drive as smoothly as ever.

Several of my buddies chipped in with advice on this:

Roy said – don't be aggressive. Don't do stupid things because you are angry at somebody. For example:

- Don't tailgate a guy, because you didn't like something he did.
- Don't stomp on your brakes because you think the guy behind you is too close.
- Don't accelerate to keep someone from overtaking you.
- Don't speed to scare other people in the car.
- Don't refuse to yield when 2 lanes merge into one – "just because you have an equal right to the lane."

Be Philosophical

One of my friends observed, "Have you ever noticed that a lot of lousy drivers are Oriental?" I said, I must admit, I had not noted that. But maybe it is true. I don't want to show prejudice, but I do understand that if nobody in your family ever had a car, then it's hard to learn how to be a good driver. If there was no culture of good driving in your family, it will take a while to learn it. And since a lot of oriental people were at a disadvantage – locked in detention camps for years, or forced to live in city slums – then no wonder they have not grown up with good drivers in their family. Give them some time. However, I do know several Chinese-Americans and Japanese-Americans who are very good drivers. So, every general rule can have lots of exceptions.

Hats?

My personal suspicion is about guys who wear formal hats. (I don't mean cowboy hats, or ski hats, but felt hats, fedoras or old-fashioned semi-formal hats.) I'm not sure why, but when I see a guy pottering along, not paying attention to what is going on around him, he is often wearing a hat. However, I know a couple guys who wear hats, and are good, competent, aggressive drivers. So again, the exception proves the rule....

More Good Philosophy

Stay away from flaky or incompetent drivers, or guys who start doing unpredictable things. Just yesterday, I was coming down from the foothills from Mariposa, CA, following 2 cars at about 60 mph, uphill and down. The car ahead of me passed the lead car. After a while the car now ahead of me slowed down to 45 mph – and not because of a curve or hill. Nor a cop. I had been on his tail – but I got back 50 yards, because I got very nervous that he was going to do something stupid. So, if a driver starts driving strangely – especially if you cannot figure out why – it is a good idea to stay away from him. Either stay 'way back, or pick a safe time and pass him, but make sure you will be able to get 'WAY out ahead of him.

When another driver behaves like an ass, I just put a little space between him and me. Sometimes I try to put a *LOT* of space between him and me. Other times, I try to get *just* far enough ahead or behind the guy, so I can see if he has an accident. I can be a witness, in case one is needed. So, if you see a guy driving badly, stay away from him, either behind or ahead.

Recently I was driving behind a friend on a gravel road. My friends in my car said, "Don't pass him, he'll be insulted. It wouldn't be right to pass him. It would not be right to make him eat your dust." – Well, he was going about 18 mph, and this was MUCH too slow a speed to drive on that road. When we came to a wide spot, I swung out to pass, bipped my horn, and flew on by him. And while for 20 seconds, he was eating my dust, within a minute, there was no problem, because the dust was all gone, and that car was out of sight. I know how to drive on a gravel road, and when you are on a 35 mph road, 18 is just absurd. If I had to stay in 2nd gear, I'd have run out of gas on my way to town. As it was, I got into 4th and rolled along fast. When I met him later, he was not insulted. He just did not want to get any stone bruises on his tires. I was not worried about that, because my tires are big and do not get bruised.

"Body Language"

So if a guy does not give you any signals – does not turn on his blinkers or hit his brake-lights – how do you know what he is going to do? And what should *you* do?

Well – if a car is getting slower and slower, he is either getting ready for a turn, or looking for a place to stop. Even if he does not signal. Sometimes you can see the driver turn his head off to the side – as if he is searching for an address. When I see that, I am likely to start to pull to the center of the road, and *bip* my horn, just in case he wants to pull right and let the rest of the world by. But I would not *just* go out to pass him – because he might be planning to turn left!!

If you see a car wandering back and forth in his lane, you can get suspicious: he is either very sloppy, very sleepy, or drunk. At midnight, or at 1:30 AM, it is probably the latter. No matter what, stay away from him. If you decide to pass him, bip your horn or blink your lights, and pass as quickly as you can. Get out a good distance ahead, and keep out of his way. Or, stay 'way back. Sometimes it is a good idea to just stay back and watch what happens.

"Defensive Driving"

This was a plan established by various insurance companies and safety authorities. It's a whole philosophy that says, don't be pushy, and watch out for other drivers who are pushy, and be prepared to concede the right-of-way to them. This is largely similar to what I have been proposing: "Watch out for the other guy."

I have not seen a lot of stuff on "Defensive Driving", recently. And I never really saw all that much about it when I was a kid, because they had not developed it at the time. When it came out, I was minding my own business, and did not see much about it. Still, I should go back and see what was written about "Defensive Driving". It does not exactly force you to be a marshmallow. It does not require you to never move confidently. But some people said that it has a weakness, because you are only able to defend, when somebody attacks your "space". I like to anticipate that somebody might do something, and I do the right thing before I have to. Still, a lot of the things I am suggesting, in this book, are variations on "Defensive Driving".

"Space Management"

One time I got talking with a bus driver named Joe. He was agreeable to talk about the art of driving. He was a good, experienced driver. His philosophy for looking at driving was, "Space Management". As you roll along the road, there is a space around you and in front of you, where things and vehicles may affect you. If you drive faster, that "space" that you have to worry about, tends to get bigger, and you still have to make certain that nobody does anything in that zone to get you in trouble. If they do, you have to slow down or steer to a different lane to avoid that conflict. That's a pretty good way to look at it. Good Philosophy.

"Four Eyes"

Another guy told me you need one eye to look at the road, right in front of you, and one to look in your mirrors, and one to look at your speedometer and dashboard. And you need one more to look way out ahead of you. Since most of us do not have 4 eyes to look in four different places, then we must time-share, and scan, and take turns at these 4 tasks. That is one of the hard things for beginning drivers to learn to do. For a beginner, each one of these tends to take almost all your time. So the art of time-sharing takes a *lot* of practice and study, until you can do it automatically.

Pointy

As I mentioned, my sister Jerrilyn once commuted to work with me, for several months. We discovered that it was useful for the "passenger" to POINT at brake-lights up ahead, and call out "brakes". We developed this so if we were talking, we did not even have to say the *word* brakes. For example, *she* would just *point* at the brake lights that were starting to light up, up ahead, and keep on talking. I would *point* my fingers also, to confirm that I got the message.

She has continued to use this system, with her family. She uses it not just for brake lights, but for any other strange happenings that are popping up, up ahead – or off on the side. Now, somebody might say, it ain't polite to POINT. But it also ain't polite to drive into an accident, and this seems like a very good way to minimize the danger of an accident. For instance if my passenger just says, "LOOK OUT!", that may be of some help, but if he says, "LOOK OUT!" and POINTS at the car who is starting to do something stupid, or points at somebody who is starting to infringe on my "Managed Space", that might be a lot better. You might try it. I think it's a good idea.

Note, this is a way to use your passenger's eyes to help watch out for things and to see things for you. It does not yet make "Four Eyes", but it is a step in the right direction. And, sometimes your passenger can see things the driver can't, as he gets a different angle. And, even a kid could be helpful at this.

TRAINED RESPONSES

I talked with an expert driving instructor, here in San Francisco, several months ago. He was writing a book, and his topic is, how a driver should be *trained* to automatically do the right thing. This is because often you do not have time to think or plan; you have to pre-plan what you will do in any case, for certain types of problems. Hey, I'll have to call him up and see how his book is coming. I bet he even has some ideas I don't. I want to read his book, and be able to recommend his book. Maybe he can say a few good words about mine. I sent him my Column on "Reflex Response Stuff", which is included here as Chapter 60. I figured that out, myself, independently. Of course, there are all sorts of cases where you cannot exactly plan in advance what you would do. But you can plan some general philosophical moves.

Well, I bet there are a lot of other "philosophical" topics, but that is all I can think of right now. Good place to quit. / rap

Chapter 31. RUDE, NASTY, UNPLEASANT DRIVERS

In the Chapter on Junk On The Road, I already told you about the guy who kept driving ahead when there was a lot of junk from a busted playpen on the road – even though I held up my hand for him to stop. When one of the sticks busted a hole in his radiator – all you can say is, justice is rarely served to a nasty driver, but when it is, and it's the driver's own nastiness that does him in – oh, that justice feels good. In that case, I did not have to kick his car, or holler at him. He just caused himself his own pain.

How to Hold Your Temper?

WHAT do most Driving Teachers tell you about this?? About Nasty Rude Drivers? They usually tell you that you should always be nice to other drivers – and not get angry.

– WHY is that not adequate advice? Because there are a lot of cases where it is NOT HUMANLY POSSIBLE. If a driver cuts you off, you can understand that. Maybe he's in a big hurry. Maybe he's just a slob. Let him go, and in a few minutes he will be far away from you.

He Cut You Off?

But if a driver cuts you off, and then makes some other moves to be unpleasant to you – has your instructor or your parent told you how to handle this problem? Maybe not. But, see my suggestions below – down near the end.

Let me tell you a story Terry told me. Terry asked me, "Bob, do you ever see a driver who zooms up when you signal for a left turn, and sits on your left, and will not let you get in the left lane?" I said, No. He said, "I sometimes see these people who zoom up and block you from getting in the left lane." I said that I really do not see people doing this. When I want to take a left lane, I check to see if this area is clear. If it is, I signal and promptly take that lane. If a guy decided to try to pre-empt that lane, he would not get there ahead of me. Or if he really is moving a lot faster than I am, I will not even try to signal or to pull out until he is past me. So, I never see another driver trying to block me off from my lane-change. Do YOU guys see that??

Rough Justice...

Anyhow, Terry explained what happened to his wife recently. She was driving down Route I-280 by Palo Alto. She signalled for a left lane change, and some idiot zoomed ahead and drove right up on her left. Not only that, but he kept looking over at her, and grinning, because he had blocked her. He kept grinning at her, and grinning... and just then – the Mercedes Benz in front of him hit his brakes hard. And the idiot who was grinning over to the right – he was not watching, and the idiot slammed into the Mercedes. Ooohh, think, EXPENSIVE.

In case you had not thought about this, the guy BEHIND is responsible if he slams into the car in front. YOU have the responsibility to not bump into the car in front of YOU. And even if you put on your brakes hard, the guy behind YOU is responsible for not hitting YOU. So, it is not very bright, to keep grinning at a driver beside you, in case the car in front of you hits his brakes....

Expensive Lessons...

Then a friend told me about another driver who was kind of nasty. When a car signalled to move to a right-hand lane, Mr. Nasty would speed up and block that car. One day, he started to block a car on his left, who wanted to get over into the exit lane. Whenever that car would speed up, he would speed up. Whenever that car would slow down, he slowed down. After a while, the car on the left was getting kind of desperate, so he floored it and cut right, even as Mr. Nasty was speeding up to block him. The frustrated driver smashed into Mr. Nasty, and both cars crashed and were totalled. Mr. Nasty was badly injured, too. Afterwards, he admitted he had made a mistake, and said he would never do it again. Well, I would not have believed anybody could be so stupid in the first place. I am kinda speechless. But I would say, if somebody tried to block me out like that, I could probably safely evade him. If there were heavy traffic, I would wait until a car blocked Mr. Nasty, and then I would ease around to get to my exit. Or, if there were no traffic, I would wait until the last second and then I could easily outbrake Mr. Nasty, and cut behind him and go down the exit. Get the picture?

Who's Too Slow? Who's Too Fast?

I am sometimes considered, by some of my colleagues, to be an aggressive, pushy driver. Maybe that is not a fair accusation, or maybe it is. I won't argue about that. Sometimes perhaps I am pushy. Other times, I am laid-back, cautious, and *not* pushy. I must say, I am in favor of progress. But I always try to move along as well as I can, and if a guy is trying to move along, I like to get out of his way.

Hey, LOOK: my VW has a 1.6-liter engine, and it goes uphill very well, and with more power, faster than 1968 VWs ever did in 1968. Okay? And still, almost EVERY CAR ON THE ROAD can go uphill faster than I can, if there are not too many curves. Every other car has more power per weight than I do. So, every damn' car in California can go up a hill faster than I can. And, if he WANTS to, I will pull over and let him. The law says that if there are 4 cars behind me, and I am struggling up a hill, I do not have to pull over and let them by. But if there are 5, I am legally required to. Yet we know that a TAIL of even 10 or 20 cars does not actually cause a stupid driver to pull over.

Let me assure you, if even ONE car shows up on my tail, and he is serious about wanting to go faster than I can go, I will cheerfully pull over and let him pass. And if a serious driver comes up behind *you*, *you* should let him pass, too. Hey, anybody who likes to drive slow, ought to let other traffic by him. I bet 40% of the unhappiness and rancor on the road (and a lot of the accidents, too) are caused by a driver who doesn't know how to go fast, but has no idea how frustrating it can be for other drivers to get stuck behind a slow driver.

Every once in a while, I get stuck behind a slow vehicle up in the Sierras. Often this is a Recreational Vehicle – a big Camper. It's not just me. It is usually about 25 other cars, stuck behind this foolish, thoughtless *slow* driver, all frustrated. One of these days, I plan to get a fast motorcycle to pull up ahead of this RV, and do a Citizen's Arrest. We will get that RV to stop, and we will get other cars to block it totally. Then we will let all the other traffic by it. Then we will let all the air out of all the tires on this RV.

THEN we will go down into town, and explain to all the RV dealers, what just happened. And we will caution these dealers to tell all the other RV owners, to NOT block the roads and refuse to let people pass. Or else.

OK?? Is that a good idea?

Are you on my side? Or do you drive a slow RV? Think about it. If you do not want to drive fast, or if you *cannot* go as fast as other people want to, and there are several cars behind you – or even just *one* car – pull over and let those guys go by. It's better for you, and better for everybody else.

Sometimes, I can't go fast, and when other people want to go faster – I let them go. I help them pass me. Who am I, to try to block them? I can't play God and tell them they should not go faster than I'm going – even if I am going over the speed limit. It suits me fine if another guy knows how to move along at a good speed.

On the other hand, sometimes I want to go faster than other slow (or fast) drivers. I have enough power to go out and pass, in most cases. I hope that doesn't bother anybody else.

– Long ago, whenever I went to pass a slow car, with my first (1962) VW, the driver would look over at me, just as I was passing him, and realize, "Oh, if that little car is going to pass me, I must be going too slow", and he would tromp on the gas, and I could not pass him. I must say, I did consider that irksome to me. But for the last 15 years, almost nobody does that. So the world is not as grouchy a place as it used to be.... Maybe people are more used to being passed by VWs.

– SO, I have seen that drivers are not, in general, as nasty as they were, just a few years ago. I think I have seen fewer nasty or unpleasant or rude drivers – and I think that is not *just* because I moved out of Massachusetts! I think that *even* in Massachusetts, there are not as many disagreeable or unpleasant drivers as there used to be.

The Other Way Around...

Hey – what do you do if somebody shows you that he thinks that *you* are a nasty person? He blows his horn – or gives you "the finger", to show his disdain for the way you drive.

Well, you could *obviously* send him back a similar reply – give him the finger, too. BUT, you know what? I do not recommend that. You do not have to be unpleasant. Even if you are driving a big truck, or an expensive car, or a pretentious car. Besides, the guy might have a gun. Some drivers might get really mad at you, or try to run you off the road. It's better to use the old dictum, "A soft answer turneth away wrath".

I recommend that you learn how to give a classic shrug.

How to Shrug...

Let's say you are stopped at a light. You just goofed up the driver behind you. Then you have to perform a shrug, to show the guy behind you that you didn't mean any harm, and you're sorry.

There are 2 basic styles of shrug:

– 1. The Mechanic's Shrug: You stare straight ahead. You hold up both hands beside your head – see Sketch A. Meanwhile you lift your shoulders up, and duck your head down, for a second, so as to say, "What could I do?" – Or –

– 2. – If you did something really stupid, put both hands over your head, on both sides, as if to say, "Oh, what I just did was really stupid". See Sketch B.

– Either way, it's much better than giving the guy the finger. If the driver is behind you, he can see you shrug. If he is beside you, turn sideways so he can see you give the shrug.

– Now, what if you are driving on the road, and you goofed up another driver – perhaps cut him off, or nearly caused an accident? You want to give the guy a shrug – but to do that takes both hands. How can you drive without both hands on the wheel? First, you have to learn how to drive with your knees for just a short time.

THE CLASSICAL "MECHANIC'S SHRUG" (REAR VIEW)

When You Should Drive With Your Knees...

First of all, you should never drive with your knees, for more than just a second or two. Second, you should never drive with your knees when you cannot move your hands back to the wheel instantly. Like, you should NOT drive with your milkshake in your left hand, and your burger in your right hand, and only your knee against the wheel. You must be able to get back to steering instantly. You should normally drive with your hands on the steering wheel. And you should not take both your hands off the wheel. Still, I gotta show you how to do this. Because if you don't hold

y

A CLASSICAL SHRUG – –"I'M SORRY" – –"MEA CULPA"– – WHILE STEERING WITH THE LEFT KNEE AGAINST THE STEERING WHEEL ....

your knee up against the wheel, then nobody is holding onto the wheel, and that would be absurd.

How to Drive With Your Knees...

If you are on a reasonably straight road, and if the car is pointing stably in its lane, and if you think it will stay in the middle of its lane for a couple seconds – lift your left leg up, and put your thigh or your knee up against the steering wheel, to stop it from turning. If the car is still stable, then lift up your hands and do a shrug for a second or two.

Meanwhile, you must always keep your eyes on the road. If you need to steer, you bring your hands down fast to the wheel, and steer. Or if you need to brake, you can take your knee off the wheel and step on the brakes, at the same time you are returning your hands to the wheel. Not a big deal, for one or two seconds. A guy behind you can almost always see this and appreciate that you are apologetic. Again, if you have to grab the wheel and steer, no problem – just keep your eyes on the road.

I am *not* saying you should not ever get mad, inside. I'm just saying that it is a good idea not to show it, and a good idea not to rant or rave at the other driver. You may try hollering, to yourself – when he cannot hear you. You can shout, when he is out of earshot, "I cannot *BELIEVE* how stupid that driver was!!!!" It might make you feel better. I think it's bad if you hold all your anger inside and do not even say a peep.

So, try not to be nasty when you don't have to. And don't get too cross at other people if they goof you up. It's OK to shout and Holler*, so long as they cannot hear you. And you'll feel better.

"Road Rage"

"Road Rage" is really nothing new, but the awareness of it is suddenly a big deal. Let's all try not to show our anger at other drivers who make rash moves or foolish mistakes. (Even if they HIT YOUR CAR, it's a good idea not to lose your cool.) If you calmly contemplate, in your head, what an *idiot* some other driver is, that's better than showing you are angry. Don't make things worse by swearing or making rude gestures. OK?

* *"What's All This Hollering Stuff, Anyhow?"*, Robert A. Pease, in ELECTRONIC DESIGN *Magazine, July 10, 1996, Penton Publishing, Hasbrouck Heights, New Jersey 07604.*

Chapter 32. RISKS

Everybody takes risks. Every time we get in a car, we take a risk. Every time we walk out of our house, we take risks. Every time we climb out of bed, we take risks. If we did not take any risks, we would get nothing done. The question might be -- what are *acceptable risks*?

Going skiing is fun – and it involves taking some risks. Driving your car vigorously involves risks. Driving in snow is more risky. Driving a small, light car like a VW is supposedly more risky than driving a heavy car. However, I am willing to take those risks. I don't find them very bad. Further, a smaller car (that is more agile) may be able to avoid certain kinds of accidents that a larger car might not be able to.

Risk per Mile?

The insurance companies seem to think there is more risk in driving a lot of miles per year – because they charge you a higher insurance rate if you drive a lot of miles per year. I disagree. Being a good driver means doing a lot of practice. Driving a lot of miles. People who drive fewer miles have less practice – and are usually not as good drivers, and have more accidents per mile. People who drive VERY LITTLE are usually lousy drivers. Think about it. I refuse to believe that drivers who drive MORE, have more accidents than people who don't drive much. Because they have a lot fewer accidents per mile.

Still, everybody wants to avoid excessive or unreasonable risks. In this book, I am trying to point out that some things that do seem not very risky, can actually be pretty dangerous. I want to teach you guys how to minimize that excess risk.

– The following text has been CRIBBED from an e-mail by Roy in Austin Texas:

"STAR TREK Probability Theory"

"If you watch much of Star Trek, you've probably observed that the mathematics of probability don't work the same in that universe. There are two significant differences:

"Things with very small probabilities happen too often. We are told that the chance of a transporter malfunction, or of the holodeck hurting someone, are better than a million to one. Yet we've seen multiple happenings of both in only a couple hundred episodes. Boy, if I was Johnny Luck (our nickname for Capt. Jean-Luc Picard) I'd have that holodeck sealed off.

"Come to think of it, this sounds a lot like NASA's Space Shuttle Probability Theory. So, was the Space Shuttle *Challenger* destroyed by TV probability theory? Too much wishful thinking?

"Conversely, things with large probabilities don't happen often enough. It seems that over and over, the probability of surviving some course of action is only 1 out of 2 or 2 out of 3. The crew (or crew person) bravely set their jaws, unselfishly choose to accept the risk, and thus save the ship. Yet they don't die or get hurt much.

"The point, of course, is that you can survive a 50% chance of death, or 10%, or 1%, but if you keep doing it, you are going to get killed. If you are going to survive years of driving, you have to make your everyday risk very small.

"Let's look at some examples. If you took a 1% risk of dying every day, how long before the accumulated risk would be 50%, 90%, 99% or 99.9%??

RISK of DEATH	ELAPSED TIME
50%	2.3 months
90%	7-1/2 months
99%	1 year + 3 months
99.9%	1 year + 10.5 months
99.99%	2 years + 6 months

"Here's another way to look at it: The population of the earth is about 5 billion people. If everybody took a 1% chance of death every day, how fast would the population decrease? (assume no births)

TIME	POPULATION
0	5,000,000,000
Day 1	4,950,000,000 *
1 year	128,000,000
2 years	3,270,000
3 years	83,700
4 years	2,140
5 years	55
6 years	1.4
6 years, 1 month	1

* Note that there would be 50 million deaths on day 1, and not a whole lot less on day 2, etc."

– Thanks for pointing out these risks, Roy!!

– If we all drove like that, the world would not be where it is today. Therefore, we must concede that very few people take a risk of 1% per day. Not even your dumb brother-in-law who has wrecked a car several times in the last 5 years!!

Can you drive and keep your risks acceptably low? I don't want a death risk of 1% per day or per year; I think a traffic death rate of 1% per 50 years is tolerable, for *me*. I'm *certainly* not going to demand a death risk of 1% in 1000 years, because I'd stay home all the time and never have any fun.

The National Safety Council...

Years ago, the "National Safety Council" used to pompously predict that on a 4-day holiday weekend, such as Labor Day, 540 people would die in car crashes, between Friday night and Tuesday morning. Scary! And by Tuesday morning, we found out they were right.

However, somebody finally noticed that since there were about 50,000 traffic deaths in a year, then we can expect about 540 deaths, on the average, in ANY 4-day period. So, if there were MILLIONS of vacationing drivers on the road on a 4-day weekend, and only 540 got killed, than a lot of people must be driving pretty safely. Finally those Safety Experts got cut off from their ability to bleat about dangerous driving.

Think of it this way – if 48 million drivers were on the road, on any given day, and 48 drivers and 90 passengers were killed, that is a chance of 1 in a million for the drivers. If you drive 300 days per year, that's a 300 ppm rate, per year, or for 50 years, 15000 ppm. HEY – that is about 1.5% per 50 years. That is just a little worse than what I said I would tolerate. Of course, I hope to do a little better than that.... After writing this book, I'd be embarrassed if I didn't live forever.

Still, as I been sayin', and I'll say it once more: anything that you do, that is risky – such as speeding, or hurrying through corners – if you get away with it for a while, and you think you are safe – if you keep it up long enough, there is some interesting chance of getting in trouble. You figure out if the risks are worth it. Now I'll shut up.

Chapter 33. PENALTIES, PAIN, and OTHER INCENTIVES

When I first started writing this book, I realized, to make any sense, I have to have rational descriptions of pain and penalties. I cannot tell a teenage driver, with a straight face, "If you speed, you will die", because we both know that is BS. We all speed. And we all die – eventually. Even people who do not speed, all die. So I can't sell you a dumb line of crap.

Yet there are penalties. It is worth a LOT of effort, and a lot of thinking and planning, to avoid accidents.

Pain

If you get into accidents, it may hurt. You may bang your head, and hurt for months – or years. Or break a leg. You might be hospitalized for days – or weeks. You might lose an arm. Or a leg. Or two. Or you might just get aches and pains that last for years. If you were in a fire, it might take many months to do the skin transplants to get your burns patched up. I am told that is very painful, and the pain is very *annoying*. And it does not go away for a LONG time.

All these things *can happen*. Not very often, but if you went into a hospital and talked to people who were really banged up, you might think, "Hey, it sure would be nice to NOT get stuck in here."

Then you might say – "But accidents happen to the other guy. I'm too smart to get into accidents." Teenagers are really good at saying that. Yeah. Sure.

Look, every one of those guys who is moaning in the hospital, used to say that, or think that, too. Arguing that "it won't happen to me" is a pretty thin argument to depend on. Even arguing, "I read all of Pease's book, and I understand it", won't help you much, if you don't abandon certain kinds of dangerous driving.

Expense

It might cost you a lot of money. You might have to replace things that your insurance does not cover. Or your insurance rates might go up. 'Way up. Or your insurance company might DUMP you, or put you into an "assigned risk" category that costs a lot more.

Time Lost...

It might cost you a lot of time. You might have to spend a lot of time, *walking*, or riding a bus, until you get your car fixed. Time talking to repair shops. Time talking to insurance guys. Time in jail. If you *really* screwed up, maybe time in prison. Even worse, you might have to spend some time talking to lawyers.

Loss of Friends...

It might cost you a friendship. If you rack up your car, your passenger might be more than a little unhappy with you. If your passenger is badly injured – maybe you lose a friend. If your boyfriend or girlfriend is killed in an accident while you were driving – YOU LOSE. Even if you did not get a scratch.

It might cost you a really good car. If you have a car that is really nice – you might have a real problem replacing it – that might be impossible.

You might get a very troubled mind, if your car hurt or killed some innocent person. I remember that line from the National Safety Council: "I couldn't see that kid, that night when he ran out in front of me. I was too drunk to see him. But I can see him now. I see him every day. I just close my eyes – and I see him...." Are you *sure* you do not have any conscience to bother you for MANY years, if you caused an accident that causes some poor guy to get badly hurt, or crippled, or killed? What if some stupid school-bus driver pulls out in front of you, and a whole bunch of kids are killed? Hey, perhaps the accident was not even your fault – but if you had made the right move, you *might have* avoided hitting that bus.

Or, you might just get killed. Hey, it won't likely hurt for long, when you SMASH into that wall. And after a short time, it won't hurt at all.

Worst Case...

And you know what would be, for me, the worst part of that? For the 4 seconds before impact, I would realize: "Everybody will come to the funeral and say, 'Bob really screwed up.'" I think that would really bother me, that they would all be thinking that. For the rest of my life – for about 4 seconds.

Positive Incentives

What are some of the incentives that are POSITIVE, as opposed to penalties? Well, other people may think you are a really nice person, because you are a good, safe driver. You may get trusted to drive to special places – which you would not get to do if you had accidents.

Sometimes, a person of the opposite sex may like you if you are a safe driver, and may decide to shun you if you hot-rod too much, or do crazy stupid things – or get into accidents. So, sometimes the friendship of a special person can make it worthwhile to cut down on certain wild tactics. You figure it out.

Right now, I can't think of any other POSITIVE incentives, but I bet there are some. You tell me. Ah – yes – now I recall. When I was 18, working on a farm, the boss set me to driving a truck. I drove it fairly competently, and did not goof up nor goof off too much. Shortly, he set me to driving the workers' bus. It was not a big deal, but it was a lot better than walking down a long hot row with a hoe, hoeing weeds.

If you are a good driver, you may get a chance to drive some interesting cars, or other vehicles. Hey, do racing sponsors give a car to a young guy who is aggressive and pushy and crazy-fast? No, generally they do not – they give it to a kid who shows some promise, and drives smoothly, and does not get into accidents. So there really are some positive incentives, not to drive like crazy.

So why do drivers do things that are not quite safe? – things that are really dangerous? Well, we try to calculate the *risks*. We think that if the chance of being penalized is small enough, it may be OK to take that risk. And sometimes we are right. BUT, sometimes we are wrong. In that case we have to reconsider – did we really botch our estimates of the risks? Refer to the Chapter on Risks.

Continued Risks...

And, as mentioned elsewhere, we often do things that are risky, because we have done them, many times, and it seems that we got away with it. So we keep doing it. We keep on until – until we get in trouble. Maybe we shoulda got smart, and learned to quit the most risky behavior, *before* we got in trouble??????????

Police, Insurance People, and Lawyers

I think I already mentioned, in the Chapters on these topics, that staying out of accidents makes it easier to avoid spending a lot of time, talking to these people. So, just in case these are *not* your favorite people, there is another good reason to try to avoid accidents....

Registry of Motor Vehicles

The Department (or Registry) of Motor Vehicles is loosely linked to the police. If the police issue a lot of tickets, and you refuse to pay, the Registry will grab ahold of you, the next time you want to register your car, or in case you want to sell it. You'll have to pay up before you can get your registration. Conversely, if you have too many accidents, the Registry can request a judge to suspend your driving license. This kind of linkage will vary in every state. It does not have much DIRECT to do with accidents, but if you have one or more accidents, they may inform you that you have certain technical problems – like – suspending your license if you accumulate too many "points", by having too many accidents. You don't have to think much about them, but it is nice to know that not having accidents is a good way to stay away from these people. Another good incentive.

Well, there's another short chapter....

Chapter 34. MAKING ASSUMPTIONS – And How They Can Get You in Trouble...

One of my friends raised the questions of *assumptions*. What if you *assume* that a car is going to turn right, just because he is signalling a right turn. You look left to see if there is any car coming – and there is not. Then you proceed straight ahead – and you find that you have crashed into that car – which did not turn, after all.

Or you *assume* you can make a sharp turn, the same as usual, even though you know that one of your tire's pressure is low. Well, with the tire low, you *can not* make the curve. Crunch.

Or you *assume* you can make a sharp curve, as usual, even though the first rain of the season is just starting. And you skid. Crunch again.

Well, that is part of this book, to remind you that a little tiny "detail", like a bit of rain, or some low tire pressure, is NOT a minor detail, and can in fact make a BIG difference in how your car corners or stops. No, you should NOT assume that your car's capability to perform well is unchanged. *6-19/22*

A friend of mine, Don, was coming down the hill on Route 17, which is a 4-lane road with a center divider in most places, but some cross traffic. Well, we all know that this is a dangerous road. But if people drive in a rational way, maybe it ain't so bad. Ah, but what if we *assume* the other drivers will be rational – and they ain't?

Don was coming down the hill in the fast lane. A car pulled out from the right, and crossed in front of him, to go up the other lane. Don assumed the car would get out of the way. And he did. However, Don was NOT expecting a second car to follow the first car. And a second car DID follow the first car. Now, everybody was assuming the first car would keep going, and get out of the way.

But he didn't. He stopped half-way across the road, leaving the second car squarely blocking the fast lane. Well, Don was assuming the first and second cars would go away. BUT they didn't. Don was *assuming* he would not have to hit his brakes. So he didn't brake – until he realized that the second car was NOT following his assumptions, but was REALLY stopped right there in front of him. So Don locked up his brakes and got stopped about a foot from the second car. I must say, that idiot in the second car probably got the scare he deserved, because he didn't know if Don could stop. And, hey, Don didn't know, either!

Be a Skeptic

I guess the general point is, if you want to make any assumptions, *assume* that the other car is NOT going to get out of your way. *Assume* that it is a good idea to put on the brakes and slow down a little, just in case the way is blocked up ahead.

Assume that if the pavement is not optimum, it will be worse, and you should go slower around the curve. Hey, I specifically like to take a little skid on a rainy freeway ramp, so the lurch and slide will remind me that the road is slippery today. That little lurchy feel in my gut, is a good reminder, all day long.

I hate to peddle old trite phrases, but it's an old saying that an ASSUMPTION makes an ASS out of U and ME. So if you want to ASSUME something, be skeptical. Assume that the worst case may indeed happen, and you want to be prepared, so you will be slowed down enough to stop. And it's not just YOU that slowed down, but, if you do it right, the guy behind you will be forced to slow down, too, and HE will not slam into you if you have to stop. OK?

Modern Cars...

I think there is one more aspect of this. Modern cars are built to perform and handle so well, that you can corner hard, and brake hard, and not even notice it. Your power steering does not even tell you how hard you were working to get around the curve. Then if the road is a little slippery, or the tire pressures are wrong, it is easy to *assume* that you are not driving very fast, and you should be OK. But actually, you were driving up near the limits of the road and the tires, and if the road gets wet, and all you are trying to do is go as fast as you did yesterday – then you get in trouble.

I think I avoid that problem, because I try to drive up near the Limits, and I think I know where the limits are, and I KNOW I have to slow down on a wet day. Does that make any sense?

Well, there's another short chapter....

I am not responsible, nor am I liable, for any driving mistakes you make because of anything I wrote

Chapter 35. JUDGEMENT

What does it take to be a good driver? It takes experience, and you have to have good judgement.

How do you get good judgement? You develop good judgement by getting in trouble, and you learn.

How do you get in trouble? By having bad judgement.

How do you break out of this cycle? This book will help, because it acts like SYNTHETIC GOOD JUDGEMENT. For a beginning driver, it will help you survive, without having to make so many mistakes. As you read this, you are *learning from the mistakes of others.* After you have some experience, you can develop your own good judgement. But before you are an experienced driver, the advice in this book can help keep you out of trouble, by minimizing bad judgement. Also, the Chapter on "Reflex Response Stuff" is good to study, as it can help you plan in advance, what your judgement will be. You can *pre-plan* what your choices will be, in many cases.

For example – if you hear a siren behind you, you might decide automatically to slow down and pull over to the right, and stop, to let the ambulance or fire engine go past. Or, in a nervous panic, you might decide to step on the gas and get away. May I suggest that the former plan is a good idea. Stepping on the gas is a *lousy* idea, because the police get very suspicious about anybody with the wrong reflex response.

Well, there's another short chapter. / rap

here – or any advice that I do NOT give. Whatever you do, DON'T break laws, and DO use good sense and good judgement, no matter what you read.

Chapter 36. SLEEPY-ness and BOREDOM

You Can't Stay In Your Lane If You Fall Asleep...

Let me tell you a new deal. In my day, I have griped a lot about the Massachusetts Turnpike, and I have said many grouchy things about that road. But I was driving down the Mass Pike last month, and I noticed something new, something they are doing right: Now if you start to veer off the 3 main lanes of the Mass Pike, *either* to the left or to the right, the pavement has blocks with grooves that will REALLY wake you up. These grooves are like 2 inches deep and 6 inches apart, and will *REALLLY* vibrate your car. Are these called RUMBLE STRIPS? I think so. I sure wish all the Interstate Highways would add these wake-up zones at the edges of their pavement. I wish they would accept this as a Federal Standard. I really believe this could cut down on "fall-asleep" accidents. Let me tell you where to write, to argue in favor of this.* I mean, have *you* ever nearly fallen asleep on the road?

"The Wages of Sin is Death"

A visitor, Mary, told about a time she missed work for a year. That's a hell of a waste of time – not to mention the pain and suffering. She was driving east near Elko Nevada, on Interstate Route 80. She told me that when she started out that morning, she was not aware that I-80 was one of the top 10 roads in the USA – *tops* for accidents because of boredom. Most drivers have not learned to drive for hour after hour and not watch anything go by in the way of scenery. If you ever get bored by 5 minutes of *the same thing,* wait until you see 5 hours. Or 10. Or 15.

When I was a kid, I was impressed by the great potential for boredom when my father drove up the new Maine Turnpike – the straightest road I had ever seen, at that time. Ah, but compared to Nevada, that is *nothing* – a very minor deal. The Maine Turnpike is a ROLLERCOASTER compared to some of the roads in Nevada. Not only is I-80 mostly a flat, boring straight road, but the alternative routes, such as US 50 and US 6, are also, in many places, rather flat, straight, and kinda boring. I really like these roads, but it calls for a special kind of thinking to survive along these roads.

BORING? You want BORING? I'll show you BORING...

Actually, I used to think that I-80 across Nevada *was* boring, but now that I have been studying the geology of the western mountains, I find lots of things to look at. My eyes *rove* from the road to a hill, then *back* to the road. Then I peruse a *line,* perhaps a fault-line or a cliff or ledge that ascends the hill – and then back to the road. Then – if there is not any traffic, and if I feel there is no problem on the road ahead – my eyes *caress* another straighter line ascending the hill – perhaps a dirt road, or perhaps an old railroad grade. Then, with no waste of time, my eyes *snap*

* to write to - Federal Highway Administration, 400 - 7th Street SW, Washington DC 20590.

back to the road. If you pretend that you can concentrate solely on the road, yeah, that *WOULD* put you to sleep. Whatever the hell puts you to sleep, STOP DOING IT.

Let me spell it out clearly: "The WAGES of SIN is DEATH". (New Testament reference). I hate to be preachy, BUT. BUT – if you are unable to stay awake, please take a nap, because if you want to live, if you want to survive, and you are sleepy, then you really ought to stop and rest.

There are ENTIRELY too many people who have died because the driver could not keep awake. So, if you do not want to kill yourself *and* all the people in your car, and the people in another on-coming car, then, *take a break.* A 10-minute nap can do you a *lot* of good. I hate to be preachy, but while I can trust every reader and every driver to follow a LOT of rules quite faithfully, I cannot trust YOU to stay awake, when your head is saying to you, "I am going to go to sleep no matter what you do". It's hard to fight with that. Don't fight. Take a break and then re-start.

I have driven across the whole USA with one other driver, in 3 days, without a lot of sleep. I have blinked. I have woken up after a calibrated 3-second BLINK, and found myself right in the middle of my lane, and wondering why I was still centered in the middle of my lane, after what seemed like a 10-minute nap. DO NOT DO THAT. DO NOT PUSH your luck. Stop and take a break. Splash water on your face. Or, better yet, take a nap, and *then* splash water on your face.

> If you are trying to drink a cup of coffee to help stay awake, or smoke a cigarette, those are well-known *stimulants.* Everybody knows that if you are a little tired or bored, a cup of coffee can help you be more alert. BUT, if you are really tired, and if you are relying on another cup of coffee to get you through the night, that coffee is just a Band Aid* and the coffee will not REALLY keep you safely awake for long.

> Sometimes, a short stop and a little water to wash your face can help you keep refreshed and awake. Sometimes a short walk is a good break. Sometimes turning on the radio or a tape can help keep you alert and awake. But sometimes a 10-minute nap is the better solution. TAKE a NAP!!!

A month ago, I was driving home from a hike. I felt really crummy, because there was so much pollen that my nose was clogged, and my eyes were very itchy. And just before I got to the on-ramp for I-80, I was feeling REALLY sleepy. It was NOT gonna be safe for me to get out on that freeway. I pulled over and took a 15-minute nap. When my watch's beeper went off, I was really surprisingly refreshed. Could I have made it with a cup of coffee or a cigarette for stimulation? Maybe, but the nap was probably better and safer.

Pills?

It's American lore that some drivers – and especially truck drivers – take "Uppers" or Bennies (Benzedrine) or similar stimulants to stay awake on long runs. I wish they didn't, because some of these pills can turn you into a Zombie. You are awake – but you aren't. Your eyes are open – but are you seeing anything? If a dangerous

* Band Aid is a registered trade-mark of the Johnson & Johnson Company.

situation happens, can you react? Anyhow, most of these pills are illegal, and probably a really bad idea, and I have to agree that the authorities are correct to condemn their use. You must avoid them. Especially while you are driving.

But, if a cup of java makes you feel alert enough to make the last 30 miles home, and you think it will, then maybe that is a good idea. (But a nap might be better.)

Back to I-80 in Nevada...

In the case of my visitor, Mary, she had started her day of driving about 8 AM. She stopped at noon, and then again at 6 PM, and took another rest-stop. And then she started out again. At 7 PM, she apparently dozed off and veered slightly off the pavement on the right. Her right wheels hooked the edge of the pavement, and she tried to veer back onto the road – and went 'way off the road on the left. She went down a shallow embankment and hit a rock. Fortunately, a truck-driver behind her car saw the whole thing, and immediately used his CB radio to call for an ambulance. The ambulance arrived in time to help her survive and recover. If she had gone off the road at night, with nobody watching, she would have died *on the spot*. Think about it. Could it happen to you? Do you know anybody who would claim that they do not keep on driving when they are a little sleepy??

YOU Should Beware of Other SLEEPY DRIVERS...

Let's say *your* car has a minor breakdown. *You* should avoid walking around in the break-down lane. Because sometimes a driver gets absentminded or sleepy, and drives down the breakdown lane. Especially at night... when he might be watching your tail-lights or reflectors, and following in the lane behind you. For example, it is not extremely wise to stand behind your car, if it is broken down, because sometimes a car will come down the breakdown lane and cut your legs off. It's safer to stand behind the guard-rail, to avoid this.

> So, I recommend that you learn to stand behind the guard rail, rather than sitting in your car, because of that thin possibility that your car may be rammed from behind. However, if it is cold or rainy, it is not realistic to expect all your passengers to stand behind the guard-rail, rather than wait in the car... you gotta use your judgement.

Examples...

I talked to a Cop. He said he had finished a long shift and was headed home about 2 AM. Half a mile from home, he apparently fell asleep and nicked a car on the right. Instinctively, he cut the wheel to the left – and went through a wood post fence into a swamp, and the car was totalled. He was a good driver and was very embarrassed at making such a silly mistake. Yet, that's what can happen to *you*. And, *your boss* will probably not cheerfully buy a new car for you....

I know another guy who was on a long trip. He drove 700 miles to get home, and fell asleep 1/4 mile from home and drove into a big stone. *Not* a good recommended procedure.

–Got the picture??? –Don't do that....

Chapter 37. PASSING

Passing another car or truck can be one of the most boring, routine, easy maneuvers you can do, on an otherwise empty road, or on an uncrowded freeway. ALSO, passing can be one of the most interesting, hair-raising, perilous things you can do, on a busy road. And, everything in-between. Let's discuss.

Passing On An Uncrowded Freeway

On a freeway, all you have to do, to pass the guy ahead of you, is to *merge* carefully into a lane that is moving faster than the slow guy ahead of you. Check to make sure it is safe to enter that lane, and signal your Change of Lane. Get out there and keep your foot on the gas long enough – this can vary from a second to over a minute – and when you get properly and safely ahead of the guy or guys that you have passed – just signal for a right-hand lane change, and pull back into your old lane. You have passed a guy. Big deal.

Passing On a Busy 2-Lane Road

NOW, let's consider another situation. You have been following a slow car for several minutes on a meandering 2-lane blacktop road. The driver of this slow car keeps waving his arm, gesticulating, pointing. He slows down for every curve – but speeds up when he comes to a straight stretch. And every time you come to a straight stretch, there is some on-coming traffic. Meanwhile, there are 9 cars behind you. They would all like to pass this guy – but you are the guy on the spot. YOU are the car behind the slow guy, and it is YOUR turn to pass, as soon as you can pass safely. Finally, you come out of a curve at about 45 mph, and approach a fairly short straight stretch, perhaps just a couple hundred yards long. You don't wait until the straight to step on the gas – you downshift to 3rd and floor it before you come out of the curve. As soon as you see that the straight stretch seems clear, you pull out to pass the slow guy. Even though that slow car is still accelerating, you are pretty sure you can pass him – even if a car comes around the corner toward you.

Just then you DO see a car coming slowly around the curve toward you. You are not quite past that slow car – and that dumb useless son-of-a-bitch is still accelerating, slowly. But you still have over 150 yards, and you judge that you will get safely ahead. You blink your headlights briefly as a caution to the on-coming car. The "slow car" is now doing well over 60, as the miserable fellow has thoughtlessly sped up as you were trying to pass him. (That WAS illegal, for him to speed up when somebody is passing him.) But you accelerated faster, and you are already a tiny bit ahead of him. Now is a good time to turn on your right-turn blinkers, to indicate that you are going to move into the right lane shortly.

Now the oncoming car is just 80 yards up, and you check your mirror to insure that you are now a small safe distance ahead of the slow car. You ease on in, back into your own lane. The oncoming car flashes past with more than a second to spare. Hey, if each of you is doing 60 mph = 88 ft per second, that is a closing speed of 176 feet per second. So a 1-second margin does not sound very big – but every good driver knows how to judge a 1-second margin.

Now you shift up into high gear and roll into the next corner. You keep your foot on the gas, and you don't lift. But you reach over and blink your parking lights on and off, so that the driver of the slow car – now 80 yards behind you – will think you are hitting your brakes, too. But you don't. You keep rolling through that curve at 59 mph.

Now that you have safely completed the pass, your heart can stop racing, and your adrenaline can relax back to normal levels. Aren't you glad your car has good passing power? When you come out of the curve, the open road is in front of you – and the slow car is nowhere in sight. At the end of the straight stretch, you look in your mirror, and the slow guy is just creeping around the curve and into the straight, 300 yards back. And some other poor guy is trying to pass him. 'Bye, bye.

And that's about the toughest job of passing that you can do.

Keep Going or Pull Back In?

At any time, when you are trying to pass, if an approaching car suddenly appears, before you are sure you can complete your pass safely, you have to make a fairly hasty decision: can you complete the pass? – or, will you have to hit the brakes, and pull back in behind that slow car?? In the previous example, if the oncoming car had appeared even 1/2 second earlier, you would have aborted your pass, and slammed on your brakes, and tucked back in behind the slow car.

How do you know whether to keep passing, or hit the brakes? This involves judgement. An inexperienced driver should not normally go out to pass, unless there is obviously enough room to pass. And even then, judgement is required.

– You have to judge:

- your acceleration: whether you can maintain it, or if you expect it is going to increase or decrease a lot;
- the slope of the hill, whether an upgrade or downgrade;
- the distance you are, behind or ahead of the car you are passing;
- the speed of the on-coming vehicle. Is it a slow tractor or a fast car??
- the length of the vehicle you have to pass. Is it an ordinary car, or a trailer truck? That makes a lot of difference;
- and the space between you and the oncoming car.

– All these spaces and speeds must be carefully judged, in about a half of a second, or preferably less. Should you keep going? Or, slow down and pull back behind the slow car? There's the judgement call.

– Of course, the guy you are passing may suddenly notice that he is being passed, and may also hit the brakes in an effort to help you pass – just when you were trying to brake and pull back into line. Then you MUST be prepared to nail the brakes harder than the other guy, and get back in. You *have to* be prepared to out-brake that guy! One way or another, you *have to* be able to get back in.

Passing on Multi-Lane Roads

– Let's go back to multi-lane roads. If the road is nearly empty, it does not take a lot of judgement to decide if you can go out to pass. As you approach the slower car, you check out in advance, is the left lane going to be clear when you want to pass? You check the mirror so it seems clear, signal for the left-hand lane, and double-check that the left lane is clear. (Check all your mirrors, or turn your head very briefly). You go out and pass. When you are done, you get back in. You do not even have to tromp on the gas, because you just maintain your constant speed.

In this case, the only major problem is, do you have enough power to pass, if the road starts up a hill? Hey, I drive a VW, and sometimes I start to pass at the foot of an upgrade, and it may take a long time to get past the poor guy. Meanwhile, I keep checking my mirror to see if anybody is getting mad because I am preventing him from passing. I sure try to minimize that. I don't want people mad at me. Bad etiquette. Also, I try to avoid staying in the other car's blind spot, any longer than I can help it. I try to get ahead of that, and get at least even with the other car, so the other driver can see my car, even if he does not have very good peripheral vision.

Other options – If the left lane happens to be full at the time I'd like to take it, maybe I can use the right lane. In most states it is now legal to pass on the right.

Passing on the Right

I remember, just a few years ago, in Connecticut, it was VERY illegal to pass on the right. So if some idiot got into the far left lane at 50 mph, it might be a trap. If you passed the guy on the right, the un-marked police car could nail you. The other trap was if a car would stop in the middle of the street, waiting for a break in oncoming traffic so it could make a left turn. Even if it was a 4-lane road, you were supposed to stop and wait for him to make his turn. If you sneaked around that car, whether in the right-lane or on the shoulder, the cop was waiting right there to do some "revenue enhancement". But not any more.... That kind of CRAP has been changed so all state laws have to conform to Federal standards, and passing on the right is now legal, even in Connecticut. The bureaucrats in Connecticut are not any longer permitted to pass obstructionist laws.

Freeway Passing Tactics

Let's say you are on a 4-lane highway, and coming up behind a slow vehicle. And there is a car on your left, rolling at the same speed as you. If you just wait until the last second, you might have to hit your brakes hard, and then wait until you get a chance to get into the left lane to pass. Very silly.

The wise thing is to take your foot partly off the gas for just a couple seconds – and do this *early*. Slow down just 1 or 2 mph, and hit your left-hand blinker. Then in a few seconds that other car will be ahead of you, and you can pull in behind him. Then you can touch the gas a little and come back up to your cruising speed. The earlier you do it, the less energy you waste, and the easier it is to pass. Waiting to the last minute is very wasteful.

Procedures to Avoid

I know a guy who traded in his VW on a big-engine Dodge. When rolling on the freeway, he would come up behind a slow car, hit the brakes, and slow down. Then he would check to see if the passing lane was clear. Then he would TROMP on the gas, and go out and pass the slow car. He loved that Dodge because it was so much faster than a VW. But he complained because the Dodge got such poor gas mileage. He did not realize that stepping on the brakes hard, and then flooring the gas, was a guaranteed way to get poor gas mileage. Further, he would still hit the brakes behind the slow car, and then check for a free lane, and then floor it – even though there was no other car on the road! If he could have checked his need for a lane, well before he had to hit his brakes, he could have driven a lot more safely and economically. And he could have kept a better average speed, too. But at the time, I did not know him well enough to explain his problem to him.

Passing in Heavy Traffic on Multi-Lane Roads

– Now, let's say you are on this same multi-lane road, and the traffic is getting heavy. You can still pass a slow car – as soon as you can get into the fast lane. Here, the main problem is, how to *merge*. If the left-hand lane is really going pretty fast, and there are not many breaks in traffic, you should plan well in advance, when to ease into that lane.

– Worse yet, if you are trying to pass a really slow truck – you may also get badly slowed down, and find it really hard to merge into a fast lane. So if you are coming up behind a slow truck, it is even more important to merge into the faster lane LONG before you catch up to the truck. You gotta plan ahead!!

When a freeway is REALLY crowded, it can be almost impossible to merge into a faster lane. You can turn on your blinkers, and *still* nobody will let you out. This is especially bad when traffic is passing you at 60 mph, and the slow truck you are following is doing 40.

You have to check your mirrors and guess if there is a person who will give you a break, and let you out. That is NOT a reasonable place for a beginning driver. Even experienced drivers find this very hard to do. Sometimes, holding your hand out the window and giving a hand-signal for the left lane can work better than just turning on your blinker.

Of course, if traffic is so heavy that you can't get over to the left lane, you may also have trouble getting back. If you have a passenger, that person may be able to give you advice on how to merge, or when it is safe to pull over. If you are on your own, you may be better off to stay in your own lane and wait. If the roads in your area get really hectic and tight and pushy, you should be aware of that. It's no fun, being on those really congested roads, like a busy Los Angeles freeway, or the Long Island Expressway on Long Island NY.

Still, no matter how miserable the clogged traffic is, passing a slow vehicle only involves selecting a faster lane, and figuring out how and when to merge with it. The multi-lane is still simpler than 2-lane roads.

Passing on the 2-Lane.

Many times, you are on a 2-lane road, and after you catch up with a truck or a slow car, in just a few seconds, you get a free shot to pass. You pull out with your wheels right up near the center-line, so you can see around the vehicle ahead. You look ahead, and there is no car out there for the next half mile. You just step on the gas and go. After a number of seconds, you get safely past that slow vehicle, and you signal with your right-hand blinker, and you pull in. Not a big deal. Even a young or beginning driver can do this, without much concern or worry. When it looks *really* clear, you can just do it. Of course, it is always best for any beginning driver, to have his teacher along to say, "Yeah, go ahead. That really is very safe. That is what it looks like when it is safe to pass." Then you can GO.

However, this is a rare situation. Usually there are complicating factors. When you pull out, you may get started in your pass, and you see an oncoming car. Is it far enough away? Is it coming fast or slow? Do you have enough power? Is the slow car being helpful, by slowing down to help you get ahead?

Will you be able to just step on the gas and pass? Is your engine running rough, or smooth? In a manual-transmission car, do you have enough torque and passing power, or will you have to downshift, to get the acceleration you need? If so, you better do it. "Shift, or get off the pot."

When you have to do it at night, can you judge the oncoming traffic adequately? Are his headlights close together, or far apart? One thing is for sure – if those headlights start out as 2 tiny specs close together, and their angle keeps getting bigger, you better be back in your lane before he gets to you! And the whole thing is a matter of judgement.

What if you look out there, and you would LIKE to pass, but you decide you do not have enough power to pass – and then the guy behind you decides HE wants to go. Then you keep in your lane and let him go, and leave some space between yourself and the car ahead, so the fast car can pull in if he needs to. He may not be able to get past both YOU and the slow car, too.

Oncoming Traffic – Cars Coming at YOU

Inga told me that she was driving her pickup truck down a long downgrade. Half a mile away she saw a car approaching her in her lane, passing on the upgrade. She was minding her own business – and rolling at about 60. When the cars got closer, the passing car pulled over into his lane, at the last minute, revealing – ANOTHER car passing. That car was really stupid and did NOT pull over and let her by – he stayed out in the passing lane. Inga had to pull over onto the shoulder. Unfortunately, she lost control, and the pickup went off the road and rolled over out in the bushes, two times.

Some of the other drivers stopped and ran over, expecting to find her killed. She was not WOUNDED, but her ribs were all badly bruised.

There were several complicating factors.

* *First, the second guy who was out passing should have known he was in trouble, and should have pulled in BEHIND the slow car (the one that was being passed), rather than keep going.*

* *Secondly, the slow car being passed should have hit the brakes and let both cars in. I suspect he was largely to blame for the accident, because he not only did not slow down. He probably kept his foot on the gas, making it hard for the cars to pass him. Pretty bad stuff. If you were in that car, if YOU are being passed, YOU had better slow down and let the passing cars in.*

* *Thirdly, Inga was not wearing her seat belt. Her injuries were worse, compared to what they might have been if she had been wearing her seat belt.*

* *Fourthly, Inga was rolling down the hill in Neutral. When she discovered that the idiot had taken her lane, she was not able to keep the pickup under control. She would have had a better chance of keeping it under control, if she had kept it in gear. Note, pickups are not usually very stable. If you put on the brakes hard, the pickup is more likely to spin or lurch than an ordinary car. So, deciding to shift into neutral was probably a contributing factor. There's a related story about pickups getting unstable and spinning badly when they try to brake hard, in the Chapter on Brakes.*

* *Fifthly, I like tall cars such as old pickup trucks and VW Busses, because you sit up high, and you can see things from a high viewpoint. If Inga had looked suspiciously, she might have realized that SOMETHING was wrong, in the traffic coming up that hill. If she were driving defensively, she should have put on the brakes fairly hard, quite early, as soon as she just SUSPECTED that there was more than one car coming up the hill. Then she also shoulda blinked her headlights ON a couple times. She might have avoided the accident even though somebody was trying to pin it on her.*

NAMELY: If somebody is trying to make an accident happen, right in front of you, you may be invited to the party, but you don't have to join in! If you think the oncoming cars in your lane are going to have trouble getting back into their lane before they get up to you, slow down and give them some room. If you have to pull 'way over on the shoulder, you'll be better off if you have slowed down *early*.

Passing on Three-Lane Roads

If you drive on roads where there is a center passing lane, you must be VERY careful about assuming nobody else will want that center lane. Don't make a dive for it, just to discover that somebody else made his dive to demand that lane, too. It's better to *ease* out into that lane and let all oncoming traffic know you have established your request for that lane. Then, while you are easing out there, if someone else makes a dive for it, you would have a chance to pull back in, before you get half-way past the car you are passing.

Passing on Three-Lane Roads With a Climbing Lane

This is a LOT different from a 3-lane road with a center lane – a lot less dangerous. It's a little bit like any other multi-lane road, except you must realize that at the top of the hill, you have to finish your passing, as the SLOW lane will disappear. If you don't have a lot of power, you may not make it. Try not to rely too much on the generosity of the car or truck you are passing, to let you ahead at the last second. You may have to drop back.

If you foresee that that will happen, and you can't complete the pass, then don't block the left lane and prevent other fast cars from passing. Don't be a dog in the manger.

Passing on Gravel or Dirt Roads

Sometimes you come up behind a guy on a dirt road or gravel road. And sometimes it is dusty. Well, it's not a lot of fun, eating the other guy's dust, but it's not nice to make him eat *your* dust, either. So if you plan to pass, you must plan to go fast enough to get 'WAY out ahead of him, so your dust will dissipate before he comes along. If you can't do that, then stay back and keep out of his dust.

If the other driver can't see you very well in his dust cloud, you will be wise to turn on your headlights, and tap your horn, to let him know you want to pass. Make sure there is room to get by, because not all gravel roads have a constant width. Most drivers will slow and let you past. Then, clear out.

Being Passed...

No matter how fast you are going, somebody will come up behind you and will want to pass you. When you come to a passing zone, the guy goes out and wants to pass. You should help him do so, if it will work – if it is safe for him to pass.

For example, if the road is really clear, you don't have to slow down – just let him go. But if there are any complicating factors – such as oncoming traffic – and the guy goes out to pass anyhow, it is polite to take your foot off the gas, or even touch the brakes, to help the guy get past. Hey, when I am going up a hill, I hate to take my foot off the gas, and I hate to touch my brakes, but if that's what it takes to get the Passing guy safely past me, I'll slow down a little.

If there are a LOT of guys behind, and I can't keep my speed up, I'll pull over and stop, so they don't get mad at me. It's only reasonable etiquette. A beginning driver often has a situation where he cannot drive as fast, on a curvy road, as everybody else wants to. Hey, pull over and take a break. Let them go. In the state of California, and probably in some other states, if as many as 5 cars pull up behind you, you are obligated to pull over and let them pass. If you don't do it, you are subject to being pulled over for a ticket.

Exceptions...

Now, there are some exceptions. If there is a guy who slows down on corners, and catches up to me on straight stretches, I may not help him pass, because if he gets ahead of me, he'll just slow me down half the time. I am not obligated to help a guy pass me, if he is then just going to slow me down. I'm not going to try to *hinder* him from passing me, but I may not *help* him. Of course, this presumes that I am fairly familiar with the road, and that I know I can keep ahead of him on the curves. But, in general, it is illegal to *obstruct* a car that wants to pass you, or to *hinder him*. Unless the road is *perfectly clear*, don't speed up when a guy is passing you.

HEY, that MADMAN back there is trying to PASS ME!!

Sometimes a driver comes up behind you, and just clings to your tail, at a really unsafe distance. You can just tell he is quite urgent about wanting to pass you. Maybe he is desperate. Well, you might keep strictly to the speed limit. Or you might speed up a little, so he will not be slowed down much while you are waiting to get to the next passing zone. But the best thing is to find a little place and pull over and let him go. Sometimes you just need a wide breakdown lane, 50 yards long. If you just pull over into there, he can usually get by OK. You may not even have to slow down! Or, sometimes you can pull off into any mini wide spot, and slow 'way down or stop, and let him go.

Why should you pull over to let a guy speed by? Well – maybe he is trying to get to a hospital, or maybe he is desperately late for a meeting. Slowing him down will not really help anybody. If he is an accident looking for a place to happen, I want him to be as far away from me as possible, when that accident does happen. And if there is a cop out there, preparing to enhance his town's revenue, then it's better for him to talk to this speeder than to talk to *me* – or to *you*.

Body English...

While you are waiting to find a safe place to pull over, you can put your right-hand blinkers on, to indicate your intention and willingness to pull over and let the guy go. Another thing is to turn your head to the right for a second, so he can see you are looking for a place to get out of his way. This is especially good when you are in the left lane, trying to complete your pass of a slower car, so you can get out of his way. Any driver in a hurry will see you turn your head and realize you are alert, and will cooperate as soon as you can.

If I am passing one car, and there is another guy pushing on my tail like that, when should I pull over to let him past? After all, it's not nice to cut right in front of the other driver. My solution is, *as soon as* the car behind me is even with the car I just passed, I turn on my right-hand signals and try to start easing right. That's a good rule of thumb. The driver I just passed can see that the car behind me is getting pushy, so he understands why I am pulling over in front of him, sooner and closer than normal.

HEY, that guy in my MIRROR must be doing 80!!

Sometimes, you look in your mirror – and this most amazing sight appears: a car coming up *really fast*. Maybe two cars. What the heck do you do? (If anything.)

First of all, changing your lane might be a really bad idea. If he is planning to go by you on the left – and if there is room for that – just staying in your lane and keeping rolling may be the best solution. If he is planning on wedging past you on the right – in the breakdown lane – then you had better let him go. If you were to pull over to the right at the last second, he might not be able to avoid hitting you. On the other hand, if you see the guy more than 100 yards off, you might be able to signal to the right, and ease to the right lane, and let him through. Hey, it might be a guy with a stuck gas pedal, who has not read this book. Or a guy running from the mob. Or if you are on a downhill, it might be a truck (or car) who has lost his brakes. If the guy has his lights on and is blinking them and blasting his horn, you might assume he needs all the help he can get. If you think pulling over will help, and you can do it early enough not to confuse him, go ahead and do that.

What if you conclude that he is gonna hit you. He is not making any effort to dodge. Should you dodge at the last second? I would not, because *he* still might dodge. But I'd get on the horn, and I'd blink my lights just a little. Maybe he is absent-minded. Would I duck down in my seat? Hey, if I am doing 40 and the guy is doing 80, I might just lie down in the front seat. I can survive crashing into a guard-rail at 35, but I can't survive just sitting up there like a little man, and letting him hit me at 80. So, while this rarely happens, this is the kind of last-second problem you may partially prepare for by thinking about it in advance. There are no easy answers.

No-Passing Zones

> ADVICE: YOU should never pass in a no-passing zone. Then YOU
> never have to worry about the cop pulling YOU over. YOU should
> ALWAYS obey the law.

However, that is not necessarily what *you* do, or what *I* do. I always consider a "no-passing zone" to be an advisory situation. The Motor Vehicle Regulations can be very strict. The law may even be enforced. Or it may not. But the laws of gravity and inertia are very broad – and they are *ALWAYS* enforced. The Laws of Common Sense have a little latitude, too. When I come up behind a slow SLOW vehicle – a truck or a tractor – or even a slow car – I have to consider – can I pass him safely, even if it is a no-passing zone? In a 40 mph zone, I probably can't pass if he is going 30 or 20. But what if he is going 10? Or, 5 mph? Or, 3 mph?? If there is a cop behind me, I may decide that that is a good reason not to pass. (In that case, I would probably just pull over and let the cop pass me, and then I would fall in behind the cop, and watch what *HE* decides to do!!)

But if it is merely a short no-passing zone, and I can CLEARLY get by safely, then I will probably pull out into the passing lane, and look at the situation. Often the truck driver is a good guy, and he may wave me on, or pull over into the breakdown lane and help me pass. If it looks safe, I may go out and pass.

You may say, "But that is breaking the law." Maybe. What if the guy is doing ZERO mph? What if he is STOPPED? Does that mean you should still NEVER pass a stopped vehicle in a NO-Passing Zone? Maybe. Maybe the oncoming traffic is too heavy. Maybe you can't see far enough ahead. Maybe the curve *is* too severe. Maybe you should walk up and ask the driver if he is planning to move. (Heck, moving vans do sometimes park illegally for *HOURS*.) So, if you come up to a vehicle that is very slow – from ZERO to 5 or 10 or 20 mph – is it really reasonable and safe to pass?

When in Rome... Do As the Romans Do?

When I was trekking in Nepal recently, we went on a couple all-day bus rides, to get to where our hikes began. To my concern and dismay, I saw our bus driver go out to pass slower trucks on blind curves and steep hills, where it was obvious he could not get past the slower vehicle if an oncoming car just happened to show up. Many times, he got out in the passing lane and struggled past slower trucks. ONLY ONE TIME did a Toyota Land Cruiser come over the hill! Then, we *all* had to hit our brakes and stop. Then we re-started and got out of the passing lane, and everything was OK. But that driver lost any chance of a tip.

On the way back from that hike, we had a different bus driver. He seemed a little more safe and cautious. He still went out to pass on some blind upgrades, but he always *bipped* his horn, and apparently it was agreed that the truck (or bus, or ox-cart) that was being passed would slow down and let us past, if there was on-coming traffic. He seemed to be driving safely, though I was not entirely at ease with the situation. But we liked the driver's attitude and style, and we gave him a good tip.

A couple days later, I took an all-day drive with Gobal, a very thoughtful and competent driver, in his old Corolla. He, too, passed on blind hills, but his car was exposed to danger for a *much* shorter time than a bus would be. I considered asking him to wait until it was REALLY SAFE – but I decided if the driver had gotten to a good old age, driving as he did, asking him to change now would be a bit silly. We had a good drive, with no incidents, except that I could not believe we kept doing that! I guess it is a good thing that in Nepal, all rental cars come equipped with a driver.... I think I would be happier, to NOT be driving, if I knew that around any corner, I could at any time see two large Tata trucks bearing down on me.

Caution...

There are a couple trick problems here. You can look around a car, and the passing lane looks clear. But a car may be hidden out ahead, in a dip in the road. If you start to pass, that car may suddenly appear and get you into trouble – you may have to hit your brakes HARD. So if you are tempted to pass in a "No-Passing" zone, be aware that this tricky situation can occur. Sometimes the signs that advise you, "UNSAFE to PASS" really do provide a valid opinion. LOOK for the possibility of a dip where a car could be hiding. Or a car could enter from a side-road, into this area of limited visibility. If a car suddenly appears from this dip, you may have to hit your brakes and pull back into line, fast.

NEW No-Passing Zones

On the other hand, out here in the west, there are many miles of very good 2-lane roads that *USED TO BE* passing zones, but Federal Standards recently required them to be converted to NO-Passing zones. This has made a lot of people very unhappy. If you come up behind a slow vehicle, and you look, and you drive along, and you look, and every place that *looks* like a good passing zone, is painted with the double yellow, you may not be dreaming. Maybe just last year it was a legal passing zone. I'm not going to tell you it is safe, and I am NOT going to tell you it is not safe. I'm not going to tell you that that car 7 cars behind you is not an unmarked police car. I'm not going to tell you what to do.

It might be entrapment. Maybe that cop is sitting back there, just waiting for you to get frustrated at being unable to pass. NOW, he SHOULD be grabbing the slow truck or RV (Recreational Vehicle) that is slowing down a lot of cars, mile after mile. But maybe he *isn't* back there... or maybe he is. Maybe he prefers to pull YOU over when, in great frustration, you decide to pass a very slow vehicle in a no-passing zone. You figure out whether it is worth the risk, explaining this to the judge.

Passing Zone Ahead...

Many times, there will be a sign on a curvy 2-lane road: "Climbing Lane 2 miles ahead" or "Passing Lane, 1/2 mile". This is an indication that you may want to wait for that passing lane. However, the guy you wanted to pass may just like to go slow on curves, and he may tromp on the gas and go up that passing lane very fast, giving you no chance to pass him. Don't be too surprised. There's not much you can do about it. Don't get mad.

Advanced Techniques

When you are behind a slow car, you usually should not hang on his bumper, waiting to pass. Often, a slow driver is a poor driver, and his unassertiveness indicates that he might make another foolish move. So, it is often a poor idea to sit just a couple car lengths off his bumper. Even if the slow vehicle is a truck, and the driver is very competent, and climbing as fast as he can, it is usually not a good idea, to drive right on his tail.

Instead, if you know the road, it is often wise to get back 20 or 30 yards, and, as you approach the next legal passing zone, downshift and start speeding up toward the slow car. Get some momentum. You might get up to 55 mph, just a few car-lengths behind the 44 mph car, just as you get to the start of the passing zone. If the way is clear, you have the guy already beat. This is sometimes called the "slingshot"

6/29/92

technique. This is a very old trick, and is often used by smart drivers who don't have as much power as they would like. It requires good judgement, to get going at a good speed, but not too fast, and not too close to the other car.

HOWEVER, if there is on-coming traffic, you'll have to nail your brakes, and bide your time. Wait for the next passing zone. Or, if it is a fairly long passing zone, you may be able to pass after the on-coming traffic goes by.

I Can't Believe I See This in my Mirror!

One time I was driving across Canada on a good 65-mph 2-lane road. A bus was coming toward me, and I could see a car speeding up behind the bus – obviously planning to do a slingshot. As soon as I was past the bus, the fast car pulled out to pass the bus, at well over 80 mph. But I remembered a little detail: there was a car coming along a hundred yards behind me. I looked in my mirror, and saw vehicles all over the road. The car behind me was throwing up gravel as he tried to get *'way over* on his shoulder without spinning out of control. The bus was 'way over on *his* shoulder, trying to get out of the way. And the fast car went right down the middle. Lord only knows what he was thinking. Hey, slingshot passing is all very fine, but you are supposed to abort if the on-coming lane is not clear. Don't bull your way through. I darn' near saw a BIG wreck in my mirror.

Problems in Passing

One problem is a lack of power. This might be especially conspicuous on up-hills. Another problem is when the passing zones are short. Another problem is poor visibility. If it were rainy or snowy, you might not be able to see if the way is clear. Another problem is if the guy you are trying to pass, is speeding up. This is very annoying, but unless you BIP your horn to let him know you really want to pass, and unless he decides to slow down to let you by, there's not much you can do. If there is a guy I just CANNOT get past, on the straight stretches, but he slows down for the curves and slows me up badly, that is why I put my HYMNAL in my checklist. If I am just getting more and more frustrated because I cannot pass this miserable fellow, I'll stop and sing 3 verses of "Nearer My God to Thee", or some such hymn, to distract me from my frustration. Nothing else does much good. Of course, if I know the road pretty well and I know there is a good long passing zone up ahead a few miles, I may just keep going.

There is one thing you can do about safe passing – if you have to do a lot of driving on roads with small passing zones, you might be sure your next car has good passing power. That can be a good safety feature, if used with discretion.

Be Careful About Relative Speed Passing – Too Fast

I put in a comment, in the Chapter on Heavy Traffic, about how it is a bad idea to pass slow traffic at a speed much faster than the slow traffic, because one of the slow cars may pull out right in front of you. Another variation on this is in the Chapter on Speeding. I gave an example of the guy driving up the M1 at 100 mph. When a guy he was passing "shied" at him – veered into his lane – he hit his brakes and spun and spun. Ignoring the fact that he was speeding, his speed was too fast relative to the car he was passing.

Be Careful About Relative Speed Passing – Too Slow

What if you are passing a car, and suddenly *he* starts to pass, or veers into your lane? Well, first you should get on the brakes. Meanwhile, it is often a good idea to ease over to the left, even if it is only over to the left side of your lane, to give you a little more space for you to brake. Simultaneously you can get your thumb on the horn, to prevent him from coming any further. You may not get hit if you back off and brake hard. But, this is a good reason to stay out of the other guy's blind spot! He might not have noticed you.

That just shows, it's a good idea to do your passing promptly, and not take all day about it. He might have noticed you, but if you stay on his left side forever, he may forget about you, and then absent-mindedly go out to pass. If he makes a *fast* dive for the passing lane, you may not be able to avoid getting hit. So this is a case of Passing where a relative speed that is TOO SMALL can cause you problems.

Similarly, when you are just planning to merge to another lane, make sure nobody else is trying to grab that lane. The general rule is, if you see a lane, and you think you can signal and then take that lane, be VERY careful that somebody else is not going to take it. In a case like that, ease into that lane slowly enough that the other guy can see that he should not make a DIVE for it. And if he *does* make a dive for it, back off and let him have it. There are times when you can be pushy, but lateral moves are a bad time.

Give Him The Lights...

If I am at all concerned about the guy I am about to pass – if I suspect the other guy may be sloppy or inattentive, or drunk, I will blink my lights as I come up behind him. If they are OFF, I blink them ON. If they are ON, I blink them OFF. I think that is more polite, and more effective, than hitting my high beams.

I recall reading an old law, in Massachusetts, that any car attempting to pass shall beep his horn to make sure he notifies the car he is passing. These days, I am sure that law has been repealed, but if you have any doubt about the alertness of the car you plan to pass, then a little beep may be wise.

Technical Aspects

My son Jonathan loaned me a book* on how roads are engineered. It has a lot of boring stuff with a few interesting tidbits. It does mention that highway engineers try to arrange the curves, hills, and crests of hills so that passing is feasible. Nothing amazing. But at least it does indicate that highway engineers do try to think about such things, and try to plan for safe roads. (If the money is not there, then safe features are not always built in, and we cannot always pass safely when we want to.)

HIGHWAY ENGINEERING, Oglesby and Hicks; see in the Appendix on Book Reviews.

Chapter 38. HEAVY TRAFFIC – and driving in it.

Now, there are many kinds of heavy traffic. When I was a kid, 2 lanes of traffic in each direction seemed kind of hectic. Now, 6 or 8 lanes can be just as scary, but not much worse than 2 lanes used to seem.

There are several basic problems. Partly I mentioned these in the Chapter on Lanes, saying that driving on a Los Angeles freeway can be VERY difficult, for any driver, and not just for inexperienced ones. In other words, Mr. Young Driver, no, you are not *imagining things* when you think that heavy traffic crap is stressful. You are quite right – this is stressful for everybody. But experience can make it a little less scary, and more manageable. And some of the tactics in this book can help, too.

I already stated, back in the Chapter on Lanes, that it can be very difficult to navigate, especially for the driver by himself. You have to plan your navigation, so you know where to turn off. Read that, there.

– If the lanes are narrow, that can be quite scary. Read about that also in the Chapter on Lanes. If you are rolling along right beside trucks – big, *NOISY* trucks, this can be pretty unnerving on a busy road, especially with narrow lanes, and especially for inexperienced drivers. Don't let anybody pretend that it is not.

If you try to stay 2 car-lengths per 10 mph behind the car ahead of you – you KNOW there will be other cars that will wedge in there. Even 1 car-length per 10 mph is often not tolerated – another car will squeeze in. So you have to live with people driving right in front of you, even if you try to avoid that. Fortunately, you can tolerate the closer spacing, in some cases, by watching the brake lights at least 4 or 6 or more cars ahead.... You must be prepared to put on your brakes as early as anybody does. Especially, before the car ahead of you! That way, *even if* the car behind you is following *too close*, and even if he has lousy brakes, and a bald tire or two, you have a chance to brake lightly, and not force him to brake too hard, and thus you may keep him off your rear bumper. Read more about this in the Chapter on Following Distance.

Choices

And if there *is* a guy behind you, who insists on driving too close, you might pull over and let him ride on *somebody else's* tail. Maybe you can politely pull over in front of a car that is keeping a safe distance behind the car ahead of him. Then in a short while, you will have a thoughtful driver behind you, and at a reasonable space, too.

Or, you might just gradually slow down 1 or 2 mph, and then after a minute, slow down a little more, so the guy behind you may decide he prefers to pass you. But I have seen a lot of drivers who are so unthinking, they will just sit behind a car and not think about passing. If you pull over, they will speed up and disappear in the traffic ahead of you, quickly. OR, sometimes they will get ahead of you – and then slow down. When drivers are *really* stupid and thoughtless, you can never tell what they are going to do.

◆ ◆ ◆

Similarly, you do often have some choice about who you are following. If there is a real *SQUIRREL* – some kind of crazy driver – slow down *or* speed up and get away from him. I don't like to ride behind pickup trucks, because they are not very stable when they have to brake hard, *and* they are hard to see over or around.

But I do not usually mind driving behind large trucks, because their drivers are usually safe and conservative, AND, they are able to see over other traffic, so they usually put on their brakes early. And, they have strong brakes, but they do not usually like to decelerate or stop *too fast*. If you don't mind their exhaust fumes, or the sandblasting they send at your windshield, then you may find that a safe place to drive. Further, other drivers may not wedge in front of you, because a lot of drivers don't like to drive behind trucks. Of course, you usually cannot see around the truck, so you are trusting the truck driver to watch out for your interests. This is not a great idea – but when you are on a *terrible* road, with *awful* traffic, this may be better than some of the alternatives. You gotta use your judgement.

◆ ◆ ◆

When I came out to San Francisco about 20 years ago, I was impressed that, in case of a big slowdown on a busy freeway, the drivers gradually slowed down, whereas in similar cases in the Boston area we often got drivers making panic stops. I sure appreciate it when other drivers show enough foresight to look ahead and ease on the brakes before the last second. I really think more drivers here are looking ahead 6 or 10 cars – paying attention. I was curious if Massachusetts drivers are really as bad as they used to be. So I asked some of my friends back East. They said, yes, no real improvements in the last 20 years.... Meanwhile, if other drivers are crashing into each other, and locking up their brakes, your best defense is to *look far ahead*, and ease on your brakes early.

◆ ◆ ◆

Often on these crowded roads, there is no room for parking in case of flat tires or breakdowns. That's no fun if you break down – and it's no fun if you are behind another car that breaks down. Squeezing 3 lanes of traffic into two, to get past a dead car or an accident, is no fun. But that's what happens when the road engineers can't get the funds to put in a proper breakdown lane. (Most bridges don't have breakdown lanes, but the eastern end of the San Mateo Bridge has 5 miles of road with 2 lanes each way – WITH some breakdown spots where you can pull over.)

◆ ◆ ◆

One time my wife and son were driving across the US. They travelled mostly on byways, but when they got further east, they had to make up some time and put on some miles fast, so they got on Ontario Route 401 to get past Toronto Canada. They were rolling through that city at rush hour. But the traffic was not slow – it was heavy, tightly-spaced traffic at 70 mph! They were not used to that, and it bothered them. But they survived it. I must say, I am not literally used to that fast, packed traffic. I'm used to people driving at 65, 70, and even a few guys at 75 – but mostly in loose traffic; if it gets heavy, it tends to slow down to 60 or 55.

◆ ◆ ◆

Another place that made me nervous was on the Long Island Expressway, east of New York City. It was 10 o'clock at night, and traffic was flowing raggedly, varying between 50 and 60 and 70 mph. The lanes were not very wide; the pavement was rough, and the lanes kept jerking to the left or right, due to construction. And the drivers all wanted to stay about 3 car lengths apart at 65 mph. And I really didn't trust the way they braked hard. A bunch of *pushy* guys! But I survived, by being cautious and conservative.

Still, that would be a MUCH harder place for an inexperienced driver to get along. Obviously, nobody likes to send a beginning driver out on a tough road like that. But eventually your teacher may get you enough experience that you can do it, without greatly endangering yourself and everybody else on the road.

◆ ◆ ◆

In heavy traffic, it can get really hard to merge, because nobody wants to give you a lane, and you can't take your eyes off the car in front of you. If you can get a co-pilot who is a good driver, that can be very helpful, if he can tell you, for example, "Okay to pull right now." Or, "Wait, don't pull right now." It requires good judgement to know when to say that. So you normally can't just get a kid to help you there.

I mean, let me remind you of the example of the driver who was waiting at an intersection, angled to the left, so he could not see to the right. He asked his passenger, "Any cars on the right?" And the passenger replied – "No . . . . . . – only a truck." Would you trust a kid in a case like that?

◆ ◆ ◆

Also, try to keep an eye on your speedometer. If everybody else is going 70, it may be safer to go with the flow, than try to impose your slow speed on everybody else. That would annoy other drivers, and may make the congestion worse.

BUT you may have a choice of a lane that is slower. If I have a choice of a slower lane where the drivers are stupid, or a faster lane where they are not so bad, I'll get in the faster lane for at least a while, and try to get away from the stupid guys, and maybe find a "pack" of drivers that are able to drive intelligently. Then I'll hang around with *them*.

The Complete Picture

And all this time, you are keeping a more-or-less safe distance from cars on the sides and ahead. But don't forget to check your gas gauge. You don't want to get absent-minded and run out! And, ultimately, you have to keep track of your progress, so you remember the place you want to turn off!

Slow Bumper-to-Bumper Traffic

Many of the same rules listed above apply to slow stop-and-go traffic. That is my least favorite kind of driving. Of course, this can happen on city streets. Or on freeways. Or bridges. I often take an alternate route, or go at an alternate time, to try to avoid this. But sometimes we have no choice.

No Brake Lights?!

The basic idea in any heavy-traffic situation is to pay attention, and don't take your eyes off the road too long. You must *assume* that the guy in front of you may stop suddenly. You just don't know *when*. He may slow down gently 7 times in a row, and then slam on the brakes. Remember, there's a 1-in-400 chance that he has no brake lights. So keep an eye on his *size*. If his tail is looking *wider* and *wider*, and he is getting *closer* and *closer* – but his brake lights are not lit – which are you going to believe? Hey, that car really is slowing down or stopping, and you have to put on your brakes. Do not DEPEND on his brake lights. In fact, you can often *assume* that a guy that does not show any brake lights, may not have any. Of course if he is just sitting on a flat road, stopped, you may soon find that, as soon as he starts and stops, he *does* have brake lights. But it costs NOTHING, to assume that he does not. Then you are a lot safer, if he really does not – because you are WATCHING for him to SHOW brake lights, and to BRAKE. And preferably both.

Now you may say – That is a stupid thing to be thinking about! But not so. When you are in stop-and-go traffic, there is not a heck of a lot else to do. One of the best things you can *do*, while waiting in traffic, is to think about *exactly that:* Does the guy in front of you have his brake lights working? I am *not* saying you cannot sing along with the song on the radio, or talk with your passengers. You can learn to do that, ALSO. But you can learn to watch actively for the proof that the guy has brake lights, using a *different section* of your brain. Then, after you have proven that he does, then you can relax a tiny bit. Reach for a tape. Change the station. Place a call *carefully* on your car phone. But it's a good idea to avoid these distracting activities until you are pretty sure the guy's brake lights are working.

What if the guy does NOT have any brake lights? Well, the sign in Appendix W can be photo-copied. Make several copies, and keep a couple in your car. Then, in most kinds of stop-and-go traffic, you can change to another lane, and try to pull up even with the driver. Hold up the sign against your window so he can see it. Beep your horn. Wave the sign. Beep again, until he sees it. He may wave or raise his eyebrows. Then give a little wave. And all the time, YOU are watching the traffic in front of you, so YOU do not have an accident. (If your passenger can help wave this sign, that's best.)

If traffic is really stopped, such as at a traffic light, you can just shift into neutral, and put on the hand-brake securely, and walk up and show them the sign. If you smile, you are not likely to get shot – even in a neighborhood where looking sideways at a guy can get you shot. Many drivers are appreciative. Some drivers don't care. Some cannot read. But, hey, it is worth a try. It's a neighborly thing to do, to warn them that they are in a dangerous car. I just set up a sign *en Espanol*, for Hispanic drivers. Sometimes that really lights up the driver's eyes, when the sign in English just draws a blank! I haven't made up a sign in Chinese or Vietnamese, yet.

The other thing you might do, if you have time, is suggest to the driver that he can blink his parking lights on and off, when he steps on the brakes, as a substitute for brake lights. It's a poor substitute, but better than nothing.

Another thing you can do is get back behind that brake-light-less car, because if YOU know they have no brake lights, YOU are the safest driver to be behind them. Stay a safe distance back, and concentrate on not screwing up. Protect his tail.

Vigilance

I know a guy who was driving on the Golden Gate Bridge. He took his eyes off the car in front of him – for just a couple seconds. Well, maybe it was 3 seconds. The car in front stopped. He looked up and saw this, and hit his brakes at the last second. He almost got stopped – he had slowed to about 5 mph at contact. But it cost him $2000 in front-end repairs. Ouch. So be careful about making assumptions of how long you can look away from the road, in stop-and-go driving. It is best to assume that a VERY short time is all you can divert your attention. If traffic is very light, and you are spaced a long way back, you may be able to look away for a second or two. If it's really heavy, half a second may be too much.

Lane-Jockeying

When the stop-and-go gets really bad, sometimes you notice that one lane is making better progress than another. So it is reasonable to ease into that lane. But if you then see another lane moving better, you might jump for *that* one. And then, another. This is called Lane-Jockeying. Or Lane-Hopping. Or, Weaving. Pretty soon you are spending all your time watching which lane you can swerve into. This is a lousy idea. Even if you are good at merging, it is not terribly polite. And it is not very safe. I mean, sometimes you might wedge in front of a guy and force him to hit the brakes. NOT nice. You might even cause an accident. And the cause of that accident will probably be pinned on YOU.

So, if you are going to lane-jockey *at all*, be VERY careful. Try to avoid changing lanes more than once per mile, or once every couple minutes, as a rule of thumb. Be VERY careful to merge politely and safely. (Just signalling your intention to change lanes, and barging in, is not enough.) If your lane is slowing down, you must either move into the other lane *before* you slow down – or you must stay in your lane and slow down a lot. Otherwise, if you are hesitant and cannot make up your mind, you'll hit the car in front of you – AND get hit from behind. In other words, we are talking about risky tactics, advanced tactics. Not for beginners.

That does not mean you cannot change lanes to choose a better one. You just want to do it carefully and thoughtfully.

For example, when I am headed to work down I-280, if there is any slow-down near South San Francisco or San Bruno, I *know* that the left lanes will slow down a LOT, and the right lane will slow a lot less. The right lane almost always makes a lot better progress – so I always merge over to the right-hand lane. (Of course, one time in a year, there will be a dumb accident in the RH lane, so occasionally the right lane is a loser.) I stay over on the right for a mile or two, until that lane slows down for a busy right-hand exit. Then I know I'm better off to ease over to the left lanes, which are beginning to make better progress past the slow traffic on the right.

But I normally do not "jockey" back and forth between lanes, trying to pick a better lane. In that area, jockeying does no good at all.

In other places, it's hard to foresee which lane will progress better. Sometimes one lane moves up really well. If you jump into this lane, it then stops and the other lanes go by you. That's what Murphy's Law predicts! So, lane-jockeying sometimes is counter-productive.

Sometimes you can *see* that there's a big crash up ahead on the right. That does not necessarily mean that the left lanes will progress much better, because sometimes a cop is out there, directing traffic. He may be making sure that each lane makes equal progress.

Still, lane-jockeying is not a great idea, and if you have to do it, be careful.

Care When Passing Slow Traffic

The other side of the coin is when you are moving, and somebody pops out of a slow traffic lane, right in front of you. First, you may expect that some foolish or absent-minded person will do this, occasionally. So you should take some precautions. There are two major strategies to avoid hitting a guy that pulls out from a slow traffic lane:

– 1. Get in a lane further from the slow or stopped traffic. On an 8-lane road, with 4 lanes each way, such as I-280 in San Bruno, that is feasible. The two right-hand lanes for the I-380 exit are typically slow, and if I stay in the far left-hand lane, there is a much lower chance of clash or conflict, than if I were rolling in the third lane. On smaller roads, it may be harder to do this. And,

– 2. If you have to pass slow lanes, slow down. If the other guys are stopped, and you are cruising free at 55, you might feel great – until some absent-minded guy pulls out right in front of you. A friend of mine, Mark, was commuting in his pick-up on the Nimitz, one of the Bay Area's infamous freeways.

The Chester Nimitz Freeway from Oakland to San Jose used to be California Route 17, and people used to have bumper-stickers on their cars: "Pray for me, I drive Route 17". Now those bumper-stickers are obsolete, because the Route number has been changed to I-880. The road has been improved a little in the

last few years. But it is still not a great road, with some unfortunate traffic
patterns and conflicts, and lots of heavy traffic.

Anyhow, Mark was rolling about 45 mph down that road, past stopped traffic in
the adjacent lane. A guy pulled out of that lane and Mark hit him. It would be almost
impossible to avoid that accident – unless you got smart and slowed down in the
first place.

I like to ease past slow or stopped traffic at a relative speed of no more than 15
or 20 mph. That means, if they seem to be rolling at 20, I don't go over 35 or 40.
Then if somebody pulls out, I have a reasonable chance to stop. I don't care if the
guy behind me flashes his headlights, I am NOT going to go faster. It's just not safe.

And in case you are getting suspicious about somebody lurching out – such as –
you see the car's front pointed into your lane – keep your foot on the brake, and
slow down even a little more, maybe.

Gawkers

Of course, you have often seen a big traffic slowdown – and when you get to the
point of the slow-down – there is nothing there – not any accident or problem on
your side of the road, at all – only an accident on the other side of the road.
Gawkers who have to go slow so they can look at that accident sure do cause a lot of
wasted time. Wish they wouldn't. A friend in Germany says they have so much of
this, at predictable places, that they build *walls* on the median, so you cannot gawk.
I guess this makes sense.

Smooth It Out...

If the car in front of you is surging ahead, and then, within a few seconds, hitting the
brakes *hard*, you are not obligated to do the exact same. You can accelerate lightly,
and then when he gets a ways up ahead, and hits the brakes, you can ease on your
brakes lightly. With a little luck, you may not even have to stop, but can follow along
behind that jackrabbit. It's better for your car, and the drivers behind you will
appreciate it, if you drive more smoothly. What if some guy wedges in front of you
while you have fallen a bit behind? He may get there ahead of you. He may also
crash into the car ahead of you. As far as I am concerned, if the car behind me wants
to crash into the car ahead of me, I do not want to get in his way.

Blind Spots

Though I mentioned this earlier, I'll repeat: When in heavy traffic, do not stay in
another driver's blind spot, as defined in the Chapter on Lanes. Also, do not let
another car stay in *your* blind spot. Further, when you are changing lanes, try to
avoid pulling into someone else's blind spot, *from the side*. This is because the other
driver cannot see you come in there, and he might not even suspect it. So if you
HAVE TO ease into another driver's blind spot, ease out of it, soon, by slowing down
or speeding up a little.

WELL... was that another short chapter – ? No... But, very few are....   ⌐

Chapter 39. FOLLOWING DISTANCE

"How to Do It Wrong..."

Once upon a time, I was driving down Bayshore Freeway – that is good old Route 101, from San Francisco down toward Silicon Valley. I was rolling at about 60, and I caught up with a trash truck.

On the back of the truck, a sign said, STAY BACK 10 FEET. So I did. After a short while, the truck driver started blinking his lights. Hey, I was only following instructions. After a short while, he tagged his brakes, and started to slow down. So I decided to stop following him – I went out and passed him. But I know that I was getting definitely better gas mileage, when I was following at 1/20 car length per 10 mph, rather than 1 or 2 car lengths per 10 mph. (Refer to "Drafting" below.)

Safer Spacing...

If you follow other traffic by 2 seconds, or 2 car-lengths per 10 mph, that is a fairly conservative way to drive safely. This is one part of Defensive Driving. Some of my buddies recommended, get back 4 (or 5) seconds. Ideally, on an empty road, that is not a bad idea, to have a good, big safety margin. But when traffic gets heavy, and you are going 60 mph, that equals 88 feet per second. So you would be 352 feet back, or about 20 car-lengths back. You KNOW that 1 or 2 other cars will wedge in there. In certain parts of the world, 3 or 4 people will wedge in there. And if you try to slow down, even more will wedge in.

So, simply trying to be conservative and safety-minded, by staying back at 4 seconds of spacing, is useless. Mostly, it just *won't* work. So, there's not much point in practicing driving 4 seconds back, because in most parts of the US – or the world – you will have to learn to drive at 1 or 2 seconds of spacing. Starting out, yes, driving in light traffic is best for a beginning driver. That is a good way to practice and build up confidence. But shortly, your teacher will have to show you how to get along at 2 seconds of spacing, and then, when you can handle that fairly comfortably and safely, at around 1 second, at least for short periods.

Keep a Good Watch

As soon as you have learned how to stay in your lane, the next priority to learn, in general freeway traffic, is to keep scanning the road ahead for problems, and likewise, keep scanning the mirror for odd things. If you see a car easing into your blind spot, ease off and make sure he continues to pass, so he does not park himself there in your blind spot.

One of the most important parts of scanning ahead, is to watch for brakelights up ahead. If traffic is light, just watch a couple cars ahead. If the traffic is closely spaced, the old rule says you should stay one car-length back, per 10 mph. Thus, at

60 mph, you should stay back at least 120 or 140 feet. It may be hard to do this, because another car will squeeze in there! Now, literally, you don't have to stay TOO FAR back of the car ahead of you, but you can compensate for that by keeping an eye on the brake lights of cars 6 or 8 or 10 cars up. If *any* of these cars start hitting their brakes, you can wisely get your foot on your brakes, and touch them lightly, just in case. If the traffic is really slowing down, you will have *your* foot ON YOUR BRAKES before the guy in front of you does, so you are really prepared. And you also have warned the car behind you. That's about as well as you can do. (If traffic is not really slowing, then you can just keep rolling.)

In The Squeeze

If you are caught in high-pressure traffic, one thing you might try, is to pull in behind a guy who is a good smooth driver. Or get behind a guy who keeps a little extra space in front of him. You usually want to avoid a guy who keeps only a tiny space, or who brakes erratically. And then, position yourself where you can see ahead at least 6 or 8 cars... And then keep watching ahead. Watch for any brake lights.

"Drafting"

Look, I used to do a lot of bicycle riding, "drafting" behind bicycles and trucks. "Drafting" is what race cars do, to get in the "draft" or "slipstream" of another car. You can do that if you trust that car's driver, a whole lot. In a race car, drafting a few feet behind another fast car improves your gas mileage and rests your engine.

Bicycle racers draft behind other bicycles, too, to rest their legs and save energy. About 4 inches behind. So, behind a truck, I would pedal along about 15 feet back at 30, 40, or even 50 mph. This cut down a LOT of wind drag, especially when there was a headwind. I never did bump into a truck, or crash. I kept my hands on my brakes, with really fast reflexes. I survived. But I don't recommend it.

Also I used to "draft" my Beetle, behind big trucks. I was getting MUCH better gas mileage, during the last petroleum crisis. But I don't recommend that for everybody. I mean, sometimes I would be drafting about 50 feet back, and the truck would hit his brakes. That's OK. But a couple times the truck had no brake lights!!! This is a situation that is not ideal. But I did it, several times, and survived, and I won't do it any more.

Other Disadvantages...

Another problem of driving behind big trucks, is the exhaust fumes. Some people really dislike diesel exhaust fumes. Myself, I can take it or leave it. But when a truck is dripping Diesel fuel and drips it on your windshield, that is a *real mess,* because if you turn on your wipers, it just smears your windshield *and* wrecks your wiper blades. Time to get away from that truck! In many parts of the world, the truck lifts up a lot of sand, and the sand will gradually sand-blast your windshield, making it very hard to see out. So there is another good reason not to "draft" behind trucks.

Now, one of my reviewers pointed out that when you are behind another car or truck, you should never stay just a few feet back, but a long ways back. However, if you are going to crash into the guy ahead of you, you may be better off if you just stay back a few feet, as I said in the first paragraph. Then if he hits his brakes, he will not slow down a lot before you hit him. Much better than letting him slow down a LOT, and then hitting him... (that's supposed to be a joke).

There is another problem with following too close behind another vehicle – especially behind a truck that you cannot see around. If he suddenly swerves to another lane, and you see a stopped vehicle – or a big pile of junk – right in front of you – and there ain't anywhere for you to go – then that's a bad problem. This is called "blind-gating" – namely, tail-gating so close that you are driving blind. It's not a good idea to do that.

Some of the other material on Following Distance has been typed up in the Chapter on Heavy Traffic, or the Chapter on Lanes, and I may just leave it there – that is not a bad place for it. So, you can check in those chapters, too. This is just the rest of the new material.

A Passenger Can Contribute to Safety...

One summer I was commuting to work with my sister Jerrilyn. I was in the habit of saying "brakes", any time I saw a lot of brake lights, 'way out in front of me. My sister was helpful and observant, and when she saw brake lights, *she* would say "brakes", and I would repeat "brakes", to acknowledge that I heard her, and that I saw the brake lights. After a while, we realized we were ruining a lot of perfectly good conversations, by saying "brakes" all the time. We got in the habit of pointing with 2 fingers, to POINT at the brakes. She would POINT at the brake lights, and I would *repeat* the pointing gesture, to acknowledge that I'd seen them. And we could continue our conversation, uninterrupted. I still do this.

My sister says she still does this, and she prefers to point *and* say "brakes" or, "Look out". She observes, shouting "Look out" is better than nothing, but shouting "Look out" *and POINTING* is much better – then the driver knows where to LOOK. A good POINT!

Chapter 40. NOISES

As stated somewhere up above, small noises are not usually serious, but you might want to check them out before they get serious. When they get louder, they may be warning you of a serious problem. You might be very close to a breakdown – or a condition that could cause an accident. Slow down and stop, as soon as you can safely do so. Check out the noise. Or, get a knowledgeable person to look into them. Interpreting a noise is usually a job for an expert. But you can help.

If you hear a strange noise, notice under what conditions this noise occurs. Only when the engine is cold? Only when it is hot? Does the noise rise in frequency or volume, as the speed rises? Does the noise rise with the ENGINE speed?? Does it CORRELATE with putting on the brakes, or NOT putting on the brakes? Left turn? Right turn? If you listen to Car Talk, you will often hear Tom and Ray Magliozzi ask questions that try to zero in on the source of the noise. They are pretty good.

If you are not sure about the noise, or if it only happens under obscure conditions, bring a tape-recorder, and tape the noise, to show the expert repair man. Often he can recognize the sound, and the conditions. I've had good luck doing that.

The tape-recorder technique is very useful if the noise is intermittent – if it is not always there, and if you cannot predict when it will happen.

Typical noises are caused by:

- *squealing* brakes.

- *ping* (see Chapter 7, on *Ping*)

- *rattling* exhaust parts

- *rubbing* wheel bearings

- *clanking* drive-shaft parts

- *roaring* sounds from muffler

- *clunking* sounds during curves - (Constant-velocity joints?)

- *thumping* sounds - (tire going bad?)

- *squealing* sounds - (fan belt? - check it out!)

- *whistling* sound - (may be your roof rack? - not a big deal).

- *sloshing, gurgling* liquids in the heater or cooling system.

- etc., etc.

When we turn this book into a *movie*, or a *video*, we can put in some real sounds and noises. But for now, this will have to do.

I am not responsible, nor am I liable, for any driving mistakes you make because of anything I wrote

Chapter 41. BREAKDOWNS

··

I have mentioned several places in this book – ideas you can use to try to avoid a breakdown. Well, nobody wants to have a breakdown, but, what does that have to do with *accidents?*

Here is a very simple LIST of ways that a BREAKDOWN can turn into an ACCIDENT:

1. You run out of gas. You park safely over on the side of the road. You climb out. Your car gets hit. Or, YOU get hit, by some sloppy driver. This is one of the most common cases. There are too many sloppy (or sleepy) drivers out there. Especially at night, but even in the daytime, too. They follow your tail lights – and don't even notice you are stopped.

2. Your brakes wear out, and it's unsafe to continue. So – you park the car. And it gets hit.

3. You run low on gas. You are out of money. You can't buy gas. You try to make it home, and you run out. Same ending.

4. Your engine runs out of oil – or water. The engine seizes when you are in the high-speed lane. You get hit trying to get to the right-hand lane.

5. You have a flat tire – but you have no jack. OR no spare. You have to try to walk in to town, a long ways. Die of thirst in the hot sun.

6. Your car breaks down out in the boonies. You freeze your feet walking in to town.

7. Your car breaks down – thief tows it away. (Don't laugh; that happened to me. My engine died, because the crankshaft broke, and I had to leave my car along the side of US 101, Bayshore Freeway, in San Mateo CA. The thieves came along with a tow truck and towed it away. They hot-wired it, and it ran so terribly, they towed it back and left it where they found it!! Is that an insult, or is that an INSULT? I got the engine fixed, and drove that car another 80,000 miles.)

8. You have a blowout, because you were too cheap to replace a marginal or dubious tire. You lurch into an accident – or hit a curb and break or bend the wheel.

9. You have bald tires, and you skid on a rainy road. Hit a tree.

10. You have 4 good tires, but then you have a flat. Your spare tire is nearly bald. It's a snowy day. You don't have any traction, and you can't get up or down hills in the snow. You slide into a ditch.

11. Your car breaks down in a bad part of town; you get mugged on your way to a pay phone, and the car is vandalized, too.

12. One brake light burns out. You ignore or neglect this. Then the other one burns out. You get rammed by a car who can't see any brake lights.

13. Your car won't start. You are late to work for the 7th time, and lose your job.

14. You have a flat tire on a big bridge, and the tow truck is required to tow you off, because you are not permitted to change a tire on the bridge. That's an expensive tow.

15. You have one accident too many, and your Insurance company makes you an Assigned Risk. Your cost of insurance doubles.

– Well – you get the picture. There are all sorts of reasons to try to avoid breakdowns, *in addition* to the cost and the waste of time. It's worth a lot of effort, and a good bit of money, to keep your car in good running condition, and avoid breakdowns. See also the Appendix on Tools and on Spare Parts. These items may not prevent an accident *directly,* but you may be able to minimize your breakdowns, and recover from them quickly. That can help you get the heck out of the breakdown lane, as fast as possible!

Chapter 42. SAFETY EQUIPMENT

Safety equipment means, anything that keeps you safe. Sunglasses. Seat belts. Anything that is especially related to preventing accidents.

Money...

Money is often the *best* safety equipment. Because if you need some other safety equipment, you can often buy it. New wiper blades. Sunglasses. Whatever. And if you haven't got cash, plastic (i.e. a credit card) usually works, in most stores. So, that's why we put it on our check-list. Important stuff. However, sometimes, if the store is *out*, or if the store is *closed*, even *money* will not get you a solution to your problem. So sometimes you should make your own safety plans.

Seat-belts...

I just tried to replace my seat-belts. They are 27 years old, which is absurd. I should have replaced them, long ago, because nylon gradually degrades when exposed to sunlight. I got 12 feet of good nylon webbing, only to discover that our sewing machine cannot sew it. So I shall have to sew it by hand. I'll put a little more than 100 stitches in each joint, and I'll be a lot better off. Within a month. Honest.

Of course, seat-belts don't do you any good if you don't put them on. In most states, it is the law; and in every place, the laws of nature tell you that you are better off in most accidents, to have your seat-belts on. In many situations, the seat belt holds you down firmly and helps you AVOID having an accident. I think that is a LOT better than, having the accident but not getting hurt. Anyhow, even for short trips, just about everybody should have their seat belt and shoulder-belt ON, before you start. No more lecturing needed. You will do it.

Improper Seat-Belt Installations...

One of my buddies Tom got a ride in the back seat of a friend's new car. The owner had made several customized modifications to the car. A few minutes down the road, Tom felt a sharp whack on his belly. He was puzzled, but did not say anything. When it happened a second time, he decided to quietly unbuckle his seat belt. A good thing. It turned out, the car's owner had installed special rear seat belts, and the length of the belt was *much* longer than needed. In fact, there were several extra feet of belt – that stuck out the door. In fact, the seat belt hung out the door so far, it was able to flop under the rear tire, and when it did, it *PULLED* really hard on the belt. Fortunately, they stopped and checked out this bad noise, and they were able to cut off the excessive length before any serious harm was done.

305

Isadora Duncan Had Problems, Too....

Tom pointed out that the noted dancer of the 1920s, Isadora Duncan, had a similar problem. She went for a drive in a sporty roadster, while wearing one of her trade-marked long scarves. UNfortunately, the scarf got wrapped up in the spokes of the rear wheels, and she was killed. The books say she was strangled. Not exactly. Actually, she was decapitated. So don't be too sloppy about straps or clothes hanging out in the breezes.

Miscellaneous Safety Equipment

Other stuff:

- Sunglasses, so you can see what's happening.

- Snow scrapers.

- A bottle of brake fluid.

- A flashlight.

- Maybe a flare, in case you come to an accident scene and have to help direct traffic.

- A fire-extinguisher is a good thing to have. I have carried one in my Beetles, for over 20 years, and have not had the occasion to use it. Still a good idea.

- I consider a shovel of good general usefulness, and I think it's good for safety, although I must admit I can't think of exactly where I would use it for safety purposes. But it DOES help me get through.

- Another good idea to have, is a small first-aid kit. A few band-aids, a couple simple bandages, and a small instruction book in case you forget your Boy-Scout or Girl-Scout merit-badge instructions.

Air Bags?

Should you buy a car with air-bags? I don't object to that. But most people never have an accident that activates the air-bags. For the driving I do, I don't feel terribly bad about not having them. But if having them makes you feel safer, that's fine, go ahead and spend your money on that feature.

HOWEVER, if having air-bags on your car just means you drive more aggressively, then you are playing games with safety. That's OK with me; go ahead and do it, but just be aware that you are playing that game.

Recently warnings have come out, in the fall of 1996, that Air Bags are so powerful that they are dangerous, not only for babies, but for children and small adults – even for small drivers. Developments in this area are not final, but it is probably a good idea for children to sit in the back seat, and avoid sitting up front if there are Air Bags there. Make sure that only forward-facing baby seats are used in a front seat where Air Bags are provided.

What do you do if there are too many kids to sit only in back? What if you have a pick-up truck, and there *is* no "back seat"? Well, if there is not any switch to let you turn off that air bag, then you might ask the manufacturer of your car what *they* recommend....

ABS?

Similarly, you can buy a car with ABS (Anti-Lock Braking System) – and you can say that provides better safety. However, the latest data on ABS indicate that it encourages people to drive more aggressively, so there are not any fewer accidents, nor are accidents less expensive. In other words, the insurance companies are NOT going to give you lower rates after you pay for ABS.

So if YOU plan to buy ABS and THEN drive carefully, slowly, and safely, you may be more safe. Just be aware that most people just use the ABS to let them go faster!

Recently I rented a car with ABS on a snowy day in Denver. Yes, the ABS did help prevent skids when you are hitting the brakes hard. You can even steer a little while braking hard. But if you get in a skid and try to hit the brakes, the ABS does no good at all. If you get a lot of confidence that ABS can help you slow down, you may start driving more aggressively – and get in trouble!

Honk, Honk...

One other safety item – your horn. You can use your horn to prevent accidents. And you should have an automatic reflex, to get your hand or thumb over to the horn ring, so you can hit it fast if you need to.

I'll tell you one place I keep my thumb on the horn: at Yosemite Park. I don't know if the other drivers are absorbed in the lovely scenery, or terrified because they do not see a guard rail. But about every 40th car I see in Yosemite is shying across the center line. And I just naturally zap them with a beep of the horn. You should be prepared to do so, too.

Well, there's another short chapter. That's OK.

6/24/22

Chapter 43. MUFFLERS and EXHAUST SYSTEMS

This is gonna be, thank God, a short chapter. At last.

What does your Muffler (and the exhaust system) do? It does about 3 things. It cuts down the noise, so the driver is not deafened, and the neighbors won't complain about the noise. It gets your exhaust out to the back of the car, so you won't be inhaling it. And most modern cars have a catalytic converter, which helps your exhaust burn clean, so you won't put out much smog.

What if you have a hole in your exhaust system? You might make so much noise that it's hard to hear. You can't drive safely if you can't hear. Things like sirens, fire trucks, etc. It's not nice to make so loud a roaring sound, that your neighbors get mad. Further, if you have a hole in your exhaust system, the exhaust leak could overheat other parts of your car, perhaps causing damages. Especially if an exhaust pipe breaks, up near the engine.

But if you keep putting off the repair, eventually a nice policeman will pull you over and explain that you have to get it fixed, this week. Of course, this will happen when you are in a hurry trying to get to the airport, to go on a 6-day trip. It's best to get your exhaust system repaired before the cop has to remind you.

Serious Stuff...

But that's not the worst. If you ignore an exhaust leak, you may get carbon monoxide poisoning. If you have any holes in the floor of your ratty old car – or even if there is just a funny air flow under the bottom of your new car, an exhaust leak can get into the car. In case you never studied chemistry, the carbon monoxide in a car's exhaust is really kind of poisonous. If you get a lot, you can die pretty quick, or pass out and drive into roadside junk, NOT good for your health. Even a low concentration can fill up your blood gradually, and make you groggy, sleepy, weird. If you start feeling at all sleepy, or weird, when there is an exhaust leak, stop and get it fixed, fast. A very serious health problem.

Problems compound...

I heard about a guy who had some rust spots in the bottom of his car, and when his tail-pipe broke, he stuffed rags in the rusty holes. After a while, he was getting sleepier and *sleepier* by the time he got to work. Somebody explained, rags are NOT capable of blocking out the carbon monoxide – just before he was going to pass out....

Patches??

I can mention that VWs' mufflers are not extremely long-lived, especially back east where the salt gets at them. So when I had "a little rust spot" on my muffler, I have tried, over the years, several different kinds of patching materials. Different kinds of goo, cement, patch kits, clamps, wires, bandages. Most of these lasted about a week and then fell off leaving no trace. So don't expect any "repair" to be worth much. Besides, in some states, trying to patch a muffler is illegal. The best, most cost-effective way is to buy a high-quality, rust-resistant muffler. Cheapies are a loser.

Cheap Junk...

In fact I twice bought a muffler from J. C. Whitney. Each time, the thing fell apart in about 2 months. I complained that their muffler was junk. They said that because I had bought it and kept it in my house for 3 months before I installed it, the warrantee had run out, so, tough luck. They thought they could safely tell me, tough luck. I always figured I would wait until I had a chance to get even with them. And here it is. I don't know if J.C. Whitney makes any mufflers that are any good, but if they sell you a piece of cheap junk that wears holes in itself because the internal baffles rattle against the shell, well, don't be too surprised. I warned you.

Rear Hatches

If you have a car with a rear door or hatch or window, you should be aware that exhaust fumes can be drawn into the back of your car, even if you do NOT have a broken exhaust system. Consult the owner's manual. If you are driving, and you do not smell a lot of fumes, you may be able to make a short trip – a dump-run, or bringing some trees back from the nursery. But keep your windows open, and your vents, to let as much fresh air blow onto the driver – and the passengers – as possible. This is NOT a popular mode for bringing home your snow-blower in January, but for a short trip, you will probably survive. Just don't push your luck.

Loose Parts Rattling...

Other problems – horrible noises when the muffler parts (or the heat shields over and under the muffler) rattle and drive you nuts. You might decide to try to bend the heat shield, but be careful as you are reaching past muffler parts that can be VERY HOT.

Don't Park Over Grasses or Stuff That Could Catch Fire!!

Your catalytic converter might be hot enough to set fire to grasses or weeds, if you park your car over grasses or stuff. So, be very careful not to let that happen. That can even happen if the heat shields are intact, but it is much more likely to happen if they are bent or missing.

That's all – a short chapter. About time.

Chapter 44. OTHER CARS & TRAFFIC on the ROAD

We drivers must be prepared to share the road with a lot of other interesting vehicles, critters, and STUFF. What does that have to do with Accidents? Well, if you come around a corner and find a herd of cows on their way home from pasture, you should not be astonished to find that there are *slippery* places on the road. If you want to stop, jamming on the brakes may not work as well as it usually does.

Slow Vehicles

If there are tractors, or trucks, they may be very slow. That does not mean they won't try to help you get past, as soon as possible. But that might take a minute or two. So you have to nail the brakes, and wait for a safe place to pass.

Motorcycles and Bicycles

Motorcycles can go very fast, but they can also be very vulnerable. And they are hard to see. So we should try to avoid crunching into them – even though they sometimes try to slice across our path.

When I first came to California, I saw a lot of people driving motorcycles and having a lot of fun. I thought it might be fun to get a motorcycle. Then I was driving along Route 9, and a motorcycle passed me, and passed the car ahead of me – and – oops. The next car decided to make a left turn, just as the motorcycle was trying to get past him. I stopped and tried to help. The cyclist said, "Just ease my cycle over to the side of the road, and call me an ambulance, because I have a broken leg." He knew his situation, and he was resigned to a trip to the hospital. Needless to say, I changed my mind about buying a motorcycle.

Now, if somebody ever invents a laser holograph, so my motorcycle would LOOK LIKE a heavy truck, then I'll buy a motorcycle. But because motorcycles are so hard to *see*, I'll have to wait a while...

Bicycles are much slower – yet they can still try to slice though our space. VERY vulnerable. Some bicyclists are kids. Others are crusty, nasty teenagers or older men who only scorn people in cars. Even though it is not easy, we should try to be nice to them because if they fall or bump us, they can be badly hurt. Give them a lot of space. Don't assume they will continue in a straight line without ever wobbling.

Other Cars

Well, we should try to watch out for all other cars. Don't jump in front of them. Be careful if they start to pull out in front of you. Beware of cars beside you, or in your blind spot. (See in the Chapter on Vision.) Be on the look-out for merging traffic, and try to help them when you can. – What else did I forget? Not much. See also, the Chapter on Pedestrians and Equestrinas. Anyhow, there's another short chapter.

Chapter 45. PEDESTRIANS and EQUESTRINAS

We drivers must also be prepared to share the road with a lot of walkers, people and other animals, walking or standing on or near the road. These people may do some very unpredictable things – not to mention what a horse might do.... I have never hit any pedestrians with my car, fortunately. I must admit, I have done a lot of my driving on roads where there are not many pedestrians.

One time I was bicycling north up Mass Ave in Cambridge, right near the center line of that busy city street. I saw a jay-walker standing in the middle of the street, right on the center line. He was looking at the southbound traffic – the oncoming traffic. He was looking AWAY from me. Suddenly, he took a step backward, to avoid some on-coming car he didn't like the looks of. He stepped back *right in front of me*, and I hit him square with my front wheel and bowled him over – knocked him down. Fortunately, I was not going very fast, and he was not hurt. We were both embarrassed. So we dusted ourselves off and went on our ways. BUT, I am glad I was not driving a car.

The point is, you must allow for a pedestrian to do some unpredictable things, and you have to allow a good bit of space. There is almost NOTHING that you can predict, or that you *cannot* predict, that you can be *sure* a pedestrian will not do. So you have to allow a lot of space.

Kids...

NOW, there are adult pedestrians – and there are kids. Kids of all sizes. While you can expect that most adults are not likely to leap into the road, with kids, you can expect that they may occasionally do *exactly* that. So, you should be *especially* careful if kids are walking along the road. They might not hear you approaching. Or a group of teen-agers might just start horsing around, and one of them might lurch out into the roadway.

I was very impressed while travelling in Nepal. Small kids as young as 5 or 4 would walk along a road with trucks and busses rolling along at 40 or 50 mph, barely 2 or 3 feet away. And the drivers were not overly worried, because they knew the kids had learned to walk very steadily, and not lurch in front of the car. I would never trust a small kid that way in the U.S.; I would *bip* my horn and slow down.

Similarly, I was impressed that these young kids would walk cheerfully along a steep trail, or along the top of a stone wall 6 feet high, with no great concern. The kid's mother would stand right there, with no concern about her little kid walking along the top of a stone wall – because she knew he was safe, and would not trip or fall. These kids really were very steady on their feet. Much steadier than any kids we see in the States.

Babies??

There is a challenging old story about a driver of an army truck. According to that story, YOU are a soldier, driving a truck full of soldiers, down a rough dirt road, in Korea, or VietNam, or some other oriental country. The road runs down along a narrow ridge, and then up another hill. You are driving this truck, and you are in a hurry, to get to the next camp to meet a schedule.

As you descend this road, you see a pile of STUFF in the road. As you approach, you see that the pile of STUFF is – a small baby. A small Oriental baby. The baby is sitting right in the middle of the narrow road, crying. You hit the brakes hard, and you have a full second to realize 3 things:

(1) You cannot stop before you hit the baby.

(2) If you try to avoid the baby, and go off the narrow road, the cliffs fall off very steeply, and many of the soldiers in the back of the truck would be badly injured, or would die. Or,

(3) If you keep straight ahead, you will kill the baby, but your soldiers will be safe. WELL, as far as I am concerned, this is a bunch of crap. It is a hypothetical story, and the person who is posing the question is trying to moralize at us. The story is not based on reality.

IF the baby is sitting in the road, then I see 3 possibilities –

(a) The person who let the baby get into the road is primarily responsible for the baby's death – NOT the driver – not YOU – not ME. Or,

(b) This may be some kind of Viet Cong trap, and if I try to stop, the VC will fire on us. Or,

(c) The VC wants me to drive off the road and kill everybody.

Anyhow, when a puzzle is posed in the form of a conundrum, so that there is no right or easy or correct answer, then we are given a problem to make us think. And if I think I have no answer, I refuse to devote the rest of my life to worrying about a hypothetical question. So I am going to set this question aside, and I hope you will, too. I won't say you have to worry about this problem forever. But it is interesting to look at the different aspects of this kind of problem – !!

If a child gets in front of my car, and is not capable of responding to my HORN BLASTS – should I sacrifice my life, to save the child's life? Maybe. I'll think about that when I get to that problem. Maybe yes, maybe no. But I would not feel justified in killing 20 men and myself, just to try to save the life of one baby, in a situation where there are not supposed to be any babies in the road.

However, if I am driving at a moderate speed, and if I hit the brakes *hard* to avoid a pedestrian, and I realize that I have to hit a parked car at 10 or 20 mph to keep from hitting that person – then I have figured out that I will do that. I may not volunteer to sacrifice my life, but I may sacrifice my car.

But as for babies in the middle of a freeway – I am amused with these people who try to play God, and pose a problem that has no good solutions, just to see us squirm. What do you think?

Critters

As I mentioned in the Chapter on Reflex Responses, it is worth a good deal of effort to avoid a dog that leaps out at us. I mean, I know a couple dogs that I really dislike, but that does not mean I would ever want to hurt them. If a dog strays into the path of my car, I will try to avoid him – but if I can't do it without smashing into another car, then I have decided in advance, the dog has a lower priority.

Read that Chapter. Plan what kind of efforts you would take, to avoid a dog in your lane. Note, I would feel badly about hitting a dog, but if a dog is stupid enough to stand in the middle of the road, I have PLANNED that I will feel less bad about hitting him, than hitting the car beside me and perhaps injuring another *homo sapiens*.

What if a deer is standing there? Hitting a deer can seriously damage your car. There are supersonic whistles that are alleged to scare deer away. I'll be darned if I know if these whistles work, despite all the claims. If a deer or moose or other large animal gets in front of my car, then I would prefer not to hit that animal, but if there is no reasonable way to avoid the damage of hitting that animal, that does not cause more cost or damage than hitting the deer – then – I have decided to hit the deer. As we well know, some deer or other large animals are mesmerized by the car's lights, so if they are not capable of moving, that is THEIR problem.

Equestrinas...

Down in Los Altos, just northwest of the intersection of Foothill Expressway and El Monte Road, there used to be a sign: "Pedestrians, Bicycles, and Equestrinas Prohibited". I don't know if an "Equestrina" is a female riding on a horse, or, somebody riding on a female horse. But I got a photograph of the sign, to prove it. An honest typo error at the sign factory. But a few years ago they replaced the sign, and eliminated the typo error.

As with pedestrians, horses and their riders can make almost any move. Worse yet, horses may be scared or "spooked" by the sound of a horn, or by a flash of reflected sunlight flashing off your car – or by just about *anything*. So, you must allow a LOT of space, so you do not get dangerously close to horses. And if your car is pretty quiet, you might realize you are sneaking up pretty close behind a horse, before the rider hears you. Even my VWs are fairly quiet, if I have my foot off the gas....

BIP?

So you might BEEP your horn, to caution the horse and rider. BUT, it is EXACTLY wrong to BEEP your horn when you are close by. You should bip your horn at a big distance – at least 60 or 80 yards away. Come to think of it, if you see kids or bicyclists on the road, and you think *they* are not paying attention, you should likewise *bip* your horn at a great distance, so you will not scare them with a blast of the horn up close. Fair enough? I mean, a lot of us drivers also walk or ride bicycles or horses, and we would not want a warning blast when the car is close by – it's much nicer to get a *bip*, at a distance.

Then, you might HAVE TO hit the horn again if you get closer to the pedestrians, and the persons make a foolish move into the roadway. But when you *bip* the horn at a good distance, you decrease the possibility that BLAST will be needed.

Further, unless you have HIGH confidence that the people are a safe distance away, well off the road, slow down and make sure you can get past with safe margins, without scaring anybody. Horses and kids, too. And this is *especially* true if there is on-coming traffic.

Advice to Pedestrians

And when YOU are a pedestrian, be thoughtful and reasonably alert, and careful, and try not to encroach on the road, and scare the heck out of other drivers – OK?

OK ... another short chapter.

Chapter 46. INTERESTING CARS

New Cars

I suppose that new cars are fun. Every once in a while, I rent a car, and the odometer indicates 14 miles. I always try to be nice to a new car, and I look up the break-in procedures in the Owner's Manual. I try not to drive too fast for the first 500 miles, and not to always drive at the same constant speed. But I usually do not buy a new car, because there are not any new cars I want to buy. I happen to like good old cars. (If I could really buy a new 1962 or 1968 VW Beetle, or a 1970 Bus, right from the factory, I'd buy a couple of each!!)

I am sure that there are all kinds of nice things in new cars – but in general, these days, I find them boring. Competent, but boring. And, fairly expensive. If I ever find an excuse to buy a new car, I'll let you know. The last time I bought a new car was 24 years ago, when I bought a 1972 VW Bus. It was a good car, but not a great engine. 1972 was a bad year for a lot of bad cars, and that '72 Bus was better than a lot, but I wouldn't buy that car again. (Its engine was too expensive and complicated, and did not have as much power as it ought to.)

Still, these days, if you buy a new car, you are likely to get a pretty good, reliable car. Not like 10 or 20 years ago, when lemons were pretty likely. I will not spend any time telling you what kind of car to buy, nor how to buy it. There are other books to tell you that. I just wish you good luck. And, break it in, carefully. Change the oil at least once every 5,000 miles if you do a lot of freeway driving, or 3,000 if you don't drive much, or if you do mostly city driving. If it is as good as it should be, you can put on a LOT of miles without much trouble. It may be reliable and economical to run for 100,000 or 150,000 miles.

Will I tell you to give up on a car because you are bored? Please refer to the section below, on Used cars... and the Chapter on Oldies. Also, read the Appendix on Rental Cars. Renting a car is a good opportunity to try out a new car – hopefully, an INTERESTING car.

New cars have advantages because of their modern design and good safety equipment. If you drive in conditions where you need Anti-Lock Brakes, or if you really expect to drive into things, and you want an Air Bag, then you want a new car.

Used Cars - or - "Pre-Owned Cars"

Let's see. I have only bought – one VW bus, and 4 VW Beetles, as used cars. In general, they have run very well. I got a good buy in each case. (Refer to Appendix E, "What's All This VW Stuff, Anyhow?")

Can I tell you how to buy a used car? No, there are other books to do that. You would surely want to bring a friend who really knows cars. Or, who really knows this particular make and type of car. I mean – would I buy a Corvette on the advice of a guy who knows *Chevrolets*?? No way; I would bring along a Corvette expert. So if you ask me for advice on how to buy a Ford or Toyota or whatever, I cannot offer any advice. Go buy somebody else's book, to tell you how to do that. Bring a buddy who knows his Fords, or Toyotas, or whatever.

But if you want to buy an old air-cooled VW, you'll want the book on How to Keep your VW Alive*. It has a whole chapter on how to shop for a VW. It can help you avoid buying a car that is *shot*, or paying more than what it's worth. I recommend that book for anybody who has an old air-cooled VW. And if you are shopping, bring along a buddy who knows his Beetles.

Old Cars

When a car gets OLD, anything can happen. Things can break, or gradually get worse. As I mentioned in my stories – when they get old, ANYTHING can happen. Parts and features that start out good can become bad or unreliable. And sometimes it is hard to buy parts. (For old VWs, that is not usually a trouble, as it is for many other cars.) Things get rusty. Welding, patching, epoxying become a way of life. Still, if you have a car that you like, you can do a lot worse than staying with it, so long as it is not losing structural strength or body integrity due to rust.

I will not recommend that you should always stay with your old car. You have to know when it is time to quit – when to give up – as I did with my '70 Beetle that was losing a pint of oil every 200 yards (not, 200 miles). But, old cars have some interesting features. They have some character – which new cars seem to be missing. If you have an old car, and if, despite its faults, you know how to drive it safely, you may be better off than with a new car.

Other Interesting Cars...

I can observe that if you drive a pickup truck, you have to be very careful about jamming on your brakes. Pickups spin around even worse than VWs do, under severe braking.

If you have a high-powered car, you can accelerate out of some kinds of accidents – but you can also accelerate into other accidents. If you are driving a slow truck or an under-powered car, you have to be careful not to get in other peoples' way. On a preliminary basis, these are most of the things that I can think about, that relate to interesting cars, and the kind of accidents they can get into.

Bad Cars

Sometimes you have an opportunity to drive a car that has something wrong with it, or, something not right. What should you do about that?

Sometimes a car may have not-so-good brakes. You might have to step on the brakes twice, before the brakes work well – pumping up the brakes.

---

* *HOW TO KEEP YOUR VW ALIVE, John Muir, 1992, John Muir Press, Santa Fe, NM. About $18. Available in many bookstores. See also in Appendix on Books.*

NOW, if you are coming up to a stop sign, you may have plenty of time to step on the brakes twice. But if a dog or a car jumps out in front of you – and you just want to nail the brakes and stop – are the brakes working well enough? Or, are the brakes really *bad* until you step on them the second time? If they are – maybe you should not drive that car until you get them fixed, because, one mile out of 1000, you REALLY need the brakes *instantly*. Are you willing to take a chance of 1 in 1000 of having an accident? Be very careful with that risk.

One time my Beetle needed some brake adjustment. The brake pedal was going too far down. But it was raining, and it was inconvenient to find a place to jack up the car and lie down and adjust the brakes. Then I noticed that if I left the handbrakes on a couple clicks, the brake pedal did not go down so far. I left my handbrake on a couple clicks (still 3 clicks away from any friction), and the foot-brakes worked fine. Then within a week, I got some good weather and adjusted the brakes properly. This trick may not apply to all cars, but it's better than driving around with badly adjusted brakes while you are waiting to get in the repair shop.

Bad Tires

What if you have some bad tires? In some cases, you can go slowly and still be reasonably safe. But sometimes that is no good. I mean, if I had a tire with a cut or a badly worn spot, I would NOT want to drive across the Golden Gate Bridge, or the Bay Bridge, because breaking down there would be a big pain for me and for a lot of other people. Fortunately, I can usually get a tire changed in just a few minutes. And I always have a couple EXTRA spares around the house. What if you find you have a low tire, nearly flat? You may be able to drive slowly to a place to add more air. But on a freeway it might not be safe to do that....   ✗

If you are out in the snow, and one of your good snow tires goes bad – what if your spare tire does not have much tread? Bad news. On dead-flat roads, if you go very slowly, you may get where you are going – but you'll have no safety margin, in case you have to stop fast. And if you have to get up a hill – even a little one – a nearly bald tire on your drive axle might leave you in the lurch – or in the ditch. So, carrying a spare tire in winter that has anything less than VERY good tread, is just skirting around an accident looking for a place to happen. You GOTTA have at least one good spare tire, in winter. Or stay home when it snows.

Bad Starting

What if your engine does not *start* very well? You may get stuck. You may get where you are going – and not be able to get back. But if your engine quits on the road – there you are in the middle of the highway – dead in the water. An invitation to real trouble. If your car *runs* but does not start, make extra efforts to only stop in places where you are sure you can start. (Park on top of a big hill?)

What if your engine stalls a lot, when idling? Well, make sure you can get it started. If you can't keep it running, and you can't get it started, why start on your trip?

6/26/22

Engine Loses Power?

If your car sometimes loses power, or runs really rough, and this is unpredictable – that is really bad stuff. Because you will occasionally need a little power, to get around a curve, or up a hill – or across a lane of traffic. If the power isn't there when you need it, that can be an annoyance, or can lead to an accident. Get it fixed.

Sloppy Steering?

What if a friend loans you an old car where the steering is loose or sloppy? If you drive pretty slow, you can learn to keep it under control. Or, if you are on a road with a crown, the slant of the road will take most of the slack out of the steering, and it will seem OK. But if you get cross-winds, you will have to move the steering wheel a good bit, quickly, to avoid being pushed out of your lane. And when the wind stops blowing, you have to move your arms *back* really fast, to avoid going out of your lane on the other side. Crosswinds that blow alternately from left or right can be a real struggle. You may have to slow down, to stay even *approximately* in your lane. I was going to include an Appendix on Dead Zone Stuff, to deal with sloppy steering. But it wasn't going to help you drive any more safely than the notes I wrote here, so I left it out. (Amazing, isn't it, that there was something I didn't include!)

Of course, if your steering is really sloppy, you have to plan to get it fixed. If the tie rods are loose, and the king-pins, or ball-joints, shot, and the steering box floppy – repairing all that stuff might cost more than the car is worth. Maybe time to retire that car, and get a newer one where the steering is not in such bad shape? Think about it. Get a mechanic's advice. Maybe there is one item that's responsible for most of the sloppiness, and that won't be too expensive to repair? At least you have to understand exactly what is wrong, so you can be sure it is not falling apart.

Anyhow, those are the kinds of things you have to think about, if you are driving an old car, or a car with something worn out or working badly (which can happen even on new cars).

6/26/12

Chapter 47. *INTERESTING* ROADS

There are all kinds of interesting roads. Some of them are a lot of fun to drive on. However, some of these roads have interesting opportunities for accidents, and I will mention them.

Dirt and Gravel...

There are a lot of unpaved roads in the USA – and in the world. Some are steep, like the Mt. Washington Toll road. There are a lot of old gravel roads in New Hampshire and in northern New England. Likewise in Colorado, and Nevada, and California. Some are steep; some are flat. I cannot say I am a true *connoisseur* of old roads, because I am a glutton. A *gourmand*, not a *gourmet*. I like a *lot* of old gravel roads.

Some of them are nice and straight, and you can cruise at 55 mph. For example, the road from Big Pine CA to Eureka Valley to Death Valley. However, at the end of one 5-mile straight stretch, the gravel turns to soft sand, and your car will wallow and plow and veer, without any warning. All you can do is take your foot off the gas and let the sand slow you down. You'll be happy you didn't push it up to 65. Some are kinky as the dickens, like the roads from Maxwell CA to Stonyford, up to Black Diamond Ridge, then up to Low Gap, and down Rice Creek Road toward Clear Lake. There's at least 3000 curves on that stretch. You'll almost *never* get above 45. If everybody on the road stays on their own side, you'll have no problem. Of course this road has no center line. But most of this gravel road is a good broad 2-1/2 lanes wide, so it's not hard to find enough room on your side of the road.

Some are in the open, soaring across hillsides, like the road from North Fork, Nevada to Jarbidge, north of Elko Nevada. Here, the vistas are so grand, it's very hard to keep your eyes on the road, and you just have to stop occasionally to take in all the views. Others are in deep woods, and *narrow*, like Jefferson Notch Road in NH. When a road is pretty narrow, I prefer to take it at night, so I can keep a watch for on-coming headlights. Others are steep, like the roads from Lake City to Silverton Colorado. If you don't have 4WD, you have to be very careful not to get hung up on steep curves.

On the other hand, Corona Pass Road has a nice easy 4% grade, because it used to be an old railroad roadbed. I think you can still get up to the Continental Divide at 11,670' from the west, using easy grades, but you can't continue all the way to Boulder, because a tunnel collapsed. Again, there are great vistas. Another impressive place – also an abandoned RR roadbed – is the road from Pitkin Colorado (just east of Gunnison) up to old Alpine Tunnel. The last time I was there, it was fairly rough and steep, and I recall holding onto the steering wheel VERY TIGHT, to make sure a rock in the road didn't nudge my course very close to the cliff edges. Still, this road was well worth the effort. Those old roadbeds really do get you up into high country.

Surprise!! Bridge out...

I just remembered another problem you may find on old roadbeds. If you start west from Promontory Point, Utah, where they have a *nice* museum, you can drive along the old abandoned RR grade. But don't get going faster than about 20 or 24 mph. Because some of the little bridges are OUT. Removed. If you are going slow enough, you can just ease down the alternate route onto the ground and around the gap. But if you were going very fast, you might wreck your car, because the outages are not marked. That route in Utah is the place I remember seeing this several times, but any old roadbed might have places where the way has a bridge missing, or a washout....

Slow Roads...

If you drive a slow car, or a heavy truck, you know that there are some long steep upgrades on high-speed highways, where you cannot keep up speed. My '68 Beetle is MUCH too fast for most flat-land driving situations, but when I drive up in the mountains – such as US 50, or I-80 over the Sierras, I get bogged down below 45 mph in some places. If I do, I put my blinkers on. Of course, if I can barely hold 40, then trucks are even slower, so I have to plan my attack for passing slow trucks, while staying out of the way for fast cars to pass me, with minimum obstruction. I recall that up on I-70 near Dillon, Colorado, there are some long upgrades where I cannot even stay in third gear; I have to shift down into second, and potter up the hill at 25 mph, at nearly full throttle – with my warning blinkers blinking. I love Colorado, but at high altitude, most car engines really lose a lot of power. So, slow speed is really a danger, on a high-speed road. If you have to drive slow, you should take precautions.

The Two-Lane...

Then there are good 2-lane *paved* roads. I saw a lot of VERY competent drivers on old Route 16, from Rochester NH up to Gorham. I used to go up Route 16 a lot, to go backpacking and hiking in the White Mountains. I remember a virtual *train* of cars, just hundreds without a break, heading back down after skiing on a Sunday evening. And all moving along very competently at about the speed limit. Pity the 7 guys waiting on a side road, waiting for a break in traffic so they could pull out and join the crowd. Because there weren't many breaks in traffic.

Desert Roads

There are desert roads. Route 50 across Nevada has been called "the loneliest road in America". Yeah, that would be a lousy place to run out of gas or water. But actually it is quite nice, once you learn to appreciate it. The road from Las Vegas to Hiko to Warm Springs Nevada is impressive. I like almost any road in the southwest or in the desert. But you have to develop the right mind-set so you don't get bored. You have to teach your eyes to caress the curves of the hills, like a woman's flank, yet bring your eyes back to the road every second or two.

Curvy Roads...

When I first came out to California, I immediately discovered curvy roads. I mean, *serious* amounts of curves, such as Page Mill Road. If you start at El Camino Real in Palo Alto, and head up Page Mill just a mile, you can visit the Hewlett Packard guys. Then if you keep on going, the road starts bending – and curving. By the time you get to the top, at Skyline Drive (Route 35) there are about 206 curves. Some are very TIGHT. I mean, you find that in some places, you are looking out the side window, to see where you are going. I know a couple guys who have been commuting down Page Mill every day for over 20 years. How many does that compute up to? 5000 days, 10,000 trips, 2 million curves??

Route 1 along the California Coast easily has 3500 curves, north of San Francisco, and easily 3000 south to LA, but that is just a guess. The route from Weaverville CA to Hayfork, Forest Glen, Zenia, Alderpoint, and Garberville has 2200 curves (counted). On all these twisty roads, you have to be careful about staying in your lane, most of the time, and avoiding oncoming traffic that may not be in their lane.... (and car-sickness).

Eastern Roads...

Back east, the Blue Ridge Parkway in Virginia goes up over some handsome countryside, but in summer or fall, and on weekends, it is often cluttered up with slow tourists, and it may not be easy to pass slow drivers. But if you get off peak tourist season, it's not bad. However, drivers from the west will be impressed that it is lined with guard rails.

Western Roads – With No Guard Rails

Conversely, eastern drivers will be impressed that there are so many mountain roads out west, that have no guard rails. That's enough to give the Eastern drivers a real set of WORRIES!! If you come from back east, and every road with a 1-foot slant beside the road is protected by a guard-rail – as you know they are – then you will be AMAZED when you come west, and there are drop-offs of 10 or 100 or 1000 feet – with no guard rail. YOU will be ASTONISHED. Or, horrified. How can the authorities have such a dangerous road, and *NO GUARD-RAIL*??????

It's really very simple. If there is a guard-rail there, at the edge of the drop-off, that's nice, but you are not going to drive into the guard rail, are you? Well, if you are not going to drive into the guard-rail, then why bother to put it up? – So, they did not put it up. Saves a lot of money.

For example, one time my wife Nancy was driving my mother down Conzelman Road, a steep scary road just a mile north of San Francisco, in Marin county. This is the road which looks down from an 800-foot hill on the 750-foot towers of the Golden Gate Bridge. A great road. But, when you start down the back side, it is steeper than any road in the east, and it has no guard rails. I bet if you got 100 VW Busses or Beetles going *really fast* down that road, and cut the wheel to roll them off the road, I bet you could put 40 of them into the ocean, a quarter mile below.

My mother said, "This road is so scary, I am going to close my eyes; I just can't look." Nancy said, "I brought you up to this road because it has such a great view. If you close your eyes, I'm going to close mine, too."

On the other hand, Going-to-the-Sun Road in western Montana is pretty hairy, but it *does* have guard-rails. (East of Columbia Falls.) A Grand old road.

Roads I've Never Seen Before...

I like most roads in England. Many roads in Colorado. Many roads in France or Germany, where the drivers really know how to drive. Switchback roads, such as Piccolo St. Bernard Pass, going from Aosta and Courmayeur, Italy to Albertville, France. All sorts of twisty curving roads – and preferably at night. Preferably in a small car, with plenty of power!! Obviously we, as tourists, are seeing these roads for the first time – so it is a challenge to come around a corner, and recognize what we want to do next – slow down for a hard curve, or speed up for a straightaway.

On the Four-Lane

Then there are a few interesting 4-lane roads. The original old Merritt Parkway and Hutchinson River Parkway used to be quite curvy – and the lanes *were* awfully narrow, as it was designed for passenger cars only, and no trucks allowed. Pretty challenging. As I remarked to my friend who was riding down to New York with me, at 62 mph, "The only thing we have to fear is fear itself". But now it has been re-built, and is so much improved, it is rather boring.

Old Route 20 from Worcester Mass. to Sturbridge and to Springfield ain't bad, a 4-lane road with interesting curves and hills, and not too many traffic lights. Since most of the traffic now takes the Massachusetts Turnpike, these old roads are not bad. When you *shun* the turnpikes, it is called *shunpiking*. Fun.

City Streets...

There are several roads in San Francisco that are fun to drive. Gough St. has synchronized lights, and it's fun to try to keep moving despite slow traffic. Some city "parkways" are kinky roads, quite challenging. One friend recommended Titus Street, in San Diego, as it is essentially a paved cliff. "It was always a thrill to drive over the edge, given that you could see nothing below as you went over. Local authorities decided that teenagers were having too much fun there, so they put a Stop sign just before the edge. However, people continued to crash and burn rather often, so they finally added a telephone booth at the bottom of the hill, so local residents would not be required to call tow trucks or ambulances."

And, More Strange Roads...

Don't forget tunnels, bridges, hills, mountain roads – and, any road with snow! Dragstrips, race courses, and ice-racing on frozen lakes....

What roads do I NOT like? City streets with a stop sign every damn' block. Roads with too much slow traffic. Roads that can move right along at 50 mph, but there is a really slow 35 mph speed limit, like some places in Connecticut. Roads that used to have passing zones, but which are now striped for NO PASSING. Roads where some idiot has an RV and is going slow and won't pull over to let anybody pass.

So, what kind of roads do you like? YOU TELL ME!! See Appendix O.

Chapter 48. HURRYING

If you don't allow enough time to make a trip, and you leave late, and you have to *hurry,* that can get you in trouble. Perhaps you drive too fast, or you don't slow down until the last second at an intersection. You may try to get through a PINK light; you *almost* come to a full stop at a stop sign (well, you really did shift down into second gear). Or you try to wedge impolitely ahead of another car, or pass a slow car in a not-quite-safe zone.

I don't have to tell you: any of these things can get you in trouble (even if a cop is NOT watching....)

It is worth some effort, to try to break this habit, because you may get away with it for a while. You may think it is OK. But if you keep it up, you are likely to get in trouble. You are VERY likely to get a ticket, because the cop is merely trying to keep you from doing harm to yourself, your car, or others. And if the cop does not educate you, you may have the "bad luck" to get into an accident.

Start Early

It is a good idea to start out early, and take something to do, something to read – maybe something to knit. In other words, read the morning paper, or that magazine article, AFTER your trip, rather than before, in case you get there early. Even more important, start getting ready for your trip *early.* Pack up the stuff you need. Make sure you find your car keys, your glasses, *and* something to read when you get there. Go to the john early. Send all the kids (if any) to the john. Leave early. It's a good idea.

The Contrarian Way

However, when I was working in Dedham Mass, I used to go to a dentist, Dr. Frolik, whose office was up in Jamaica Plain. The route went up Sprague Street and Turtle Pond Parkway and Roxbury Parkway, and a few other odd roads, and up Route 1, and it went around (or past) 7 traffic circles. I made my plans to leave work at the *last possible minute,* so I had to drive as fast as I safely could, up these curvy roads and around these rotaries, to get to my dental appointment. This not only saved time. But if a policeman were ever to ask, "WHY are you driving so fast?", I would say, "I am sorry, but I am just trying to get to my dentist's office – SEE, here is my appointment slip." I figured that would make a good excuse. But in 8 years, a policeman never asked me why I was in a hurry. I never had an accident. Heck, at 2 PM, those roads were nearly empty. So I just had a good time, hurrying up around these 7 rotaries. Unfortunately, on the way back to work, I could not hurry very much, because my "excuse" would not work!

6/14/22

Avoid Hurrying

These days, when I want to get to work early, I may take US 101. But when there is an important meeting, and I really sort of HAVE TO get there on time, I take I-280, and go up Sunnyvale-Saratoga Road to get there. On the average, that route is a little slower, but its worst case is a LOT better than the worst case when taking 101. And I leave early, and if I actually get to work early, there is always something I can work on.

> SO when it is important to get somewhere on time – so you don't arrive after the boat has sailed – you should plan, not to take the "best", fastest route, but the *least bad,* least-likely-to-jam-up route.

Similarly, I often drive pretty fast down by the airport. But when I have to catch a plane, I leave good and early. Then I consciously drive *right down at* the speed limit so I won't be delayed, arguing with a cop.

One of my buddies pointed out, Murphy's law always applies when you start your trip early. The traffic is light and the lights are all green. But if you leave at the last possible minute, the lights will all turn red when you get to them. Ain't it the truth!

Well, there's another short chapter.   ⋇

Chapter 49. SPEEDING

"SPEED KILLS"

I never took a formal "Driver's Education" class, so I never ran into this directly, but everybody who ever took these courses says they always used to include a lecture on "Speed Kills". Or, "SPEED KILLS!" They were trying to teach kids to drive safely, with an emphasis on "Speed Kills". The lecturer usually had a canned speech about how driving too fast will get you killed, and is terribly dangerous. Sometimes they had a little movie about how speeding will get you killed first, and arrested and thrown in jail, second.

Well, there were a lot of young drivers who did drive fast, very fast, and too fast. And some of them had lousy cars, and some had fast cars, and some had fast, lousy cars. And some had mediocre tires. And crummy brakes. And lousy judgement. And some of these guys got killed. I heard that one of my old classmates was doing over 85 on a straight stretch near Ellington, Connecticut, and was killed when trying to pass a slow car. But people drive 80 mph and a lot more, all the time on the Autobahns. And they used to do it on the Kansas Turnpike. I see people doing it on Route 280, almost every day. All those people are going to DIE – sooner or later – but they are not likely to die because of speeding in a car.

Finally, after too many people laughed too hard, some sense was brought into those "Driver Ed" programs, and "SPEED KILLS" was de-emphasized. People got a little smarter: It is not SPEED that kills, but, SPEED DIFFERENCE. If most of the drivers are doing 63 mph on a 55 mph road, and one guy is poking along at 41, the wise policeman will not stop the guys at 63, but will stop the guy doing 41 and ask him why. He will try to get that slow driver out of there – put him on the Old Road, or demand that he get his engine fixed, if it will not go any faster, or lock him up if he is drunk. But the guy doing 41 is the real danger to safe driving, because other people are not expecting to have to pass such a slow driver. (If you ever drive a slow car, or a heavy truck, you know that there are some high-speed highways where you cannot keep up speed – such as, on upgrades. If you ever have to drive slower than 45 mph on a high-speed road, turn on your 4-way flasher signals, so people will be cautioned that they will have to pass you).

Speeding Laws...

If everybody else is going 10 mph over the limit – and you are going only 4 or 5 mph over the limit, you are not likely to get tagged – UNLESS – all the 10 mph guys are gone over the hill, out of sight. Or, the cop is hungry and needs to fill his quota. Or, if you are an out-of-state driver. Or, suddenly it starts to rain. Or, if the cop is grouchy. In other words, you can never be sure.... Refer to the Chapter on Tickets.

BUT even if you know that the only cop in town is off at a picnic, or in court, you STILL have to watch out for other laws – the Laws of Physics, and the Laws of Human Nature. If you break those, you can get into even more trouble.

How Speed Limits Are Set

In some cases, the posted speed limit really *is* "reasonable and proper". Sometimes the road engineers do try to set a speed that is safe for the curves and for the road conditions. Sometimes the highway engineers take account of blind curves, or blind intersections that the driver cannot foresee. So, sometimes the posted speed limit is quite reasonable. Often, in enlightened times and places, the speed limits are set by experts at the observed speed that 85 per cent of drivers do not exceed – at the 85th percentile. This encourages the slow drivers, that it is safe to go a little faster, and encourages the faster drivers to go a little slower, so that not everybody has to pass everybody else. This is a reasonable goal, and it works pretty well, if the traffic engineers are permitted to do it.

However, most speed limits are set by political plans, and you are supposed to drive at 35 mph through a quiet little town, or in a school zone, even at 2 AM when nobody is about. Other times, speed limits are set arbitrarily low to make life simple for the cops and the judge. It makes revenue enhancement easy.

And we all know why the 55 mph speed limit was enforced along most US highways for 20 years, even on roads that were designed to be safe at 65, 70, or, in the case of the Kansas Turnpike, 80 mph. All for the politically correct reasons spouted by our politicians in Washington DC, most of whom do not even have to drive a car. They have turned us all into speeders – and hypocrites. To discuss later.

"Speeding" in Bad Weather

One time I nearly got ticketed for doing 55 mph on an empty 55 mph freeway – just because it was raining. The story is in the Chapter on Tickets. Now, 55 mph might be a scary speed if the rain is coming down in sheets, and there is heavy traffic, and you can't see where you are going because your wipers won't do a good job, and there's a stream of water an inch deep under your tires, so you are really floating on the water. That does happen, sometimes, and when it does, I tend to slow down below 55, or sometimes much lower, depending on the traffic and the conditions. But, barring those problems, 55 mph ain't very unsafe on a good road, with light traffic, even if it is raining a little. Neither is 64, not necessarily.

NOW, while I have stated that high speed, by itself, does not "kill", does not necessarily CAUSE accidents, still, we must be aware that driving fast (too fast?) can CONTRIBUTE to accidents. It can make a little accident into a big one. And, there are certain accidents that just do not happen at low speeds, but get serious at high speeds.

Example: SPEED as a Contributing Factor

Once I was talking to a guy in England. The speed limits on motorways are supposed to be 70 mph, but that does not stop people from driving at 80, or 90, or 100 mph, or even a little faster. This guy was driving his twin-cam Escort* up the M1 in light traffic, on a dark rainy night. He was rolling at about 100 mph, in the fast lane. As he went to pass a slower driver, that car *shied* at him – drifted into his lane. He hit his brakes HARD. His car spun and spun and bounced off the centre guard rail – and then into the ditch. He was not injured – but it sure scared the hell out of him. And it wrecked the car. Totalled it.

◆ ◆ ◆

Now, does this result mean the guy should not have been going 100? Well, yes, now that we think about it, maybe he should have slowed down to 90. But, even more important, he probably should have blinked his lights so the slower car would not be asleep, or sloppy. Personally, I prefer to blink my headlights OFF AND ON, rather than blinking on the high beams. Could he have hit his horn? Well, maybe by that time it was too late. The "slow" guy was probably doing about 65 or 70, and if you are going 70, if a guy blows his horn at you, it's unclear if you could stop drifting into his lane.

Would it have helped if the guy's car had anti-skid brakes? I asked a friend who has worked on the design of anti-skid brake systems. He said, yes, most of these systems actually will work at 100 or 120 mph. There is not really much of a speed limitation on ABS. So that might have been one of the accidents where ABS might have prevented an accident. On the other hand, maybe if the guy knew he had ABS, he would have been driving even faster.

Still, speed did contribute to that accident. If the guy had been doing 65, passing a slow driver doing 40, he could much more likely have avoided a severe skid. So, let's not be silly: Speed can help cause some accidents. It can be a *significant* contributing factor. If you insist on having the advantages of going fast – the time-savings and the thrills, too – you must be aware of the risks. You must keep alert. You must know how to not just hit the brakes, but *ease them on*, because a high-speed skid on a wet road can be very scary.

AND, if you are doing 100 mph on a German Autobahn, you usually want to keep out of the fast lane, most of the time, because Porsches and BMWs are likely to be blowing right on by you, at 120 mph or more, and you do NOT want to get in THEIR way.

One of my reviewers said he thought that this fellow was really very dangerous, a very selfish person. Well, that may be true, but it should be noted that it was rather late at night, and traffic was very light. And even though he spun and wrecked his car, he did not hit any other car, on the empty road.

Rather, the point I want to make is, that he took some risks that night, as he had been taking them for a long time. And when he gambled and lost, he lost enough time and money to cancel out all the time and money he had saved for a whole lot of years. Yes, the insurance company replaced the car. But you would not want to bet that his insurance rates did not go up. As near as I can guess, the scrapes against

* Not at all the same as the Ford Escort sold in the USA, but a competent, powerful little sports-sedan.

the guard-rail would indicate to the insurance company that he really was going quite fast.

What Is Speeding?

Juan Manuel Fangio was known as one of the great racing car drivers of all time, especially in the era 1948-1953. He won races with many different kinds of cars. And he was held up as a good example for young drivers – because he never got into accidents, and he always obeyed the speed limits. Oh, yeah, sure, a polite, mild-mannered driver. (He died in the summer of 1995, as I was writing this.)

One day Mr. Fangio was driving a sedan on a good 2-lane road in Italy, with some friends. He came around a sweeping curve at 120 mph, and there in front of him was – !!! – a moving van, making a U-turn, broadside across the ENTIRE ROAD. Mr. Fangio knew that the brakes on this car were not adequate to stop at that speed – they would fade. So, he hit the brakes and *cut* the wheel and got the car sideways. With a horrifying shriek, the car slid to a safe stop, broadside, about 20 feet short of the moving van.

Thus we should always follow the example of Mr. Fangio. He was a safe driver – because he knew how to stop, even though he had mediocre brakes. Since he wasn't killed, then by definition, he was a safe driver. AND, he was always a safe driver and he obeyed the speed limits – sure – because there were not any speed limits in that part of Italy.

So, just be sure that when somebody starts telling you stories, you are not fooled into believing the wrong parts of the story. If you start driving at 120, and you are not a world-class driver, the tiniest error can cause you to DIE.

Come to think of it, even if you are reasonably smart, you can drive at 55 mph – or 45 mph – and you can STILL get into a serious accident where you can DIE. The main idea of this book is to minimize your chances of getting into that serious accident. And preferably, we want you to get into, no accident at all. Not an accident caused by speed, or by anything else.

Conspiracies...

Also – speed can COMPOUND an accident – almost any accident. Speed can *conspire* to CAUSE an accident, or make a bad accident worse.

If you are driving *a little* too fast, and you have to make an emergency stop because there is a boulder in the road, or a muffler, or a dead animal – and you just *barely* bump into a guard-rail, or a car, because you were going *just a little* too fast – then this is a reason for not going too fast.

On the other hand, driving slow can be boring.

What Is Too Fast?

Let's say YOU and I are driving through a town, and we are coming around a curve into an intersection where it's hard to see what is happening. YOU are being very careful and driving at 30 mph. I am being pushy and doing over 45, and I am passing your car, but as we come into this intersection, I put on my brakes and slow down to 37 mph.

Suddenly a trolley-car jumps out in front of us. You and I each see it at the same time, and we are at the same distance from the trolley, and we both get on the brakes as quickly as possible.

But, YOU stop as hard as you can, and bump into the side of the trolley. The trolley crunches the front end of your car. I stop with the same braking effort, and stop just a couple feet short of the trolley.** No damage. How can that be? Very simple: when you see the danger, and you have to move your foot from the gas to the brake pedal, to step on the brakes, there's a 0.6-second delay – your response time in getting onto the brakes.

I was driving a little too fast, SO I already had my foot on the brakes. When I saw the danger, I was able to hit the brakes hard and stop shorter than YOU could – because my foot was already ON THE BRAKES. About 3 feet shorter. That could be the difference between an accident, and no accident. I am NOT saying that driving faster is better or safer. I am saying that driving fast and safely can be safer, if it keeps you alert. Driving slowly can bore you into inattention. That's pretty dangerous, in my book.

So, if you are driving a little faster than other people, but you come into an intersection or other potentially dangerous place, with your foot already on the brakes, that may be a better way to keep out of accidents. It is certainly a lot better than assuming that following all laws and speed limits mean you do not have to THINK, or PAY ATTENTION, when you are driving. That is NOT the same as driving safely.

"Never Speed" as a Policy?

Now, maybe your parents think that you should not talk about what happens if you exceed the speed limit. They do not even want to think about this, because I will just INSTRUCT you to never speed.

Well, if you just tell me that your parents are persons who NEVER exceed the speed limit, I'll have a chuckle. Because I do not know anybody who does not exceed the speed limit, occasionally. And if there is anybody who does not exceed the speed limit, they probably drive MUCH too slow. And that is not a good idea, either.

I consider the speed limit as an advisory statement. If I am in a good mood, and I think I can handle the road conditions, and there is nothing wrong with my car,

---

** *The computation for the actual distance s to decelerate is*
   $$v^2 = 2\,a\,s.$$
Let's assume we can each achieve a deceleration rate A = 0.7 G or 22.5 ft/second². If MY velocity is 37 mph, I'll need 65.4 feet to stop. If YOUR velocity is 30 mph, you can stop in 43 feet. But in the case where there is a 0.6-second delay, YOU travelled 0.6 x 44 feet per second, or 26.4 feet, BEFORE YOU EVEN GOT YOUR BRAKES ON. I was going faster, but because I had my brakes on right away, I was able to stop shorter.

nor its tires nor its brakes, then I am likely to go as fast as about 80 or 90% of the other drivers. But there are cases where I am likely to go slower than that. It depends on what is safe for conditions.

But the notion that the speed limits were set by people who knew anything about anything, is pretty weird. And the concept that we are sinners all going to go to hell if we exceed a posted speed limit, or get a speeding ticket, is just too silly. However, we DO want to be careful not to go too fast and get into accidents. THAT is a serious matter.

One case where it is unsafe to speed, is where you may have trouble stopping for ordinary road conditions. In case of rain or snow, maybe the effective speed limit for *you* should be *slower* than the POSTED speed limit, which is normally intended for dry conditions. And, as I said in the Chapter on Vision, if you cannot see what is coming up, you had better slow down. For example, if there are black cows lying on the road, you had better slow down below 55, at night. However, if there are only *white* cows that may wander out on the road, 65 may be safe. *You* think about it.

If you are on a strange road and you come to a curve, it might be dangerous to come into such a corner at a high speed, because any problem – a little sand on the road, or a patch of ice, or a dog crossing the road, or a bicycle – could cause you to have a near accident, or a real accident. If you slow down coming into the corner to a more reasonable speed, you have a good chance of not having an accident. If you have already slowed down *some*, you will be able to slow down some more, in case some of those problems arise.

"But I Was Not Expecting Him To Be Going That Fast…"

The other reason not to speed, is where the Laws of Human Nature apply. If you are trying to ease through a town at 57 mph, and the speed limit is only 40, you may find that somebody pulled out in front of you. He saw you coming, but he assumed you were going about 40. And because you *were* going 57, you may find it hard to slow down for him. I just hope you don't hit him. I mean, a lot of older people are not experts at judging speeds. He made a reasonable assumption that you were 80 yards away, at 40 mph, and he could get across the street before you got that far. I hope he was right about that.

Similarly, another *class* of people who are not very good at judging speeds, are *kids*. That little boy might never have *seen* a car at 57 mph coming down his little street. He probably thought he could run across the road before you could get there. I sure hope he was right. I sure hope you did not choose that second, to peek down at the radio and try to tune in a new station.

Vandalized? – no – Mandallized

If your car has been vandalized by unpleasant people, that's unfortunate. But if it is Mandallized, that is serious. One of our friends, whose name we shall call Mandall, had an interesting problem. He was travelling on the Maine Turnpike, a good 4-lane highway, at only about 125 mph in his fast Porsche 911. Some foolish person decided to make an illegal U-turn across the median, on one of the dirt crossover

roads that are intended for only the police to use. He looked in his mirror and saw
Mr. Mandall coming, quite a ways off, and thought he had time to make his illegal
turn from the right lane into the crossover. Bad move. Both cars were totally
destroyed – in fact, by definition, you can say they were Mandallized. And both
drivers were badly injured. Unfortunately they both survived.

The basic problem is, if you are going a LOT faster than the speed limit, and
other drivers are simply expecting a driver at normal speed, they may easily pull out
in front of you. And when YOU compound the problem by driving QUITE fast, you
may not be able to stop. Or if you can stop, maybe there is a guy behind you, and *he*
can't stop.

James Dean and his Porsche...

I just read recently in the newspapers that some Failure Analysis Experts had
analyzed the accident where actor James Dean died in 1955. This accident has been
very widely publicized and very thoroughly studied. Most studies show that Mr. Dean
had left Los Angeles in his Porsche Speedster at a specific time, and he must have
been *averaging* well above 80 mph over some tough twisty roads, to reach the
accident scene when he did. Mr. Dean was a competent driver on a race-track, and
he could keep the car on the road at high speeds. The top speed for that Porsche
was over 125 mph. Police estimates were that Dean's car was doing 70 mph at the
instant of the crash.

Yet the Failure Analysis Experts said that after a COMPLETE analysis, they could
show that Dean was only going 55 mph when he hit the car that pulled out in front
of him. Thus, they said, Mr. Dean was not speeding. Yeah, sure. I do not have the
facts on this, but I am sure Dean's Porsche was braking hard for well over a hundred
feet (even though it might not have left skid marks), as he tried to slow down from
110 mph to 55. Maybe he did get down to 55 mph, but when the Ford sedan pulled
out in front of him, he was still braking — apparently did not have a place to dodge.
The driver of that Ford sedan, Mr. Donald Turnupseed, who survived the crash, (but
who died recently in 1995) said he did not see Dean's car.

◆ ◆ ◆

If YOU were in a situation like James Dean was – what could YOU have done?

– First of all – if you are travelling at a good speed along a highway – and there is
somebody out in front of you on a side road, who MIGHT be thinking about pulling
out in front of you – turn on your high beams, and *blink* them. FLASH your
headlights ON and OFF. This can help a person SEE you. Not only will he SEE you,
but when you flash your high beams a couple times, he can see that you are
INSISTENT on wanting to come through. You don't have to be doing 120, or even 55
– even at 40 mph you can properly request your right-of-way. That does NOT mean
you should count on GETTING your right-of-way – but it is fair to ask. It will
improve your odds.

– Secondly, whether you are going 55 or 65 or 125, coming into a difficult
intersection, it MIGHT be a good idea to SLOW DOWN. There is no ABSOLUTE

RIGHT to go at any particular speed. YOU do not have a RIGHT to go 65 or 55 on an interstate highway or freeway, if it is not safe to do that. James Dean did not have a RIGHT to go 125. Even if he had been in Nevada, where there were no speed limits in effect at the time, he would not have had a RIGHT to go as fast as he wanted, if his speed were conflicting with the safety of himself or others.

– Lastly, if you are headed into an intersection where some foolish person is pulling out in front of you, and you are heading for a crash – it is NOT always the best strategy to *just* stand on the brakes. It did not work for James Dean, and it often works just as badly for other people.

NOW, if a Goddamn' FREIGHT TRAIN pulls out in front of you, and there is NO WAY to dodge around it, then you HAVE TO hit your brakes as hard as you can, and if you judged it right, you stop in time. If not, that's your basic problem.

But if you are headed for a collision with a mere CAR, it is USUALLY a better idea to try to veer around the car. Dodge it. Evade it. Now, you have to guess whether the car will keep going, and continue to cross in front of you, and perhaps get out of your way – or whether it will stop in front of you. In either case, you have a good chance to evade it by steering *behind* it. (Sometimes a car pulls out in front of you and just STOPS, and it's hard to guess that he will do that.) Barring that, you are better to dodge and bounce across the shoulder or the bushes or the ditch, than to just HIT that car. As I said in the Chapter on Reflex Responses: if you plan IN ADVANCE, what you will do in some of these cases – such as a car pulling out in front of you – you have a much better chance to survive.

And this is just about as true for a guy speeding at 40 mph in a 45 mph zone, as it is for a guy doing 125 on the open road. However, when you are gambling at 125 mph, that is a gamble with a poor ratio of risk to reward....

The CONSPIRACY Theory

It is my opinion that any one factor is not likely to cause an accident. It is a *conspiracy* of factors, or events, that causes accidents. Speed, by itself, does not usually kill, nor does it usually cause accidents. But speeding can *conspire* with other factors to cause accidents. If visibility is lousy, that, combined with speed, can easily cause an accident. If traction is poor – ice, snow, or mud – that can help cause an accident. If there is inattention, or sleepiness, or sloppiness, or bad brakes, or poor tires, or booze, or rudeness – or ANY factor – that can combine with speeding, or with any other factor, to make an accident. Don't you agree? It is very rare that a single factor causes an accident. It is almost always a combination of two or more factors. Don't you agree?

And if an accident *is* going to happen, speeding does tend to make the accident worse. Don't you agree?

Accidents Will Happen – ???

NOW, ideally, we would have very few accidents. But in fact, because of human imperfection and sloppiness, we have a lot more accidents than we should. And

8/30/22

most of these are preventable. And my primary objective, in this book, is to help you guys avoid all those accidents that we possibly can.

I mean, if a guy is driving along in a very good quality car (not just a junk car), and the steering gear breaks, and the car goes off the road and crashes, I will be regretful. BUT, if I cannot prevent that kind of accident, I will not worry about that. I mostly want to prevent the preventable accidents. Fair enough? Will you join me?

Familiarity Breeds Contempt?

The other point I want to make is that any driver can do something wrong and get away with it. You can speed down a quiet road 99 times, with no problems. But maybe the 100th time, a dog or a deer might run across the road, and you might go out of control trying to dodge the animal. If you were not speeding too fast, you would not have gone out of control.

Or I might go down an exit ramp rather fast, 87 times, and the 88th time one of my tires was going flat (OR, there was a little oil on the pavement), and I spin out and bang the guard-rail. (NOW, that has not yet happened to me, but it could.)

My warning is, if you do stretch the rules, you may be able to avoid accidents MANY times – up until the point when the accident happens. The key point is to realize that, just because you have bent or broken a rule or law, many times, and apparently you got away with it, does not mean you can keep on bending that rule. You have to be careful not to press your luck.

"Let's Stop And Eat A Peach..."

Once upon a time, one of my teachers told me about the time he was working at a summer camp, many years ago, up in New York's Catskill Mountains. He had to go in to New York City to do some business. After he was done, he bought a couple bushels of peaches for the campers, and then he headed north out of town. As he went up Broadway, he saw a couple cars moving right along, so he followed them. As they got a little further north, they were really clipping along at a good speed, on old Route 9. (This was *long* before the days of Throughways.) When they finally got out on the open road, these cars stepped it up to 75 and 80. He stayed right with them. They really seemed to know where they were going! He was really making good time!

After about an hour, he decided that this high-speed driving was really very hard work and he was not used to it. He decided to stop and take a break, and eat a peach. So he took his foot off the gas, and slowed down, and stopped, and ate a peach. Then he started out again. About a mile up the road, there were the two fast cars, surrounded by 7 police cars and dozens of cops. He was too nervous to even wave; he just kept on rolling at 40 mph. Ahem.... If only *we* knew when not to press *our* luck....

Avoid Speeding

So I gotta give you this advice: at all times, avoid speeding. Avoid exceeding the speed limit. That's the only really safe thing. Get your speedometer calibrated, and avoid speeding past the posted speed limit. It's the only safe thing you can do, and it's the only safe thing I can tell you to do.

Reality

But we all know that if you have a car in good shape, and you are alert, and the road is not bad, and you want to drive fairly fast, then you will use your judgement, and do what you are going to do. I mean, I know you are going to do that anyhow. I do not know any driver who does not rely on his judgement to go faster than the posted speed limit. But, you really should also use good judgement in knowing when to take your foot off the gas *early*, or put on the brakes *early*, and slow down. That I also recommend.

If your traction is dubious, or if you know your brakes are poor, or if you cannot properly see where you are going, or if any other factor is gonna make it dangerous, then I definitely recommend that you go slower. That safe speed may be above the speed limit — or it may be below the posted speed limit. It may be faster than a lot of other people want to go – or it may be *slower* than a lot of other people want to go. But you have to learn to use your judgement, and you have to figure out how to drive safely. OK? Now, I will not waste a lot of breath telling you, "Never go faster than the Speed Limit set by bureaucrats, BECAUSE Speed Kills." That would be a waste of breath.

But I will tell you, at any time, *whether or not* you exceed the speed limit set by bureaucrats, you may STILL be breaking the Laws of Physics or the Laws of Human Nature, and you may get in trouble. So, don't be too damn' pushy, OK? And refer to the Chapter on Tickets. And the Chapter on Accidents.   ⋏

Inexperience

By definition, every new driver is inexperienced. Now, some drivers learn faster than others. Some have learned by watching other people drive. Some find it hard to judge speeds and curves, hard to pick a good safe speed. So it is fair to say that most young drivers are less good at picking a safe speed than they will be, in a few years. Therefore, new or young or inexperienced drivers should be a little less pushy about speeding. Just because you see a car going fast, does NOT mean you can do that. That might be a very sharp driver, or he might have some VERY good tires. Or, he might be drunk and headed for a BIG CRASH. In all these cases, you will probably be wise not to try to keep up with that car. You have to learn what is a good speed for YOU.

Speed on Ramps...

One time a friend of mine was cruising up Route 2 in Lexington Mass in his new Corvair, headed for a ramp onto Route 128. He was starting to slow down from 68 mph to 48 for the ramp, when a Ferrari came *booming* up the road at about 85, and passed him, and slowed down to 68, to go down the same ramp. My friend decided, what the hell, he had good tires, and he would follow that Ferrari through the ramp. The Ferrari went into the ramp at 68 and just kept hammering his way through the curve at about 68. My friend tried to follow, and had to slow down to about 56. He just could not push his car any faster. So he slowed down to what the car would do, and as he came out of the curve at about 60, he saw the Ferrari off in the distance, accelerating from 68 mph up past 85 again. So, just because you see somebody else going fast, does not necessarily mean *you* can do it. He might even be the judge's nephew....

New Speed Limits

IN December of 1995, just as I was trying to finish this book – the rules changed. The Federal 55 and 65 mph speed limits were retracted. So most states are upping their maximum speeds to 65 or 70 mph or maybe even more. Well, if they did that just AFTER I got this book out, I'd be really grouchy. But, as it happened, that just means a minor re-write, a few minutes more at my word-processor. Here we are:

ISN'T IT AMAZING that just "yesterday" a guy got a ticket for driving at 66 mph in a 55 mph zone – and now it's "Okay". H'mm. All I can say is, the laws written by humans are arbitrary. Sometimes they make sense. Sometimes they don't. I will not comment on the absolute wisdom of this.

But the Laws of Human Nature and the Laws of Physics haven't changed a doggone bit.

If your car cannot do 70 mph without breaking down, then you should drive a little slower. If your tires are crummy or dubious – or your brakes – you do not HAVE TO drive at 65 or 70. Go a little slower.

Ancient History...

In 1938, when the Pennsylvania Turnpike first opened with its speed limit of 70 mph, all sorts of cars broke down because they were not designed to run reliably at 70 mph. So some drivers learned that they could not go at 70 – especially on those long upgrades. Not on a hot day.... Hey, most cars in 1938 did NOT have very good radiators, NOT very good brakes, NOT very good tires. Your car may be a lot better than those old cars, but there may *still* be reasons for you to not go so fast.

Conflicts...

And, especially, watch out for the contrast between fast cars and slower traffic. If there is a heavy truck that can only hold 50 mph on an upgrade, it does not make any difference to him if the cars can go 55 or 65 or 70. But if YOU are behind him, and you want to pass him, YOU have to be very careful not to pull out in front of a car doing 70. The speed DIFFERENCES between the slowest cars and the fastest ones may be bigger than previously, and there is a lot of potential for danger in that difference. So you have to be *very* careful on these high-speed roads with slower traffic. Check your mirrors. If you want to pass, get out and do it early. Don't wait until the last second to pull out. Remember, the speed DIFFERENCE between the

6/30/22

faster and slower vehicles is the source of danger, not the maximum speed. You want to be really *alert*, to avoid problems.

Specifically, some of the "safety experts" say that 5,000 or 9,000 more traffic deaths will occur in 1997 due to the raised speed limits. I want to make them liars. I want us all to drive on our best behavior, and be alert, and NOT have accidents. Can this book make a difference? I hope to get it published early in 1997. Before too long, it can make a difference.

AND, if you have recently been getting away with driving at 64 on a 55 mph road, do NOT think you can get away with driving at 74 on a 65 mph road. The police will not be giving such a big margin of error. They will not be so generous or charitable.

"Last Instant" Problems

I have one last comment about speeding. I was reading in a magazine[1] about some young drivers who got into bad accidents. One young guy went out on a four-lane road and *perhaps* he was going a little faster than the speed limit. When he came to an intersection, the light changed red. He avoided one car in the intersection, but crashed into a second car, and was killed. The story *said* that the police concluded, "the light changed red at the last instant".

H'mm. Do traffic lights change red, really, "at the last instant"??? No, they really do not. The cops should not have said that. On a 45 mph road, most yellow lights are at least 3 seconds long, which gives you plenty of time and distance to stop, after you first see the light turn yellow. Ah, but what if you are not travelling at the speed limit? What if you are much, MUCH above the speed limit?

If you were rolling at not *just* 60, but 70 or 80 mph, coming into that intersection, you might say, *if* you survived, "The light changed at the last instant...." – but that is a bad rationalization. *Bad* move.

And if you are coming up to a light, AT WHATEVER SPEED, and the light turns yellow, you HAVE TO be prepared to stop. If you are a long ways back, travelling at high speed, and a light turns yellow, and you think, "AW, I can make it through before it goes red" – that may be a *very* bad idea. Meanwhile the light goes red and cars start easing out into the intersection. And you are still saying, "I did not have enough time to stop, so I hit the gas and kept on going". *Bad move.*

Judgement...

It does require good judgement to know, when you ought to hit the brakes and stop, and when it is safe to keep on going. For a learning driver, it is hard to get really good at this judgement, so it is a VERY good idea for a beginning driver to not exceed the speed limits, coming into critical locations like intersections. Okay? Because speeding makes it harder to make the right choice, even as it makes it harder to stop.

REALLY *SPEEDING*

If you are going to exceed the speed limit, for Pete's sake, don't exceed the hell out of it. If you want to go 100 mph, go out to the wide open roads of Montana, where there is now no legal speed limit in the daytime – just a "Reasonable and Proper" rule. But if you are on such a fast road – just like on a German Autobahn – that is a very dangerous place, and you have to be really alert. I'm not sure if I would be comfortable on those roads, if my car will only do 72 or 82 mph, comfortably.

If you think you want to speed at 65 mph through a small town at midnight, or at 110 mph along a seemingly-deserted Interstate, or at 85 along a back road – and you think your odds are fairly good – just think how much you will enjoy your joy-ride if a deer pops up in front of your headlights. Or a cop.... Note, on some occasions, you can talk a cop out of some arguments. But you can't talk a deer out of *anything*. So, I recommend taking it easy, and *not* over-doing it. Not speeding EXCESSIVELY.

Other High-Speed Driving: High-Speed Etiquette

– Even on US roads, watch out for an occasional guy rolling up the fast lane at 85 or 90. I mean, if a guy has a full-blooded Ferrari or Maserati, sometimes the cylinders get all *carboned up*, and he'll argue that he sorta *has to* clean out the carbon by revving it up for a little distance. If you see this guy coming up in your mirror, pull over and let him by. He has his problems, and you have yours. Let him go. Don't try to slow him down. Besides, if a cop is talking to *him*, he won't be looking at *you*.

Besides, how many of you have your speedometer calibrated? If I went down the road thinking I am doing 60 in the fast lane, and I am ACTUALLY doing 53, I would make a number of people unhappy! I have a GPS receiver and have calibrated my speedometer pretty accurately. I marked the speedometer at 60, so on a 55 mph road, I try to not exceed that, and on a 65-mph road, not much more than that. But there actually *is* a 7 mph error in my speedometer, so the real speed *is* 53, at 60 mph indicated, and 60 mph at 67 indicated. Do *you* know the calibration of *your* speedometer?

> If you drive on a road with mile-markers beside the highway, you can calibrate your own speedometer. Drive at a constant speed, such as 60. If you go 1 mph over 60 for a few seconds, try to drive 1 mph below it for a few seconds, too, so you get a fair average. Get your passenger to note the time it takes to travel just one measured mile, per the roadside markers. If it is about 62 seconds, then you are going about 58. If the time is about 65 seconds, you are doing 55 mph. Don't take just one reading, take an average of several miles, so long as you can keep a constant speed. It's a little harder at 40 mph, because most 40-mph roads do not have mile markers. My GPS receiver can indicate accurately any speed from 4 to 1485 mph.
>
> If you do not have a passenger, you can do this calibration yourself if you are a good driver, and VERY careful, and if there is minimum traffic on the road. It's good to know what your speedometer error is. Like, on a rental car....

Etiquette on English Motorways

– Now in England, an awful lot of cars drive at 75 or 85 mph or more, on the motorways. Even a lot of the trucks do 70. If you are driving over there, you can roll at any one of those speeds, if it feels right to you. Most cars that you rent are extremely competent at 80, although they may not have a lot of acceleration. Just be polite, and don't go out to pass a 70-mph slowpoke, unless you can do it and pull back in before that 95-mph Mercedes (with his high beams on) gets on your tail. It's not polite to slow him down. Even if the maximum speed limit on the motorway is just 70, it is not enforced. You won't get hassled by the police at 80 or 85, unless you are also doing something stupid.

After you have learned how to keep your little RH-drive rental car on the left side of the road, it is not hard to remember to keep over on the left-hand lane (slow lane) unless you are passing. And apply for a faster lane if you are going to need it, and be sure that when you are through passing, you pull back left. It's a constant debate: how should I pass a truck who is doing 70 but is starting to slow down on this upgrade? Can I get past him before that Rolls-Royce catches up with me? Or should I wait? Hey, it's worth a sporting try! I enjoy that challenge.

Etiquette On Autobahns

– When you get to Germany, the same basic rules apply. There are still a lot of the 4-lane Autobahns that were built in the 1930s, and there are a lot of really fast Porsches, BMWs, and Alfas cruising in the range of 160 to 200 km per hour (100 to 125 mph) or more. Why don't they enforce the speed-limits? Don't be silly, there are not any speed limits on the Autobahns, at least for most of the last 50 years. The fast German drivers are used to driving safely at these speeds. Just don't get in front of one and make him slow down – that's VERY *gauche*. Actually, I find most rental cars are very competent for cruising at 80 mph (130 kph) and you rarely have to go out to pass anybody, because almost everybody is rolling at 75 to 80 or more.

Etiquette on Autostradae

– I have driven a little in Italy, but never on an Autostrada. I understand it is like the German highways, with no limits, and a good number of cars rolling up around 120 mph. (Over there, that is 190 kph.) And even *these* guys have to watch out, because when the really fast cars come through at 150 mph and up, they have to stay out of the way, too.

General Cautions...

– I am recommending that you *not* over-do it, on these high-speed roads. If you go *almost* as fast as 'most everybody else, you will probably get along just fine, in any foreign country. I am just observing that some people roll *really* fast, and if you told them, "Speed Kills", they would not waste their breath laughing at you. They would just look at you scornfully. And demand that you get out of their way.... Don't try to keep up with *them*.

So Don't Be Pushy...

A good general rule, overseas, is, you still do not want to be the fastest car on the road, because it is easy for the Highway Patrolman (or the local cop, whoever he may be) to enhance the local revenue by ticketing YOU. In fact, you usually do not want to even be the second or third-fastest guy, because if the other fastest guys disappear over the horizon, *you* are the guy that the cop wants to talk to. On the other hand, if almost everybody else is doing 65, it is a little silly to insist on doing 54.

If I am doing 64, and there are always people passing me at 65 or 70, I consider that a safe speed. Going so slow that traffic has to SPILL around me, is NOT a safe speed, even if you are doing 56. If everybody is travelling about the same speed, that is probably the best, safest speed.

And Be Prepared to SLOW DOWN...

And if you are going to drive fast, no matter where you are going fast, be prepared to slow down. If you insist on getting up to 70 on an isolated, lonely stretch of 45 mph road, be sure to slow down to 49 before you come back into town, or up to that traffic light or intersection. And don't be too surprised if there is a speed trap at the end of the isolated stretch, to help slow you down....

Lots of luck!! And if you get yourself killed by going too fast, I'll never speak to you again.

6/30/22

---

1. *READER'S DIGEST, They Never Came Home, by Per Ola and Emily DAuaire, December 1995, pp. 86-93.*

Chapter 50. TRAFFIC TICKETS

Parking Tickets...

Of course, people get a lot of tickets for illegal parking, but I am not going to talk about that. Illegal parking does not usually have anything to do with having accidents, even though some people who disregard parking regulations also break other traffic laws.... I am going to comment mostly on tickets for speeding, illegal turns, and other "moving violations".

Speeding Tickets...

I'm not sure about your area, but in California, for a long time, the speeding ticket was some kind of an occupational hazard. The speed limits were pulled down artificially low, causing a great amount of hypocrisy. Thus, here is my list of things you can do –

How to Get a Speeding Ticket:

1. Drive more than 4 mph over the speed limit (9 mph in many places.)

2. Drive 4 mph over the speed limit AND do something else squirrelly such as –

    a. change lanes real sharply or quickly.

    b. when passing, cut closely in front of the guy you are passing.

    c. neglect to signal when changing lanes.

    d. be sloppy and don't stay well-centered in your lane.

3. Neglect to slow down when coming into a small town. A number of small Southern towns get recognized as "speed traps". Or,

4. When you come off a high-speed road, speed up well over the local speed limit. (It's easy to neglect to notice that, even though you are going a lot slower than 55, you may still be doing a lot over 35 mph.)

5. Drive faster than anybody else on the road – even if you are under the speed limit.

6. Drive 5 or 7 mph slower than the fast guys, BUT, have an out-of-state license plate. Just because you are not the fastest guy, does not mean you are really safe from a ticket....

7. If everybody else is going 10 mph over the limit – and you are going only 4 or 5, you are not likely to get tagged – UNLESS all the 10-mph guys have gone over the hill, out of sight.

8. Drive at the front of a pack of fast drivers. The radar will spot you first, and the patrolman is obligated to pull you over, even though the guy who wanted to pass you may get off scot-free. OR,

9. Drive at the back of a pack of fast cars. The patrolman who pulls up behind this pack will be obligated to pull you over – even though the cars in front of you are pulling away.

10. Drive a car with out-of-state license plates and exceed the speed limit by more than 2 mph – especially in the southeastern USA.

11. Drive a car of a model that the cop JUST HAPPENS to be in a Grouchy Mood about. This might be *my* VW – or *your* Corvette.

12. Drive a red car. Or a bright yellow Camaro. Or a fluorescent green car.

13. Drive a car for which you have to make a vague guess as to the accuracy of the speedometer. This is especially easy if you drive a car with over-sized wheels, so the speedometer reads low. If you have to drive such a car, be sure to get your speedometer calibrated. One time, many years ago, I was ticketed for "speeding" while driving a rented Mustang GT-350H, which had over-sized wheels. It would have been kind of inconvenient for me to show up in California (while I lived in Boston) to contest this.

14. Drive a car with a license plate such as "2-2-FAST", or,

15. A car with a license-plate frame, "Faster than a Speeding Ticket". I have seen a couple of such cars driving along *very carefully* at 54 mph, presumably because they have been ticketed so many times.

16. Drive in the vicinity of a cop who is behind his quota, or in a town where the budget is behind schedule. If you are an outsider, you might not know this. But if you happened to read in the local paper that the next town over has a budget shortage, you would not be surprised if you see a lot of "law enforcement" activity.

17. Drive at, or near, the posted limit, when it is very rainy or snowy.

18. And here's a comment about the new *higher* speed limits: If you have recently been getting away with driving at 64 on a 55 mph road, do NOT think you can get away with driving at 74 on a 65 mph road. The police will not be giving such a big margin of error. They will not be so generous or charitable. The 65 mph speed limits will be enforced a *lot closer* than 55 was. If your speedometer is well calibrated, keep your speed down to 68 on a 65 mph road, and watch the guys who fly past you get pulled over.

  – Note, many of these things have very little to do with driving safely, or getting into an accident. Whereas, peering into your rear-view mirror, watching for a cop, may distract you from what is going on in front of you. It can help you avoid a ticket – but may help get you into an accident...

Fifty-Four?

One time I nearly got ticketed for doing 55 mph on a 55 mph freeway. I was driving south at about 64 on Route I-280, with light traffic and light rain. And I spied a

Highway Patrol car, 'way out ahead, doing 54. I eased my speed down to 55 and kept on rolling, steady at 55 – a true, calibrated 55. As I passed the cop, I heard a loud *SQUAWK*. I was so surprised, I took my foot off the gas – but I did not realize there was a problem. I started to speed up to resume 55 – and I heard another *SQUAWK*. This time, I realized, it was coming from the police car, and the cop was trying to tell me with his loudspeaker, not to go so fast. I eased back to 53.5 mph, and kept on going. A couple miles later, the Cruiser pulled off, and he stayed off. Then I went back to 64, with no problems. Now, 55 mph might be a scary speed if the rain is coming down in sheets, and there is heavy traffic, and you can't see where you are going because your wipers won't do a good job, and there's a stream of water an inch deep under your tires, so you are really floating on the water. BUT, barring those problems, on a good road, with light traffic, 56 ain't very unsafe. Neither is 64. After all, there are a lot of people who can still remember when the speed limit on I-280 used to be 70 mph. If there is not a lot of slow traffic, the guys who do 70 out there are not causing any particular danger.

In other words, you can never be sure *exactly* what you have to do to get a ticket....

How To Get OTHER Tickets: Too Slow...

You can get a ticket for going too slowly. Because, it is not the speed of the fastest drivers on the road, that causes danger, but the speed DIFFERENCE between the fast majority and a slow minority (or *vice versa*).

Namely, if most of the drivers are doing 64 mph on a 55mph road, and one guy is poking along at 41, the wise policeman will not stop the guys at 64, but will stop the guy doing 41 and ask him why he's going so slow. He will try to get that slow driver out of there – put him on the old road, or demand that he get his engine fixed, if it will not go any faster, or lock him up if he is drunk. But the guy doing 41 is the real danger to safe driving, because other people are not expecting to have to pass such a slow driver. (If you ever have to drive at 41 mph on a high-speed road, turn on your 4-way flasher signals, so people will be cautioned that they will have to pass you).

Slowdowns on Upgrades...

If you drive a slow car, as I sometimes do, you should know that there are some high-speed highways where you cannot keep up speed. My '68 Beetle is MUCH too fast for most flat-land driving situations, but when I drive up in the mountains – such as US 50, or I-80 over the Sierras, I get bogged down below 45 mph in some places. If I do, I put my 4-way blinkers on. Of course, if I can barely hold 40, then some trucks are even slower, so I have to plan my attack for passing slow trucks, while staying out of the way for fast cars to pass me, with minimum obstruction. I recall that up on I-70 near Dillon, Colorado, there are some long upgrades where I cannot even stay in third gear; I have to shift down into second, and struggle up the hill at 25 mph, nearly full throttle – with my warning blinkers blinking. I love Colorado, but at high altitude, most car engines really lose a lot of power. So, slow speed is really a danger, on a high-speed road. If you have to drive slow, you should take precautions.

Momma Bear, Baby Bear, Papa Bear....

– Just as with the 3 Bears, where one bowl of porridge was too hot, and the second was too cold – and a third was "just right" – you can get a ticket for driving at exactly the "just right" speed.

Ron was driving along on his way to work, very carefully – because he had forgotten to bring his wallet and driver's license. The cop pulled him over – "because he was driving too carefully". When he found out that Ron had forgotten his license, he gave Ron a little citation. He also gave Ron an education.

Now, it is often a good idea to drive carefully. But if cops are looking for people driving "too carefully", because these people often *do* have a guilty conscience – then you have to think about it. If you had your driver's license, and everybody else is doing 59, and a cop goes by – if you REALLY want to have a nice chat with that policeman, all you have to do is tag your brakes to slow down from 58 to 54, and the cop will be curious why you are so nervous. He may just decide to have a chat with you.

– If you are minding your business, and not going faster than anybody else, and less than 8 mph over the speed limit, and not breaking any other laws, then you must realize: you will appear less suspicious if you keep on rolling at 62. And if the cop pulls you over anyhow, well, you can still be polite.

Miscellaneous...

One of the most common things you can get a "ticket" for is having a light burned out. At least twice a year, we read of a cop who tries to stop a guy to tell him one of his lights is not working – and the guy goes ballistic, and leads the cop on a high-speed chase and crashes. The guy had a guilty conscience – and the cop was only going to tell him he had to replace a burned-out bulb. So, if you are not in a mood to spend a few pleasant moments discussing light-bulbs with a patrolman, check the bulbs and replace any burned-out bulbs.

If you aren't speeding, or going too slow, and you don't have any lights burned out, and you keep in your lane, it's fairly hard to get a ticket. Yes, you might foolishly make a U-turn in an illegal place, or make an improper turn, but in general, that covers over 95% of all traffic tickets.

Pink Lights

After a traffic light goes yellow, it does not instantly go red. It stays yellow for a while. Then it starts turning pink. It turns PINKER and PINKER. After a while, it turns red. So if you want to avoid driving through a red light, be careful to not let it get too pink, as you are entering the intersection. But you can get a ticket for going through the intersection if the light is even a little pink as you enter.

Chapter 51. POLICE – or, Highway Patrol Officer

If I had to think of all the tough jobs in the world, I think being a policeman, or a highway patrolman, or a COP, would be the toughest. Everybody would hate me and fear me. Everybody would be expecting me to persecute them. Nobody would appreciate that I, as a policeman, am trying to protect THEM from doing things that are not just illegal, but downright stupid and dangerous to their safety and their *lives*.

The policeman has to contend, not only with the citizen who is nervous and has a burned-out tail-light, but the bank-robber who is nervous as hell and has 3 guns under his seat, and also has a burned-out tail light. He has to be polite with the first citizen, and he has to be very careful that the second guy does not kill him. Then, in case any one of us should get into an accident, the cop has to brave the dangers of fire or wreck, and try to pull us out of the wreckage, and give us first-aid or artificial respiration, and try to save our lives despite our stupidity. You know anybody who wants a nice easy job like that?

THUS – we, as honest citizens, should try to be as easy-going as possible when we are stopped by a policeman, and not make any "fast moves", even though we may inwardly be rather nervous.

A Pull-Over

Let's say you are driving along, minding your own business, and you see a red light blinking behind you. *WHO, ME?????* Sometimes, it is just a policeman or fire-truck or ambulance who wants to pass you on very important business, to go elsewhere. If that turns out to be true, what a relief!! Turn on your right-hand blinkers, pull over as much as you can to the right, slow down, stop, and let the guy by. If he goes by, fair enough.

But suppose he wants YOU. Then you have already turned on your right-hand blinkers, and eased on the brakes. Now, try to find the first safe place to stop. Then I usually put on the 4-way blinkers, get out of the car, and hold up my right hand as a sign of peace, and walk slowly back to the policeman. Presuming there is significant traffic, I try to walk over to the curb-side of the cars, so as to not be near traffic. I tried that back in Massachusetts one time, when my headlights were going bad, and the cop ordered me to go back and sit in my car. I'm not sure why that is their policy, but apparently sometimes they like you to sit in your car.

Wonder Why...

Usually the cop will ask you whether you know what you were doing wrong. Or, you can ask him, what is the problem. Try to keep a cool head. Don't panic, and don't get mad. Eventually, he will explain.

344

Then, of course, the policeman will want to see your Driver's License, and Registration, so they can check your papers. In California, they also want to see the card that proves that you have insurance. I keep a lot of junk in my Glove Compartment, but I always try to keep those documents easy to find.

It would not do any harm, to mention to the policeman, "Hey, my Registration is in my Glove Compartment – let me go in there and find it – OK?" Then he will not think you are diving for a gun...

How to Talk to a Cop...

I have heard many stories from many people that think they know how to talk to a cop. They think they know how to talk their way out of a ticket. Well, they did it *once*. Well, that's what they *say*. But I have never heard of any particular way that is supposed to be effective, to talk yourself out of a ticket. I think it is always a good policy to be polite. It may do no harm to be apologetic or repentant. "Gee, I'm sorry, I guess I was going a little faster than I should have." Or you might observe, "Can you help me calibrate my speedometer, when we leave here, because I really don't think I was going as fast as you said. Maybe my speedometer is reading wrong." One guy thought this last statement was just too dumb and obsequious. But, hey, if you are not sure your speedometer is reading correct, you might want to get the cop's opinion of what 55 mph is. I don't think that's too dumb a thing to say. But at least, try to be polite.

Protecting US from OURSELVES...

If the cop was trying to help prevent you from doing something that you realize is dangerous, you might tell him, "Thank you". For example, nobody wants to spend a lot of time talking to the cop. But if he was able to warn you that you had no brake lights, or no tail lights, he may have saved you from a serious accident. You better say *Thank you, SIR*. (Or, *Thank you, MA'AM*.)

If you can't be really sincere, then try faking it. But usually the cop has made up his mind, if he is going to give you a ticket. However, if you argue a lot, and insult him, he might easily change his mind and give you a ticket, after he had first planned not to. So, arguing and hollering may be very counter-productive. Resisting arrest is almost ALWAYS a bad idea.

And What If You Disagree?

That is not saying you have to agree with him. You may say, "But, officer, that is NOT what happened, and I do NOT agree with what you said." You don't have to agree with him, but you should still try to be polite. If you get the cop all pissed off at you, that will make him CERTAIN to show up and tell the judge why he should find you guilty. If you are polite, you have a better chance of getting fair treatment – at least in most places. Most cops try to be fair and honest. If you happen to run across one that is NOT, arguing at the scene of the pull-over or arrest, is NOT usually the right place. Maybe it is better to shut up, take notes, and see an attorney later. Arguing with a disagreeable cop is usually a losing deal.

In Case of an Accident...

If you have an accident, or if you come to an accident scene, the cop has a high priority to save people's lives, and prevent further accidents. He might ask you to help. If you can help your neighbor, as the cop instructs, that's a neighborly thing to do – even if being around a cop makes you nervous. Hey, cops are real people, too, and they are professionals. A large amount of their time is spent, trying to prevent people from hurting themselves and others. Maybe you can help.

A Reviewer?

I was able to get at least a couple highway patrolmen – not just from California – to comment on this book. They had a number of very useful comments, which I have sprinkled into the appropriate places in the book. These cops were REAL PEOPLE, who had REAL opinions on things. And, intelligent people, and people who had a lot of EXPERIENCE.

Police Problems...

Sometimes cars start into intersections when they KNOW they cannot get through. And they just block the intersection so nobody else can get through. Pretty dumb, and not very helpful. NOW, as a friend pointed out, sometimes a cop stands *right there* and says NOTHING. When pedestrians or drivers complain, the cop just shakes his head. I mean, the cop might at least walk over to these people who are blocking the intersection, and tell them to cut it out. But the cop might not want to do that.

How to fix this? Or, any other situation where it seems that you cannot get the cop to perform his duty? Well – here is one possible solution – get the cop's badge number and name, and report him to the police station, to his supervisor. Of course, it's kind of hard to make an anonymous complaint and get much results. Or if you sign your name, the policeman might be grouchy. I haven't figured out that problem yet.

On the other hand, I have heard of a good number of cases where a Neighborhood Association complained to the police that the speed limits are not being enforced in their neighborhood. When the speed trap was put into operation, the first guys they caught were – the complaining members of the Neighborhood Association. Ahem....

Chapter 52. INSURANCE

Just as we have to put up with police – even though we are not big fans of everything they do – we have to put up with insurance companies. In almost every state, you are required to carry some minimum coverage. You gotta pay. It ain't cheap.

Of course, some types of insurance are required, and other types are optional. You *have to* buy liability insurance, so if you hit a guy, you can pay for his car repairs and his medical bills. But there are many other kinds of insurance. Health insurance, insurance against other un-insured drivers, etc. Sometimes you'll want to pay for this. Sometimes it is a poor bargain. For example, I could insure my old Beetle in case I drive into a rock. But if I did, they would pay me only as much as $800 or $1000, and the insurance would cost me $300 per year. So only if I planned to drive my car into a ruinous accident every 3 years, would I break even on that insurance. In other words, I am wise to self-insure. The other place I self-insure is on my deductibles. If I had just $100 of damage to my car, every year, my insurance company would be GLAD to sell me insurance with no deductible. But if I am paying $300 for coverage that benefits me only $100 per year, that's a losing deal, too. On my '85 Bus, I think I have $500 deductible. That is, the first $500 of damage, I pay for. If it's more than that, the insurance company has to pay. That is a LOT cheaper than $0 or $100 deductible. And it's a good incentive to drive safely!

There is one area where I am willing to pay for extra insurance: The minimum insurance required in California is about $15k/30k, namely, $15,000 for one person, and $30,000 for one accident. Hey, if you hit one BMW and the guy spends a week in the hospital, that could easily use up all of the $15k/30k. If you have any assets at all – a house or furniture or savings – it is very reasonable to pay for $100k/300k of insurance, because in these days of inflated claims, and a deflated dollar, that is about the minimum amount you will be safe with. And the extra cost is fairly reasonable. That I can recommend.

What To Do With It...

Now that you have paid for this insurance – what do you do with it? I recommend – AS LITTLE AS POSSIBLE. I have not filed any claims for quite a few years. There's nothing I have run into that caused any damage, compared to the $300 deductibles.

I know some people who agree, even if you did run into another car, it is cheaper to pay off the expense out of your pocket, rather than let the insurance company pay. Example – let's say you bumped into another car, and there was a $650 repair bill on the other guy's car, for which you were largely to blame. If you pay it, that's the end of it. But if you require your insurance company to pay for it – they *appear to pay*. But you will probably pay for it the rest of your life.

And if you then get into 1 or 2 more accidents – even if they are not your fault – the insurance company will accuse you of being a bad driver, and will try to double your rates, or try to put you into an "assigned risk" pool, where you'll pay DOUBLE – or TRIPLE. Doesn't THAT sound jolly? Or they will try to CANCEL YOU! No, insurance is mostly for people in cases where they don't need it.

It's a good thing I haven't got all the checks in one place, that I've paid for my car insurance. I'm sure it would add up to $40k for the last 20 years. And I haven't had any claims, not to speak of..... Sigh.

If you are suspicious that you are not getting a good rate on your insurance, shop around. Different companies' rates vary a lot.

Good News?

OK – after all this negative stuff I've said, is there any good news? Yes, there is. I can say that most insurance companies do a pretty good job of promoting safety. I think my long-time insurance company, Liberty Mutual, does a very good job.

They promote driving safety. They will try any reasonable scheme to teach their customers to not get into accidents, which they hope will lead to not making claims. They give out literature, advice, and even a loan of a video that was not half bad.

But of course the thing they do best, to keep accident rates down, is scare the hell out of us, in case of what will happen in case of accidents. Yes, the advertisements for every insurance company tries to assure you that they will stand by you, and defend you. Yes, they will. But they are only doing what you pay them to do. And if you goof up, you can be assured that you will pay dearly.

So – good. Our insurance company really wants us to NOT get into accidents. And so do I. I guess I'll call it a draw. I guess they are on my side. And, now that I am writing a book to prevent accidents, I guess they will agree I am on their side. Maybe they will even promote my book. We shall see.

Norwegian-American Steamships??

Once upon a time, there was a Norwegian lad who immigrated to the USA. He worked hard and saved his money. He decided to buy a Steamship, so he could sell travel to Norwegians coming to the US, and also sell tours to Norwegian-Americans who got prosperous and wanted to travel back to see the Old Country. He made such good profits that he was soon able to buy another steamship. Now, did this smart fellow buy insurance from an Insurance company? No, he self-insured. He took the risk on himself.

One foggy day, two ships loomed out of the murk – and crashed into each other – and sank. No lives were lost. Which two steamships?? You guessed it – the two ships – the only assets of this steamship company crashed into each other, and sank, and that was the end of the Norwegian-American Steamship Company.

When I lived in Wilmington Mass, a couple police cars crashed into each other. They were self-insured. Of course, because I do not know any insurance company that wants to insure police cars. A similar problem.

Don't let it happen to you.

Chapter 53. LAW and LAWYERS

I am not going to say much bad about lawyers. I am not going to tell any "lawyer jokes". Some of my good friends are lawyers, and they often do good work.

If you do NOT like lawyers, and you do NOT like working with lawyers, then that *right there* is a good reason to avoid having an accident. Because if you have certain kinds of accidents, you may spend a LOT of time with one or more lawyers. Now, if you just damage your car on a rock, then you may just have all the fun of arguing with your insurance agent. That is not always fun, but it's usually not as bad as arguing with a lawyer.

What If?...

What if somebody hits your car, and it's not your fault? You may still have to testify in court, in case they are trying to convict the guy of dangerous driving. Dealing with lawyers in this situation is still not bad, because nobody is really threatening *you*.

If YOU Need Help?

Conversely, if *you* were the guy who *allegedly* drove dangerously, *you* might have to hire a lawyer, to avoid being convicted, or try to get you a minimum fair sentence. I've never been in this situation, but I can tell, THIS is surely no fun, as you may read about this.

In some cases, it is not a matter of criminal law, but of civil law. You might have to sue another driver, or another person, to force them to pay for your damages. In many cases your insurance company will take care of this, but there are always some cases where you have to go out and hire a lawyer, to protect your interest. You may have *formerly* thought bad things about lawyers, but after your lawyer got you a settlement of a bunch of thousands of dollars, you will be thinking *GOOD THINGS* about lawyers for *months*.

ON the other hand – if some miserable bastard is suing you, you may need a lawyer to defend yourself. If your lawyer can prove that the other guy is full of baloney, and if he can defend you successfully, again, you'll feel pretty good. But maybe you won't feel *quite* so great, because you may have to pay the lawyer's bills. Still, it beats the hell out of *losing* the suit and *still* having to pay the lawyer's fees.

Anyhow, if you run afoul of the *law*, you may be dealing with *lawyers*. If you really GOOFED, and did something really stupid, and somebody got badly hurt, the state may try to put you in prison. You would need some help from a lawyer, to try to minimize your damage – get you the right legal advice so you don't get a worse sentence than you deserve. The only good thing about this is, after you had the accident, you will have plenty of time to talk to lawyers. No rush. You can read books on this. But, that is somebody else's book. This is all I have to say on this topic.

Chapter 54. WHEN TO BREAK THE LAW

When YOU, as a young driver, first run into this situation, you will be puzzled: You are in heavy, slow traffic, and the cop points at the five guys ahead of you, and motions, GO! He sends them right through a STOP sign. You follow them right up to the STOP sign – and your instincts tell you to stop – because you wouldn't want to drive through a STOP sign with a Cop watching you, would you?? And the cop blows his whistle louder and louder, and motions for you to keep going! He does NOT want you to stop there!! He wants you to keep going, right through the STOP sign.

When a cop tells you to do something that is normally illegal – it ain't illegal, if you follow his instructions. Obviously, when you come to an accident scene, and the cop directing traffic motions you to drive right across the center line – watch what you are doing – and then do it, carefully. Driving straight through a red light – even though we have all learned to not do that – is another thing a cop can tell you to do. He can also motion you to stop at a green light. So, now that you know these kinds of things, don't be surprised at anything! A cop could commandeer your car and tell you to drive as fast as you can, in pursuit of some outlaw. Now, if you wait for this to happen, it will be a long wait. Still, anything can happen. Never say never.

When to Break the Law?

– Even when a cop did not specifically tell you to do it, there are other times when you can break laws. If you do it to speed somebody to a hospital, the cop may even provide an escort. One time I had to drive my wife to the hospital because she had bad trouble breathing. A cop saw me roll through a STOP sign, and turned on his blinking lights, and asked why I did it. When I explained, he let me go on to the hospital, and did not even escort me!

– When you are driving like that, in an emergency, easing through stop signs and red lights, you are, of course, obligated to be EXTRA careful not to get into an accident.

Reporting a Fire

One time I had to drive up 8 miles to the nearest phone, to report a fire in a Gift Shop, up in the White Mountain National Forest. I drove full-out. But the upgrades were so tough, going up Crawford Notch in NH, I don't think I ever did get faster than 60 mph, in my old 1962 Beetle. Anyhow, the Gift Shop burned to the ground, but we saved the gas station next door.

Avoiding a Car Coming at You

If following the law would cause an accident, then breaking a law may be permissible. For example, if you are passing a car and it "shies" at you, you may be justified in crossing over the center line, to avoid getting hit – if there is no on-coming traffic. Just don't over-do it – such as, getting in the way of on-coming traffic.

Help Traffic to Merge

If a car is trying to merge into your lane, you might consider slowing down for a second, to let him in. But if slowing down would not help, and speeding up would help let him merge, then you are justified in speeding up for a brief time, over the speed limit, to help the guy merge, and avoid an accident.

Get the picture?

Chapter 55. NEAR MISSES – and LUCK

When people talk about the role of good luck in avoiding accidents, I like to think of the words of the great old baseball coach of the 1940s, Branch Rickey:

"Good Luck is the Residue of Design".

Good luck does not just *happen*. Often you EARN it. You work for it. You do not always just get "good luck", by being lucky. That is what this book is about. If you INVEST a dozen hours reading this book, it will pay back a good investment, in future safety, and in hours you do not have to spend in a hospital, or in paying for accidents.

You may marry a damn' fine woman (or man) next year, and that may be the best investment of your life. But this book may be the best investment you make this year. I don't like to just trust to luck, but to plan for many situations.

What do we Learn from a Near-Miss?

Sometimes we see a near miss and we just figure we were lucky. For example – the time the hand-truck fell off a truck, and did not jam into me or the car ahead of me, but instead kept rolling and rolled off the busy highway!! There's not much you can say about that. BUT, I suppose I *should have* caught up with the truck driver and blinked my lights at him and beeped at him, and hollered to him, and made him stop, and explained that he should be more careful how he stows his hand-truck, in the future. Because that could have caused a very messy accident.

But other times, a near miss should tell you that you are *really* pretty stupid, and you should wise up, or next time you won't be so "lucky". For example, if you just missed a car in an intersection, maybe you need to be more careful in intersections. If you find you cannot stay in your lane properly on bad curves, or on a rainy night, you should probably slow down. Even if the cheapest way is to learn from the mistakes of others, or from this book, you must *still* learn from your own mistakes. Okay?

Angels???

Angels? You think Angels are watching over you?? Maybe they are. But if you start depending on that, you may have some real problems. I must plan to see that angelic lady, who had so many near misses on the highway that she thought angels were watching over her....

Another short chapter....

Chapter 56. OLDIES

··

When drivers live long enough, hopefully, they get smart. They get better judgement. They know what to look for. They learn how to avoid situations that cause accidents. They know when and where to be cautious. GOOD! Many drivers achieve really good judgment when they get to middle age, and are very safe drivers.

However, when drivers KEEP getting older, sometimes they have problems. Sometimes they get TOO cautious, and drive TOO slow. Sometimes they cannot see so well at night, so they wisely choose to drive mostly in the daytime. But sometimes they cannot see very well in the daytime. When you cannot see well, you are likely to have problems.

In the Family

As my mother got older, she realized she could not see well at night, so she drove only in the daytime. She drove very cautiously and safely – right up to the time she started out into an intersection, and bumped into a trash truck. Fortunately, she was not hurt. She had been pretty independent, for many years, but after she got the car repaired, she did not get her license renewed because she knew she could not see well enough to pass the tests.

> So all of you young drivers out there must be prepared for the eventual day when you gotta hang up your driver's license. It may be 50 or more years ahead, but it's probably out there somewhere. The alternative may be, if you get killed in an accident, or die of something else, and I certainly don't wish that on you. Or to win the lottery, and hire a chauffeur – which is statistically VERY UNLIKELY.

In MY Family

Right now, I am just 56, and my eyesight is just as good as it was 40 years ago. I can still see perfectly well at night, and I can still deduce the speeds of other cars, and see little tiny things at distances. But I bet in 20 years, I won't be able to see this well. So eventually, I will probably have to quit driving. I damn well better follow the advice in this Chapter, and not stupidly drive until I become an accident looking for a place to happen. Right?

In Your Family

If one of the people in your family is getting old, and is beginning to drive badly, watch out. Your mother might pull right out in front of another car – that she didn't even see. Or your Uncle Harry might not notice that he was across the centerline, forcing the other driver to swerve to avoid him, at night.

Helping the Older Driver

NOW, you do not just have to take the car keys away from such a driver. There are driving courses that older drivers can take, that can help renew their ability to drive competently. If this older driver is a member of AARP, or similar organizations, they offer refresher courses that can help an older driver be sharper and aware – and can save you several percent on insurance premiums. But in a serious case, you could get some advice from other responsible persons. Maybe that older driver should go in to be re-tested for his license. Then if he cannot pass the tests, he might be "reasonable" and decide not to drive any more. OR, he might just insist he can still drive OK, even without a license. (Some older people are predictable as to being unreasonable.) Of course – he might just pass the tests – and then where would you be?? Obviously, many older drivers will argue that they can still drive just fine. But, what would you expect them to say?

Absentminded?

Some people get really senile. Alzheimer's disease can set in, at varying ages. At first, you may just say, "Dad sure is getting absent-minded." Then, "Really forgetful." But after a few months of realizing that he can't even find his car or his keys even when they are right in front of him, right where he expects them, then it may be necessary to separate the driver from his keys. You may have to volunteer to drive your Uncle Harry.

> This is a very difficult stage of life, and I do not know any way of making things easier for you. But if an older person starts getting really absent-minded and sloppy, it is not safe to just let them go out onto the road until their car is wrecked. That's not fair to them, or to the innocent driver they run into.

Forgetful

Sometimes when older people get old and forgetful, they get lost. Just last week, an old-timer was spotted parked in his pickup truck, down at the beach. He had been missing from his home for a few days. He was kind of disoriented. It sounds like this fellow was nearly at the end of his driving career. If this is happening to somebody you know, maybe you can get expert help in getting this older driver off the road. Or maybe they are mis-medicated, and after some good medical care, they may be able to renew their license again.

I don't have all the answers on this, but at least I have asked some of the questions, and this is a good start.

Old Cars

– If you have an old car – when should you give up on it? Well, if you can't get parts for it, and can't repair the brakes – or the engine – that should tell you something. If rain water leaks in, and you have to punch a little hole in the floor to let it run out, that's one problem. If the water runs right out through big holes in the floor, as fast as it runs in, that's not so good, because the exhaust might get in and poison you with carbon monoxide. Refer to the Chapter on Mufflers. Or, if the floor is falling out, that is not very safe.

Let's say the Muffler shop wants to charge you $400 to fabricate a new exhaust system, because nobody sells mufflers for your car any more. If the car's total value, after you put in the muffler, wouldn't be much over $400 – maybe you want to park it. I'm not saying you have to send it to a junk yard, but you might want to put it out to pasture – at least until you can afford to get good parts, and restore it and get it running safely. Get another car that runs safely, to drive until you have enough money to fix the old car right.

Leaks...

If you have an old car, it may be leaking or burning oil. In that case, before you start out, it might be IMPORTANT to use the dip-stick and check the oil level, and make sure you have a few quarts of oil with you, in case you need to add some. You may find it a good idea to set up REMINDERS to make sure you remember to do this, every time you get in the car.

Similarly – any car (but especially an older car) may be leaking water – or brake fluid – or power steering fluid – or Automatic Transmission Fluid (ATF). So be sure to set up adequate reminders, to make sure you don't run out, or run too low. Avoid breakdowns.

Sloppy Steering...

Older cars sometimes have a lot of "play" or "slack" in the steering. This is also called "dead zone". If the steering play is more than an inch, at the steering wheel's rim, that's not so good. Maybe you can get it fixed. You might have to get the steering box adjusted – or replaced. Or there may be tie rod ends that are getting loose. You really should get it fixed – OR at least, get a good mechanic to check it out to make sure the steering gear is not on the point of falling apart.

Sometimes I get to drive an old car. When the road has a consistent crown (slanting off to the right) then that means you'll turn the steering wheel against that side force. But if there are crosswinds gusting from both sides, you may have to turn the wheel back and forth a lot, to take up the slack. If you get on a bumpy road, with curves and twists, it is really hard to take up the slack and drive safely. If the road is narrow, or if there is heavy traffic, that makes it even harder. If your steering is sloppy, you may have to slow down considerably, to let you keep your car where you want it on the road. Or, get it fixed. Admittedly, some cars never had good, precise steering in the first place, so you can't expect perfection.

Mature Drivers?

Now, how about grown-up drivers? OK -- we are not "thrill-crazed kids" any more. But we are not yet so old that we cannot see, nor is our reaction time too decrepit. So -- why do WE still drive into accidents? I'll have to guess: goofing off, not paying attention -- and making bad ASSUMPTIONS. Eh?

Chapter 57. WHAT IF YOU HAD AN **ACTUAL ACCIDENT?**

NOW – despite all the advice I have given you – in 57-odd chapters – what do you do if you get into a real accident in your car? Your car hits something – or somebody hits you. What do you do, NOW?

First of all, don't panic, and don't do anything stupid.

FIRST of all, make sure you do not cause a BIGGER accident. Let's say you got into a rough fender-bender in the middle of a freeway. Your car is badly dented, but it is still able to move. It has been turned around sideways on the road. You might think, "This is a very dangerous place, so I'll get turned around straight on the road." If you pull ahead just a few feet – you might hit a car going past in the next lane. That might cause a REAL wreck. So, driving to a safer place is rarely the right thing to do. (I won't say never. If there were an accident with a gasoline tanker, and a big puddle of gasoline was likely to catch fire, driving the heck out of there might be EXACTLY the right thing to try.) In general, though, take it easy, and do not try to drive away to a "safer" place. Sometimes "leaving the scene of the crime" is considered a bad thing.

SECOND, it is usually a good idea to climb out of your car, and check things out. If another driver was involved, you could say, "Are you OK?" Do not blurt out, "I'm sorry I hit you". Your insurance company will greatly prefer you to NOT say that.

Do not holler, "That was pretty stupid of you to smash into me like that, you idiot," even though you may be thinking that. Even if it is mostly true, it is not a good idea to say that. Not nice, and not *helpful*.

Second, check and make sure that things are roughly under control, as much as is possible. Make sure nobody is likely to be hit by an on-coming car. If the scene is hard to see, and traffic might soon arrive around a blind corner, or if there is fog, or some other vision problem (if it was dark, and your lights were not working) be sure to get out and flag down traffic, so they won't crash into your wreck. This was largely covered in the Chapter on Vision. You remember *that*; it was only about 170,000 words back. Anyhow, since no advice can cover every possibility, the general guideline here is – if possible – make every reasonable effort to warn traffic to not smash into the scene. As soon as you can get another driver to stop, you can get him to help you stop and direct traffic, while you go about the next phase.

THIRD: make sure nobody is hurt, or, give first aid as may be appropriate. Hey, I got my First Aid Merit Badge with the Boy Scouts about 40 years ago, and I remember a few things. Maybe you never took a good First Aid course, but here are some pretty good guidelines.

– A. If somebody is really badly hurt, try not to move him. Moving them may do more harm. This is especially true if he seems to have a back or neck injury. If that is the case, you should NEVER move the person, with one exception: If there is a lot of gasoline around, and a little spark could endanger the whole scene, sometimes you have to move, drag, or pull an injured person away from the immediate area. Since this will require snap judgement, you figure it out, on the scene. Just remember, danger of fire is usually the only reason to move a person. Although if he was knocked unconscious, and sitting on the railroad tracks, I think that might be a good reason to move him. You know the train schedules in your area, I don't.

– B. If somebody is bleeding badly, don't worry about "pressure points" or a tourniquet that they taught you in Boy Scouts. Apply a little DIRECT PRESSURE to the wound. If a guy has a cut on his arm, get HIM to hold his other hand over his arm, and hold on tight, and this can often slow the flow of blood, and help the natural clotting mechanisms to work. Maybe you are squeamish about blood. Maybe you pass out at the sight of blood. So, all the more reason to get the guy to hold his own arm, so you don't have to do it.

– C. In general, try to minimize the pain. Maybe a person with good medical skills will show up in a few minutes. OR, maybe you know that out on this road, nobody is likely to come along for *hours*. You gotta use your own judgement.

FOURTH, after all emergency problems are under control, try to report the accident to the police and other authorities. If you are in the middle of nowhere, and a car comes along, you could ask him to report the accident at the first town – or the first house with a phone – or whatever is appropriate. Tell him to call the police, and tell the police you will (or will not) need an ambulance – or a fire truck – or a tow truck – or whatever. Sometimes, it is a good idea to stop another car going the other direction and ask them to report the accident at the first phone, too. Sometimes the first house or phone in the OTHER direction is a lot closer.

FIFTH, if any other person was a witness to the accident, try to get their name and phone number before they go away. A witness's statement could be very valuable to you, if there is a dispute over what caused the accident. Some people will volunteer to be a witness; others are a little shy and you might have trouble getting them to agree to giving you that information. In such a case – you might just discreetly get their license number. Your insurance company can find them later. They are pretty good at getting a statement from a witness.

SIXTH, offer to exchange insurance information with the other driver. You will want to get his driver's license info, address, and phone. Also, his car's registration info. Also the name and address or phone of HIS insurance company. And he will want to get *your* info, likewise. If the accident was a small one, you might decide to self-insure, and you might volunteer to pay for part of the accident yourself, without

7/2/2*

reporting it to your insurance company. Make sure you do that right, and make a clear understanding, and, better yet, write it on paper.

It is STILL not a good idea to admit that it was YOUR mistake. Even if it was *partly* your mistake, it may have been partly somebody else's mistake. You CAN say, "I'm sure sorry this accident happened". You can say this even if it was the other guy's fault.

Try not to holler at the other guy or throw a lot of blame on him. If it was his fault, he feels lousy enough already. You might, though, ask some questions of fact. "Didn't you see that yellow car?" "Did you put on your brakes? You didn't seem to slow down much." You may try to learn a little more about what happened just before the accident. If he was trying to dodge a deer, and swerved across the center of the road, just as you came around a corner, that might explain something.

Or, if YOU have some information on why the accident happened (the deer ran out in front of *me*, and *I* had to swerve, and then the car skidded into *your* lane) be sure to mention it, so they will not have to guess. Of course, in that case, the deer has probably left the scene of the accident, but if deer do often cross the road at that point, this can be verified later.

> SEVENTH, if and when a policeman shows up, talk it over. If you need help, the cop can provide a lot of backup. He can call for an ambulance or tow truck, if one is needed. He may tell you some things to do; he may set you to directing traffic. When he gets there, he is *in charge*, and mostly you have to do what he says. Be sure to get his name, if it is a serious accident. He may insist on getting yours. Or, if the accident is minor, he may just ask if you need his help, and shrug and go away if you assure him you don't need help.

> EIGHTH, as soon as you have a chance, write down what happened. Write down some notes, real soon. I will include a little form that I carry around in my car. It's a standard accident report form, from an insurance company. It can help you remember what info to note down. Write down the *time* of the accident. Write down the weather and road conditions. Was it just starting to rain? Was it hard to see? Write down all the facts, at least some notes, preferably before you leave the scene of the accident. This form is in the front, at page ii. You can make copies of it.

And, if you can, before the vehicles or persons are moved, take a photograph of the scene. Any skid marks? Can your photo show that there were conditions that caused the accident? I heard of a case where a guy came through a stop sign and hit a car. The tree limbs were blocking the view of the stop sign. When he came back the next day with a camera, the tree branches had been trimmed! So if there is any question, go to a store and buy a little camera. There are an AWFUL LOT of drugstores and "convenience stores" that will sell you a $9 camera. This might be a very good investment, if the evidence at the scene needs to be confirmed. Judges and insurance companies are known to be well impressed by clear pictures of a problem.

NINTH, if it is safe, get your vehicles off the road. This may be very simple, or it may involve pushing, or a tow-truck, or whatever. If there is a policeman around, he will tell you when and how to do this. And, if this was all just a minor fender-bender, you might actually be doing this in the first minute after the accident. You might be able to do this before you exchange paperwork. It all depends. Fortunately, most accidents are minor. That does not mean they are *fun*.

TENTH, after you have checked out all these details, and answered all the questions to your satisfaction, you may be able to go on your way. Make sure the other drivers are satisfied they have enough information.

Of course, if your car has been damaged, you'll have to assess if the damage was serious enough that you should not drive, or should drive slowly. This may depend on how far you have to go. Does your steering work? Do you have a cut on a tire? Do you have enough lights working? You check it out.

ELEVENTH, when you get home, or wherever you are going, write down *complete* notes on what happened. Then, get a photocopy of the accident forms. Write down all the facts, all of what happened. You may want to make a first draft, and correct it, and write a second draft. You might or might not want to put the first draft in a separate place where you can burn it...

TWELFTH, if you think the damages may have been more than $300 or $500 or whatever the rules are in your state, you may be REQUIRED to file an accident report with the police. In California, I think the law states you may be sent to *jail* if you fail to do that. You might check that out. In general, you would use the facts and statements from item 11, the "What Happened" story.

THIRTEENTH, you may wish to contact your insurance company. Or, you may wish to contact the other driver's insurance company. I know a driver who was *dropped* by his insurance company because he was involved in 2 accidents in one year, that were NOT his fault. Refer to the section on Insurance. You figure it out. Does your insurance company *require* you to contact them?

FOURTEENTH, in case there was a lot of blame, or accusation of serious blame, on YOU, you might want to contact a lawyer. Maybe your insurance company will help on this. Maybe you want to do it independently. You figure it out.

FIFTEENTH, you might look in some books to see all the details of what you want to do next. The book on Accidents in my book-review section could be useful. I just hope you don't need it. Or, your insurance company may be able to give you some "free" advice.

SIXTEENTH. You might have to go to a doctor, or hospital. This might be item number 16, in a minor bump where you just sprung your thumb, or banged your head. OR, this might be item number one, if you are in a severe crash. In that case, it will be decided for you.

7/ 3/ 72

Hey, I hope that just *thinking about* all this STUFF is enough to encourage you to drive safely, responsibly, and sometimes even *cautiously*. I am not trying to scare you. I am just listing all the factors and ideas you may have to deal with, if you get in an accident. In a small accident, many of these 16 items can be ignored. But, what if you were in a "small accident", and you got a little blood on your chin when you bumped it on a door frame. The other driver gets out of his car, sees the blood, and passes out. He hits his head on the ground and is in the hospital for a week with a concussion. Is this gonna be a messy, expensive problem for your insurance companies to sort out? You bet. There is almost no such thing as a "small accident", if the complications get messy.

WELL – this is the last Chapter I wrote. I jumped in at 6 AM on Sunday January 21, 1996, and I finished it at 9 AM. I didn't look in any books, I just sat and typed, with my cup of Yuban coffee. Hey, this writing stuff is fun, and challenging, and a lot of work. Man. I'm glad I have finished off all the text. / R. A. Pease.

Chapter 58. YOUR First Accident

Wellll... I hope you never have to go back and read this Chapter. But if you wait long enough, most people will admit – this Chapter does apply to them.

Is your first observation: – "Where the hell did HE COME FROM?"

Or, is your first observation: – "This can't happen to ME – – I was being pretty careful...." followed by, "Well, I was being at least a LITTLE careful...."

– I won't even waste my breath with trying to guess in what sequence you will want to use some of these next comments....

- "What will my father say?"

- "What will my Mom say?"

- "What will my wife say?"

- "I wonder what my Insurance guy will say?"

- "What kind of story am I going to tell my Insurance Agent?"

- "I wonder how I'm going to pay for this? Hey, I haven't GOT $300, and the insurance is $300 deductible...."

- "I'm glad it was only the left side that got scraped."

- "I wonder if I get a big hammer, I can get the gas filler open, so I can put in some gas."

- "Why wasn't I watching for that guy that came around the corner?"

- "I'll be more careful, next time, after I get it fixed...."

Here's one you will probably not use –

- "Gee, I am glad my buddies have volunteered to help pay for the repairs."

Anyhow, when you get home, you might want to read my Chapter 57: What to do if you had an accident. You might have to read the Chapters on Insurance, and on Lawyers. I hope all your Accidents are TINY LITTLE ONES, and, not very often.

OK? Good luck. / rap

Chapter 59. RAP's Accidents

OK, how can I expect YOU GUYS to tell me about your accidents, when I have not listed *my* accidents? So, I realized I have written down lots of lists of other important items – but not, until now, a list of my own accidents. Does this represent an ego trip? Or am I bragging about how stupid I am? Maybe some combination of the two. But I am listing these here, in the interest of honesty. And maybe you can learn from *my* stupidity. Here you go:

Accident #0, 1958.

I bought an old 1939 Chevy, just to drive on farm roads, not on public roads. It was a functional car, but the brakes were not very good, so the first time you hit the brakes, nothing happened; you had to step on them twice to get any brakes. Most of the time I remembered to do this just right. One day I was driving around in my father's orchard. I wanted to turn around, and I backed up, and hit the brakes once, and nothing happened. (Not very bright.) I hit a little peach tree, and bent its trunk. I think the tree did recover, but it was not very happy for a few years. My father was not very pleased, either, but I never did any more harm than that, with that car.

> WHAT DID I LEARN FROM THIS? It is stupid to drive around with brakes that do not work. My father should have instructed me to take my brakes apart and repair them. But he didn't. Maybe he was smart. Anyhow, the tree recovered.

Anyhow, that was not on a road, and not with a registered car, so I won't count it. Let's move on to –

Accident #1, 1961.

I had an old 1951 Studebaker. It was not a great car, but it did run OK – except the handbrakes were not very good. We went out hiking in Vermont, and when we started back, I neglected to release the handbrake. I drove 4 miles down the dirt road and 4 miles up the highway before I noticed the smoke. After that, the handbrakes and the rear brakes were really bad. I eased home really gently, about 150 miles, without any hurrying, so I did not have to rely on my brakes much, and I didn't work my brakes hard at all. The next day, I took it in to a brake shop to be repaired. OK, for $75 or so, I got good brakes.

The next Sunday I was driving up Route 1 at 40 mph, and I felt a small lurch and heard a big scraping sound. I had no trouble in getting the car to ease to a stop on the shoulder. The right rear wheel had fallen off and was sitting there in the wheel well – it did not roll down the road past me. The wheel nuts did not come loose, but the big rear axle nut had come off.

I scouted around an adjacent junkyard, and found a rear axle nut from some other car. It was just a little smaller than the one I had. I started to screw it on my

Studebaker's axle. I screwed it on and off about 50 times, until it made some new threads. I was amazed that the metal of the axle was soft enough to let me cut new threads by just screwing that nut onto it. I got it screwed on tight. I wired it up tight. I drove home 15 miles – slowly, and picking a route that avoided all big bridges. The next day I took it down to the brake shop, and told them the story. I barely had to remind them that they had been the most recent people who had taken off that rear axle nut, when they repaired the brakes. They fixed it. I did not ask them *how* they fixed it.

> WHAT DID I LEARN FROM THIS? The next day I went down and placed an order for a 1962 VW Beetle. In 2 months, my Beetle came in, and I traded in that 1951 Studebaker for $50, and never looked back.

On some of my cars, I have installed a beeper to *beep* when the ignition is on and the handbrake is on. I think a beeper is better than a buzzer. Because sometimes you do have to leave your handbrakes on, and the buzzer gets annoying. I have never put one of these beepers on my Beetles, because when you shift out of first gear, if you left the handbrakes on, you will *definitely* notice it. It ain't got enough power to go anywhere if the handbrake is on.

Accident #2, 1963.

I was in ordinary traffic in Boston, on Berkeley Street. When the light went green, I turned left. A city bus also turned left, but was not watching where he was going, and put a 2-inch deep dent in my left front fender. I settled with the city's insurance agent for about $18. I told him $18 would pay for a bucket of undercoat, to paint over the bump on the sheet-metal. I still have the bucket of undercoat.

> WHAT DID I LEARN FROM THIS? I guess it is hard to be sure you do not get in front of anybody. Bus drivers do not have an easy job. Actually, this driver was pretty alert, because he stopped pretty quickly. If he hadn't been alert, he coulda put a 27-inch dent in my fender.

Accident #3, 1963.

I was driving north in Medford on Massachusetts Route 28, a city parkway, 3 lanes each way. Heavy commute traffic, accelerating from light to light. SUDDENLY, in the middle of nowhere, traffic was stopping! A police car had noticed a pedestrian standing at a cross-walk, and he decided to stop traffic and let them cross – even though they could have easily crossed when there was a break in traffic. So he put on his brakes, and held out his hand and "volunteered" to make all traffic stop. I stopped OK. The guy behind me almost stopped. He whacked my rear bumper and bent it a little. I think I settled for $10.

> WHAT DID I LEARN FROM THIS? I learned that if there is some ridiculous traffic pattern, it is a good idea to have your thumb on your horn, and let out a good beep, if you have to make an emergency stop. Because if the guy behind you is not alert, it is a good idea to hit your horn and wake him up. But, I must admit, I only figured this out in 1995.

Accident #4, 1964.

We were hiking up in New Hampshire, in May of 1964. We were up near Franconia Notch, but we decided we wanted to go over to Conway and go south down Route 16. We knew that the Kancamagus Highway, a good wide gravel road, was not yet open officially, but maybe we could get through. First, we came to the chain with the official sign saying "ROAD CLOSED", and as my wife held this up, I drove under the chain. We went up 10 miles to the big snowdrift at the top of the pass. Yes, there was about 200 yards of a big snow-bank, as deep as 3 feet. If we could shovel our way through this, we could get to Conway.

I drove around the left side of the first big snowbank, right next to the road's shoulder that slanted down steeply. I could see that there was only 60 yards of snowbank, less than 3 feet deep. Could I dig through that? I decided to retreat, temporarily. I started backing down the way I had come.

As I was backing, the rear of the car started to veer left. I cut the wheel left, naturally, to get the rear back on track. BUT, I was at the edge of the steep shoulder, and the front AND the rear of the car dropped down a foot. STOP!

I reviewed the situation. 30 miles from town. Sun would set in 3 hours. I started digging and jacking. I got rocks and chunks of log out of the woods. I got the car jacked up and just about level.

Then I tried to drive ahead, back onto the roadway. I tried 3 or 4 times. It lurched and slipped. Fell off the pile of wood. I was making progress, but the sun was getting lower. Finally a couple other drivers arrived, and with a little more shimming up, and with a couple people pushing, I got the Beetle back on the flat, on the road.

NOW, we *all* agreed we wanted to get across that snowfield. Some of us wanted to get from the east to the west, and others from west to east. We had only one shovel, my shovel. But we had about 5 people prepared to dig. We took turns. We each dug very hard for a minute, and then passed the shovel to another guy.

Along came a Vermont farmer, in his pickup truck. He was going to Portland, and he wanted to get through, too. He helped us shovel. (By this point it was obvious that 35 more minutes of shovelling would get all our cars through, a LOT faster than driving around.)

I will never forget the contribution of that Vermonter. He could dig more in 1 minute, than ANY of the rest of us could do in 2 minutes. Then he passed along the shovel to the next person.

Normally, I know how to shovel at a pace that I could work at for hours. I mean, I am good at pacing myself. If I am hiking, I will hike at a pace I can hold that is appropriate for the distance I know I have to go. I do not burn myself out. But, I am not very good at working REALLY FAST and HARD. I tried to do that, as the Vermonter was doing, and did not do well. He had exactly the right strategy for this task, as we had to take turns. All the others tried to do that, and they were not successful, either.

Anyhow, after about an hour of digging, we broke through the snowbank, and I got my Beetle through, and parked it. Then we made sure each of the other cars got through – as some of them were considerably wider than a Beetle, and they got stuck, and we had to dig a little to get them through. We all got through.

> WHAT DID I LEARN FROM THIS? Be careful when you are backing up, near an edge or drop-off. The natural move of steering your front end LEFT, does NOT bring your back end right, if you are near an edge or drop-off. Life is sometimes nonlinear. Things don't always work the way you expect.

AND, if you think you are wiser than an old Vermonter, you gotta be a *smart* sonofabitch. I am smart, and I am almost wise, and I am almost old, and yet I do not think I am smart enough to shovel as fast or effectively as that Vermont guy.

Accident #5, 1966.

I was driving along in my 1965 Bus on Route 3A, in Billerica Mass, and when a light went red, I stopped. But the guy behind me gave me a good whack in the tail. He said his brakes failed. No damage to the car, but my wife had a neck-ache for a few days. (Obviously, those old cars did not have head-rests.) The insurance company gave my wife $50 for her pain.

> WHAT DID I LEARN FROM THIS? I guess you can't be sure the guy behind you has good brakes. And if your car has head-rests, as all cars have these days, you are less likely to get a serious whip-lash incident.

Accident #6, 1967.

I was hurrying down Woburn Street, a narrow country road in Wilmington Mass, to do an errand on the way to work. I came up behind a slow dump truck. At the first straight stretch, I went out to pass the truck. However, he was going to turn left. I never could recall if he *did* put on his blinkers to turn left, and I failed to notice them, OR, if he neglected to turn on his blinkers – ? I hit my horn and braked hard and went off the road to the left, and by the time I got slowed down to about 2 mph I hit a big boulder that was set there to mark the road. A minor crumple, just a few inches. No insurance claim. No cost. When I retired that car, the value of the car did not differ by 2 cents, compared to its value if I did not hit that rock.

> WHAT DID I LEARN FROM THIS? When you are going to pass a guy, you can never be too sure he will see you. Maybe I shoulda turned on my headlights. That probably woulda have been a good idea. Maybe I shoulda hit my horn. I really cannot recall it precisely.

Accident #7, 1968.

I was driving up in my old blue 1962 Beetle, to buy groceries in my old town of Wilmington Mass, in the first snowstorm of the year. There were about 5 inches of wet snow on the ground. I went up a couple back streets to Demoulas' Market. But that was just an excuse to check out my skidding skills. Were my tires any good? I turned down a side street and nailed the gas. As I expected, I skidded a little, and then again, and then a little more skid, and I kept feeding the gas – and slid off the road onto the shoulder, which was about 5 inches down. (Not *nearly* as bad as when I slid off the Kancamagus Highway.)

I got out and dug with my shovel for a minute and jumped back in. Almost got it out. I had to jump back out and dig for another 40 seconds, before I could get off of that shallow but depressed shoulder.

> This is not a big deal, but my 4-year-old son Benjamin was quite disconcerted that we got stuck, even if it was just a little. I bet he still remembers this. Still, these 2 times were the only times I got off the road and got stuck.

WHAT DID I LEARN FROM THIS? Even on a rural snowy road, you can waste quite a few minutes sliding to a harmless place you did not plan to. And, try not to scare your kids too much.

Accident #8, 1976.

As I mentioned in the Chapter on Skids, in January of 1976, I was running about 50 mph down Mass Route 128 on the way to work, on an inch of hard-packed snow. I passed a diaper truck who was doing 45, and I noticed that he then followed me out into the passing lane.

As I started up a grade, I looked over on the right and saw a car trying to accelerate up his entrance ramp. I noticed he was fish-tailing a little on the up-hill.

Suddenly, this klutz swung left across all 3 lanes, and crashed into the center divider – right in front of the car in front of me! As we saw this absurd situation unfolding, I and the car in front of me both eased on our brakes and stopped. However....

However, that damn' diaper truck did not do a very good job of stopping. He was still doing about 20 when he hit me, and gave me a good SHOVE forward. Fortunately, I was not too close to the car ahead of me. I steered to the left, and shoved my nose into the snowbank, rather than hit the other car. But my engine got crunched. I had to get a ride to work with a friend, and had to buy another car.

> WHAT DID I LEARN FROM THAT? Beware of skidding or fishtailing drivers. Any guy who lets a fish-tail skid continue is REALLY STUPID – stay away from him!! I guess I might have figured out a way to stay a little further away from that car, and I might have gone a little slower until I got well past him. But I figured if he was going to goof up, he would goof up 'way over on the far right, not across all 3 lanes. WRONG.

If I had slowed down, I might have forced that diaper truck to slow down. But, if I had to hit my brakes at all, he STILL would have been right on my rear bumper. Then I would have just had to go slower!

Accident #9, 1976.

I was coming down Sir Francis Drake Boulevard, in Kentfield, ten miles north of the Golden Gate Bridge. It was heavy, slow stop-and-go traffic, and I was stopped. A woman started to drive up out of a store's driveway. She got within 10 feet of me and stopped. Then she started up and, at a majestic speed of 1 mph, drove into my right front wheel. Of course, I beeped my horn – and she just kept on coming. She must have been on tranquilizers or something. She was so placid, it didn't bother her. Fortunately, she barely put a dent in my hub-cap. No real harm.

> WHAT DID I LEARN FROM THAT? I guess there are some accidents you can't avoid, but you can be thankful they happened at a very slow speed.

Accident #10, 1994.

We were coming back from a hike along the California coast in 1994. I was at the corner of Main Street in Half Moon Bay, waiting to turn right onto Route 92 to go home. I was debating with my wife, whether I should turn left to buy some salmon at the very good fish store there. Finally I said, "Ok, I'll buy the fish." I checked; the light was still red, ahead of us, so no traffic was coming toward us. I cut the wheel and turned lef... ooops. Chrcunch. Some unfortunate lady was coming up behind me, in the lane left of me. I did not *suspect* she could be there. I wrecked her tire. She was not happy. In fact, she was really a little unhappy and displeased that her car was accidented. So I apologized.

Now, in a case like this, your insurance company tells you that you are not supposed to say, "I am sorry, I goofed." But, I told her, "I am sorry, I goofed." I changed her tire for her. I gave her $70 to replace her tire. I promised to pay for her damages – which eventually amounted to more than $400. But, since it was clearly my fault, I figured that was wiser than demanding that my insurance company should pay for my mistake. If you don't see the logic, read my Chapter on Insurance.

So the other driver, after being a little shaky because I scared the hell out of her, and bashed one corner of her car, went on her way, considerably delayed, but not TOO mad at me. And I went over and bought my salmon.

> WHAT DID I LEARN FROM THIS?
> 1. Do not assume that you can turn left, just because there is no oncoming traffic. There may be an empty lane on your left. That may be a legal lane, for somebody else to drive on. Somebody who is rolling along legally and cheerfully, about to pass you.... And,
>
> 2. Boy, that was an expensive piece of salmon! Impulsiveness is all very fine. But if you are in a strange place, be careful how you assume there is a clear lane or path to go somewhere.

That's all. Ten little accidents in a million miles. If you are a cautious, conservative driver, you may do better than that. If you are a slob, or aggressive, you can do a *lot* worse than that. My primary suggestion is: LEARN from the mistakes of OTHERS, including, MY mistakes. If any of you get into the accidents that I did, I will be really pissed off at you. (That is a technical phrase.) By now, YOU should be smarter than I was. So, don't do what I did. Okay?

Now, if I were really smart, I could stop there. But just after I thought I had finished this chapter, we had a severe rainstorm in California, on Dec. 12, 1995. Very few people were killed, but it made a mess for a few days – and some people lost power for a week.

I commuted down 101 and back on 280, cruising at 55 and 65 mph, forging my way past messy traffic, and braving strong winds and torrents of rain. Dodging other slow drivers. I safely travelled 83.999 miles of my 84-mile commute. I was backing into my driveway. I must admit, it *was* kinda dark. Maybe the street lights were out? Yeah, the nearest street light was out. But I really thought I was lined up with my driveway. Rolling backwards at 2 mph, the last 5 feet. WHUMP. Just like the Norwegian-American Steamship company – I backed into my other car. It did no harm to the Bus, but it bashed in my Beetle's engine compartment lid. Fortunately I was going quite slowly, and it did not cause any harm to any engine parts. Just embarrassing. I got a guy to bang out the big dent on the engine-compartment lid, and I slathered some paint on it, and the car is worth as much as it ever was.

> WHAT DID I LEARN FROM THIS? There ain't no alibis for pretending you know what you are doing. And there ain't no substitute for decent vision. I thought I could see where I was backing – but I must admit that my windows were fogged worse than usual, as some traffic was slow. (If you have never driven an old VW, I can explain that the heater and defroster are adequate only if you can keep rolling above 50 mph.)

That had better be ALL, for a long, long while.

OOOPS! - Accident #12, 1998.

I was hoping to get this book all published and printed in 1997. Then I could say, "As we go to press, my good old VW is still running strong at 361,000 miles. No more accidents." But I went on a trek in Nepal, and that killed a month, and cleaning up my mail took a month when I got home. Thus I did not have the book finished in February of 1998.

I was easing through a parking garage. There was a single steel cable, 3 feet off the ground, with no sign, no warning. I hit it and wiped out the front pillars of my good old Beetle, and bashed in the windshield. The car was totalled. I got some cuts on my fingers — not a bump or cut on my head. That good little car got me to 365,200 miles, but no further. Had to buy a newer car - a red 1970 Beetle with only 112 k miles on it.

> WHAT DID I LEARN FROM THIS? — I guess it's impossible to be absolutely certain that you can see every hazard — even when you are trying very hard to be careful.

PEASE PORRIDGE*

CHAPTER 60 – WHAT'S ALL THIS REFLEX RESPONSE STUFF, ANYHOW?

I must have been quite small, when I learned that if I dropped something heavy, I should jump so as to pull my feet out of the way of the falling object. For example, if I dropped a brick that fell toward my right foot, I didn't have to worry about my left foot, but my right foot had better clear out quickly. Obviously, just about everybody learns this early enough that you have no recollection or memory of how you learned it.

At a somewhat later age, I learned that if I dropped my glasses, or my watch, or any delicate object, it was pretty easy to swing one foot underneath that object. Even if I could not entirely prevent my glasses from hitting the floor, I could deflect them so it would only be a glancing blow. And I have developed that knack, so it is pretty automatic for me.

Then, the other day – in the summer of 1990 – I dropped something, and I did not move my foot either to catch nor to avoid the object. Well, I asked my leg, what is this that you are so blasé about? – I reached down and picked up – a stick of butter. My leg had apparently made a decision that a 4-ounce stick of butter was not worth worrying about, one way or the other. Smart leg!

I mentioned this at work, and a friend (who has a lot of experience as an auto mechanic) said, "Okay, here's the fourth situation – the fourth quadrant. Let's say you are working on a Porsche, and you leave the starter motor up on a bench. Suddenly you notice that the starter has just rolled off the bench and is on its way to the floor. It weighs 30 pounds. It costs

$900. NOW, what do you do with your leg?"

After some consideration, I figured that I would try to kick the starter with my toe, pretty hard, about 16 inches off the ground, so my toe would not get crushed, but it would have a chance of slowing down that heavy object. But I haven't gone to try it out.

Now, there is a very good and very serious application for this kind of pre-planning, pre-judging what kind of a reflex reaction you will make, instantly, in a particular situation. Let's say you are driving along a freeway, and suddenly you spot a dog in front of you. You may blow your horn, but some dogs really don't pay much attention (some of them are deaf, and others are stupid enough, they might as well be deaf.) Okay – what do you do? You might hit the brakes – but if there were a truck on your tail, he could do *lots of damage* to you.

You might swerve – that's a better way to avoid the dog (unless the dog dodges in the same direction as you do – I've seen that happen). But what if there is a car passing you? You could easily wreck your car and any number of other cars, too, depending on how many cars are around you. Or, if you dodge really hard, you could go off the road and cause additional trouble. A woman was observed trying to dodge a dog on Route 93 in Medford, Mass, about 20 years ago. She missed the dog but went off the road, down an embankment, and was killed. Bad move.

Now, I am not suggesting that you just hit the dog. In many states, if you hit a dog, you have to file a report with the

*Reprinted from ELECTRONIC DESIGN/ December 5, 1991

police, and you might have to cart in an injured animal to the vet – no fun at all. Nobody really wants to cause pain to the dog, even if the dog is out where it shouldn't be. So, it is worth some effort to try to avoid the dog. But, what is the right answer?

The answer is, I am convinced, to keep aware at all times of how much traffic there is behind you and beside you. If you are convinced there's nobody beside you, you can cut the wheel hard and avoid the dog. If the road is empty, you can also brake. Just try to avoid losing control. You might damage your car if you hit a big dog, but you might wreck it if you lose control completely.

And if you know there's heavy traffic all around you – well – you can try squeezing to one side of your lane, to give the dog a chance to miss you. And all the time you must have your thumb on the horn. Maybe the dog isn't deaf, just a little hard of hearing. And, after all that, well, if you do hit the dog, you have tried your darnedest to avoid hitting it. You did your best. But you can't do your best without being aware of traffic, and without planning in advance.

Now, if you are really aware of what's around you, you will also be prepared to dodge a deer – or a concrete block, or a loose wheel – or a child. Obviously, it is worth a lot, to try to avoid a deer, because at 50 mph, almost every car will have several thousand dollars of damage if you nail that deer. And you'll be lucky if you don't wind up with the deer in the front seat with you. And, as for dodging a child – well, I hope you never have to do it. But just in case, I hope this column helps you to plan what to do. I know that in Massachusetts there's a truck line (the Crystal Freight Co., Wakefield, Mass.) and on every truck they have painted a scene with the caption: "Crystal says: After the bouncing ball... comes a running child." The scene shows a kid about to chase a bouncing ball out into a busy street. I used to laugh at that because it seemed so far-

fetched. Then one day, *two times* a bouncing ball sprang out from behind a parked car, into the street, right in front of me. In each case, a kid stood hesitantly by the car, wise enough not to run into the street. But I stopped laughing at Crystal and her silly saying, after that.

Here's another angle on safe driving. Suppose you think you see *something* up ahead in your lane, and you're not sure if it's a blob of cardboard, or a dog, or whatever. As soon as you get at all suspicious, bring your foot over and give the brakes a tiny *tap* and start looking around for a clear lane behind you or on one side. If there's somebody behind you, it will catch their attention pretty quickly, so if you *do* have to hit the brakes hard, the driver behind you will be alert, too. Sometimes this is called defensive driving, and it sounds a little silly, but if you can use these techniques on the rare occasion there really *is* a dog or large object blocking your lane, you won't feel so foolish about tapping your brakes a little early, before you get all your plans made up.

When the New York Giants played the San Francisco 49ers in December 1990, the football experts said that Giants quarterback Phil Simms was playing much better that year, because he had learned to throw the ball away or take a sack, rather than throw the ball into a crowd and give up a lot of interceptions. Now, that's a sensible reflex reaction. But on the last play of the game, Mr. Simms could not find an open receiver, and wound up getting sacked.

The wisdom of refusing to throw into a crowd is imperfect if there is only one play, and you don't have any chance to win, other than to throw into a crowd on the last play of the game. Every habit should be accompanied by an awareness that there are times when it doesn't apply.

Now, at this point, I wanted to give you some sage advice on how to use pre-planning and reflex response to help you in the electronics business. I had written this far, and could not think of a good example. But Frank Goodenough read my first draft and came to the rescue. He pointed out an old saying, "Never try to catch a falling knife." No matter how fast you think you are, it's very unlikely that you can grab for a falling knife 10 times without getting your hand seriously sliced at least once. Even if the knife isn't moving very fast, your hand is coming over rapidly, and it's astonishing how deep a cut you can make in that situation. In other words, it ain't worth it, and you had best plan your reflex response in advance so your head will automatically tell your hand, "Don't try it."

In the electronics business (see, I told you I would get there eventually) there's a good analogy: "Never try to catch a falling soldering iron." The odds are about as poor as trying to catch a falling knife, and the payback is equally painful. So, it's worthwhile to have a holster where the iron can be kept safely without likelihood of falling. Then drill the idea into your head, that if the soldering iron *does* fall, well, *let it*.

Frank related the story of the technician who was kneeling on the floor in front of his bench, looking for a part he had dropped. When he found it, he reached up and set it on the bench. Then, being an agile and sprightly fellow, he decided to *spring* to his feet. He put his hands on the bench, and gave a great LEAP — followed by roars of pain. He had inadvertently put one of his hands down really hard on the business end of his soldering iron, which was not in any holster. He was lucky to get out of the heavy bandages in a few weeks, but he got a very painful lesson about leaving hot items where they can be contacted accidentally.

Frank also proposed that I extend the analogy to a stack of lab equipment – a pulse generator on top of three power supplies on top of a scope on a cart. If you live in California, you know there's always a 0.05% chance of having your set-up topple in case of a 'quake. Even if you don't work out here, someone could stumble and bump into the cart. And then you have the privilege of diving to see if you can *intercept* a couple of those valuable pieces of equipment before they hit the floor. It's a little outrageous, but valuable things do sometimes take a dive. Just make sure that your head *automatically* decides that if there is a soldering iron, *that* is not a good thing to try to grab. And perhaps you could set up your equipment so that the stack is unlikely to topple. Maybe you can wire it together, or tape or strap it up so it cannot fall.

Once upon a time, when virtually all electronic equipment ran on vacuum tubes, it was easy to remember that you could get a shock from almost any node of a circuit you were troubleshooting. So the rule developed: When probing or trouble-shooting a circuit, *always* keep one hand in your pocket, rather than hold onto a chassis or rack. Then if you brush against a high voltage, you may still get a shock, but it will not cause a lot of milliamperes to flow *right past your heart*. The odds of being electrocuted used to be greatly reduced by this simple precaution.

These days, the new transistorized circuits are all at low voltage – except when they aren't. There are line-operated switch-mode power supplies, and high-voltage boosters that can put out 160 volts peak-to-peak – and suddenly that old precaution of keeping one hand in your pocket is beginning to look pretty smart again.

So, whenever I start work on a high-voltage circuit, I tack in a neon lamp in series with a 100k resistor across the high-voltage busses. Then when I see this neon's glow, I'm graphically reminded that this really *is* a high-voltage circuit, and that the power is still ON (I don't care what the power switch says) and I should revert to the mode of High Voltage Cautions. If I grab onto a really hot wire, the shock may not injure me, but I might convulse and jerk backwards. That's not a good idea if I'm standing on top of a ladder, for instance. So, looking for the glow of a neon lamp is a way to remind me to be serious, and I recommend it for you, too.

Please do try to keep aware at all times while you're driving, whether there's anybody beside you or behind you, so if you do have to make an emergency swerve, you will know if it's safe. It may save your life, or it might save your car. Be careful out there! And, keep one hand in your pocket when working on high-voltage circuits.

Comments invited! – RAP / Robert A. Pease/ Engineer

This Column was originally published in Electronic Design Magazine, December 5, 1991, and is reprinted here with the kind permission of Penton Publishing.

P.S. – If a person – or a child – jumps out in front of me, I might, if I have room, just step on the brakes. But if there is not enough room or time to brake, I might have a much better chance to miss the kid if I *swerve*. Maybe there is no on-coming traffic. But what if my only choice was to swerve and hit a parked car? I'd sure hate to wreck my car, and risk serious injury. But if that was the only way to avoid hitting that kid chasing the bouncing ball – then I am prepared to hit the car. How about you? However, to avoid hitting a dog, I am NOT going to crash into a parked car. I've planned that in advance.

– You might discuss with your Driving Teacher: what other situations should *you* think about in advance, to plan what *you* would do as a Reflex Response?

P.S. Sometimes I work under my car, for minor repairs or adjustments. I never just jack it up and climb under. I jack it and then block it VERY SECURELY, so even a moderate earthquake could not drop it onto me. Even if you don't live in earthquake country, this is a good idea for you.

P.S. One reader suggested that just holding your thumb on your horn button will not be as effective as beeping the horn rapidly. He said that beeping your horn 4 times per second is even better than once or twice per second. I wouldn't have guessed that, but maybe so. Maybe my horn should be able to *toot* itself 2 or 4 times per second, automatically? Maybe a good idea..../RAP

Chapter 61. CONCLUSION

After 60 other Chapters – what do we know?

– We know that breaking any one rule may not cause an accident – not right away. But breaking TWO rules or laws can get you in trouble much quicker. You might call that, a *conspiracy* of events.

Speeding...

We know that Speeding can get you in trouble if there are other problems like traffic, or intersections. Speeding alone often does not cause any trouble, but if you ARE headed into an accident, speeding can sure make things worse.

Vision

Vision is, I think, the most important factor in most accidents. If you think you can see, and you can't, it's only a matter of a short time before you get into trouble.

Be sure your LIGHTS are all working correctly, because if they are not able to transmit your intentions to other drivers, and they can't see what you are doing, you might get in trouble. Lights are important! Not to mention, letting YOU see where you are going.

Paying Attention...

Now, if you *could* see, but you are goofing off, and looking at other things, just NOT paying attention – that is sure to get you in trouble too. There are some places where goofing off is not a big deal. But when you are driving – that is not a place to goof off.

Slow Down Early!!

As my friends who have ridden with me know, I am always interested in better ways to get me where I am going. I am always interested in a short-cut, or a way to go faster. Fine.

BUT, at an even higher priority, I am always looking for a way to stay out of ACCIDENTS. And that means I am always looking for reasons to slow down – and especially, reasons to slow down *early*. You should be, too.

So if you avoid breaking these very basic rules, and keep an eye out for other strange places – and if you slow down early, when you see trouble ahead – then you are likely to stay out of accidents.

– Okay? – Okay!

Advice From Parents To Parents

It's probably a good idea to avoid letting your young, inexperienced driver go off on un-planned trips. Make sure they understand where they are going, and how they will get there. Try to minimize the amount of "joy-riding" they do. Because drivers without much experience can get in trouble if they have not made proper plans. If they have to make a sudden turn because they were not planning, that can cause an accident. That's basically different from when they have a well-planned errand. Sending a young driver on a useful errand is a good way to get the young driver to appreciate the responsibility of driving. I'm not saying a kid going on an errand cannot ever take an option, but spur-of-the-moment (hare-brained?) changes in route can really get you in trouble. Refer back to Accident #10 in Chapter 59 – RAP's Accidents. Heck – that little (expensive) goof was caused because I made a last-second decision to go to the fish market.

"Kids Driving Kids"

Try to avoid "kids driving kids". Yes, socializing is wonderful, and fun – but it can distract the driver from paying attention to the road and other traffic. When the driver is laughing and talking with friends, and isn't paying attention, that's when he can get in trouble. Am I right? Do you remember what *you* were like when you were young? There's a time for goofing off, and a time for paying close attention to the task at hand. Like I said, in the Chapter on Distractions... it's a bad idea to send an inexperienced driver into situations where he might not be paying attention – might be talking busily or giggling, when he needs to be paying attention to serious problems.

Here in California, a recent law came into effect, forbidding drivers under 17 from driving without adult supervision. I am sure that it drives some young drivers *NUTS!* – yet it may save their lives. I read a newspaper story about some 16-year-olds who thought it would be *terrible* to not be able to just drive anywhere they wanted, any time of day or night. Of course, one of the young drivers admitted that all her 16-year-old friends had had at least one accident... Ahem...

Best wishes to you.

And if you read the Appendices too, it won't do much harm. / R.A. Pease

◆ ◆ ◆

P.S. Jean-Marc Coblence, a French lawyer who was involved in the investigation of the accident that caused the death of Princess Diana, made this general statement:

"An accident is the perfect sum of unbelievable events".

He may be right, but I would have said that most accidents are the perfect sum of *believable* events.

Another ancient sage, who probably never saw a car accident, said, "Against stupidity, the Gods themselves contend in vain." I think that's another good way to think about most accidents. /rap

Appendices

....

Here are more than 20 topics that may be of some interest, even though they may not be strictly related to accidents or safe driving....

Appendix A – FLYING

WHY do we have a Chapter on Flying, in a book about safe driving? Because the problems that drove me to write this book arose from light-plane accidents, as you will see. Also, drivers should be aware that problems that affect you in a car, can be *much* more serious in a plane – but they can still cause problems for drivers on roads.

Flying a small plane is a very simple concept, quite intuitive. Many young adults and mature children learn to fly before they learn to drive. Many aspects of flying are easy and fun. And just think of the joy of soaring in the sky, the freedom to fly almost anywhere, and the pleasant views looking down on the ground. However, I want to also mention some of the difficult and dangerous parts of flying.

Learning to Fly

About once a year, I used to read a newspaper story about a couple kids sneaking into an airfield, and finding a plane with the keys in it. They would climb in, start the engine, and roar off down the runway. They would fly for a while until they get bored, and then find an empty road, and land the plane safely, and walk away, leaving the authorities puzzled. Where did these kids learn to fly? "We learned from reading a comic book." Well, I don't *recommend* this as the right way to learn to fly, but it does indicate that the rudiments of flying a light plane are not that terribly hard to pick up.

One time I was down in Phoenix, cooling my heels at the airport, waiting for a flight back to San Jose. And an old friend, Chuck Everhart, said, "Hey, why not fly back to San Jose with us?" I knew Chuck was a good pilot, so I said, "Sure."

We took off, with me in the right-hand seat. After a while, Chuck was looking at some maps, and talking on the radio. He said, "You take the controls, Bob." So I did. After a while, Chuck indicated I was controlling the plane pretty well, and asked, "How long have you been flying?" And I replied, "About 5 minutes...." Well, I flew the plane about half the way back to San Jose, with a lot of advice from Chuck. I learned a lot of *practical* things about flying. But keeping the nose level, not too far down, and not too high, was easy, and keeping the speed about right, was easy. Holding the right altitude was not too hard. And keeping the wings level was just as natural as riding a bicycle – if the left wing dips a little, just turn the wheel a little to the right, *gently,* to bring it back up. Of course, if I had to run the radios, that would have been MUCH too complicated for me. I can't even *hear* what the radio says, and even if I heard the words, I don't understand what they mean. And I don't know what to reply. So I am a long ways from being a pilot. Still, flying a plane can be deceptively simple. A *lot* of it is just like the comic books say....

Takeoffs and Landings

I have some friends who went on a trek to Mt. Everest's base camp, in Thangboche, Nepal. And to return home, they flew back from Lukla to Kathmandu, on a small 2-engine plane. Everybody looks at their pictures and agrees, "It must be really scary to take off from Lukla. The runway is slanted downhill, and as soon as you take off, you are out over cliffs and then over jungles...."

I looked at these pictures, and I thought, "Gee, even *I* could take off safely from Lukla. The downhill slope makes the take-off run really fast and easy to pick up air speed. The runway is just 1600 feet long. And after you come off the runway, you are already 'way up in the air, so even if you lost one engine, you have a lot of altitude. Even if you had poor visibility, after you take off and turn left a little, you can fly in almost any direction, because there are no hills or mountains in front of you. So these guys obviously don't understand flying very much, because Lukla must be one of the safest places in the world to take off from...."

Then I began to think – on the converse, if Lukla is such an easy place to take off, it is NOT a very easy or safe place to *land*. If you come in to land, and you are right on target, you touch down at the very bottom of the runway, which then slants up and slows you down really easily.

BUT, if you are too LOW, there are cliffs. If you are too high, there are – MORE CLIFFS. If there are strong crosswinds, the pilot has to make sure he is not blown off course. No, Lukla is a MUCH more scary place to LAND, than to take off. Fortunately, the Air Nepal pilots are very skilled, and they do not make many mistakes. I've flown on one of these Air Nepal Twin Otters, and the pilots were very crisp and professional. And these small planes are very safe and maneuverable, and their turboprop engines are very reliable. So, no big problems.

The fact remains that in general, takeoffs are pretty safe and easy. It is LANDINGS that are tricky. Every takeoff starts with the plane lined up with the runway, at a perfectly safe speed – 0 mph. For a landing, you need to line up with the runway, and come in at a reasonable altitude – but that is often much harder to do! The only tough things about take-offs is that the plane is usually heavy, fully loaded with fuel. And the engines are just warming up. If they started to misfire, skip, or lose power for any reason, that could be an extremely serious problem. Fortunately, engines are very reliable these days.

> I wrote a Chapter on Starting out in your car, and you know that even
> though there are some things to be careful of, it is not *nearly* as critical
> as taking off in a light plane. Likewise, parking your car, no matter how
> difficult, is never is hard as landing a plane.

Engine Reliability

The other day I was working on my car, putting some new breaker points in the ignition. I got distracted by a request to fetch some heavy things to the back yard. But I finished my work, buttoned up the engine, and started to drive to work. I got a mile down the road, doing 62 mph in the passing lane, and my engine just QUIT. I kicked in the clutch, turned off the key, shifted into neutral, and rolled half a mile, and easily got over to the breakdown lane, and parked. I checked the area that I had last been working on – the points. They were sitting there, flopping around, because I had not tightened up the screw properly. I re-set them, tightened up the screw *tight*, and went to work.

> If you have sloppy work, or a loss of power, or run out of gas in your car, that is not usually a big deal. But in a plane, that can be very very serious. Now, it is true that if you lose power, you may be able to get the plane to an airport, or land on a road, or on a field. BUT you have a pretty good chance of wrecking the plane. So, any mechanic that works on a plane must be methodical, careful, precise, and use checklists meticulously. Still, there are many other "mechanical" problems that might cause minor problems in a car – but disaster in the air. Dirty fuel, carburetor icing, bad spark, an oil leak, or loss of coolant – these can really imperil your little plane. But they might cause a breakdown in your car – perhaps leading to an accident.

Weather and Visibility

There are several other kinds of problems for flyers. If the weather is too bad, and visibility is poor, a flyer may have trouble getting down to a safe landing. May not be able to see the ground. May not be able to find the airport. There are two basic kinds of flying – VFR, or Visual Flight Rules, and IFR, or Instrument Flight Rules. If you do not have a full Instrument Rating, you are definitely not supposed to fly where you cannot see where you are going. This not only means you cannot fly *through* a fluffy little cloud, it means you are not even supposed to fly *near* clouds. (Not within 500 vertical feet, or 2000 feet horizontal.)

Even if the plane has all the instruments you need to "fly blind", and navigate through clouds, it is not safe and not legal for the pilot to try to do so, if he has not passed all the tests and completed his IFR training. Because it is too easy to get disoriented and confused when engulfed in clouds.

So, in concept, if you have your IFR rating, you can fly a little plane right into a cloud or fog bank at 100 mph – whereas I have pointed out that that is dangerous as death, at 55 mph in a car. Still, you have to know that there are not any rocks or trees in that cloud. And you have to know exactly how you will come out of that cloud.

Chuck Everhart was commuting from San Jose CA to his home in Pine Mountain Lake in the Sierra foothills, in December 1994. He had made this commute several thousand times, over 15 years. He knew what to do when the weather was good, and what to do if the weather was bad. In this case, he got a radio report of bad weather around the airport. He circled once NEAR his home airport, to confirm that the clouds were really low. Then he radioed the next airport north, at Columbia, and checked in with them, to get clearance to land, as that airport was lower and had adequate visibility.

But he never made it. For some completely inexplicable reason, he did not maintain a safe 4000 foot altitude, but he somehow got lower. With clouds all around, he hit the top of one of the very few tall pine trees on a ridge at the 2900-foot level, on Paper Cabin Ridge, just a few miles north of Pine Mountain Lake. The plane might have kept flying, but for some reason, it came straight down, and Chuck and a passenger were killed instantly. Bad show.

We always thought Chuck would be a survivor. All of Chuck's friends, at the funeral services, agreed that Chuck was very careful, serious, never did stupid things, and never took chances. There is a well-known pattern, that new pilots are pretty careful, but after they get in the vicinity of 600 to 1000 hours of flying time, they get cocky, sloppy, nonchalant – and careless. Many flying accidents occur out in that time frame. But Chuck had 5,000 flying hours.

Chuck *knew* how important it was to keep plenty of altitude. And he *knew* that the hills just north of Pine Mountain Lake were about the same height as at the airport, so he would naturally stay high and not descend until rather close to the Columbia airport. And Chuck *knew* that if he lost power, or had engine problems, he could easily descend to the west, where the hills were lower, and the visibility was better. But he didn't do that, so we can assume that he probably did not have engine problems.

So the whole thing was quite inexplicable. I hate to belabor the point, but, a bunch of Chuck's friends sat around and drank a beer, and we could not think of any way that we would EVER expect Chuck to make that mistake. But it did happen. We lost him.

In a few months, we may get the Accident Report from the NTSB, the National Transportation Safety Board. Those guys are extremely good at analyzing things, and we may find out what happened. There may be clues. But small planes like that do not have a "black box". So it is a little harder to figure out what happened.[1]

> Do you ever drive in bad visibility? Do you ever guess that you can get through, despite bad weather, and bad visibility? And you usually get through. But if you are in a plane, bad visibility may get you into a place that causes a serious accident. You can't stop and wait out the weather. Even very good flyers can be fooled by tricky conditions. (Even when all their friends say they are not likely to be fooled or bamboozled by complicated conditions and bad visibility.)

So at least, when you are driving a car, you know that you can slow down or stop and check things over. Maybe you will decide that you should leave your car parked. Or maybe you can clean your windshield off, and start out again. But even in a car, these things can cause trouble, serious trouble. You don't have to crash at 130 mph to die – you can get in a big wreck even at just 30 or 40 mph. You can get killed, or seriously injured, even when you are trying to drive slowly and carefully. People do it every day.

Still, in a plane, you do not have many options, such as to slow down, or stop and park. When Charles Lindbergh was first flying the mail, his mother told him, "Now, be sure to fly low and slow." She wanted him to play it safe. He was too polite to tell her, that "low and slow" is NOT the right way to fly safely. High and medium-fast is much safer for flying. But in a car, if you have a tough situation, low and slow is feasible, and it may be a good way to stay out of trouble.

Mid-Air Collisions

Some friends have assured me that mid-air collisions are NOT the major cause of light-plane crashes. But I read a book, *Avoiding Mid-Air Collisions*, by Ms. Shari Stamford Krause.* She pointed out that there are SO many ways that another plane can sneak up behind you, that one should not make any assumptions about collisions, unless you are really good at looking all around. Even then, in grey or hazy conditions, a plane can get surprisingly close before you see it. You look at your instruments for 3 seconds, or poke at your radio, and look up – and there is another plane really MUCH too close. How does that happen? Ah – all too easily.

After reading Ms. Krause's book, I decided that I would not want to take up flying unless I could get a couple car headlights mounted on my plane, to make it easier for other pilots to see me. But that does not help visibility from other angles....

Another friend of mine, Ron Brown, was giving a student some flying lessons, flying over the Connecticut River in clear weather. Another plane came up behind him, at an angle, and did not see him, and ripped off his tail. Ron's plane went out of control and crashed, and he was killed.

I saw the NTSB report, a big thick document. Basically it said, if somebody comes up behind you, and is not paying attention, you don't have much of a chance to avoid an accident. You have to have some confidence that the other pilot will see and avoid you.

> Watching out for other cars is a very important part of driving. But at least you don't have to look out for cars coming at you from below or above, or at bad angles. Most cars are either behind you or ahead of you, or coming in on a side street. AH – but when you are in a parking lot, another driver may be cutting across the lot at an angle! Be EXTRA careful in such a case!!! And, YOU should avoid cutting across that parking lot, unless *YOU* can clearly see that you are not going to imperil another car.

Dead-End Streets

Have you ever driven your car up a street, and discovered that it was a dead-end street? Well, you put on the brakes, and make a U-turn, or back up a couple times, and get turned around, and go back and try another street. But, in an airplane it is not that easy.

Kathy Raphael was learning to fly, and she already had her private Pilot's license. She had 109 hours of flight time. She was working on her instrument ratings, and she was planning to be an airline pilot. We joked with her about "Royal Kathy Airlines".

She went up with her instructor and one other student, to practice mountain flying. They were going to make a few landings, and then fly over the Sierras, and land at Bridgeport CA, on the east side of the Sierras, and then fly back.

They made some practice landings up at Columbia Airport, and then continued up into the higher foothills, northeast of Columbia California, up toward Sonora Pass. Their plane was last sighted by a hiker, flying about 3,000 feet above Kennedy Meadows.

UNFORTUNATELY, as they continued east, they must have descended – inexplicably – and then got headed up into a canyon. The canyon got narrower, and narrower, and they tried to climb out. But the walls of the canyon kept rising faster than the plane could climb. Then the canyon took a turn, and they saw – a solid wall. No way out.

The instructor apparently tried a hammerhead stall – a wingover – to zoom up, and stall, and then fall back, under control, and return the way they had come in. But it did not work. They did not have enough air-speed, nor enough altitude, and all three people were killed instantly.

Very sad. Because all three pilots, the instructor, and the two students, ALL knew that it is unsafe to fly up a canyon. Heck, even *I* know *that*. If there is something in a canyon worth looking at, then you fly DOWN the canyon. Yet the fact remains, inexplicable, that they DID fly up the canyon, and they paid a very high price.[2]

◆ ◆ ◆

There is another slightly similar story; I read the book, and I saw the story on TV: "And I Alone Survived". A woman decided to fly with a couple friends, over to Bishop California, which, again, is on the east side of the Sierras. They started out in pretty good weather, and ascended to get over Independence Pass. Unfortunately, they got diverted into the WRONG valley. When they approached the pass, it was a higher pass than they expected, and it was, again, too narrow to turn or circle. The plane crashed about 40 feet below the pass. One person was killed instantly, one person died after a few hours, and the lone survivor decided she had better walk out, rather than wait at the pass to be rescued. She could see the lights of cars and towns, just 15 miles away to the east.

(Note, the western slopes of the Sierras are typically fairly shallow, and wooded, and extend for dozens of miles. The slopes on the East are normally much steeper and shorter. Tougher for hiking, but not so far to hike.) She hiked down some very steep mountainsides, and negotiated her way around cliffs and difficult vegetation, and walked out to civilization that next day. Tough lady, walking 20 miles over uncharted countryside with no maps, no trails, and a broken arm....

Still, the situation was similar: The pilot started up a valley where he did not want to be, and got trapped in a narrow canyon, and could not climb enough, and could not turn back or circle. Crunch. Ouch.

So I'll repeat: the next time you find yourself on a narrow dead-end street, and you have to turn around, be glad you are not in a light plane.

The Right Way?

I read another book, about mountain climbing: "Eiger Dreams", by Jon Krakauer.
The author pointed out that to get to most of the challenging mountain climbing in
Alaska, you have to hire a bush pilot to fly you in. So he thought it was important to
explain some of the essential rules of mountain flying.

FIRST of all, the pilot must not ASSUME that he can cross any ridge or pass.
There are so many variables – weather, icing conditions, power or lack of power,
headwinds, tailwinds, and downdrafts, that every attempt to fly over a ridge or
mountain or pass should be assumed to be unlikely. If you think you have 800
pounds on board, but it's actually 950, you won't be able to climb as well as you first
thought you were doing. Or, a crummy little downdraft may cause you to be just a
few hundred feet lower than you thought you should be. Even a little tailwind,
which is normally considered helpful, may cause you to arrive at a ridge before you
had time to ascend as much as you wanted....

CONSEQUENTLY, you should never approach a ridge or wall or pass, straight-on.
You should angle up to it. Then, if there are not bad headwinds, or downdrafts, and
if you have a safe margin of altitude, you veer *toward* the pass and go over it, and
down the far side. But if you do NOT have enough altitude, or if you do NOT like
the downdrafts, then you just veer AWAY from the pass, and go back, and circle, and
get a little higher, and try again. But any assumption that you will get over that ridge
is very dangerous. So this wisdom should be added together with the rule, "Never fly
up a canyon". Maybe some more of this kind of planning could help avoid several
kinds of accidents.

A Weighty Problem

In April of 1996, little Jessica Dubroff took off from Half Moon Bay, California, and
flew a light plane to Cheyenne Wyoming. If you didn't count a couple hours when
she took a nap and her flying instructor took the controls, she might have been the
youngest person to fly across the USA. But shortly after the take-off from Cheyenne,
the plane crashed, and Jessica and her father and her flight instructor were killed.
And there was a LOT of criticism in the newspapers about anybody who would let a
little kid fly a plane.

As the facts became clearer, the cause of the accident began to make at least
some rational sense. The plane did *not* crash because it was just too heavy. And it
did not crash because Jessica was a lousy pilot, or stupid. It crashed partly because
she was a little kid, and because she was inexperienced, and because several other
mistakes were made.

The plane was heavily loaded, but its gross weight was not appreciably over the
limit for the elevation and other conditions. However, there was a good bit of heavy
camping equipment in the back of the plane. And what was up front? Little Jessica,
along with one adult. So while the total weight of the plane was not excessive, the
plane *was* tail-heavy. The center of gravity was so far back, it was outside the
allowable limit for that plane. The plane was too tail-heavy too fly efficiently, and it

was not able to climb. When it hit rough weather and stalled, it was impossible to control.

If Jessica had been sitting in back, and an adult up front, would that have made the plane more controllable? Sure. Would a more experienced pilot have recognized the tail-heavy condition? Possibly. Still, it was a *conspiracy of events* that led to this unfortunate crash.[3]

> Most automobile accidents are not caused by a single reason, but by a combination or conspiracy of events. That's one of my major arguments. A car that is too tail-heavy can also be difficult to control. And an inexperienced driver may fail to recognize the problems as they develop. But at least in a car, if it starts to feel weird, you can drive slowly.

WHY ARE WE INTERESTED IN THIS?

Why am I mentioning all this junk about flying? Why am I so concerned about a couple of young people dying?

First of all, I have always been interested in flying, and several times I have thought about taking up flying. So I was very concerned about these accidents that took smart, competent people away from us. How did they happen?

Air Safety

And then, how could we keep it from happening again? Could we set up a radio transmitter to blast away at any plane that approaches that canyon, to warn them to stay out? No, that probably would not work. Could we set up a tall sign-post? No. A sign on a long rope stretched across the canyon? Not feasible! Flashing lights? Maybe, but unlikely.

I remember that *Flying* Magazine used to publish pilots' stories of how they did something stupid, and got into an accident, or a near-accident. I still remember pilots' stories from 30 years ago: "I took off with my ailerons locked, and I had a heck of a time maneuvering back to land, with no roll control." Or, "I took off and assumed I could get through under the weather – or – if I couldn't – at least I could get back to my home field. Bad idea." These stories really were impressive. Scary and impressive. They really made an impression on me.

What Can I Do for Air Safety?

I thought and thought – what can I do to promote air safety? And I realized – not a hell of a lot. I can't write those stories – only the pilots can do that. But then I thought, well, could I help young drivers avoid car accidents? And I decided, yes.

I am a good enough writer, and I can tell the stories about car accidents. I can list a lot of things a young driver should know – how to avoid doing dumb things that can cause accidents. And I can illustrate this with stories of actual accidents – the kind of stories that young people will listen to (rather than dumb preaching). So that is what I am doing. So, as I *veered* away from trying to improve air safety, I wound up writing this book. That's why these stories are important. Also, I plan to contribute 1/3 of the net profits from this book to Air Safety. Heaven only knows what that will amount to.

Conclusions...

So, I wrote down several ideas, in this Appendix, to illustrate that certain problems are really somewhat SIMILAR, between flying and driving a car. But in fact the real level of danger is quite DIFFERENT. Most problems or mistakes are *a lot* more serious and dangerous, in a plane. Many of the mistakes you can make in an airplane will immediately kill you, but if you are really lucky and clever you might survive. In a car, most of the mistakes will not kill you, but if you work really hard or are extremely clever, only then can you kill yourself.

◆ ◆ ◆

1. Chuck Everhart's plane hit a couple pine trees fairly high, about 40 feet off the ground. The NTSB investigator climbed up a tree and said he saw paint on the tree, at a level where the trunk was snapped off, about 5 inches in diameter. Then, 100 yards in horizontal distance beyond the ridge-top, the plane hit the ground 300 feet down (lower). All of Chuck's friends could not think of any obvious reason why the plane would not glide a LOT further than that. Perhaps the controls jammed and caused the plane to put in extreme negative G's. Or maybe it pulled up and stalled and flopped down. So we had to wait for the NTSB report, to find out what really happened.

When we read the NTSB report, we saw that the crash site was just 100 yards west of the ridge, but 250 yards from the trees. That explained why the plane was so close to the ridge – it was not flying perpendicular to the ridge, but at an angle.

The NTSB Investigators found a cellular phone near the crash site. Telephone company records showed that Chuck had made several phone calls just before the crash, and was just dialling another call at the time of the crash. So there's another way a portable phone can get you in trouble. In your car, as in a plane, don't let a phone call distract you from paying attention to your driving.

2. There was also another plane crash site in that same canyon where Kathy died, right near by. I still need to check out the exact location of the crash site. I want to take a hike up there. Of course, the planes' wreckage has been removed. But I just want to look at that damned canyon.

3. I got a "Brief Of Accident" from the NTSB, File No. 1514, 04/11/96, concerning the crash of "Jessica Dubroff's plane". It did not provide a lot of new information EXCEPT to note that the plane was 84 pounds overweight! That's serious!! If you combine that with poor weather, gusts and rain and windshear, PLUS a serious tail-heavy condition (which was not mentioned in the Brief), you can just tell why the plane could not stay in the air. Sigh....

If YOU were teaching a student to drive, and he got into an accident because you didn't teach him right – you'd feel terrible, right? So how can you make your student smarter than you are? Maybe it would take CRITICAL THINKING, which involves teaching the student to QUESTION everything his teacher says. Of course, even if your students QUESTION YOU a lot of the time, YOU should try to be correct, most of the time.

Should Jessica Dubroff have questionned her Flying Instructor's computations of the plane's weight? In retrospect, yes, that probably would have been a good idea. Yes, it's a bit improbable, to expect a 6-year old kid to correct her teacher. Maybe every good teacher should purposefully insert little "mistakes" into his teaching, to encourage the students to catch and correct their teacher's errors. Is that too much to expect? Maybe, but, hey, it's worth a try. / rap

– Note: this Appendix was reviewed by R. Dobkin, R. Sleeth, J. T. LoSciuto, W. Baroudi, T. Myers, and J. Duelks.

Appendix B – LEARNING TO DRIVE

Preliminary Education

Many young people learn how to drive a bicycle. After a number of years of bicycling, you have learned a lot of the things you should know for driving a car. You learned that there are limitations on acceleration, and on traction. You learned that braking is important, judgement and timing are important, judging a curve and your speed as approaching it are important – and if you goof, it hurts. I rode my bicycles several thousand miles before I got to drive a car.

When I was young, a lot of people lived on farms, and learned to drive tractors or farm trucks. If you can drive around on back lots and farm roads (as many of my friends did), and if you can keep your speed down so you don't get hurt, you can learn a lot. But these days, not many people live on farms, nor in the country. Unfortunately.

Learning to Drive a Car...

When it really comes time to learn to drive a car, legally, that is a slightly different art. Let's say you start studying the motor vehicle rules. Do you learn in school, in a driving school, or from a parent, or from some other person?

Many people point out that if a kid learns from his father or mother, this can be a VERY stressful situation, so, you shouldn't do it. This may be true. If you have a good relationship with your kid, you might think that you can teach this reasonable young person to drive. However, if all does not go well, the good relationship might go bad. There are as many ways for a relationship to go bad, as one can IMAGINE. "He burned up the clutch because he didn't do what I told him...." "My mother told me to turn left, but she meant right, and I turned left and the truck hit us...." Any number of things COULD happen.

Yes, I Did Some Teaching...

Now, I have to say, I *did* teach my sons to drive. I was driving an old Beetle, and it's not really hard to learn to slip the clutch with such a low first gear. It's not too hard to steer or to shift. Just an ordinary challenge. They were reasonably good learners, and we never really had any trouble. We never really got mad at each other, because we were able to choose some fairly low-stress locations to learn to drive – empty parking lots, etc.

Come to think of it, I did also teach my wife to drive, 30 years ago. She was a good bicyclist, with many thousands of miles on fast touring bicycles. Thus I was not surprised that she quickly learned to be a good driver and a good learner, and did not get mad at me – well, at least she did not admit to getting mad. Not very much.

One day down by Barnstable Mass, we were sitting at an intersection, with the engine idling, debating and deciding which way to go next. We decided. She shifted into first gear. Now, she forgot to put in the clutch. But she did it so NICELY, that the gearbox went into first, without any graunch. Away we went. I suggested she might want to put in the clutch next time. Now she does.

(Note, the cars SHE drives get their gearbox to last at least as far as MY cars. I think that might have something to do with the fact that most of my cars, for 28 years, have been pre-owned. Pre-driven. Put it this way, if some guy bought a brand new VW, and mistreated it for 80,000 miles, I can drive it 170,000 more by nursing it.)

Steps of Learning...

Since first gear in most cars is a fairly jerky gear, and hard for anybody to drive smoothly in, we got into second gear as early as possible. Then, sometimes into third. But, these young guys did know how to ride a bicycle pretty well. They knew how to steer, and how to put on brakes. Would I be nervous about taking on the task of teaching somebody to drive, if they did not know how to ride a bike?? Yeah, I would. If I ran into problems, I would stop fast, and go to a professional teacher. Maybe that is a good rule.

After the basic skills are reasonably well learned, and after a suitable learner's permit is obtained, it may be a good time to go out on the road. You want to choose some VERY empty roads, preferably on an early Sunday morning, so the driver can learn about LANES. You should be able to go as slow as needed. Fortunately, these days it is easy to get good brakes. If in danger or in doubt, stepping on the brakes solves a LOT of problems.

I will not say that there is any *one way* to teach a beginner to learn to drive that is necessarily good, or BAD, but you have to plan so that errors will not cause serious problems. You have to figure out how to get that done. Maybe a driving school with a teacher with a good reputation is a good choice. I would not want to choose any procedure, randomly.

Automatic Shift?

If you only have an automatic shift car, that is not necessarily bad. Driving schools will teach a person whichever gearshift they want. Or both. Most young people are coordinated enough to learn on a stick-shift. But I have seen some drivers whose co-ordination is so marginal, and their thinking is so awkward and easily flustered, that I would not recommend stick-shift driving, at least not at first.

First Things First

Of course, as I said in my first Chapter, it is important to know how to STOP before you get started. Now, if a kid has ridden bicycles a lot, then braking is just a simple variation on something they already know. If the kid has never driven anything with brakes, well, maybe you just start at the top of a slanted parking lot, and practice braking even before you put the car in gear, before you start the engine.

Steering is the same idea: If I had to teach a kid who has never ridden a bicycle or any other vehicle – that would be a real challenge!! I could probably do it, but the younger a person learns an art such as steering, the better.

Who is a Teacher?

Let me tell you one thing about kids learning to drive. For one reason or another, you might decide that you should not go out and teach your kid how to drive. BUT you have ALREADY taught your kid a lot about driving, by your example. If you never come to a full stop at stop signs, your kids MIGHT have already learned to do that. Or they might learn to rebel and to stop at every stop sign. But your attitudes are put into their heads, from a very early age. So you should almost ALWAYS try to set a good example. Got the picture?

I mean, my father was a professional truck driver, and I think he was pretty conservative, careful, and cautious. But if he ever had to drive vigorously, I have NO DOUBT that he could have done that well. But I almost never saw him drive in a pushy or aggressive way – because he did not have to.

The Driving Test

When a young person has been driving, that tends to lead to "the driving test". What car to drive? Whatever, make sure all lights and equipment are working, before you go in for the driver's test. And, insurance, too!

Insurance?

Of course, a MAJOR question is, can the adult get the appropriate insurance? Or can the kid help pay for his insurance? Will the driver's license permit the kid to get a job that he could not get without it? This is a VERY complicated area. Insurance costs when a young driver is added, can cost THOUSANDS of dollars in additional costs, in many city locations. In other places, just hundreds. Either way, a very serious consideration.

When I got my license, my father obtained a statement from our insurance company that it was OK for me to drive our family car (a 1955 Packard Clipper) ONLY on rare occasions. And that is what I did. OK, I survived that. Mostly, I was permitted to drive a pickup or truck or bus at work. I never really had any problems at work. I drove fairly carefully. And I still rode my bicycle a few miles to get to work. Good exercise. I did not buy a car, and buy insurance, until 5 years after I had my license.

What This Book is NOT...

One thing I think I should remind you about this book: This is NOT a do-it-yourself book, for a person learning to drive. This book is not a substitute for a good teacher. This book is not a substitute even for a pretty good teacher.

But it is intended to go beyond the first teacher. After you have learned everything you can from one teacher, it is usually time to go on to another teacher, so you can get a new slant on things, and so you can learn more things. This book can be that teacher. Or, a guidebook for that teacher. Or, even better, this book *plus* another person – an adult – or even another young driver – can help bring a fairly green driver, up to a reasonable level of awareness. Of course, there is no substitute for practice. And, no substitute for THINKING.

– That has covered most of the topics I planned to cover. This mini-chapter, or Appendix, is NOT a course on how to teach driving, but notes and comments on any course of teaching or learning you may plan or consider. This is not a completely-covered topic, but just some notes on the *philosophy* about learning to drive, and notes on teaching.

P.S. — A Note to Driving Teachers:

Do you know all the ideas and techniques in this book? You may be a better Driving Instructor than Bob Pease is — but you'll probably be better yet if you read this book. Obviously, you can't teach every advanced driving topic to every student. There's not time to do that. But you can recommend to every student that they ought to understand some of these advanced topics. Or, include the book as part of your course. Make some of it required reading. Some of Pease's suggestions are very basic — not just advanced.

Appendix C – THINKING

Nobody has to read this. It's just for fun. But I thought it would be good to write about the philosophy of THINKING. At first I was going to write a book showing people how to stay out of accidents. But then I realized that while you can *train* people on some topics – and you should – there are many situations that you can not train for. You have to educate people, and teach them how to think. I wrote a Column on Critical Thinking, a few years ago, and it was pretty straightforward: You teach young people how to ask questions, in a skeptical way, and get them in a mood to search for a thoughtful answer. I'll paraphrase that Column, 1000 words into 2: "Question Authority".

But I liked my Reflex Response Column, too – (Chapter 60). I pointed out that in some cases, you just cannot sit around in the middle of intersections and ponder what to do while traffic is bearing down on you. You have to categorize things into cases that you can analyze in advance, and if you then see this situation materializing, you will know what you should do. I mean, at what age do young children learn to move their feet away, if they drop something sharp or dangerous, like a pair of scissors? And at what age do they learn to put a foot out to catch a valuable or delicate item, such as a watch? Surely, at a young age. And, that's a pretty fast amount of reflex response! An object falls 3 feet in less than 0.5 seconds. That is pretty fast response, considering that it is hard to pull your foot off the gas-pedal, and get it on the brake pedal, in less than 0.6 seconds!

Driver Training?

NOW, the notion of training yourself to do certain things, on a programmed basis, sounds pretty dreary and depressing, even if it is a necessary and valuable part of driving a car. BUT, the good part is, you are supposed to do your thinking and arguing and planning and debating, before the fact. So some of these cases can bring young drivers to do a lot of thinking. I like that.

Recently I ran into a quote allegedly from Henry Ford: "Thinking is very difficult. That's why very few people do it." I am still trying to verify this quote, but it sure does sound like Henry. Anyhow, I hope to add a few more comments in here, to encourage thinking.

That is one of the functions of Quiz Number Two – to get the young drivers to think about situations. If a parent wants to think about these questions, too, that is fine. And then you might even discuss it with your kid.

I guess I may have finally gotten the last of this chapter written. For a long time, I had no idea what I would write. I hope I have been able to suggest the right kind of attack on some rhetorical questions.

Because if you are playing baseball or driving a car, you do want to be well primed and trained to do the right thing, in many particular cases. The quote from Branch Rickey, "Good luck is the residue of design" is a good one. BUT, every once in a while, when you are driving along, you run into a situation that nobody ever thought of before. THINK FAST!! Can you act decisively and do some good, and perhaps save a person's life, and not cause problems? – and avoid an accident? – or not cause an accident? That's where the thinking comes in – the training of yourself to think, and analyze problems, and come to a reasonable solution – a good decision.

Note, I did not say, a PERFECT solution. If I wanted this book to be PERFECT, it might take 2 more years to get it out, and that would be WRONG. If I had done it PERFECTLY, I would have had it out 5 or 10 years ago, and saved a lot more lives. But that's not possible. So I plan to get this book, as good as possible, as quickly as possible. I'm not waiting until I get it "perfect". OK?

Thinking versus Driving...

One time, when I was a kid, I heard that intelligent people do not make good drivers. At that time, I was the valedictorian of my class, and I got high grades on most of my classes, and I did well at taking tests. So I was a little disappointed that I was gonna be condemned to be a lousy driver.

But I think I have become a very GOOD driver. Not perfect, and maybe not excellent, but much better than average. After all, if I was an average driver, my insurance claims would be AVERAGE. But my actual claims over the last 30 years have been about 2% of what I pay the insurance company. Yet I think I am also an intelligent person. So, was that old pronouncement wrong?

Yeah. I think that old statement, that "intelligent" people will be bad drivers, is too vague. Maybe "intellectuals" or "theorists" or people who do a lot of conceptual work, are not such good drivers. Maybe they get distracted while thinking about things. Maybe they do not pay attention to the road. But I do not usually have those problems. Even when I am deep in thought, I do not ignore what is going on ahead of me. So, maybe that explains why I am not as bad a driver as that old dictum indicated.

I may add in some more ideas later. But if I can teach your kids to drive safely, I've done a good job. If I can teach them to THINK, then I did a *very* good job.

– Your comments are invited...(See Appendix O.) / RAP

Appendix D – REVIEWS of OTHER BOOKS

1. *Sportsmanlike Driving* by the American Automobile Association, with Dr. Francis C. Kenel, coordinating Author. Ninth Edition, 1994. ISBN: 0-07-001338-1 or 0-07-001338-X (paperback). About $24. Glencoe Division of Macmillan/ McGraw-Hill School Book Publishing Company.

– This is a pretty good classbook, and has been updated about 7 times since its first edition in 1955. It is well written for 5th graders, or people who read (or think) at the fifth grade level. It is very basic and does not cover much intermediate or advanced material. I mean, when it covers "short trips" or "long trips", it does not even mention the word *money*. For a beginning driver, it should take about an hour to read this book and prove you know and understand everything in it. Plenty of nice pictures. It's not a bad book, for basics. I've seen worse.

2. *Wild In the Streets: The Boston Driver's Handbook*, by Richard Gerstman and Richard Trachtman, 1982. ISBN: 0-201-11000-8. Yes, still in print!! Addison Wesley. 1 Jacob Drive, Reading, Mass. 01867. Send $8.61, which includes tax and mailing. The outrageous ideas in this book are partly true – and partly tongue-in-cheek. You figure it out, which is what! Still, true or not, those of you who have driven around Boston will agree that most of this is consistent with the Boston driver's mentality.

3. *In the Driver's Seat*, Davis, Maryott, and Stiska, Houghton Mifflin, 1978. ISBN: 0-395256-87-9, out of print. This has some better insights than *Sportsmanlike Driving*. It seems to be written for the 7th to 9th-grade level. But, like most driver's education books, it is full of platitudes and oversimplified situations.

4. Tom and Ray Magliozzi – the Car Talk Guys. They call themselves, "Click and Clack, the Tappet Brothers". They have published a book – and they write a column in some newspapers – and they have a weekly radio program on National Public Radio. Check your local radio stations to find the NPR station, and ask the station when their show, "Car Talk", is on. It's kind of wacky, but you may learn to like it, if you are interested in cars. Also they have a booklet. "Ten Ways you may be Ruining Your Car Without Even Knowing It!" (Send $3.00 and a stamped self-addressed envelope Number 10 envelope with 55 cents (1.9 ounces worth) postage.)

Tom and Ray Magliozzi also have a CD-ROM and/or a Cassette tape of "The Best of Car Talk". To order, call (303) 595-5905.

5. Is their old book still in print? Yes! *Car Talk*, by Tom and Ray Magliozzi. Dell Books, a division of Bantam Doubleday Dell Publishing, New York. 1991. ISBN: 0-440-50364-7. About $14.

– These guys are mostly concerned about keeping your car running. But they do give good advice on how to avoid doing stupid things that can cause accidents. I do NOT agree with everything they say, but I do tune in every weekend. Fun. Zany. Wild sense of humor. I love them, even if they sometimes seem to ignore various true or reasonable answers.

6. *High-Performance Driving*, Paul Petersen, Simon & Schuster, 1974; ISBN: 671-27117-2. Good ideas for moderate-to-high performance driving. Tips on best performance, cornering on race courses, maximum speed on the race course, etc. Most hints are, "Avoid doing *this*, to avoid going out of control and running off the road at high speed and damaging your car." This will be of limited value to most of my readers. This covers mostly advanced topics, for people planning to do off-road racing. I might recommend a book like this, for advanced drivers who have a reason to do high-speed stuff – with a mention of the risks.

7. *Surviving an Accident*, 1994, by Robert Saperstein, J. D., and Dana Saperstein, Ph.D. Pathfinder Publishing of CA, 458 Dorothy Avenue, Ventura CA. 93003. (805) 642-9278. ISBN: 0-934793-55-7. How to handle legal, psychological, and medical aspects of your accident after you have it. Good Lord!! They tell you that you may want to read this book before you have an accident, so you can know how to behave after the accident. Bleeah!! People ought to mostly read MY book, so they have a better chance to AVOID the accident, which these authors never even *thought of*. I list this book as a reference, but I recommend that you should think and plan so as to not have to use it. Of course, I have a short chapter on this topic, what to do after you had an accident, but not a lot – just enough to keep you out of trouble.

8. *Zen Driving*, K. T. Berger, Ballentine, 1988. ISBN: 0-345-35350-1. Lots of platitudes and philosophical truisms. Maybe if you are already a follower of Zen, this might be helpful, but otherwise it is just annoying.

– "Zen never explains but indicates".

– "Think of you and your car as one unit."

– "A clear mind, No – thought".

– "You also want to be clear of all the *shoulds* and *should-nots* of driving."

– "Don't think about it, just do it." (NOTE: this is what I recommend in my Chapter on Reflex Response. I teach you how to do that, but these book gives you no plan, just the platitude....)

There are a few good ideas in here, but not much helpful to a young or inexperienced driver.

9. *Hit Me – I Need the Money*; Marjorie Berte, ICS Press, 243 Kearney St. SF CA 94108. 1991. ISBN: 1-55815-152-4. A lot about the insurance industry, and legal/insurance problems. They wanna cut down on the cost of insurance – so do I,

but from a slightly different angle. These guys want to add lots of laws and regulations to inhibit bad driving. Largely, that's ineffective, as we already have a whole bushel of doggone laws that we break all the time. What's the point in having MORE laws that we'll just break? I just want to make it easier to obey the laws, especially when it is important.

If you are really interested in the interactions between lawyers, insurance companies, and law-makers – if you are interested where your insurance money goes – you can read this one. The rest of us will pass.

10. *A Policy on Arterial Highways in Urban Areas*, written and published by the American Association of State Highway Officials, Washington DC, 1957. This is kind of fun to read, because it explains the policies and guidelines of how a lot of our highways got built. In a case like the "mixmaster" in Hartford, (see in my Chapter on Lanes) where traffic has to enter on the right, and cross through heavy traffic trying to exit on the right in a short distance – which this book calls "weaving" – it recommends several hundred feet of separation be provided between the entrance ramp and the exit ramps, *depending on* the amount of traffic volume. On page 490, it states, for example, "Weaving sections often simplify the layout of interchanges and result in right-of-way and construction economy. Weaving movements of small volume, as well as certain weaving volumes with proper length and width of weaving sections, operate satisfactorily. Their use at minor interchanges often are appropriate but for large volume weaving movements during peak hours, probable results are traffic stream friction, reduced speed of operation, and lowered capacity." In other words, highway engineers knew 40 years ago that making a "mixmaster" would make a mess, but sometimes they didn't want to believe it, so they built a bad one, anyhow. Perhaps they wanted to pretend the traffic volume would be small, so they tried to build the road on the cheapest format. Ahem....

11. *Highway Engineering*, Clarkson Oglesby and R. Gary Hicks, John Wiley & Sons, 1954 & 1982 (Fourth Edition). ISBN: 0-471-02936-X. This is a textbook for college courses. A lot of this is rather detailed and technical info for the design and engineering of roads, but there is a good chapter on how the design of highways affects traffic safety. There is a nice chart on page 285 that shows the recommended length of a passing zone at speeds such as 30 mph (100 feet), 40 mph (1500 feet) or 60 mph (2200 feet).

12. I have also talked a little with Derek Scott at Apex Driving School (San Francisco) – (415) 566-4999 – he had some fair ideas on the philosophy of safe driving.

My next attack was to call on the Calif. Auto Assoc'n, to ask their advice on what's a good book on learning how to drive safely – "for my nephew". They just recommended *Sportsmanlike Driving*, see above.

Also I'll look into driving schools. And "traffic schools". I may even show up by bicycle at a Driving School and pretend to be a dummy, and see what I learn – see what they teach me.

X

13. *Avoiding Mid-Air Collisions*, Shari Stamford Krause, PhD., 1995, TAB Books, a Division of McGraw Hill, New York. ISBN: 0-07-035944-X. About $16.95. This mostly deals with the problems of flying a light plane in the case of various problems – weather, other planes, poor visibility, and "the myths and realities of mid-air collision avoidance". If I were a beginning flyer, I would want to take this book out of the library every year or two, even if it did scare the hell out of me. It analyzes actual case studies of mid-air-collisions – what went wrong and how they could have been prevented.

14. *Avoiding Common Pilot Errors – An Air Traffic Controller's View*, John Stewart, Tab Books, Blue Ridge Summit PA; 1989.

If you are really taking up flying, you'll want to learn about all the standard procedures for talking to an Air Traffic Controller (ATC). Then, when you think you know what you are doing, read this book, and you'll learn about how intricate and confusing life can be. A bunch of little problems and confusions and miscommunications. Man, you gotta be *smart* to talk to these guys, and avoid confusion! Here's an example: A guy with a lawn-mowing tractor wanted permission to cross a runway. When he transmitted his request to the tower, there was apparently a lot of static on the radio, as another aircraft was transmitting on the same channel. He waited and got no reply. So he transmitted his name, location and identity again. The tower controller asked him to explain his request, saying, "Go ahead", as in, "Go ahead and state your request". Of course the lawnmower began to "Go ahead" and proceed across a busy runway, until he looked up and saw planes headed his way....

Tab Books puts out a whole series on Flying, including:

– *Mountain Flying*, by Doug Geeting and Steve Woerner.

– *ABCs of Safe Flying*, by David Frazier.

– *The Art of Instrument Flying*, by J.R. Williams.

I'll check into these.

15. *I Learned About Flying from That*, Vol. 2 (out of print) and *I Learned About Flying from That*, Vol. 3, by the editors of Flying Magazine; Tab Books. About $15, paperback. A friend informed me of this, and I immediately went out and ordered Vol. 3. As I mentioned in the Appendix on Flying, these are very educational, and scary, and entertaining to read. I was alternately amused, but mostly horrified about how easy it is to get into trouble in a small plane.

16. *Motorcycling Excellence: The Motorcycle Safety Foundation's Guide to Skills, Knowledge, and Strategies for Riding Right*, Whitehorse Press, about $20. ISBN: 1-884313-01-9. This is a pretty good book for motorcyclists to get educated about safe riding practices. I'm not an expert on motorcycling (though I did try it, one weekend in Kathmandu).

But I know that motorcyclists need all the help they can get, to avoid accidents. There are a lot of things you can do to get in trouble on a motorcycle, that you don't have to worry about in a car. The worst problem, as I see it, is that many drivers just don't see or notice a motorcycle. Sometimes they just drive out in front of a motorcycle. I'll buy a 'cycle as soon as I can buy one with this accessory: a laser hologram that makes my motorcycle *appear like* a large dump truck – then other drivers would beware and respect me. But that is not going to happen, not very soon.

17. *The Book of Expert Driving*, E. D. Fales, Jr., Bantam Books, 1971, out of print. This was a pretty good book for its day. I didn't find any good ideas in this book that I hadn't covered. But it had a lot of silly old-fashioned statements. Such as – "The only safe rule for controlling skids is never get into one. They are terribly dangerous." Needless to say, Mr. Fales never teaches you how to practice your skidding!

18. *Superdriver*, Sir John Whitmore, Motorbooks International, P. O. Box 2, Osceola, WI 54020. ISBN: 0-87938-315-1, about $20, out of print. - This book encourages the driver to be alert and a master of (British) highway driving. Go faster without accidents. Safer and swifter, on the open road and on the race track. Liberate the driving skills within your mind. Not a bad book, but a little different emphasis than the beginning driver needs, especially in the USA. Emphasis on avoiding accidents is secondary. But the emphasis on staying alert and aware, is excellent.

19. *How to Keep Your VW Alive*, 1992, John Muir Press, Santa Fe, NM. About $18. The late John Muir wrote this – a classic book. If you want to buy and drive an old VW, that is the book you need. I do not know how many Beetles and Busses are still running, but there's a LOT, out here in California.

◆◆◆

– Are there any good books on how to drive safely and avoid accidents? Not until right now!! I hope you are enjoying reading *my* book. / R. A. Pease

Appendix E – What's All This VW Stuff, Anyhow?

Why do I like VWs? Well, I have gotten a lot of reliable miles, and a lot of enjoyable miles, in the last 40 years in VWs. I don't want to bore you, but I have some good feelings about them. They are fun and interesting and challenging to drive. I mean, if you like to just climb into a car, and step on the gas and go, well, that's a different car. I like to shift. I like to think. I like to feel the road under me. I like to feel the torque rise up. Even old VW Beetles had some of this *"Fahrvergnugen"*. All that word means is, Enjoyment (vergnugen) of driving (fahren). Not Boring.

I have driven a bunch of cars recently, and when you step on the gas, they are BORING. (See the Appendix on Rentals.) Yes, they will eventually go fast. But when you get in a VW Rabbit or Golf, or an *interesting* car, as you start out in first, and shift into second, and *nail it* – really floor it – in just a couple seconds, the acceleration really turns on, and the torque is coming up, and you have to get ready to shift really soon. Then in third, you have to think, and plan – where is the first curve? – when do I have to ease my foot off the gas? I really like that. Even a VW Beetle accelerates crisply enough, to make you think.

The Shape of the Acceleration Curve...

Y' know – I built an accelerometer. I should have taken some *curves* on the acceleration of different cars – but I did not have time to do that right.

If *you* like to drive a big Chrysler or a Chevy Caprice or a Ford Taurus, they may have *more* acceleration. But if a VW Rabbit has a better torque curve, you may have more fun driving it. You may be more alert and interested in driving. I happen to think that is good. Whatever you prefer, well, you drive it.

Meanwhile, here is a list of the VWs I have owned:

LIST of RAP's VWs...

	MILES ...	CONDITION ...	# OF ENGINES
1. 1962 Btle, Blu,	0 to 169k.	Retired, running w/ bad bearings, rusty.	1 Engine.
2. 1965 Bus, Wht,	0 to 160k.	Traded in, running ok. (rusty)	2 Engine.
3. 1968 Btle, Tan,	35k to 115k.	Accident when running strong. (rusty)	1 Engine.
4. 1970 Btle, Blu,	79k to 249k.	Automatic. Retired, Running, leaking oil.	4 Engine.
5. 1972 Bus, Red,	0 to 162k.	Retired with smoking exhaust. Not rusty.	2 Engine.
6. 1968 Btle, Tan,	47k to 365k.	Still running strong. Retired.	2 Engine.
7. 1969 Btle, Red,	95k to 218k.	Still running strong.	1 Engine.
8. 1974 Btle, Tan,	45k to 90k.	Still running strong.	1 Engine.
9. 1985 Bus, Blu,	9k to 110k.	Still running strong.	1 Engine.

Total number of miles (air-cooled) – 1,214,000 *plus*

Total number of miles (all VWs) – 1,315,000 *plus*

◆ ◆ ◆

– Hey, I won't say I have never had any troubles with my VWs. I can't say I never had to spend any money on repairs. But I have had a lot of fun, and a lot of good miles, and pretty good luck. I got no gripes. VWs have run pretty well for me. I don't baby them too much, but I do try to treat them fairly as I work them hard. Note, if you divide 1,214,000 miles by 14 engines, that's better than 80,000 miles per engine – and still rolling, on at least 4 or 5 of them. And a lot of miles to go. Not bad, considering I bought some used cars with a good bit of miles on them, and still got good service.

Old Joke:

Question: Why do VWs not slow down for corners?
Answer: Because if they did, they would never be able to get up to speed again....

– That may be some kind of old joke, but VW drivers have always found it fun, and challenging, to get through corners as fast as they can. Slowing down for corners is for other drivers to do. A VW Beetle is not exactly a "sports car", but it can be driven as a sporty car. The steering is light, so you can tell if you are getting into trouble by going too fast. Of course, if you try to be the fastest car on the road, you can spin out and get in real trouble. On the other hand, on a snowy day, it is easy to be faster than 99% of the cars on the road, and quite safely. That is a lot of the fun of a VW.

Obsolete?

Are VW Beetles obsolete? You might say that. Many cars are obsolete the day they are made. But there are still a lot of old VWs running strong, out here in the West. So there are a lot of people who enjoy their VWs, and we don't care if some people think they are "obsolete". Hey, there are MILLIONS of Fords and Chevys and you-name-its that were built after my '68 or '69 or '70 Beetle, and a lot of them have been junked. And of all those other old cars that were *not* junked – how many of those cars are better than mine? How many of them have a lower operating cost? How many are fun to drive? I rest my case.

When is a VW not a VW?

– You might say – "Pease – you only know how to drive old junky cars." Not exactly true. One time I was invited by Porsche of America, to test-drive some of their cars. The instructor showed us a test of driving in a loop around some cones. He got a Porsche 911 around these cones in 5.4 seconds. When it was my turn, I got the 911 around those cones in 5.4 seconds, also. That 240-hp car, on good pavement, had the same *feel* as a VW on snow – except faster and quicker. I figured that out *fast*, as soon as I floored the gas on a machine I had never driven before. I have driven Corvettes and hot Mustangs, and a Chevy Corsica that really liked to MOVE. And I even managed to keep them all on the road....

Buying a Used Car?

If you wanted to buy an old VW Beetle or Bus, I would caution you where to look to see if there was rust – such as, under the spare tire. And you would need an experienced guy to drive it and see if it feels right. The late John Muir wrote the book – *How to Keep Your VW Alive*. See in the Appendix on Book Reviews. That is a classic book, and if you want to buy and drive an old VW, that is the book you need, as it has a Chapter on How to Buy a Used VW. I do not know how many Beetles and Busses are still running, but there's a LOT.

Non-Polluting Cars?

– Pease, you drive all these miles – but these old cars are all a lot of polluters. You must be responsible for smogging up the whole San Francisco Bay area – eh?

   – Not really – I keep my car tuned up, and it rarely falls below 28 mpg. My car almost always passes its smog test with no problems, on the first try. So, it's not so bad.

My Next Car?

– OK, Pease, you drive this old 1968 clunker. When it gives out, you can't buy another one – so what are you going to buy? Well, it is NOT true that I cannot buy another one. Every week I see 3 or 4 advertisements for a 1968, 1969, or 1970 Beetle in very good shape, with prices in the range $900 to $2000. So if an elephant comes along and sits on my good old 1968 car – I'll just buy another one. Really!

                                                                                        ┼

Appendix F – ECONOMY

If you have to go on a short trip, to run an errand, or to buy a small chunk of groceries, or go to a nearby restaurant, the best mode – the one that will cost the least – is often, to leave the car and walk, or take a bicycle. Sometimes that is excellent exercise. Sometimes it will take no more time, if you count the time looking for a parking space. So, please consider that. Because it's not only good for the environment, and will not only save you on gasoline, but it will greatly decrease the wear and tear on your car.

Short Trips

Because short trips do not warm up your car's engine. An occasional short trip does no harm. But if you take only a short trip or two, every day, you get these problems:

– Water condenses in the engine, and never gets boiled off.

– Water and acids and other contaminants condense in the oil, and never get boiled off.

– Water condenses in the muffler, causing the muffler to start rusting faster than normal.

– When your engine is cold, it runs rich, and the actual engine efficiency is poor. Also, tires, gearboxes, engine oil, etc., are cold, and these all contribute to poor efficiency. So if you take one drive to do 4 errands, each time you move along on the next leg of your trip, the engine will be partly warmed up, and you will get better efficiency and fuel mileage compared to 4 separate trips. Much better economy. And you may be able to travel fewer miles, and spend less time, compared to doing each errand separately.

So if you are going to do some errands, try to do several at one time, in sequence. Or maybe you can do them on the way home from work.

Economy is not just gas consumption. It is usually related to overall vehicle cost. If you buy a car that is a lot more car than you need, or an engine that is much bigger than you need, that will cost you. If you get an engine that is too small, and flog it really hard, and wear it out, that's poor economy. If you get a car that is too small and over-load it more than on just a rare occasion, that's foolish, too.

Idling – versus Turning Off The Engine

When you come to a long traffic light, it is usually wise to turn off your engine. In the Silicon Valley area, (anywhere south of San Francisco, down to San Jose), many of the red lights in the daytime, (and especially at rush hour) are as long as 2 or 2-1/2 minutes or more. If you arrive at a light, just after it went red, it is *definitely* more economical to turn off the engine, and wait for the light to go green. It also generates a lot less smog.

Of course, at night, if your battery is weak, and you turn off your engine, the lights might run the battery down. Bad idea. Don't turn off the engine in that case.

If the red light is likely to stay red less than 10 or 20 seconds, or if you do not know how long it has been red, it is not usually wise to kill the engine.

If your engine does not start very well, then of course these rules do not apply. If your battery is weak, don't fool around. Let the engine idle. But these guidelines were checked out by Porsche *and* Volkswagen *and* by one of the Japanese car makers. They all researched the design of cars that automatically turned off their own engines if allowed to idle more than just a few seconds, and then re-started automatically as soon as you step on the clutch. I am not sure if I need such a car, but it might be an interesting idea to save fuel in places where there is a lot of stopping at traffic lights. It might cut a lot of air pollution and smog, too. But, you do not have to buy a car that does this for you – just do it yourself.

Now, the long-term economy says, if you are pretty sure the light will be red for more than about 20 seconds, shut off the engine. If you figure it will stay red *less* than about 20, let it idle. You may burn a little more gas, but you will decrease the wear and tear on the starter motor. On the other hand, I can say that the starter motor on my 1968 Beetle is running just fine after 335,000 miles – I have probably used the starter 20,000 times. However, since the engine starts fairly promptly, typically less than in 3 seconds, then that is only 60,000 seconds or 17 hours. And most electric motors will last more than 17 hours, if you do not abuse them or overheat them.

BUT, there is another case. If you are very low on gas, you may turn off your engine even for 6 or 8 seconds, and burn less gas. It may, in the long run, cost you a trifle more, because you may have to replace your starter motor a little sooner, but you may get a little closer to home, or you may get to the gas station. So the 20-second rule does not apply to this case.

I know one guy who was running very low on gas. He pulled into a gas station that was closed. He tipped each of the 20 spouts into his gas tank. He got about a pint, which was enough to get him home.

Another guy was going on a rock-climbing trip, and was running very low on gas. He had no spare gallon. It was late at night, and all the gas stations were closed. He might have kept going until he ran out of gas, but that would have been stupid. So what did he do? He stopped and parked at a closed gas station. He rolled out his sleeping bag and went to sleep. When the gas station opened up, the next morning, he bought some gas and continued on his way.

Put On The Brakes – To Save Energy

It is common knowledge that when a traffic light turns red, you have to stop – – – WRONG!! If a light turns red in front of you, you do NOT necessarily have to stop.

But on the other hand, you are not supposed to drive through it. The wise thing is to slow down.

If a light turns red, a good ways out in front of you, and you just take your foot off the gas – that may not be the best procedure. Because it's wasteful to keep rolling at speed, if you just have to stop when you get to the light – and then the light turns green. Instead, if you have any guess as to how long the cycle of greens and reds is going to take, then you can make a good-judgement economy move:

– When you see the light turn red, a moderate distance ahead of you, get on the brakes fairly early, and slow down a little, *early*.

– Cut your speed to the best speed at which you will probably not have to slow down again, before the light turns green.

– Just slow down, and then hold that slow speed. You might even take your foot off the gas. You might leave it on the gas, lightly.

– Then, when the light goes green, you will not have to accelerate so much. The *maximum minimum speed* you can go down to, early, is best, and most economical. This may save a little bit on brake wear, and a good bit on clutch wear, if you do not have to stop at all. It will also save on gas.

If I am on an upgrade, I often slow down to as slow as 5 mph, so I can just idle along up the grade in first gear, waiting for the light to turn green. This technique can lead to ZERO wear on the clutch, because you never have to slip the clutch to start on the uphill. While this is most advantageous for cars with manual transmission, it still saves energy and wear on automatic-shift cars. And when the light turns green, you are already rolling.

Of course, if you judge that you are a *long* way from the light, you just keep rolling and as you get closer, it may turn green for you. You can't always time every light just right. There is one red light I often come up to, at a freeway exit ramp, that is virtually *never* green for me, because it is a trip light. If I am just rolling along alone, I just *have to* slow down and stop and wait for the light to trip. Tricky strategies do not help here! However, if there are cars ahead of me, I can go up near the light, and slow 'way down, and wait for THEM to trip the light, and then I can follow them through on the green. So sometimes I do not have to stop at that light....

CAUTION: If you are approaching an intersection and trying to go slow until the light turns green, DO NOT get sloppy and roll into the intersection before the light is really green, AND before you are sure the traffic is really clear. (Those are not the same thing!) If you are within a few yards of the light, and it is still red, you have to plan to stop. It is not OK to pretend and hope the light is going to be green only a small part of a second after you enter the intersection. Because you might have a close-encounter of the fourth kind, with a guy who is going across the intersection, kind of late on the yellow light, as the yellow light goes red. Watch out for that guy!

So when I am driving along and approach a red light, if I think it will turn green *soon*, I slow down and ease up to the light, in hopes that if I go slow enough, it will turn green before I have to stop. But if I am pretty sure it will not turn green, then I stop and turn off the engine.

EXCEPTION:

If I come off a 60 or 65 mph freeway, my engine is good and hot. I have figured out that it is best for the longevity of the engine, to leave the engine idling for the first mile or two, or the first couple minutes after I come down from highway speeds. So I let it idle at the first one or two stop lights, rather than turning off the key. But further along, I turn off the key.

Economical Driving

Here are some good GENERAL suggestions for economy: Don't accelerate REALLY HARD; don't step on the gas really hard; don't hit the brakes REALLY HARD; don't corner REALLY HARD. Also, don't accelerate too slow – try to shift into top gear as early as you can without "lugging". Try to avoid excessive speeds. Don't let your tires get underinflated. Don't idle more than you have to. When you start the car, except at extremely cold temperatures, don't idle or warm up the engine, but start right out, gradually and slowly. When you have a new car, follow the break-in instructions, for the first 500 or 1000 miles, as the owner's manual recommends. And read the entire owner's manual every year or two, just in case there is some other advice or special feature that is important for long life or economy.

Change the oil every 3000 miles in cases of ordinary driving, or perhaps every 5000 miles if you put on a lot of easy highway miles. (That's what I do.) If you have to do a lot of short trips in cold winter weather, consult your owner's manual, to see if it recommends oil changes at 1,000 or 2,000 miles in those conditions. Keep the engine tuned up, so you avoid getting lousy gas mileage. Check your gas mileage, so in case your gas mileage starts getting worse, you can spot it right away.

– Got the picture? There are a lot of things you can do, that make for good, safe, smooth driving, and help your overall costs, and help the car run long and reliably.

5th Gear...

If you have a car with a 4-speed gearbox, then we are talking about the 5th gear – that is, free-wheeling, or coasting, by shifting into neutral, also called "Mexican Overdrive". NOW, this is probably illegal under the motor-vehicle laws of every state, as it is in California. But the laws of nature also state that if you keep your engine running when you do not need your engine, that wastes fuel. During the last petroleum crisis, I had optimized my route, and refined this ability to roll down hills, with the engine off and the gearbox in neutral, as much as 3 or 4 miles per day. *Free* miles. And if we have another energy crisis, I might do it again.

Down at the local Masonic Temple, there is a sign with an arrow:

"Scottish Rite Parking". Well, if turning off your engine and rolling the last half mile to work, and pulling into your parking spot, with no energy wasted, is not a frugal kind of "Scottish Rite", then, I don't know what is.

Why is this illegal? In the old days, if you shifted out of gear, you might not be able to shift back in. These days that is usually not a problem. What if you have power brakes, and if you shut down the engine, your brakes work lousy? Then you should not shut down your engine. What if you have power steering, and your steering gets very heavy and difficult if the engine is off? Then you should not shut off your engine. What if your car does not start very well? Then you should not shut off your engine. What if your transmission does not shift very well? Then you should not shift out of gear. Okay?

Keep Under Control

Refer to Helga's accident, in her pick-up truck, in the Chapter on Passing, where she was free-wheeling (coasting) down a hill, and could not easily slow down, and lost control. I believe the coasting was a definite contributing factor to the accident. If she had not been coasting, she probably could have braked a lot better, and kept her vehicle under control. So if you were free-wheeling down a hill, and coming into some kind of problem area, you must be aware that you are vulnerable. Step on the brakes early, slow down early, get your speed way down, and get back in gear, with your engine on.

This section is going to be an Appendix, because the topics mentioned here are mostly related to saving you money, and not to avoiding accidents. So it will not be a Chapter.

Appendix G – JUMP-STARTS

This information about Jump-Starting is an Appendix, because it is a Special Circumstance. This does not mean it is not important to read, and it does not mean that you can't have a lovely stupid accident when trying to jump-start your car. But you will probably NOT be using it every year – unless you and your friends have old cars....

An Urban Legend?

Okay – what the heck is an "Urban Legend" ??? It's a little bit like the story of Little Red Riding Hood and the Wolf, but it happened in a city – or on a highway.

For example, a man had a car that broke down, and a woman with Rhode Island plates stopped and asked if she could help. The guy said, "Yes, I need a push-start. I need to get up to 30 mph to start." The woman backed up about a quarter mile. And as the guy watched in great puzzlement, she got a nice running start, up to 30 mph. In perfect horror, the guy watched her come up behind him. There was nothing he could do except lie down on the front seat. She hit him at 30 mph, and destroyed both cars, and nearly got killed herself. And he did *not* get his engine started....

NOW, in Rhode Island, or North Dakota, or any of 48 other states, this PROBABLY NEVER HAPPENED. In other words, this was NOT a real occurrence – but it holds a little element of truth – even though it never happened. The story has been sent in to magazines, from many people, from many places – but it probably never happened, in any state.

HOW to do Push-starts

– FIRST of all, *that* is the WRONG way to help a guy get a push-start. DO NOT do that. Probably nobody ever DID misinterpret that as a way to start a car – but that story sure had LEGS.

– SECOND, jump-starting a car with a manual transmission is pretty easy to do, even at 6 or 8 mph – but to get an Automatic-Transmission (AT) car going, you may need to push it slowly up to 25 or 30 mph, so it is not trivial. You can't just do it on a city street unless everything is very clear.

– THIRD, some AT cars are not recommended for a push-start. So you better read your Owner's Manual. I would not give you a push-start unless you are SURE it's permitted. The Owner's Manual has to say you can do it.

– FOURTH, in general, a jump-start with jumper-cables is generally better and safer, depending on what's wrong. The other day, I came across a guy whose starter motor would not work, so he needed a push-start. (His battery was perfectly OK.)

But his fan-belt was ALSO not working. So we gave that up, as a bad try. He had 2 failures in the same hour: his fan-belt *and* the starter motor.

Starting with Jumper-Cables

I hate to waste so much print to tell you how to do it right, but if you do it wrong, you can get an explosion. So let's list briefly how to do it right.

   – Let's assume the battery on one car is dead, and you know why – such as – you left some lights on. (If you don't know why it went dead, that is a matter for caution.)

   – Get the cars close together and get access to the batteries – but do not put on the jumper cables yet.

   – If possible, turn off the equipment that caused the battery to go dead.

   – Connect the HOT, POSITIVE, RED wire of the Jumper Cables, to the HOT terminal of one car's battery, and the other red to the positive terminal of the other car's battery. This is normally the terminal with the insulated wire. This is the one marked "+".

This is the one that does NOT have the plain, un-insulated braided ground strap going to ground. If there is any question at all, stop and check, because any goof can cause a terrible explosion. It can rip your battery open. NOTE, all cars for the last 20 years have a positive hot voltage, and thus a NEGATIVE GROUND. Besides, car batteries are labeled, for + and –, but if you don't have a flashlight, that may be hard to see on a dark rainy night.

(The only exceptions to this, "negative ground" convention, are a very small number of old (20- or 30-year-old) British cars. Anybody who has such a car should know it.) (Some old cars may have 6-volt electrical systems. You cannot normally jump-start a 6-volt car from a 12-volt car, so don't try it.)

   – Next, connect the black (ground) cable to a bumper of one car.

   – Next, just *touch* the other end of the ground cable to the bumper of the other car. If the one battery is low, there may be a medium-sized spark, but if it starts to draw a big ARC, that's time to stop and reconsider what's wrong. If the spark is pretty small, then clip it on the bumper.

The REASON you attach this ground wire to the BUMPER, and NOT to the battery, is that if you are making a goof, and the battery is going to *explode*, you want to be standing over by the bumper, not with your nose stuck above the battery. You want to be a reasonable distance away from the batteries. Okay??

   – After you get the cables connected, start up the good car, and run the engine at a fast idle – a slow roar – about half speed – for about 5 minutes. This is to let the good car put charge into the bad battery. I have seen cases where the bad battery is so poor, that the wires start to smoke. Time to stop, undo the ground wire, and reconsider. Sometimes, that poor car is so sick, it cannot be started.

– After 3 to 5 minutes, there should be enough charge in the low battery. Turn the engine down to a low idle, to prevent the chance of damage to the charging system in case of a goof-up. Better yet, turn off the engine.

– Now the battery should have enough charge, to start an engine that *wants* to start. Give it a try. It may start. If it does, rev the engine a little, and let its charging system put some more charge into the battery. Do NOT turn off the engine!!!! (I did that, once.)

– Now, disconnect the ground wires, from the bumpers. Keep them away from the red wires. Then carefully disconnect the hot wires. Stow them. Rev the engine a good bit, to get a little more charge in, before starting to move (see below for Automatics.)

After You Started It – for MANUAL Transmissions –

– Then if you are in a car with a manual transmission, be *extra* careful not to stall the engine, when you are getting going. Rev the engine, and *slip the clutch*, good and plenty, carefully, to get going. Pick a route where you do not have to stop and start often.

Make Sure It Likes to Start...

– Here's what I do, in a manual transmission car, after a jump start. I get rolling on the road, and after a mile, on a nice quiet straight street, at about 30 mph, I step on the clutch and turn off the engine. Then I put it in neutral, and turn the key, and LISTEN. Usually it cranks and fires, pretty well, because the battery has gotten a pretty good charge. Then I continue on my way, knowing I have a safety factor.

What if it won't crank decently? That might be telling me, my battery is SHOT, or the charging system IS NOT WORKING! Still, I am rolling at 20 mph, so I shift into 2nd, pop the clutch, the engine starts, and I head for emergency service.

For example, if I am 20 miles from home, and my battery won't crank, I know I probably would not make it home. I would try to find a service station that can give me 20 minutes of fast charge. If I do that, then I should be able to ease home. If I didn't do that, I might run out of power, half-way home, with an absolutely dead battery. I'd need to get the car towed, and I'd need to take a bus to get home 3 hours late. Stopping to get some fast charge might save me all that grief and money. I still might have to get a new battery, or a repair of my charging system, in a few days, but at least I don't want to get stranded.

After You Get It Started – For AUTOMATIC Transmissions

– Some automatic transmission cars have a tendency to stall when put into DRIVE. If that is what your car does, you will know it. If that happens, maybe you don't stow the jumper cables right away! Try to get rolling and pick a route that does not require many stops or shifts.

– If I had an automatic transmission car, that could be started at 30 mph, I would get up to 35 or 40, shift into neutral, and turn off the engine. I'd try to re-start with the key. If it wouldn't start with the key and starter, I would shift from neutral into LO, and let it start. As I said, above, I would get to a repair shop to get a fast charge.   ✗

Won't Start?

– But, if the reason the battery was dead was because the engine did NOT want to start – then – maybe it just WILL NOT start? Here are a few examples: the starter is SHOT, and pulls the battery down by pulling 1000 amperes. (In case this happens, you were wise not to leave the other car charging!)

Or, if the coil is *shot*, or the carburetor is *clogged*, or the fuel-injection computer is *on the Fritz*, or if the ignition is *inoperative*, or the car is out of *gas* – you could crank all night long, and the engine will not start. So, you *have* to know when to give up. You probably need professional help. I mean, some things can be fixed – but not everything can be fixed by a couple enthusiastic amateurs, standing out in a dark, cold parking lot. Still, you gave it a try.

Rolling Starts

Basically, there are 3 *kinds of* cars, and 4 *modes* of rolling starts.

– As we mentioned above, there are manual transmission cars, which are almost always able to be started with a push; automatic transmissions that have to get up to 30 mph to start; and automatic cars that are NOT supposed to be push-started.

THEN, there are 4 *modes* – a hand-push-start, a push with a car, a tow with a rope or a chain, and a roll down a hill.

– Then there are several modes of failure. If you know you just let the lights drain down the battery, you know it should start.

– Or, if the starter is shot, you can get the engine going with a push-start.

– BUT if the motor is kinda sick – sometimes you do not KNOW if the engine can be made to start – but it may be worth a try.

– FIRST of all, for a car with an AT that is NOT supposed to be push-started – either use jumper cables, or get it towed in to a repair shop. That's simple.

– SECOND – a car with AT may need to get up to 25 or 30 mph. A car-push-start is not preferable, because any goof can cause a little accident.

– THIRD – a car with manual transmission can easily get going with any mode as listed here:

What mode of rolling start?

Rolling Down A Hill...

– If you have a hill, like I do in front of my house, that is the best, safest method, because you don't have two cars pushing or pulling on each other. Almost any

✗

9/9/22

downgrade is good for 6 or 8 mph; if the hill is enough for 30 mph, as mine is, you'll know it, pretty quick.

Push by People...

– A push-start, with people, is often pretty easy, but it helps to have 2 or 3 people, PLUS a little downgrade. If you are at the bottom of a grade, you need some friends to push it up to the top of the grade; then, it's pretty easy to push the car back down.... But if you are out on a street, you have to be careful that traffic does not endanger the guys who are pushing!

Push by a Car...

– A push-start from a car may or may not be fairly safe – depending on how the bumpers match up. If one bumper slips over the other, you can get the pushing car with its front bumper shoved into the trunk of the pushed car. Sounds expensive. I'd recommend this only if one of the bumpers has "bumperettes" or over-riders, to prevent the bumpers from getting past each other.

An alternative idea is to take an old tire, not on a rim, and tie it up so it hangs down over the bumper, so the bumper is pushing on the tire, not directly on the bumper. Then a couple inches of up/down misalignment will not let the bumpers cross past each other. Still, a bit risky. I wouldn't want to screw around with that, with a nice new car.

A Tow by a Car...

– A tow from another car is less risky. Try to get a nice long, strong rope. Fifteen feet is kind of short; 30 is better. I usually carry around a few chunks of strong rope. If you had to go to a hardware store or grocery store, and buy 100 feet of clothesline, that can be used to make five 20-foot strands, which should be plenty for a light car. For a heavier car, it may not be enough unless you are very careful, so you might need a heavier rope. Or a chain. Or a strap.

When you fasten the rope, try to wrap it around suspension frames, not just the bumpers. Try to arrange it so it will not tend to cut on bumpers or other sharp metal parts.

– PROCEDURE for PUSH-STARTING – Manual Transmissions

– Get the car up to at least 6 or 8 mph. The driver should jump in at 4 or 5 mph, to make sure he does not slip and fall and fail to get in!! There's a small danger!

Immediately turn the key on. Then, with the clutch in, shift into second. When the car is going "fast enough", *pop* the clutch – let it out *quickly*. Stab the gas. If the engine catches, rev it up, and warm up the engine appropriately. Be careful not to let the engine die. If there is any chance it would stall, the driver should stay in the car and keep the throttle depressed enough so it won't stall, while the other guy undoes any ropes. As soon as you are clear, keep the engine going, being careful not to stall it. Then if you have a chance, after a mile or two, check to "Make Sure It Likes To Start" (see above).

NOTE – any car can push another car up to 6 or 8 mph, without very much likelihood of getting the bumpers over-ridden, if you are pretty careful. This is NOT TRUE for a car with an automatic transmission, that has to get up to 30 mph....

NOTE – as soon as I got my first VW, I checked out how easy it is to push-start. I figured out that on a flat road, I can just about push it up to 5 mph all by myself, hop in, pop the clutch in second, and start it. If there is any downgrade, or any person helping, that makes it a lot easier. You might check out your own car, perhaps on a slight downgrade, to see how easily you can do it, and to get a good feel for, "How fast is, 'fast enough'?"

– PROCEDURE for PUSH-STARTING, for Automatic Transmissions

– First, you are going to have to get the car up to 30 mph. Unless one of the cars has really massive bumpers, to make sure they will not get crossed up, it is NOT a good idea to push a car up to 30 mph. One thing you could do is push the car UP a slight grade, very slowly and gently, and then push it down a little faster. That makes it a lot easier.

If the car pushing has an automatic transmission, it can get up to 30 mph pretty easily. But if the pushing car has a manual transmission, that driver has to be very careful not to fall behind when he shifts, and then bump the car hard when he gets in second. This is a time for a gentle speed shift, not for a leisurely double-clutched shift. Shift as quickly and smoothly as you can, while applying a minimum amount of gas.

– PROCEDURE for TOWING, for Automatic Transmissions

If the car is towing, or pulling with a rope or chain, many things are a lot easier. Even for a manual shift car, it can tow a big car easily. For example, in my little gutless VW Beetle, I can easily tow a bigger car up to 30. I ease on the clutch and get up to about 5 mph in first, and then speed-shift gently into second, to make sure I do not get any slack. Then I can pull it easily up to 30, in second. Not hard – and, MUCH easier than a push. Safer.

When the car that is towed gets about around 30, he THEN shifts from (neutral) to LOW. The engine will start, if it is going to. CAUTION – if the engine starts to race, the towed car could run into the car in front. You have to be ready to step on the brakes to make sure you do not run into the tow-car! And, remember, you are still linked with a rope or chain. You have to slow down VERY CAREFULLY, to make sure you do not yank too hard on a bumper, or break the rope! Normally, the best procedure is for the car in back to put on the brakes very gently, first to get the slack out of the rope, and then to slow down both cars. It is not reasonable to let the car in front try to avoid pulling hard on the rope – he can't see it. Further, you do not want to let the rope develop much slack, because then the towed car might run over it! This towing stuff is very complicated!! Not recommended for beginners!

All this time, you are wandering across a mall parking lot, or a quiet street. If it is dark, or raining, and the visibility is lousy, you can be doing some pretty dangerous stuff. In that case, it might be wise to wait and get it started in the morning. Walking around in bad visibility with heavy traffic going by is NOT very safe. These are Advanced Techniques, for special circumstances, and normally for experienced drivers. I should probably not even be telling you this, but if you were going to do this anyhow, I may as well warn you what parts are safe, and what are dangerous. OK?

SPECIAL SECTION...

Sometimes old VW's don't like to start because the wires to the starter solenoid are too long, with bad connectors. Sometimes the solenoid gets old. If you turn the key and get only a tiny click, a horn relay can help. Send me a SASE for the solution: Robert A. Pease, 682 Miramar Avenue (Apt. V), San Francisco, CA 94112.

7/10/12

Appendix H – FOUR-WHEEL DRIVE (4WD)

I'll repeat here what I said back in the Chapter on Manual Transmissions: I am not an expert on 4WD. But even if I were, I would not tell you everything I know, because this is not the right place. Still, I'll throw in a brief set of comments.

The best part about a 4WD car is that you can drive it just like an ordinary car. You can just leave it in 2-wheel drive and leave the transmission in HIGH range, and DRIVE. Whether manual transmission or automatic, you can just drive it like any other car. To a large extent, a study of 4WD is not relevant to this book, but the types of accidents you can have with 4WD vehicles are discussed here.

Difficult Places

What gets interesting is when you start driving on difficult roads, that are steep, or tilted, or have poor traction – sandy or snowy.

Even in high range, if you leave it in low gear, you can really make amazing progress, nice and slow and deliberate. As I have mentioned in a few places, sometimes I can force my Beetle up a very steep hill by hurrying into the hill. If I get going slow, and lose power, or lose traction, I'll get bogged down and stopped. But the 4WD can ease through difficult places, and does not have to hurry, because the low gear is typically rather low, and the engine's torque is quite strong.

Get INTO Trouble With 2WD, and Get OUT with 4WD

The best thing about 4WD is, if you go onto moderately bad roads, and get stuck in 2-Wheel Drive, you can then shift into 4WD and use that to get out. But if you use 4WD to get into trouble, you can get MUCH deeper into trouble. Then, maybe you can use your WINCH, or your friends' car, to help get you out. It's a well known statement, and painfully true, that using 4WD, you can get REALLY STUCK, much further back in the hills, than with 2WD.

My wife has a Mitsubishi Montero. (Back in Massachusetts, this car gets labeled a Dodge Raider, but that does not change what it really is.) She didn't just get it because she needed 4WD, but the car was sitting there, and the price was right. So she bought it, and it runs quite competently. I have tried to get it stuck in the snow, in 2WD, so I could then shift into 4WD and get unstuck. But I couldn't get it stuck. I have tried just lurching into big snow-banks, to get stuck. I couldn't get stuck. The big knobby tires just kept churning, and turning over, and it kept moving. Never got stuck. So I guess I just have to accept that it's a really adequate machine to go in fairly difficult places.

Kinds of 4WD

There are several variation on 4WD. Some modern cars (like Audi) come with full-time 4WD – sometimes called "All-Wheel Drive". You never have to shift out of it. It has a fluid coupling between the front and rear wheels.

The oldest version had a transfer case to connect in High range, for normal driving, or Low range, for all slow steep driving, and then you have your choice of 2WD or 4WD. But, to get the front wheels connected, you have to go out to each front hub, to switch each hub to LOCK, to get it connected. Many people find this objectionable, if you are, for example, situated in a big mud-puddle. With other 4WD systems, you just stop, and then shift from your seat, and then go. The most modern type lets you shift while rolling, such as climbing a steep snowy road, where you would rather not have to stop.

What Can Go Wrong?

The 4WD parts themselves are quite reliable. They may be expensive to buy, and expensive to maintain, but they do WORK. The major 4WD problem is, you can get into trouble on difficult roads. You can get on a steeply slanting road, and tip over. You can get on a road that is too steep, up or down, and skid, and flop over. You can get into a deep hole and need a lot of help, winching out. (Just because you have a winch, does NOT mean there is anything to hook onto.) And most tall 4WD vehicles now get a warning label, that if you just *cut* your wheel too hard, at any speed, you can tip it over. After all, a high ground-clearance is great – but it goes WITH a high center-of-gravity.

You can get out on rough roads and slash a tire on a sharp rock. There are all sorts of things you can do, to get into trouble with 4WD. The antidote for all these things is, to take it easy and don't do too many rash things, on back roads where you may not be able to get out. One of my reviewers observed, however, that when you look over the side of a cliff, to see where the 4WD vehicles fell off the road, it is mostly new, shiny 4WDs, not old, experienced ones.

One friend observed that a lot of people get into trouble because they drive into a sticky place, and try to shift into 4WD – and it does not go. This is sometimes because a pneumatic hose or cable fell off. If you are headed into serious places, make *sure* your 4WD really is working, when you turn it on. Put your bumper against a heavy post, and make sure all 4 wheels will turn, when they are on a patch of sand. Or get the advice of an expert, to make sure your 4WD is all there.

Most 4WD vehicles do not have "Positraction", so trying to go up a steep road with one lane of ice may not work even as well as a car with a "limited slip" differential. Whatever you have, make sure you know what you have, and that it is working the way you want it.

Make SURE You Can Walk Out...

Pilots in Alaska have all learned one rule, for well over 60 years – make sure you can "walk out of it". If you fly from one town to another one, just a couple dozen minutes away, and something goes bad – dirty fuel, rotten weather – etc. – there are plenty of places to land – lakes or swamps. But you have to have, in the plane, the right clothes and boots to walk out. And a sleeping bag. And some food. Even if you do not crash or get hurt, you have to be prepared to wait a week or two, to get rescued, in case of bad weather. You may have to walk out along a 50-mile river valley, to get to a town only 10 miles away. So, there is no substitute for having the right boots and equipment – even though you plan to be only a few minutes, by air, from civilization. Moccasins won't cut it. Tee-shirts ain't enough. Boots and Parka are correct.

Similarly, when YOU drive in the back-country, YOU should have boots and equipment so you can walk out. If you are in dry country, bring *plenty* of water. If it is cold, keep lots of warm clothes – and sleeping bags. Either way, bring a couple spare gallons of gasoline in a safe container. Even if you are travelling with friends, you might get separated from them.

Snowmobiles, Off-Road Cycles, and ATVs

There are LOTS of ways to get in trouble with these vehicles – similar to troubles with a 4WD. Some of these are related to the fact that you can get going fast on rough terrain, and tip over, or hit a ditch. But the other problem you can have with any of these vehicles is very basic – you can get *so far* into the Back Woods or Boondocks in just 5 minutes, that it may take you ALL DAY to get back out, in case your vehicle breaks down or runs out of gas or has an accident. And if that accident occurs at sunset — you may be spending a long cold night. So, be reasonably careful, and travel with a buddy. And, be prepared to walk out.

You don't need to have a 4WD, or a VW, or a snowmobile, to get in trouble, in the back country. There are LOTS of places you can drive with an ordinary car, and get WELL back up in the hills. You might do this in October, when the first 2-foot snow-fall means your car will not be rescued until next June (and your remains may not be found nor recovered until then, either). But in any other month, we read about somebody who busted his gas tank and had to walk out 40 miles in very cold (or, very hot) conditions. Any time you get off the highways, be prepared to walk out. And tell somebody where you are going, so if you get stranded, they will know where to come look for you....

Be prepared to walk out –

Appendix I – TOOLS

Everybody has his own ideas on what's a good set of tools. Somebody might say, "A cellular phone, a credit card, and my AAA membership." That may be exactly right for him.

Other people may want a full set of 50 wrenches and 6 kinds of pliers and 8 types of screwdrivers. Feeler gauges. Shovel, 2 kinds of jacks, and tire-patching kits. I tend to operate like that. But everybody has their own opinions.

I'll list a couple different levels of tool-preparedness:

Minimum Tools:

- Car Jack, and lug-nut wrench
- Ordinary screwdriver
- Phillips-head screwdriver
- Vise-grip pliers
- Jack-knife
- 3 feet of 2-by-4
- Snow scraper
- A couple dollar bills, plus a few dimes
- Flashlight
- Paper towels, for cleaning up
- Plastic spoons, forks, knives
- Wet, soapy towelettes in sealed packages – for cleaning up your hands
- Placard: You Have No Brake Lights

– There are always occasional things that get loose on a car, or have to be adjusted. The screwdrivers are good for that. And, the vise-grip pliers are one of the best ways to grab THINGS. Actually, they are NOT very good on nuts or bolts, because they tend to beat them up, but in an emergency, they do *work*. The 2-by-4 can be used under the jack, or under a tire, or can be used as a hammer to *whack* things.

◆ ◆ ◆

Next Level: Add on:

- One adjustable wrench

414

- Spark-plug wrench
- One set open-end wrenches, metric or SAE
- One cheap set of socket wrenches ($7.00 on sale)
- Large, medium, and small screwdrivers, BOTH ordinary and Phillips-head
- Slip-joint pliers
- Electrician's pliers with cutters
- One or 2 chunks of 2-by-6 plank
- Small or medium-size shovel
- Big snow-scraper
- Carpenter's hammer
- Two 3' lengths of iron pipe (1") for extra leverage on lug wrenches

◆ ◆ ◆

Expert's Collection:

All of the above, PLUS:

- Any special kind of wrenches, Allen wrenches, pliers, screwdrivers (as you prefer)
- Good socket wrenches
- Large screwdriver (2' long) for prying and leverring

◆ ◆ ◆

Next I will add a list of SUPPLIES that will occasionally be useful.

STUFF – supplies (Minimum):

- One or 2 wire coat hangers
- Quart of oil
- Pencils, pens, paper
- Spare glasses?
- Maps
- Paper towels, cloths, rags
- Kleenex

Add On, for the Next Round:

- 1 gallon can of gas, secured in a safe place
- 1 or 2 quarts of water
- Can of brake fluid
- 4 feet of baling wire
- A set of old spark plugs

- A set of old spark-plug wires
- Bottle of compressed gas to inflate a flat tire
- Alligator clips
- Insulated wire
- Jack-knife with cork-screw
- Flares
- More pencils, paper, maps
- Hymnal, Bible
- Windex or window-washing fluid, in sprayer
- Windshield-washer solvent
- Cord, small ropes
- Heavy rope
- Tire chains
- Fan belt
- Fire extinguisher

♦ ♦ ♦

Other Items:

- Small ice-box (for stowing your camera, or your gas-bottle for inflating your tire, and/or food on the way home from the grocery store.)
- Spare bulbs for brake lights, parking lights

♦ ♦ ♦

Most of these are listed in the index, so if you have to ask, "Why do I need to bring that stuff?", the answer is buried in my text, somewhere. It's not just a check-list, but a thinking list.

ν

Appendix J - SPARE PARTS

Everybody has his own ideas on what's a good set of spare parts.

Here's a good basic list. And I'll explain why.

- OLD spark plugs
- OLD spark plug wires
- Ignition parts. ("Breaker points", or whatever you use.)
- OLD fuel filter
- NEW fuel filter
- OLD air filter
- NEW air filter
- Spare fan belt
- Old fan belt
- An assortment of fuses
- A 6th tire on a rim, to keep at home, so you have a spare when you come home after a flat.

◆◆◆

Why??

Even if you are a guy who says, "My repair facilities are a cellular phone, a credit card, and my AAA membership", I will recommend that you should carry these parts. Even if you are a guy who deals with problems by using just those tools, there are times when you need some specialized parts. And if the AAA guy does not have them, you are hung up. If you break down on a Saturday night, and there are no parts stores open, you may not MOVE until Monday morning. So if you carry a small amount of spare parts, then you are much less likely to be stranded on the road. This is especially true if you have a car that is not common – such as a Jaguar or Alfa – that uses not-standard spare parts. This list is not a Chapter, because having Spare Parts does not keep you out of accidents. But having Spare Parts helps you keep out of Breakdowns, so I put it in as an Appendix.

There is one other item that you might consider. I have not been able to get any opinion whether this is a useful or a silly item. But if you were going to drive across Africa, you would certainly bring along – a spare electronic ignition module. Because without it, you are not going to move. Am I wrong?

Another Reason...

The other reason to carry all these parts – the old ones and the new ones – is that somebody might flag you down and say, "I have a car just like yours, and it won't run. Can you help me?" If you have extra spare parts, you can give that person a chunk of wire, or a filter, or a fan belt, and still have one for you.

I mean, if I were driving on a dirt road in the middle of nowhere, and a guy with a Chevy or a Ford seemed to be having car trouble, I would definitely stop and see if I could help. But if it's along a freeway, I normally would NOT stop to help a Ford or Chevy, because I know nothing about the procedures or parts or tools that a Chevy or Ford needs, to get going.

But I usually DO stop to see if I can help a guy with a VW, because I often DO have the info, the parts, and the tools needed. And I carry a spare (old) fan-belt that I can give away. And a spare fuel filter. And a spare gallon of gas. And a spare set of points. Sometimes I am *exactly* the guy to help him get going again.

Now, if *you* know anything about fixing a Ford like you drive, *you* should stop and help a guy with a Ford. I will, too, but only in the boonies. And if you stop to help a VW, but only in the boonies, I understand that completely.

P.S. – I don't know about YOUR car, but If I put on MY spare fan belt, I should go and buy another fan belt, RIGHT AWAY. Because the new one I just put on may fail in a short time. I think that may be because the fan-belt I carried around several years has gotten degraded, so it will not last long. Plausible?

7/11/22

PEASE PORRIDGE*

APPENDIX K — WHAT'S ALL THIS DEAD CAR STUFF, ANYHOW?

Every year, in January, I compile a list of all the Dead Cars I have seen over the last calendar year, along the highways. If you want to see it, send me a <u>SASE</u> and I'll mail you a copy. This year will be the 22nd annual list, going back to when I lived in Massachusetts in 1969. It lists every car according to their manufacturer, and sometimes by type.

For example, I try to keep the GMC cars separate from the Fords or the Chryslers, but I can't possibly segregate the Chevys from the Buicks – for all I know, they have the same engine anyhow.

I do separate the Volkswagens from the SAABs, which was my original intention. Back in 1969, I was trying to show some of my buddies that the SAABs of that era were less reliable than VWs, even though the SAAB engines had "only 7 moving parts". I found that there were lots of dead or abandoned Volkswagens along the roads, but there were also quite a few dead SAABs. It seemed that there were more SAABS than one would expect from the number of SAABs on the road. Over the years, I kept on listing all the cars I saw, dead or accidented or abandoned, foreign or domestic.

Now, what's the significance of these lists? Do they prove that one car is more reliable than another? No, not really, because even though you could tell how many cars of any particular make are registered in any state, that does not tell you the number being *driven*. But I have had a lot of fun, keeping notes on the Dead Cars. And my friends find it amusing to look at these lists.

Just the other day, I was writing down the data for one dead Mercedes Benz, and 1 abandoned Ford with a flat tire. My passenger asked, "You mean, every time you see an abandoned car, you write down a note?" I replied, "Sure... doesn't everybody?..."

In the last 5 years, I began to keep a list of the cars I saw with no brake lights. I carry an envelope that I can hold up to warn a driver, "YOU HAVE NO BRAKE LIGHTS". I really don't like to see cars driving around with no brake lights.

Because it is all too easy for them to collect an innocent car on their rear, when they hit their brakes, but the following driver cannot tell this. So an accident can happen, and in my neighborhood, insurance rates go up even tho many of us had no accidents at all.

On the other side of the placard, it says "YOU HAVE ONLY ONE BRAKE LIGHT" – because after one brake light burns out, what happens next? The other one burns out, and the car is left with none. So I like to warn these guys to get their brake lights fixed. In 1990, I notified 69 cars that they had no brake lights, and 144 cars that they had only one brake light.

There were about 6 guys with no brake lights that got away – sometimes they turn off in traffic before I can catch up with them, or sometimes a light changes against me. Still, I think I'm doing something useful, even though my wife

419

sometimes gripes that I beep my horn too much, just to tell a guy he has only one brake light.

But think about this: A guy has only a right brake light. He starts to signal for a right turn. Then he hits his brakes. In many cars, the brake light and the blinkers are connected to the same bulb, so when he hits the brakes, no change occurs, and the driver behind cannot tell he is hitting his brakes. So in some cases, one brake light burned out is as bad as no brake lights at all.

What do I do about brake lights? On each of my four cars, I've rigged extra brake lights up high, so that they're really noticeable to the drivers behind me. If 1 or 2 bulbs burn out, I still have a couple left. Best of all, I can look in my mirror and see if the extra bulbs light up when I hit the brakes, so I can tell if the brakes' pressure-switch is working. Now, if *you* want to take a broad pen and print neatly on a blank envelope, or a piece of paper taped to an envelope, *you, too,* will be able to warn drivers: "YOU HAVE NO BRAKE LIGHTS" and "YOU HAVE ONLY ONE BRAKE LIGHT".

Now, just what kind of car do *you* drive, Pease, to get good reliability? Ah, yes, I drive a car with exactly the right amount of modern electronic, computerized equipment – a 1968 VW Beetle. (My wife drives a newer car, a 1969 Beetle.)

Now, as an engineer, I suppose I should say good things about all the fancy electronic fuel injection and spark computers and diagnostic computers and Lambda sensors. But I get 31 mpg and the car goes just as fast as I want, and that's good enough for me. The bottom line is that I prefer a car that has proven itself by running reliably for 244,000 miles. (*Ed.: now up to 340 k.*) In fact, until a couple months ago, it was still running on the Original Engine, the original crank and pistons and cylinders (though it is true I had replaced the cylinder heads).

Sometimes I do connect a Heathkit

electronic ignition system to minimize wear and tear on the breaker points. But right now it's on the blink, so I just went back to the old conventional (Kettering) ignition system, points and coil and distributor and "condenser". I set my own timing and I adjust my own valves. That is one good thing about old, simple cars – if something does go wrong, (which is rarely) you can fix it yourself.

Do you ever count your own car, Pease, when it's dead? Yes, but that is not very often. One time my coil burned out. One time my distributor got loose and lifted out of its spigot, and it took me a full hour to figure out that when the engine turned, there had to be a reason why the distributor and its rotor did not. Another time a fuel hose fell off, but I fixed that and got going quickly, so I only counted it as 1/2.

There are several cases where I count a car as 1/2. For example, if a guy with a Volvo is talking to a guy with a Datsun, and they both have their hoods up, I may count 1/2 Datsun, 1/2 Volvo, 1 Helper. I count people who are obviously helping out as a Helper, not as a Dead Car. If I'm not sure it's a Rabbit on the other side of the road on a rainy night, I may count 1/2 Rabbit, and 1/2 Modern Boxy Car (1/2 Modbox). If I can't even tell if it was probably foreign or U.S.-made, it gets scored as "1 car".

Do I think that electronic systems are going to improve the reliability of vehicles? Well, maybe. I recall the story of one of the first trucks that had an anti-lock brake system. They were driving innocently down the road when a nearby driver keyed the transmitter on his CB radio, and the truck immediately locked up all its brakes. It turned out, somebody had decided it would *hurt* the reliability to add bypass capacitors across all of the sensors and the inputs of the sensor amplifiers.

That's what you learn from MIL HDBK-217, remember? So when the transmitter went on, all of the amplifiers went berserk. Oh, the *amplifiers* were perfectly "reliable", but the system had not been engineered properly. It was a miracle that nobody was behind the truck when it locked up all its brakes.

Are the new electronic system better for the environment? Maybe so. Maybe a new sedan can travel down the road emitting even less smog and emissions than my VW, so long as its computer is working right. But 10 years down the road, what happens when you can't get parts for the computerized systems? My car will still be running just fine. I think I'll stand pat.

After all, I have all of the tools and techniques I need to keep old VWs running forever. *Forever?* Well, there are old VWs around here that are over 35 years old, and if I can keep my good new Beetles running 35 more years, they may outlive me. You would not want to bet that I can't keep them running. Meanwhile, if I see another VW broken down on the road, I stop and see if I can help.

Sometimes I have a tool or a gallon of gas, or the spare part they're in need of – a fan belt, or some points, or a clamp for a fuel hose. So I try to help solve their problem. If we can't figure out what's wrong, I leave them a SASE so they can write to me and explain what was the problem once they find out.

For example, one guy sent me a letter stating that the 1969 Bus he had just bought was merely out of gas. The gas gauge was broken, but the previous owner, of course, had not warned him about that. (Not very nice.)

So, when I see a dead, abandoned, or broken-down car along the freeway, I score it. I categorize and count it. Now, if a guy is just changing a tire, or pouring in a spare gallon of gas, I list that problem, but I do not count the car as dead or abandoned. In 1990, I saw 24 people that ran out of gas, 139 with a flat tire, 211 pulled over by a cop, and 16 with a broken drive-shaft (remember, none of my cars has a drive-shaft). I counted 293.5 GMC cars, 146 VWs, and one Citroen. What are the corresponding totals for 1991? I'll let you know as soon as I have them all added up.

Comments invited! / RAP /
Robert A. Pease / Engineer
National Semiconductor Corp.
M.S. D2597A
P.O. Box 58090
Santa Clara, CA 95052-8090

This Column was originally published in Electronic Design Magazine, February 6, 1992, and is reprinted here with the kind permission of Penton Publishing.

Afterthoughts... I was too busy writing, to compile the 1994 and 1995 Annual Dead-Car lists. I had a big BOX full of envelopes with little lists of dead cars, but I did not have time to add them up. Finally in January of 1997, I got out a composite list for 1994-1996. I'll send you this if you send me a SASE (Self-Addressed Stamped Envelope). My friends at work always waste a lot of time, reading these lists of Dead Cars. So to make sure everybody in the Industry gets equally goofed up, I send copies of my List to engineers at other companies on the east coast, and overseas, too.

I can mention that, five years after I wrote this, my Beetle is still able to get through smog checks, with low emissions, with no problems. A lot of cars are having problems passing the 1996 smog tests – but not me. /rap

– You do not have to draw up your own placard saying "YOU HAVE NO BRAKE LIGHTS" – you can just photocopy the one in this book. See the following pages. Or, if you want to, of course you can make up your own....

7/11/2²

PEASE PORRIDGE*

APPENDIX L – WHAT'S ALL THIS STUPID, DANGEROUS STUFF, ANYHOW?

Recently, I was remarking to a colleague about a small write-up I saw in one of the IEEE publications, about some college professors who were trying, many years ago, to make a hard disk. They had somebody fabricate a 36-inch diameter disc of 1/2 inch aluminum, and tried to bring it up to 3600 rpm. The air drag was so much that they had to resort to outrageous amounts of power to pull it up to speed.

I said I had seen an old hard disk, retired from service at Singer Librascope. It was 4 feet across, and it ran at the synchronous speed of 3600 rpm. They must have run that one in a vacuum, to avoid the terrible drag losses. My old hiking friend Les Earnest told me this was one of 6 disks on a horizontal spindle, each 47.5 inches in diameter, 16-inch inside diameter, 7/16 inch thick, and weighing 70 lb. Les has one suspended from his living-room ceiling, and uses it for a coffee-table. I have heard of such a disk getting loose, and starting to spin on the floor, until it gathers up speed and smashes into things....

My friend looked around and, seeing it was a quiet time, started to tell me about his long-ago experiences at a Defense Contractor. He had a ball-bearing which had gotten kind of dirty and crummy, so he washed it in solvent, and got it nice and clean. Then he took it over to an air hose, and opened up the nozzle, to clean out the solvent. He held the bearing by the outer race, and as he played the air on the bearing, it began to spin, pretty fast. Wow

– it got up to a really good whine. He called over to a couple of his pals – "Hey, come over and look at this." They went over and watched him turn on the air. The bearing began to whine – faster – faster – Suddenly there was only the hiss of the air, and then silence. The inner race of the bearing was GONE. The balls were gone. Where did they go? They looked all around. They never did find any pieces, and they never did find any holes where pieces had gone through a wall or ceiling. They decided they were very lucky, and shut up, and went back to work. Later, they learned that company regulations (although unpublished) specified that anybody blowing air onto a ball-bearing like that could get fired – even though this offense was not listed nor defined.

Anyhow, the guy computed that with 100-psi air, you could get the inner races up to about 140 mph. On a 1" radius, that's about 20,000 g's, and that is not a safe area to expect a steel member not to rip itself to shreds. Those guys were VERY lucky.

Now, this falls into the category of telling your kids, "Don't put beans in your ears." Or, "Whatever you do, don't put those beans up your nose." Needless to say, telling a kid to not do something, is to almost ensure that they can think of nothing else. About 19 years ago, Lois Lee, our premier mask designer, told me, "Shouldn't you worry about this problem, Bob?" I told her, "Don't think about it. Also, don't think about Annapolis, Maryland, and don't think about Pensacola, Florida." To this day, if I tell Lois, "Don't think about it", Lois says,

*Reprinted from ELECTRONIC DESIGN/ October 24, 1995

"Which one should I not think about, Annapolis or Pensacola?"

So, I'll tell you that you should probably never blow air onto a ball bearing so it can spin at any appreciable speed, to blow out the cleaning solvent. Blow squarely, transversely, down onto the bearing, or, hold both races. Let it turn over, *real* slow. If you insist on doing stupid things, and you want to over-rev a ball bearing, make sure there is no person and no car for at least a half mile, in the plane of rotation of the bearing. Make sure the fragments are not likely to ricochet and hit YOU. Are there any other precautions? Oh, yeah, make sure you don't get caught. Also if you goof, have a buddy who can apply artificial respiration, and put on a tourniquet, and drive you to the hospital.

The other classical stupid, dangerous thing to do was proposed by Longfellow: "I shot an arrow into the air. It fell to earth, I know not where." THIS is the story of the kid who takes his new bow and arrows outside. After his parents warn him not to shoot at cats or other people, he figures out – he can make the arrow disappear! He aims STRAIGHT UP IN THE AIR, and lets it fly! For the first 3 or 4 seconds, he looks up in wonderment and satisfaction. Wow – he has done it! The arrow is OUT OF SIGHT. Then after a second of delay, he realizes in horror: that arrow is surely not going to stay up there. It will come back down. And perhaps, *quite nearby*.

He tries not to panic. Maybe he can wait until the arrow comes into sight, and then dodge it. But after two seconds, he realizes it's *much* too risky, trying to dodge an arrow coming at you head-on, nearly invisible. So – should he run? – which way? After a couple seconds of panicky indecision, he runs upwind as fast as he can. He almost always survives. But still, it's scary. Under what condition would I shoot an arrow up in the air? Only if I knew of some VERY sturdy beams I could stand under. Or a cave, or a couple feet of earth. I just do not want to fool around with this. (Just standing under a *roof* would not make me feel safe, not at all.)

Now, what if I fired a gun straight up in the air? Well, the bullet is sure to fall back down at a velocity much lower than the muzzle velocity of 400 to 1000 ft/second. So if I could find a large, sturdy tree limb, I would guess that is not an unsafe place to stand, waiting for the bullet to come back down. A while back, I inherited an old rifle, a Remington single-shot .22 rifle. The first thing I did was to install a lock on the trigger, so it could not be fired. Then I tried to take it down to the police station to register it, but they said they could not register the gun as it had no serial number. Maybe I should try again?

Anyhow, after I carefully cleaned the barrel, I tried a couple test shots. I shot at a 2-inch-thick old telephone book. I was impressed when the bullet came out the other side with still a little velocity. I have not yet set up a ballistic pendulum to measure its muzzle velocity. I have not yet shot a bullet straight up in the air. I have not yet put any beans up my nose. You better not, neither....

Then a story came rambling through the Internet, about the "Darwin Award" nominee.

"You all know about the Darwin awards — it's an annual honor given to the person who did the gene pool the biggest service by killing themselves in the most extraordinarily stupid way.

Last year's winner was the fellow who was killed by a Coke(tm) machine, which toppled over on top of him as he was attempting to tip a free soda out of it.

And this year's nominee is:

The Arizona (U.S.) Highway Patrol came upon a pile of smoldering metal imbedded into the side of a cliff rising above the road, at the apex of a curve.

The wreckage resembled the site of an airplane crash, but it was a car. The type of car was unidentifiable at the scene. The boys in the lab finally figured out what it was, and what had happened.

It seems that a guy had somehow got ahold of a JATO unit (Jet Assisted Take-Off, actually a solid-fuel rocket) that is used to give heavy military transport planes an extra 'push' for taking off from short airfields. He had driven his Chevy Impala out into the desert, and found a long, straight stretch of road. Then he attached the JATO unit to his car, jumped in, got up some speed, and fired off the JATO!!

Best as they could determine, he was doing somewhere between 250 and 300 mph (350-420 kph) when he came to that curve.

The brakes were completely burned away, apparently from trying to slow the car. Note: Solid-fuel rockets don't have an "off" ... once started, they burn at full thrust 'til the fuel is all gone.

P.S. – what a ride, can you imagine the excitement? – Actually I know someone that did something similar with a Racing go-kart engine and a minibike. These engines have a very peaky Torque vs. RPM curve. There was lots of blood, a helmet worn down to the lining, and 6 months of healing."

Well, I have not yet gotten any confirmation on whether this really did take place, but it *does* sound plausible. But I want to make this point: if a buddy told you he was planning to do this, would you be able to talk him out of it? Would you be able to convince him, by computing that 10,000 lb. of thrust for 20 seconds is probably enough to get him in REAL TROUBLE? I would hope so. I checked in some books to find out what ratings are available for JATO bottles. In general, they are MUCH too big and powerful to put on a car. That would give you about 2 G's. Even from a standing start, your speedometer would go past 120 mph in about 6 or 7 seconds, and past 180 in 10 or 12 seconds. And Impalas never did have brakes worth a darn – not to mention, enough braking to hold back 10,000 lb. at 100 mph. I did find one cute little JATO unit listed, weighing just 85 lb.,

that put out 5,000 lb. for 2 seconds. A unit that can put out 5,000 lb. for 20 seconds weighed about 650 pounds – not exactly easy to strap on the back of an Impala. The story begins to sound a little unlikely....

I once read that the young Thomas Edison found a hillside with a road cut into it. He measured the hillside and the cut. He went home and computed that if he came down the hill on his sled, he would have enough speed and trajectory to be able to LEAP over the cut. He tried it. The sled smashed into the lower side of the cut, and he was, luckily, only very badly bruised. He went home and discovered that he had dropped a decimal place in his computations.

So don't get sloppy with your math, when the answer to the problem is not just a point on your grade, but, WILL YOU LIVE OR DIE? And don't put too many beans in your ears. (Long needle-nosed pliers, which most of us electronics guys own, can get the beans out, without TOO much pain.)

Dennis Monticelli told me about a third-hand account he heard, which he suspects did really happen. There were 2 amateur radio enthusiasts who wanted to rig up their antenna for better DX, more distance and better reception. They wanted to put it on the highest place around. Where was that? On top of a power tower. So one guy climbed up the tower, carrying his antenna. UNfortunately, about 80 feet up, he bumped the antenna against a high-voltage wire, was horribly shocked, badly burned, and was dead when he hit the ground. His buddy watched thoughtfully. What an unfortunate error. So he took the antenna, climbed up the tower, and *very carefully* eased the antenna past all the high-voltage wires, and mounted it on the top of the tower. When the ambulance arrived to carry the first fellow to the morgue, the second fellow was enthusiastically exclaiming about the *great* reception his radio was now getting!

Darwin only got one of *them*.

Chester Simpson told me about a duck hunter who was a real cheapskate. When a duck was shot out of the sky, wounded but not dead, flapping and flopping on the ground, the guy was too cheap to use a shell to dispatch the bird. Rather, he turned the shotgun around and clubbed the bird to death with the butt of the gun. This went on for several years until... you guessed it. The gun went off and finished *him* off. Revenge?

All this is not exactly the same as SMWISICDI,[1] or, "Show Me Where It Says I Can't Do It", but rather more like, "Let Me Show You Why You Had Better NOT Do That". Those of us who are engineers have some responsibility to caution people when something they are proposing to do is REALLY stupid and Dangerous. OK?

Comments invited! / All for now. /
RAP / Robert A. Pease / Engineer
Address: M/S D2597A
National Semiconductor Corp.
P.O. Box 58090
Santa Clara, CA 95052-8090

◆ ◆ ◆

[1] Robert A. Pease, "What's All This SMWISICDI Stuff, Anyhow?", Electronic Design, May 9, 1991, p.133.

This Column was originally published in Electronic Design Magazine, October 24, 1995, and is reprinted here with the kind permission of Penton Publishing.

◆ ◆ ◆

P.S. – I never did hear any feedback from any of Electronic Design's 165,000 readers, to indicate that that car crash really happened. Add that to the difficulty of mounting a 650-lb rocket on the back of a car, and the difficulty of mounting it so several thousand pounds of thrust will not cause it to tear loose, and I have to believe that never really happened.

Still, I made my point that engineers have some responsibility for cautioning their friends that some actions may have really dangerous consequences. Even if you are not an engineer, you have to think about this. If you wanted to try an experiment with your car, could a certain problem arise, that would get you in real trouble? FOR EXAMPLE, when you get in a skid on an icy road, and while you are sideways, then if you came to a bare stretch of pavement – how fast would you have to be going to make your car roll over? Refer to the Chapter on Skidding....

α

PEASE PORRIDGE*

APPENDIX M – WHAT'S ALL THIS DOUBLE-CLUTCHING STUFF, ANYHOW?

Recently, a pair of California Condors were released into the wilds of the San Gorgonio mountains of southern California. This was a significant event, because there had been Condors flying around those mountains from the year 60,000,000 B.C. to 1986 A.D. But in 1986, the naturalists convinced the California Fish and Game Dept. that to prevent the Condors from going extinct, they had to capture all the Condors and put them into protective custody until the breeding stock had gotten up to a viable level. For 6 years, these naturalists tried various approaches to bring the number of Condors to a healthy status, and they did finally succeed. One of the important tricks they used was to sneak in via a trapdoor, and every time Mama Condor would lay two eggs, they would remove one and put it in an incubator. The Mama would look down and decide to lay another egg, as the number of eggs did not look like a very large number. (Apparently Condors are not as smart as crows, which can count up to 5 or 6, fairly consistently.) Anyhow, by this procedure, the condor families were tricked into raising two clutches of eggs – one that the family would raise, and another clutch of eggs that would be hatched and raised by the naturalists, behind the scenes. This trick was called, "Double-clutching".

Now, if you have driven old cars, or trucks, or sports or racing cars, you will be amused at this play on words, because double-clutching is a procedure to save wear and tear on your gearbox, and also on your clutch, at the expense of a little

extra work for your left leg. What is double-clutching, (or, as the British call it, "double de-clutching") and why is it significant?

– Let's say you are accelerating in 2nd gear, and when you are ready to shift into 3rd, you decide not to use the standard approach, which is just to tromp on the clutch, take your foot off the gas, shove the shift lever into third, and let the clutch back out. You decide to double-clutch properly:

First, you take your foot off the gas and kick in the clutch. You shift into neutral, AND let the clutch out. You wait perhaps 0.3 to 1.0 seconds for the engine to slow down from its high revs, depending on how fast you were revving when you started to shift, and how much inertia the engine has to slow down. THEN you kick in the clutch and shift into 3rd, and let the clutch out quickly, and feed the gas appropriately. If you have judged it right, when you let the clutch out, there is not any JERK, and when you shove the lever into third, the gears and engine are at a synchronized speed, so there is minimum wear on the synchronizers, which are the tiny clutches that bring the clutch plate and the gears into smooth synchrony. Also there is usually less wear on the clutch plates.

What's the big deal? The main point is that when you try to shift into 3rd gear, the engine has slowed down itself and the clutch plate to the right speed, just about the same speed as the gearbox, so it saves wear on the synchronizers and the clutch. It can also save shock and strain on the whole drive-train, as the speeds are just

426

about synchronized when you let out the clutch.

Well, big deal. Cars have not needed double-clutching since the synchromesh transmission was popularized 50 years ago. Why bother?

Why fool around with anachronistic motions? Isn't it just buying trouble? Even Tom and Ray Magliozzi* claim that double-clutching is silly and stupid and wasteful of energy. Ah, but I can tell you the reasons.

First, in most cars, the actual gears are always in constant mesh, and the synchronizers only decide which pair of gears to connect to their shaft. But many trucks are still set up with a non-synchromesh gearbox, and so are some racing cars. With trucks, because they have so many gears, it is noticeably more efficient not to have all the gears in mesh, all the time, so with this "crash-box", you HAVE TO double-clutch, or you will not be able to shift. The same is true for racing cars, in which to gain the last couple percent of efficiency, only one set of gears is in mesh at any time, and you have to actually synchronize their speeds OR you can't get it in gear. Despite the obvious drawbacks of having to double-clutch, the gearbox is stronger than a comparable synchromesh one, and more efficient, and has less tendency to overheat.

Other reasons for double-clutching: because it is the right way to do it. Because it saves wear and tear on your synchronizers, in the long run, if you are planning to run your car over 200,000 miles, as I do. Because it is fun to do. Because in *very* cold weather, (–10 degrees F, for example) you may *have to* double-clutch to shift gears at all, at least for the first few miles.

But the most important reason is, if your clutch linkage ever fails, you can still shift and get home, by double-clutching, getting the engine and gears' speeds synchronized and then just EASING the shifter into the right gear. In the last 1,050,000 miles of driving VWs, I have lost

my clutch about 3 times, and each time, with careful planning, I have been able to drive home safely. One time I pulled into the Customs House at Calais, Maine, and discovered my clutch was out. I eased along carefully and managed to get all the way home, 350 miles, to Boston, where it was convenient to put the car in the shop to have the clutch repaired – much more convenient than in the middle of a vacation, or the middle of Maine.

Another reason is that on some old cars, first gear is not synchromesh, so if you need to shift into first without coming to a full stop, you have to double-clutch. Also, a lot of cars these days are made with weak, chintzy synchros, so they soon wear out, and to drive them gracefully, you need to double-clutch.

Note, when down-shifting, you have to shift into neutral and then *blip* the throttle momentarily before you shift into the lower gear. It requires practice and a good feel, a good touch, to do it right. Especially considering the embarrassing noises you make if you miss your shift into a low gear on a crash-box. For example, you should aim to have the revs just a little high, so if you miss, the engine will soon slow down, and the gears will then be at the right speed to mesh, and then the cogs will slip in....

OKAY, Pease, I'll try this double-clutching some day; but why do you bring up all *this* stuff in an electronics magazine? Ah, there is an excellent analogy: In most conventional switching regulators, the power transistor turns on while there is a lot of voltage across it, and after it turns off, the voltage usually increases to a large voltage. When the transistors turn on, the diodes are already carrying significant current, and the transistors have to turn the diodes OFF. This is all somewhat stressful, and causes the transistors and diodes to have large turn-on surges and turn-off surges – pulses of power on every cycle. Of course, diodes and transistors have been designed to withstand these stresses and surges with excellent reliability; we see them all the time.

Still, people have designed "resonant mode" switchers which are especially designed to have zero-voltage and zero-current switching. In these regulators, most of those turn-on and turn-off stresses are eliminated, because the transistor is at a very low voltage when you turn it on, and at a very low current when you are ready to turn it off. Consequently, most voltage and current transients are greatly decreased, so that less filtering and shielding is required to enable the complete regulator to have low Radio Frequency Interference (RFI). Now, to design such a supply takes a more complicated controller IC, and more expensive parts, and a very careful layout, and a lot of expertise in the electrical design. So while you get some advantages, you have to pay for them.

Now, when you want to build a compact high-performance switch-mode regulator at switching frequencies up to about 1 MHz, conventional switchers can do at least as well as resonant ones, in terms of cost, size, and performance. But if you need a switcher even smaller and faster than that (as most users do not), then when the switching frequency rises above 2 MHz, the resonant mode switchers begin to show real advantages.

At this time, National does not make these resonant-mode switchers, so I cannot offer you any detailed info about all of their advantages and their disadvantages. But I have explained most of their key features. And now you can see why the smooth, stress-less turn-on and turn-off of the transistors and diodes in these resonant-mode switchers are analogous to double-clutching your shifts.

P.S. – even if you double-clutch your shifts most of the time, as I do, do you know when is it a good idea NOT to double-clutch? My primary answer is, when you are in complicated traffic, and you don't want to fool around; or when

you are really struggling on an upgrade, and a speed-shift prevents you from losing speed. So, with every rule, you should be aware that there are times when the rule does not apply. Some day I'm going to write a book about that topic...

Comments invited.

RAP/ Robert A. Pease
Mail Stop D2597A
National Semiconductor Corp.
P. O. Box 58090
Santa Clara, CA 95052

* CAR-TALK, on many National Public Radio stations, is a wild mixture of automotive wisdom, and entertaining banter about cars, from Tom and Ray Magliozzi. I tune in nearly every Saturday morning. Ask your local NPR station for their broadcast time – if you like *my* stuff, and if you are interested in cars, you'll probably like *their* stuff.

This Column was originally published in Electronic Design Magazine, August 5, 1993, and is reprinted here with the kind permission of Penton Publishing.

♦♦♦

One of my readers pointed out that the transmissions for many sports cars and racing cars and trucks are NOT made with gears out-of-mesh. The gears are always in mesh, and they actually have cogs similar to synchronizers. They just do not have the synchronizer clutches... He's probably right.

♦♦♦

Another reader pointed out that many modern racing cars have computerized transmissions that shift, complete with double-clutching, in 50 milliseconds, with minimum stress on the parts, as all throttle errors and human errors are eliminated. Thus you avoid the possibility of missing a shift and busting your gearbox or over-revving your engine. I believe it.

Appendix N – ADVANCED TOPIC: HEEL-AND-TOE BRAKING

What the heck is THAT? A square-dance step? A ballet move? No. Heel-and-Toe braking is a tricky, delicate procedure – an advanced procedure. Specifically, when I am braking into a corner, I do not just brake, and I do not just down-shift. And I do not just double-clutch. I do all three.

Now, *how* can you keep your brakes on, and simultaneously downshift and double-clutch? (You guys with Slush-boxes can laugh – or you can be be jealous, but that is your problem.) *How* can you *blip* the gas, hit the clutch twice, and keep a steady foot on the brakes? Well, that is a good question. And the answer has been around for many years – it's a good trick.

First of all, let's assume you know how to downshift. Then let's assume you know how to double-clutch for a down-shift. That means – as described in the preceding Appendix on Double-clutching – you want to BLIP the throttle in the middle of your shift procedure, while the shifter is in neutral, and the clutch pedal is momentarily up. Well, it has been well known for 50 years that you can HOLD your toe on the brake pedal, and BLIP the gas pedal with your heel. This means you can use two feet for 3 functions – and that is what is needed.

EXACTLY How To Do It...

As you are braking fairly hard into a corner, when it is time to shift, *keep* your right toe on the brakes, and kick the clutch in, and shift into neutral. And, as you are double-clutching, let out the clutch while you are in neutral. THEN reach over with your right heel and *blip* the gas, just momentarily, to rev the engine a bit, as required. Then shift promptly into your lower gear, and if you did it right, let out the clutch quickly – and there will be no jerk. And all this time, you kept your right toe smoothly on the brakes, so the brakes do not lurch, either. Then, when you approach the apex of the corner, you are ready to get off the brakes and feed the gas, and as you come out of the corner, you can step hard on the gas and accelerate.

If you hadn't downshifted, you would be stuck in a high gear, with the engine at low RPMs, and would not have enough power to accelerate out of the corner. You might lug the engine to get up speed – or you might waste time, down-shifting, as you come out of the corner. Since you did your down-shifting coming *into* the corner, you are all set.

Now, it is true that if you don't know how to shift very well, and if you don't know how to double-clutch, really quite proficiently, then you are not ready to do this. But when you have your double-clutching down pat, then you can try heel-and-toe braking.

♦ ♦ ♦

Boy racers like to do this kind of stuff with great aplomb. And I do, too. But, race-car drivers do this at very good speed and excellent proficiency. They do this while racing at more than 9/10 of full braking effort, and I do not. Still, if you can do this exercise smoothly, you can get your car to make better speed through a corner, go faster, and slow down more smoothly, and accelerate more smoothly, and not abuse the car. If you do this right – you will put less wear on the car – and less wear on the brakes. The budget for auto racing in Formula 1 has been over $50 million dollars per year for the last 40 years. Therefore, the art of heel-and-toe has been around, and reinforced by $$$$, for a lot of years.

Anybody with a good car, with a stick shift, can see if this is a good way to drive. I'm not saying you want to practice this while taking your Aunt Tillie to the Opera – but if you are very smooth, she may not be able to tell. I mean, I do it 5 or 10 times per day. Sometimes I am just in a hurry – but other times it is just the right way to play the game, fast or slow. Even if I am not braking hard. Other times, I *alternate* between braking and downshifting. (That is not bad, either.)

What If You Didn't?

The point is, if you did NOT heel-and-toe, when you are braking really hard, if you downshift and suddenly let out the clutch, the extra force of bringing the engine up to speed when the clutch is let out, can cause the wheels to skid – because you had the brakes on so hard, that the wheels were on the point of sliding. OR, if you were not racing, then when you let out the clutch, the car will *jerk*. OR, if you just use your brakes, and you do NOT downshift, you will use your brakes more – and when it is time to accelerate, you will be in too high a gear.

– OR, if you DON'T use heel-and-toe, then you might have to brake early, and then shift down, and then brake some more. That's not a bad idea, as it rests your brakes. But when you really have to brake hard, and you are braking into a corner, it is a good idea to downshift, so you will be ready to accelerate coming out of the corner.

So if you want to be a good, fast, *SMOOTH* driver, and you are already good at double-clutching your down-shifts, then heel-and-toe work is the next thing to study, and practice, until you get it right, and smooth, too. And that's the FINAL DETAIL, the final refinement, for Brakes and Braking, and using your Clutch and Downshifting – all in one merged procedure.

Practical Uses for Heel-and-Toe

I already mentioned, back in the Chapter on the Clutch, that a guy with bad handbrakes and a sick engine was able to get out of a bad predicament on a steep hill, by stomping on the gas *and* the brake, too, both with his right foot. That is a form of Heel-and-Toe procedure.

Also, when my engine is not quite warmed up, in the first half mile, it may idle roughly and try to stall when I am coming to a stop sign. By using heel-and-toe technique, I can reach over and blip the gas, and prevent it from stalling, as I stay on the brakes. So this is not just an abstruse, exotic concept for fast, hard, sporty driving. It can be useful in a real-world setting. However, your brake pedal has to be adjusted reasonably low, so your right toe can rest on the brakes and the heel can reach over to hit the gas pedal.

When NOT To Use Heel-and-Toe?

When you are driving on snow or ice, it is quite important to drive smoothly. However, simply braking without downshifting is usually OK, as you are not braking very hard, so your brakes are not going to overheat. So, when driving on snow or ice, heel-and-toe technique is not important. Not a big deal. I usually do *not* use heel-and-toe on snow. And if you are driving very moderately or gently, you can alternate with braking and down-shifting, so you don't have to do both at the same time.

And a friend pointed out that some race-car drivers in Grand Prix Cars (Formula 1) do not have to double-clutch because they have computers that shift the gears of the "manual transmission", automatically, in 50 milliseconds, less than 1/10 of a second. The computers do the double-clutching, and they *blip* the gas all automatically, on some of the most modern race cars. Since you or I will never get to drive one of those cars, then we may still find double-clutching a useful technique to learn....

Appendix O – INVITATION to READERS

Now, I've been telling you a lot of my ideas about good driving and safe driving. It's time for you to turn the tables on me, if you want to.

1. If you think I said anything stupid, or *wrong*, in this book, please write to me. I promise to read your letter and think about it. I'll try to reply. I mean, you could be right, and I could be wrong. Or maybe the other way. I can't guarantee to get every debate settled, but I'll try. Send to the address below. Please include a return address, if possible. If you want to argue with me, and you got some facts on your side, it would be nice if you could include a copy of those facts.

2. Likewise, if there is something that I forgot to put in, that I should have put in, let me know. And I'll try to comment.

3. I may someday have a follow-up book with more educational examples of accidents. If you saw an accident, or had one happen to you, or a near miss, that was *interesting* or *educational* or *enlightening*, I would not mind hearing about it. I don't care whom you blame the accident on – you can blame it on the other guy, if it was really your fault. You can tell this from any viewpoint you want. But try not to bend or stretch the facts very much. As you may have noted, I think real examples are some of the best, most educational ways for learning. Permission to publish will be obtained. All stories will be kept anonymous. Identity will be destroyed before any publication. If you want to tell the story with a code name (as I have done with every accident in this book) that would simplify things.

4. I would be interested in hearing about any roads that you think are interesting or pleasant or amazing. That may make a fun list, too.

5. If this book keeps you out of an accident, tell me about it!

I can observe that there were a dozen topics that I did not know, and my reviewers told me about them, and I put them in the book. There were a dozen *other* topics, that I *DID* know, and I forgot to put them in, and when the reviewers reminded me, I put them in, too. I am sure there are some more topics of both of those classes, and I will add them in – as soon as you tell me. OK?

– Thank you. / R. A. Pease

– Send your comments to: Robert A. Pease
682 Miramar Avenue
San Francisco CA 94112-1232

432

Appendix P – CHECKLISTS

If you are going to drive, you might as well do it competently.

If you are going on a trip – you might as well do that competently, too. If airplane pilots need a checklist, maybe you need a checklist, too, for your driving and for your trips. These checklists are NOT copyrighted. Copy a dozen, and keep several in your car. Copy as many as you want. Give one to a friend – it is supposed to be useful. *These two pages are not copyrighted.*

If you start out on a trip without any one of these things, you could either get into trouble, or have an accident, or have a breakdown, or waste your whole trip, and have to repeat it. Most cars cost at least 5 or 10 cents per mile to drive, so repeating a mere 20-mile (round-trip) journey will cost you at least $1 or 2, not to mention the time you wasted. Just the other day, I went to a store to buy cream – and forgot to buy coffee. Had to go back later. Dumb!

If I myself start out to buy groceries, and I run out of gas, or have some kind of breakdown, I am at worst either 1/4 mile from my house, or 1/4 mile from the store. Any place, in-between, I can roll downhill to a gas station. Maybe if YOU leave YOUR house (or ranch) to buy groceries, and run out of gas, you might be stuck 10 miles from any road, and 2 hours of walking from the nearest house or car. So YOUR checklist would be a little different from MINE. I like to go out on drives in the back country, and when I do, I have to be pretty well equipped, but I don't have to be terribly well equipped just to go to the grocery store. But maybe you do.

CHECK LIST for Small Trips

- ❑ Can I walk?
- ❑ Take a Bicycle?
- ❑ Enough gas?
- ❑ Enough money?
- ❑ Wallet *including*
  - ❑ Driver's License?
  - ❑ Credit Card?
- ❑ Glasses?
- ❑ Sunglasses?
- ❑ Seatbelt on?
- ❑ If you are going on an errand to bring SOMETHING to SOMEBODY, did you BRING IT?

- ❑ Address?
  (If you are going to a new place)
- ❑ Phone Number?
- ❑ Map ? (If you are going to a new place)
- ❑ Shopping list?
  (If you are going shopping)
- ❑ Diapers?
  (Don't leave them on top of the car!)
- ❑ Baby food?
- ❑ The baby? (Don't forget HIM)
- ❑ Quart of Oil
- ❑ Water
- ❑ Spare gasoline
- ❑ Spare key

If you like this book, send $21.95 to Robert Pease, 682L Miramar Avenue, San Francisco, CA 94112.

CHECKLIST for Longer Trips – Vacation Trips

- ❏ Money, travellers' checks
- ❏ Airline tickets
- ❏ Reservations
- ❏ Maps
- ❏ Check tires
- ❏ Check Belts
- ❏ Check hoses
- ❏ Check oil?

♦♦♦

BIGGER CHECKLIST: for Big Long Trips:

– All of the above, PLUS:

- ❏ Water
- ❏ Ice-chest, ICE
- ❏ Food
- ❏ INSPECT 5 tires
- ❏ Check all 4 tires
- ❏ and spare tire
  for good pressure.
- ❏ Jack
- ❏ Planks
- ❏ Check hoses
- ❏ Check fanbelts
- ❏ Change oil?
- ❏ More money
- ❏ PLASTIC

CHECKLISTS for Winter Trips

Warm clothes,

- ❏ Hat
- ❏ Coat
- ❏ Mitts
- ❏ Boots
- ❏ Sleeping bags?
- ❏ Snow scraper?
- ❏ Shovel?
- ❏ Chains?

♦♦♦

Check fluids:

- ❏ power steering
- ❏ oil
- ❏ antifreeze.

Spare parts:

- ❏ Fan Belt
- ❏ Plugs, wires
- ❏ Tools
- ❏ whatever...
- ❏ Special items you want to bring. (Quilt for Aunt Bessie, Cigars for Uncle Jack...etc. – Don't Forget – !!)
- ❏ Camping gear – as you prefer –
- ❏ SEE Checklist for Backpack Trips.
- ❏ SEE Checklist for Business Trips.

♦♦♦

I *wanted* to include my favorite old Check-lists for equipment and *stuff* to bring on Business Trips and on Mountaineering (Hiking or Backpack) trips, but they didn't fit into the book. If you want a free copy of the lists, send a SASE.

You are permitted to have a good expanded list. And if you send me your ideas, I would be delighted to hear them. R. Pease, 682L Miramar Ave., San Francisco CA 94112.

Appendix Q – HUMOR

If we are going to be as serious as possible, about how to avoid accidents, we must also consider the idea of *humor*, and humorous stories about accidents. Somebody may say, "That's terrible, Bob – we don't want to laugh about that. That's no laughing matter." Well, anybody who always takes everything too seriously, and has no sense of humor, does not have to *read* this Appendix. Just skip 5 pages, and you won't even have to think about it. OK? But, if you want to read it, just keep reading....

◆ ◆ ◆

One of my favorite stories is about the guy who drives into a service station and says – "Hey, have you got a P215SR14 tire?"

The garageman says, "Sure, I got them."

The driver says, "Okay, I got a flat; put a tire on this rim."

The garageman says, "Pretty bad cut there."

The driver says, "Yeah, I cut it on a milk bottle."

The garageman says, "Didn't you see it?"

The driver says, "Naw, the kid musta had it under his coat."

◆ ◆ ◆

One of my friends told me this next story, which he says happened to a friend of his family:

The father of the family came down to breakfast and announced, "If you notice the big scrape mark on the car, don't worry, I did it."

So of course everybody went out to look, and there was a big scrape mark.

The mother asked, "How did you do that?"

And he replied, "My headlights went out, and I had to drive home with no lights."

She asked, "Where were you driving, to get such a scrape?"

And he replied, "Down on the bridge on River Road."

And she asked, "How come the scrape is on the *left* side of the car?"

And he replied, "I was passing another car, on the bridge...."

435

The guy who told me this story says that driver was a Minister, and he believes it is the actual truth of what was said. I dunno, I wasn't there.

♦ ♦ ♦

A couple years ago, I sent in a question to Doctor Science: "Those Sierra-Club members are always complaining that the air is so polluted. If we just let the air out of the tires on their Volvos and SAABs, all that air that is impounded would expand, and there would be a lot more fresh air. Don't you think it would be a good idea to go to a Sierra Club meeting and let all the air out of the tires of all the cars in the parking lot?"

Doctor Science had his assistant Rodney read this question, on the radio, and then he replied, "That's a great idea... Go ahead and do it, Bob."

But, I don't think I'll do it. First of all, my wife would get ticked off, because she is a Sierra Club member, and she'd just make me pump them up again. Secondly, the amount of air in all the tires in the world is about 0.000 000 000 03% of all the world's air – less than one millionth of a millionth of all the air – so the dilution we would get by letting all the air out of *all* tires would be negligible. Third, the air in tires usually smells AWFUL, so it would probably make the pollution WORSE.

This situation is not exactly an *accident*, but if this happened, it sure would be a catastrophe! Imagine how long it would take to get all our tires pumped up again!!

♦ ♦ ♦

A friend, Richard, told me this story about an old Vermont farmer. I won't hardly try to tell this in a good Vermont accent, but you can try:

Ephraim had been driving for 70 years, tractors, and Model T's, and farm trucks, and pick-up trucks. But he had never quite bothered to get a driver's license. Finally the town policeman, another old-timer, decided to help old Ephraim get his license. He took Ephraim down to Montpelier, to the Registry of Motor Vehicles, to help Ephraim get through the test. Now, Ephraim did not really know all the laws, nor the exact correct answer to every question, but he was getting along OK.

Finally the policeman asked him a test question: "Now Ephraim, let's say you are driving up Thompson's hill in your old pickup. And you see a hay-wagon going up the hill really slow. And you come up behind him. What would you do?"

Ephraim replied, "Why, I guess I would go out and pass that hay wagon." (Now, *you* know and *I* know that is not the correct answer to that question.)

Then the policeman said, "But now, suppose there is a big semi-trailer coming over the top of the hill at 55 mph. What would you do?"

Ephraim scratched his chin, and then his face lit up. And he said "Waaall, I'd reach over and wake up my brother Gus."

The policeman was dumb-founded. "Why would you do that?"

And Ephraim said, "Ayup, I would reach over and thump my brother Gus. And I'd tell him, 'Wake up, Gus.' Because Gus hain't never seen a big wreck before."

◆ ◆ ◆

– When you tell it like that, it's funny. If you can tell it with a good Vermont accent, it is even better. But when a big wreck really happens, it ain't funny, McGee.

◆ ◆ ◆

What's all this White Horse Stuff, Anyhow?

(This is another esaeP's Fable....)

One time, a mountain guide was driving in Switzerland. He had to drive over a high pass, to get to the place for the next day's climb. He was driving a little rented Renault.

As the day began to get late, and the sun began to set, the guide started up the pass. But it was a very high pass, and the little Renault began to run rough, and lose power, and then it ran even rougher. Finally, just a few kilometers short of the pass, the engine coughed and quit altogether.

The guide got out, and opened the engine compartment. It was cold, and getting dark, and it was windy. And he did not know very much about fixing cars. He peered into the bowels of the engine compartment. He tried to see if anything obvious was wrong. Nothing obvious. Then he heard a gust of wind behind him. It sounded like a deep voice, mumbling – "Turn the screw on the carburetor." He turned and looked behind him – there was a white horse, just standing there. He stared at the horse. The horse stared back.

After a moment, he looked back at the engine. The voice came again – "Turn the big screw on the carburetor." He whirled and stared at the horse incredulously – there was no other being or person for miles, on that barren mountainside. The horse just stood there, impassively.

He looked back at the car. And he reached in his pocket for his Swiss Army knife. He looked in the engine compartment – there was something on the left corner that looked like – a carburetor. And there was – a screw, a big one. A muffled voice came – "Turn the big screw clockwise." He gave the screw a full turn clockwise, and looked around. The white horse was cantering away.

He climbed in the driver's seat and turned the key. The engine fired – and ran smoothly. He put it in gear, and the little car ran smoothly, up over the pass, and then easily down the far side.

When he got down to town, he went to buy some *essence* (the French word for gasoline). He passed a few dozen francs to the garage man, and as he pumped the gas, the guide said, " You know, the strangest thing just happened to me, up on the pass. My car was running badly, and I couldn't get over the pass. And when I was trying to fix it, it seemed like a horse told me to turn a screw on the carburetor." The garage man nodded his head. "Aye, and that was a white horse?" The guide's eyes bugged out, and he nodded, yes. The garage man shrugged, "You were lucky. Another kilometer up the road, there's a black horse, and he doesn't know anything at all about Renaults."

◆ ◆ ◆

– Okay, that was more of a breakdown than of an Accident, but, I couldn't resist it.... I have to give credit to Steve Aisthorpe for this story.

◆ ◆ ◆

– Now, this next story is a SIGHT gag, so I will have to write out for you, some long dumb instructions in words, that represent what you will act out, when you tell the story. When you tell it, and act it out, it won't be nearly so awkward and dumb – literally. This story I also heard from Steve Aisthorpe, our hike leader with *Wilderness Travel* in the Swiss Alps in September of 1991. The reference to British Football is of course what we Yankees would call soccer, so you can insert a reference to your favorite Football team – or, to your least favorite team, as you please. Note, if you have a good reason to tell the joke about any other nationality, go right ahead. But the story works well when told BY a Scotsman, with a Scottish accent, so, ENJOY:

The Scotsmen and the Monkey

One time a Scotsman acquired a Monkey. This was really a very bright animal, and he soon found he enjoyed taking the Monkey to Football games, and the Monkey enjoyed it too. In fact, the Monkey enjoyed the games a good deal more than the man's wife did. So the Monkey went to the Football games, and the wife was delighted to be able to stay home.

One day the Scotsman went for a drive to an away game, in his van, with three friends and the Monkey, too. Unfortunately, while they were travelling, they had a terrible wreck, and all 4 men were very seriously injured – but the Monkey was not harmed. The man's wife was called, and she was very concerned. The policeman told her that there was no indication what caused the accident, because all of the men were still unconscious. The wife observed, "But the Monkey – he is very intelligent. He can't talk, but if you ask him questions, he may be able to show you what happened."

So the policeman began to question the Monkey. "Did you see what happened at the accident?" The Monkey nodded his head, yes. "Aha", says the policeman.

"What were the men doing?" The Monkey moved his hands, side-by-side, to indicate a person dealing cards. "So, they were playing cards?" The Monkey nodded yes. "Aha", says the policeman.

"What else were they doing?" he asked the Monkey. The Monkey held up his hands to his mouth, as if with a sandwich, and started to make chewing motions. "Aha – they were eating?" And the Monkey nodded his head, yes.

"What else were they doing?" The Monkey held an imaginary beer bottle to his lips and hoisted it up and tipped back his head. "Aha, so, they were drinking?" The Monkey nodded yes. "Aha. I thought so. That explains a lot. Thank you very much for your help."

Then the policeman thought for a second. "And what were YOU doing at the time of the accident?" And the Monkey grinned, and held up his hands – as if to a steering wheel – and turned the imaginary steering wheel back and forth.

◆ ◆ ◆

– OK, guys, if you know any funny stories about accidents, better than those, or even *nearly* as good – send them in and I may include them in future versions. Hey, if we wanted to pretend that gallows humor has no merit, well, you pretend what you want to. I still think an example – even a humorous example – is the best way to teach. Since hearing that story about the hay wagon, I have never passed a hay wagon on a steep hill.... / R. A. Pease

Appendix R – RENTAL CARS

Most of the time, when you rent a car, you are in a strange place, a strange city. And in a strange car. So you have to be pretty careful.

Are you on your own? – or with a passenger? Maybe your passenger can help you navigate, and read the maps, and watch out for strange traffic patterns. If you can do that, that's great.

Choice?

What kind of a car do you get? About 350 years ago, a guy named Hobson was in the business of renting horses to people. You could rent any horse you wanted, *so long as* that was the horse Mr. Hobson wanted to rent you, which was, the horse nearest the door. Thus, "Hobson's choice" is – no choice at all.

These days, if you rent a car, you usually have a much better choice than that. If you want a small car, or a mid-size car, or a big car, you can usually get what you want, when you make your reservation. When you get to the desk, you can still ask what kind of small cars they have available, or, big, or sporty, or whatever you are interested in. The car they previously told you was NOT available, might just be available. Or, perhaps you want to rent a car *with* a cellular phone? Some people consider that a useful piece of safety equipment, or necessary for business.

In Europe, rentals are moderately priced for manual-shift cars, but quite expensive for an Automatic Transmission (20 to 60% extra).

When I used to rent cars a lot, 20 or 30 years ago, I would try to rent a cheap VW Beetle, every other time, and then alternately I would rent a sports car like a hot V-8 Mustang, or a Corvette. The *average* cost was about the same as renting a dumb big sedan. But it was a lot more fun. So, if you shop wisely, you may be able to rent an interesting car.

Young Drivers...

But one of my buddies pointed out that some agencies will not rent certain kinds of cars to under-25-year-old drivers. Sporty cars, for example. This may vary with location, or with different rental companies. Also, young drivers – anyone under 25 – may have problems renting a car. Inquire in advance. If you are travelling on business, it may be better to get your company's travel agent to reserve a car, rather than rent it yourself. That way, they can see that you are a responsible person. Either way, make sure they do not think you are too young to rent their car. Ask before you leave.

Older Drivers...

In some European countries, car rental companies may reject drivers over age 75 or even 70, despite good driving records. Ask your travel agent to ensure this is OK, before you depart.

– If you are an independent businessman, your business insurance might not cover car rentals. Your personal insurance will not cover business rentals. To avoid being whip-sawed, ask your insurance agent.

"We Have No Reservation in Your Name..."

– This is not a paragraph on *car crashes* or *collisions*, but when the computer crashes, that sure can be a *disaster*. You show up at the rental counter, and they claim they never heard of you. At this point, I sure hope you brought your Reservation Number with you. (I went for years without even knowing the advantages of having a reservation number, but then some rental companies started to *give me* a reservation number, and I figured out that was a valuable item.)

Even if you do show them your reservation number, they may say, "Oh, our records show that *you* cancelled your reservation a week ago." At that point, you may have to call in the supervisor, or demand to talk to the rental agency's General Manager, or call up your Travel Agent and get THEM to intercede for you. Because *sometimes*, computers do get funny ideas in their heads. You might try arguing, "MY reservation Number is ABC994587. *I* certainly never cancelled that reservation. Can you show me that the person who cancelled my reservation used that Reservation Number? I bet you cannot do that. You had better find me a car, real fast!" You have an argument on your hands! Good luck!! And, if you are at all concerned about being hung up at a rush season, you might call up the rental agency a couple days before you start your trip, and ask them if they still have your reservation correct – just to be safe.

Rental Contract Problems...

I just saw on a rental agreement that one company may refuse to rent to you if you have "a bad driving record". I'm not sure how the rental company would find out if I had a bad driving record, but I'm glad I do not have to worry about that. Maybe if you had an accident in one of their cars, they would refuse to rent to you, next time....

Not all cars are priced similarly. The agency that gave you the cheapest rental rate, last month, may be a very expensive choice, this week. You should plan to shop around to avoid getting a poor price.

Safety Checkoff

Before you leave the rental car yard, be sure to check out several items, which will take, literally, just a minute. Make sure you can find the horn, the hand-brake (or emergency brake), and the release for the hand-brake. Make sure you can find the windshield wiper control, and the headlights. Even if it's not raining, you might hit a puddle, and you'll need the wipers. Even if it's daytime, you may come upon a tunnel or a dark underpass. Also, make sure you know how to get the key *out of* the ignition, as sometimes there is a fiendish hidden lever that will trap your key and puzzle you for many minutes.

If you are mostly familiar with old cars, you may be puzzled in your rental car, because you can't get it to shift from Park into Reverse or Drive. Most new cars have an interlock, so you have to step on the brakes before you can shift out of Park.

If the car is quite new, you can assume its tires have decent tread. But if there are a lot of miles on the odometer, you might check to see if the tires have good treads. This would be especially important if you expect to run into snow. Also, you might check that the tires do not have any cuts. Just to be safe.

Strange Traffic Patterns...

Navigation in a STRANGE town, with strange traffic patterns and strange driving culture (like Boston or New York), can be very challenging. Or Paris, where it is a little harder to read the street signs. So at least before you leave the yard, make sure you know what are the names or numbers of the first few roads you will be taking. Check your map. AND, even if you have to go back to ask the clerk at the counter, make sure you have adequate instructions to find your way back to the rental place! Usually, for a mainstream rental place, you just follow the signs to the airport, and then look for the signs for car rental return. But for some of the smaller agencies, you need a good map and a good sense of direction.

◆ ◆ ◆

Now, GO, and have fun. Just keep an eye out for the weird local traffic patterns and driving customs. I mean, it's hard for a Yankee to comprehend that in Paris, they drive around at night with only their parking lights on! If you turn on your headlights, they can tell *you* are some kind of weirdo!

– Just as you may drive from your home town to a place you have never been before, you can get to a strange place in a rental car. So you have to watch out for strange traffic, in a strange car. You have to be careful to avoid all sorts of odd potential accidents, from roads you may have never seen before, with drivers doing strange things you have never seen before. You have to keep your eyes open, and be alert for strange drivers coming at you from strange directions.

Strange Traffic?

I was recently driving a rented car in a strange place – it just happened to be Jackson Wyoming. I found myself driving VERY cautiously at intersections. Maybe it was because this little car was so low that its visibility was poor, when looking past other cars at corners? Maybe I was just nervous about traffic patterns, with strange vehicles coming at odd speeds? But it kept me being nervous and cautious at intersections, until I left town.

In this town, one of my friends stopped at a stop sign. He checked for traffic, and then started into the intersection. A car materialized out of nowhere and he hit the car, which set off his air bags. The airbags slammed and bruised him. The first view of the damages seemed to be not too bad. But when it was time to pay, it added up to $6000.

7/13/22

So maybe I was not too foolish about being extra-cautious. This may be wise, in any strange territory where traffic patterns seem odd – even if you cannot put your finger on WHY they are strange.

◆ ◆ ◆

Even when you are just returning to your old town, your old stamping grounds sometimes can be tricky for navigating – because sometimes they have changed. Some roads do not go through where they used to. Some roads may be new, and signs change, and exit ramps or entrance ramps may have been closed, and route numbers get changed. So be cautious.

Sometimes it is fun to go Shunpiking – take the old road. If there is a new road that takes most of the traffic off the old road, the old road may be pleasant, and a good way to go. I usually take old Route 20 from Worcester to Sturbridge Mass, because the Mass Pike takes all the heavy traffic away.

Strange Kinds of Cars...

NOW, if you are USED TO driving a Ford, you might decide to rent a similar Ford. But it's often more fun and adventurous to rent another make of car. You might learn something. Just remember that the light switches might be in a *completely different* place than you are used to!! You might also have to be careful also about strange gear-shift patterns.

Cruise Control

Many people run into Cruise Control for the first time, on a rental car. Fortunately, you never *have to* use it. Thus, you can postpone your familiarization until you are on an empty open road. Basically, there are just a few controls: ON; RESUME (resume the Previously Set Speed); OFF; Increase Speed; and Coast, or, Decrease Speed. So, in general, you can figure out these controls as you go along. Also, you'll be relieved to find that if the Cruise Control is on, and you touch the brakes, it turns off the Cruise Control, automatically.

You may not need Cruise Control to drive safely on any road. The main need for Cruise control is to keep you from going too fast on the wide open roads. If you set your Cruise Control at 69 mph on a 65 mph road, you are MUCH less likely to get a ticket than just driving at a speed that seems safe. It's entirely too easy to get up to 75 or 80, as many rental cars run smoother and quieter than what you left at home. That might not be a completely unsafe speed, but you won't get very far arguing with the Revenue Enhancement Officer.

Back Roads?

One of my buddies observed that if you rent a car, you never have to worry about four-wheel drive, because you can drive anywhere and never worry about dragging the under-side of the car over rocks – because it's just a rental car. That might seem true, but if you really get hung up, and badly stuck, or bust a hole in the gas tank, you'll be sorry you have to walk out and hire a tow-truck. So, don't make too many assumptions that you can drag a rented car over rough ground with impunity.

I just rented a car where the contract's fine print stated that I must not drive it off any paved road. No gravel roads. Even if my friend had a gravel driveway, I would have to park on the street, and walk up the driveway – ? Fat chance!! Still, I can see that the rental people have to protect themselves from idiots who take their cars on back roads and bash the heck out of them.

List of Rental Cars

Now, some people might say, poor Bob Pease, he has driven VWs so much, he doesn't know what a good car is. Well, yes and no. I have driven a lot of rental cars that were pretty interesting. A few had pretty good handling. Some had poor handling. Others were just mediocre. Most of them would go pretty fast if you just stepped on the gas long enough. But a lot of them sure were boring.

LIST of Good, Interesting Cars I have Rented:
- 1968 Corvette
- 1968 Mustang 350GTH (225 HP V-8, from Hertz)
- 1969 VW Beetle
- 1979 VW Rabbit
- 1965 VW Pickup
- 1993 Rover Metro 1.7 Liter
    (this is basically a Honda Civic, assembled in England.)
- 1990 Mazda 323 Protege
- 1995 Corsica

– I sure had a lot of fun in these cars!! Amazing!!

NEXT, a LIST of adequate (but not very interesting) rental cars:
- 1965 Ford Galaxie (my first rental car; in SF)
- 1970 Plymouth Fury III
- 1985 Ford Van (drove it 12,000 miles)
- 1967 Ford Mustang
- 1993 Ford Tempo
- 1996 Ford Escort
- 1967 Chevy Nova
- 1982 Chevy Vega
- 1990 Chevette
- 1994 Dodge Sedan (heavy but stable at 65 mph on packed snow)
- 1995 Pontiac Sunbirds
- 1988 Oldsmobile
- 1987 Buick
- a few Chevy Cavaliers
- assorted Fords

- assorted Chevys
- assorted Chrysler products

– *and* various foreign cars:
- 1992 Nissan Sentra
- 1989 Renault Alliance
- 1969 Triumph TR-6
- 1992 Geo Prism
- 1990 & 1994 Toyota Corollas
- 1969 Toyota Corona
- 1993 Mazda 323
- 1967 & 1966 VW Beetles
- and a few others....

– THEN, in Europe:
- 1994 Vauxhall Corsa (England)
- 1975 Ford Escort Estate Wagon (England)
- 1994 Peugeot 204 (France)
- 1994 Opel Astra (France)
- 1994 Siat (England)
- 1972 Fiat (France)
- 1993 Rover Metro 1400cc
- 1992 & 1995 Fiestas (England)
- and a few others....

THEN, a Short List of really BAD rental cars:
- 1970 GMC Vauxhall (England) (The Starter failed, AND the engine would not keep running on a misty evening; 23,000 miles on it.)

- 1976 Vega (The engine would not start at 20 below zero. The local garage could not get it to start, and the Rental company could not get it to start, so I asked them to tow this (brand new but useless) car away....)

Also I have driven various Fords and Chevys and Chryslers, Porsches and BMWs and Audis, Toyotas and Subarus and Mazdas and Datsuns, Peugeots and Saabs and Packards, pickups, trucks, and busses. So don't try to pigeonhole me as guy who only drives crummy slow cars!

– Now, have YOU driven an assortment of cars as broad as that?

– I have rented from dozens of Rental Agencies, but I have never rented a car from Rent-A-Wreck ... it was never convenient to do so.

Appendix S – SPARK

This was *going to be* a real Chapter, but it turned into an Appendix, because problems with your spark do not happen every day, and they are not likely to cause an accident. However, some problems with Ignition can be serious, and can lead to serious (that is, *expensive*) engine damage, which you want to avoid. So I rearranged this into the Chapter about Ping, and I put the rest of the information about Ignition into this Appendix on Spark.

Ignition problems can also cause breakdowns, and can be fairly hard to trouble-shoot. So, read this Appendix for general advice, in case your engine is running badly, and you suspect it may not be a fuel problem.

How Does Your Ignition System Work?

– In particular, how does your ignition system provide a spark to the right plug, at the right time? In the old days, cars had a simple set of breaker points, tungsten metal contacts that touched momentarily to get some current going through the *coil*, which is a sort of transformer. When the engine turned over far enough, typically just before the piston got to the top of the cylinder, the *breaker* points stopped making a contact – they *broke* the circuit – and the coil would convert that current into a little high-voltage energy, which is enough to make a spark. The *distributor* has a *rotor* that steers that high-voltage energy to the correct spark plug wire, and the spark occurs across the gap of the *spark plug*, inside each *cylinder* of your engine, at the right time. This system was invented in the 1920's, and is called the Kettering system. (Before *that*, cars used *magnetos*.)

These days, most cars have electronic spark computers, and magnetic timing sensors, rather than breaker points. On a good day, they are very reliable – but nobody said they are cheap, if you have to replace them. And most engines still do have a "coil", to generate the high voltage, *and* a distributor, to steer the spark to the right plug.

These days, good spark plugs (typically made with platinum tips) can run a long time, as much as 50,000 or 100,000 miles. But the spark plug wires do not usually last as long as the plugs. The rubber degrades, and the insulator can break down, and your engine starts *skipping* or running rough at high speeds. The last time this happened on my Beetle, I measured the resistance of the center conductors of the wires. It was about 1,000 ohms, on good wires *and* on bad ones, so the series resistance of the wire is not what gets bad. Apparently it is the insulation of the wire that breaks down.

Checking for Good Spark.

How can you tell if you have a weak spark? If your spark is just about gone, or you have no spark, that is easy to tell. With the engine turned OFF, pull the wire that

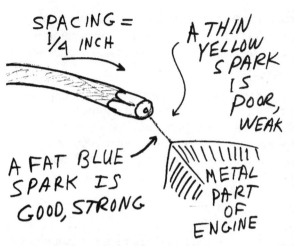

SPACING = 1/4 INCH

A THIN YELLOW SPARK IS POOR, WEAK

A FAT BLUE SPARK IS GOOD, STRONG

METAL PART OF ENGINE

comes from the coil, out of the center of the distributor. The distributor is the sort of round thing with 6 (or 4 or 8) spark-plug wires coming out of it. Take the center wire OUT of the distributor, and hold it near a piece of metal that is part of the engine, that is grounded. (A metal hose clamp that is just on a couple hoses is not suitable; it has to be part of the metal of the engine.) Hold the wire with a thick wad of cloth or paper, or use an insulated-handle (plastic-handle) screwdriver, to pin down the wire so its metal-tipped end is about 1/4 inch away from ground, and hold it securely so it won't move. Do NOT use your hand to hold the wire, or you'll get some lovely shocks. Keep your hand away from any fans or fan-belts. Your neck-tie, too.

Make sure the car is not in gear, and the handbrakes are on. Then you need a helper or accomplice to turn the key and crank the engine for just a few seconds. The engine will NOT start. If you have "good spark", the spark will jump the gap with a nice fat blue spark. See at *sketch 1*.

This nice fat spark indicates the ignition system has a lot of voltage and current, and puts a lot of energy into each spark. If you get no spark at all, stop cranking, and move the end up to about 1/8 inch away from the ground. Crank again. If you still get no spark, that explains why your car won't start at all. If you get a thin yellow spark, that is probably a good explanation why you are losing power at high speeds. It indicates your coil may be bad, or your ignition computer may be weak. Or maybe your breaker points are bad, in case of an older ignition system. At least you know that you have an ignition problem, and it's not your gas that is bad.

How Far Does The Spark Get??

Even if you get a good strong spark coming out of the center of the coil, that does NOT mean it is getting a good spark to the spark plugs. You can take one of the spark-plug wires off a spark plug, and use the cloth or whatever, to hold the metal tip of that wire 1/4 inch from the ground. NOT with your fingers, remember. Make sure your hands and nose and clothes and necktie and all parts of you are not near the fan belt or the fan or any other moving parts. Then crank the engine.

In this case, the engine WILL probably start. If there is no spark there, or only a weak one (barely 1/8 inch), that can explain why the engine runs so badly – bad wires, or a bad distributor. If your engine is just running slightly badly, you may have only 1 or 2 wires bad, so you may have to check all of them. But at least your engine is running well enough to get you to a place where you can get out of the rain, and get decent lighting.

√

While there are many kinds of work that you can best do in a well-lighted place, ignition problems can sometimes be best detected in the dark. Let your engine run in the pitch dark, and you may be able to see a spark arcing over. Or, you may not.... Just be careful.

> NOTE, many electronic ignition systems can be damaged if a spark gap gets too big, or if a wire falls off. So if there is one wire not connecting well, or one plug not firing at all, drive a minimum amount, and not too fast, because it could wreck the (expensive) ignition computer. Also, the unburned gas could badly overheat your (expensive) catalytic converter. So, get it fixed as soon as you can.

Checking Wires

There is one more trick you can do to detect one bad spark plug (or, bad wire). Let's pretend you have 4 cylinders in your engine. If you use an insulated-handle screw driver to short each individual spark-plug wire to ground, when the engine is running badly, then in 3 cases, the engine will run *worse*, but when you short one plug, it will not get worse. *That* is the plug that is firing badly. So the process of elimination is not always a difficult problem. (But on a VW, the plugs are so inaccessible that you can't easily do that.)

The Distributor

You might have a crack on your distributor cap. The spark may just jump down the crack at high speed. So if you carried along a spare old distributor cap, that is a good idea. Or if the weather is really wet, there may just be too much water on the distributor cap. Or there might even be moisture *inside* the distributor cap. Paper towels can help. And after you get the distributor cap and the high-voltage end of the coil *dry and clean*, there is a spray lacquer called "Wire-Dri", that you can spray on the end of the coil, and on the distributor cap, to keep them dry and insulated. After that lacquer dries a few minutes, your engine will run much better.

As I mentioned in the Appendix on Rental Cars, I once rented a little Vauxhall car in England. The starter motor quit the first day. But that did not bother me, because I could always park it on a top of a hill, and start it on the roll. I was headed back to the nearest city, to turn in the car, but it was a very foggy night, and the engine ran weaker and weaker. It finally quit at the bottom of a hill. I walked back to the nearest village pub, and bought a pint of ale. I was talking with some of the local men, and when I explained my problem, one fellow said, "Oh, I bet my Wire-Dri can help you out." After we finished our pints, we walked down to the car. We dried off the distributor and he sprayed some lacquer on it. Then we pushed the car back up the hill a few dozen yards. When the lacquer was dry, we pushed the car down the hill and it started fine. I thanked the guy, and drove into town where I was able to get the car swapped in the next day for a car that would start and run. But people who live in damp climates really have to know about tricks like Wire-Dri. Here in San Francisco, it gets fairly foggy at times, but I rarely have problems with bad spark or moisture on the distributor.

After all, my VWs have the engine in back, under cover, and the rain does not fall on the distributor. As a paraphrase of Chuck Berry's immortal song, *Maybelline*, "Rain-water blowin' all under my hood; I knew that was doin' my motor no good." I prefer to have all my ignition parts in out of the rain. I think that is *much better* than having them out in front with the rain blowing on them.

In May of 1996, my Beetle began to lose power and run rough. Then it began to run on just 2 cylinders. After I limped the last 4 miles to work, I did some troubleshooting. I spent almost an hour checking why cylinders number 1 and 2 would not fire. I was about to give up, and get it towed, when I spotted a crack on the *inside* of the distributor, a crack between wires 1 and 2 – not a crack to ground. It was causing the spark for the number 1 plug to try to fire both plugs 1 and 2. And it couldn't do it. I drilled a hole in the side of the distributor, to interrupt the path, and it ran fine. So I went over and bought a new distributor. And I kept the old one for an emergency spare.

Spark Plug Problems?

Maybe your spark plugs are dirty. You might take them out and see. When you put the wrench on, apply torque as evenly as possible so you don't put much *bending force* on the plug. Otherwise, you might break a plug.

Sometimes plugs get fouled or oily on the inside, near the tip; other times they might be dirty on the outside, on the insulator, or the insulator might be cracked. I take out my spark plugs occasionally and clean off the outside with a paper towel, and scrape away the debris and dirt on the inside, using the awl point of my pen-knife. If the outer electrode is worn or missing, that also will explain why it is misfiring. Maybe the gap has worn to be *a lot more than* 1/32 inch. Then you can tap lightly on the outer electrode, to bend it down to about the right space – in the ball-park of 0.028 to 0.032 inches, for most cars, or, whatever is recommended in your Owner's Manual.

THIS is the time when you are glad you carried along some of your old spark plugs, as I mentioned in the Appendix on Spare Parts. Old plugs that were running fairly well when you removed them, can be a LOT better than a plug you pull out of your engine that is REALLY FOULED, or busted.

When you are ready to replace your plug, make *sure* to thread them in carefully, by finger if possible, to make sure they do not get cross-threaded. And try to unfasten just one spark-plug wire at a time, to make sure you don't cross them up!

Spark Gap ?

I recall one time when I returned from a month-long trip, and my good old '62 Beetle did not want to start, at + 10 degrees F. It cranked OK, perhaps a little weakly, but did not want to fire at all. I solved the problem by pulling out just one spark plug – which was worn to a gap of about 0.042 inches – and I gapped it down to about 0.022 inches. I figured, if I did not have a strong spark, not enough to jump a gap of 0.042, it might be much happier to jump a gap of 0.022 inches. I was right. The first spark-plug fired, and then the others fired OK, too. The engine started and ran just fine, and I drove home. Then, later, I took out the other plugs and gapped them all down to the correct value of 0.028 inches.

WHAT IS WRONG with a gap a lot *larger* than the value listed in your owner's manual (for example, 0.028 inches) – ? It may be too hard for the spark to jump the gap, so you might get a high-speed miss. What is wrong with a gap *smaller* than the correct value? Your spark would not have enough energy to fire the fuel-air mixture properly, so you might get poor economy, and you might lose power at high speeds. So, while there is a range where a small variation in the spark gap is not absolutely important (perhaps in the range 0.025 to 0.031 inch; consult your Owner's Manual) sometimes if the gap is much TOO wide, or much TOO narrow, you may get poor performance – maybe a high-speed miss, or poor gas mileage.

Why Is a Weak Spark a Problem At High Speeds?

Very simple: It takes more voltage to fire a spark when the pressure is high. When your car is just idling or running at low speeds, there is not much air in the cylinder – even at the peak of the compression stroke, which is roughly when the spark has to fire. That is because the throttle is mostly closed, so there is a vacuum in the intake area. Even though the piston draws as much air and fuel mixture as it can, out of the intake manifold, there is not much air in there, so there is not much pressure in the cylinder.

When you press the gas pedal down – you open the throttle, and the cylinder can fill up with air very nicely. Then when all that air is compressed in the Compression stroke, there is a LOT of pressure, and it takes more voltage to fire a spark at high pressure. So if there is something weak in your ignition system – bad wires, or bad coil, or spark plugs dirty, or gapped too wide – the engine will run OK at light throttle settings, but will misfire at higher speeds, when the throttle is open and there is more *pressure* inside the cylinder. Depending on where the trouble is, it may misfire a little on one cylinder – or on many or all cylinders.

Also, if your coil is weak, or your points are bad, the current in the coil may not have enough *time* to build up properly in the short time at high revs – and the weak spark may not be able to fire a plug. In practice, bad spark can be caused by either one of these – or a combination of both.

So if that's the problem you have, somebody has to trouble-shoot the system, as mentioned above. You may not want to do all this trouble-shooting yourself – let the repair shop do it. But, at least it should make sense, now.

On the other hand, if you are in the middle of nowhere, with no repair shops for miles, you may be able to figure out what is wrong. You may be able to swap in an old wire or an old plug, instead of a bad one – or put in an old distributor cap that is not as bad as the one that is working badly – and maybe get out of trouble – and keep from being stranded!

Timing...

One of my friends likes to tell this joke. He says, "Did you know that I am the greatest comedian in Poland? Go ahead, ask me why I am the greatest comedian in Poland". So, I start to say, "Tom, tell me wh..." and he interrupts, "TIMING!".... It's a dumb joke, but I like it.

Likewise, your car may have a good spark, but if it fires at the wrong time, your car can run badly. Sometimes I notice my VW is not running very *strong*. It will still go fast, and it still gets good gas mileage, but it seems to be deficient in torque at moderate speeds. After a few more weeks, it even begins to skip or cough a little – and a VW never should do that. And the mid-range torque really is weak. When I check the timing, I find the spark is firing very late – perhaps 15 or 20 degrees after top-dead-center. When I re-adjust the ignition timing – the car runs fine again. So this is the kind of problem you can have with old-fashioned (Kettering) ignition systems. The points can wear, and the timing can go out of adjustment. It is true that modern ignition systems do not tend to wear out of adjustment. But I am not always pleased with them. I'll stay with what I got.

If you invest in a timing light, you can easily check your timing and see if it is bad. A timing light costs about $20 or $30. If you want to keep your car in good running condition, it's a good investment.

Specifically, when you send your car into the shop for ignition work, then when you get it back, use your timing light. See what you see, when the timing is supposed to be *right*. Then if you ever have to adjust it, you know where the timing should be set. And you can tell if it is set wrong.

"Ping"

The converse of timing the spark too late is, your ignition timing might be firing too early. OK, what's wrong with THAT? Simple: the engine will start to *ping*. Refer to the Chapter on *Ping* to solve that problem. If you don't solve the *ping* problem, you can damage your engine.

What if the Spark is OK?

If your Spark seems to be OK, but your engine is running badly, then your problem may easily be bad fuel flow – maybe a bad fuel pump or fuel filter. Jump back to the Chapter on Gasoline, and see if you can do a test on fuel flow, to pin down the problem. Still, there are times when a number of tests indicate that the Spark is OK, and then you go study fuel problems, and after a while, you come back and discover an ignition problem, after all.

Keeping your ignition system working properly means following the maintenance procedures listed in the Owner's Manual, reasonably carefully. Make sure plugs and wires and any other parts are cleaned or replaced as required. And do NOT throw the old parts away, but keep them in a bag or box, in case you need them, or in case somebody else does. If you do not maintain your car properly, you will probably find it running really rough on a cold rainy night when you are on a long trip, with 200 miles to go... and no repair shops open.

7/17/22

Appendix T – QUIZ NUMBER ONE

....

The purpose of this Quiz is to make sure your young driver has really read the book. There is another quiz, but that one is different. You can feel free to SNIP these Quiz Questions – and the Quiz Answers – out of the book. You can make extra copies of these Questions (you have my permission to copy them). If you have more than one young driver, make enough photocopies so you can spring the quiz on each kid. I am not trying to be unfair about this. You can tell your Young Driver about the Quiz, or you can spring it on him if you don't believe he could possibly have read this book that fast. It might make a good oral quiz – or maybe you believe in written tests....

This Quiz may also be useful for parents who say, "After the stupid thing you did with your car last night, you have to read this entire book, and understand it, before I ever let you drive that car again. I have the keys locked up. If you can show me you read the book, I may change my mind and not flush them down the toilet...."

1. (DISTRACTIONS) What was Ben trying to eat, that got him into trouble? What did he crash into? How would you avoid an accident if you had to eat that? Show me.

2. (SKIDS) If you are trying to accelerate up a slippery, snowy or sandy hill, list 2 or 3 things you might notice to tell you if your wheels are slipping.

3. (BRAKES) If you step on the brakes, and the pedal goes to the floor, name 4 or 5 things you could do to help you stop – and put them in order of which ones you would do first.

4. (STEERING) If your engine quits, can you still steer your car?

5. (VISION) If your hood flops up in your view, what do you do, to see where you are going?

6. (VISION – FOG) If you are rolling at 58, and the guy ahead of you hits his brakes 3 times and disappears into a heavy fog bank, what should you do?

7. (SPEEDING) Your buddy is driving home fast, at night, on a deserted freeway. Can you explain to him why not to go 85 mph ?

8. (VISION) Your buddy is driving fast, and he keeps looking in his mirror to make sure there is not a cop behind him. He does not keep looking at the road, and he starts to veer off the road. Should you reach over and turn off the key, to slow him down?

9. (GASOLINE) What if you see gas dripping out from the bottom of your gas-tank. What kind of tool should you use to plug the hole?

10. (BREAKDOWNS) If you break down along the freeway, should you stand in front of your car, or behind your car?

11. (ENGINES) Your buddy is driving along a 2-lane road, and as he approaches a curve he says, "The gas pedal is stuck! I can't slow down!" What do you tell him?

12. (BRAKES) You just burned up your handbrakes, by leaving them on. What do you do next? You have to drive 200 miles to get home, and you can't waste a lot of time.

13. (VISION) The snow is coming down fast, and you don't have a scraper. What do you do, to clear the snow off the windshield?

14. (SNOW) You don't have any gloves or mittens, and your heater is not working very well. How do you keep your hands warm? They are very cold, but in an hour you will get home.

453

QUIZ ANSWERS.

1. Ben was trying to eat a piece of tomato dangling from a sandwich. But he drove into a telephone pole. If you had to show how to eat some tomato dangling from a sandwich, you might cock your head to the left, and bring your sandwich down from the right, AND keep both eyes on the road.

2. You might hear the engine's speed rise a lot. You might hear the tires whine. You might feel the car's tail pointing in a different direction. You might see the speedometer needle suddenly rise a lot.

3. PUMP the brakes – step on the brakes a couple times. Pull on your handbrake. Turn off the key, just a little way left of the RUN position. OR, leave the key on, but downshift; then turn off the key. If none of these things are working well enough, and you really need to slow down, scrub the car gently against the guard-rail. Or try to spot some good bushes to drive into.

4. Yes, if the engine stops, you can still turn the wheel, but it will probably get very HEAVY, as your power steering will not work. But, if you turn off the KEY, to the OFF position, you will not be able to steer AT ALL. Never turn off your key more than a small distance, when you are rolling.

5. Peer under the bottom of the hood. OR, open your window fast and put your head out the window.

6. YOU should HIT YOUR brakes 3 or 4 times and slow down at least as much as the guy ahead of you did. Cut your speed roughly in HALF before you enter the fog-bank, so the car behind you can see that you are slowing a LOT. Turn on your headlights. If it is really hard to see in that fog, turn on your 4-way blinkers. Follow him carefully into the fog. OR, pull over to the right, and STOP, to avoid going into the fog.

7. This is not easy, but it is worth a try. Explain that cops may be lurking. Explain that there is no great hurry to get home. If he says he is trying to keep awake, give him a back-rub, to help keep him awake. Convince him to stop for a minute, to get a drink of water or coffee, or to wash his face with some water.

8. No, do NOT turn off the key. But you should explain to the driver, firmly, that he is getting too sloppy, and, drunk or sober, he has to wake up and drive competently.

9. You should not use *any* tool to plug the hole. Do not touch the hole. Park in a safe place, outside, and put a pan under the drips. It is POSSIBLE that a fuel line has gotten frayed or broken. Sometimes you can shove a pencil into a rubber fuel line to close it off.

10. Neither. Stand far off the road, behind a guard rail or even further. Of course, if it is pouring or freezing cold, you may have to stay in your car. That is better, slightly, than standing *behind* your car.

11. Tell him, "Hit the brakes, hard" and then, tell him to turn off the ignition key, just a little. Make sure he does not turn off the key all the way.

12. If your front brakes are working OK, then you may be able to drive home if you go rather slowly and carefully. Don't get close behind other cars. Downshift. Use lower gears. Pick a route where braking and stopping are likely to be the minimum. If your front brakes are poor, you may barely be able to drive to a repair shop. Or, if it is really bad, get it towed in.

13. Have you got a credit card? Or your wallet will work better than fingers.... Paper or a stick. NOT metal tools. Not a tin can. Then, go to a store and buy a scraper. Money is a good tool.

14. One way is to drive with one hand, and hold your hand in the air-flow from the heater or defroster. Or sit on one hand. Put it under your armpit. (We guys with old VWs know a lot of ways to warm up our hands, because our heaters do not put out much heat in really cold weather.)

These questions are not perfect. Some are not even very good. Likewise, the answers. But still, OK.

Appendix U – QUIZ NUMBER TWO ...on various Provocative Topics...

We already had one quiz, just to make sure you read the book.

But, *this* Quiz is different. The purpose of *this* quiz is to encourage the new driver to think, and to bring up discussions that will make better drivers. Discuss some of these ideas with your Driving Teacher, and with each parent. Maybe even with your friends. If you are driving somewhere, or riding with somebody else, and you see something stupid or dangerous, discuss it with other people.

You can feel free to SNIP these Quiz Questions out of the book. You can make extra copies of the Questions (they are not copyrighted.) But, don't worry about making extra copies of the answers. The "answers" just refer you to the pages of text that talk about this question.

There are not necessarily any "right answers" or "wrong answers" for these questions. In fact, if you and your TEACHER come up with new ideas on how to drive safely, write them down and send them in to the address on page 432. If you think the quiz questions are not perfect, or lousy, send me your new question, that you think is better.

1. (DISTRACTIONS) When is it OK to eat when driving?

2. (SKIDS) Around your neighborhood, where and when is it a good time, and place, to practice skidding on the first snowy day?

3. (BRAKES) If you step on the brakes, and the brakes don't seem to work very well, what would you do? If you normally drive an automatic, what would you do in a manual-shift gearbox? And, vice versa?

4. (STEERING) What do you do, if your steering starts feeling weird?

5. (STEERING) What do you do if you start hearing bad noises when you turn the steering wheel?

6. (VISION) What if you turn on your lights, and they don't seem to go on?

7. (TRANSMISSION, MANUAL) If you are shifting in normal traffic, and suddenly you get a lot of grinding sounds when you shift, what do you do?

8. (SPEEDING) Your buddy is driving home fast, at night, on a deserted freeway. Can you explain to him why not to go 85 mph ?

9. (VISION) Your buddy is driving fast, and he keeps looking in his mirror to make sure there is not a cop behind him. He does not keep looking at the road, and he starts to veer off the road. Should you reach over and turn off the key, to slow him down?

10. (SLEEPY) You start getting really sleepy. How do you choose a good place for a nap?

11. (DRUGS) You thought you only had a couple beers, but you realize somebody must have got more booze into you than you expected. Maybe they spiked your beer with booze. You feel really weird. Maybe Sleepy. Maybe a little – ill. Time to stop driving, FAST, and sober up for a while. Where is a safe place to stop, on a summer evening, if you are on –
    – a. A Freeway?
    – b. A City street?
    – c. A country road?

12. Same as 11, but on a cool winter evening?

Appendix V – APOLOGIA

– Now, an "apologia" is just an old Greek word that means, "an explanation of how things got to be the way they are...." Maybe when you read this, some of the things in this book will make sense.

– PEASE – What can you say about the length of the book?? – Well, it's like the clerk who asked, "Do you want this pizza cut in 6 pieces, or 8 pieces?" and the customer says, "Six, because we could never eat 8 pieces."

When I started to write this book, some people said, "Gee, Bob, 37 Chapters sounds like too much." So I said, "Good, then I'll make 61 Chapters – plus a dozen appendices." I did this because some of the Chapters were so big, they were getting too long and awkward. So I split some of the bigger Chapters into 2 Chapters.

– PEASE, why so much *stuff*?? – Well, I coulda put together a cute little book, and left out half the *stuff*. I could pretend that driving is pretty simple, and that it is *easy* to learn to drive safely under all conditions. But that's *bullshit*. Driving is NOT that easy. There are many little topics or problems that you don't run into every day – and that is EXACTLY what this book is about. A Driving Instruction Course that has 16 hours of classroom training, just *cannot* teach you all the important things. It cannot begin to teach you the important little tidbits.

– NOW, PEASE, in this book, there are a lot of funny little details. Are they important?? – Well, if you don't have that problem, then it may not be important – not right away. You may never have your brakes fail, or you may never have your gas pedal stick at full throttle, but I'll be damned if I will leave out little things just because they are not *likely* to happen.

HEY, on any given week, of all the cars in the USA, only 2 cars in a million may lose their brakes; and only 2 cars in a million may have a stuck gas pedal. Two in a million sounds like small odds, eh? But since there are about 88 million cars, that would say that 176 cars lose their brakes. If you are one of the 176 unlucky people, you might decide it is *very important*. So this book may have turned into an "Encyclopedia". Longer than any of us expected – because there are more kinds of trouble than we anticipated. After we wrote the problems down, and the suggested defenses against them, the text got kinda long. That's okay. It can't be helped.

– PEASE, couldn't you have made the book shorter, if you left out all the examples of accidents?? – Well, it might have been shorter – but the whole point of bringing up these EXAMPLES, is for teaching – to get the idea EMBEDDED in your head. If I just spouted a lot of theory and platitudes and fancy concepts, and listed some rules, and said, "ALWAYS do *this*, and NEVER do *that*" – I think it is hard to learn from books like that. Even if the book would be very short, it would not be very good. The examples are EXACTLY what I designed the book around, as the primary educational approach. If you know a guy who wants to write a book, without examples, well, he can write any book he wants to, but that is not THIS book. And I don't think it would work very well. It would not teach the young drivers in a way that would make the ideas STICK.

– PEASE, could you fit the info into a Comic book??

– Maybe I should do that next. That's a popular way to get a message across! Also, I won't say a video-tape or a CD-ROM is a bad idea. I thought about these, but I figured they would take a LOT more time to do well, and if I wanted to bring them out with the book, the book would be delayed a lot, and I did NOT want to do that.

– PEASE, you ought to apologize for talking so much about VWs.

– Well, maybe I should, but there is not anything much I could do about it. Most of my driving experience is in VWs. So I have written about what happened to me in my car. But I have driven a lot of other kinds of cars, too – rented and borrowed. So I know a good bit about assorted American and Foreign cars. And I asked my friends to talk about their experiences with their cars. I put in as many such items as I could.

Besides, if you have a car that is BIGGER or BETTER or FASTER (or crummier) than a VW, most of what I write will be directly applicable to your car, too.

– PEASE, shouldn't you apologize for writing mostly about driving in Massachusetts and California??

– No, not really. I mean, there are mountainous roads in the east and the west, but there are flat roads and straight roads, and towns and cities, too. So most of the driving in the midwest or south is not really much different from some of the driving in California. I have, after all, driven across the US about 12 times. I have probably driven 100,000 miles outside of California or New England. I have driven in every state except Florida, and in most provinces of Canada, too. So I know a good bit about *most* kinds of driving, in most parts of America.

And also around the world. I have ridden as a passenger and observer in cars in Japan, Nepal, Thailand, and India. I have driven in England and Scotland, France, Germany, Switzerland, and a little bit of other European countries. And I have friends in those countries whose comments are very educational. So while I am not an expert on driving everywhere, I know quite a bit, and I am good at writing it down. And I hope this info is useful to you.

– PEASE, you talk about RIGHT and LEFT. But there are millions of potential readers in other countries who drive on the opposite side of the road. Aren't you going to confuse these readers??

– Eventually I'll make a reverse-image text, to help drivers in England, Japan, Australia, etc., and to avoid confusing them. Right now, they will have to read this first edition and do their own mirror-image conversion. Not a big deal. If they don't want to wait for the second version, they can take a pencil to my text.

– Could I have made a book with all short, easy words?? – No.

– Could I have written the whole book with no cuss-words?? – No.

– Could I have made a book all politically correct, with all he/she and him/her? – Hey, if somebody else wants to try writing that book, I'll let him/her do it. But I think that's wrong, and I say the hell with it. If YOU want to read a politically-correct, namby-pamby book that was written for 5th-graders, go ahead, but I don't think you'll learn anything.

– Pease, why do you write like that?? – Well, I write like I talk. I put in more commas than most writers do, because I put in a comma where there is a *pause*, to make it easier to read. And I put in a lotta *italics*, and a lot of CAPITALS, to indicate my emphasis. That's how I talk.

So, this is the book I wrote, and I hope you find it educational and entertaining. / RAP / Robert A. Pease / 1996 and 1998.

you do, DON'T break laws, and DO use good sense and good judgement, no matter what you read.

Appendix W – YOU HAVE NO BRAKE LIGHTS

I am not responsible, nor am I liable, for any driving mistakes you make because of anything I wrote here – or any advice that I do NOT give. Whatever

Here are 4 pages that are not copyrighted. Please feel free to make several copies – one for each car that you drive, and make a couple spares, too. Just shove the corner of the book into a photocopier, and make one copy first to see that the orientation is right. Make a few copies for friends, too! Glue or tape these sheets to the front and back of a big old envelope. Make sure you get them right-side up. Then when you hold it up and see the one message, you know that the other message is on the other side, where an adjacent driver can see it. Refer to Chapter 27 and Appendix K. Just be very careful that *you* don't drive into an accident while beeping and holding it up for another driver to see.

AMEN

PEASE'S BOOK *"HOW TO DRIVE INTO ACCIDENT.*

COPY ME • THIS PAGE IS *NOT* COPYRIGHTED • COPY ME • THIS PAGE WAS COPIED FROM ROBERT

YOU
HAVE

OPY ME • THIS PAGE IS *NOT* COPYRIGHTED • COPY ME

NO BRAKE LIGHTS

Here are 4 pages that are not copyrighted. Please feel free to make several copies – one for each car that you drive, and make a couple spares, too. Just shove the corner of the book into a photocopier, and make one copy first to see that the orientation is right. Make a few copies for friends, too! Glue or tape these sheets to the front and back of a big old envelope. Make sure you get them right-side up. Then when you hold it up and see the one message, you know that the other message is on the other side, where an adjacent driver can see it. Refer to Chapter 27 and Appendix K. Just be very careful that *you* don't drive into an accident while beeping and holding it up for another driver to see.

COPY ME • THIS PAGE IS *NOT* COPYRIGHTED • COPY ME • THIS PAGE WAS COPIED FROM ROBERT PEASE'S BOOK *"HOW TO DRIVE INTO ACCIDENTS*

YOU HAVE ONLY

COPY ME • THIS PAGE IS *NOT* COPYRIGHTED • COPY ME

ND HOW NOT TO" • COPY ME • MAKE EXTRA COPIES & KEEP IN YOUR CAR • COPY ME • TAPE ONTO A HEAVY ENVELOPE • COPY ME • THIS PAGE IS *NOT* COPYRIGHTED • MAKE COPIES FOR YOUR FRIENDS • COPY ME • COPY ME • MAKE LOTS OF COPIES • COPY ME • COPY ME • MAKE LOTS OF COPIES

ONE BRAKE LIGHT

Appendix X – THE LAST WORD....

I realized that I would surely have a number of last-minute ideas to add, after the whole book was type-set. If I added a few paragraphs to Chapter 2, it might move every page number up by one, and make a shambles of the Index. Disastrous. Unacceptable.

To avoid that, I planned to insert any such late ideas into this "last-word" section. A whole bunch of "PS's". That's how I planned this....

Reckless What?

If you see somebody driving recklessly – speeding or driving sloppily, or acting as if drunk – or if you see an actual accident – you might report them by your car phone or CB radio, or at a pay phone. Call 911 or equivalent. Conversely, if *you* are "joyriding", goofing off, "hotrodding", driving too fast or sloppily – somebody might report YOU by car phone. These days, don't be surprised at ANYTHING. So, don't drive recklessly – drive wreck-lessly.

Racing or Drag-Racing

I almost forgot to put this in: Accelerating vigorously away from a stop light is something we all do, sometimes. But racing to get ahead of another car is NOT a good idea. Yes, you want to get up to the speed limit, promptly, and if the other car is a slow-poke, you might want to get ahead of him. But... don't accelerate wildly, not up past the speed limit. This goes with the previous paragraph.

Pedestrian Safety

It's a bad idea to assume that other people will see you, as you walk along the side of a road. Especially at night. Do not assume that you can safely cross a road at a cross-walk, even though such a crossing is "protected" for pedestrians. (Myself, I prefer to jaywalk, and cross against the lights, to make sure I am paying attention to traffic. I want it to be MY responsibility to know a car will not hit me.) - Imagine how lousy some driver would feel if he hit you! Imagine how bad YOU would feel!!! Try to avoid walking where sleepy, sloppy, or drunk drivers might hit you, if they did not notice you....

Mal-Adjusted Brakes

Sometimes brakes get mis-adjusted, either by a person, or by the automatic adjusters. Or a stuck caliper. If they start dragging, they can get extremely hot. Then they could cause the brake fluid to boil, or the brakes to pull to one side, or fade, and any of those could cause an accident.

So keep alert when driving. When you roll up to a stop on a very shallow grade – make sure that when you take your foot off the brakes, the car will roll a little. If it

464

won't roll as it normally does, that could be the clue that your brakes are dragging. After a hard stop, your brakes might heat up a lot. But all 4 brakes should heat up about the same amount. Is one set of brakes a lot hotter than the rest, with no provocation? That's a clue that your brakes may be dragging, or goofed up. (But be careful not to burn your fingers. If you just put your hand *near* hot brakes, you can feel the radiant heat.)

Slowpoking

On a recent program about "Road Rage", I heard a cop say that slow drivers were not a serious problem. Don't you believe it. You may want to drive slowly and cautiously – fine – but if even ONE driver seems annoyed because he is BLOCKED by your slow driving – even if you think your slow speed is justified – pull over and let him by. For example, on a snowy day, you might think traction is poor. But the guy behind you might have good snow tires, and you should not try to block him from going faster.

Retrofit of "Rumble-Strips"

Recently on I-93 north of Boston, I saw new "Rumble-Strips" at the edge of the shoulder. These were not newly cast into new concrete, as on the newly-rebuilt sections of the Mass. Pike, but were just ground and sawed into the asphalt. A great retrofit!

Cigarettes and Ashtrays

Smokers: Please don't throw your cigarette butts out the window. It's too easy in California (or in other places) to set the countryside on fire. Use an ashtray, or other metal container, to hold the butts. Later, discard in a proper trash bin – do not litter.

Cellular Phones?

Some people say they are happy they have a cellular phone, so they can call for emergency help in case of an accident. But when you are out in the boondocks, will the cellular phone get through? Next time you are headed into a sparse area, make a call. See if it gets through. Useful to know.

Accident-Related Crime

TOUGH NH

I'm sure you've read how some thugs drive their cars into accidents, and then when the unsuspecting driver gets out of his car, he is robbed. So in some tough neighborhoods, maybe you would want to just roll down the window a crack, to exchange information. But I doubt if that would stop a determined robber.

Trick to Prevent Speeding

A couple guys told how to avoid speeding in a slow zone (such as a school zone) – by downshifting to second. Then if you started to absent-mindedly speed up, your engine revving too high would remind you to slow back down. Fair idea.

LAST last word: check my website: http://www.transtronix.com ĸ

Section Y - INDEX

Robert, Ilino, Erik, Bill, Ralph, &ENEE

Beam   p423

EPHRAM   P436

HORSE   P437

Appendix Z - BUY ME

This page is not copyrighted.

You can make as many copies as you want of this page. – In fact, please DO make photo-copies of this page! – There is no limit to the number of copies you can make of this page!! *VAUX HILL   448*

You can buy this book –

How To Drive Into ACCIDENTS – And How NOT To

from the author, Robert A. Pease.

This price will be held for you until July 31, 1999. After 1999, there is no guarantee the price will not go up (or down). Send for details.

To buy this book in paperback – send a check or money order for $21.95 which INCLUDES tax, postage, and U.S. shipping, to:

Robert A. Pease   *Do not go back roads*
682 B Miramar Avenue   *farther than you can*
San Francisco, California 94112-1232   *walk out.*

Be sure to include your address.

If this book is for another person or young driver, list that name too, at the end.

Send book to: _____ *CORSICA* _____ *p 444* _____

_____ *Magnelis* _____ *p 446* _____

Street Address: _____

Town or City: _____ *3 Current flow to spark plug* _____

State: _____ *1 modern car timing* _____ ZIP: _____

Name of Student Driver: ___ *Page 454* ___ *Hood up* _____

Page 459   Go to H.

- Books will be shipped by 4th Class Book Rate; allow about 2 or 3 weeks for delivery.

- Volume discounts are available for quantities larger than 10 books.

- Hardcover version may be available for $31.95 (including tax and shipping).

- For Shipments to Foreign addresses:
  – Send International Money Order for $24.95 US;
  – price includes shipping by slow surface mail.

- For walk-up sales, $18.95 (no shipping costs; sales tax included).